AVOIDING WAR
Problems of Crisis Management

AVOIDING WAR
Problems of Crisis Management

EDITED BY

Alexander L. George

WITH CONTRIBUTIONS BY

Yaacov Bar-Siman-Tov   Theodore J. Ralston
Kurt M. Campbell   J. Philip Rogers
Arthur A. Cohen   Scott D. Sagan
M. Steven Fish   Richard Smoke
Christer Jönsson   Janice Gross Stein
Jack S. Levy   Stan A. Taylor
Jerrold M. Post   Allen S. Whiting
Phil Williams

Westview Press
BOULDER • SAN FRANCISCO • OXFORD

Copyright © 1991 by Westview Press, Inc.

Published in 1991 in the United States of America by Westview Press, Inc., 5500 Central Avenue, Boulder, Colorado 80301, and in the United Kingdom by Westview Press, 36 Lonsdale Road, Summertown, Oxford OX2 7EW

Library of Congress Cataloging-in-Publication Data
Avoiding war : problems of crisis management / edited by Alexander L.
  George ; with contributions by Yaacov Bar-Siman-Tov . . . [et al.].
    p. cm.
  Includes bibliographical references and index.
  ISBN 0-8133-1232-9 — ISBN 0-8133-1233-7 (pbk.)
  1. Military history, Modern—20th century. 2. War—Case studies.
3. Crisis management. I. George, Alexander L. II. Bar-Siman-Tov,
Yaacov, 1946–   .
D431.A86 1991
327.1′6—dc20   90-27581
                                                                    CIP

Printed and bound in the United States of America

The paper used in this publication meets the requirements
of the American National Standard for Permanence of Paper
for Printed Library Materials Z39.48-1984.

10   9   8   7   6   5   4   3   2

For David Hamburg
with respect and affection

Contents

Preface

This book attempts to provide a comprehensive and systematic analysis of the phenomenon of "inadvertent war," which we define as a war that neither side wanted or expected at the outset of a diplomatic crisis but that nonetheless occurred during the course of crisis developments. The book links the analysis of such developments with the role that crisis management can play in preventing inadvertent war.

My interest in these problems was initially aroused by having observed and later studied the outbreak of the Korean War in June 1950 and the war with the People's Republic of China that followed in November. Both of these wars can be regarded as instances of inadvertent war. The North Korean government did not want or expect its effort to achieve a quick military victory over South Korea to lead to war with the United States. The United States did not expect the North Koreans to launch an all-out attack against South Korea and did not plan to intervene militarily should that unexpected contingency occur. In fact, prior to the outbreak of the war, U.S. policy did not include coming to the defense of South Korea, and Washington gave numerous indications, which were available to the North Korean government and its patron, the Soviet Union, that it was not committed to doing so. Having failed to attempt to deter an attack against South Korea, U.S. leaders quite unexpectedly reversed their policy of no commitment once the attack occurred, and the United States intervened to prevent the overrunning of South Korea.[1] (The reader will note the similarity in these respects between the outbreak of the Korean War and the U.S. response to the Iraqi attack against Kuwait, which Washington failed to anticipate and did not attempt to deter but nonetheless felt it must oppose after it occurred!)

My interest in the problems and requirements of crisis management was aroused by observing, with the benefit of hindsight to be sure, the mistakes that President Harry S. Truman and Secretary of State Dean Acheson committed in misjudging and mismanaging the threat of Chinese communist military intervention in the Korean War after Gen. Douglas MacArthur's forces succeeded in routing the North Korean army from South Korea. The U.S.-China conflict, too, was an avoidable and unnecessary war.[2]

My interest in crisis management developed further in a 1971 study of the uses and limitations of the strategy of coercive diplomacy. In doing the research for this study, I became aware of the fundamental tension that can arise between some of the most important requirements of crisis management and some of the most salient aspects of coercive diplomacy.[3] This was strikingly the case in President John F. Kennedy's efforts to persuade Premier Nikita Khrushchev to remove Soviet missiles from Cuba. It was evident in this and other historical cases I examined that in some confrontations a prudent approach to crisis management may require policy makers to slow down the momentum of events and to deliberately create pauses in crisis developments in order to give both sides time to make careful, well-considered decisions and engage in serious diplomatic communication to explore acceptable ways of terminating the crisis. But it is precisely these important "requirements" of crisis management that conflict with the emphasis that some variants of coercive diplomacy place upon creating a sense of time urgency for the adversary to comply with the demands made on him.

I derived fresh stimulation from participation in a Pugwash workshop on crisis management and crisis prevention that was organized by Dr. David Hamburg and held in 1978.[4] Some years later I did additional research on crisis management when Dr. Hilliard Roderick, then Tom Slick Professor of World Peace at the University of Texas (Austin), organized a conference on "Avoiding Inadvertent War: Crisis Management," which was held in February 1983. On this occasion, drawing on my earlier work and on writings on the requirements of crisis management by Phil Williams, Ole Holsti, Charles Hermann, and other scholars, I discussed some of the problems policy makers encounter in attempting to meet these requirements.[5] After viewing parts of a videotape of the University of Texas conference, Dr. Richard Beal, special assistant to the president for crisis management planning of the National Security Council (NSC), invited me to discuss with him some innovations in crisis management procedures that had been introduced into the NSC during the Reagan administration. My discussion with Dr. Beal and, particularly, the talk he gave when we appeared together on a panel on crisis management at the American Association for the Advancement of Science (AAAS) annual meeting in New York in May 1984, familiarized me with a sobering list of problems he and others had identified in attempting to improve White House capabilities for crisis management.

Among the impediments to effective crisis management identified by Dr. Beal were the following: (1) Information during a crisis tends to "crowd" the judgment, prudence, and wisdom of policy makers; (2) sophisticated information technology recently introduced into the White House crisis management facility makes unusual and severe demands on decision makers and their advisers; (3) crises typically include important idiosyncratic events that are difficult to generalize about, which handicaps and limits the development of useful general theories or plans for crisis management; (4) there is no adequate institutional memory at top levels in the White House for crisis management purposes; (5) much learning is possible from managing crises, but such learning is neither easily codified nor readily available for use in planning for or dealing with new crises; (6) presidential control is essential for crisis management, but it is equally necessary to avoid possibly harmful effects from attempts at micromanagement by the White House; (7) in a tense, fast-moving crisis, decision makers are likely to suffer from too much or too little information—during the Grenada invasion, for instance, Beal's office did not know what was going on for eight hours; (8) "information uncertainty" as to crisis developments is an inherent problem in crisis management.[6]

Immediately after Beal's talk at the AAAS meeting, Dr. Hamburg, who was now president of the Carnegie Corporation of New York, and I discussed with him the possibility of organizing one or more small meetings with former high-level crisis managers to discuss some of the problems Beal had identified. Beal was receptive but within a month or two he developed a serious illness, which led to his untimely death.

The University of Texas conference not only led to additional meetings between scholars and officials responsible for crisis management but it also stimulated the International Institute of Strategic Studies (IISS) in London to organize a meeting on crisis management, which took place in 1984. The IISS conference focused on the question of whether current crisis management concepts and procedures are robust enough to withstand the pressures of a tense U.S.-Soviet confrontation in which strategic and theater forces begin to go on alert. In a paper presented to this conference, I emphasized that in a crisis fundamental tensions are likely to arise between military "logic" and political-diplomatic "logic," tensions that can severely complicate the policy maker's dual task of safeguarding his country's most important interests while at the same time avoiding actions that could trigger unwanted escalation.[7]

Drawing upon the IISS paper, I gave a talk on this subject at each of two annual conferences organized by the Workshop on Political-Military Decision Making at which high-level military officers and political officials met with academic specialists in decision making and organizational behavior to discuss ways of achieving better integration of political and military considerations in the management of foreign policy. The first of these meetings was held at Stanford (March 1985), and my paper, "Crisis Management: 'Lessons' from Past U.S.-Soviet Crises," appeared in a subsequent publication of conference proceedings.[8] The second meeting, held in England in June 1986, was cosponsored by Gen. John Chain, USAF, Chief of Staff, Supreme Headquarters Allied Powers Europe (SHAPE). It brought together many high-level officers from a number of NATO countries whose responsibilities include planning and operational duties in some aspect of crisis management.

In other ways as well, I tried to inform myself on what was being done and what might be done to improve our capability for crisis management and to find out what well-informed persons believe are significant gaps in knowledge and procedures. In the spring of 1985, I discussed these matters with officials in the National Security Council staff. These and other conversations led me to organize a conference of persons engaged in crisis management planning, operations, and research within and outside the U.S. government. The purpose of the meeting was to take stock of the state of the field, identify problems and gaps, assess research needs and opportunities, and, more generally, discuss who was doing what in this field and consider where different kinds of research projects could best be carried out—whether within government itself, in think tanks, or in academic research centers. Dr. Hamburg sponsored this meeting, held in September 1985, as part of Carnegie's program of support for research on "Avoiding Nuclear War."

The Carnegie-sponsored meeting and the other experiences I have described helped me to define and delimit the research reported in this volume. Some important studies discussed at the Carnegie meeting can be done well only with benefit of access to classified information. There was general agreement at the meeting, however, that historical case studies and conceptual and analytical studies of the kind reported in this book, which do not require the use of classified materials, can be useful and in some respects can be better done at academic research centers.

I should briefly mention that the National Academy of Sciences (NAS) has sponsored useful reflection on crisis management problems. The NAS Institute of Medicine held a symposium on the medical effects of nuclear war in September 1985, at which I gave a paper on "The Impact of Crisis-Induced Stress on Decision Making."[9]

The National Academy of Sciences subsequently undertook another initiative to improve understanding of the problems of crisis management and to highlight its importance. A two-day symposium on this subject, in which I participated, was held at the annual meeting of academy members in April 1986. The symposium was organized and sponsored by two NAS committees: the Committee on Security and Arms Control, and the relatively new Committee on the Contributions of the Behavioral and Social Sciences for Avoiding Nuclear War, of which I was a member.[10]

Scholars in the United States have discussed problems of crisis management and crisis avoidance with Soviet academicians in a number of forums since the early 1980s. In 1983, Dr. Hamburg presented a paper we had coauthored at a meeting in Moscow sponsored by the Soviet Academy of Sciences.[11] These problems have received careful attention in a series of unofficial joint U.S.-Soviet meetings of the Dartmouth Conference Task Force on Regional Conflicts, sponsored by the Charles F. Kettering Foundation and cochaired for many years by Harold H. Saunders and, until recently, Yevgeny Primakov.[12] Problems of crisis avoidance have also been a central concern of a joint U.S.-Soviet study group that has focused on avoiding nuclear war. This study group has involved a series of meetings since 1983 between a U.S. group chaired by Graham T. Allison, then dean of the John F. Kennedy School of Government at Harvard, and a Soviet group chaired by Georgy Arbatov, director of the USA and Canada Institute, Soviet Academy of Sciences.[13]

I want to convey a deeply held appreciation to my collaborators in the volume for their willingness to draw upon their special knowledge and to undertake original research for the study, and to express my admiration for the quality of the chapters they have contributed. Indeed, a project with so ambitious a scope could not possibly have been accomplished by a single individual. I was fortunate to have been able to draw so many talented scholars into the project.

I would like to express my appreciation to the John D. and Catherine T. MacArthur Foundation and the Carnegie Corporation of New York for funding the project.

I was fortunate once again to have the ever-helpful and cheerful administrative support provided by Arlee Ellis, the highly professional and thoughtful editing of the entire manuscript by Rachelle Marshall, the efficient typing and secretarial services of Willa Leonard, and the services of Eliska Ryznar, who had the challenging task of preparing the index.

Finally, it gives me great pleasure to acknowledge my long-standing indebtedness to David Hamburg, a valued friend and wise counselor for the past thirty-five years. He was among the first to recognize the need for scholarly research and serious planning for managing U.S.-Soviet rivalry in order to avoid war-threatening confrontations such as the Cuban Missile Crisis and to help decision makers manage and terminate such crises without allowing the nations involved to plunge into war. The Pugwash workshop on these problems that Hamburg organized in 1978 did much to stimulate others as well as myself to give serious attention to these urgent tasks. Even before assuming the presidency of the Carnegie Corporation of New York in 1982, and since doing so, he has worked imaginatively, constructively, and tirelessly to organize and encourage many activities directed toward achieving these objectives. Indeed, a great deal of the important research accomplished during the 1980s on better understanding the risks of nuclear war and devising ways of controlling and eliminating such wars owes much to his inspiration and support.

Alexander L. George
Stanford, California

NOTES

1. For a fuller analysis, see A.L. George and R. Smoke, *Deterrence in American Foreign Policy: Theory and Practice* (New York: Columbia University Press, 1974), Ch. 6, "The Outbreak of the Korean War."
2. For a fuller account see the case study provided in Chapter 7 of this volume by Allen Whiting.
3. A.L. George, D.K. Hall, and W.E. Simons, *The Limits of Coercive Diplomacy* (Boston: Little, Brown, 1971). This strategy of coercive diplomacy is also discussed in Chapter 16 of this volume.
4. For a brief discussion of the workshop proceedings see the Foreword by David Hamburg in Graham T. Allison and William L. Ury with Bruce J. Allyn, eds., *Windows of Opportunity: From Cold War to Peaceful Competition in U.S.-Soviet Relations* (Cambridge, MA: Ballinger, 1989), pp. ix–xi.
5. Hilliard Roderick with Ulla Magnusson, *Avoiding Inadvertent War: Crisis Management* (Austin, TX: L.B. Johnson School of Public Affairs, 1983).
6. Beal's talk has not been published, so far as I know, but it was taped with his permission. A brief summary appeared in "Crisis Management Under Strain," *Science* (August 31, 1984): 907–909. Information problems and efforts to improve White House capabilities are also discussed in some detail by former members of the Crisis Management Center in the National Security Council; see Ronald H. Hinckley, "National Security in the Information Age," *The Washington Quarterly* (Spring 1986): 125–139; and Rodney B. McDaniel, "C³I: A National Security Council Perspective," Center for Information Policy Research, Harvard University (no date).
7. This paper was subsequently published under the title "Crisis Management: The Interaction of Political and Military Considerations," in the IISS journal *Survival* (September/October 1984). See Chapter 3 of this volume.
8. In J.J. Chain, R. Dixon, and R. Weissinger-Baylon, eds., *Decisionmaking in the Atlantic Alliance: The Management of Political-Military Crises* (Menlo Park, CA: Strategic Decisions Press, 1987).

9. Published in *The Medical Implications of Nuclear War*, Institute of Medicine, National Academy of Sciences (Washington, D.C.: National Academy Press, 1986), pp. 529–552. For additional discussion of the possible impact of crisis-induced stress, see Chapter 20 by Dr. Jerrold Post in this volume.

10. Lynn Rusten and Paul Stern, staff members of the Academy's National Research Council, drew on the symposium and other materials in preparing *Crisis Management in the Nuclear Age* (Washington, D.C.: National Academy Press, 1987).

11. David A. Hamburg and Alexander L. George, "Reducing the Risk of Nuclear War: An Approach to Crisis Prevention." A brief adaptation of this paper, "Nuclear Crisis Management," was published in the *Bulletin of the Atomic Scientists* 40, 6 (June/July 1984).

12. For an account of these meetings that focuses on discussion of the Middle East conflicts, see the special issue of *AEI Foreign Policy and Defense Review*, "The Superpowers in the Middle East," 6, 1 (1986), edited by Harold H. Saunders. To this special issue I contributed a paper, "Mechanisms for Moderating Superpower Competition."

13. A report on some of these discussions appears in *Windows of Opportunity*. To this collaborative U.S.-Soviet volume I contributed a chapter, "The Search for Agreed Norms."

Editor's Note

As this book goes to press, the war in the Persian Gulf is officially concluded. The crisis that preceded the war offers a wealth of opportunities to apply and illustrate the relevance of the analytical framework presented here. A fully developed case study will have to wait for the perspective that time will bring and the sources that will open up over the coming years. In the meantime, the provisional account presented in the Epilogue is offered in order to demonstrate the immediate and continuing usefulness of the principles and strategies of crisis management in analyzing confrontations and crises in the post-Cold War world.

A.L.G.

PART ONE

FRAMEWORK OF THE STUDY

CHAPTER 1

Is Research on Crisis Management Needed?

Alexander L. George

It is unusual to begin a study, as we do here, by asking whether research on the subject of the study is really necessary. One may well question whether there is any longer a need to be concerned about the problems of managing U.S.-Soviet crises. Such an optimistic view need not rest solely on the dramatic improvement in East-West relations and the shift toward moderation in Soviet foreign policy under Mikhail Gorbachev. In addition, optimists can cite the record of highly successful crisis management by the superpowers in the past, which is indeed a remarkable one. The fact of the matter is that there has been no shooting war of any kind directly involving the military forces of the Soviet Union and the United States.

From the beginning of the Cold War, the leaders of both countries have generally behaved with enough caution, prudence, and good sense—and, one may add, with an indispensable element of good luck—to survive a series of tense confrontations in Berlin, Cuba, the Middle East, and Asia without plunging into war. The shared fear that such crises could get out of hand and result in catastrophic nuclear war has provided powerful motivation in both Moscow and Washington for restrained behavior and tacit cooperation in managing their confrontations.

It is important, too, that from the very first of their Cold War confrontations U.S. and Soviet leaders intuitively grasped the essential principles of crisis management; even more important, they have generally acted in ways that were consistent with these principles or at least not flagrantly in violation of them.

There have been several other favorable developments in U.S.-Soviet relations as well. Over the years, the two sides have developed a set of basic tacit "rules of prudence" to govern their relationship.[1] And the superpowers have made considerable progress in working out cooperative arrangements in many components of their overall security relationship.[2]

Admittedly, the history of superpower relations since the onset of the Cold War shows that Moscow and Washington have been much more successful in managing crises than in avoiding them. Still, it may well be correct, as some observers believe, that over the years the two superpowers have also gradually learned to better understand and respect each other's vital interests, to regulate and somewhat restrain their global rivalry, and to deal with specific conflicts of interest in ways that do not plunge them into new war-threatening crises. Indeed, one cannot fail to be impressed with the fact that there has been no war-threatening crisis in U.S.-Soviet relations since the unexpected twenty-four-hour confrontation between them toward the end of the Arab-Israeli War of October 1973. And, despite the brief alert of U.S. strategic forces during that crisis, most observers agree that the danger of war at that time was much more remote than during the Cuban Missile Crisis of 1962. Significant, too, is the fact that no new war-threatening crises erupted during the deterioration of superpower relations in the late 1970s and early 1980s.

Why, then, should we be concerned over the possibility that a crisis of an unexpected kind might occur in the future that might draw the superpowers close to the brink of war once more? We must remember that such a crisis need not be one that is initiated by one of the superpowers or that initially threatens either superpower's vital or important interests. Although such possibilities cannot be excluded, much more likely are scenarios of a U.S.-Soviet confrontation that develops, as in past Middle East wars, from a regional conflict involving local states, each of which is supported by one of the superpowers. As Phil Williams notes in Chapter 21, a war-threatening crisis is not even inconceivable in the new Europe, remarkably altered as the security picture has become since the erosion of the Warsaw Pact and the unification of Germany.

Certainly any new crisis would confront leaders in Moscow and Washington, and perhaps in other capitals as well, with significant new challenges that would have to be mastered to avoid escalation to a shooting war. The fact that crisis management was successful in the past would offer no guarantee of similar success in a new confrontation.

Various obstacles and threats to effective crisis management will be described in this study. Although surmounted in past crises, such threats and obstacles may prove more difficult to overcome in a future crisis. It cannot be taken for granted that individuals who come into top-level policy-making positions in the future will be familiar with the general principles and requirements of crisis management. In any case, new policy makers will face the challenging task of applying these general principles to the specific, distinctive configuration of a new crisis.

It should be noted, too, that general lessons drawn from the study of past crises typically do not address the many specific operational aspects of crisis management that are of critical importance. The operational skill, know-how, and judgment that one set of decision makers acquires from personal experience in successfully managing crises cannot be easily transferred to a new set of leaders. Moreover, as former officials have frequently lamented, "institutional memory" on matters of direct importance for the management of crises is disturbingly inadequate at the highest levels of the U.S. government.[3]

In any case, past experience in crisis management and lessons derived from it will have to be adapted to the many important changes in the strategic-military context of U.S.-Soviet relations and in the rest of the international system that have occurred since the Cuban Missile Crisis and the October 1973 war in the Middle East. Particularly worrisome to many well-informed strategic analysts have been developments in military technology and force postures over the past ten or fifteen years that would pose serious threats to crisis stability in future U.S.-Soviet confrontations. Improved accuracy of strategic missiles, forward deployment on land and sea of forces with first-strike capabilities, shortened warning times, a tendency to rely on launch-on-warning, and the development of interlocking warning and alert systems have combined to raise concern about the possibility of so-called "decapitation strikes" by either side against the other's command systems. As a result, it is feared, one or both sides would feel substantial pressure to initiate a preemptive strike during a tense crisis that is threatening to escalate. Moreover, the possibility of unauthorized and accidental military actions during a crisis that might trigger escalation cannot be excluded.

Thus, while mutual strategic deterrence seems quite firm in peacetime, with neither side worrying that the other would attempt to launch a surprise attack, well-informed specialists on both sides in the 1980s expressed concern lest confidence in the stability of strategic deterrence be shaken during a tense confrontation. In both the United States and the Soviet Union,[4] serious attention has been given to these new developments affecting crisis stability. In sum, even if the probability of new war-threatening crises involving the Soviet Union and the United States can be judged to be quite small, such a seemingly remote contingency cannot be ignored, as the possibility of escalation to war would then arise. An attitude of complacency must not be allowed to develop. History warns us that hypothetical catastrophes that seem quite implausible even to informed observers can and do repeatedly occur.

Hence, one need not assign substantial probability to the danger of a nuclear war between the superpowers in order to justify efforts to learn more about how an inadvertent war—one neither side expected or wanted at the beginning of a crisis—might come about, how crisis management could break down in a future confrontation, and how improved planning and training, prudent policies, and timely actions could prevent or further reduce the likelihood of such a catastrophe. Any new Soviet-U.S. crisis would confront decision makers on both sides with severe policy dilemmas and fateful choices. It is necessary for new leaders who will have to manage any new crisis to acquire an understanding of the kinds of policy dilemmas and difficult choices they will confront in that event.

The present study draws on past experience with crises to identify and analyze the challenging tasks of crisis management. Our aim is to contribute to the development of better *generic* knowledge about the requirements of crisis management and to illuminate the major obstacles and threats that are likely to be experienced in attempting to manage and terminate crises before they escalate to war. If generic knowledge about the phenomenon of crisis management is properly formulated, as we hope this study will succeed in doing, it should be applicable not only to U.S.-Soviet and East-West relations but to crises among other states in the international system as well. In the Addendum to this book we apply our analysis to the events that led to the Persian Gulf War.

NOTES

1. For a detailed discussion, see Graham T. Allison, "Primitive Rules of Prudence: Foundations of Peaceful Competition," in G. T. Allison and W. L. Ury with B. J. Allyn,

eds., *Windows of Opportunity: From Cold War to Peaceful Competition in U.S.-Soviet Relations* (Cambridge, MA: Ballinger, 1989), pp. 9–27. An important historical-analytical perspective is provided by John Lewis Gaddis, "The Long Peace: Elements of Stability in the Postwar International System," *International Security*, 10, 4 (Spring 1986).

2. For a comprehensive analysis of U.S.-Soviet cooperative security efforts since World War II see A. L. George, P. J. Farley, and A. Dallin, eds., *U.S.-Soviet Security Cooperation: Achievements, Failures, Lessons* (New York: Oxford University Press, 1988).

3. This weakness was noted, for example, by the then special assistant to the president for crisis management planning, Dr. Richard Beal, in a talk at a panel on crisis management at the annual meetings of the American Association for the Advancement of Science in New York, May 28, 1984. For a summary, see R. Jeffrey Smith, "Crisis Management Under Strain," *Science*, 31 (August 1984), pp. 907–909.

Informed accounts of innovations in crisis management technology and procedures during the Reagan presidency by other participants are provided by Ronald H. Hinckley, "National Security in the Information Age," *Washington Quarterly* 9, 2 (Spring 1986): 125–139; and Rodney B. McDaniel, "C³I: A National Security Council Perspective," Seminar on Command, Control, Communications, and Intelligence, Center for Information Policy Research, Harvard University (no date).

4. In Soviet writings in the late 1980s a new emphasis appeared on the danger that inadvertent war might occur as the result of the rapid escalation of a regional crisis, erroneous political decisions under severe time constraints during a crisis, and technical accidents that would have a magnified impact during tense crisis situations. For detailed discussion see Stephen M. Meyer, "Soviet Perspectives on the Paths to Nuclear War," in G. T. Allison, A. Carnesale, and J. S. Nye, Jr., eds., *Hawks, Doves, and Owls: An Agenda for Avoiding Nuclear War* (New York: Norton, 1985), pp. 167–205; Bruce J. Allyn, "Towards a Common Framework: Avoiding Inadvertent War and Crisis," in G. T. Allison et al., eds., *Windows of Opportunity*, pp. 185–219; and Jeffrey Legro, "Soviet Crisis Decision-Making and the Gorbachev Reforms," *Survival*, 31, 4 (July/August 1989), pp. 339–358.

CHAPTER 2

Plan of the Study

Alexander L. George

This study focuses on the possibility that a diplomatic crisis involving the United States and the Soviet Union either directly or indirectly might conceivably get out of hand and escalate to war. While the central objective of the study is to indicate how improvements in crisis management can help prevent such a disaster, its findings should also be applicable to a variety of crises involving other actors in the state system.

Specialists in both the United States and the Soviet Union have shared the view for many years that if war should occur between the superpowers, the most likely scenario for such a disaster would be a tense crisis that spins out of control rather than a premeditated attack launched out of the blue by one superpower against the other. Both President Reagan and General Secretary Gorbachev agreed at their very first summit in November 1985 that "a nuclear war cannot be won and must never be fought." In addition, the two leaders emphasized "the importance of preventing any war between them, whether nuclear or conventional," a statement of particular significance in that it implicitly recognizes the danger that any shooting war between the military forces of the two superpowers might escalate to nuclear war.

Quite clearly, avoidance of an unwanted, inadvertent war is of the highest priority for both superpowers. It is an objective that deserves the most thorough study so that adequate safeguards can be developed to prevent any new crisis from escalating to war.

ACCIDENTAL AND INADVERTENT WARS: DEFINITIONS, CAUSAL FACTORS, AND SCENARIOS

There is no substantial consensus in the literature on how to distinguish between different types of unwanted, unexpected wars. The terms "accidental" and "inadvertent" war are employed in different ways by different analysts; additional confusion is created by some writers' contention that this is not a meaningful distinction, by other analysts' preference for the term "unintentional" wars, and by still other specialists' argument that none of these terms has any real significance because all past wars reflected a decision to go to war.

7

Our own position can be summarized briefly. Definitions of a complex phenomenon, as in the present case, are often of limited value; they should not be
allowed to constrain open-ended empirical analysis of the phenomenon but should
be used flexibly as starting points to facilitate such analysis. Our research objective
after all is not to provide definitions that will command consensus but to identify
causal factors and sequences that lead to wars neither side wanted or expected. Two
types of unwanted war, we believe, can and should be distinguished for purposes
of analysis and policy making. These are "accidental war" and "inadvertent war."
First, let us note that what these two types of war have in common is that neither
is a premeditated war, as exemplified by the classical case of preventive war. In the
modern nuclear era, the preventive war option is associated with the hypothetical
possibility that one of the superpowers might plan and initiate an unprovoked
nuclear war, most likely in a peacetime environment in order to achieve surprise.
The objective of preventive war is to destroy or substantially weaken an opponent's
military capabilities and warmaking potential and thereby eliminate the opponent's
ability to threaten or compete in the international arena. Other types of preventive
war employing conventional arms and involving states other than the two superpowers are also possible. There are various motivations for preventive war.[1]

We make our distinction between accidental and inadvertent war as simple as
possible. Basically, the distinction is between a war that starts as a result of actions
not properly authorized either by central decision makers or their legitimately
predelegated command to those lower in the chain of command (accidental war)
and a war that *is* authorized during the course of a crisis, even though at the outset
of the crisis central decision makers did not want or expect a war (inadvertent war).

This simple distinction leaves open the possibility that an accidental war can
occur during the course of a crisis, though it might occur also in a noncrisis
environment. It also recognizes the possibility that accidents and unauthorized
actions of various kinds that take place during the course of a crisis can play a role
in the origins of an inadvertent war by adding to the momentum of events that
finally lead central decision makers to initiate war. These two additional possibilities
do not invalidate the basic distinction proposed here between accidental and
inadvertent war.

Since the possibility of accidental war is not the subject of the present study, we
will not discuss in any detail factors that might trigger this type of a war. One such
trigger that has received a great deal of attention would be an accidental or
unauthorized launch of strategic nuclear weapons. (The recipient of such an attack,
of course, must still decide whether to retaliate.) In addition, an accidental war
could conceivably occur when a wholly erroneous interpretation or significant
misinterpretation of tactical warning leads one side to assume that an opponent has
already launched a substantial nuclear strike, and this assumption, in turn, triggers
a decision to promptly launch a major nuclear retaliatory blow. Such an accidental
war scenario, it should be noted, differs from one type of inadvertent war that
occurs when one side initiates a preemptive war on the basis of an erroneous
strategic warning that the opponent has decided to attack and is making what
appear to be preparations to launch war in the very near future but has not yet set
the attack into motion. Strictly speaking, by definition, preemption is undertaken

in the latter case solely on the basis of erroneous strategic warning, before any tactical warning that the opponent's attack is already underway. In practice, of course, a preemptive war can be initiated on the basis of a combination of strategic warning and some partial but inconclusive tactical warning or on the basis of a mixture of equivocal strategic and tactical warnings.[2] And, of course, preemption may be resorted to on the basis of correct warning that the adversary is preparing to attack.

We do not want to leave the reader with the impression that there is only one type of inadvertent war—the scenario of preemptive war just noted—or that this is the only type of concern. In fact, as we shall see, there are many possible inadvertent war scenarios and many different contributing causes.

RESEARCH OBJECTIVES AND RESEARCH STRATEGY

The research objectives of this study are, quite simply, to add to the knowledge of how inadvertent wars can occur in order to understand better how to avoid them. To this end we shall employ a research strategy that focuses on two types of historical cases: crises involving the United States and the Soviet Union that threatened to result in war but that were successfully managed and terminated without war's occurrence, and crises between states other than the two superpowers that led to inadvertent war.

These historical cases, carefully interpreted, will provide relevant material for our study. Since there has been no instance of an inadvertent war (or for that matter any shooting war) between the Soviet Union and the United States, only inadvertent wars that developed between other states are available for study. Five historical cases of inadvertent war will be analyzed: three are taken from the post–World War II era (the war in Korea between the United States and the People's Republic of China, the Suez War of 1956, and the Arab-Israeli War of 1967); and two are drawn from earlier historical epochs (the Crimean War and World War I).

In each of these case studies, the investigator addresses two questions: (1) What were the critically important developments during the crisis that led to the war, and (2) why did these critical events occur? The answer to the first question provides an analytical description of the path to inadvertent war. The answer to the second question provides an explanation for the critical steps in the path to war.

We do not expect to find identical or even highly similar paths to inadvertent war in these five cases. There are different paths and different causal dynamics associated with inadvertent war. In fact, we share with other investigators the starting premise that inadvertent war can occur in several different ways. One can usefully distinguish different types of inadvertent war by the type of reasoning that leads to decisions to initiate such wars. Part Seven of this study will provide a typology of inadvertent wars and identify paths to such wars.

In addition to doing the job of the historian as best as we can in explaining how a particular crisis escalated to war, we use these specific case histories to develop *generic knowledge* about the phenomenology of inadvertent war—that is, how it develops under different conditions—and the causal dynamics of crisis escalation to inadvertent war. To move from specific historical explanations to generic knowledge requires the use of a general framework of variables that catches at least the most important concrete characteristics of each historical case.

In using historical case studies to develop generic knowledge, an investigator has to decide at what level of generality and abstraction to formulate variables that will comprise the framework. This is not an easy judgment to make. Too abstract a framework may result in generic knowledge that is so far removed from the realities of the phenomenon as experienced by decision makers that the findings may lack practical value for policy making. At the other extreme, purely descriptive studies of historical events that make no use at all of general variables are likely to result in lessons that are highly specific to each case and, in consequence, are likely to have policy relevance only for new cases that are similar to the historical case from which the lessons were derived. A general theoretical framework makes it possible to aggregate, cumulate, and differentiate the lessons of many cases.[3]

One of the analytical frameworks we will employ to develop generic knowledge about inadvertent war consists of a set of general crisis management principles (or "requirements") that we derived some years ago from examination of past crises. This framework, which can be regarded as a provisional theory of crisis management, will be outlined in Chapter 4.

The working assumption of the study is that an inadvertent war—regardless of the specifics of a crisis and the context in which it occurs—is more likely to be avoided if both sides adhere reasonably well to these general principles of crisis management. Conversely, failure to adhere to these principles may well result in a war (or the expansion of a war) that neither side wanted or expected. It is at the level of generality of these crisis management principles that we will develop generic knowledge of the phenomenology and causal dynamics of inadvertent war.

However, for several reasons, we must avoid too narrow a focus on the importance of adhering to general crisis management principles. Such general requirements must always be operationalized—that is, implemented by means of specific actions that are appropriate to the special configuration and development of the particular crisis at hand. This is a challenging task in any crisis and, as we shall see, the choices of strategy and tactics for managing a crisis are often a matter of sharp disagreement within a policy-making group. Then, too, we want to avoid explaining too much—either when crisis management succeeded or when it failed—exclusively in terms of whether decision makers adhered to general crisis management principles. Explanations at this level of analysis can be somewhat shallow or even misleading. We need to deepen and enrich explanations of crisis management outcomes by considering why and under what circumstances decision makers sometimes apply general principles effectively and fail to do so at other times. For this purpose we shall also make use of a broader theoretical framework suggested by Phil Williams during the course of our study, which emphasizes the importance of three additional variables: the strength of the incentives for crisis management in any particular case, the opportunities for managing that crisis, and the skills and capabilities for doing so demonstrated by the participants. This broader framework is described more fully in the Introduction to Part Two.

Empirical data for theory development can be provided not only through the study of historical experience but also by means of realistic games that are designed to simulate the crisis dynamics that may lead to inadvertent war. Crisis simulations are conducted on a classified basis in several different parts of the government. Unclassified games have been carried out by a number of research organizations, including the Rand Corporation in its Avoiding Nuclear War project.

We noted earlier that our research strategy also draws upon historical cases in which the two superpowers successfully managed and terminated a number of tense crises without plunging into war. Five such cases are included in our study: the Berlin Blockade Crisis of 1948–1949; the Cuban Missile Crisis in 1962; and the Arab-Israeli Wars of 1967, 1970, and 1973. A number of other crises in which the United States and the Soviets were directly or indirectly involved were not included in the present study in order to keep it from becoming unmanageable.

Cases of successful U.S.-Soviet crisis management are useful for our study in two ways. First, they provide a contrast to the five cases of inadvertent war. Contrasting cases of successful and unsuccessful crisis management should give us a better understanding of the relevance of the general principles of crisis management and the broader theoretical framework of incentives, opportunities, and skills. Second, since various threats to crisis management were indeed experienced in these five cases, analysis of these cases in which war was nonetheless avoided will be useful for the purpose of identifying severe difficulties that crisis management encountered in the past that may arise again in future crises.

Identification and analysis of such threats and obstacles to effective crisis management are important parts of the generic knowledge that our study attempts to develop. Part Seven of the study will discuss these generic problems of crisis management. Awareness and anticipation of such possible threats can improve contingency planning and heighten readiness to deal with the threats.

In addition to crises in which Moscow and Washington confronted each other, we have included one other case—the Sino-Soviet border clash of 1969. Study of this case enables us to enrich and extend our observations regarding challenges to crisis management and how they were dealt with by nuclear powers. To anticipate some of our findings, this case indicates that Moscow and Beijing displayed the same kind of adherence to crisis management principles when confronting each other as was the case when they confronted the United States in other crises. Analysis of the Sino-Soviet crisis of 1969, therefore, gives added support for the relevance of our provisional crisis management theory.

The study will also analyze special crisis management problems that arise in regional conflicts, such as in the Arab-Israeli Wars of 1967, 1970, and 1973, when the two superpowers back local actors that are on the verge of war or are already engaged in warfare. Regional conflicts of this kind create major policy dilemmas for Moscow and Washington. To what extent should a superpower provide its regional ally with military weapons, encourage or condone its initiation of war, and pressure it to accept a ceasefire or to make concessions? In other words, how can a superpower support its ally in such regional conflicts without allowing its regional ally to drag it into a war with the rival superpower that is backing the other regional actor? Quite clearly, while the general principles of crisis management are also relevant for such regional conflicts, they may be less salient insofar as the regional actors directly involved are less interested in avoiding war than are their superpower patrons. When this is the case, the superpowers encounter additional difficulties in trying to make crisis management work.

Finally, while we believe that our theoretical framework of crisis management is relevant and can be useful, we do not believe that crisis management is easy or that inadvertent wars could be easily avoided if only policy makers understood crisis management principles and implemented them skillfully. Indeed, our case studies will illustrate in various ways why crisis management is often difficult and why emphasis should be placed on crisis avoidance and crisis prevention.

Before outlining our provisional theory of crisis management in Chapter 4, we shall discuss in the next chapter the tension often experienced in crises of this kind between "military logic" and the often quite different imperatives of diplomatic efforts to achieve crisis management objectives. An understanding of the tension between these two competing "logics" clarifies some of the policy dilemmas experienced in crisis management that are a central focus of the study.

NOTES

1. For an analytical discussion see Jack S. Levy, "Declining Power and the Preventive Motivation for War," *World Politics* 40 (October 1987): 82–197. For a comprehensive review and assessment of various theories regarding the causes of war, see the same author's "The Causes of War: A Review of Theories and Evidence," in Philip E. Tetlock, et al., eds., *Behavior, Society, and Nuclear War*, Vol. I (New York: Oxford University Press, 1989), pp. 209–333.

2. For additional discussion of the distinction between inadvertent and accidental war, and of scenarios and variables associated with accidental war, see for example Michael D. Intriligator and Dagobert L. Brito, "Accidental Nuclear War: An Important Issue for Arms Control," and Alexander L. George and Kurt Gottfried, "Workshop Summary and Discussion," both in *Accidental Nuclear War*, Proceedings of the Eighteenth Pugwash Workshop on Nuclear Forces (Toronto: Science for Peace/Samuel Stevens, 1990), pp. 6–30, 31–56. A concise discussion of accidental war and various hypothetical scenarios is presented by Paul Bracken in Chapter 2, "Accidental Nuclear War," in Graham T. Allison, Albert Carnesale, and Joseph S. Nye, Jr., eds., *Hawks, Doves, and Owls* (New York: Norton, 1985); pp. 25–53.

3. For general discussion of the challenging task of utilizing historical cases for theory development, see Alexander L. George, "Case Studies and Theory Development: The Method of Structured, Focused Comparison," in Paul G. Lauren, ed., *Diplomatic History: New Approaches* (New York: Free Press, 1979); also, "Case Studies and Theories of Organizational Decisionmaking," with Timothy J. McKeown, in *Advances in Information Processing in Organizations*, Vol. 2 (Greenwich, CT: JAI Press, 1985).

CHAPTER 3

The Tension Between "Military Logic" and Requirements of Diplomacy in Crisis Management

Alexander L. George

The proposition that force is an instrument of diplomacy is part of the conventional wisdom of statecraft. Moreover, historical experience supports the view that in many—though certainly not all—conflicts of interest between states, efforts that rely solely on diplomacy may prove ineffectual. However, this observation leaves unanswered a central and difficult question in the theory and practice of statecraft: How, and under what conditions, can military force be used most effectively in support of diplomatic efforts to achieve a given objective? Any responsible answer to this question must take into account the fact that attempts to use force as an instrument of diplomacy are often not only ineffective but can seriously aggravate conflicts of interest or even trigger unwanted wars that might otherwise have been avoided.

In addressing these questions, this study focuses on diplomatic confrontations between militarily powerful adversaries in which both sides wish to advance or protect their interests without having to initiate combat or inadvertently provoke it; that is, they wish to manage and terminate the crisis as acceptably as possible without triggering escalation to warfare. In crises of this kind, policy makers withhold authorization of combat missions by their military forces, and they focus instead on determining which movements and alerts of military forces are necessary or desirable and how they can be coordinated with diplomatic moves.

NONCOMBAT MILITARY OPTIONS FOR CRISIS MANAGEMENT

What, then, are the various noncombat actions that political leaders can authorize their military forces to take in crises of this kind? We can identify various noncombat actions that have one or another of the following purposes:

1. Reduce the vulnerability of theater and strategic forces

2. Increase readiness of forces for defensive and offensive combat operations if war occurs
3. Use forces in appropriate, nonprovocative ways to demonstrate resolution in support of crisis objectives
4. Use forces to signal limited intentions and to reassure opponent[1]
5. Use forces in noncombat missions to aid in preventing damage to one's interests without engaging in or threatening escalation
6. Use forces to deter adversary from escalating the crisis or initiating combat
7. Use forces to neutralize coercive threats by adversary
8. Use forces to exert coercive bargaining pressure on adversary

While military leaders are prepared to use their forces in any of these ways in a crisis, the first two—reducing the vulnerability and increasing the readiness of forces—will generally have particular relevance for professional military officers. We must remember that whenever a war-threatening crisis erupts, military leaders regard it as their most urgent task and highest priority to get ready to fight if war comes. Such readiness requires more than merely reducing the vulnerability of those forces that might become targets if the adversary initiates war or increasing the readiness of forces for defensive operations. In addition, military doctrine and "military logic" provide powerful arguments—such as the importance of seizing the initiative—for increasing the readiness of one's forces for offensive operations as well.

Although the logic of these imperatives is understood and appreciated by political decision makers, they may be quite unwilling to authorize some military alerts and readiness measures. Their reluctance to do so may stem from a concern (one, in fact, that military leaders may share) over the possibility that military alerts and movements required to reduce the vulnerability and improve the readiness of one side's forces may be perceived by its adversary as preparations to initiate hostilities or as efforts to bring coercive pressure to bear in crisis bargaining; as a result, the adversary may feel obliged to authorize alerts and movements of its own forces, which, in turn, trigger additional moves by the other side. Indeed, the possibility of a vicious cycle of interacting alerts became a matter of acute concern to specialists in both the United States and the Soviet Union beginning approximately a decade ago. Studies have been made and much has been written in both countries about the possible destabilizing and escalatory consequences of the interaction of military alert measures that the superpowers might feel obliged to take in a crisis.[2] Prudence may indeed require each side to take certain measures to reduce the vulnerability and increase the readiness of its military forces. However, some alerting measures of this kind may not be free from ambiguity as to one's intentions, and they may be perceived by the other side as threatening.

What is at work here is a particularly acute and dangerous version of the well-known "security dilemma" in international relations—namely, the perverse phenomenon whereby defensive measures one side undertakes to enhance its own security may be judged by the other side to have possible offensive purposes that endanger *its* security and hence require it to take additional defensive measures of its own. In other words, an initial misperception of the opponent's motives for alerting its military forces can trigger an action-reaction cycle that can result in a breakdown of mutual efforts to manage the crisis.

A particularly dangerous possibility of this type was discussed by Paul Bracken. He noted that the increased complexity of the U.S. command-and-control system, with its procedural checks and balances, does indeed make the likelihood of accidental nuclear war very low in peacetime. However, the likelihood of nuclear war increases significantly as a result of alerting procedures in crisis situations because (1) in both the United States and the Soviet Union, warning systems have been integrated and tightly coupled with alerts of nuclear forces, and (2) because the warning-alert systems of the superpowers have tended to become interlocked.[3]

Similarly, John Steinbruner has called attention to the danger that arises from the fact that one side may regard its opponent's command system as the target of greatest opportunity in the event of war.[4] Other analysts as well have expressed concern that circumstances of this kind could create unbearable pressure on political leaders to take preemptive military action before the adversary decides to do so.[5]

THE REQUIREMENT FOR PRESIDENTIAL CONTROL AND "USABLE" MILITARY OPTIONS

It has long been recognized that a fundamental tension exists between political-diplomatic and military considerations in efforts to manage certain kinds of crises and, similarly, in efforts to keep limited conflicts from escalating.[6] This problem was forced upon the consciousness of U.S. leaders during the course of the Korean War and quickly led them to recognize the necessity for the president to exert control over and impose some constraints on both the strategy and, often, the tactical operations of a theater commander. Prior to that time, the traditional practice had been to give a theater commander considerable authority to determine the most appropriate strategy and tactics for achieving the objectives assigned to him with the forces placed at his disposal. Quite understandably, theater commanders relied on basic military doctrine and the criterion of military efficiency in choosing their strategy and tactics.

The Korean War taught not only President Truman but all succeeding administrations that a president's responsibility does not stop with establishing political objectives and allocating resources to be employed in a conflict; he must also maintain firm control over the level of costs and risks that is acceptable in pursuing those objectives. He must do so when the strategy and tactics preferred by a theater commander increase the likelihood of escalation to levels of warfare that central decision makers in Washington wish to avoid. For this reason, the president must be willing to intervene on a timely basis in the determination of military plans and in aspects of their implementation. To the extent that presidents choose to do so, however, such intervention brings into play the possibility of serious tension between military logic and the often competing requirements of diplomacy and foreign policy.

We must recognize that presidential intervention in military strategy and tactics, however well-intentioned, raises the danger of micromanagement of crises and adds to the dilemmas of crisis management. Military professionals, civilian strategists, and other civilians have all expressed grave concern that micromanagement can contribute to ineffectual military performance that prolongs warfare and that may also prevent a successful outcome.

Since the Korean War, it has often been said that these problems can be minimized by achieving better integration of political and military considerations in force planning, as well as in contingency plans for use of force. The need for better integration was recognized and explicitly emphasized in President Kennedy's doctrine of flexible, controlled response. Indeed, important general requirements for integrating political and military factors for purposes of crisis management were explicitly suggested in Kennedy's Special Message on the Defense Budget, submitted to Congress on March 28, 1961. He emphasized that response to attacks against any part of the free world would have to be "suitable, selective" as well as "swift and effective." Kennedy proceeded to identify general guidelines for the design and use of military forces: "Our weapons systems must be *usable* in a manner permitting *deliberation* and *discrimination* as to *timing, scope and targets* in *response to civilian authority*" (emphasis added).

The doctrine of flexible, controlled response asserted the need for a greater variety of force options that would enable the United States to use *limited force* and credible threats of force to achieve a variety of *limited objectives* in pursuing its foreign policy. Clearly implied was the distinction between what may be called "gross capabilities" and "usable options" that had emerged from the critique of massive retaliation. A power such as the United States has ample military forces for attacking and destroying any number and variety of targets. Gross military capabilities of this character, however, do not necessarily provide a president with options he will be willing to draw upon in a diplomatic crisis or low-level military conflict. Rather, gross military capabilities provide only the ingredients from which planners must develop usable options—that is, options a president will be willing to use, or threaten to use, only if they promise to accomplish his whole purpose, diplomatic as well as military, in the way he thinks appropriate and necessary. As the Cuban Missile Crisis was to demonstrate, military options—such as the proposed air strike against missile sites—that do not meet these complex criteria are likely to be less acceptable to a president, particularly at the critical opening stages of diplomatic crises that are laden with dangerous escalation potential.

THE NEED FOR POLITICAL-MILITARY STRATEGY IN CRISIS MANAGEMENT

Thus, the Kennedy administration attempted to develop a more complex concept of strategy that would enable planners to generate a variety of credible, appropriate threats and available military options to be used, if necessary, in a controlled, discriminating manner in order to achieve limited foreign policy goals. This objective in turn required the development of a somewhat novel concept of strategy, one that combined and integrated both diplomatic and military considerations.

A *political-military strategy* of this kind differs in important respects from *conventional military strategy*. Conventional military strategy focuses upon the task of making the most efficient use of available military forces to achieve assigned military objectives. The criterion of efficiency, so defined, gives military logic its special character and focus. In contrast, diplomacy seeks to achieve political objectives, and it works with a concept of strategy that is appreciably broader and more complex than conventional military strategy. In the practice of diplomacy, strategy consists of utilizing a variety of resources, not just military forces, in attempting to get an opponent to do something he would not otherwise do. Diplomatic strategy relies upon some mix and sequencing of persuasion, coercive threats or actions, and accommodative offers and concessions. In short, while diplomacy may make use of threats of force and may even employ limited force, it seeks to make force a flexible, refined psychological instrument of policy instead of employing force as a blunt, crude instrument.

Nowhere can this be seen more clearly than when policy makers employ *coercive diplomacy* as their strategy for managing a crisis created by an adversary's effort to change a status quo situation in his own favor. Faced with the need to press the adversary to stop or to undo his provocation, the policy makers use coercive diplomacy to persuade him to acquiesce instead of bludgeoning him into doing so. Coercive diplomatic strategy focuses upon the task of affecting the opponent's will and his utility calculations rather than negating his military capabilities. Thus, coercive diplomacy has an essentially *signalling, bargaining, negotiating* character— a feature that is absent or much diminished in traditional military strategy—which the policy maker attempts to build into the conceptualization and conduct of military operations. In coercive diplomacy the use of military force to inflict damage may be deferred and merely threatened, or it may be employed in modest increments to signal resolution and to intimidate. Moreover, and again unlike their use in traditional military strategy, force and threats of force may become part of a carrot and stick approach to influencing the opponent's behavior. In some cases the carrot offered may be of equal or even greater significance than the stick that is threatened.

It is not surprising that in many situations a country's leaders prefer to employ diplomacy rather than a purely military approach for resolving disputes created by an adversary's encroachment. Relying upon a combination of persuasion, accommodation, and coercion, diplomatic strategy offers the possibility of achieving one's objectives more economically than does traditional military strategy. But herein also lies a danger: Coercive diplomacy becomes a beguiling strategy, one with risks and limitations that are not always appreciated and properly weighed by policy makers. For in fact, as we shall indicate later in this study, coercive diplomacy is often quite difficult to implement successfully, whether because the logic of diplomacy is not easily reconciled with the logic and requirements of military strategy or because the conditions for making successful use of coercive diplomacy simply do not exist in a particular situation.

THE IMPORTANCE OF RULES OF ENGAGEMENT[7]

The military component of crisis management strategy will vary from case to case. Some aspects of it incorporate standard practices governing the management of combat forces and other aspects are tailored to the peculiarities of the particular crisis situation.

In developing contingency plans for dealing with possible crises, military planners formulate provisional standing orders for the forces that may be employed. Orders of this kind consist of (1) actions that can be taken under specified circumstances at the discretion of different levels of command unless negated by countermanding orders from higher command or political authorities ("command by negation"), and (2) actions that can be taken by military units only if expressly authorized by higher command or by political authorities at some point in the development of the crisis ("positive command"). Together, actions controlled via command by negation and positive command constitute the rules of engagement under which military forces operate in a crisis.

It is important to recognize that the ability of top-level political authorities to maintain control over the moves and actions of military forces is made difficult because of the exceedingly large number of often complex standing orders that come into effect at the onset of a crisis and as it intensifies. It is not easy for top-level political authorities to have full and timely knowledge of the multitude of existing standing orders. As a result, they may fail to coordinate some critically important standing orders with their overall crisis management strategy. Similarly, lacking adequate sophistication and experience in military matters, political authorities may fail to understand the military rationale for some standing orders or may not be aware of the possible harmful consequences of altering these orders ostensibly for the purpose of managing the crisis—in other words, the danger of micromanagement to which we alluded earlier.

This problem is compounded by the fact that important changes in authorized rules of engagement may automatically go into effect as higher levels of alert are declared by the national political authority. These alert-induced changes in rules of engagement are worked out in peacetime with general crisis requirements in mind; as a result, they may not prove to be sufficiently sensitive to the special characteristics and requirements of a particular crisis. Accordingly, some elements of preprogrammed rules of engagement triggered by successively higher alerts may be dysfunctional for the crisis at hand and, therefore, be in need of timely alteration. But this requires that top-level political and national command authorities have at their disposal (1) full data on existing and programmed rules of engagement, and (2) specialized staff officers capable of quickly identifying appropriate modifications of rules of engagement in order to better meet crisis management requirements.

Moreover, since crises often develop in unexpected ways, it may be difficult for central decision makers to quickly reconsider and revise standing orders; as a result, synchronization of political-diplomatic and military components of strategy may suffer. Citing several possible examples of lack of coordination and synchronization of military actions with overall crisis management imperatives during the Cuban Missile Crisis, John Steinbruner draws an important lesson:

> Though there is reason to be concerned about the implications of these incidents, they cannot be explained away simply as unusual mistakes or aberrant behavior on the part of a few individuals. *They reflect rather the sort of thing that must be expected to happen when high crisis strikes the very complicated, inevitably decentralized, very large organizations that constitute modern strategic forces.*

Once military command channels perceive that actual combat may be in prospect there are a large number of organizational preparations which must be made. *It is not possible for the President or any other single individual to control or even be informed of all aspects of this activity.* In order for the complex organizational system to work at all a great deal of authority to make preparations necessarily resides at low levels of the command structure. *This very basic fact unfortunately provides ample means for the events of a crisis to exceed the control of central political authorities and the decisions they made.*[8]

Information on other crises provides numerous other examples, sometimes of lesser potential significance, of the difficulty central decision makers experience in attempting to infuse political-diplomatic desiderata into the management of military forces. President Johnson's tight control over bombing targets during the Vietnam War led to considerable criticism by military leaders of "overcontrol and overmanagement" of tactical operations. General Lucias Clay's assertive actions in the tense Berlin Blockade Crisis of 1961 were regarded by some in Washington as provocative and capable of triggering escalation, and they led to reinforcement of constraints on his discretion. "It was because of such problems," Richard Betts notes, "that the McNamara regime in the Pentagon put so much emphasis on preventing subordinate links in the chain of command from taking initiatives that might have dangerous political ramifications."

Earlier, in the Lebanon crisis of 1958, the U.S. ambassador, Robert McClintock, was repeatedly frustrated in his efforts to orchestrate the deployment and use of U.S. forces with what he regarded to be the political requirements of the situation. As Betts notes, in this crisis military authorities had the advantage. What the ambassador wanted was inconsistent with standing orders through the military chain of command. In circumstances of this kind, "force and diplomacy can become disjoined, and implementation can distort policy." At the same time, it is understandable, as Betts further observes, that "[m]ilitary officers are reluctant to be placed in positions where they are answerable to people outside their normal chain of command because this reduces the clarity of their responsibility."[9]

It is often difficult for political authorities to decide the merits of the case when military leaders assert that "tactical necessity" requires rules of engagement that allow them discretion in employment of military options—that is, they argue for command through negation rather than positive command. Indeed, such decisions often entail difficult trade-off questions and genuine policy dilemmas that cannot be easily resolved. During the Quemoy-Matsu Crisis of 1958, as Betts notes, Eisenhower was repeatedly faced with pressures of this kind. Later, in his memoirs, Eisenhower complained, "I was continually pressured—almost hounded—by Chiang on one side and by our own military on the other requesting delegation of authority for immediate action to United States commanders on the spot in case of attack on Formosa or the offshore island. . . . I insisted that I would assess developments as they occurred."[10]

This discussion of the tension that often exists between military and diplomatic considerations should serve to make more comprehensible some of the "requirements" for crisis management discussed in the next chapter, requirements that attempt to reduce such tensions and to achieve some degree of integration of the political and military dimensions of crisis management.

NOTES

1. Indeed, it should not be forgotten that military forces can be used to give *reassuring signals* to an adversary during a crisis.

The ability to signal limited intentions via military measures may be particularly important when, as is often the case, a crisis is accompanied by a great deal of "noise" in verbal communications and other warning indicators. Paul Bracken cites several examples of efforts by political leaders in an acute crisis to "dampen the internal and mutual dynamics" of a possibly "overstimulated warning and intelligence system(s)." Thus, "during the Soviet invasion of Czechoslovakia in 1968, NATO cancelled routine reconnaissance flights over West Germany to avoid giving the Soviets the impression NATO was increasing its military activities." During the Cuban missile crisis, "President Kennedy reportedly ordered the fuses and warheads removed from American *Jupiter* missiles in Turkey to forestall any sort of accident in the tense environment." And "during the Soviet-inspired crackdown in Poland in 1981, NATO cut back its intelligence collection efforts in order not to provoke Soviet counteractions." Bracken, *The Command and Control of Nuclear Forces* (New Haven: Yale University Press, 1983), p. 72.

McGeorge Bundy questions the report that President Kennedy ordered the fuses and warheads removed from the Jupiter missiles in Turkey. [*Danger and Survival* (New York: Random House, 1988), fn. 80, pp. 689–90.] Scott Sagan has called my attention to another example of a reassuring signal; during the Cuban missile crisis General Lauris Norstad decided not to place NATO and EUCOM on DefCon3 alert and advised component commanders to avoid taking actions that could be considered provocative.

2. See, for example, Richard K. Betts, *Nuclear Blackmail and Nuclear Balance* (Washington, D.C.: Brookings Institution, 1987); Paul Bracken, *Command and Control of Nuclear Forces;* Bruce G. Blair, *Strategic Command and Control: Redefining the Nuclear Threat* (Washington, D.C.: Brookings Institution, 1985); Ashton B. Carter, John D. Steinbruner, and Charles A. Zraket, eds., *Managing Nuclear Operations* (Washington, D.C.: Brookings Institution, 1987); Kurt Gottfried and Bruce G. Blair, eds., *Crisis Stability and Nuclear War* (New York: Oxford University Press, 1988); Robert Jervis, *The Meaning of the Nuclear Revolution* (Ithaca: Cornell University Press, 1989); Richard Ned Lebow, *Nuclear Crisis Management: A Dangerous Illusion* (Ithaca: Cornell University Press, 1987).

3. In consequence, Bracken notes, "A threatening Soviet military action or alert can be detected almost immediately by American warning and intelligence systems and conveyed to force commanders. *The detected action may not have a clear meaning, but because of its possible consequences protective measures must be taken against it.* The action-reaction process does not necessarily stop after only two moves, . . . the overall effect of both Soviet and American actions might be to aggravate the crisis, forcing alert levels to ratchet upward worldwide. Although each side might well believe it was taking necessary precautionary moves, the other side might see a precaution as a threat. . . . Few people would disagree that *operating nuclear forces at such high levels of alert . . . could easily tip over into preemptive attacks and all-out war.* Each nation might not want war but might feel driven to hit first rather than second." Bracken, *Command and Control of Nuclear Forces*, pp. 59–60, 64–65 (emphasis added).

4. In this circumstance "both nuclear establishments . . . are subject to potentially fatal stress under crisis conditions. . . . If war should ever appear unavoidable, military commanders on both sides charged with executing their assigned missions would inevitably seek authority to initiate attack whatever prior security policy may have been. . . . The pressures on political

leaders at that point would be extreme. . . ." John Steinbruner, "Launch Under Attack," *Scientific American*, January 1984, p. 47.

5. See the sources cited in note 2.

6. The next few pages draw on chapter 1, "The Development of Doctrine and Strategy," in A. L. George, D. K. Hall, and W. E. Simons, eds., *The Limits of Coercive Diplomacy* (Boston: Little, Brown, 1971); and A. L. George, "Crisis Management: The Interaction of Political and Military Considerations," *Survival*, 26, 5 (September/October 1984), pp. 223–234.

7. For a fuller discussion see Chapter 19 by Scott Sagan.

8. John Steinbruner, "An Assessment of Nuclear Crises," in Franklin Griffiths and John C. Polanyi, eds., *The Dangers of Nuclear War* (Toronto: University of Toronto Press, 1980), pp. 39–40 (emphasis added).

9. For a detailed discussion, see Joseph F. Bouchard, "Use of Naval Force in Crises: A Theory of Stratified Crisis Interaction," Ph.D. dissertation, Department of Political Science, Stanford University, September 1988.

10. Richard K. Betts, *Soldiers, Statesmen, and Cold War Crises* (Cambridge, MA: Harvard University Press, 1977), pp. 146, 149, and 150.

CHAPTER 4

A Provisional Theory
of Crisis Management

Alexander L. George

Drawing upon earlier research on past crises and discussion with persons who have acquired experience in crisis management, I have formulated a theory of crisis management that served as the starting point for the present study.[1] This chapter begins with a discussion of the basic paradox and policy dilemma of crisis management and then outlines political and operational requirements to which policy makers must be sensitive in deciding how to deal with a war-threatening crisis.

THE BASIC PARADOX AND POLICY DILEMMA
OF CRISIS MANAGEMENT

Confrontations between adversaries can be easily managed and terminated—indeed, avoided altogether—if either side is willing to back away from a confrontation and accept damage to its interests. This is the basic paradox of crisis management: There need be no crisis if only one side backs down. Indeed, in many situations it requires a deliberate policy decision to transform a conflict of interest between two states into a crisis. President Truman, for example, was urged by important advisers not to take action to oppose the Soviet blockade of ground access to West Berlin in 1948 on the grounds that it would be highly disadvantageous for the United States to get involved in military operations to defend an isolated outpost lying 100 km inside East Germany. Secretary of Defense Robert McNamara reportedly remarked shortly after the discovery of Soviet missiles in Cuba that "a missile is a missile" whether placed in Cuba or the Soviet Union, implying that since the strategic balance was not thereby significantly altered, perhaps the United States should not respond to the missile deployment in ways that would create a dangerous crisis.[2] Neither Truman nor Kennedy accepted advice that would have avoided converting the opponent's action into a crisis. Similarly, in October 1973, Nixon and Kissinger decided that they could not ignore Brezhnev's threat of unilateral intervention in the Middle East War, coupled as it was with knowledge that Soviet airborne forces had been placed on alert; in response they ordered an alert of U.S. strategic forces, thereby moving the two superpowers into a possibly dangerous confrontation. In the summer of 1979, as the result of an erratic decision-making process, the Carter administration drifted into a minicrisis over the "discovery" of a Soviet combat brigade in Cuba, a crisis from which it later had to retreat.[3]

As these examples illustrate, it is only because neither side is willing to back down initially that a perceived conflict of interests results in a crisis. Some crises arise in ways that leave one side no choice but to oppose its adversary; other crises emerge only because one side decides to accept a challenge from the other and to oppose it. Still other crises, as will be noted in Chapter 16, are deliberately initiated by one side in an effort to bring about a favorable change in the status quo.

Once a crisis is set into motion, each side feels impelled to do what is needed to protect or advance its most important interests; at the same time, however, it recognizes that it must avoid utilizing options and actions for this purpose that could trigger unwanted escalation of the crisis. This is the *policy dilemma* of crisis management.

The tension between these two objectives—protection of one's interests and avoidance of measures that could trigger undesired escalation—creates a dilemma that is the basic challenge policy makers engaged in crisis management must try to resolve. Some months after the Cuban Missile Crisis, Secretary of Defense McNamara observed in testimony before a congressional committee, "Today there is no longer any such thing as strategy; there is only crisis management."[4] In this statement, McNamara exaggerated and oversimplified the "lesson" of the missile crisis in order to make the point that to avoid war in crises of this kind, policy makers must be prepared to give priority to the requirements for prudent crisis management at the expense of some of the standard requirements of conventional military strategy.

The sharp antithesis between strategy and crisis management in McNamara's statement, however, is misleading. For, in fact, strategy is a necessary ingredient in crisis management. It is only by developing a *political-military strategy* appropriate for the situation at hand that policy makers can hope to deal effectively with the policy dilemma that confronts them in such crises. A variety of crisis management strategies—both offensive and defensive—will be identified and discussed in Chapter 16.

THE POLITICAL AND OPERATIONAL REQUIREMENTS OF CRISIS MANAGEMENT

It is useful to distinguish between political and operational requirements to which policy makers must be sensitive in managing a war-threatening crisis. The term "requirements" is not employed here in the strict sense of *necessary* conditions for successful crisis management. Rather, the term is used to refer to general principles and desiderata that are relevant for effective management of such confrontations— that is, requirements that, if met, are likely to facilitate achievement of one's objectives in a crisis without unwanted escalation. Not all of these requirements are equally important in any given crisis, and the importance of a given type of requirement is likely to vary in different crises. One reason for this is that crisis management tends to be highly context-dependent. By this I mean that the prospects for and outcomes of crisis management are subject to the interplay of many variables that are likely to present themselves in somewhat different configurations in different confrontations. Moreover, the outcomes of crises—whether they end in peace or in warfare—are determined not only by the fidelity, or lack thereof, with which one side adheres to these requirements but by the behavior of the other side as well and, in the last analysis, by the interaction between the two sides. In other words, a certain amount of mutual restraint and cooperation between the two sides may be necessary for effective crisis management. In any case, the prior questions, as noted in Chapter 2, concern the strength of the actors' incentives for avoiding war, the opportunities available to them for crisis management, and the level of skill they bring to bear in efforts to manage crises.

Because of these and other variables, one cannot expect to develop a robust theory of crisis management, one that encompasses knowledge of all possible patterns of behavior and interaction and therefore enables us to generate confident predictions as to whether crisis management will succeed or fail in any particular situation or to offer advice that will guarantee success. As international relations theorists generally recognize, outcomes of strategic interaction between states tend to be indeterminate and not easily predictable. The outcomes of crises are not an exception in this respect.

Nonetheless, it is possible to articulate a more modest theory that codifies experience gained in past efforts at crisis management. Such a theory should be useful to policy makers as a kind of check-list of general principles and "requirements" to weigh and take into account in dealing with new confrontations. The theory can be useful to policy makers in other ways as well. It articulates the types of policy dilemmas they may experience and the difficult choices they will be called upon to make. It highlights the tension to be expected between military logic and political-diplomatic logic when deciding how to deal with crises. It identifies the major threats to one's ability to avoid unwanted escalation and alerts policy makers to the sources of misperception and miscalculation of the actions and intentions of the adversary.

In brief, the type of crisis management theory to be developed in this study is offered as an aid to the judgment that policy makers must inevitably exercise in diagnosing and dealing with crisis situations; it is not a recipe book that can substitute for such judgment.

The two *political* requirements for crisis management are limitation of objectives pursued in the crisis, and limitation of means employed on behalf of those objectives. The possibility of terminating diplomatic confrontations without war may depend on whether one or both sides have carefully limited their crisis objectives. Why is this important? The more ambitious the aims pursued at the expense of the adversary, the more strongly motivated the adversary will be to resist. The danger of escalation is heightened if both sides pursue ambitious objectives, for that will tend to make the conflict of interests appear to be irreconcilable or, certainly, more difficult to resolve without escalation of the crisis to war.

Even prudent limitation of objectives, however, may not suffice. In addition, careful limitation of the means employed on behalf of those objectives may also be necessary. In the Cuban Missile Crisis, as we shall see, President Kennedy limited both his objective—confining it to the removal of the missiles and rejecting

advice that he aim at removal of Castro or removal of Soviet influence in Cuba—
and also the means he employed to secure removal of the missiles—a blockade
rather than air strikes against the missile sites or an invasion of Cuba. Kennedy
acted as he did in order to maintain control over the danger of escalation to war
and to give diplomacy an opportunity to resolve the crisis peacefully. In contrast,
as Allen Whiting's case study makes clear, after the Chinese had intervened with
substantial forces in Korea, President Truman did not see fit either to reduce the
war objectives the United States had been pursuing, which were to eliminate the
communist North Korean government and to unify the two Koreas by force, or to
limit the means for achieving that ambitious objective—the resumption of General
MacArthur's march to the Yalu even after substantial Chinese forces had entered
North Korea and engaged in combat with U.S. and South Korean forces.

Limitation of objectives and means, however, will not ensure control over the
danger of unwanted escalation. In addition, a number of operational requirements
for crisis management may have to be met by the two sides. These operational
requirements arise from the necessity for policy makers to integrate as best they
can the military and diplomatic measures they employ in order to deal with the
crisis. These requirements attempt to deal with the tension that often exists between
military logic and diplomatic logic, which was discussed in the preceding chapter.

Seven operational principles or "requirements" have been identified from earlier
studies of some past crises.

1. Each side's political authorities must maintain informed control of some kind
   over military options—alerts, deployments, and low-level actions, as well as
   the selection and timing of military movements.
2. The tempo and momentum of military movements may have to be deliberately
   slowed down and pauses created to provide enough time for the two sides
   to exchange diplomatic signals and communications and to give each side
   adequate time to assess the situation, make decisions, and respond to proposals.
3. Movements of military forces must be carefully coordinated with diplomatic
   actions as part of an integrated strategy for terminating the crisis acceptably
   without war or escalation to higher levels of violence.
4. Movements of military forces and threats of force intended to signal resolve
   must be consistent with limited diplomatic objectives—that is, "noise" must
   be avoided or minimized.
5. Military moves and threats should be avoided that give the opponent the
   impression that one is about to resort to large-scale warfare, thereby forcing
   him to consider preemption.
6. Diplomatic-military options should be chosen that signal, or are consistent
   with, a desire to negotiate a way out of the crisis rather than to seek a
   military solution.
7. Diplomatic proposals and military moves should be selected that leave the
   opponent a way out of the crisis that is compatible with his fundamental
   interests.

The relative importance of these operational requirements varies in different crises, as does the difficulty of incorporating them into a strategy for coping with the crisis.

Another limitation of the provisional theory outlined here arises from the fact that it is a two-actor model. Crisis management encounters additional difficulties when more than two actors are involved in a crisis. This is the case when, as in the Middle East, the United States and the Soviet Union support different regional actors whose conflict is at the core of the crisis. Multiple actors were involved in quite a few of the other crises that are examined in Parts Two, Three, and Four. The analyses of these multi-actor crises will highlight the special difficulties of meeting the political and operational requirements of crisis management.

Efforts to impose crisis management requirements on military forces often exacerbate the latent, built-in tension between competing diplomatic and military considerations. Indeed, crisis management strategy requires novel concepts of military planning, operations, and control of forces that strain the experience, imagination, and patience of military professionals and civilians alike.

Of course, the requirements for crisis management listed here provide only general guidelines for policy planners and decision makers. The challenging task they face in any confrontation is to devise and employ a version of crisis management strategy and tactics that takes these requirements into account in ways tailored to the special configuration of that crisis. Since crises differ substantially in structure and dynamics, in the importance of what is at stake for the two sides, in the larger diplomatic-military context, in the level of risks and opportunities posed for each side, and in the domestic and international constraints operating on the policy makers involved, different variants of strategies for managing crises need to be improvised for each case. These strategies will be discussed in Chapter 16.

The political and operational requirements identified comprise my provisional theory of crisis management. It will be the framework employed in the historical case studies reported in this volume. The authors of the case studies have been asked to judge how useful the provisional theory is for their analyses and to make whatever additions or modifications to the framework are needed to describe and explain the crisis in question. Thus, while the case studies will be informed and sensitized by the provisional theory, they should also serve to assess, refine, or alter that theory. In other words, my provisional theory is only a starting point for developing the analysis of crisis management. Part Seven will amplify and refine the theory, drawing on the findings of the study.

NOTES

1. This was reported in several previous publications; see particularly Alexander L. George, "Crisis Management: The Interaction of Political and Military Considerations," *Survival* (September/October, 1984). Important contributions to developing a theoretical framework of crisis management have been made by a number of other scholars, including Coral Bell, Michael Brecher, Dan Caldwell, Daniel Frei, Charles Hermann, Ole Holsti, Irving Janis, Richard Ned Lebow, Richard Smoke, and Phil Williams.

2. I am indebted to Scott Sagan for calling my attention to the possibility that the remark "a missile is a missile" commonly attributed to Secretary of Defense McNamara is a

somewhat inaccurate paraphrase of what he said in the meeting of President Kennedy's advisers on October 16, 1962. However, according to the excerpts of the audiotape of this meeting McNamara did explicitly state that the deployment of Soviet missiles into Cuba did not at all change the strategic balance, and that they did not constitute a "military problem" but, rather, "a domestic, political problem." ("Documentation: White House Tapes and Minutes of the Cuban Missile Crisis," *International Security* 10, 1 (Summer 1985): 184, 192.)

3. This case is described and analyzed by Gloria Duffy, "Crisis Prevention in Cuba," in A. L. George, ed., *Managing U.S.-Soviet Rivalry: Problems of Crisis Prevention* (Boulder: Westview Press, 1983), pp. 285–318.

4. As quoted by Coral Bell, *The Conventions of Crisis* (London: Oxford University Press, 1971), p. 2.

INADVERTENT WARS

Introduction to Part Two

Alexander L. George

We examine five cases of inadvertent war in the pages that follow. (The concept of "inadvertent war" was defined and distinguished from "accidental war" in Chapter 2.) In most of these cases, at the beginning of the diplomatic crisis neither side wanted or expected the war that followed, and it is for this reason that we label them as instances of "inadvertent war." (World War I is a special case of inadvertent war in that no one wanted or expected a *world* war.) In several other cases, the available historical data do not fully establish that both sides wanted and expected to avoid war. Developments that led to war in the five cases do not follow a single pattern, which confirms an expectation held at the outset of this study that there is no single path to inadvertent war. This is an important finding in and of itself, as it warns against overgeneralization and oversimplification in describing the causes of inadvertent war and the paths that can lead to it.

As Jack S. Levy emphasizes in his study of the origins of World War I, not all diplomatic crises are equally manageable by leaders. In fact, some crises are peculiarly resistant to even the best efforts of statesmen to avoid war either because of the structure and dynamics of the international system, the balance of power considerations, or the domestic and alliance constraints on the parties to the dispute, or because the interests of the two sides are so fundamentally antagonistic that they cannot be easily reconciled, even with effort, during the course of a crisis. An inadvertent war may occur because during the course of the crisis, one or the other side reaches the conclusion that initiation of war has become necessary in order to secure its objectives or avoid an unacceptable diplomatic outcome, or because one or the other side decides to embrace more ambitious objectives than it entertained at the outset and is willing to accept the risk of war or resort to force itself for this purpose.

It is important, therefore, not to permit our interest in improving crisis management to lead us to exaggerate its potential for avoiding war or to overstate the significance of crisis mismanagement as a causal factor in accounting for inadvertent war. At the same time, however, we reject as a starting point for this study that all of these inadvertent wars were inevitable and that no opportunities were present for avoiding war. Therefore we regard it as useful to examine these cases of inadvertent war in order to (1) identify failures to adhere to any of the political and operational requirements of crisis management outlined earlier in this book, (2) assess as best we can what role such failures played in the path to inadvertent war in each case, and (3) address the admittedly difficult counterfactual question of whether better adherence to these crisis management principles might have made it possible to bring the crisis to a peaceful resolution.

This is the approach taken by the authors of the case studies that follow. They were asked, and agreed, to use the crisis management framework employed in this study as a heuristic tool. Familiarity with the list of political and operational principles of crisis management enabled them to sensitize their analyses to possibly relevant factors in the path to war. Moreover, analysis was not to stop with identification of specific failures by statesmen to adhere to one or another of these crisis management requirements but was to determine as accurately as possible the causes of such failures. Nor was the task of analysis to be satisfied by brief observations to the effect that war might well have been avoided had this or that requirement been met. Instead, we wanted the analyst to employ a more detailed and disciplined form of counterfactual analysis to support a judgment that war might have been avoided had certain crisis management principles and practices been more effectively employed.

It should come as no surprise, therefore, that in two of our cases—World War I and the 1967 Arab-Israeli War—the analysts' sober conclusion is that opportunities for timely, effective crisis management were quite limited. Even so, the conclusion drawn by the analysts in these cases is that while the probability of war was high, it was not certain; there were at least a few missed opportunities for more effective crisis management that, had they been exploited, might have enabled the participants to avoid war. In our other cases, better opportunities for crisis management presented themselves but were not effectively utilized.

It may be helpful in reading these five case studies to keep in mind the following questions:

- What were the *incentives* to avoid war—that is, the interests, threats, and opportunities for gain perceived by the actors—and did these change during the crisis?
- What were the *opportunities* for constructive crisis management at different points, and were these perceived and utilized by the participants?
- What *level of skill and capabilities* for crisis management did the participants display at critical decision points during the crisis?[1]

It seems self-evident that when incentives to avoid war are very weak, opportunities for avoiding war quite limited, and relevant skills lacking, then the likelihood of a crisis developing into inadvertent war is very high. Conversely, when incentives to avoid war are strong, good opportunities for crisis management are available and are recognized, and the participants have well-developed skills and capabilities for crisis management, then the likelihood of a crisis escalating to war is relatively low. This observation will be particularly relevant in the next part of the study, which examines cases of successful crisis management.

As these remarks suggest, incentives, opportunities, and skills are variables that differ from one crisis to another. The strength of one's incentive for getting through a crisis without war is particularly important, for in the absence of a pronounced desire to avoid war, the actors are less likely to look for and utilize opportunities for crisis management. Similarly, their skills and capabilities for doing so are less likely to be called upon to the fullest extent. At the same time, an initially strong incentive to avoid a war may erode as the crisis develops. In any case, as Allen S. Whiting's account of U.S. policy making in the confrontation with China illustrates, a disincentive for war by no means suffices to avoid a conflict when opportunities for crisis management are neglected and the actors are unskilled in the modalities of crisis management.

It is particularly noteworthy that in several of our cases the incentive to avoid war was relatively weak to begin with or eroded with the development of the crisis. In the Crimean War case, as Richard Smoke shows, although the British government initially neither expected nor wanted war, nonetheless it decided to initiate war *after* the Russian government accepted the terms for a peaceful settlement. It did so in response to strong domestic pressure for a military victory and was influenced in this direction by a concern that the image of British naval superiority might be damaged by the overwhelming defeat the Russian navy had inflicted on the Turkish fleet.

In the World War I case, the importance of incentives to avoid war is not so easily analyzed, as several different types of wars were possible—a localized war between Austria-Hungary and Serbia, its escalation into a continental war involving Germany and Austria-Hungary against Russia and France, and further escalation to a general European or world war involving Britain as well. As Levy's analysis indicates, the five major powers differed significantly in the ranking of their relative preferences among a negotiated peace and each of these three types of war. Critical in the end was the German misperception of British preferences and the British decision, however reluctantly arrived at, to join in a general war rather than to stay out of the continental war that erupted between Germany and Austria-Hungary on one side and Russia and France on the other.

The disincentive for a general world war in 1914 that characterized to some extent all of the major powers was, however, not of an overwhelming nature. Although it was recognized that such a war would be painful, very few anticipated that it would develop into the kind of costly, prolonged total war that it became. On the contrary, in 1914 the *image of war*—a psychological variable that strongly influences the strength of incentives to avoid it—was that for one hundred years, all European wars had been terminated through a negotiated settlement within a reasonably short period of time. Moreover, the prevailing image endowed war with a noble, heroic character that offered psychological and political compensation for the sacrifices that would be entailed.

War developed in Korea between China and the United States in 1950 as a consequence of Washington's miscalculated escalation of its objectives after the North Korean army was defeated. Washington did not want a war with China; however, its disincentive for such a war proved to be irrelevant and ineffectual because U.S. leaders misconstrued Beijing's perception of the threat to its security interests entailed by U.S. policy and actions. The lesson is an important one: Even when leaders do not want war, this is not a sufficient condition for avoiding it. Opportunities for crisis management must be seized or created, and skill in meeting the requirements for crisis management is also necessary.

In the 1967 case of inadvertent war, as Janice Gross Stein emphasizes, Israel was not at all inclined to go to war in the early stages of the crisis. But its incentive to do so became overwhelming as a result of Gamal Abdel Nasser's provocative actions in challenging Israel's deterrent posture and its security position. Ironically, Nasser did not want war at the outset. His initial objective, in which he succeeded, was to deter possible Israeli action against Syria. However, Nasser then succumbed to domestic and alliance pressures to challenge Israel further. He realized that his provocative actions now made war virtually inevitable, but his distaste for war at that stage was not powerful enough to cause him to retreat from the challenges he had mounted to Israel.

Turning to the opportunities that existed for constructive crisis management in these confrontations, our case studies offer a diverse picture. In the Crimean case, as Smoke notes, a number of opportunities presented themselves for managing the crisis, very possibly in ways that would have enabled the participants to avoid war. But these opportunities were missed or ineffectively utilized. The opportunities in 1914, Levy notes, were few and of a limited and problematic character. Had Austria-Hungary mounted its punitive action against Serbia more promptly, it might have achieved a successful fait accompli without a wider war. Had Berlin imposed its "Halt in Belgrade" demand on its Austrian ally more decisively, it might have weakened the Russian incentive to deter or oppose the Austro-Hungarian action against Serbia and paved the way for a negotiated settlement. Had England conveyed, in a more timely and credible manner, its commitment to enter the war were France and Russia to become embroiled, the German disposition to avoid such a general war might have motivated Berlin to moderate its support for Austria-Hungary so as to avoid getting into war with Russia and France, which in turn might well have deterred Austrian action against Serbia.

In the 1950 confrontation between the United States and China in Korea, Whiting notes that opportunities for crisis management to avoid war with China were indeed recognized by China specialists in the U.S. State Department but that their urgent advice was not heeded by central decision makers. Whether Mao saw or was interested in opportunities for managing the confrontation to avoid the big war that followed is uncertain, given his perception of the acute U.S. threat to China's security; also uncertain is how China would have responded had Washington seized the opportunity in early November to shrink the ambitious political objectives it had adopted earlier and proceeded to limit the means employed on their behalf while signaling a credible desire for a negotiated settlement.

In the 1967 clash between Israel and Nasser, as Stein notes, opportunities for crisis management were quite limited and occurred only early in the crisis. This case strongly reinforces the conventional wisdom that early action is needed to stabilize and terminate a crisis before the dynamics of escalation come into play.

Turning to the role of skill and capability in crisis management, not surprisingly these cases indicate that when incentives are weak and opportunities limited, skill in crisis management is less relevant and cannot easily halt or prevent the movement toward war. Nonetheless, the analysis of each of these cases reveals glaring violations of crisis management principles that contributed to the escalation to war. Perhaps foremost among them was the failure to *limit objectives*—one of our political requirements for effective crisis management—in the Crimean, Korean, and Arab-Israeli cases. And in the 1914 case, Austria-Hungary's unwillingness to limit the objectives and scope of its demands on Serbia was certainly a contributing cause of the escalation that followed.

We have saved for last a discussion of the complex crisis leading to the Suez War, as it is a somewhat borderline example of inadvertent war. At the inception of the crisis between Egypt and the British and French, as Christer Jönsson indicates, while the United States and its two Western allies were still ostensibly considering the possibility of Western financing for a new Aswan Dam, neither they nor Nasser wanted or expected that a war would follow should they decline to do so. Even when he proceeded to nationalize the Suez Canal, Nasser had a number of seemingly good reasons for assuming that his action would not provoke war. His miscalculation proved to be a critical step in the development of inadvertent war. In response to the takeover, the British and French quickly concluded that while they should try coercive diplomacy and negotiation in attempting to persuade Nasser to back off, the resort to force was very likely to become necessary. Since British and French leaders now adopted the additional objective of getting rid of Nasser, it is not surprising that they should conclude that they would have to resort to war to achieve this objective.

Thus, while Nasser's incentive to avoid war was strong, the same certainly cannot be said of the British and French after he nationalized the Suez Canal. Thereafter, opportunities for avoiding war were quite limited and depended largely on how well the United States would manage the deteriorating crisis.

Washington's incentive to avoid a war was pronounced, but it was not matched by skill in managing the crisis. In fact, as Jönsson amply documents, the heavy-handed and humiliating fashion in which John Foster Dulles withdrew the U.S. offer to finance the Aswan Dam helped provoke Nasser into nationalizing the canal. Later, Eisenhower's and Dulles's efforts to dissuade the British and French from resorting to force while the United States attempted to find some peaceful way of dealing with the canal issue foundered as a result of incredibly inept signaling and ambiguous communication by Washington to its two allies with regard to the critical question of whether the United States would condone and accept, or strongly oppose, an attack against Egypt. As a result, the opportunity to deter the British, and thereby the French and Israelis, from proceeding was lost. Jönsson identifies a number of other serious flaws in this early effort to apply crisis management concepts and procedures in an admittedly complex multi-actor crisis.

Finally, it should be noted that more than two states were also involved in three other of these cases of inadvertent war. In multi-state crises of this kind, opportunities for miscommunication and misperception increase, and it becomes more difficult to localize the initial conflict between two parties and to carry out the precepts of crisis management. We shall see further evidence of this difficulty in Part Four, which focuses on three multi-actor crises in the Middle East.

NOTES

1. I am indebted to Phil Williams for this three-fold framework of incentives, opportunities, skill and capabilities.

CHAPTER 5

The Crimean War

Richard Smoke

Although the Crimean War was fought nearly a century and a half ago, the crisis that led to it still offers valuable lessons to the contemporary analyst. The crisis repays study for it offers striking lessons in how policy makers' failure to come to grips with the difficult tasks of crisis management can lead to tragically costly outcomes. The Crimean War is often remembered today for the many blunders committed by both sides after the war began. It is especially remembered, of course, for one of the most famous military blunders of all time—The Charge of the Light Brigade. But the blunders that were committed before the war began were at least equally consequential and are a good deal more instructive for us today. Unlike the military blunders, their relevance has not been obscured by advancing technology.

To analysts today, the most striking and instructive overall feature of the Crimean War is that it was a war that not one of the participants wanted and not one of them expected throughout nearly all of the crisis period leading up to it. As such, it is one of the best examples in modern history of an almost entirely inadvertent war. Of course, it was not inadvertent in the sense of being a pure accident, as might happen today if, for example, nuclear missiles were launched by a malfunctioning computer. It was inadvertent in the sense that policy makers found themselves, at the last, "driven" into a war they had been confident they could avoid. They were "driven" into it by force of circumstances. But the circumstances were ones that the policy makers themselves had created at earlier stages of the crisis. As we shall see, there was not just one opportunity but several, during the events leading up to the war, for good crisis management to halt the crisis short of war. Every one of these opportunities was lost.

In this historical case, then, the failures of crisis management are at the very center of the story. They are not adjacent to, or peripherally part of, or one minor thread in, the sequence of events by which war came—they are the central theme of those events.

This chapter draws heavily from Chapter 7 of my book, *War: Controlling Escalation* (Cambridge, MA: Harvard University Press, 1977); used by permission. Here I have reanalyzed the Crimean case study presented in that chapter from the viewpoint of crisis management.

My assessment of the crisis period leading to the Crimean War begins with a succinct overview of its main events. As we shall see, the crisis did not erupt all at once but unfolded through stages. With this overview in mind, I will then return to the most important decision points in the sequence and examine them one by one. Each of these is a point at which the developing crisis was thrust, by some decision, into its next, and more dangerous, stage. Before beginning the historical overview, let me offer some preliminary observations about the effect of the time factor in this case.

The Crimean War began in September 1854. The crisis leading up to it began some two years earlier and developed in stages. To analysts of today, this seems like a slow, even leisurely, pace for an escalating crisis. In our era we are used to thinking of crises that erupt quickly, last for a time measured in days, and then end one way or another. Either they boil up into war, or they are resolved or at least reduced back down to some lesser, precritical level of conflict.

Thus a crisis that develops over two years might not even seem, at first glance, to be sufficiently similar to potential crises of our own era to make its analysis worthwhile. In particular, the factor of *time pressure* seems to be missing. Time pressure can easily increase the stress on decision makers and thus degrade their capacity for processing information and exercising calm judgment. Many of today's analysts are used to thinking of time pressure as being the very essence of crisis, indeed as being perhaps the thing beyond all others that makes a crisis potentially so difficult to cope with.[1]

To this possible complaint that a two-year-long crisis of the nineteenth century may be scarcely relevant today, three rebuttals may be made. One is that time pressures on policy makers, and other serious factors involving time limits, can arise at certain moments within what is, in its totality, a two-year crisis. We shall see that such moments occurred on several occasions during the Crimean crisis.

A second rebuttal is that a striking feature of this crisis is precisely that it escalated step after step to war in spite of the availability of a great deal of time. Months—even years—were available, and policy makers still made the faulty decisions that drove the crisis forward into war. So far from rendering this crisis irrelevant, then, its long time span makes it all the more relevant, for it teaches us that severely limited time alone is not what makes crises dangerous and difficult and that gaining more time (however helpful) is not a panacea for resolving crises.

Understanding this, in turn, leads us to the third point: If time pressure is not the heart of the matter, what is? This brings us to the basic theme of this book, which addresses the fundamental dilemma of crisis management for policy makers: how to meet simultaneously the strong need to protect threatened national interests and the strong need to avoid war. Of course, it is true that severe time pressure may, as a practical matter, make it harder to find a creative way out of this dilemma. But even if ample time is available, the dilemma remains and may not be successfully resolved—as the Crimean crisis amply illustrates.

HISTORICAL OVERVIEW OF THE CRISIS

The crisis years from 1852 to 1854 (and the next year-and-a-half, to the end of the war in 1857) were a period of intense diplomatic activity. An unusually large number of active participants was involved. They changed their policies repeatedly and at times pursued several, even conflicting, policies simultaneously. The result was an intricate maze in which "the strangest cross-currents confused relatively simple issues."[2] The politico-military events surrounding the Crimean crisis and war are the most complicated of any one period in the nineteenth century.[3] This chapter's focus on crisis management will permit some simplifications, but even so, we will be unable to avoid a certain amount of complexity.

In one sense, the underlying cause of the crisis and war was basically straight-forward. The Ottoman Empire, which once had threatened to overrun all of Europe, had been undergoing slow decay for centuries. The Russian Empire to its north had been enjoying an equally gradual growth in power and had the ambition, reaching back almost a millennium, for unconditionally free access to the Mediterranean Sea. The predictable results were Russian impulses for southward expansion and a series of Russo-Turkish conflicts, most of which had resulted in Russian advances. Since the late 1600s, "for nearly two centuries there had been a war between Russia and Turkey about every twenty years."[4] By the 1850s, another was due if the traditional schedule were to be maintained.

But the initial stage of the crisis in 1852 involved something else. The first step was a competition between Russia and France for influence over the Ottoman government in Constantinople, which called itself "the Sublime Porte" or simply the Porte.

The patriarchs of the Orthodox church, under the protection of the Russian czar, had long controlled the keys to the "holy places" in Palestine—sites such as the church at Bethlehem, considered sacred to Christianity but lying deep within the Ottoman Empire. In 1850 Louis Napoleon had begun a diplomatic effort aimed at bringing these holy places under Roman Catholic control. After assuming the imperial crown and becoming Napoleon III, he needed to consolidate his domestic position by winning the active support of French clerics and by demonstrating to audiences at home and abroad that he was a vigorous leader in the Bonapartist tradition. Determined to press the holy places issue as a way of accomplishing both objectives at once, he soon obtained partial concessions from the Porte. Nonetheless, he sent an impressive new battleship through the Dardanelles and also threatened to bombard Tripoli, an Ottoman possession, to back up his insistence on obtaining his full demands. Slowly the Turks gave in—and this was taken as a serious challenge in St. Petersburg, where the czar felt he could not allow the Orthodox patriarchs to be deprived of their traditional rights.

Russian policy makers had operated for decades on the assumption that Turkey could serve as a buffer state to protect the security of the Black Sea. But they considered as an essential prerequisite that the Ottomans should be more afraid of Russia than of any other power. Now the Turks were demonstrating that they feared France more. In February 1853, Czar Nicholas I mobilized two army corps on the southern frontier and sent Prince Alexander Menshikov to Constantinople as a plenipotentiary extraordinary with a set of demands that would extend the czar's influence within the Ottoman Empire.

These vigorous moves were intended primarily to restore the Russian conception of the status quo ante, but they upset the British government. British policy makers felt that the balance of power in the eastern Mediterranean (conceived to be an essential British interest) was being affected. As a sign of their concern, they appointed a new ambassador to the Porte who was known to have strong anti-Russian feelings. Meanwhile Menshikov began his mission by demanding that the Turkish government dismiss the present foreign minister and appoint a more Russophile one. This plus the Russian military preparations led Napoleon to order the Mediterranean fleet to Salamis in Greece. The Turks, emboldened by these visible signs of support from the Western great powers, refused the more far-reaching of Menshikov's demands and claimed that to grant them would turn Turkey into a Russian satellite. The prince left Constantinople, breaking off relations as he went.

Anticipating that a Russian military stroke was now likely, and unable to obtain assurances from St. Petersburg that Menshikov's demands were intended to be more limited than the Turks claimed, policy makers in London turned to stronger measures. Earlier they had refused to send the Royal Navy to the area on the grounds that such a move would be provocative. Now they ordered a fleet to Besika Bay, just outside the Dardanelles. The French immediately advanced their own fleet to join the British one.

The Russians felt that they had to execute the military threat that had backed Prince Menshikov. In July 1853, troops occupied the almost undefended Ottoman principalities of Moldavia and Wallachia (much of what is now Romania), and it was announced in St. Petersburg that the troops would remain until Menshikov's demands had been met. There was no significant fighting in the principalities, and the Porte held off counterattacking with major army units until it could ascertain the Western reaction. A period of about three months of "phony war" ensued while Britain, France, Austria, and Prussia sent representatives to a conference in Vienna to try to find a peaceful solution. The resulting Vienna Note, declared the Turks, did not adequately protect Ottoman sovereignty. After the British and French advanced their fleets through the Dardanelles to Constantinople and after riots in the city demanding action, the Porte struck back at the Russians in October. The ninth Russo-Turkish War got underway in earnest.

In the two principalities, the Turks made a surprisingly effective counterattack, and far to the east they opened a second front in the Caucasus. But in November a Turkish squadron was utterly annihilated by a Russian fleet while anchored at Sinope, a Turkish Black Sea port. The "Sinope massacre," as it was promptly called in the West, generated extreme public reaction in Britain and France. The entire British press called for military action, and in December a cabinet reshuffle brought more militant ministers to the fore. Napoleon declared that the joint Franco-British fleet must sail into the Black Sea. In January 1854, it did. Shortly thereafter the czar withdrew his ambassadors from Paris and London. The British and French signed an alliance with the Turks, delivered an ultimatum to Russia that demanded a troop withdrawal from the principalities, and when this went unanswered, declared war and began to prepare expeditionary forces for a campaign in the Balkans.

Now there was another phony war period, through the spring and early summer of 1854, while these preparations went forward. The Western powers made intense diplomatic efforts to bring the Austrian Empire into the conflict as an ally, and policy makers in Vienna finally agreed to join in demanding the withdrawal of Russian forces from the principalities. Czar Nicholas recognized that Russia was far more vulnerable to an Austrian attack than to an Anglo-French one and decided to comply with the Austrian demand. The Russian troops were withdrawn from the principalities over the summer.

The military status quo ante had now returned, and the Western allies were left with no obvious reason to fight. But public opinion in France and Britain demanded a military "victory." For this reason and others, it was decided that the Anglo-French expeditionary force would assault Sebastopol, an important Russian city in the Crimea and the principal Russian naval base on the Black Sea. So, almost a year after the outbreak of the Russo-Turkish War, the conflict entered a new and much enlarged phase as the Crimean War proper began in September 1854.

Due to endemic mismanagement on both sides, no early decision by arms could be reached. Finally, in January 1856, Russia—largely at Austrian insistence— accepted outline terms for a settlement. A peace conference was convened in Paris in February and a final peace treaty concluded in March. For various reasons, the Russians obtained lighter terms in the treaty than the British, in particular, had wished.

The events of the 1850s have haunting familiarity for Americans who remember their war in Vietnam. Both times, a large force of Western troops got bogged down in an excessively drawn-out war on the edge of Asia. Victory proved elusive for reasons that were not obvious. In the end, the costs of the war were vastly higher than anyone in the West had guessed beforehand and were vastly higher than could be justified by the original, half-forgotten issues at stake. And no one was very clear on just how they had gotten enmeshed in the war.

Let us now examine the chief decision points in the escalating crisis of 1852 to 1854.[5]

STEPS IN THE CRISIS

The Holy Places Dispute

During the nineteenth century, the great powers of Europe routinely made demands on various weaker states, and France and Britain often backed up these demands with displays of naval power. There was nothing unusual about Napoleon III demanding concessions from the Ottoman Empire regarding the Christian holy places and demonstrating his seriousness with a naval display. French policy makers expected a minor crisis with Turkey, not the beginning of a major international crisis. At this stage, the French were applying an offensive strategy of *controlled pressure* in pursuit of their national interest (as Napoleon perceived it). This offensive crisis strategy was routine in that era and for the great powers was frequently successful. And indeed, in this case, it was successful for the French in the short term.

However, the French erred in considering only the short term. More exactly, they erred in failing to appreciate how their strategy of controlled pressure might trigger other latent conflicts embedded in the situation. Several latent conflicts were relevant; the most important involved a delicate balance between Russia and Great Britain. For decades the British had been suspicious not only of Russian expansionist tendencies generally but in particular of Russia's desire to increase its naval power in the Mediterranean. Policy makers in London also recognized that Russia had a legitimate security interest in maintaining a real, if rather informal, influence over the Ottomans. However, they considered that Britain had an equally legitimate interest in maintaining British naval supremacy in the Mediterranean and, thus, in preventing Russian influence over Turkey from reaching the level of hegemony.[6]

The balance between Russian influence and British resistance was a delicate one, and the French upset this balance. They did so by (1) injecting themselves into Ottoman affairs in pursuit of objectives not previously considered legitimate French interests, (2) employing fast-paced and belligerent tactics, and (3) scoring a highly visible success. In coping with the French initiative, the Russians took actions that activated British suspicions. Subsequently the British found themselves gravitating toward France in search of an ally, and both assumed a gradually more hostile posture toward the Russians as the latter continued to try (as they saw it) to regain their previous influence with the Turks.

The French could have improved their offensive strategy of controlled pressure by credibly communicating to the Russians (and others) the limits of their objectives. In fact, Napoleon at this stage was interested chiefly in the holy places and did not, at the time, seriously entertain larger objectives vis-à-vis the Turks. The French could have, but did not, communicate this effectively to St. Petersburg. By not doing so, they allowed the Russians to conjecture that French designs on the Ottoman Empire might be extensive and that the step so far taken was merely an opening gambit. This inference significantly increased Russian motives to respond strongly.[7]

The Menshikov Mission

The next stage of the crisis is defined by Prince Menshikov's mission to Constantinople. As perceived by the Russian Foreign Ministry, this step was an exercise in defensive crisis management and largely a defensive exercise in *coercive* diplomacy. Menshikov's instructions from the Foreign Ministry were to make certain coercive threats, partly with the goal of regaining for the Orthodox patriarchs their previous privileges in the holy places. If his instructions had been confined to that goal, this crisis management effort would probably have succeeded in defusing the crisis. On the advice of the British ambassador in Constantinople, the Porte agreed to restore those privileges; and the French, having no British support, had already decided not to pursue the issue further.[8]

However, Menshikov's instructions were more complicated than this. His demands mixed two strategies: coercive diplomacy and a form of limited escalation. He not only demanded back control of the holy places, but he also made substantially larger demands that amounted to giving the Russian czar an unprecedented degree of control over the political status of Christians living within the Ottoman Empire.[9] It was these larger demands that alarmed the Western great powers, who saw them as an offensive move by Russia against the Porte. The Western powers felt they had to respond, which carried the crisis on to its next stage.

From the Russian viewpoint, it was not at all clear that an offensive strategy was being attempted. Here we arrive at an important analytic concept for understanding crises and their management: *ambiguity*. The meaning of one player's step may not be clear to other parties; it may be ambiguous. More intriguingly, it may be ambiguous even as perceived by the very party taking the step.

Understanding the powerful role of ambiguity requires us to carefully dissect this moment in the crisis. First, the Russian Foreign Ministry did not have a predominantly offensive motive for a strategy of limited escalation. As Alexander George notes in Chapter 16, limited escalation can be a defensive strategy. The Foreign Ministry believed that regaining control of the holy places was not sufficient to restore the status quo ante. Something more fundamental had changed when the French had won that control, and this more fundamental element had to be changed back as well. The French had wielded new naval capabilities. As the Russians saw it, the Turks now believed that "a French fleet would beat a Russian fleet even combined with a Turkish one."[10] Since the Turks would favor the country they feared most, the Russians now had to come up with some other, non-naval device to restore the traditional Turkish fear of Russia—hence the larger Menshikov demands. A larger role for the czar in "protecting the Christians" would give back to the czar the predominant external influence within the Ottoman Empire. This influence, although different in form, would restore approximately the previous correction of forces—as the Russians saw it.

This Russian calculus was, by itself, sufficiently subtle that one might doubt whether it would be entirely clear in London and Paris. But Russian policy was much more ambiguous than this.

In addition to this defensive motive, the Russians had some offensive motivation as well. A limited escalation can, of course, be an offensive as well as a defensive strategy, and Menshikov's limited escalation was meant as both. The Russians, much more than the Western powers, believed that a complete breakdown of the Ottoman Empire might be imminent. Should that occur, the Russians intended to be well-positioned to take advantage of the situation. Thus from St. Peterburg's viewpoint, Menshikov's demands—precisely because they were ambiguously both defensive and offensive—represented an excellent way to achieve the minimum objective of restoring the status quo ante and to set the stage for achieving much larger objectives in the contingency of an Ottoman breakdown.[11]

The effect of this ambiguity in Russian motives and strategy was compounded by the way the strategy was perceived in the West. This brings us to another of the most difficult aspects of crisis management. Policy makers in the Western capitals evaluated Russian behavior within a different framework of perceptions and expectations. They did not have the same expectations as the Russians that a collapse of the Ottoman Empire might be imminent. On the contrary, they believed the empire might well last. They had reasons to fear but, unlike the Russians, few reasons to welcome, an Ottoman collapse. And they did not have well-developed contingency objectives should a collapse occur, although they were keenly aware that the Russians did. Therefore, the Westerners tended to see any Russian move that seemed related to the possibility of an Ottoman collapse as more of an effort to bring it about than did the Russians. In short, the Russian demands made by Menshikov, already highly ambiguous even in Russian eyes, became even more ambiguous in Western eyes. Menshikov's demands were seen by the Russians as somewhat more defensive than offensive, but the West saw them as more offensive than defensive.[12]

The French advanced their fleet to Greece, the British ambassador in Constantinople advised the Porte to reject Menshikov's demands, and the Porte did so. Menshikov departed, breaking diplomatic relations.

Military Advances

The British and French, anticipating that the Russians would now make a military move, sent fleets to Besika Bay, just outside the Dardanelles (June 1853). The Russian troops already poised on the border occupied the almost undefended Turkish principalities. Let us consider these military moves.

The Western crisis managers took their step as a strategy to convey commitment and resolve and saw it as essentially defensive. They were making no new demands, merely signaling a reinforcement of a message already communicated—namely, that they opposed an increase of Russian influence over the Porte.

At this time British and French policy makers considered that a war with Russia was a remote contingency; indeed, they did not yet see the situation as a full-fledged European crisis. We may observe, then, that they were not yet experiencing, to any significant extent, the central dilemma of crisis management—the tension between protecting national interests and preventing war. War was not considered a substantial possibility.

During this era, the deployment of a naval squadron to a trouble spot was a device frequently employed (especially by Britain and France) for signaling to a diplomatic opponent a nation's seriousness of intent and depth of involvement in a situation. The device hardly ever led to war; it was essentially a standard diplomatic maneuver, which is how British and French policy makers meant it this time. They perceived (correctly) that Czar Nicholas did not want (or expect) a major war. They expected that the outcome of their signal would be fresh negotiations. When the czar realized that the West was getting seriously involved, he would find some face-saving way of withdrawing the more extreme Menshikov demands, and negotiations to resolve the crisis would begin.

Meanwhile, the Russians felt that if they did not carry out the military threat that had implicitly backed Menshikov, they would be in an even weaker position than before. They saw their bloodless occupation of the principalities as the next feasible step toward achieving existing Russian objectives—not new ones. The Russian strategy was again one of limited escalation, based on the same ambiguous mixture of defensive and offensive motives.

The crisis managers in St. Petersburg were also not yet anticipating a major European crisis. They, too, were not yet experiencing the tension between protecting interests and preventing war. Of course, a war with Turkey was obviously possible, perhaps likely. The Russians contemplated this possibility with equanimity and were unsurprised when the Turks finally struck back some months later. The ninth in the long series of Russo-Turkish Wars had been anticipated as a possibility all along and was not feared.[13] The possibility of a war with the British and French was assessed as remote.

The full reasons for this misinterpretation of the Anglo-French fleet movement are complicated, but they might be summarized this way. The Russians perceived correctly that that French, by themselves, would not allow the crisis to escalate seriously but would be happy to act in concert with the British. The Russians thus perceived correctly that the key factor was the British attitude. "[Czar] Nicholas always had said that he did not care what France thought or did as long as England was in agreement with him."[14] He also knew that normally the British were at least as suspicious of the French as of the Russians. But the czar and his advisors misunderstood how and why the British attitude might change. The explanation for this misunderstanding is complex, but most important was a lack of adequate and objective reporting to high-level policy makers in St. Petersburg, both at lower levels of the bureaucracy and in the embassies abroad. For reasons of bureaucratic politics, among others, the information delivered to the policy-making level was skewed and inaccurate. The result was that Russian policy makers believed, in the late spring of 1853, that the British sent their fleet largely for reasons of their own domestic and bureaucratic politics and thus concluded that the gesture should not be seen as a serious warning signal. St. Petersburg dismissed the significance of a signal that Paris and London had thought was plain.[15]

By summertime the Russians were fully in position in Moldavia and Wallachia, while powerful Western fleets were at anchor just outside the Dardanelles. But still nobody expected a major war or even an intense European crisis. There was as yet no fighting between Russians and Turks. And major negotiations were now under way.

Negotiations

With Austrian assistance, the Western powers drafted a negotiating document called the Vienna Note. In this fashion, the British and French crisis managers were attempting to defuse the situation. Czar Nicholas said he was willing to agree to the note. But the Turks were not, claiming it did not sufficiently protect them. Negotiations continued.[16]

In this phase of events, the Turks had settled on a subtle course of action— one that was to serve them well. They did not counterattack in the principalities at this time, thus postponing actual fighting. But neither did they agree to anything that would move the situation toward a negotiated resolution. They simply took no action and decided on nothing.

It is difficult to know, even in retrospect, whether this inaction was a masterly policy or a mere accident. The internal governmental politics of the Turkish capital were as Byzantine as ever, and the net result of the many-sided policy struggle was frequently zero. On the other hand, at least some Turkish officials may have insightfully grasped a Western cultural bias. There is a tendency for Westerners to believe that deciding on an action in a problematic situation is "doing something about it," while not acting means that one is "not doing something about it."

If the Ottomans had promptly counterattacked in the principalities, this action would have tended to define the situation as another in the series of Russo-Turkish Wars. Britain and France would—at this time—have had little reason to intervene. By not attacking and also not agreeing to any resolution, the Turks held open what late twentieth-century analysts often call the definition of the situation. They gave the Western powers an extended opportunity to become more deeply involved in the problem, which would probably (as turned out to be the case) define and formulate their interests in a way that de facto favored the Ottomans.

THE DEVELOPING WESTERN COMMITMENT

Contrary to an assumption sometimes made by contemporary analysts, commitments that are intended to deter a potential opponent from taking action in some gray area are often not made in one clear and explicit decision but develop gradually over time. It would be hard to find a more eloquent example of this than the development during 1853 of an Anglo-French commitment to the Ottoman Empire. Nearly a year passed between the haziest beginnings of this commitment and its appearance in full-fledged form, with the entrance of the Anglo-French fleet into the Black Sea in January 1854. Yet so gradually did it develop that it is impossible to pick any moment during this period and say definitely that before then there was no Western commitment to the Turks and afterward there was. The masterly, or accidental, behavior of the Turks, which helped draw the Western powers deeper into the situation, represents one strand in the explanation of this process. A second strand, of course, involves the fact that the Russians were continuing to pursue an ambiguous mixture of defensive and offensive goals. Another strand was a failure by the Western powers to recognize some of the implications of their own crisis management decisions.

Perhaps the simplest failure involved what might be called the purely technical side of crisis management. The Western squadrons could not remain in Besika Bay past October because winter storms would be dangerous to ships there. By October the squadrons would either have to be advanced—for instance, to Constantinople—or pulled well back—for instance, to Greece. One step would look like an escalation, the other like a retreat. This problem had not been weighed in the late spring, when the fleets had been ordered to the bay. Here, incidentally, is an example of how the element of time can enter even into what seems like a slow-motion crisis to late-twentieth-century eyes.

A more complicated failure came a little later. On October 8, policy makers in London ordered the British fleet to advance to the harbor at Constantinople. They did so knowing, of course, that the French fleet would sail with it. (And, indeed, a secondary motive was to demonstrate to the French, who had generally been taking the stance that London was being too cautious, that Britain could be a good ally.) This step was intended as a limited escalation. The British felt this strategy to be desirable because they had fresh information. To be exact, they had fresh *mis*information.

In late September, Czar Nicholas had held a personal meeting with the Austrian emperor. The British were correctly informed that, in addition to the ostensible agenda, the two emperors had secretly discussed the topic that was often on the czar's mind—the potential breakup of the fragile Ottoman Empire, which the czar thought might be imminent. However, the British were misinformed about the significance of the conversation. They took it to mean that the two emperors were conspiring to reach a mutual agreement for carving up Ottoman territory, to be added to their own respective empires, and perhaps for taking active steps to destabilize the Ottoman Empire. In fact, the predominant motive and emphasis of the conversation was different. The sprawling Austrian and Russian Empires both had long, vulnerable borders with the Ottoman Empire. The czar wanted to make sure that, in the contingency of an Ottoman collapse, he and the Austrian emperor were in agreement about necessary measures and would not misunderstand each other's behavior. The czar saw himself as trying to *avoid* a European crisis, in a contingency he believed all too likely. The British saw him as conspiring to *create* a crisis, in a contingency that was unlikely—or that would be unlikely were it not for his own constant meddling in Turkish affairs.

For this chief reason, the British decided it was time to send Czar Nicholas a much stronger signal. (There were other, secondary factors in this decision as well.[17]) Advancing the squadron to Constantinople would be a clear (but limited) escalation. Because it was a violation of international law[18] and because the Russian ambassador in London had explicitly warned against this very move, British policy makers believed that this escalation should finally make it unmistakably clear to the czar that Great Britain opposed his Turkish policy.

In this, the British succeeded. However, their action also made something unmistakably clear to the Turks as well—namely, that the greatest naval power in the world was starting to line up on their side. The British fleet arrived in the harbor at Constantinople on October 22. On October 23, the Turkish army advanced into Moldavia and Wallachia and engaged the enemy. The ninth Russo-Turkish War had begun in earnest.

THE NEXT STEP: SINOPE

A war on the edge of Europe, with a Western fleet close by and symbolizing a degree of Western involvement, did constitute a major European crisis. Policy makers in all the major capitals did consider, from this point on, that a larger war was possible. However, for some time yet they continued to assess it as unlikely, and most of them also wanted to avoid it. (There were several individual exceptions, and, of course, the Turks avidly wanted strong allies.) Policy makers among the great powers continued to believe that good crisis management would enable them to avoid any larger war.

Because winter would be arriving shortly in the principalities, there could be only a few weeks of fighting until spring. Policy makers in all the capitals believed that the five months or more of winter would allow them to find some negotiated resolution to the crisis.

However, the Turks did not confine themselves to engaging the Russians in Moldavia and Wallachia. They also opened a second front, far to the east at the other end of the Black Sea, where the Ottoman and Russian Empires also bordered each other in the Caucasus Mountains. This action helped set the stage for the next—and, in its consequences, most severe—escalation of the crisis.

When the British moved their fleet to Constantinople, they also sent Czar Nicholas a message warning him not to attack any Turkish port on the Black Sea and indicating that Britain would respond if he did. This message was intended to help confine the fighting. In late twentieth-century parlance, it was meant as an escalation-control measure. The czar saw it as such, accepted it, and so ordered his Black Sea navy. However, as the order was passed down the Russian chain of command, it was interpreted narrowly rather than broadly.

During November, the Turks sent ships along the southern edge of the Black Sea, carrying supplies to their troops in the Caucasus region. At the end of the month, a flotilla of these ships was at anchor in the harbor of Sinope, a Turkish port city some three hundred miles east of Constantinople. Russian Black Sea naval commanders perceived what they regarded as a perfectly legitimate military opportunity. Avoiding any attack on the port city itself, they attacked the Turkish ships in the harbor. The Russians had superior naval technology and they annihilated the Turkish flotilla.[19]

Policy makers in London and Paris were staggered. The French public and even more so the British public was utterly inflamed. In the following days, the press in these countries dubbed this event "the Sinope massacre." Every major newspaper in Great Britain vehemently demanded a strong British counterstroke.[20] As one historian has written, "Few governments have ever been subjected to pressure so sudden and so severe, and few ministers would have dared to resist it. In fact most of them did not want to."[21]

In reality, according to international law the Russian action had been strictly legal. A naval squadron had simply intercepted a military convoy carrying military supplies toward a war front in a declared war. The fact that the battle was one-sided merely reflected the military situation on the spot. But that is not how the British and French saw it. The action had taken them utterly by surprise. It seemed to violate the ground rule that the British had laid down. It was an attack on the Turkish navy, which they saw as implicitly under some degree of protection by the Anglo-French squadrons at Constantinople. And it was a sharp escalation in the fighting: Previously all hostilities had been on land, but now the Russians were extending them into a new domain—the sea.

In the psychology of the British and French, perhaps the worst fact of all was the easy and total victory scored by the Russians. The complete, almost costless, annihilation of an enemy fleet was an action typical of a distinctly superior naval power. In this era, France to some extent and Britain almost entirely based their international positions and strength on their naval power. Russia had never been a great naval power, and in fact the real effectiveness of the Russian navy, compared to that of the British or French fleets, did not significantly change because of Sinope. Both the Western navies remained, in fact, incomparably superior. But now the appearance of Russia as a great naval power was being created, or might be created, in the eyes of the rest of the world and perhaps in the eyes of the Russians themselves. What the British and French feared most was that Russia might now begin to act like a major naval power and that other nations might accept Russia in that role.

Thus, the most important impact of Sinope on the developing crisis was on perceptions, and on perceptions of a particular kind. The intense Western response, both among policy makers and the public, came from the fear of a basic change, internationally, in perceptions of national power and national roles, with possible political and politico-military consequences that might follow for decades. This is a different kind of "perception" from what late-twentieth-century analysts sometimes mean by that term. The Western response at this moment was not based on any concrete, analytic concern, such as the implication of the Sinope victory for the British or French admiralties' technical "threat estimates." Rather, it was more global, more public, more diffuse, more political, and more long-term.

What of the Russian viewpoint? Their naval action at Sinope had not been intended by Russian policy makers as any kind of step in their management of the crisis with the West. The action was in no sense a crisis management strategy. They did not even perceive it in the terms of management of the larger international crisis. They saw it merely as a simple military action within the local war. Analytically, this is a striking example of how the same event can be perceived in radically different ways by different players. The British and French perceived the Sinope "massacre" as a dramatic intensification of the European crisis. The Russians did not perceive the Sinope naval action in crisis management terms at all; they saw it merely as an event in the local context.

FURTHER ANALYSIS

An adequate assessment of crisis management in this case should approach the Sinope event from another analytic viewpoint as well, namely an assessment of the preconditions that made it possible. Of course, one precondition involved the Russian pursuit of an ambiguous mixture of offensive and defensive objectives. Another salient point to observe is the way in which British and French crisis managers failed to think through the potential implications of their decision to advance their fleets to Constantinople. Granting, for the sake of analysis, that this questionable decision was to be made at all, we may observe that some of its implications could have been avoided by taking certain other actions in accompaniment. These accompanying actions, needed for sound crisis management, were not taken.

The chief reason given publicly by London and Paris for the fleet advance was to protect the city of Constantinople and its European residents. Policy makers could have explicitly excluded any intent to provide blanket protection for the Turkish navy or any general commitment to the defense of Turkey. (In their own minds they certainly had not yet made such a commitment.) Explicit public statements on these points would have gone far toward forestalling the later interpretation by the public of what the Sinope attack meant.

A more ambitious step was possible in addition. The Western powers could have made their fleet advance contingent upon good behavior by the Turks. Constantinople could have been told that this step was meant only defensively and that the ships would be withdrawn if the Turks opened hostilities in Moldavia and Wallachia. Doing this might have headed off the outbreak of the Russo-Turkish War. Conceiving of the matter this way, however, would have required a capacity (perhaps unusual) on the part of Western policy managers to think along two tracks at once. This step would have required them to regard the fleet advance as serving a dual purpose: simultaneously to reinforce the signal to Russia and to manipulate strongly the Turkish risk calculus.

If this is asking too much, a lesser, but still valuable, step was also possible. At the minimum, the British and French should have made their naval advance contingent upon Turkey taking hostile action only to regain its principalities. Constantinople could have been made to understand clearly that the West did not want to back any general Turkish revanche and would not sanction attacks on additional fronts. Such a message would probably have deterred the Turks from opening the Caucasus front, far to the east. Even if it did not, this message would have relieved the West of any obligation to respond to Sinope.

None of these accompanying steps was taken when the fleets advanced to Constantinople. Instead, the worst of all possible kinds of commitments was created—a commitment that was felt to be real by both the deterring parties (Britain and France) and the protected client (Turkey) but that was nonspecific and inexplicit. In October, London and Paris made no explicit commitment to the Turks to defend them in the event of any particular, identifed contingency. They merely sent a fleet that was vastly more powerful than that of any conceivable foe to the harbor of the Turks' capital, as a general support of the Turkish position.[22]

By offering a commitment that was at once so powerful and so unspecified, the British and French unwittingly created a state of affairs that made Sinope possible. They put in place the preconditions by which an event such as the Sinope attack could occur, as well as the extreme Western reaction it provoked.

The British and French also unwittingly constricted their own future options. After Sinope and the resultant Western reaction, London and Paris found that they had few options left.

THE NEXT STEP: NEW WESTERN MILITARY ACTION

The obvious Western military response to the Sinope "massacre" was to send the naval squadrons harbored at Constantinople into the Black Sea. This was also the only strong military step that could be taken promptly.

Some members of the cabinet in London (in contemporary language, "doves") initially balked at this step for fear that it would lead directly to war with Russia. These policy makers were now experiencing strongly the central crisis dilemma of advancing and protecting interests or preventing war, and they preferred to prevent war. Others in the cabinet ("hawks") experienced the same dilemma and preferred the opposite choice. But before the cabinet could thoroughly debate the issue, it received a message from Paris.

Napoleon III insisted on a joint, immediate advance of the fleets. His message informed the British that if they would not agree, he would either send the French fleet into the Black Sea unilaterally or withdraw it all the way back to France.

The message was actually a bluff, but it was potent nonetheless. The cabinet calculated that if the French withdrew, Britain would be left holding the Near

Eastern bag, including some degree of commitment to the Porte and a public that would not stand for any similar withdrawal. On the other hand, if the French advanced unilaterally, the cabinet would be left having to explain to an inflamed public why the French could do so but the greatest naval power in the world could not. In fact, Napoleon was not really in a position to carry out either of his threats. The cabinet guessed as much, but it also saw him as an unpredictable quantity and felt it could not be sure. In any case, what he demanded might be in the British interest. Many argued that it was.

A device was hit on that yielded a consensus between hawks and doves in the cabinet because it seemed to promise a possible outcome other than war. The French had been laggard in pressing upon the Turks the latest of a long series of peace plans. So London could propose a quid pro quo to Paris: Napoleon's active support for the latest peace plan in exchange for a joint advance into the Black Sea. Napoleon promptly agreed.

We may observe analytically that the Western crisis managers were able to settle on this option because it appeared to offer a resolution of the central dilemma of crisis management. They hoped to take two actions at once in order to cope with each half of the central dilemma. The need to protect and advance national interests was met by advancing the squadrons. The need to prevent war was met by strongly pressing the new peace plan. At this moment, then, they hoped that a two-track policy would resolve the central dilemma, or at least loosen it sufficiently to provide more time and breathing room.

The advance of the fleets represented a strategy of *limited escalation*. At this point, the British saw their chief interest as being the restoration of the previous international perception that Russia was not a major naval power and that Britain was the world's greatest naval power. Naturally they saw this restoration of the perceptual status quo ante as being defensive in nature. Thus, the limited escalation was seen as a defensive strategy. The Western fleets advanced into the Black Sea in the first days of 1854, with orders to bar any use of the sea by the Russian Black Sea fleet.

The Turks had been doing fairly well in the ground war[23] and now had every expectation of receiving active support from the Anglo-French fleets. They had no reason to pay much attention to the peace plan, and it soon died.

THE NEXT STEP IN THE WESTERN COMMITMENT

Czar Nicholas now comprehended that the British were determined to preserve the status quo ante, as they conceived it, in the Ottoman Empire. The czar decided to try to control any further escalation of the crisis and avoid any wider war. This decision was not an easy one, for in the meantime the Russian population had also developed a strongly pro-war mood in reaction, on the one hand, to Russian troops being attacked on two fronts and, on the other, to the great victory at Sinope. Nonetheless, St. Petersburg made no hostile response to the Western entry into the Black Sea and kept the Russian fleet in port.

The only immediate Russian response was to make an inquiry of Britain and France: Would the Western fleet prevent the Turkish navy from sailing on the Black Sea as it was preventing the Russian navy from doing?

Such were not the Western fleet's orders, but they could have been. In January 1854, the crisis managers in London and Paris lost another opportunity to control the escalating crisis. The superiority of the combined Anglo-French fleet over the Russian and Turkish fleets was so complete that its deployment could have been used to bar both belligerents from using the Black Sea. Doing so would have helped greatly to control the crisis. It would have confined the fighting to land, and more important, have demonstrated to the Russians that the Western powers were prepared to limit the degree of their hostility.

Analytically, this was essentially the same error that the Western policy makers had made the previous October, when they had advanced their squadrons to Constantinople. On both occasions, they failed to take advantage of the full potential for crisis management that their enormously powerful squadrons gave them. They did not couple one purpose of their action—to oppose Russia—with another purpose that could also have been served by the same action—to better control potential escalation of the crisis. Again, however, conceiving of the matter in this way would have required the capacity to think along two tracks at once. Instead, they identified their interests more and more, through these months, with just one side in the conflict—the Turks.

The Anglo-French action to close the Black Sea to the Russians while allowing the Turks to use it also further deepened the Western commitment to the Turks de facto. Indeed, this one-sided intervention in an ongoing war would have been sufficient justification, in international law, for Russia to declare war on Britain and France (that is, it would have been a lawful *casus belli*). However, the czar had nothing to gain by doing so, and he merely recalled the Russian ambassadors from London and Paris.

LAST CHANCES

It is not often that history is kind enough to offer policy makers who have already commited a *casus belli* a last chance to pull back from the brink and find a resolution to the crisis. In this case, history offered several chances.

The first came almost at once. An unusual military standoff existed in the local theater. The Russians could not hope to defeat the Western fleets in the Black Sea. But the fleets also could not intervene in the fighting on the land. Thus, neither side could successfully strike at the other. To remedy this situation, the British and French began preparations to create an expeditionary force of troops to be sent to the theater if necessary. But it would take months to prepare this force and, in the meantime, French and some British policy makers wanted to reopen negotiations. At the end of January, Napoleon sent a new peace offer to St. Petersburg.

Unfortunately, this diplomatic opportunity lasted only a few weeks. The Austrians injected themselves into the situation by suggesting to Britain and France that if they delivered an ultimatum demanding (on threat of declarations of war) Russian withdrawal from the principalities, Austria would support it. This was done, but the czar refused to budge. The British and French felt they had no choice but to follow through on their declarations of war.[24]

Two months passed (April and May 1854) during which the great powers were formally at war but actual fighting took place only between the Russians and the

Turks. Anglo-French preparations for an expeditionary force were pressed forward, and it was generally expected that there would be a military test of capabilities between the Russians and the West when that force was sent to Moldavia and Wallachia. The outcome was not at all certain. However great the Western naval power might be, there was a real question as to whether the West would be able to deploy to a distant theater ground forces that would be able to defeat the Russians, who were nearly on the border of their own homeland. Negotiations were largely suspended, pending the outcome of this test of capabilities.

However, that test never materialized, for the Austrians acted again. They sent St. Petersburg a unilateral ultimatum of their own, demanding that the Russians withdraw from the principalities or face Austrian intervention. Now the czar was faced with a far more potent threat, for the Austrian Empire bordered directly on that of Russia. The border was long and an attack could come at many places. The czar backed down and began withdrawing his troops from Moldavia and Wallachia. (The Austrians could claim a measure of moral legitimacy for their action because the principalities bordered on their own territory and both the Russian occupation and the fighting had—inadvertently but unarguably—harmed Austrian interests.)

By agreement with Constantinople, the Austrians peacefully occupied the principalities, the Turkish troops withdrawing to allow them to do so. Analytically, this served as a sophisticated crisis management measure. In the terminology of the late twentieth century, the Austrians were providing "third-party peacekeeping forces" whose principal missions were to keep the belligerents' troops separated and to remove the contested territory from the fighting.

The stage was now set for a renewal of general negotiations. Czar Nicholas had been unpleasantly surprised by the Austrian ultimatum and was now ready to be moderate in his expectations regarding a resolution of the crisis. The ostensible Anglo-French objective of obtaining Russian withdrawal from the principalities had been achieved. This was also the ostensible Ottoman objective. The Russians and Turks were militarily engaged only on the Caucasus front, where the fighting was not very active. From the viewpoint of a logical assessment of all parties' stated objectives, an excellent basis existed for a negotiated resolution of the crisis.

THE LAST CHANCE IS LOST

Psychologically, however, the situation was not so simple. The Ottomans saw themselves as having nearly obtained something they had not enjoyed for a very long time: an alliance with powerful Western nations, that might help them achieve a victory that would not merely restore the status quo ante but allow them to regain some part of the territory lost to Russia in previous wars. Thus, the Ottomans did not want to call off the crisis at this stage. However, they could not block its resolution without the assent of the great powers. The decisive psychology, therefore, was that of the British and French.

From the viewpoint of policy makers in London and Paris, it was awkward, to say the least, that their main stated goal—Russian retreat from the principalities— had been achieved not by themselves but by someone else. Worse, by the time it was clear that the Russians were complying with the terms of the Austrian ultimatum, the Anglo-French expeditionary force had already departed for the war theater. The troops had set sail accompanied by great popular enthusiasm and exciting departure festivities.

The powerful popular reaction to the Sinope "massacre" had been partially satisfied by the entry of the Anglo-French fleet into the Black Sea in January. But after the declarations of war, the public had avidly followed every detail of the preparations for the expedition to the war theater. After the expedition had left, the British and French publics strongly demanded a victory.

At this point, the policy purpose and the psychological effect of the declaration of war and the preparation of the expedition had become separated. For policy makers, the policy purpose of both steps was to increase the pressure on the Russians to withdraw from the principalities. However, these steps created a domestic psychological effect, which, once in existence, carried its own force. In different ways, the somewhat fragile government of Napoleon III and the democratically elected government in London were dependent upon public opinion. Once that opinion was aroused and demanding a military victory, it would have been difficult for policy makers not to comply in some fashion, even if they did not particularly wish to do so.

However, many now wanted a military victory themselves. The hawk wing of the cabinet had been increasing in influence since the previous autumn. In the perception of the hawks, the British interest in the region was not merely to restore the status quo ante for the Ottoman Empire and forestall any immediate increase in Russian influence. They conceived of a larger British interest in the region: a significant reduction of Russian power and influence.

The British hawks and doves had been having an argument that bears a marked similarity to the argument between hawks and doves in the West a century later regarding Russia. The argument in the 1850s, like that a century later, turned on this question: Were Russian objectives fundamentally aggressive? Was Russia basically an expansionist power? Or were Russian objectives fundamentally defensive? Were the Russians occasionally taking local, merely tactical initiatives to defensively bolster and strengthen what they saw as a fundamentally weak position? In the 1850s, the British debated these questions with respect to the region around the straits of the Bosporus and Dardanelles. A century later, Westerners debated similar issues with much larger scope. But the questions themselves were closely analogous.

During the late autumn, winter, and spring, the hawks gained increasing ascendency in the British cabinet. Their overall policy conclusion was that restoration of the status quo ante was not enough. In addition, Russian power in the region must be reduced. After Austria removed the principalities from the war, this wing of British opinion (which was supported by many elements in the bureaucracy and among British military officers) began casting around for other ways to diminish Russian influence. The expeditionary force had already sailed. The public was demanding a victory. Why not give them one by taking some military action that would also meet the policy objective of reducing Russian power?

Analytically we should observe that this policy stance is no longer one of crisis management. Those holding this viewpoint no longer saw themselves as managing a crisis. War had already been declared. They saw themselves as intending to win a war. They intended, of course, to have a brief, limited war with quite limited objectives. Once those were obtained, peace could be restored.

At this point occurred one of those unpredictable accidents that so bedevil the school of thought that "history is determined by great social forces, not individuals." The British and French military planners made a simple mistake, but one that was to have enormous consequences.

The military planners knew that Britain and France had a fleet in the Black Sea that was easily supreme over all possible challengers. The two countries also had an expeditionary force on the way whose capabilities were only moderate, but significant. This force could not be used in the principalities, which had been neutralized by the Austrians. The chief base of Russian power in the Black Sea area was Sebastopol, a city and port on the Crimean peninsula. Although Sebastopol was the major Russian naval base in the area, the city and the peninsula around it were only lightly garrisoned by troops.

The peninsula is connected to the Russian mainland by only a narrow neck of land, about five miles wide at its narrowest point, with the roads not in the center but somewhat near the sea. It seemed evident that, with their total command of the sea, French and British squadrons deployed on both sides of the narrow neck could sweep the roads with their guns, thereby effectively choking off the peninsula. Then no Russian reinforcements could be sent to the Crimea. The expeditionary force, landed amphibiously on the peninsula, could then attack Sebastopol from the nearly undefended landward side. Planners expected the force to capture the city, and the Russian Black Sea fleet anchored there, in just a few weeks. The orders went out. Analytically, this can be seen as a *fait accompli* strategy: an offensive strategy intended to accomplish a specific objective quickly and certainly.

Only when the Western squadrons and the expeditionary forces arrived in the vicinity did they discover the terrible error that had been made. The water on either side of the narrow neck was quite shallow. The warships could not get close enough to shore to interdict the roads with their gunfire. The Russians therefore could send reinforcements and supplies down the peninsula to their forces in the Sebastopol area. The Anglo-French expeditionary force, already being landed, would not be able to defeat the reinforced Russian units (if they could defeat them at all) before Sebastopol had time to erect major defenses on its landward approach. Yet the expeditionary force could not be taken off the peninsula without risking heavy losses on the beach and without the entire operation representing a disastrous Anglo-French defeat.

Analytically, we may observe the way in which the stunning planning error interacted with the bellicose public (and official) opinion. On the one hand, the planners' expectation of a quick, inexpensive victory made it unnecessary for high-level policy makers at home to try to resist or change public enthusiasm. On the other hand, the public enthusiasm for the war (strongly shared within the governments and military ranks) provided one of the least supportive psychological atmospheres imaginable for cautious and careful intelligence gathering, planning, and analysis.

Thus began the war in the Crimea. In September 1854, the Western troops found themselves bogged down in a land war on the edge of Asia, which turned out to last much longer and to be far more costly than anyone in the West had anticipated.

ANALYTIC CONCLUSIONS

The Crimean War was the product of a lengthy crisis, which escalated through a number of steps. Throughout most of the sequence, policy makers in the major capitals neither wanted a major European war nor doubted their ability to manage the crisis. Nonetheless they lost control of it.

Two early steps in the sequence were initiatives that had offensive objectives. Napoleon's original effort to secure the keys to the holy places was an attempt to change the status quo in France's favor and was generally recognized as such, including in Paris. Czar Nicholas's effort, via the Menshikov mission, to assert Russian influence within the Ottoman Empire was also partly offensive in motivation and was generally seen as offensive outside Russia. But this effort was also partly defensive, especially as viewed by the Russians, and thus included an important element of ambiguity.

After these two early steps, all others were motivated defensively until nearly the end, when the hawks in London and Paris chose a new and offensive objective. Throughout much of the sequence, the crisis escalated for a number of other reasons. These included an institutional failure of the Russian Foreign Ministry to report information accurately; a deliberate effort by the Turks to draw, by their own inaction, the Western powers deeper into the situation; an asymmetry between Western naval power and local Russian predominance on the ground; and the role of public opinion in the West. In addition, some of the most important strands in a causal explanation of how the crisis escalated into war concern important failures of crisis management. Six significant failures can be identified that have generic significance for crisis management today. This chapter closes with a brief discussion of each of them, in roughly ascending order of importance.

1. Possibly the simplest lesson is that technical mistakes, as they might be called, can arise and have serious consequences for crisis management, even under circumstances where a priori one might expect that such errors would not arise. There was a technical mistake, of a sort, made in the advance of the Anglo-French fleets to Besika Bay (a step decided upon and carried out initially by the British, subsequently joined by the French). Policy makers did not consider in the spring the fact that the fleets would have to leave the bay in the fall, either by advancing or retreating. A far more serious technical mistake was made at the climax of the crisis, when planners assumed that the Western fleets could get close enough to the Crimean peninsula's narrow neck to interdict the roads, thus choking off the peninsula. (This error was also made primarily by the British.)

Analytically, it is not enough to observe that these errors occurred and thus conclude that technical mistakes may play an important role in crises. We should go on to make the further observation that these errors in naval affairs were made by the greatest naval power in the world. By the mid-nineteenth century, Great Britain had ruled the seas for more than two hundred years and for most of that time had staked nearly its entire national security policy (as we would call it today) on its naval prowess. A priori one might imagine that if there were ever a country whose policy makers and national security establishment would not make technical mistakes of this kind, it would be Great Britain. Britain made them. The policy conclusions for the national security establishments of today's great powers, regarding carefulness and professional humility rather than hubris, are obvious.

2. It is highly relevant to the world of the late twentieth and early twenty-first centuries to observe the complexities that arise in the context of multipolar, regional situations. (Many of today's analysts are more familiar with the analysis of essentially bipolar crisis situations.) Here is another reason why the Crimean case, despite being so old, is a relevant and significant one for contemporary analysts.

The entire Crimean crisis, from first almost to last, is a demonstration of the complexity of multipolar regional problems. Two points not yet made in this study might be stated now. One is that an outside great power may face genuine dilemmas in trying to gain its objectives by way of support for a regional ally. One such dilemma is that it is difficult for a great power to take steps in the region without creating opportunities for the regional ally, making its own moves, to draw the great power in further. The steps taken by Britain and France created situations the Ottomans could exploit to draw them deeper into the situation. A related dilemma is that steps taken by the great power to further its own objectives by giving support to the regional ally may create situations that the regional ally can then use for *its* objectives—objectives that may not serve the interests of the great power. Britain's advances of the fleet, which were intended to deter and coerce the Russians, allowed the Turks to pursue their own objectives through actions that did not necessarily help Britain's interests. Similar dilemmas were experienced by the superpowers in the Arab-Israeli wars, as the chapters on the Middle East conflict point out.

The second point is that multipolar regional situations—especially fragile, easily destabilized ones—need to be assessed (in part) in terms of the bipolar disputes embedded within them and the possible effects of the strategies of the bipolar players. Outside great powers may hope to adopt the well-known policy of localizing conflicts. But the dynamics of regional, bipolar disputes and potential strategies available to the regional players may instead have the opposite effect: The regional conflict becomes not localized but internationalized if the outside great powers are not extremely careful. Clearly this occurred in the Crimean case, and we might observe the similarity of the Crimean case, in this respect, to the scenario that led to World War I.[25]

3. Although it was alluded to earlier, the psychology of perceptions is a theme that should be stressed. There is a tendency for analysts, inside and outside government organizations, to give too narrow a meaning to "perceptions." Understandably, they tend to interpret perceptions in an analytic sense that, much of the time, is indeed the most useful interpretation. But at times perceptions come into play in a much larger way and acquire political importance which the familiar analytic meaning may not entirely capture.

Two examples of such political perceptions from the Crimean case have been noted in this chapter. One involved the Sinope "massacre." For crisis managers in London and Paris, this easy Russian victory did not change any perceptions of the power of the Russian navy in the professional, technical sense. Sinope did not change the "admiralty threat estimates." But it did change the more global, political perception of Russia in the sense that countries around the world, and Russia itself, might now start to see Russia as a naval power and this might alter the future behavior of Russia and other nations. Political perceptions in this sense can be out of line with technical realities, but the insistence by naval analysts that nothing had really changed in the global balance of naval power would not necessarily forestall this political effect. Public opinion is usually responsive to political effects, not to technical perceptions, and it was for this reason that British and French public opinion reacted so strongly.

The other example of larger perceptions and psychology involved the Western expeditionary force. The analytic perception was that this force had been dispatched to remove the Russians from the principalities. From the literal viewpoint, this was correct. But after the British and French declarations of war, a political and public perception had arisen that this force had been dispatched to bring the war to the Russians and, of course, to win. In the context of this larger political perception, arguments in favor of new, elevated Anglo-French objectives took on a new force and meaning. The same arguments had been raised months earlier with far less effect. Over the months their analytic merit had not changed, but the perceptual context had.

This elevation of Western objectives violated the political requirement discussed in Chapter 4, calling for the limitation of objectives. As that discussion pointed out, important limits on objectives may be essential for successful crisis management. When the Western powers abandoned their earlier, defensive, political objective of restoring the status quo ante and adopted an offensive objective, they also ceased to control the crisis.[26]

4. Although mentioned earlier, another theme deserves reiteration. Opportunities may arise for policy makers to integrate actions taken to control the intensity of a crisis with actions aimed at achieving national objectives. Such coupling may greatly improve the quality of crisis management.

One of the major failures of crisis management in the Crimean case was the repeated failure of the British and French to take advantage of opportunities for this kind of coupling. Their several advances of the fleets offered them repeated opportunities to employ the fleet in ways that would control the behavior of the Turks as well as deter and coerce the Russians. Exercising these options might well have kept the crisis from escalating into a European war. These options were passed up.

5. One of the most familiar ideas to late-twentieth-century analysts is the idea of signaling one's intentions. For specialists in crisis management, this importantly includes adequately signaling the *limits* of one's objectives. The simplest lesson from the Crimean crisis is the importance of undertaking this signaling. Early in the crisis, for instance, the French made no major effort to communicate to St. Petersburg the limits of French intentions regarding the holy places, thereby leaving open the formation of grave Russian suspicions.

Analysis of the Crimean crisis also underscores a lesson that many other crises can also teach—the lesson of just how difficult that task can be. In this crisis, as in others, signals that seemed plain to the signaler were seriously misperceived or were not perceived at all. An example is the advance of the Anglo-French fleet to Besika Bay. Evidently, successful signaling may not be an easy matter. And it may not be easy for crisis managers, who believe that they have sent a clear signal, to realize that in spite of their effort, the signal may not have been correctly perceived.

The reason may be simply that the signal has not been delivered strongly enough and, hence, the answer is to make it stronger, in some crude sense of that term. A more basic reason why signals may not succeed is that the intended recipient is comprehending the world through a different set of lenses. Making a signal stronger is not necessarily the best way of coping with this difficulty; making it stronger could even backfire. The advance of the fleet to Besika Bay did not fail as a signal because the step was insufficiently strong. Doubling the size of the fleet or advancing it a little further would not have made the signal successful; viewed from the perspective of strength alone, this rather dramatic step was ample. It failed as a signal not because it was too weak but because the Russians perceived it in a context different from the intended one.

Something similar applies to the Russian step of occupying the principalities, a step that was taken, among other reasons, as a signal to the West of the seriousness of Russian anxiety. The signal did not succeed. It did not fail because the step was too weak; a stronger step would not have succeeded either. The signal failed because the West perceived the step through different lenses. Already concerned about Russian expansionist motives, the West saw the step as confirmation of the validity of that concern. (And if the Russians had taken a stronger step, that increase in the strength of the signal would have backfired, for to Western leaders it would only have confirmed the West's concern—not the Russian one—even more strongly.)

6. The role of other players' "lenses" or perceptual frameworks has a significance far beyond the problem of signaling alone. Indeed, it would be difficult to over-emphasize the importance of differing frameworks of perceptions among nations involved in international crises. Differences in underlying perceptions have diverse effects, which can be fundamental to failures of crisis management.

The Crimean case offers striking examples. The naval operation at Sinope was perceived in completely different ways in Russia and in the West, not because there was any disagreement about the facts of what had happened but because those facts were assessed within different frameworks of perceptions of the overall situation. The original French initiative regarding the holy places was perceived in very different ways in Russia, in Constantinople, and in the West, again not due to any disagreement about the facts but because the facts were assessed within differing perceptions of the larger context. And there may be no more all-pervasive causal factor underlying the entire crisis than the differing perceptions on the part of the Russians and most others regarding the fragility of the Ottoman Empire. The fact that the Russians saw the empire as nearing collapse and others did not continually created situations in which the Russians perceived themselves as acting defensively to handle that contingency, while others saw them as acting offensively to generate that contingency.

Nothing is more common among policy makers trying to manage a crisis than for them to say, "Of course, we must understand the other side's point of view."

For an analyst to repeat this again would be seen by policy makers as redundant. But the real question, as analysts can hardly stress too strongly, is what that phrase means. The Crimean crisis and many others demonstrate that it is often interpreted too shallowly by policy makers. Too often they seek to understand, and indeed do understand, the other side's point of view in certain specific respects, while failing to grasp more basic, underlying differences in the other side's view of the situation as a whole.

The maxim "we must understand the other side's point of view" was already a cliché in 1852. Policy makers in London, Paris, and St. Petersburg knew it well and thought they were carrying it out. But they carried it out only in some ways, not in others, and so they stumbled into a war that not one of them originally wanted.[27]

NOTES

1. Many researchers have emphasized that the limited time available for response to a crisis can severely constrain the quality of decision making. Some regard short response time as an inherent characteristic of crisis and include it as part of the definition of international crises; others prefer to regard it as a variable, which may or may not be present in all crises, rather than a component of the definition.

For a discussion of the importance of time pressure in crisis decision making, see for example: Charles F. Hermann (ed.), *International Crises: Insights from Behavioral Research* (New York: The Free Press, 1972), ch. 1; Michael Brecher, *Decisions in Crisis* (Berkeley; University of California Press, 1980), ch. 1; Ole R. Holsti, *Crisis, Escalation, War* (Montreal and London: McGill-Queen's University Press, 1972), ch. 1; and Alexander L. George, "The Impact of Crisis-Induced Stress on Decision-Making," in National Academy of Sciences, *The Medical Implications of Nuclear War* (Washington, D.C.: National Academy Press, 1986), pp. 529–552.

Some policy-oriented researchers have proposed specific devices for gaining time in crises; see for instance William L. Ury and Richard Smoke, *Beyond the Hotline: Controlling a Nuclear Crisis, a Report to the U.S. Arms Control and Disarmament Agency* (Cambridge, MA: Harvard Law School Nuclear Negotiation Project, 1984), pp. 38–43.

2. Cyril Falls, *A Hundred Years of War* (London: Gerald Duckworth, 1953), p. 21.

3. An exception to this generalization was the Congress of Vienna in 1814–1815, but this lasted only a few months. The diplomacy directly involved with the Crimean War extends over a period of more than four years. The extremely terse and compact treatment of this diplomacy in the *New Cambridge Modern History* takes up twenty-two pages.

4. Agatha Ramm, and B. H. Sumner, "The Crimean War," in *The New Cambridge Modern History* (Cambridge, U.K.: Cambridge University Press, 1960.), Vol. 10, p. 468.

5. The analysis that follows focuses on the crisis-management aspects of this period. As such, it explicitly contains elements that were left implicit in the original case study from which this one is drawn, and also omits other points that were developed explicitly in that original case study. For the reference to the original study, see the text note at the bottom of the first page of this chapter.

6. John Marriott, *The Eastern Question* (Fourth ed., Oxford: Clarendon Press, 1958), ch. 9; and Vernon J. Puryear, *England, Russia and the Straits Question 1844–1856* (Berkeley, CA: University of California Press, 1931), chs. 1–4.

7. Alternative Russian policies at the next step are speculative but as we shall see it is clear that St. Petersburg had useful options that were less aggressive than the one chosen. It was the more plausible for the Russians to conjecture that French designs might be far-

reaching, because the Russians themselves had far-reaching designs, however ones conceived to be applied only in certain contingencies.

8. At this time the British and French were not allied, and indeed London was at least as suspicious of French intentions as of Russian ones. The British ambassador in Constantinople was not unhappy to have an opportunity to advise the Porte to squelch the French initiative. The French decided not to pursue the matter further because they were encountering Russian, not just Turkish, resistance; Napoleon needed cheap and easy victories, not expensive ones.

9. For example, under Menshikov's program Christians involved in some kinds of judicial disputes would be able to appeal their cases to the Russian czar and receive an enforceable ruling.

10. From a dispatch from the British chargé in Constantinople to the British foreign minister in London. Quoted in A.J.P. Taylor, *The Struggle for Mastery in Europe 1848–1918* (Oxford: Clarendon Press, 1954), p. 49.

11. A further element of ambiguity, probably not relevant in the late twentieth century, was created by an additional fact: the more extreme of Menshikov's demands were made without the knowledge or approval of the Russian Foreign Ministry, at the personal order of the sovereign, Czar Nicholas II.

12. The complicated web of behavior, perception, and expectation at this point is examined somewhat more extensively in the original version of this chapter.

13. A war with Turkey was not inevitable The same two principalities had been occupied by Russian troops some years earlier, in a previous diplomatic dispute, and there had been no war.

14. Puryear, *England, Russia and the Straits*, p. 244.

15. St. Petersburg's interpretation was not completely wrong. There was an element of truth in it, and British fleets had been moved around for essentially domestic reasons before. But the weight of British policy makers' attitudes was shifting in an anti-Russian direction, and St. Petersburg did not realize it until substantially later. For a fuller assessment of the Russian misperception, see the original chapter from which this paper is drawn.

16. I do not mean, by entitling this passage "the next step," to imply that this was the first occasion at which negotiations were attempted, or that negotiations were opened only now, as a next step. In fact complicated negotiations were going on throughout this entire period among many parties. I mean, rather, that for a period in the summer of 1853, negotiations became the chief focus of crisis managers' attention, and an especially large and important effort was made.

17. Other factors included these: Turkish policy makers had repeatedly requested the arrival of the British fleet, to "calm the people," who (it was claimed) did not understand why their government was not counterattacking in the principalities. In September, there had been a leak of an internal memorandum of the Russian Foreign Ministry. That memorandum seemed to show that St. Petersburg was cynically manipulating the diplomatic negotiations then going on for its own purposes. The leaked memorandum was widely publicized in the British press, which reacted violently to it and demanded that Britain take strong action. The democratically elected government in London felt it had to pay attention to this expression of British public opinion. Behind these factors lay others, in the intricate diplomacy and politics of this period.

18. Specifically, the Straits Convention of 1841, which all the great powers including Russia and Britain had signed.

19. The Russian Navy had been equipped with a new type of shell that readily pierced the heavy outer hulls of the Turkish ships. The Turks did not have such shells.

20. In these days before public opinion polling, newspaper editorials were the chief gauge of public opinion. There is no reason to think that a modern-style polling would have yielded any different result.

21. Harold Temperley, *England and the Near East: the Crimea* (London: Longmans Green, 1936), p. 375. The Western reaction to Sinope is discussed by Temperley, pp. 371–378; by Ramm and Sumner, "The Crimean War," p. 477; and by Alyce Edythe Mange, *The Near Eastern Policy of the Emperor Napoleon III* (Urbana, IL: University of Illinois Press, 1940), pp. 34–35.

22. Strictly speaking, I should say the West made no explicit commitment to the Turks to defend them in any specific, identified contingency that was at all probable. There was a reasonably clear commitment to protect the city of Constantinople from direct Russian attack. However this possibility was so remote as to be nearly meaningless. The city had its own defenses and there was a strong Turkish army between it and the Russians. Russian forces in the principalities were not nearly large enough to contemplate such an attack. And there was no reason to suppose that Czar Nicholas was contemplating such a thing (and indeed, he was not).

23. In spite of the disaster at Sinope, the Ottoman campaign in the Caucasus had succeeded in advancing into Russian territory and capturing a key Russian fort before winter made further fighting impossible. The Ottoman counterattack in the principalities had also proven stronger than the Russians or many others had expected.

24. The czar calculated correctly that Austrian support was only diplomatic and that the Austrians were not in a position to threaten force. The account presented here of events during this period is necessarily simplified. For a fuller account, see the original version of this chapter.

25. I am indebted to Alexander George for the points made in this paragraph and the two preceding ones. A simpler, related point is that an outside great power may undertake some localized initiative for its own ends, which have the unintended consequences of upsetting delicate, regional balances of power. France's Holy Places initiative did this in the Crimean case.

26. It would also be valid to say, as I did earlier in this chapter, that at this point the British and French policy makers decided that they no longer wished to manage a crisis; now they wished to win a war.

Much earlier, the Russians had also adopted an offensive political objective, vis-à-vis the Ottomans. It was partially that (coupled with the Western determination not to allow it) that was driving the crisis all along. However, the Russians also had defensive objectives, and they were prepared to negotiate their political objectives, as they proved both by accepting the Vienna Note and by accepting the Austrian ultimatum that they withdraw from the principalities.

27. The importance of the underlying framework of perceptions, not just of specific, concrete perceptions, is stressed in many chapters of the book from which this case study is adapted: *War: Controlling Escalation*. (See in particular ch. 9.) That book also stresses the importance of an element that, due to limitations of space, I have not discussed here: expectations about the future, as distinct from perceptions (of the present). The fundamental role played by differences in perceptions also is a familiar theme in many studies of international crises and of the origins of wars, and its importance is stressed by many authors.

CHAPTER 6

The Role of Crisis Mismanagement in the Outbreak of World War I

Jack S. Levy

In this study I analyze the extent to which the outbreak of World War I can be explained by the mismanagement of the July 1914 crisis by political and military leaders.[1] I begin by identifying the preferences of each of the great powers over the set of most likely outcomes of the crisis, along with the assumptions, interests, and expectations that help shape these preferences. I then specify a number of critical decision points in the processes leading to the war and the diplomatic, military, institutional, and domestic constraints facing political leaders at each point. This provides the framework for an analysis of whether this combination of interests and constraints precluded political leaders from taking alternative actions that might have avoided a major war without sacrificing their vital interests.

World War I is the most frequently cited illustration of "inadvertent war" and is the source of many hypotheses on this phenomenon.[2] For this reason it is essential that we understand precisely in which respects (if any) World War I was inadvertent. Such understanding is especially important in light of the current debate over the validity of Fritz Fischer's argument that German political and military elites seized the opportunity created by the assassination of the Austrian archduke to provoke a great power war in order to secure Germany's position on the continent, establish its status as a world power, and solve its domestic political crisis.[3] I will argue that the images of World War I, either as inadvertent or as the deliberate outcome of Germany's drive for world power, are each exaggerated and that a hypothesis based on a belligerent Germany is not necessarily inconsistent with a crisis management/ inadvertent war perspective.

This study was supported by a Social Science Research Council/MacArthur Foundation Fellowship in International Peace and Security. It has benefited from the comments and criticisms of Michael Adas, Raymond Duvall, John Freeman, Alexander George, Scott Sagan, Stephen Van Evera, John Vasquez, Phil Williams, and various participants in international relations colloquia at the University of Minnesota, Washington University-St. Louis, and Rutgers University. This chapter is an expanded version of my article entitled "Preferences, Constraints, and Choices in July 1914," *International Security* 15, 3 (Winter 1990–91): 151–86; used by permission of MIT Press.

THEORETICAL CONSIDERATIONS

One point that has received inadequate attention in the theoretical literature is that not all international crises are equally amenable to crisis management by political leaders. Some crises are structured in such as way—in terms of the preferences of the actors and the diplomatic, geographical, technological, and organizational constraints on their freedom of action—that they are likely to escalate to war in spite of the desires of statesmen to avoid it.[4] In other cases, political decision makers may give far higher priority to securing their objectives than to avoiding war and may be willing to accept a high risk of war for that purpose. Or, they may actually prefer war to other possible outcomes. The outbreak of war under such conditions should not be treated as a failure of crisis management but instead as the result of antithetical interests of states.

Because of their exclusive focus on short-term considerations, applications of crisis management frameworks often underestimate the importance of the underlying interests and structural constraints that generate the crisis, shape the context within which decisions are made, and, to a great extent, determine the interests of the actors and the strategies available to them. The result is often an exaggeration of the causal importance of the management or mismanagement of the crisis by decision makers. In order to avoid this, a study of crisis management must begin by specifying the underlying preferences of each of the actors and the structural constraints on their actions.[5] This analysis of preferences must incorporate a set of outcomes that is sufficiently differentiated to reflect accurately the definition of the situation by the actors themselves. The common dichotomy between war and nonwar is not useful in all cases, for political leaders often have significantly different evaluations of the desirability of different *kinds* of war based on their assessments of likely outcomes. For example, they may prefer a limited war to a negotiated peace but prefer peace to a larger war involving outside intervention. The failure to incorporate a differentiated set of possible outcomes into the analysis is a serious limitation of many studies of the causes of World War I and other wars, and it has led to some unproductive debates about whether or not decision makers really "wanted war."

The existence of irreconcilable interests between states is not necessarily inconsistent with a strategy of crisis management. A state may prefer the military defeat of an adversary through war to any reasonable negotiated compromise but still wish to conduct the war in such a way as to minimize the likelihood of hostile intervention by third parties. This may require a strategy of intrawar crisis management and intrawar deterrence, and Alexander George's political and operational requirements for successful crisis management are still relevant. We can continue to speak of political limitations on the decision makers' objectives and on the means employed to achieve those objectives in wartime as important criteria for intrawar crisis management designed to secure one's interests without provoking a costly escalation of the conflict. If central decision makers preferred a limited war, yet for whatever reasons fought the war in a way that triggered an undesirable escalation, then the outcome could be attributed in part to the failure of crisis management.

My analysis of the role of crisis mismanagement in the outbreak of World War I will begin with an analysis of the preferences of each of the great powers over various possible outcomes of the crisis.[6] I will then identify a number of critical decision points in the processes leading to war. At each point I specify the options available to each of the great powers; identify the expectations of political leaders (and differences among them) regarding the probable intentions of their adversaries and the likely outcomes of various courses of action, including the chances of victory or defeat and likely diplomatic and domestic consequences; analyze whether the actions of political and military leaders contributed to the escalation of the crisis to war and whether those actions deviated from the political and operational requirements of crisis management; and assess the extent to which departures from these principles of statecraft were compelled by the interests and expectations of political leaders and the structural constraints under which they operated, and the extent to which those actions can be better explained by flawed information processing, decision making, and crisis mismanagement.

I will also attempt to evaluate whether the probability assessments of the political leaders were reasonable given the information available, whether more timely actions might have had more favorable consequences, and whether more creative statecraft might have generated new options and changed the structure of incentives in a way that could have led to a less costly outcome. Because my primary concern is to evaluate whether the combination of interests and constraints prevented political leaders from acting in a way that might have avoided a major war and to do so within a reasonably parsimonious framework, I will not give much attention to the psychological factors and human limitations that affected the behavior of decision makers.[7]

I want to emphasize that the question of the role of crisis mismanagement in the processes leading to war is not equivalent to the question of the causes of war. Whereas the latter question is concerned with both the underlying (or remote) and immediate (or proximate) factors contributing to war, the question of crisis mismanagement is concerned primarily with the immediate causes. Focusing on these proximate causes directs attention away from the broader structural forces that shape the military, political, social, and economic context within which the crisis occurs.[8] These factors are not ignored in this study but are incorporated into the interests and preferences of each of the great powers and the structural constraints of their choices.[9]

Because of the complexity of the crisis leading to the outbreak of war in 1914 and the critical importance of the timing of actions, I have included a timeline of key events in the appendix.

THE INTERESTS, PREFERENCES, AND EXPECTATIONS OF THE ACTORS

In the aftermath of the assassination of Archduke Franz Ferdinand, the leaders of all of the European great powers expected that Austria-Hungary would seek some form of compensation from Serbia. Serbia had been suspected of some complicity in the assassination, and its actions had become an increasing threat to the internal stability of the fragile Austro-Hungarian empire. There was little fear in the immediate aftermath of the assassination that war or even a major crisis would inevitably follow, for it was generally assumed that significant Serbian concessions would be forthcoming and sufficient to maintain the peace.[10]

The fear of war increased dramatically on July 23 and 24 with the news of the Austrian ultimatum to Serbia and its extreme demands.[11] The sense of danger was intensified by the fear that because of interlocking alliance agreements, there was a good chance that an Austro-Serbian war might draw in Russia in support of Serbia, Germany in support of Austria-Hungary, and France in support of Russia, along with the respective Balkan allies of each of the great powers, creating a continental war. It was also feared that the war could expand further into a general European or world war through the intervention of Britain on the side of the Entente.[12]

Thus, most of the leading political decision makers in July 1914 perceived four possible outcomes of the July crisis:

1. A peaceful but one-sided *negotiated settlement* based on Serbian acceptance of most of the Austrian demands
2. A *localized Austro-Serbian war* in the Balkans
3. Expansion of the Austro-Serbian conflict into a *continental war* involving Russia, Germany, and France as well as Austria-Hungary and Serbia
4. Expansion of the continental war into a *world war* through the intervention of Britain[13]

In the decision-theoretic framework that will guide this study, these four possibilities constitute the set of feasible outcomes of the crisis.

First let us consider *Austria-Hungary*. Faced with increasingly intractable ethnic problems and internal decay in its multinational empire, the increasing strength and hostility of Serbia, and the deterioration of the dual monarchy's position among the great powers, Austro-Hungarian leaders had become increasingly desperate and saw only two alternatives: the preservation of the dual monarchy through the reconstruction of the Balkans under its own domination, or the collapse of the monarchy.[14] They believed that the assassination of the archduke provided the perfect opportunity to move against Serbia, that immediate military action would be perceived as legitimate by the other powers, that although Russia and France were gaining in strength they were not yet ready for war, and that a preventive war against Serbia to arrest both external and internal decline was necessary while the military and diplomatic contexts were still favorable.[15]

The only concessions that Vienna would have accepted in lieu of war were those that provided an opportunity to check Serb nationalism and break Serbia's hold on the loyalties of the minorities of the dual monarchy, which would have required Serbia's total and humiliating acceptance of all Austrian demands. Austrian leaders recognized that no Serbian government could accept the demanded infringement on Serbian sovereignty without soon being overthrown, and in fact they constructed the ultimatum in such a way that it was too humiliating for Serbia to accept. When Serbia surprisingly accepted the vast majority of the terms of the ultimatum, Austria-Hungary still proceeded with a declaration of war, which revealed its preference for war over a settlement involving anything short of unconditional Serbian capitulation.[16]

The evidence is mixed regarding the extent to which the risk of Russian intervention was acknowledged and incorporated into Vienna's decision-making calculus. Although they recognized some risk of Russian intervention, Austrian leaders (and particularly Chief of Staff Conrad von Hötzendorf) believed that an intervention could in all likelihood be avoided by a *fait accompli* against Serbia backed by firm assurances of German support (just as German threats had forced Russia to back down in the Balkans crisis of 1908).[17] Though Austria clearly preferred a local war to a continental war, the status quo was so intolerable that a continental war was prefereable to a negotiated peace. Thus, Austria was willing to risk a larger war through Russian intervention, particularly as long as Russia was perceived to be unready for war.[18]

Although Austria perceived British intervention to be highly unlikely, it would have been very costly, for by putting more pressure on Germany in the west, British intervention would further delay Berlin's ability to divert its armies to the east and therefore leave Austria-Hungary in a vulnerable position with respect to Russia. If Austrian decision makers had been faced with the choice between a negotiated settlement or a world war, they probably would have preferred the former. But because they preferred a local war to a negotiated settlement, they pursued a policy of crisis management only to the extent that they believed a *fait accompli* against Serbia would minimize the risks that a local war would escalate.

There is little doubt that the Austro-Hungarian preference for a local war over a negotiated settlement based on unilateral Serbian concessions was not unconditional but was contingent on German support. Austrian leaders needed German support for both diplomatic and domestic political reasons. Both Foreign Minister Leopold von Berchtold and Chief of Staff Conrad feared being abandoned by Germany and strongly preferred a negotiated settlement to an Austro-Russian/Serbian War without German support for Austria. Austrian leaders also believed that their decaying monarchy could embark on war only if it was united internally, and this was problematic. Emperor Franz Joseph wanted to wait for the results of the official investigation of the assassination to prove Serbian complicity, and Hungarian Prime Minister Stephan Tisza also opposed war, perhaps for domestic political reasons.[19]

The German blank check of July 5 and 6 was sufficient to satisfy Conrad and (after some negotiation) to persuade the political opposition within Austria-Hungary that war was a desirable solution. Luigi Albertini concludes that if Germany had not wanted Austria to move against Serbia, "neither Francis Joseph, nor Berchtold, nor even Conrad would have gone ahead with the venture." Thus, German support was a necessary condition for an Austro-Hungarian war against Serbia.[20]

Serbia contributed more to the onset of the crisis (by failing to prevent the assassination) than to the escalation of the crisis to war. Serbia preferred peace to war with Austria and was willing to make significant concessions in order to preserve it, but only up to a point. The Serbian documents show that Serbian Prime Minister Nikola Pasic intended to accept no demands that infringed on Serbian sovereignty, in part because extreme concessions would be politically impossible. Although Russian support and, in fact, encouragement of Serbian firmness were undoubtedly helpful, Belgrade's hardline position predated the ultimatum.[21] This suggests that Serbia's rather conciliatory reply to the ultimatum[22] represented its maximum concessions, that it was not inclined to be more flexible in extended negotiations with Austria-Hungary, and that the concessions likely to appease Vienna would probably have been unacceptable to Belgrade.[23]

Russia's leaders believed that their strategic and economic interests in the Turkish Straits depended on maintaining Serbia and Romania as buffer states and that Russia's influence in the Balkans and indeed its great power status depended on its influence among the southern Slavs and its patronage of Serbia. Yet the tsar and other officials were appalled by the assassination and could not risk alienating Britain. On balance, they were willing to allow Serbia to be chastised severely as long as Austria removed from the ultimatum "those points which infringe on Serbia's sovereign rights."

Thus, the tsar preferred peace based on some Serbian concessions to an Austro-Serbian war, but he also preferred a continental war and even more a world war with British intervention against Germany to a local war in the Balkans, for Russia could not allow Serbia to be crushed by Austria. This position was reinforced by public opinion and the press, which was strongly pro-Serbian, and by the belief among many Russian leaders that an assertive foreign policy was necessary for their own domestic political purposes and for the internal development of Russia.[24]

Russian leaders also believed that Russia's reputation was at stake, both as a great power in Europe and as the traditional protector of the Balkan Slavs. They were particularly sensitive to its recent humiliations in the annexation crisis of 1908–1909 and the Russo-Japanese War and believed that to back down again would seriously undercut its future power and influence in the Balkans and in the European great power system as a whole. Foreign Minister Sergius Sazonov spoke for most Russian leaders, including many moderates without panslav leanings, when he stated that if Russia were to abandon the Slavs now, "she would be considered a decadent state and would henceforth have to take second place among the powers."[25]

Nearly all factions within *Britain* preferred a negotiated settlement, based on Serbian concessions, to any war, and British leaders made considerable efforts to discourage Austria-Hungary from attacking Serbia. British Foreign Secretary Edward Grey had no sympathy for Serbia, and although he preferred a negotiated settlement based on significant Serbian concessions to an Austro-Serbian war, he was willing to tolerate some Austrian military action against Serbia. Grey was more concerned with localizing the war and preventing escalation than with avoiding Austrian action per se, and hence he strongly preferred a local war to a continental war as long as Austrian actions were kept within limits.[26] He believed that the best way to avoid a continental war was to prevent a local war, and to that end, Grey undertook several diplomatic initiatives. These included his July 26, 1914, proposal for a four-power conference in London and his proposal on the 29th that Austria halt its military advance in Belgrade.[27] But if the war were to escalate to a general continental war, Grey, other Liberal Imperialists, and Unionists believed that British interests in the integrity of France and the maintenance of the balance of power in Europe would be sufficiently threatened that British intervention would be necessary. Thus, they preferred a world war to a continental war. But the radicals, Labour, middle-of-the-road liberals, and many in the cabinet preferred neutrality, and it took the German violation of Belgian neutrality to sway the idealists on the left.[28] Thus, British preferences between a continental war and a world war were context dependent, unstable, the source of considerable internal debate, and they only emerged over time.

France had no direct strategic or reputational interests in the Balkans and had not given her Russian ally much support there in recent diplomatic crises. But the alliance with Russia was the cornerstone of France's security policy and its only protection against Germany. France had to support Russia in any war with Germany, but for domestic reasons it was highly desirable that the war be over an issue that was perceived to involve a direct threat to France and that Russia not initiate the war (as specified in the alliance treaty).[29] President Raymond Poincaré and Premier René Viviani hoped that Austria would not push too hard and that Russia could tolerate some Serbian concessions; they thus preferred a negotiated peace to a local war and a local war to a continental war. They did their best to restrain Russia without alienating it and to support plans for the localization of any Austro-Serbian war (including the Halt in Belgrade Plan), though their absence from France during much of the crisis limited their influence in the other capitals.[30] But if Russia insisted on war, French leaders knew they would be forced to follow rather than risk the disintegration of the alliance, and in that case they preferred a world war with Britain on France's side.

The critical case is that of *Germany*, for key Austrian and particularly Hungarian decision makers were unwilling to move against Serbia without German support. The early revisionist view in the 1920s was that Germany did not want war of any sort but needed to maintain Austria-Hungary as its only great power ally in Europe, and that in spite of its best efforts to restrain Vienna, Germany ultimately allowed itself to be dragged unwillingly into a world war by its weaker ally.[31] After the path-breaking work of Fischer, it is now generally agreed that Germany preferred a local war in the Balkans even to a one-sided negotiated settlement, that it exerted sustained pressure on an already eager Austria-Hungary to initiate a war, and that it was willing to tolerate a high risk of a continental war in the process.[32] But the outcome that German political leaders feared most, and almost certainly did not expect, was the expansion of a continental war into a world war through British intervention.

In response to the assassination of the archduke and Vienna's subsequent proposal "to eliminate Serbia" as a key actor in the Balkans, the kaiser informed Austrian Ambassador Count Ladislas Szogyeny on July 5 that Austria-Hungary could "count on Germany's full support" even in the case of "grave European complications," including Russian intervention. This infamous "blank check" was formally issued by Chancellor Théobald von Bethmann-Hollweg the next day, and there is substantial evidence that Germany not only gave Austria-Hungary a free hand but actually encouraged it to move militarily against Serbia. Many German leaders doubted Vienna's resolve and urged Vienna to move as quickly as possible in the hope that a *fait accompli* would minimize the likelihood of the expansion of the war. Germany also insisted that the ultimatum to Serbia be framed in such strong terms as to make Serbia's acceptance virtually impossible, which only reinforced Vienna's determination. Two weeks later, when Grey and Sazonov were trying to buy time and manage the crisis, Germany gave no support to proposals for mediation between Austria-Hungary and Serbia, did all that it could to sabotage them, and continued to press Austria-Hungary to act quickly. Thus, the evidence is fairly clear that Germany preferred a local war even to a one-sided peaceful settlement of the Austro-Serbian conflict.[33]

Although German political leaders were willing to accept the risk that a local war would escalate into a continental war, they actually preferred a local war to a continental war. They hoped and expected that an Austrian *fait accompli* against Serbia, backed by German threats against Russia, would enable the central powers to manage the intrawar crisis in such a way as to minimize the risk of escalation, though they recognized some risk of Russian intervention and were willing to tolerate that risk.[34]

Austria would almost certainly emerge victorious from a localized Austro-Serbian war. Such an outcome would do more, however, than strengthen Austria at the expense of Serbia and reduce the Slavic threat in the Balkans; Bethmann-Hollweg and others believed that if France were economically and militarily unable or unwilling to come to the aid of Russia, there was a good chance it might be divided from Russia. In Fischer's words,

> the central objective of [German] diplomacy . . . was to split the Entente, and this Bethmann-Hollweg meant to enforce at any price, with or without war. In any case the Serbian crisis would bring about a re-grouping of continental power relationships in a sense favorable to Germany and without intervention by Britain. The conflict must be localized . . . and Germany hoped to bring about a new grouping of forces in both the Balkans and the Mediterranean.[35]

Jarausch makes a similar argument:

> A local Balkan war would bring a diplomatic triumph, a realignment of the south-eastern states and the breakup of the Entente. Equally likely seemed a continental war, engulfing Russia, Austria, France, and Germany. In such a conflict, the general staff promised a good chance of winning. Less desirable than a localized conflict, a continental struggle might ease the Russian pressure from the east, revitalize faltering Austria and regain the diplomatic initiative in the Balkans. In Bethmann's mind only the last alternative was fraught with unacceptable danger: world war.[36]

Jarausch concludes that Germany wanted a "quick punitive strike, but *not* . . . a continental or world war. . . . Bethmann clearly preferred local war, was willing to gamble on continental war, but he abhorred world war."[37] There is little doubt that world war was the last preference of all German leaders. Even Fischer and Imanuel Geiss, the strongest supporters of the German war guilt argument, do not go so far as to argue that Germany sought a world war and argue instead that the neutralization of Britain was a central aim of Bethmann-Hollweg's foreign policy.[38] It would be much easier to handle Britain after either a defeat of France and Russia or an Austrian smashing of Serbia that left the Entente in shambles.

The question of German preferences between a continental war and a local war is more difficult to establish, though the bulk of the evidence suggests that most German political leaders preferred a local war but were willing to risk a continental war. The view of Fischer and his associates that Germany preferred a continental war[39] is based in part on the view that Germany wanted a preventive war against Russia before the completion of Russia's military reorganization and the modernization of its railroad system. Support for a preventive war among German civilians as well as the even more hawkish military is thoroughly documented,[40] though the question of whether they actually preferred continental war to a local war is rarely addressed. My argument is that the fear of Germany's relative decline led German political leaders to prefer a continental war to the status quo, but that their expectations that a localized Austro-Serbian war would lead to the splitting of the Entente and the regrouping of European diplomatic alignments (as well as an Austrian victory) led them to prefer such a war as a less costly means of achieving Germany's larger security interests. It was in part for this reason that Bethmann-Hollweg opposed a preventive war against Russia.[41]

The incentive for a continental war might have been further enhanced by the hope of German political leaders that a major war would bolster their domestic political support and give them added time to deal with the internal crisis arising from the consequences of industrialization and the rise of the Social Democracy movement.[42] Although German political elites recognized the domestic benefits of an external war, they also recognized that such a war carried substantial risks; a victorious war by Austria against Serbia, on the other hand, would bring domestic benefits with a minimum of risks.[43] Thus, because of a combination of preventive and scapegoat motivations, German political leaders preferred a local war to a continental war and the latter to a negotiated settlement but were willing to risk the second in pursuing the first so as to avoid the third. These motivations were strong enough to increase the critical risk of escalation the Germans were willing to accept in encouraging Austrian military action against Serbia but not so strong that they actually preferred Russian intervention and the continental war that would follow.

We can now summarize the preferences of the five leading great powers plus Serbia in the set of the four most plausible outcomes of the crisis: a negotiated peace based on significant but not unconditional Serbian concessions (NP), a localized war in the Balkans between Austria-Hungary and Serbia (LW), a continental war involving Germany on the side of Austria, and Russia and France on the side of Serbia (CW), and a general European or world war with Britain joining the war against the central powers (WW). Here the symbol > means preferred to and ? indicates that a definitive preference cannot be established.[44]

Austria-Hungary	LW	>	CW	>	NP	>	WW
Germany	LW	>	CW	>	NP	>	WW
Russia	NP	>	WW	>	CW	>	LW
France	NP	>	LW	>	WW	>	CW
Britain	NP	>	LW	>	WW	?	CW
Serbia	NP	>	WW	>	CW	>	LW

Thus, all of the European great powers plus Serbia preferred a negotiated settlement to a world war. Yet they found themselves entrapped in a world war that resulted in enormous human and economic costs, profound social and political changes, and the collapse of three empires, but that achieved few of their goals, settled little, and set the stage for another cataclysmic world war two decades later. How could this happen? Was the crisis structured in such a way that each state's rational pursuit of its own interests led inevitably to a world war, or did statesmen fail to manage the crisis in a way that might have avoided a world war while preserving their vital interests?

It must be recognized that political leaders were not confronted with a single decision as to whether or not to go to war in 1914 but, instead, with a series of decisions at a succession of critical decision points as the crisis unfolded over time. Their preferences concerning outcomes were relatively stable over time, but their policy options, strategic constraints, available information, and policy dilemmas were often different at these successive decision points. Moreover, each decision altered the constraints that decision makers faced at the next critical juncture and further narrowed their freedom of maneuver. Consequently, it is necessary to examine the calculus of choice at each of these critical decision points.[45]

CRITICAL DECISION POINTS

The key decision points were as follows:

1. The Austro-Hungarian decision of whether to attack Serbia or to accept a negotiated settlement based on extensive but not unconditional Serbian concessions.[46] An Austrian declaration of war was a necessary condition for war of any kind.
2. The German decision of whether to support or encourage an Austro-Hungarian attack against Serbia. German support for Austria was a necessary condition for war of any kind.
3. The Serbian decision of whether to give an unconditional acceptance to the Austrian terms. Unconditional acceptance of the ultimatum would have been sufficient for peace and the absence of a war of any kind.
4. With the Austro-Hungarian declaration of war, the decision for each of the great powers as to whether to accept the Halt in Belgrade proposal. Austrian (and German) acceptance of this proposal would probably have been sufficient to prevent a continental war (and therefore a world war) and to terminate the Austro-Serbian conflict in its early stages.
5. The Russian decision of whether to intervene in support of Serbia or to allow her to be crushed by Austria. Nonintervention by Russia was a necessary and sufficient condition for the localization of the conflict.
6. The German decision of whether to stand aside in an Austro-Russian war, intervene against Russia alone, or initiate a war against France as well as Russia.
7. The British decision of whether to intervene or not in the continental war. Intervention meant world war.

The choices made at several of these critical junctures are fairly easily explained in terms of the preceding discussion of the various great powers' preferences and their expectations regarding possible actions and their consequences. Austria wanted to reduce Serbia to the status of a vassal either through war or through Serbia's total capitulation and, once assured of German support, refused to compromise. Germany's support for Austria follows from its preferences for a local war and its assumption of British neutrality in the event of a continental war. Serbia was willing to compromise but not to the point that would infringe on its sovereign rights. Because both Germany and Austria wanted a local war, in one sense crisis mismanagement played essentially no role in the outbreak of the Austro-Serbian war on July 28. In another sense, however, the two countries did engage in intrawar crisis management, for they believed that an Austrian *fait accompli* in conjunction with German deterrence of Russia would be sufficient to secure their objectives while at the same time minimizing the risks of Russian intervention and the expansion of the Austro-Serbian war. Their willingness to risk a continental war was contingent, however, on the critical assumption of British neutrality, to which we now turn.[47]

THE ASSUMPTION OF BRITISH NEUTRALITY

Because German support of Austria was a necessary condition for an Austro-Serbian war and German expectations of British neutrality in a continental war were a necessary condition for its support of Austria, German perceptions of the strong likelihood of British neutrality emerge as the key to the escalation of all stages of the crisis. I will argue that Bethmann-Hollweg and other German political leaders were quite confident of British neutrality, that they based their policy on that expectation, and that only with the shattering of their assumption on July 29 did they reverse their policy and attempt to manage the crisis to avoid war. I will then attempt to explain why Germans clung to this dubious assumption, focusing both on the British failure to give a clear commitment to intervene and on the German failure to recognize the warnings that did exist.

The kaiser had been convinced from the beginning of the crisis that Britain would stand aside from a European conflict. Later in the war he exclaimed, "If only someone had told me beforehand that England would take up arms against us!" The evidence is less clear concerning Bethmann-Hollweg, who at times appeared to waver on the question of the likelihood of British intervention and who recognized the degree of uncertainty involved.[48] But the bulk of the evidence seems to suggest that Bethmann-Hollweg was generally confident of British neutrality and that he had based his entire policy on that assumption. He assured the kaiser (July 23) that "it was improbable that England would *immediately* enter the fray," implying that if England did intervene it would probably be too late. Bethmann-Hollweg remained convinced of British neutrality until the night of July 29, when the German ambassador to England, Karl Lichnowsky, conveyed an unequivocal warning from Grey that although Britain would stand aside in an Austro-Serbian war, it would probably be forced to intervene if France were involved.[49]

The German military, perhaps reflecting a tendency toward worst-case military planning, generally did not share the assumption of British neutrality. Alfred von

Schlieffen's original plan was based on the expectation of British intervention in response to a German attack against France, and this assumption was shared by Helmuth von Moltke and most other military leaders. The Germany military had little respect for the British and discounted the impact that their intervention would have on the war. The Germans expected a short war that would be decided before the British had time to make an impact and for that reason did not push the civilian leaders particularly hard to secure British neutrality. There is no doubt that Bethmann-Hollweg, even in his most pessimistic moods, accepted this minimum assumption that Britain would not intervene early in a continental war.[50] In any case, the German military did not begin to have a decisive influence on key decisions until July 30, and by that time perceptions of British intentions were fairly uniform among German civilian and military leaders.[51]

The assumption of British neutrality by Bethmann-Hollweg, the kaiser, Foreign Secretary Gottlieb von Jagow, and others was the cornerstone of German policy throughout the July crisis up until July 29. Albertini concludes that there is little doubt that in allowing Austria to attack Serbia, "Germany started from the assumption that, if the attack developed into a European war, England would remain neutral." The importance of British neutrality is suggested by Bethmann-Hollweg's efforts throughout the crisis to secure a formal commitment of neutrality from the British. He believed that British policy could be influenced by German diplomacy and concessions and that the likelihood of Britain's neutrality depended upon its perception that Germany was fighting a defensive war in response to Russian aggression.[52]

This concern for British neutrality was reinforced by domestic political considerations. Bethmann-Hollweg wanted to ensure a united front at home and was uncertain of the intentions of the Social Democrats, who had vacillated between a socialist-internationalist and a socialist-patriot position (they had supported the Army Bill in 1913). Bethmann-Hollweg believed that the Social Democrats were virtually certain to support a defensive war for which Russia could be blamed. Thus, for both diplomatic and domestic political reasons, he went to great lengths to ensure that Germany did not mobilize before Russia so that Russia would bear the onus for starting the conflict.[53]

The importance of British neutrality to the Germans is also demonstrated by their reaction to Lichnowsky's reports beginning July 26 that Grey had changed his position (after Austria's rejection of Serbia's response to the ultimatum). The kaiser was the first to take these warnings seriously (July 27), and within a day he made his compromise Halt in Belgrade proposal.[54] It was not until Lichnowsky's telegram on the 29th that others' expectations of British intentions began to shift, but the response in Berlin was immediate, drastic, and quite revealing. As Fischer argues, German political leaders, especially Bethmann-Hollweg, were "shattered" by that telegram, for "the foundation of their policy during the crisis had collapsed." Bethmann-Hollweg responded with a flurry of six increasingly urgent telegrams that night. He proposed that Vienna accept mediation and the Halt in Belgrade plan, and warned that Germany would not allow itself "to be drawn wantonly into a world conflagration by Vienna."[55] These efforts by the chancellor appear to represent a sincere effort to find an acceptable resolution to the crisis that would avoid the one outcome he had always feared but had recognized was likely only on the 29th. In a span of several hours, Bethmann-Hollweg reversed the policy that had guided Germany throughout the July crisis.[56]

Berchtold's first response was to reject the chancellor's proposal, though he delayed a formal response. After three weeks of German pressure to move against Serbia, Austria-Hungary had made the politically difficult decisions to issue the ultimatum, declare war, and begin the bombardment of Belgrade and the mobilization for war. Once these actions were taken it was difficult to modify and redirect them. This would involve an enormous loss of credibility, the upsetting of a coalition of domestic political interests that had not been easy to construct, and the undoing of a psychological commitment. As Lebow argues, "[H]aving finally crossed their psychological Rubicon, the Austrian leaders obviously felt a tremendous sense of psychological release and were hardly about to turn back willingly."[57]

This episode demonstrates the importance of the timing of actions designed to reinforce crisis management. Had Germany pressured Austria-Hungary for restraint prior to the declaration of war on the 28th, it would have been far more difficult for Vienna to resist, particularly given Tisza's likely support for the peace proposals and the consequences of his defection for the internal unity that Austrian leaders perceived to be essential for any war effort. Austrian acquiescence would have been even more likely had the German pressure come before the ultimatum was delivered on the 23rd, and there is every reason to believe that an earlier warning from Grey would have been sufficient to trigger a German warning to Vienna. Albertini concludes that "if Grey had spoken before 23 July, or even after the 23rd but not later than the afternoon of the 27th, as he spoke on the 29th, Germany would very likely have restrained Austria from declaring war on Serbia and the European war, at least for the time being, would have been averted."[58]

It is conceivable, however, that even as late as July 30 the war could have been avoided, though the margin for maneuver was admittedly thin. Berchtold continued to delay a response to Bethmann-Hollweg's proposal, and the chancellor continued his pleas for peace but with less enthusiasm. He refrained from intensifying the pressure on his Austrian ally, perhaps because of an increasing fatalism, a sense of narrowing options, and a loss of control induced by the psychological stress of the crisis.[59] This restraint was unfortunate, for stronger German pressure on Austria-Hungary probably would have worked at this point. In spite of the diplomatic, domestic political, and psychological costs to Vienna of reversing course after a declaration of war, the prospect of being left to fight Russia and Serbia alone would have been even less desirable. In addition, strong German pressure might have provided Hungarian Prime Minister Tisza with an excuse to back out of a decision he had undertaken only with the greatest reluctance, and his defection would have undermined the internal unity necessary for a successful war effort.[60]

It is easy to say that Germany should have known that Britain would intervene in any continental war involving its French and Russian allies, particularly if Belgium's neutrality were violated. A German victory in a two-front war would give Berlin a position of dominance on the continent and control of the channel ports that were so critical for British naval security, leave Britain without strong allies on the continent, and provide Germany with a strategic and industrial base from which it could challenge Britain on the global level. British support for France in the 1905 and 1911 Moroccan crises was a clear indicator that no British government was likely to stand aside while Germany increased its influence at the expense of France. The naval agreements with France, of which the Germans had some knowledge, created an additional British obligation, and British reputational interests were also at stake. Thus, Moltke had argued (in a 1913 memo) that Britain would intervene in a Franco-German war "because she fears German hegemony and true to her policy of maintaining a balance of power will do all she can to check the increase of German power."[61] Moreover, there had been numerous warnings from Britain in the past that it would not stay neutral in a continental war.

Although the dismissal of these warnings by German leaders and their failure to appreciate British strategic interests can be explained in part by their motivated psychological biases and wishful thinking,[62] they did have some reasons to believe that the British might remain neutral. There were multiple signals (or noise) coming out of London, and these were not all consistent with the warnings from Lichnowsky. Though Grey repeatedly refused to give Berlin an unconditional commitment of neutrality, he also refused to give France and Russia a commitment to come to their defense. Thus, the uncertainty generated by the failure of British leaders to give a formal commitment was exacerbated further by their statements and actions. Given the equivocal nature of incoming information and its low signal-to-noise ratio; prior expectations of German leaders, which had been reinforced by an overall improvement in Anglo-German relations over the previous three years; and the strategic dilemmas, political difficulties (particularly in terms of civil-military relations), and psychological stress that would have been generated by a different interpretation of the evidence, it was perhaps not surprising that German political leaders concluded that Britain would stay out of a continental war, particularly if British decision makers perceived the war as being initiated by Russia.[63]

That German misperceptions were the product of the inherent ambiguity of the incoming signals as much of their own motivated biases is suggested by the fact that officials in France and Russia, whose motivated biases would have led in the opposite direction from Germany's and who had constantly pressured Britain for a clear commitment, were also uncertain of British intentions.[64] Even the British were uncertain as to what they would do. Chancellor of the Exchequer David Lloyd George and Winston Churchill, first lord of the admiralty, were both skeptical regarding whether the government would intervene on the continent,[65] and Grey himself was uncertain. On the 29th, Grey told Jules Cambon (French Ambassador to Berlin) that "[i]f Germany became involved, we had not made up our minds what we should do." On August 1, the cabinet rejected a proposal to dispatch the British Expeditionary Force to the continent and forbade Churchill from ordering the full mobilization of the navy.[66]

The British failure to give a clear and timely commitment in support of its allies was a critical step in the process leading to an Austro-Serbian war and its expansion into a world war, for it eliminated the one threat that would have led German political decision makers to restrain their counterparts in Vienna. Yet British leaders were faced with some serious diplomatic and domestic political constraints, and it is not clear that they could have acted differently. Diplomatically, they were confronted with a difficult strategic dilemma: While a clear commitment would reinforce deterrence against Germany, it might at the same time encourage Russia to pursue a riskier course against Austria-Hungary. Many British leaders assumed that by leaving their commitment ambiguous, they could maximize the likelihood that they could restrain Russia without alienating it and deter the Germans without provoking them.[67] This reasoning was undoubtedly less compelling after July 27–28, for the German rejection of Grey's proposal for a four-power conference and the Austrian declaration of war greatly reduced any remaining doubt regarding the intentions of the central powers.

Another factor contributing to Britain's failure to make commitment from the beginning of the crisis was the optimism generated by the general improvement in Anglo-German relations over the previous three years. Although the naval rivalry between Britain and Germany remained unresolved, in other respects relations were much improved. This led Grey and others to assume erroneously that the July 1914 crisis could be resolved through Anglo-German cooperation, as had the earlier Balkan Wars, and therefore they chose to dilute and delay their deterrent threat in the hope that a more accommodative policy might achieve their desired goals with fewer risks.[68] Evidence suggests that Grey perceived that Berlin was divided between a war party and a peace party (headed by Bethmann-Hollweg), that his hesitancy to issue a deterrent threat was motivated by his fear that it would only strengthen hardline elements in Berlin, and that his conciliatory actions were aimed at strengthening Bethmann-Hollweg in his internal political struggles with the military.[69] By July 28, however, it became increasingly clear that Germany had no intention of restraining Austria-Hungary, and therefore these considerations cannot explain Grey's continued failure to issue an unequivocal warning to Germany after that date.

By July 27, but probably not before, the primary factor precluding Grey from issuing a clear warning to Germany was cabinet politics in England. A majority of the liberal cabinet was opposed to British involvement in war, and Grey knew that it would be difficult to secure any commitment from them.[70] At a full meeting of the cabinet on the 27th, Grey asked if Britain should intervene if France were attacked by Germany. Five ministers warned that they would resign if such a vote were taken. On July 29, the same day as Grey's informal warning to Germany through Lichnowsky, the cabinet agreed that "at this stage we were unable to pledge ourselves in advance either under all circumstances to stand aside or on any condition to go in." On August 1, Grey stated, "we could not propose to Parliament at this moment to send an expeditionary military force to the continent."[71] As Churchill later argued with regard to a possible warning to Germany that Britain would declare war if Germany attacked France or violated Belgian territory, "I am certain that if Sir Edward Grey had sent the kind of ultimatum suggested, the Cabinet would have broken up, and it is also my belief that up til Wednesday (29th) or Thursday (30th) at least, the House of Commons would have repudiated his action. Nothing less than the deeds of Germany would have converted the British nation to war."[72]

It is significant that Churchill refers to *German* deeds. Austrian action against Serbia was not sufficient to bring in Britain, for, as I argued earlier, if a negotiated peace were not possible, Britain preferred a localized war in the Balkans, whatever its outcome, to a continental or world war. But what specific German deeds were necessary and sufficient to bring Britain into the war? For Grey, any Franco-German war was enough of a threat to British interests to require intervention. This was probably not true for the cabinet, unless the course of the war were to pose such a threat to France that only British intervention could block German hegemony on the continent. Although it is difficult to know for sure how the cabinet would have responded under various contingencies,[73] it appears that the critical trigger for cabinet approval of British intervention in the early stages of the war was the German violation of Belgian neutrality, which was an integral part of the Schlieffen Plan.[74] The significance of Belgium for Britain, and particularly for the radicals in the cabinet, was more political than strategic, for the balance of power on the continent and the future of Belgium and its channel ports would ultimately be dependent upon the outcome of a Franco-German war quite independently of whether Belgian neutrality was violated at its outset. For years the radicals had refused to be swayed by balance of power arguments, and in the end they need a moral justification, which was provided by the 1839 guarantee of Belgian neutrality. As Zara S. Steiner argues, "[T]he issue of Belgium was all-important because the radical conscience needed a *raison d'etre.*"[75]

Grey's domestic political constraints did not leave him bereft of means of influencing Germany. Although a formal threat to Berlin was probably precluded by cabinet politics, an informal warning was not. Recall that although Grey's warning of July 29 through Lichnowsky was not approved by the cabinet, it had a tremendous impact on Germany, and that a similar informal warning could have been issued much earlier. As I argued above, such a warning probably would have been sufficient to maintain the peace, at least for a time. But Grey perceived other constraints during this period, including the fear of giving too much encouragement to Russia and not enough to what he saw as the peace party in Berlin. Although we now know that Germany was more in need of restraint than was Russia and that earlier pressure from London on Berlin would probably have avoided war, it is more difficult to say that Grey should have known this for certain in July 1914.

I have argued that in the absence of a German violation of Belgian neutrality, the probability of British intervention in a continental war would have been considerably less. Such intervention would also have been delayed, for British radicals would probably have needed to see severe military setbacks to France in order to be convinced of the strategic necessity of military action. Thus, the Schlieffen Plan and the envelopment of France through Belgium not only precluded German decision makers from effectively managing to avoid the world war they feared but also ensured that the British would enter the war at an early stage and thus maximize their impact. Thus, part of the explanation for the erroneous assumption of British neutrality by German political decision makers must be traced to their miscalculation of the consequences of the Schlieffen Plan, to which we will return.

Although the erroneous assumption of British neutrality was a necessary condition for German support of an Austrian invasion of Serbia and, consequently, also a necessary condition for a continental or world war (at least until the Austrian declaration of war on July 28), it was not a sufficient condition. It is conceivable that a continental war could have been avoided if Austria had undertaken military action immediately following the assassination, for under some conditions a *fait accompli* strategy involving quick and decisive military action may be optimum in terms of securing one's objectives with minimum risk of escalation.[76]

THE DELAY OF AUSTRO-HUNGARIAN MILITARY ACTION

Although Austria did pursue a *fait accompli* strategy, it waited for a month after the assassination of the archduke, and the timing may have been critical. The combination of universal outrage over the assassination, the belief that some Austrian response in defense of its honor would be legitimate, the fear of a wider war, and German deterrence of Russia might have been sufficient to localize the war. Thus, Taylor asserts that "[t]he one chance of success for Austria-Hungary would have been rapid action." Ritter concludes that "Swift action would have been politically much more effective and less dangerous to the peace of Europe than the endless delay that did take place." Samuel R. Williamson, Jr., writes that "What had appeared in early June to be a calculated, acceptable risk—a local war with Serbia— would loom more dangerous and provocative two weeks later."[77]

The assumption that a larger war might be avoided through immediate action was held by most German leaders and was a major rationale underlying their pressure on Austria-Hungary to move as quickly as possible. It was also accepted by Grey.[78] There is less evidence regarding Russian decision makers, and their views, of course, were critical. For the tsar, the principle of monarchical solidarity may have outweighed strategic and reputational interests in the immediate aftermath of the assassination. The greater the delay, however, the more the punishment of Serbia would be decoupled from the assassination and the indignation it generated, and the legitimacy it might have provided. A punitive strike against Serbia that did not involve extensive territorial acquisitions would have lessened Russian (and British) concerns. Hungarian Prime Minister Tisza's demand that Austria-Hungary renounce any territorial annexations at Serbian expense, and the acceptance of this renunciation by the Austro-Hungarian Council of Ministers, was in fact designed to minimize the likelihood of Russian intervention, though it came too late.[79] Perhaps a major consequence of the delay was to transform the possibility of an early punitive strike into a local war that was much more likely to escalate.

How do we explain the Austro-Hungarian delay? Immediate action was not possible because of the necessity of securing German support. There were several reasons for the extensive delay after Germany issued a blank check on July 5–6. One reason concerned military constraints. Berchtold had initially wanted to attack Serbia without first mobilizing and was distressed to learn from army chief of staff Conrad on July 6 that an invasion could not begin until two weeks after mobilization.[80] Although this explains the delay in military action, it does not explain Austria's delay in issuing the ultimatum or declaring war. One important factor here derives from Austria-Hungary's domestic structure and internal political situation. Tisza opposed any form of military action, and the risk of a major war with Russia required a united monarchy. Tisza was not won over until July 14, when others accepted his demand for a renunciation of territorial annexation at Serbia's expense.[81]

Two additional factors combine to explain the additional ten-day delay in the issuance of the ultimatum. One was organizational constraints imposed on the army by the timetable of the harvest leaves, which Conrad had agreed to in response to agrarian pressures. Early in July, Conrad learned that sizable numbers of Habsburg troops were dispersed throughout the empire on harvest leave and were not scheduled to return until July 21–22. An early recall of the troops would disrupt the harvests and possibly the railroad-based mobilization plans and would eliminate the possible benefits of surprise associated with the ultimatum.[82] A second factor was diplomatic: Austrian decision makers did not want to deliver the ultimatum to Serbia until after the state visit of French president Poincaré and Premier Viviani to St. Petersburg on July 23, for they feared that the French might encourage a stronger Russian response.[83] The ultimatum to Serbia was delivered that day, followed by Serbia's reply on July 25 and Austria's declaration of war on the 28th.

By this time, any Austrian military action would be so decoupled from the outrage following the assassination that it would have lost the halo of legitimacy that might have accompanied earlier action. Moreover, once the unprecedented terms of the ultimatum became known, Serbia was no longer perceived as the primary violator of international norms. At this point, it was more likely that the best hope for peace lay in a *delay* in the declaration of war. The timing of the declaration of war was absolutely critical and deserves more attention in the literature. First, it led directly to a partial Russian mobilization, which initiated a rapid and nearly irreversible sequence of mobilization threats and actions over the next four days.[84] Second, it made it much more difficult for Vienna to give in to German pressures for restraint, which began on the night of July 29–30 after Lichnowsky's warning from Grey. Why the rush to declare war if an invasion could not begin for two weeks?

The matter was addressed by Berchtold and Conrad on July 26. Conrad wanted to delay a declaration of war until August 12, when a crushing military *fait accompli* against Serbia could be carried out. But Berchtold insisted on an early declaration of war to pacify Germany, which had been strongly pressing for immediate action. In addition, he now seemed to welcome the lapse between the declaration of war and the beginning of military operations and hoped that it would provide time for additional pressure on Serbia from its allies.[85] That is, his preferred strategy (and that of Emperor Franz Joseph) apparently had switched from military victory over Serbia to securing its "unconditional submission" through a particularly strong variant of coercive diplomacy.[86] But Berchtold's strategy backfired, only strengthening Serbia's resolve and that of her allies and accelerating the conflict spiral.

This is not surprising, for a declaration of war is rarely an effective instrument of coercive pressure, particularly in the context of a refusal to provide the adversary (or its allies) with a face-saving way out of the crisis. The more general problem lies in the inconsistency in Austrian policy. Vienna deliberately designed the ultimatum so that it could not be accepted and would therefore provide a justification for war.[87] Finding that it lacked the means for an immediate *fait accompli*, Austria switched to a highly coercive policy but did not combine it with diplomatic measures that might have made it effective. Austrian leaders did not soften the degrading terms of the ultimatum to provide Serbia with a face-saving way out of the crisis and only compounded matters further with a premature declaration of war that could only lead to the further escalation of the crisis.

In retrospect, one can probably conclude that Conrad's preference for a delay in the declaration of war until military operations could begin would have increased the probability of a peaceful settlement, though perhaps not by much. Austrian mobilization would still have begun, so that countermobilizations by Russia and then by Germany could not be far behind. But that might have taken a few days and would have provided additional time for some important new developments to have an impact. Bethmann-Hollweg's efforts to restrain Vienna would have been more likely to succeed in the absence of an Austrian declaration of war, which put its credibility at stake and in so doing increased the domestic political and psychological costs of backing down. In this different diplomatic context, the combination of German pressure and the new Halt in Belgrade proposal might have been sufficient to delay, at least temporarily, a world war that none of the great powers wanted.[88]

THE HALT IN BELGRADE PROPOSAL

Europe learned the details of Austria's 48-hour ultimatum on July 24. The Russians concluded that Austria-Hungary was deliberately trying to provoke war, and the next day the tsar authorized preparatory military actions (short of mobilization) in order to deter an Austrian move against Serbia and, if that failed, enable the army to intervene in Serbia's defense. Grey began exploring the possibility of British mediation on the same day and on July 26 invited France, Germany, and Italy to send their ambassadors to London for a conference. Austria refused, as did Germany, which continued to press for immediate military action as a means of localizing the war.

By July 27, the kaiser had begun to fear British intervention and at the same time believed that after the conciliatory Serbian reply, "every cause of war has vanished." On the 28th, he instructed Jagow to request that Vienna accept "a temporary military occupation of a portion of Serbia (Belgrade)" as a "guaranty for the enforcement and carrying out of the promises." Grey's proposal the next day was nearly identical, asking for mediation under the following conditions: Russia would suspend military operations against Serbia, while Austria would occupy Belgrade and "hold the occupied territory until she had complete satisfaction from Serbia. . . . [but] not advance further," pending great power mediation between Austria and Russia. These proposals for a halt in Belgrade demonstrate a sincere effort by the kaiser, Jagow, and Grey to manage the escalating crisis and to localize it in the Balkans. Their basic aim was to allow Austria to gain a significant diplomatic victory and to demonstrate its military prowess and prestige without damaging Russia's reputation.[89]

Austrian Foreign Minister Berchtold's immediate response to German Ambassador H. L. Tschirschky was that it was too late to change course, and his formal response was then delayed and deliberately evasive. Berchtold believed that the temporary occupation of Belgrade would not be sufficient to achieve Austria's initial crisis objectives—the removal of the threat from Serbia and the southern Slavs. He feared that although a temporary occupation of Belgrade would provide leverage against Serbia, it would also generate diplomatic pressure on Vienna to soften its demands. Moreover, even if Russia were willing to tolerate an Austrian occupation of Belgrade, it would be "mere tinsel," for the Serbian army would remain intact, see Russia as its savior, and provoke another crisis in two or three years under conditions much less favorable to Austria. He was also concerned about the reputational and domestic political costs of reversing course after an earlier declaration of war.[90]

In spite of the costs to Austrian leaders of reversing course and scaling back their objectives, the costs of defying German pressure would also be enormous, particularly if such pressure were accompanied by explicit threats that Germany would withdraw its support from Austria if the Austrians did not accept the proposal. There is a good chance that additional German pressure would have been sufficient to compel Vienna's acceptance of the Halt in Belgrade Plan and deter more extensive military action at that time. Albertini concludes that on the day of the order of general mobilization, "Berchtold was assailed by doubts and hesitations, so that it remains an open question whether he would actually have put the order into execution if he had received further strong pressure from Berlin in favor of the 'Halt in Belgrade' and mediation." Similarly, David Kaiser argues, "the Vienna government could not possibly have held out against united pressure to accept some variant of the 'Halt in Belgrade' plan."[91] A critical reason for Vienna's failure to accept the proposal was the fact that German pressure on Vienna was only moderate in intensity, accompanied by mixed signals, and withdrawn prematurely.

Although the Halt in Belgrade proposal was fully consistent with many basic principles of crisis management, it failed in part because of the violation of the principle that top-level decision makers maintain centralized political control of diplomatic and military actions and ensure that their diplomatic signals to allies as well as adversaries are not subverted by subordinates. The kaiser's proposal was ready for delivery early on July 28 (before the declaration of war), but Bethmann-Hollweg delayed its delivery to Vienna for twelve hours and distorted its contents in significant ways to reduce its impact. Whereas the kaiser insisted only that Austria had to have a "guaranty that the promises were carried out," the chancellor emphasized in his telegram to German ambassador Tschirschky that the aim of the temporary occupation was "to force the Serbian Government to the complete fulfillment of her demands," and he deleted the phrase about war no longer being necessary. Bethmann-Hollweg also told Tschirschky "to avoid very carefully giving rise to the impression that we wish to hold Austria back." Tschirschky delayed further and, in fact, may have encouraged Austrian belligerency. In addition, Albertini concludes that Tschirschky and Berchtold "were in league" to deceive Berlin, deflect German pressure for restraint, and delay a response to German pressures.[92] The ambiguous signals from Berlin continued even after Bethmann-Hollweg reversed course on July 29 and began pressing Vienna to accept Grey's Halt in Belgrade proposal. At the same time that Bethmann-Hollweg was urging Berchtold to consider the Halt in Belgrade proposal, Moltke was urging Conrad to press forward with mobilization and warning that any further delay would be disastrous. This led Conrad to complain, "Who actually rules in Berlin, Bethmann or Moltke?"[93]

Not only was Berlin's pressure too weak to impress Austrian leaders with the urgency of an immediate acceptance of the peace proposal and with the potentially serious consequences of their failure to do so, but the pressure was not sustained. Bethmann-Hollweg reversed his position and effectively withdrew German support from the Halt in Belgrade proposal on the evening of July 30, after receiving reports that Russia was about to begin general mobilization, that Belgium had begun preparations for war (which could bottle up the German invasion of France and therefore disrupt the entire war on both fronts), and that Austria was concentrating its forces against Serbia (which would leave inadequate strength in Galicia for an offensive against Russia).[94] These reports had led to an abrupt shift in Moltke's position, a general uneasiness among the military, intense pressure for the declaration of a "state of imminent war," and increased military influence on the political decision making process, which up to that point had not been significant.[95] Thus, a real opportunity for peace was lost. Albertini concludes that "if on the 30th Bethmann had not let himself be overruled by Moltke, had insisted with Berchtold, on pain of nonrecognition of the *casus foederis*, that Austria should content herself with the Anglo-German proposals, and had then waited for Sazonov to follow suit, the peace of the world might have been saved."[96]

With the announcement of the Russian mobilization on the morning of July 31, political as well as military decision makers came to perceive that a continental war was inevitable, and these perceptions soon took on a self-fulfilling character. Efforts to deter war gave way to concentration on how to prepare for an unavoidable war. Military requirements came to dominate the agenda, and the military acquired a leading role in decision-making processes. The sequence of events from July 28 to August 4 seemed to follow an inexorable pattern, and political leaders came to believe that they had lost control of events.[97] This loss of control is often traced to the rigidity of the Austrian, Russian, and German mobilization plans, which we now consider. We will find that these rigidities provided some interesting and often unrecognized opportunities as well as constraints.

THE AUSTRO-HUNGARIAN MOBILIZATION

The nature of the Austro-Hungarian mobilization and war plans derived largely from the strategic dilemma confronting the dual monarchy—the need to be able to fight a two-front war against both Russia and Serbia. The plans were designed to permit a certain degree of flexibility, allowing for partial mobilization against either or both of these adversaries and for offensive action against one and defensive action against the other, depending on the nature of the threats to Austrian interests. But once a partial mobilization was initiated against Serbia, the troops involved could not easily be shifted back to the Galician front to meet a major Russian attack. If Vienna moved with two of its three groups against Serbia, it would have difficulty dealing with a major offensive from Russia. Thus, the constraints on Austria-Hungary, which are often attributed to the rigidity of the army's mobilization plans, actually stemmed from the inherent difficulties of fighting a two-front war, the poor quality of the Austro-Hungarian railway system, and the inability and unwillingness of the Germans to provide significant help against Russia in the early stages of the war because of the requirements of the Schlieffen Plan.[98]

These constraints provided military incentives for Vienna to speed up the flow of events rather than slow them down once mobilization had been initiated. Conrad insisted that he had to know by the fifth day of mobilization whether the Russians were planning to intervene, else his plans would go awry. In fact, an early Russian decision to intervene might have been better for Vienna than a delay accompanied by uncertainty regarding Russian intentions.[99] The Austrians' dilemma was that the longer they delayed mobilization against Serbia, the more time they would have to learn of Russian intentions and plan accordingly, but this would also mean more time for external diplomatic pressure on Austria to show restraint and soften its demands on Serbia.

THE RUSSIAN MOBILIZATION

These constraints on Vienna provided an opportunity for Russia that is rarely acknowledged in the literature. Russian leaders hoped that a mobilization, in conjunction with diplomatic pressure from the other powers, would deter Austria from an all-out military attack against Serbia, limit the concessions Serbia would have to make, and improve its own ability to defend Serbia in the event of war. But it is not clear that Russia had to mobilize in order to deter Austria from sending more than a minimal defense force to the Balkan front and, therefore, limit the damage to Serbia from an Austrian attack. These objectives could have been accomplished through a mere *threat* to mobilize. And there was no immediate threat to Serbia, for an Austrian invasion could not begin until August 12. Thus, Turner argues that "it was very much to Russia's advantage to delay any mobilization until a substantial part of the Austrian army was entangled in operations against Serbia."[100]

This suggests that a Russian partial mobilization was not really necessary to support Russian interests in the Balkans and that it could have been delayed for several more days, perhaps accompanied by coercive threats against Austria. Such restraint would have presumably delayed the alarm felt by Moltke and the German generals, eliminated the need for German mobilization or even preparatory military action, and thus provided more time for Bethmann-Hollweg to continue his pressure on Vienna to accept the Halt in Belgrade Plan. It is in this sense that the Russian mobilization was the critical action leading to the war. Turner suggests that it was taken in part because "Sazonov and the Russian generals failed to grasp the immense diplomatic and military advantages conferred on them by the Austrian dilemma."[101]

But protecting Serbia was not Russia's only aim. Russian leaders recognized that if deterrence failed and they were forced to intervene on Serbia's behalf, Germany would certainly follow and be led by the Schlieffen Plan to attack France first. It was imperative for Russia to come to the aid of its French ally before it was crushed by Germany.[102] Russian leaders also perceived that speed was of the essence, that a few days' delay would put France in an increasingly precarious position, and, therefore, that they had to mobilize as quickly as possible, particularly once war appeared inevitable. They also thought they could get an additional jump on Germany by conducting some mobilization measures in secret, and, in fact, the initiation of "the period preparatory to war" on July 26 is best seen as the first stage of mobilization.[103]

For technical military reasons, it was not feasible for the Russians to order a partial mobilization against Austria-Hungary and then wait before mobilizing against Germany. A partial mobilization would disrupt railway transport and delay for months a systematic general mobilization against Germany. It would not only leave Russia dangerously exposed to a hostile and war-prone Germany but also leave it unable to come immediately to the aid of France. Thus, the tsar, after some wavering and intense pressure from the military, decided to order general mobilization for July 31 rather than a partial mobilization against Austria-Hungary alone.[104]

THE GERMAN MOBILIZATION

In order to increase the likelihood of securing the support of the Social Democrats at home and the neutrality of Britain abroad, German officials wanted to shift the blame for the war to Russia and had a strong incentive not to be the first to mobilize. Thus, some form of Russian mobilization was a necessary condition for German mobilization, and general mobilization by the Russians was a sufficient condition for German mobilization. The question is whether a Russian partial mobilization was also a sufficient condition for a German mobilization. Although Albertini and others may be correct that a Russian "partial mobilization would have led to war no less surely than general mobilization,"[105] the causal linkage was delayed and indirect rather than immediate and direct: A partial mobilization by Russia would eventually have led to a German mobilization because of the Russian threat to Austria, not because of the direct threat to Germany. In fact, the threat to Germany would have been lessened somewhat as Russian partial mobilization measures progressed because these measures would have delayed and interfered with a subsequent Russian general mobilization.

The historical record suggests that German military and political leaders were cautious in reacting to Russian military actions prior to the general mobilization. On July 29, three days after Russia had begun pre-mobilization measures, Moltke refused to support the proposal of War Minister Erich von Falkenhayn for a proclamation of a "threatening danger of war." After hearing of Russia's partial mobilization, Bethmann-Hollweg refused to order an immediate German mobilization, a decision that generated only slight opposition from Moltke. Bethmann-Hollweg believed that the *casus foederis* had not arisen and that Germany must wait for a state of war between Russia and Austria-Hungary "because otherwise we should not have public opinion with us either at home or in England." For the same reasons, it was imperative that Austria should not appear as the aggressor.[106] The German military began pressing hard for mobilization only on July 30, after new information regarding the intensity of Russian military preparations, but the German's demand was rejected by Bethmann-Hollweg. It was only with the news of the Russian general mobilization the following day that the chancellor agreed to a German mobilization.

Once both sides had mobilized, however, Germany had a strong incentive to strike first because of the Schlieffen Plan. Because the capture of Liège and its vital forts and railroad lines was necessary before the invasion of France could proceed, the Schlieffen Plan required that German armies cross the frontier and advance into Belgium as an integral part of the mobilization. The perception that even small leads in mobilization would have significant military benefits and that small delays could be catastrophic created additional military incentives to move as quickly as possible.[107] Thus, once Russia moved to a general mobilization, the German decision for war was determined entirely by the structure of the alliance system and existing mobilization plans. Military requirements for preparing for war took precedence over political requirements for avoiding one, and there was no feasible role for crisis management in avoiding a continental war. And because the Schlieffen Plan involved the movement through Belgium, a world war was almost certain to follow.[108]

It is important to note that the Schlieffen Plan made it inevitable that any war involving Germany would necessarily be a two-front war in which Britain would be forced to intervene, regardless of the particular issues at stake or the political conditions under which war occurred. This was particularly tragic because a world war was the outcome German leaders most wanted to avoid. The reliance on the Schlieffen Plan in spite of its escalatory dynamic can be explained in part as a result of the separation of military planning from the political objectives it was presumably designed to serve. German mobilization and war plans in general, and the Schlieffen Plan in particular, were constructed exclusively by the military, with minimal consultation, with civilian leaders, and on the basis of technical military considerations rather than political ones.[109] The sweep through Belgium, for example, did not take into account the impact on England of the violation of Belgian neutrality. Jagow's request in 1912 that the need to violate Belgian neutrality be re-evaluated was rejected by Moltke, and, until 1913, there was not even an inquiry into the feasibility of alternative operational plans that might carry fewer political risks.[110]

Taylor concludes that the military mobilization plans "aimed at the best technical results without allowing for either the political conditions from which war might spring or the political consequences which might follow." They reflected the traditional military priority placed on winning any war that breaks out, rather than doing everything possible to prevent it from occurring. The plans were also rigid and were very difficult to change at the last minute in response to changing political circumstances. Ritter concludes that "[t]he outbreak of war in 1914 is the most tragic example of a government's helpless dependence on the planning of strategists that history has ever seen"; and Albertini concludes that the primary reason that Germany "set fire to the powder cask" was "the requirements of the Schlieffen Plan, which no doubt was a masterpiece of military science, but also a monument of that utter lack of political horsesense which is the main cause of European disorders and upheavals."[111]

The problem of the separation of military planning from political objectives was exacerabated further by the lack of knowledge on the part of political leaders of the details of their military plans and those of their adversaries. The basic problem was decision makers' ignorance of the discrepancy between their foreign-policy objectives and the limited range of military instruments available to support them. Whereas the military generally conceived of mobilization as a means of preparing for a certain and immediate war and designed military plans with that in mind, political leaders generally conceived of mobilization as an instrument of deterrence or coercive diplomacy. They had little conception of how few options they had, how inflexible and indiscriminate they were, or of the extent to which their room to maneuver had been limited. In particular, although political leaders were vaguely familiar with the idea that "mobilization means war," they lacked a profound understanding of what this really meant, how quickly one would follow from the other, and how their freedom of action to conduct policy would be affected. They were unaware that diplomatic options would be foreclosed and war begun before mobilization had been completed. They took certain actions in all sincerity to manage the crisis and avoid war, assuming that the risks were limited or at least manageable, only to find that they had forced their adversary to escalate and that their subsequent choices had been narrowed even further.[112]

If political leaders had only understood the consequences of certain mobilization measures, it is conceivable that at certain critical decision points they might have acted differently. At a minimum, they might have delayed taking certain actions for as long as possible in order to provide more time for managing the crisis through diplomacy to protect their interests without war. Like many others, Foreign Secretary Grey did not realize that German mobilization meant war. Perhaps more important, he failed to recognize the dangers of the Austrian and Russian mobilizations and the chain reactions they would trigger. He made no effort to restrain his Russian ally and, in fact, initially thought it reasonable that Austria, Russia, and France mobilize while he continued to work for peace.[113] Because of the importance to Russia of securing a British commitment to enter the war, British pressure would have reduced the likelihood of Russian intervention or at least delayed the critical Russian mobilization, though by how much it is difficult to say. Such a delay would have reduced the probability of a continental war, but in so doing, it would have increased the probability of an Austrian move against Serbia.

Until fairly late in the crisis, Russian Foreign Minister Sazonov perceived partial mobilization as a usable and controllable instrument for the purposes of coercion and did not realize that it would undercut the process of negotiating for peace. On July 24, he proposed the mobilization of the military districts of Kiev, Odessa, Moscow, and Kazan (but not Warsaw, Vilna, or St. Petersburg) as a means of pressuring Austria while at the same time not alarming Germany. He did not realize that Austria would be forced to order a general mobilization, which would involve the Austro-German alliance, and therefore require a general mobilization by Germany and lead to war. Nor did he realize that a partial mobilization by Russia would seriously interfere with a subsequent general mobilization.[114]

Albertini concludes that if Sazonov had understood these aspects of the mobilization process and known that for Germany any mobilization was equivalent to war, there is "no doubt" that he would have acted differently. He "would never have got the Council of Ministers on 24 July or the Tsar on 25 July to approve it [the partial mobilization] in principle, nor would he have proclaimed it on the evening of 28 July with incalculable consequences."[115] He would have attempted to delay a partial mobilization (even more so if he had understood the strategic dilemmas faced by Austria-Hungary and the potential military advantages to Russia of a delay in its own mobilization), and the tsar would probably have gone along. This would have delayed the point at which the military in Germany and Russia began to exert a significant influence on their respective political processes. Beth-mann-Hollweg's pressure on Vienna to accept the Halt in Belgrade Plan could have continued, and the likelihood of a peaceful settlement would have been increased, although by how much is uncertain.[116]

CONCLUSIONS

I have argued that the political decision makers of each of the great powers in the 1914 crisis preferred a peaceful settlement, based on extensive Serbian concessions, to a world war. Yet they ended up with the war that none of them wanted and none deliberately sought, and, in this sense, World War I was inadvertent. The primary explanation for this outcome lies in the irreconcilable interests of the great powers, the structure of power and alliances that created difficult strategic dilemmas, the military mobilization and war plans that were designed to deal with those dilemmas, some critical assumptions on each side regarding the likely behavior of its adversaries, and miscalculations by each great power as to the consequences of its own actions and those of others. Thus, the causes of World War I are to be found primarily in the underlying economic, military, diplomatic, political, and social forces that existed prior to the onset of the crisis and that created a mutually irreconcilable set of political interests among the great powers. Although the perceptions, decisions, and actions of statesmen during the July crisis increased the probability of war, that probability was already fairly high immediately following the assassination of Archduke Franz Ferdinand.

To say that war was likely in July 1914, however, is not to say that it was inevitable. There were several critical points in the July crisis at which political leaders could have behaved differently without seriously threatening their vital interests, and thereby they might have facilitated other attempts to manage the crisis. The set of actions that would have been mutually acceptable was not only quite small, however, but was critically dependent on timing, for the windows of opportunity in July 1914 were not only narrow but were constantly changing, and at different times for each of the great powers. I have argued that the failure to undertake the necessary actions can be interpreted as the failure to follow some basic principles of crisis management. Although many of the departures from these principles can be explained in terms of strategic necessities following from underlying preferences, others were due to strategic miscalculations and failures of individual judgment that might have been avoided and to domestic and bureaucratic pressures that might have been finessed.

One opportunity for a local Austro-Serbian conflict to be contained occurred in the two weeks immediately following the assassination. Because of the hostility the assassination aroused toward Serbia, the perceived legitimacy of a modest Austrian response, and the concern to avoid a great power war, it is conceivable that an Austrian *fait accompli* might have been successful without provoking

Russian intervention. The prospects for localization would have been enhanced if the Austrian *fait accompli* had been limited to the weakening of Serbian military power without significant territorial readjustments, particularly if it were accompanied by a great power agreement based on something comparable to the Halt in Belgrade proposal. But Austrian action was delayed because of Vienna's need to secure absolute assurance of German support and then to overcome internal political divisions in the dual monarchy. An additional cause of delay was the technical military constraints deriving from the cumbersome Austro-Hungarian mobilization process. Great power consensus on a halt in Belgrade was probably impossible until the crisis had intensified to the point that Grey realized the need to warn Germany and Bethmann-Hollweg realized that Austria must be restrained. Thus, the opportunity for localizing the conflict at this stage was probably slim.

Adequate German pressure would almost certainly have been sufficient to restrain Austria and prevent war, but such pressure was not forthcoming prior to July 29 because German political leaders wanted a local war and were willing to risk a continental war as long as they were fairly certain of British neutrality. Their erroneous assumption of British neutrality resulted not only from wishful thinking but also from the inherent ambiguity of the signals coming from London and the absence of a firm British commitment. This lack of firmness was due to (1) Grey's fear that an explicit threat to Germany would only encourage Russian meddling in the Balkans and, at the same time, undermine the assumed "peace" party in Berlin; (2) his hope that the crisis could be managed through cooperation with Berlin; and (3) opposition from radicals in the British cabinet. The terms of the July 23–24 ultimatum, the preliminary mobilization measures by Austria, Russia, and France beginning on the 26th, and the German rejection the next day of Grey's four-power conference proposal should have been enough, however, to convince Grey of the need to issue an earlier warning to Germany. Had this come before the Austrian declaration of war, German pressure would probably have been enough to force Austria to accept the Halt in Belgrade Plan rather than launch an all-out invasion of Serbia.

The Austrian declaration of war was itself premature and unnecessary on strictly military grounds, for Austria could not begin an invasion of Serbia until August 12. Had Berchtold followed Conrad's preference to delay the declaration of war, the few extra days before Austrian mobilization triggered a Russian mobilization would have provided additional time for Bethmann-Hollweg to force Austria to accept the Halt in Belgrade Plan and for Grey to solidify Russian and French support for the plan. The timing of the declaration owes more to pressure from Germany than to strategic calculations, and German pressure itself was based on the erroneous assumption that the likelihood of localization would be enhanced by immediate military action. But the time for a successful military *fait accompli* had long passed. A strategy of coercive diplomacy based on the ultimatum was probably more likely to succeed. Berchtold seems to have been thinking along these lines, at least by the 26th, but his failure to soften the terms of the ultimatum to make it consistent with his new strategy precluded the successful use of coercive diplomacy.

Even if the declaration of war had not been delayed, however, a major war might have been avoided. Adequate German pressure would still have been sufficient to restrain Austria and force it to accept the Halt in Belgrade Plan. But only modest pressure was forthcoming from Bethmann-Hollweg, and that was diluted further in Vienna's eyes because of independent actions by Moltke and Tschirschky, which encouraged an immediate attack. Bethmann-Hollweg's pressure ended prematurely on the 30th because of Russia's partial mobilization and fears that a general mobilization would soon follow, the requirements of the Schlieffen Plan that German mobilization and war must eventually follow a partial mobilization and must immediately follow a general mobilization by Russia, the underlying assumption regarding the superiority of the offensive and the incentive this created to strike first, and perhaps by the belief that war had become inevitable.

A Russian mobilization immediately after the Austrian declaration of war was not necessary to protect Serbia, however, for Austria could not begin an invasion until August 12, and Russia should have recognized that technical constraints on Austrian mobilization meant that Russia would reap some strategic advantages by delaying mobilization. Given the certainty of German intervention in an Austro-Russian war and the nature of the Schlieffen Plan, however, Russia had an incentive to get a jump on Germany in order to aid France. Nevertheless, had the Russians known that Germany would almost certainly not mobilize before a Russian partial mobilization and perhaps not even before a general mobilization, they could have delayed action without weakening Russia's own position or Serbia's. This would have provided a few extra days for Bethmann-Hollweg to coerce Austria to accept the Halt in Belgrade Plan, and to do so in a context in which the German military was not forced to respond to Russian mobilization efforts and in which Grey could attempt to restrain Russia and France.

We can conclude that there were several points at which decision makers could have done more to manage the July crisis in a way that secured their vital interests without the costs of a world war that none of them sought and few really expected, and, in this sense, the mismanagement of the July 1914 crisis contributed to the outbreak of World War I. It is necessary to repeat, however, that the primary explanation for the outbreak of the war lies in underlying diplomatic, political, economic, and social forces at work long before the emergence of the crisis in July 1914. These forces largely shaped the preferences of key decision makers and the structural and domestic constraints on their choices. Because of these preferences and constraints, the window of opportunity for successful crisis management was fairly small and placed enormous demands on the intellectual, diplomatic, and political skills of leading decision makers. Moreover, the structure of the European system in 1914 and the set of interests it fostered provide little grounds for believing that a negotiated settlement arising from successful crisis management would have been stable and that another equally intractable crisis would not have arisen in the next few months or the next few years.[117]

CHRONOLOGY OF THE JULY 1914 CRISIS

June

28   Assassination of Austrian archduke and heir apparent Franz Ferdinand by Serbian nationalists.

July

5   Austrian cabinet chief Hoyos mission to Berlin.
Kaiser gives "blank check" to Austria.

6   German Chancellor Bethmann-Hollweg formally issues "blank check."

7   Hungarian Prime Minister Tisza opposes war.
Austrian Ministerial Council adopts plan for ultimatum.

14   Tisza agrees to war without territorial annexations.

19   Austro-Hungarian council approves ultimatum to Serbia.

20–23   French President Poincaré and Prime Minister Viviani visit St. Petersburg.

21   Text of ultimatum sent to Berlin.

23   Austria-Hungary delivers 48-hour ultimatum to Serbia.

24   Austria informs France, Russia, and Britain of ultimatum.
Russia warns Austria not to crush Serbia.
Germany requests that the conflict be localized.
British Foreign Secretary Grey proposes mediation.

25   Russian tsar authorizes pre-mobilization measures.
Serbia mobilizes against Austria; replies to ultimatum
Austria-Hungary rejects Serbian reply, breaks diplomatic relations, decides
   to mobilize against Serbia (to begin July 28), and assures Russia that
   no Serbian territory will be annexed.
Kaiser orders return of fleet.
Grey again proposes mediation.
German Foreign Secretary Jagow forwards Grey's proposal to Vienna.
France assures Russia of its support.

26   Russia asks Germany to restrain Austria.
Russia begins "period preparatory to war."
Germany learns of Russian military preparations.
Grey proposes four-power conference of British, French, German, and
   Italian ambassadors.
Austria rejects British proposal.
France takes precautionary military measures.

27   France accepts Grey's proposals.
Bethmann-Hollweg rejects Grey's proposal for conference.
Grey asks Berlin to request Vienna's acceptance of Serbian reply.
Russian pre-mobilization measures extended.
Austro-Hungarian Chief of Staff Conrad reluctantly agrees to Foreign
   Minister Berchtold's request for Austrian declaration of war.

28 Kaiser requests Jagow to call for halt in Belgrade (10 A.M.).
Austria-Hungary declares war on Serbia (11 A.M.); bombards Belgrade;
begins mobilization.
Kaiser appeals to tsar.

29 Russia mobilizes Kiev, Odessa, Moscow, and Kazan military districts and
Baltic and Black Sea fleets (12 A.M.).
Tsar appeals for kaiser's help in averting war (1 A.M.).
Vienna refuses to enter into negotiations with Serbia.
Poincaré and Viviani return to Paris.
Grey calls for halt in Belgrade.
German ambassador to Vienna Tschirschky transmits kaiser's Halt in
Belgrade proposal.
Germany warns Russia against general mobilization.
Bethmann-Hollweg requests British neutrality.
Russian army prepares to order general mobilization.
Tsar decides against general mobilization.
Tsar proposes Hague Conference.
German general staff learns of Belgian military preparations (4 P.M.).
Jagow (5 P.M.) and Bethmann-Hollweg (much later) learn of Russian
partial mobilization.
Arrival of Ambassador Lichnowsky's report of Grey's warning that Britain
could not remain neutral in a continental war (9:12 P.M.).

30 Bethmann-Hollweg urges restraint (3 A.M.).
German Chief of Staff Moltke presses for general mobilization; encour-
ages Austria to mobilize.
Bethmann-Hollweg rejects (12 noon and again at 9 P.M.) Moltke's request
for declaration of "state of imminent war"; promises decision by noon
on July 31.
Conrad note (delivered later) that Austria will stay on defensive against
Russia.
Bethmann-Hollweg agrees to declaration of imminent war (9 P.M.).
Tsar orders general mobilization for July 31 (5 P.M.).

31 Berlin learns of Russian general mobilization (12 P.M.).
Austrian general mobilization.
Kaiser proclaims "state of imminent war" (1 P.M.).
Germany sends 12-hour ultimatum to Russia to stop military measures
on German frontier; rejects British request to respect Belgian neu-
trality.
France orders mobilization for August 1, 10 km withdrawal.

August

1 Lichnowsky report of possible British neutrality.
British cabinet refuses to dispatch expeditionary force.
French mobilization (3:55 P.M.).

German mobilization (4:00 P.M.).
Germany declares war on Russia (7:00 P.M.).

2   British cabinet agrees to protect north coast of France and Channel against German attack.
Germany invades Luxembourg; demands free passage from Belgium.

3   Italy declares neutrality.
Germany declares war on France.
German-Turkish treaty concluded.
Britain mobilizes army; cabinet issues ultimatum to Berlin.

4   Germany invades Belgium.
British ultimatum to Berlin.
Britain declares war on Germany.

6   Austria-Hungary declares war on Russia.
British cabinet agrees to send army to France.

12 Austria-Hungary invades Serbia.

NOTES

1. More complete documentation and references in support of the arguments made in this paper can be found in my 1988 paper (same title) for the American Political Science Association.

2. See Barbara Tuchman, *The Guns of August* (New York: Dell, 1962); Miles Kahler, "Rumors of War: The 1914 Analogy," *Foreign Affairs* 58 (Winter 1979/1980):374–96; Richard Ned Lebow, *Nuclear Crisis Management* (Ithaca, N.Y.: Cornell University Press, 1987), chs. 2–4; Paul Bracken, *The Command and Control of Nuclear Forces* (New Haven: Yale University Press, 1983), pp. 2–3, 65, 222–23. For a critique see Marc Trachtenberg, "The Meaning of Mobilization in 1914," *International Security* 15, 3 (Winter 1990/91): 120–50.

3. Fritz Fischer, *Germany's Aims in the First World War* (New York: Norton, 1961/ 1967); Fischer, *War of Illusions: German Policies from 1911–1914*, trans. by Marian Jackson (New York: Norton, 1975); Fischer, *World Power or Decline* (New York: Norton, 1974). On the debate see H. W. Koch, *The Origins of the First World War: Great Power Rivalry and German War Aims* (London: Macmillan, 1972); John A. Moses, *The Politics of Illusion: The Fischer Controversy in German Historiography* (London: George Prior, 1975); David E. Kaiser, "Germany and the Origins of the First World War," *Journal of Modern History* 55 (September 1983):442–74.

4. If the crisis is structured as a single-play prisoners' dilemma, for example, decision makers prefer peace but feel compelled by circumstances to take actions which lead to war.

5. This is implicit in George's emphasis on the political as well as operational criteria for successful crisis management. These ideas are developed more fully in my 1988 APSA paper. I use the concept of *preferences* in the formal decision-theoretic sense of preferences over possible *outcomes* of the crisis, not preferences over alternative *strategies* to achieve those outcomes. On the theoretical importance of both system structure and state preferences see James D. Morrow, "Social Choice and System Structure in World Politics," *World Politics* 41 (October 1988): 75–97.

6. I will also note significant differences in preferences among key factions within each country.

7. On the psychology of decision making in 1914 see Ole R. Holsti, *Crisis, Escalation, War* (Montreal: McGill-Queens University Press, 1972) and other studies associated with the "1914 Project" directed by Robert North; Peter Lowenberg, "Arno Mayer's 'Internal Causes and Purposes of War in Europe, 1870–1956,'" *Journal of Modern History* 42 (1970): 628–36; Richard Ned Lebow, *Between Peace and War* (Baltimore: Johns Hopkins University Press, 1981); Jack Snyder, *The Ideology of the Offensive: Military Decision Making and the Disasters of 1914* (Ithaca, N.Y.: Cornell University Press, 1984).

8. For good analytically organized summaries of the underlying causes of World War I see Sidney B. Fay, *The Origins of the World War* (New York: Free Press, 1966), 1:32–59; James Joll, *The Origins of the First World War* (London: Longman, 1984), chs. 3–9. Interpretations of the July 1914 crisis in terms of structural theories can be found in Manus I. Midlarksy, *The Onset of Systemic War* (Boston: Unwin Hyman, 1988); Charles F. Doran, "Systemic Disequilibrium, Foreign Policy Role, and the Power Cycle," *Journal of Conflict Resolution* 33 (September 1989):371–401; and Paul W. Schroeder, "World War I as Galloping Gertie," *Journal of Modern History* 44 (1972):319–45.

9. In fact, an examination of the preference structures of the various actors will go a long way in assessing the extent to which the most important causes of the war can be found in the underlying forces which shape these preferences rather than in the mismanagement of the July crisis by political leaders.

10. Fischer, *War Aims*, pp. 51, 66; Joll, p. 9; Herbert Butterfield, "Sir Edward Grey in July 1914," *Historical Studies* 5 (1965):7–8.

11. Fay, *Origins of the World War*, 2:286–91; Luigi Albertini, *The Origins of the War of 1914*, 3 vols., trans. by Isabella M. Massey (Westport, Conn.: Greenwood Press, 1980), 2: ch. VII; Bernadotte E. Schmitt, *The Coming of the War, 1914*, 2 vols. (New York: Howard Fertig, 1966), 1: ch. X.

12. On the interlocking alliance systems see Joll, *Origins of First World War*, ch. 3; Scott D. Sagan, "1914 Revisited," *International Security* 11 (Fall 1986):151–75.

13. It would be possible to identify additional outcomes, such as an unconditional Serbian acceptance of all the terms of the Austrian utimatum, a limited Austro-Hungarian invasion of Serbia based on the Halt in Belgrade Plan, or an earlier punitive strike. For the sake of simplicity and parsimony such complications would be better saved for a subsequent and more thorough analysis of the World War I case.

14. L. L. Farrar, Jr., "The limits of choice: July 1914 reconsidered," *Journal of Conflict Resolution* 16 (March 1972):10.

15. On the general decline of Austria-Hungary see Oscar Jaszi, *The Dissolution of the Habsburg Monarchy* (Chicago: University of Chicago Press, 1964); Paul Kennedy, *The Rise and Fall of the Great Powers* (New York: Random House, 1987), pp. 215–19; Joll, *Origins of First World War*, pp. 92–94. On the importance of Austrian prestige see Fischer, *War Aims*, pp. 51–52, 59. On pressure for preventive war in Austria see Gerhard Ritter, *The Sword and the Scepter*, 4 vols., trans. by Heinz Norden (Coral Gables, Fla.: University of Miami Press, 1969–73), 2:227–39; Fischer, *War Aims*, p. 33; Fischer, *Illusions*, p. 398; V. R. Berghahn, *Germany and the Approach of War in 1914* (New York: St. Martin's, 1973), pp. 171–72, 193–94; Fay, *Origins of the World War*, 1:43, 390, 466–67; 2:9, 13–14; Joll, *Origins of First World War*, p. 87; Schmitt, *Coming of War*, 2:217–18; also Jack S. Levy, "Declining Power and the Preventive Motivation for War," *World Politics* 40 (October 1987): 82–107.

16. Albertini, *War of 1914*, 2: 168–69; Fischer, *War Aims*, p. 64; D.C.B. Lieven, *Russia and the Origins of the First World War* (New York: St. Martin's, 1983), p. 147. British Foreign Secretary Grey described the ultimatum as "the most formidable document

I had ever seen addressed by one State to another. . . ." In G.P. Gooch and Harold Temperley, eds., *British Documents on the Origins of the War, 1898–1914*, vol. XI (London: H.M. Stationery Office, 1926), No. 91, p. 73. On Austria's dilemma in formulating the ultimatum, see Farrar, "Limits," p. 14, and for the text of the ultimatum see Albertini, *War of 1914*, 2:286–89.

17. Norman Stone, "Moltke and Conrad: Relations between the Austro-Hungarian and German General Staffs, 1909–1914." In Paul M. Kennedy, ed., *The War Plans of the Great Powers, 1880–1914* (Boston: George Allen and Unwin, 1979).

18. Samuel R. Williamson, Jr., "The Origins of World War I," *Journal of Interdisciplinary History* 18 (Spring 1988):610; Joll, *Origins of First World War*, p. 10–11; Geiss, "Outbreak," p. 86.

19. Fischer, *War Aims*, pp. 52, 56; Ritter, *Sword and Scepter*, 2:236; A.J.P. Taylor, *The Struggle for Mastery in Europe, 1848–1914* (New York: Oxford University Press, 1971), p. 527. An intriguing hypothesis is that Tisza feared that a victorious foreign war would increase the power of Vienna within the monarchy and enable Austrian leaders to restructure the monarchy, and perhaps even concede some power to the Slavs at the expense of the Hungarians.

20. This proposition is more problematic after the Austrian declaration of war on July 28. Albertini, *War of 1914*, 2:162. A German veto would have been even more compelling in conjunction with four-power agreement on some variation of the Halt in Belgrade Plan. Imanuel Geiss, "The Outbreak of the First World War and German War Aims," *Journal of Contemporary History* 1 (1966):86; Kaiser, "Germany," p. 471; Albertini, *War of 1914*, 2:466–527, 651–73; 3:232–36. Williamson ("Origins," p. 807) suggests that without German support Vienna might have taken some limited military action short of war.

21. Williamson, "Origins," p. 811, 813n; Lieven, *Russia*, p. 147. It has been argued that Russian promises of support led the Serbian cabinet to adopt a less compromising response to the Austrian ultimatum than they otherwise would have done (Albertini, *War of 1914*, 3:352–62; Lieven, *Russia*, p. 114), but this has been questioned by Williamson, "Origins," pp. 811–13.

22. Serbia held out only on the demand that Austro-Hungarian officials participate in the Serbian inquiry into the assassination plot. The kaiser believed that the Serbian reply was sufficiently conciliatory that "on the whole the wishes of the Danube Monarchy have been acceded to. . . . Every cause for war falls to the ground." Karl Kautsky, *Outbreak of the World War: German Documents* (New York: Oxford University Press, 1924), no. 293, p. 273. He insisted, however, on a "temporary occupation of Belgrade" to ensure Serbian compliance and perhaps to appease his own military. Geiss, "Outbreak," pp. 82–83.

23. With regard to other outcomes, Serbia preferred a continental war with Russian support (and therefore also a world war with British intervention) to a localized war with Austria-Hungary, but her role in the expansion of the war in negligible.

24. Taylor, *Mastery*, p. 517; Kaiser, "Germany," p. 471; Albertini, *War of 1914*, 2:403–5; Imanuel Geiss, ed., *July 1914, The Outbreak of the First World War: Selected Documents* (New York: Scribner's, 1967), pp. 230–31, 241–42, 303–34; Geiss, "Outbreak," pp. 82, 87; Farrar, "Limits," p. 14. Joll, *Origins of First World War*, pp. 102–6. The Russian elites' incentive for diversionary action was modified by the fear that war could lead to revolution. Lieven, *Russia*, pp. 122, 153; Joll, *Origins of First World War*, p. 105.

25. In Lieven, *Russia*, pp. 141–47. Also Joll, *Origins of First World War*, p. 55.

26. Butterfield, "Sir Edward Grey," (p. 7) quotes Grey as saying that "if [Austria-Hungary] could make war on Servia and at the same time satisfy Russia, well and good." See also Fischer, *War Aims*, p. 66. Note that Grey's threat of intervention in his July 29 warning to Lichnowsky was conditional upon French involvement in the war.

27. The kaiser made a similar proposal the previous day.

28. Zara S. Steiner, *Britain and the Origins of the First World War* (New York: St. Martin's Press, 1977), chs. 7–10; Taylor, *Mastery*, pp. 525–26; Arno J. Mayer, "Domestic Causes of the First World War," in Leonard Krieger and Fritz Stern, eds., *The Responsibility of Power* (New York: Doubleday, 1967), pp. 298–300; K. M. Wilson, "The British Cabinet's Decision for War, 2 August 1914" *British Journal of International Studies* 1 (1975):148–59; Paul Kennedy, *The Realities Behind Diplomacy: Background Influences on British External Policy, 1865–1980* (London: Allen and Unwin, 1981), pp. 136–39; Joll, *Origins of First World War*, pp. 97–98.

29. Joll, *Origins of First World War*, p. 99. It was also necessary for France to maintain the good will of Britain, and therefore it could not behave too provocatively.

30. John F. V. Keiger, *France and the Origins of the First World War* (New York: St. Martin's, 1983), ch. 7. The absence of Poincaré and Viviani also resulted in a somewhat greater role for Maurice Paleologue, the revanchist French ambassador to Russia.

31. Fay, *Origins of the World War*, vol. 2; Harry Elmer Barnes, *The Genesis of the World War* (New York: Knopf, 1926).

32. What most differentiates Fischer from others is his argument that German political leaders actualy preferred a continental war to a local war in the Balkans. See fn. 44.

33. Fischer, *War Aims*, pp. 53–64, 69; Konrad H. Jarausch, "The Illusion of Limited War: Chancellor Bethmann-Hollweg's Calculated Risk, July 1914," *Central European History* 2 (March 1969):56; Taylor, *Mastery*, p. 522; Farrar, "Limits," p. 13; John Rohl, ed., *1914: Delusion or Design* (New York: St. Martin's, 1973).

34. Jagow to Lichnowsky, July 18, in Geiss, *July 1914*, pp. 122–24. Albertini, *War of 1914*, 2:159–64; Schmitt, *Coming of War*, 1:321; Stephen Van Evera, "The Cult of the Offensive and the Origins of the First World War," *International Security* 9 (Summer 1984):83.

35. Fischer, *War Aims*, p. 60.

36. Jarausch, "Limited War," p. 58. Both Jarausch and Bethmann-Hollweg expected that a local war would split the Entente, but neither explains why. Bethmann may have assumed that France would support Russia if and only if Russia were directly threatened by Germany (as stipulated by the terms of the Franco-Russian alliance), and that the absence of French support would not only prevent Russia from coming to Serbia's aid but also lead it to drop France as an unreliable ally. But I have argued that although France preferred to stay out of a local war, and might try to convince Russia that it was in its interests to do the same, France would follow Russia if necessary and give whatever support it needed.

37. Jarausch, "Limited War," pp. 61, 75. See also Berghahn, *Approach of War*, pp. 192, 196.

38. Fischer, *War Aims*, ch. 2; Geiss, "Outbreak," pp. 84, 88; Jarausch, "Limited War," pp. 58, 75; Berghahn, *Approach of War*, p. 196; Michael R. Gordon, "Domestic Conflict and the Origins of the First World War: The British and the German Cases," *Journal of Modern History* 46 (June 1974): 194–95; Stephen Van Evera, "Why Cooperation Failed in 1914," *World Politics* 38 (October 1985): 100, and "Cult," p. 83; Sagan, "1914 Revisited," p. 168; Sean M. Lynn-Jones, "Detente and Deterrence: Anglo-German Relations, 1911–1914," *International Security* 11 (Fall 1986): 142–43; Tuchman, *Guns of August*, p. 95.

39. Although this is a standard interpretation of Fischer, he is not perfectly consistent on this point. See *War Aims*, p. 60 and *Illusions*, pp. 480, 515. Geiss ("Outbreak," pp. 79, 86) states explicitly that Germany preferred a continental war even to a local war which succeeded in splitting the Entente.

40. Fischer, *War Aims*, p. 49; Fischer, *Illusions*, pp. 377–79, 402, 427; Geiss, "Outbreak," pp. 77–78; Berghahn, *Approach of War*, chs. 6–10; Schmitt, *Coming of War*, pp. 321–25; Kaiser, "Germany," p. 469; Joll, *Origins of First World War*, p. 114; Jarausch, "Limited War," p. 48; Farrar, "Limits," p. 12; Evera, "Cult," pp. 79–85; Paul M. Kennedy,

"The First World War and the International Power System," *International Security* 9 (Summer 1984): 28.

41. Wolfgang J. Mommsen, "The Debate on German War Aims," in Walter Lacqueur and George Mosse, eds., *1914: The Coming of the First World War* (New York: Harper Torchbooks, 1966), p. 60.

42. Fischer, *Illusions;* Berghahn, *Approach of War,* ch. 6–9; Gordon, "Domestic Conflict," pp. 191–226; Mayer, "Domestic Causes"; Wolfgang J. Mommsen, "Domestic Factors in German Foreign Policy before 1914," *Central European History* 6 (March 1973):3–43; Jack S. Levy, "The Diversionary Theory of War: A Critique," in Manus I. Midlarsky, ed., *Handbook of War Studies* (London: Allen & Unwin, 1989), pp. 259–88.

43. Bethmann-Hollweg feared the revolutionary consequences of a major war, particularly if Germany were to lose. Mommsen, "Domestic Factors," p. 33; Mayer, "Domestic Causes," p. 293.

44. The primary differences among Fischer, the "inadvertent-war" school (Fay, Tuchman, etc.), and myself can be summarized by our respective views of German preference orderings:

Fischer	CW	>	LW	>	NP	>	WW
inadvertent war	NP	>	LW	>	CW	>	WW
Levy	LW	>	CW	>	NP	>	WW

Note that some in the inadvertent-war school concede that Germany may have actually preferred a local war, so that LW > NP. Van Evera ("Cooperation," p. 100) and Jarausch ("Limited War," p. 75) each shares my characterization of German preferences but not my overall interpretation of the causes of the war.

45. Thus the attempt to model the 1914 case as a 2 × 2 game in normal form (e.g., Glenn H. Snyder and Paul Diesing, *Conflict among Nations* [Princeton, N.J.: Princeton University Press, 1977], ch. 2) is flawed on several counts: the situation cannot be reduced to two coalitions because preferences were not congruent within each alliance, to two strategic options for each actor, to dichotomous outcomes of either war or peace, or to a single choice in a one-play game.

46. It will be useful to distinguish between the decisions to issue the ultimatum, declare war, and begin the invasion.

47. I recognize that one must be careful in using post-1945 concepts like deterrence and crisis management to describe and explain the perceptions, motivations, and behaviors of earlier states and state officials. Although statesmen had no concept of "deterrence" in 1914, German leaders hoped that the threat to intervene against Russia would be sufficient to keep Russia from moving against Austria, and in this sense they attempted to deter Russia.

48. Tuchman, *Guns of August,* p. 143; Fischer, *War Aims,* p. 63; Albertini, *War of 1914,* 2:517; Lebow, *Between Peace and War,* p. 132. Steiner, *Britain* (p. 126) emphasizes that Bethmann and Jagow both wavered between optimism and pessimism on this issue.

49. Jagow agreed, and told French Ambassador Cambon on July 26 that "We are sure of English neutrality." Bethmann had earlier (December 1912) expressed confidence that Britain would stand aside "If the *provocation* appeared to come directly from Russia and France." Albertini, *War of 1914,* 2:429, 520; Bethmann to William II, July 23, in Jarausch, "Limited War," p. 62. Lichnowsky to Jagow, received July 29, 9:12 P.M., in Geiss, *Outbreak,* pp. 130–31; Albertini 2:508–27; Fischer, *War Aims,* pp. 31, 63, 78–82; Fischer, "The Miscalculation of English Neutrality: An Aspect of German Foreign Policy on the Eve of World War I," in Soloman Wank, et al., *The Mirror of History* (Santa Barbara, CA: ABC-Clio, 1988), pp. 369–93. Schmitt, *Coming of War,* 2:159–61; Lebow, *Peace and War,* pp. 133–34. Mommsen ("Domestic Factors," p. 38n) disagrees.

50. Gerhard Ritter, *The Schlieffen Plan* (New York: Praeger, 1958); Tuchman, *Guns of August*, pp. 41, 144–45; Fisher, *War Aims*, p. 49. The main exception was Tirpitz. Lebow, *Peace and War*, p. 130n.

Bethmann's view was probably the following: Britain might intervene, but only if France were on the verge of being crushed by Germany, and such intervention could be avoided by Germany's guarantees that it sought no territorial annexations from France. Thus in spite of some disagreements among German civilian and military leaders about the likelihood of British neutrality in the abstract (let me call this the "strong neutrality assumption"), there was consensus that Britain would not intervene early in the war (the "weak neutrality assumption"). It is clear that Bethmann would not risk a continental war if he doubted the validity of this weaker assumption. Thus my earlier proposition that the German assumption of British neutrality was a necessary condition for war of any kind should be interpreted in terms of the weak neutrality assumption. See my "Preferences, Constraints, and Choices in July 1914," *International Security* 15, 3 (Winter 1990–91): 165n.

51. Ritter, *Schlieffen Plan*, pp. 71, 161–62; Van Evera, "Cult," p. 92; Lynn-Jones, "Detente," p. 144; L. L. Farrar, Jr., *The Short-War Illusion* (Santa Barbara, Calif.: ABC-Clio, 1973); Steiner, *Britain*, p. 125; Kaiser, "Germany," p. 469; Geiss, "Outbreak," p. 84; Trachtenberg, "Meaning of Mobilization," pp. 137–43. Moltke wavered on this point, and on August 2 said that "England's neutrality is of such importance to us that a promise of moderation in case of a victory over France . . . could be made unconditionally." Fischer, *War Aims*, pp. 33, 85; Geiss, *July 1914*, pp. 350–51.

52. Albertini, *War of 1914*, 2:502–8, 514–20 (quote). This assumption is also critical for Fischer and his associates. Fischer, *War Aims*, ch. 2, *Illusions*, p. 496; Geiss, "Outbreak." Also Lebow, *Peace and War*, p. 133; Lynn-Jones, "Detente," pp. 143–44. The German bid for neutrality, which goes back to the Haldane mission of 1912, failed because it insisted that German *involvement* in war be sufficient for British neutrality, whereas Britain insisted that it could offer neutrality only in the event of an *unprovoked* attack on Germany. Fischer, *War Aims*, p. 27.

53. Fischer, *War Aims*, pp. 70–76, 80–81, 85, *Illusions*, pp. 162, 495; Geiss, "Outbreak," p. 86; *July 14*, pp. 269, 350; Joll, *Origins of First World War*, pp. 20, 26–29, 116; Jarausch, "Limited War," pp. 63–68; Albertini, *War of 1914*, 2:502.

54. Albertini, *War of 1914*, 2:431–45; Lebow, *Peace and War*, pp. 131–2, 140–1.

55. Fischer, *War Aims*, p. 78; Bethmann-Hollweg to Tschirschky, 2:55 A.M., 3:00 A.M. 30 July 1914, in Geiss, *July 1914*, pp. 91–93; Albertini, *War of 1914*, 2:504, 520–25; Fischer, *War Aims*, pp. 78–82; Schmitt, *Coming of War*, 2:161–72; Jarausch, "Limited War," pp. 65–68; Lynn-Jones "Detente," pp. 143–44. The critical impact of British intentions is also demonstrated by the German response to Lichnowsky's August 1 report of Grey's offer that if Germany "were not to attack France, England would remain neutral and guarantee the passivity of France." Albertini, *War of 1914*, 3:380–81. The kaiser, chancellor and others were elated, and the kaiser announced "Now we can go to war against Russia only. We simply march the whole of our army to the East." Tuchman, *Guns of August*, p. 98. Moltke objected strenuously on grounds of the rigidity of the mobilization and war plans, but he was overruled, and German acceptance of what they thought was the British proposal was sent to England. It was soon revealed that the offer of neutrality did not represent British policy, and German plans for the invasion of France through Belgium continued. Albertini, *War of 1914*, 3:380–86; Jack S. Levy, "Organizational Routines and the Causes of War," *International Studies Quarterly* 30 (June 1986):199; Tuchman, *Guns of August*, p. 98.

56. Fischer, and to a lesser extent Geiss, argue that Bethmann's policy shift on July 29–30 was temporary, and that "peace moves" later that day were simply tactical expedients to deceive Britain and ensure that the blame for the conflict which Germany still sought could

be shifted onto Russia. Fischer, *War Aims*, pp. 79–82; Geiss, "Outbreak," p. 84; *July 1914*, p. 269. Lebow (*Peace and War*, pp. 135–39) emphasizes the importance of psychological stress, emotional turmoil, exaggerated confidence and pessimistic fatalism, and hypervigilant coping behavior in Bethmann's shifts in policy on July 29–31. See my letter to the editor, *International Security* 16 (Summer 1991).

Trachtenberg ("Meaning of Mobilization," pp. 134–36) argues that Bethmann shifted course on July 29–30 because of the Russian partial mobilization rather than the warning from Grey. Although the evidence for the importance of British neutrality for German leaders goes far beyond the events of the evening of July 29–30, my review of the sequence, timing, and content of Bethmann's telegrams to Vienna that night suggests that Lichnowsky's message from London had a greater impact on Bethmann than did news from Russia.

57. Lebow, *Peace and War*, p. 136. This argument is buttressed by psychological evidence which suggests that the reluctance to reopen a decision is proportionate to the difficulty of making it in the first place. Robert Jervis, *Perception and Misperception in International Politics* (Princeton: Princeton University Press, 1976), pp. 383–406.

58. Albertini, *War of 1914*, 2:514, 3:643; Lynn-Jones, "Detente," pp. 139, 144; Kaiser, "Germany," p. 471.

59. Lebow, *Peace and War*, pp. 136–47.

60. A German threat that was combined with certain face-saving compromises for Austria (such as the Halt in Belgrade Plan) would have been even more likely to succeed.

61. Tuchman, *Guns of August*, p. 144. Also Trevor Wilson, *The Myriad Faces of War: Britain and the Great War, 1914–1918* (Oxford: Basil Blackwell, 1986), ch. 1; Sir Llewellyn Woodward, *Great Britain and the War of 1914–1918* (Boston: Beacon Press, 1967), pp. 19–20.

62. See Lebow, *Peace and War*, pp. 130–31.

63. Schmitt, *Coming of War*, 2: 52–53; Albertini, *War of 1914*, 2:425, 429, 687–88; Lynn-Jones, "Detente," p. 142; Alexander George and Richard Smoke, *Deterrence in American Foreign Policy* (New York: Columbia University Press, 1974), pp. 572–80.

64. French Chief of Staff Joseph Joffre was so uncertain of British intervention that he did not include that assumption in the formation of the French army's war plan, and Sazonov warned the Russian Council of Ministers on July 24 that any escalation of war would be dangerous "since it is not known what attitude Great Britain would take in the matter." Samuel R. Williamson, "Joffre Shapes French Strategy, 1911–1913," in Kennedy, *War Plans*, p. 146; Lieven, *Russia*, p. 142; Sagan, "1914 Revisited," pp. 169–70; Lynn-Jones, "Detente," p. 141; Joll, *Origins of First World War*, pp. 19, 26.

65. Wilson, *Faces of War*, pp. 149–50; Sagan, "1914 Revisited," p. 170.

66. *British Documents*, XI, no. 283, p. 180; Wilson, *Faces of War*, p. 150. Here I am using the "third party" criterion to assess the extent to which misperceptions are determined by the inherent uncertainty of the situation as opposed to the motivated biases of decision makers. See Jervis, *Perception*, p. 7; Lebow, *Peace and War*, p. 91; Sagan, "1914 Revisited," p. 170; Jack S. Levy, "The Causes of War: A Review of Theories and Evidence," in Philip E. Tetlock, et al., eds., *Behavior, Society, and Nuclear War*, vol. 1 (New York: Oxford University Press, 1989), pp. 287–88.

67. Grey's attempted balancing act in a combined "alliance dilemma" and "adversary dilemma" has been described as a "straddle strategy" by Glenn H. Snyder, "The Security Dilemma in Alliance Politics," *World Politics* 36 (July 1984):461–95. See also Joll, *Origins of First World War*, p. 20; Albertini, *War of 1914*, 2:515; Farrar, *Illusion*, p. 15; Woodward, *Great Britain*, p. 21. This strategy was based on the idea that "If both sides do not know what we shall do, both will be less willing to run risks" (Joll, p. 20), which makes the debatable assumption that both Russian and German decision makers were risk-averse and would act more cautiously when faced with uncertainty.

68. Lynn-Jones, "Detente," pp. 125–40; Steiner, *Britain*, pp. 145–215. On the naval rivalry see Paul Kennedy, *The Rise of the Anglo-German Naval Rivalry, 1860–1914* (London: Allen & Unwin, 1982), ch. 22.

69. Michael Eckstein, "Sir Edward Grey and Imperial Germany in 1914," *Journal of Contemporary History* 6 (1971):121–31.

70. Steiner, *Britain*, ch. 9; Wilson, *Faces of War*, pp. 148–59; Lynn-Jones, "Detente," p. 139. Grey's aims were not only to prevent a continental war if at all possible, and not only to bring Britain into such a war if it did occur, but also to ensure that his divided country be brought into the war united. The risk of an early warning to Germany was that the cabinet and perhaps Parliament might react so strongly as to undercut both the second and third objectives.

71. Wilson, *Faces of War*, pp. 149–50; Steiner, *Britain*, p. 233; Michael G. Eckstein and Zara Steiner, "The Sarajevo Crisis," in F. H. Hinsley, ed., *British Foreign Policy Under Sir Edward Grey* (Cambridge: Cambridge University Press, 1977), p. 404; *British Documents*, XI, no. 426, p. 253; Woodward, *Great Britain*, pp. 21–22.

72. Quoted in Albertini, *War of 1914*, 2:515.

73. Samuel J. Williamson, Jr., *The Politics of Grand Strategy* (Cambridge, Mass.: Harvard University Press, 1969) argues that Britain would have intervened in the absence of a German invasion of Belgium.

74. The Schlieffen Plan was based on the assumptions that any continental war would be a two-front war for Germany, that its Russian and French enemies had to be dealt with one at a time, that the offensive was the dominant form of warfare, that France could be quickly defeated more easily and more rapidly than Russia but only by an enveloping movement through Belgium, that any advance through Belgium required the rapid and preemptive seizure of Liège, and that consequently the move into Belgium had to come early in the mobilization process itself (the third day). Ritter, *The Schlieffen Plan*; Snyder, *Ideology*, chs. 4–5; L.C.F. Turner, "The Significance of the Schlieffen Plan," in Kennedy, *War Plans*; Levy, "Routines," p. 197.

75. Steiner, *Origins*, p. 237; Wilson, *Faces of War*, p. 25; Tuchman, *Guns of August*, pp. 113, 137; Butterfield, "Sir Edward Grey," p. 1; Berghahn, *Approach of War*, pp. 208–09.

76. See George, "Strategies for Crisis Management," in this volume.

77. Taylor, *Mastery*, pp. 522–23; Ritter, *Sword and Scepter*, 2:236; Samuel R. Williamson, Jr., "Theories of Foreign Policy Process and Foreign Policy Outcomes," in Paul Gordon Lauren, ed., *Diplomacy* (New York: Free Press, 1979), pp. 151–53. See also Schmitt, *Coming of War*, 1:393; Berghahn, *Approach of War*, p. 195; Butterfield, "Sir Edward Grey," p. 11; Dwight E. Lee, *Europe's Crucial Years: The Diplomatic Background of World War I, 1902–1914* (Hanover, N.H.: University Press of New England, 1974), p. 382.

78. Fischer, *War Aims*, pp. 53–61; Jarausch, "Limited War," pp. 60–68; Joll, *Origins of First World War*, p. 15; Lee, *Crucial Years*, p. 382; Butterfield, "Sir Edward Grey," pp. 10–11.

79. Albertini, *War of 1914*, 2:175; Butterfield, "Sir Edward Grey," p. 10. It is not clear that Austria-Hungary planned to fulfill this promise. See Pierre Renouvin, *The Immediate Origins of the War*, trans. by Theodore C. Hume (New Haven: Yale University Press, 1928), pp. 128–29; Williamson, "Origins," p. 810.

80. Albertini, *War of 1914*, 2:455.

81. Albertini, *War of 1914*, 2:175; Schmitt, *Coming of War*, 1:345–57; Norman Stone, "Hungary and the Crisis of July 1914," *Journal of Contemporary History* 1 (1966):147–64. Minor frontier adjustments were permitted.

82. Williamson, "Theories," pp. 152–53; and "Origins," p. 808; Levy, "Routines," p. 202.

83. Tschirschky to Bethmann-Hollweg, 14 July, in Geiss, *July 1914*, pp. 114–15.

84. Although the Russian "period preparatory to war" beginning on July 26 generated concern in Germany, it was the partial mobilization on July 30 and particularly the general mobilization the following day that triggered a German response.

85. Albertini, *War of 1914*, 2:455–56; Joll, *Origins of First World War*, pp. 14–15. Domestic public opinion and the press had also become increasingly belligerent. Albertini, 2:453–58.

86. This may not be a significant change, however, for Berchtold's preference for an unconditional capitulation over war was ever so slight, and he was unwilling to make any further compromises to gain a one-sided diplomatic victory without war.

87. It is difficult to determine whether this strategy of coercive diplomacy had been adopted at the time of the ultimatum, and whether the ultimatum was designed as a justification for war or as a highly coercive instrument to secure Serbia's submission. It appears that the decision makers involved in the process each had a different conception of the purpose of the ultimatum.

88. This assumes that the combination of the ultimatum, Bethmann's rejection of Grey's proposal for a four-power conference, and Russia's early preparations for war would have been perceived by Grey as threatening enough to issue a strong warning even in the absence of an Austrian declaration of war.

89. *German Documents*, no. 293, p. 273; Grey to Goschen, July 29, *British Documents*, no. 286, p. 182; A.J.P. Taylor, *War by Time-table*. In *History of the 20th Century*, vol. 2 (New York: Purnell, 1974), p. 445.

90. Fischer, *War Aims*, p. 73; Albertini, *War of 1914*, 2:656–57; Schmitt, *Coming of War*, 2:217–18; Renouvin, *Immediate Origins*, p. 193. It has also been argued that Vienna was constrained by the absence of contingency plans for the occupation of Belgrade apart from a general invasion of Serbia. Holsti, *Crisis*, pp. 157, 216. But Serbia had decided not to defend Belgrade (Taylor, *Time-table*, p. 445). If Austria had possessed more timely intelligence, it could have occupied the city without interfering with any subsequent mobilization against Russia.

91. Albertini, *War of 1914*, 2:659, 669–73; Kaiser, "Germany," p. 471.

92. *German Documents*, no. 323, pp. 288–89; Fischer, *War Aims*, p. 72; Geiss, "Outbreak," p. 83; Albertini, *War of 1914*, 2:653–61. Tschirschky also delayed notifying Berlin of the Austrian declaration of war.

93. Albertini, *War of 1914*, 2:673–74; Turner, "Schlieffen Plan," p. 215.

94. Ulrich Trumpener, "War Premeditated? German Intelligence Operations in July 1914," *Central European History* 9 (March 1976), p. 77; Albertini, *War of 1914*, 2:500; Turner, "Schlieffen Plan," p. 215.

95. The military in general and Moltke in particular had not exerted much pressure on Bethmann throughout most of the July crisis, and had accepted Bethmann's efforts to restrain Vienna early on the 30th. The military's demand for a proclamation of "imminent threat of war" was accepted late on July 30 after being rejected earlier that day. Just before it was to be announced at noon on the 31st, however, Germany received news of Russian general mobilization. Berlin sent a 12-hour ultimatum to St. Petersburg demanding that all military preparations be stopped. The Russian rejection of this demand was followed by a declaration of war on August 1. Albertini, *War of 1914*, 2:502, 3:13, 31, 232, 236; Fischer, *War Aims*, pp. 85–86; Trachtenberg, "A Reassessment," pp. 62–63.

96. Albertini, *War of 1914*, 3:31.

97. Joll, *Origins of First World War*, pp. 21, 107, 203; Lebow, *Peace and War*, pp. 254–56.

98. Conrad's defense plan called for minimal defense forces in both Galicia (A-Staffel, thirty divisions) and in the Balkans (Minimalgruppe Balkan, ten divisions). An additional

twelve divisions (B-Staffel) could be sent either to the Balkans (where they would add sufficient strength to destroy Serbia) *or* to Galicia (where they would combine with A-Staffel to provide for a powerful offensive against Russia). Stone, "Moltke and Conrad," pp. 225–26, 233, 243–44.

99. This was recognized by both Conrad and Moltke. Conrad described a delayed Russian intervention as "the most difficult yet most probable case." Stone, "Moltke and Conrad," pp. 228–35; Fischer, *War Aims*, p. 74; L.C.F. Turner, *Origins of the First World War* (New York: Norton, 1970), pp. 92–93, and "The Russian Mobilisation in 1914," in Kennedy, *War Plans*, p. 258. Albertini, *War of 1914*, 2:482.

100. Turner, *Origins*, p. 92; Turner, "Russian Mobilisation," pp. 258, 266; Albertini, *War of 1914*, 2:482.

101. Turner, *Origins*, p. 93, "Russian Mobilisation," pp. 258, 266, Kennedy, *War Plans*, p. 15. Sazonov's original plan was to wait until Austria actually invaded Serbia before initiating partial mobilization. Albertini, *War of 1914*, 2:538.

102. This belief was reinforced by Russia's fear that Germany was looking for an opportunity to launch a preventive war against Russia. Van Evera, "Cult," pp. 87–88.

103. Turner, "Russian Mobilisation," pp. 261–62; Baron M. F. Schilling, *How the War Began in 1914: The Diary of the Russian Foreign Office* (London: Allen & Unwin, 1925), pp. 62–66; Albertini, *War of 1914*, 2:565–72; Snyder, *Ideology*, chs. 6–7; Van Evera, "Cult," pp. 72–78. Trachtenberg, "Meaning of Mobilization," pp. 145–47.

104. Russian General Danilov even suggests that the military, given a choice, might have preferred no mobilization to partial mobilization. Albertini, *War of 1914*, 2:293, 543; Turner, *Origins*, p. 92, "Russian Mobilisation" (1979); Schilling, *How War Began*, p. 117. A general mobilization had been ordered and cancelled on July 29, and a partial mobilization was ordered the next day.

105. Albertini, *War of 1914*, 2:292–93, 485n (for quote). Also Turner, *Origins*, pp. 92, 104; Snyder, *Ideology*, p. 88; Kennedy, *War Plans*, pp. 16–17; Van Evera, "Cult," p. 88; Levy, "Routines," p. 198.

106. Albertini, *War of 1914*, 2:496–503; Trachtenberg, "Meaning of Mobilization," pp. 137–39; Fischer, *Illusions*, pp. 495–96, *War Aims*, p. 85. Late on July 29 Moltke (with unanimous support from political and military leaders) instructed Conrad: "Do not declare war on Russia but wait for Russia's attack." Fischer, *Illusions*, p. 496.

107. Van Evera, "Cult," pp. 71–79; Snyder, "Dilemma," p. 177; Levy, "Routines," pp. 195–96; Turner, "Schlieffen Plan," 216.

108. Albertini, *War of 1914*, 2:480; Turner, *Origins*, p. 63; A.J.P. Taylor, *War by Time-Table* (London: MacDonald, 1968), p. 25; Levy, "Routines," pp. 197–98. For analyses of the feasibility of a German offensive in the east while maintaining a defensive holding action in the west, see Snyder, *Ideology*, pp. 116–22; Tuchman, *Guns of August*, p. 100. The Franco-Russian alliance made it unlikely that France would stay neutral in a Russo-German war, but if Germany had fought defensively in the west and avoided Belgium, the chances of British intervention would have been much less.

109. Ritter, *Schlieffen Plan*; Ritter, *Sword and Scepter*, vol. 2, ch. 9; Turner, "Schlieffen Plan," p. 205; Gordon A. Craig. *The Politics of the Prussian Army, 1640–1945* (London: Oxford University Press, 1955), pp. 195, 277; Snyder, *Ideology*, ch. 4; Kennedy, *War Plans*, p. 17; Levy, "Routines," pp. 207–9.

110. Snyder, *Ideology*, p. 121; Ritter, *Sword and Scepter*, 2:205. One can also find examples of the dominance of technical military considerations in the Russian mobilization and war plans and the influential role of the military in the political decision-making process. See Lieven, *Russia*, pp. 63, 122. The military had far less influence in France and in Britain during the July crisis. Steiner, *Britain*, p. 220; Keiger, *France* ch. 7; Kennedy, *War Plans*, p. 7.

111. Taylor, *War by Time-Table* (1968), p. 19; Taylor, "Time-table" (1974), p. 444; Ritter, *Sword and Scepter*, vol. 2, ch. 9, *Schlieffen Plan*, p. 90; Albertini, *War of 1914*, 3:253; Snyder, *Ideology*, chs. 4–5; Van Evera, "Cult," pp. 85–86; L.C.F. Turner, "The Significance of the Schlieffen Plan," in Kennedy, *War Plans*, p. 205; Tuchman, *Guns of August*, pp. 94–101; Levy, "Routines," pp. 198–201, 209.

112. Albertini, *War of 1914*, 2:479–85, 579–81; 3:195, 391; Ritter, *Sword and Scepter*, 2:266; Turner, *Origins*, pp. 92, 99, 108; "Schlieffen Plan," p. 213; Levy, "Routines," pp. 209–10.

113. Albertini, *War of 1914*, 2:332, 480, 3:391; Turner, *Origins*, p. 99.

114. Albertini, *War of 1914*, 2:480–81; Turner, "The Mobilisation" (1979), p. 260. This incentive to mobilize was reinforced by the hope that mobilization might help diffuse internal unrest. Fay, *Origins of the World War*, 2:305; Turner, "The Russian Mobilization in 1914," *Journal of Contemporary History* 3 (January 1968):65–88; Hans Rogger, "Russia in 1914," in Laqueur and Mosse, pp. 229–53. Sazonov's ignorance is explained in part by the fact that Janushkevich had been chief of staff for only five months, was not familiar with the details of mobilization, and therefore failed to warn Sazonov of the implications of partial mobilization. This tragedy is compounded further by the failure of Germany to warn Russia of the risks involved. In fact, on July 27 German Foreign Secretary Jagow erroneously assured both the British and the French ambassadors to Berlin that "if Russia only mobilized in the south, Germany would not mobilize." Albertini, *War of 1914*, 2:481–82.

115. Albertini, *War of 1914*, 2:294, 480–82, 624, 3:43; Van Evera, "Cult," p. 76; Turner, "Russian Mobilisation" (1968), p. 71; Lebow, *Crisis Management*, p. 111. But see Trachtenberg, "Meaning of Mobilization," pp. 145–47.

116. Many German political leaders were also ignorant of key aspects of the mobilization plans. But because they had no choice but to mobilize in response to a general mobilization by Russia and because the mobilization process would be so difficult to reverse, their ignorance of the consequences of mobilization was probably less critical than the nature of the plans themselves. It is interesting to speculate, however, whether Bethmann would have behaved differently had he realized that his central policy goal of British neutrality would be undercut by the demands of the Schlieffen Plan. Bethmann knew of the invasion of Belgium, but did not learn until July 31, *after* the ultimatum to Russia, that it must begin on the third day of mobilization (Turner, *Origins*, p. 213), which would reduce the diplomatic advantages to Germany of allowing Russia to mobilize first.

117. A subsequent crisis would have been all the more serious because of the tendency for states' bargaining tactics to become increasingly coercive and intractable in successive crises with the same adversary. See Russell J. Leng, "When Will They Ever Learn? Coercive Bargaining in Recurrent Crises," *Journal of Conflict Resolution* 27 (September 1983):379–419; John A. Vasquez, "The Steps to War," *World Politics* 40 (October 1987):138–40.

CHAPTER 7

The U.S.-China War in Korea

Allen S. Whiting

In November 1950, U.S. and Chinese armies locked in major combat for the first time in history. Their engagement in the mountains of North Korea confounded policy makers in Washington and raised grim prospects in Peking. The subsequent war lasted two-and-a-half years, inflicted at least 300,000 Chinese casualties, and drove the Democrats from office for the first time in two decades. Collision in Korea blocked official relations between the People's Republic of China (PRC) and the United States for twenty years.

Numerous studies have attempted to explain how this collision occurred, with special attention given to U.S. decision making, for which far better evidence is available than is the case for the Chinese side. Single cause and multiple factor analyses offer a rich menu from which to select plausible answers to the question: How could war inadvertently occur between two major powers with ample time to communicate their intent and no plan or preference for war?

My primary purpose, however, is not to select one or another of the existing explanations or to offer still another reconstruction of the events as giving "the real reason" Washington and Peking stumbled into war. Instead I will focus on the political and operational requirements for crisis management outlined in Chapter 4 in order to assess their relevance in this situation.[1] First, to what extent did U.S. policy makers meet the political requirements of crisis management once Chinese forces had actively engaged U.N. forces in North Korea? And, to the extent that informed inferences permit reasonable speculation about the Chinese side, how did Peking handle the circumstances of crisis management?

PROLOGUE TO WAR: SEPTEMBER–NOVEMBER 1950

As U.N. commander, Gen. Douglas MacArthur brilliantly reversed the tide of war unleashed by Pyongyang's June 25 attack across the 38th parallel. In September, his surprise landing of major forces behind enemy lines at Inchon threatened to cut off North Korean troops in the south from reinforcement and supply. With communist fortunes clearly shattered and the future ominous, Peking commenced a series of systematically increased warnings against a U.S. invasion of the north.[2] On September 25, the acting chief of staff informally told the Indian ambassador that China would not "sit back with folded hands and let the Americans come to the border." On October 1, South Korean units crossed the 38th parallel, and the next day Premier Zhou Enlai summoned the Indian ambassador at midnight for a formal démarche, warning that should U.S. troops do likewise, China would intervene.

On October 7, U.S. troops entered North Korea as the U.N. General Assembly passed a resolution that endorsed "all appropriate steps to ensure conditions of stability *throughout Korea*" (italics added). This indirect language was chosen to transform the initial U.N. objective of repelling aggression into the goal of uniting the entire peninsula by force if necessary. Thus, the first political requirement of crisis management, the limitation of objectives, was virtually precluded by positing a maximum goal for U.N. operations. Only if U.S. policy makers had reviewed this goal later within the new context of active Chinese intervention and assessed both its feasibility and its cost could the situation have remained open for averting a wholly new war.

Within a week the Chinese People's Volunteers (CPV) began secretly crossing the Yalu River while Peking's Foreign Ministry spokesman publicly declared, "The Chinese people cannot stand idly by with regard to . . . the invasion of Korea by the United States and its accomplices and to the dangerous trend toward extending the war." The first fighting occurred on October 29 between the CPV and South Korean troops at the Yalu River some forty miles below the border. The initial clashes between the CPV and the United States took place November 2 on both the western and eastern fronts. Three days later, General MacArthur notified the United Nations that "Chinese Communist military units" were in Korea. On November 7, North Korea officially acknowledged that Chinese forces had crossed the Yalu on October 25 (they actually had moved ten days earlier). The same day, in an important development that U.S. policy makers would have to assess correctly, the CPV broke off all contact for three weeks, disappearing into the mountain vastness.

On November 16, President Harry Truman publicly endorsed a draft Security Council resolution of November 10, which pledged to "hold the Chinese frontier inviolate, to protect fully legitimate Chinese and Korean interests in the frontier zone and to withdraw the U.N. forces as soon as stability has been restored and a unified, independent, and democratic government established *throughout Korea*"[3] (italics added). His final point made fully explicit the maximum objective conveyed more discreetly in the October 7 U.N. resolution, despite the fact that Chinese forces had since entered the battle and thereby changed the situation. Nevertheless, no private Sino-U.S. exchanges occurred to test the sufficiency of President Truman's assurances or the risk in his goal of unifying the peninsula without the Pyongyang regime.

No diplomatic relations existed between the PRC and the United States because of Washington's previous refusal to transfer recognition from the Republic of China represented by the Nationalist forces on Taiwan to Mao Zedong's new regime in Peking. In mid-October, an isolated effort by the U.S. ambassador in New Delhi to reach his Chinese counterpart through Indian channels was rebuffed.[4] Although the ambassador's overture had not been intended to probe Peking's intentions, much less to explore possible negotiations to avoid conflict, it might have opened up such a possibility had it succeeded.

Prior to actual contact with the CPV, Washington had dismissed Peking's warnings as bluff, with the exception of Asian specialists in the Department of State who gave them serious weight.[5] The Central Intelligence Agency (CIA) concluded on October 12 that "there are no convincing indications of an actual Chinese Communist intention to resort to full-scale intervention in Korea."[6] Meanwhile on October 9, the Joint Chiefs of Staff (JCS) had granted General MacArthur considerable latitude in deciding when to engage Peking's forces should they come in contact.

> Hereafter in the event of open or covert employment anywhere in Korea of major Chinese Communist units, without prior announcement, you should continue the action as long as, in your judgement, action by forces now under your control offers a reasonable chance of success. In any case you will obtain authorization from Washington prior to taking any military action against objectives in Chinese territory.[7]

This directive threatened to counter the second political requirement for crisis management, namely limitation of means in pursuit of goals. By leaving it to MacArthur's "judgement" when "a reasonable chance of success" justified engaging "major Chinese Communist units," Washington passed a key decision to the field commander without any required review that might serve political means. Moreover, this directive was never revised or rescinded after combat occurred between the CPV and U.N. forces in late October and early November.

INTELLIGENCE REPORTS AND ESTIMATES: POST-CONTACT

The setting for White House decision making includes intelligence reports and analyses from the field as well as those made in Washington. In early November, this setting established a crisis context radically different from that which had prevailed prior to contact with the CPV. Thus, on November 3, the Far East Command (FEC) estimated Chinese strength in Korea as between 16,500 and 34,000 troops but on November 8 raised the minimum figure to 34,500.[8] This became 30–40,000 in the National Intelligence Estimate (NIE) of November 8.[9] But the next day Tokyo headquarters gave the probable Chinese force as 76,800.[10] Then on November 10, MacArthur's spokesman publicly declared that 60,000 Chinese troops were in Korea "with an equal number of reinforcements on the way" from a reserve of up to 500,000 in adjacent Manchuria.[11]

Thus, within a week, the Far East Command had doubled its force estimate and pointed to a massive buildup just across the border. Yet subsequent deliberations in Washington seemingly took no notice of the sudden increase in force estimates. There was no further NIE to update the earlier one before MacArthur's final offensive on November 24, which triggered the massive Chinese counterattack of November 25.

The general's personal view remained sanguine despite his intelligence reports. In a conversation of November 16, he reportedly put the Chinese strength at only

30,000, claiming that only those troops who could have entered covertly, avoiding open deployment, would have gone undetected by U.S. air and intelligence capabilities.[12] Although this report did not influence views in Washington, as it was not received there until December, his gross contradiction of FEC estimates suggests that MacArthur refused to acknowledge the potential seriousness of Chinese intervention.

MacArthur's influence on U.S. decision making can only be speculated upon. However, the official army history dwelt at some length on this question, noting that standard operating procedure leaves tactical intelligence to the field while responsibility for strategic intelligence and political estimating is jointly shared by theater headquarters, the CIA, and the Department of the Army.[13]

Two constraints implicitly inhibited Washington from challenging MacArthur's estimates and judgment. First, his daring gamble at Inchon had been opposed or questioned by virtually all of his peers and superiors in the Pentagon, yet it had succeeded. Second, the general's aggressive political style had been demonstrated in late August by his public warning against "misconceptions currently being voiced concerning the relationship of Formosa [Taiwan] to our strategic potential in the Pacific."[14] He had called Taiwan "an unsinkable aircraft carrier" possessing "a concentration of operational air and naval bases potentially greater than any similar concentration on the Asiatic mainland between the Yellow Sea and the Strait of Malacca." President Truman ordered this statement to be withdrawn as unauthorized, but MacArthur's compliance came too late to prevent press publication.

Thus, any military questioning of MacArthur had to confront his consistently successful record in Korea, from the initial intervention in June to the shattering of North Korean resistance and near-total occupation of the peninsula in November. Politically, MacArthur's open challenging of administration policy on Taiwan had strengthened the administration's opponents on a volatile issue in the November 7 off-year election. We will return to this latter aspect in our review of options in the post-election context. At this point, it suffices to note the bureaucratic and political factors that, while undocumented, almost certainly influenced the handling of his views in Washington.

The general's optimism flagged only once during this period. On November 7, a JCS query on Chinese intervention evoked his warning that "such forces will be used and increased at will, probably without a formal declaration of hostilities. If this enemy build-up continues, it can easily reach a point preventing our resumption of the offensive and even force a retrograde movement."[15] But two days later MacArthur reverted to form, declaring, "I believe that with my air power . . . I can deny reinforcements coming across the Yalu in sufficient strength to prevent the destruction of those forces now arrayed against me in North Korea."[16] The official army history notes, "This reliance on air power . . . was probably the crucial factor in MacArthur's calculations."[17]

Combat with the CPV jolted Washington into making its first serious assessment of Chinese objectives. On November 1, O. Edmund Clubb, head of the Office of Chinese Affairs in the Department of State, warned that intervention was unlikely to be limited, judging from Chinese domestic propaganda, and it was unlikely to have been undertaken without Soviet agreement and assistance.[18] He did not think its aim was to protect the Yalu River Dam and power plant, about which much speculation had occurred, because Chinese media had made no reference thereto. Moreover, communist ideology put politics above economics. Therefore, Clubb concluded, intervention would be aimed at helping North Korea and protecting China from a perceived threat of U.S. aggression.

Two days later, Clubb's office sounded a louder alarm, noting "with deep concern . . . the growing possibility that we may be drawn into warfare with Communist China . . . a tragedy to the American and Chinese peoples [that] might lead to a disaster for the United States, should war with China spring World War III."[19] The same day the assistant secretary of state for public affairs expressed deep concern in a memorandum to Assistant Secretary of State Rusk: "At the very least the Chinese are building up to very large numbers (perhaps a hundred thousand or so) . . . in Korea, with the probable purpose of keeping us bogged down in Korea for many months. At the most they are building up to open employment of hundreds of thousands . . . with a full expectation that this will mean general war between the Chinese and ourselves (for which they are preparing their own people psychologically)."[20]

Another sober assessment of the significance of the Chinese intervention was cabled by the U.S. consulate in Hong Kong: "Not yet prepared to accept interpretation that decision means early all-out war . . . but Chinese Communists undoubtedly fear time is running out for North Koreans and may well feel it necessary take risk of sending in more of own units as less dangerous in long run than permitting U.N. forces consolidate position in Korea and thus from Chinese Communist point of view posing threat to their border."[21] This was a sharp change from Hong Kong's previous estimate of October 13, which had seen military intervention as "not likely."[22] On November 4, Clubb provided Rusk with a fuller analysis, which concluded with a somber prediction: "The minimum Chinese Communist objective must be considered to be either the restoration of the *status quo ante* June 25 in North Korea or the expulsion of U.N. forces from the entire Korean peninsula."[23]

This concatenation of estimates, all but one from China specialists, conflicted with MacArthur's response of November 4 to a JCS query. The general argued that while overt intervention was possible, "there are many fundamental reasons against it and sufficient evidence has not yet come to hand to warrant its immediate acceptance."[24] However, another China specialist, John Paton Davies of the Policy Planning Staff, directly countered MacArthur's logic by postulating four motivations behind intervention: (1) China seeks "ideologically . . . to foster Korean Communist resistance and, ultimately, expansion on the peninsula"; (2) Peking sees the U.N. forces "as hostile" because the United States is the major actor and is viewed "with morbid distrust and hatred . . . [after] five years of intensely bitter civil war in which they regarded us as allies of their enemies, culminating in the galling frustration of our action this summer with regard to Formosa"; (3) the Kremlin is actively urging China to support the Korean Communists; and (4) the invasion of Tibet "shows that Peiping is willing to forgo membership in the U.N."[25]

In another memorandum to Rusk on November 7, Clubb sharpened Davies's reference to the U.S.–Chiang Kai-shek tie: "The Chinese Communists undoubtedly look askance at support of the National Government, our efforts to keep Peiping out of the U.N., our guerrilla contacts (which very probably have become known to the Communist side), our avowed anti-Communist position."[26] This allusion to CIA operations may have evoked discussion recorded in more restricted documents, but no such impact is evident from available materials.

The aforementioned NIE of November 8 settled on two primary motivations for Chinese intervention, namely "to halt the advance of U.N. forces in Korea and to keep a Communist regime in being on Korean soil."[27] The forecast was grim: "A likely and logical development . . . is that the opposing sides will build up their combat power in successive increments to checkmate the other until forces of major magnitude are involved. At any point in this development . . . the situation may get out of hand and lead to a general war." Moreover, "the Chinese Communists . . . have accepted a grave risk of retaliation and general war. They would probably ignore an ultimatum requiring their withdrawal."

As the most authoritative statement of the intelligence community, this NIE presumably carried considerable weight. It did not pull punches or hide behind bureaucratic obfuscation. It did not try to determine how many Chinese forces were already in Korea. It agreed with the China specialists' views and rejected MacArthur's. Apparently by coincidence, its issuance was immediately followed by the Far East Command doubling its estimate of probable CPV strength in Korea, implicitly validating the forecast, although there is no record of the NIE being transmitted to Tokyo either in summary or in full.

At this point, Chinese forces broke off all contact along the entire Korean front, not resuming action until MacArthur's November 24 offensive. I will examine possible explanations for this withdrawal below. A paradoxical situation resulted. On the one hand, the conjuncture of an NIE forecast with the enemy disengagement afforded optimum conditions for the systematic reassessment of U.S. goals and political-military options together with the potential risks and gains, a key condition or requirement in crisis management. On the other hand, the mysterious disappearance of Chinese forces reduced a sense of crisis and seemingly relieved the necessity to reconsider U.S. goals. As we shall see, no such reassessment or reconsideration occurred, despite the consensus of China specialists that Peking was prepared for a major war. These experts not only did not revise their sober estimates during the CPV disengagement but, on the contrary, formulated them more strongly.

One final point must be noted in connection with the determination of Chinese objectives. Not until November 14 did a draft National Security Council (NSC) memorandum in response to the NIE declare, "It is of the utmost importance that the real intentions of the Chinese Communists be ascertained as soon as possible."[28] Recommendations toward that end included (1) "intensify covert actions to determine Chinese Communist intentions," and (2) use "other available channels . . . to ascertain Chinese Communist intentions and, in particular, to determine whether there is any basis for arrangements which might stabilize Sino-Korean frontier problems on a satisfactory basis."

Rusk, however, in responding to a November 10 proposal from Clubb, had already anticipated the NSC recommendation. On November 13, he asked the

Swedish ambassador to ask his government to have its ambassador in Peking probe for the regime's "present intentions and any basis for the peaceful settlement of their legitimate anxieties."[29] The probe failed to elicit any response.[30]

According to an editorial footnote, the NSC memorandum was circulated for consideration with further action noted on November 30, by which time, of course, a new war had erupted. Its call for action "as soon as possible" won a slow response. On November 20, Ambassador Philip Jessup recommended that "methods . . . to determine Chinese Communist intentions . . . should include . . . contacts with the Chinese Communist regime through friendly governments and private channels."[31] If any covert action or exploitation of political channels to Peking occurred other than the single Swedish effort, it is not mentioned in the available documentation.

GOALS AND OPTIONS

The strategic goal of unifying all of Korea under U.N. auspices was stated in the General Assembly resolution of October 7. At no point was this goal specifically challenged or reassessed as a consequence of Chinese intervention. No top official suggested that the United States reconsider the objective of a united Korea. The reiteration of this goal in internal memoranda and externally directed communications by Secretary of State Dean Acheson and others remained consistent down to the time of MacArthur's final offensive, contrary to the first political requirement for crisis management of limiting objectives.

The second political requirement, limiting the means used in pursuit of those objectives, received some consideration but without any change in the policy that had existed prior to combat with Chinese forces. Halting U.N. forces well short of the Yalu River so as to leave a border zone roughly twenty miles deep posed a possible alternative to total military occupation of North Korea. But the first systematic exposition of this option did not come until November 20, four days before MacArthur launched his "home by Christmas" offensive. Moreover, the earlier treatment of this proposal suggests it had already been ruled out for all practical purposes.

The concept of a demilitarized zone along the Sino-Korean border was advanced by London in reaction to the initial Chinese engagements. It accorded with widespread speculation concerning the importance of the Suiho Dam and power plants on the Yalu River to Manchuria, China's main industrial base. But as early as November 4, Clubb explicitly dismissed this factor as "without major political or economic significance" for Peking.[32]

Far more important, MacArthur unleashed a blistering attack against stopping short of the Yalu, using both military and political arguments. The tenor of his attack was significant, not only for its rationale but for its possible impact on discussion of the proposal in Washington. On November 9, he informed the JCS that he planned an offensive on November 15 "with the mission of driving to the border and securing all of North Korea. Any program short of this would completely destroy the morale of my forces and its psychological consequence would be inestimable."[33] He nonetheless proceeded to estimate the consequences.

First, halting short of the border "would unquestionably arouse such resentment among the South Koreans that their forces would collapse or might even turn against us. It would therefore necessitate immediately a large increment of increase in foreign troops." Second, to suppose China "would abide by any delimitations upon further expansion southward would represent wishful thinking at its very worst." Third, "to give up any portion of North Korea to the aggression of the Chinese Communists . . . would bankrupt our leadership and influence in Asia and render untenable our position both politically and militarily." Fourth, "it would impose on us the disadvantage of having inevitably to fight [a general] war if it occurs bereft of the support of countless Asians." Fifth, it "would entirely reverse the tremendous moral and psychological uplift throughout Asia and perhaps the entire free world which accompanied the United Nations decision of June 25 and leave in its place a revulsion against that organization bordering on complete disillusionment and distrust."

MacArthur excoriated London in terms that carried political weight in the current U.S. debate over "who lost China":

> The widely reported British desire to appease the Chinese Communists by giving them a strip of Northern Korea finds its historic precedent in the action taken at Munich. . . . Of that settlement our own State Department has this to say . . . 'The crisis occasioned by the German occupation of Austria in March 1938 was followed by the Munich crisis in September, when the weakness of peaceful efforts toward just settlements in the face of determined aggression was unmistakably demonstrated.'
>
> This observation of the State Department points unmistakably to the lessons of history. I am unaware of a single exception which would cast doubt upon the validity of this concept. . . . It is tribute to aggression which encourages that very international lawlessness which it is the fundamental duty of the United Nations to curb.

As a parting shot, MacArthur claimed that "to yield to so immoral a proposition . . . would follow clearly in the footsteps of the British who by the appeasement of recognition [of the People's Republic] lost the respect of all the rest of Asia without gaining that of the Chinese segment."

Logistical problems delayed MacArthur's offensive. In the meantime, support for slowing up military action and weighing negotiations with Peking came from China specialists in the State Department. On November 7, Clubb argued that there was still

> time to consider the possibility of some *detente*. . . . The [forthcoming] attendance of the Chinese Communist delegation at the U.N. in connection with the case of Formosa would offer . . . a major opportunity . . . both in respect to Formosa and otherwise, if such be possible, . . . this should be a period for some slowing up of military operations to permit political estimates and discussions with our allies, to the end that, in our haste to win a battle, we shall not lose a war.[34]

Clubb's memorandum fits important operational as well as political requirements of crisis management concerning the reduction of military momentum, the exploration of political alternatives, and the exploitation of reduced hostilities for probing the enemy's flexibility. Davies expanded on Clubb's proposal on November 17 with a recommendation that was uniquely detailed compared with all other papers during this period.

1. Sponsor a U.N. resolution announcing the conclusion of full scale U.N. military action and calling for (a) the demilitarization of the northern fringe of Korea, (b) the withdrawal of all foreign military elements from that zone, (c) its administration by a U.N. Commission pending the holding of elections throughout North Korea and the establishment of normal civil administration, and (d) the phased withdrawal of U.N. forces from Korea;
2. immediately begin the retirement of all U.N. forces to a defensive position at the neck of the Korean peninsula [roughly the 39th parallel above Pyongyang and Wonsan];
3. cease military air action over the demilitarized zone but elsewhere continue whatever military action is deemed necessary;
4. accept in our planning the likelihood that part of North Korea will remain under effective Kremlin control and be a constant threat to the ROK;
5. build up the ROK armed forces to a condition where they can within a year hold at the neck of the peninsula anything short of a major Chinese or Soviet attack.[35]

Davies's memorandum, emanating from the Policy Planning Staff, presumably circulated at Acheson's level where it apparently influenced Ambassador Jessup's memorandum of November 20 advising Acheson for the upcoming discussion with Secretary of Defense George Marshall and the JCS. Jessup argued that the general objective "of the unity and independence of Korea . . . does not necessarily require the military occupation of all of Korea to its northernmost boundaries . . . at least ninety percent of the Korean population is in territory under the control of U.N. forces."[36] He then posited "three courses of military action" to be considered: go to the border, stop short of the border, and withdraw to a defensive line south of extant positions.

Jessup suggested that the first course be questioned in terms of its military capability to deny penetration and infiltration, its comparable advantage compared with a line distant from the border, its possible increased risk of expanding the conflict, and its maintenance should China fully commit its capabilities. Pending determination of these questions, he proposed consideration of "support in the U.N. for the U.K. proposal for . . . a 'demilitarized zone' or 'security zone' . . . with a U.N. commission to assume responsibility for this zone and for the negotiation of border problems between the Koreans, the Chinese, and the Russians."

Despite the obvious parallels, Jessup's memorandum differed from those of Clubb and Davies in one crucial respect—namely, the timing of political and military moves. He proposed "to couple [further military] advances with some type of political negotiations. . . . Naturally such negotiations should be conducted in such a way as not to suggest weakness." This accorded with Acheson's well-known dictum of "negotiation from strength." But it contradicted the crisis management requirement of limiting military means and subordinating them to diplomatic means in pursuit of political objectives. Jessup also avoided challenging the continued pursuit of Korean unification and the limiting of political objectives.

On November 21, top-level State and Pentagon officials held the fullest discussion to date of the border zone question. Acheson's agenda included two items pertaining to our inquiry: "to support U.N. and U.S. political action directed toward the withdrawal of the Chinese from Korea" and "to avoid being drawn by the Korean situation into major hostilities against Communist China."[37] These occurred in the context of the U.N. resolution of October 7, "looking toward the unification of the country."

Secretary of Defense George Marshall questioned the concept of a demilitarized zone and declared that such a zone would have to be established on the Chinese side of the river if it existed on the Korean side.[38] Moreover, the latter would require military protection for the U.N. commission there. In any event, Marshall assumed that MacArthur's successful offensive would precede any political proposals. Acheson countered that the offensive might be only partially successful and that it would be difficult to win agreement to establishing demilitarized zones on both sides. He emphasized the need to terminate Chinese intervention and to meet the concerns of U.N. allies.

Generals Omar Bradley, J. Lawton Collins, and Hoyt Vandenberg discussed the military feasibility of alternative positions, agreeing that the Yalu bank would be hard to hold but that the high ground behind it could be defended.[39] A lengthy discussion followed over whether to announce this line in advance or to negotiate its arrangement, but its precise location was not identified. Acheson emphasized the advantage of negotiating Peking into accepting a position that the United States intended to take anyway, while Marshall favored an announcement by MacArthur that he would stop at the high ground and then negotiate the details.

At this point, Acheson, Marshall, and Averell Harriman withdrew from the discussion, leaving the JCS to pursue other matters. Jessup's record laconically notes, "There was a brief discussion of what would happen if General MacArthur's offensive bogged down. There was no consensus on what could be done at that time." So much for contingency planning.

No actionable decision emerged from the meeting, despite the apparent agreement that securing an area just short of the Yalu River would meet the general U.N. objective and that this would be made known at some point with possible negotiations to follow. That evening, Acheson cabled the London embassy to head off Foreign Minister Ernest Bevin's proposal for a demilitarized zone. Acheson gave four reasons for opposing it: (1) it would confuse MacArthur, whose offensive was about to begin; (2) the Chinese delegation was about to arrive at the United Nations and would take the proposal as a commitment from which they could bargain for something more; (3) the proposal "will present grave military problems and danger which have not been adequately explored"; and (4) "until results of the forthcoming offensive are known it is impossible to ascertain what course can and should be safely adopted."[40]

Judging from the consistent U.S. opposition to the U.K.'s proposing this idea at the United Nations and the desultory handling of it in Washington, it seems clear that the idea of stopping any significant distance short of the Yalu River won no serious consideration. Moreover, to the extent that the issue was raised at all, MacArthur's offensive gained first priority over any alternative political-military options. No authoritative voice called for postponement of the offensive, either pending further information on Chinese capabilities and intentions or in order to probe for a negotiated settlement. Last but not least, the JCS was unwilling or unable to define what course of action would follow should the offensive fail.

Acheson concurred with the Pentagon in accepting MacArthur's plan as being plausible. In his planning session before meeting with Marshall and the JCS, he declared that there should be no change in MacArthur's orders to advance against the Chinese until it was evident he could not succeed.[41] The general needed to "probe" the situation and, if he were successful in driving the Chinese across the Yalu, the ROK might take over the border area. If MacArthur met strong resistance, however, and a long struggle were inevitable, "we must turn again to the field of negotiation."

Likewise at the November 21 meeting, according to David S. McLellan's review of Acheson's minutes, he "seems to have shared the prevailing confidence that MacArthur could accomplish his mission and that Chinese intervention, if it did occur, could be contained within a buffer zone along the border."[42] This refusal at the highest level to posit a worst case contingency and to explore alternative courses of action that weighed costs against gains effectively eliminated reconsideration of objectives and allowed for only a minimal reconsideration of means. Consequently, the original policy survived intact. The option of withdrawal to a defensive position in the neck of the peninsula received no attention. The U.K. proposal for a demilitarized zone received delayed study with informal agreement on a drastically reduced version. Finally, military options prevailed over political ones, leaving U.S. policy what it had been before contact between Chinese and U.N. forces had occurred.

To be sure, the nearly daily cables from Seoul reporting little or no contact with Chinese forces for nearly three weeks after their initial battle with U.S. troops could have induced complacency as a comfortable alternative to a worst case prognosis. Typical was the November 18 dispatch from the U.S. chargé, which offered the "main conclusion is they fighting delaying actions and not committed to all-out intervention. Reasons . . . not clear . . . but information currently available leads us to believe . . . will in end fall short of all-out war."[43]

Yet the NIE based on "information as of November 21" delivered a clear warning that if Peking failed to win "U.N. withdrawal from Korea . . . [there] will be increased Chinese intervention in Korea. At a minimum the Chinese will conduct, on an increased scale, unacknowledged operations" to immobilize U.N. forces and inflict attrition.[44] The NIE could not say whether Peking was "yet committed to a full-scale offensive effort," but it pointed out that "eventually they may undertake operations designed to cause the U.N. to withdraw from Korea." Although the estimate was not signed off until the eve of General MacArthur's new offensive, its drafting far preceded that event. Furthermore, it reflected the summary judgment of the intelligence community, which clearly cautioned against taking any reassurance from the Chinese disengagement.

DOMESTIC POLITICS

Nowhere in the published documents or official analyses is reference made to the effect of domestic politics on decisions regarding Korea. This is not surprising, given the tacit understanding within the Department of State and the Department of Defense that such considerations must be left to the president and not enter into deliberations outside the White House.[45] However, it is impossible to ignore the political context within which Chinese intervention was discussed, given the off-year election and its specific impact on the public reputations of both Truman and Acheson.

On November 7, 1950, over forty million voters went to the polls, more than had ever voted in an off-year election.[46] Supporters of the administration suffered badly, with Far East policy the dominant reason in several races. The losers included Senator Scott Lucas, majority leader, and Senator Millard E. Tydings, chairman of the Armed Services Committee and opponent of Senator Joseph R. McCarthy.

The next day, Acheson responded to press conference questions by stoutly insisting he would not resign or change policies.[47] However, James Reston's analysis was headlined "Democrats' Election Losses Weaken Acheson's Position—Some Senators of Party Now Believe That Secretary Is a Political Liability."[48] The text not only amplified the headline but also emphasized "the suspicious attitude of the country toward him and his department." Reston condemned the ruthlessness of the attacks on the Truman administration, writing that "suspicions in the public mind . . . have been increased by as ignoble a series of political tricks as this country has seen since the Al Smith campaign in 1928. And Mr. Acheson's head has been through the hole most of the time." Arthur Krock amplified on this theme in noting that "of the conspicuous Democratic candidates who ventured to defend Secretary Acheson vigorously from charges growing out of the loss of China, the Korean war and the incidents centering on Alger Hiss, only Senator Lehman and—on the face of the returns—Senator Benton survived the polls."[49]

It was only two days after the election that MacArthur's message to the JCS attacked the U.K. proposal to limit the advance of U.N. troops as a "desire to appease" consistent with "its historic precedent taken at Munich." He charged that "to give up any portion of North Korea to the aggression of the Chinese Communists would be the greatest defeat of the free world in recent times."[50] After MacArthur's open challenge in August to the Truman-Acheson policy on Taiwan, the implication of these words in the election's aftermath could not have been overlooked by the White House. The logic of the situation indicates that domestic politics provided one constraint on consideration of any options other than a full advance to the border and Korean unification as U.S. goals. How serious that constraint was cannot be determined, but its probable presence must be noted in examining Washington's failure to react to Chinese Communist intervention with effective crisis management.

THE CHINESE POSTURE

We have no such access to archives in Peking as we do to those in Washington. In particular, Mao Zedong's policy is difficult to assess because it behooves others to blame him for shortcomings in the intervention, whatever may have been their actual responsibility at the time. Accepting this caution, however, we can still draw inferences from indirect evidence to speculate on the likely range of Chinese Communist intentions and behavioral motivations.

According to an interview with an authoritative military source in Peking, the secret military history of the Korean War portrays the CPV as largely unprepared to cope with the logistical demands of fighting in the Korean mountains in winter.[51] Mao allegedly ordered the Yalu River crossing without having staffed the operation in advance. As a result, except for those units permanently stationed in Manchuria, the troops lacked adequate clothing and suffered more casualties from frostbite than from combat.[52] But Mao was adamant about the necessity to prevent the United States from occupying all of Korea and thereby posing a direct threat to China's industrial base in the northeast.

Whether Mao countenanced a greater offensive objective at the outset, namely the expulsion of U.N. forces from the peninsula and its unification under a communist aegis, cannot be determined from the available sources. However, the aforementioned military historian denied that the suspension of combat on November 7–8 was aimed at testing U.N. resolve or determining U.N. objectives with a readiness to negotiate a compromise division of control in the north. Instead, he insisted, the three-week pause was to build up troops and supplies for counterattacking the next U.N. offensive. In addition, the withdrawal would lure U.N. forces into a trap to be sprung when the CPV moved down from concealment in the surrounding mountains.[53]

As has often been noted, Mao's strategy and tactics followed the classic military analyst, Sun Tzu, whose aphorisms include, "All warfare is based on deception. Therefore when capable, feign incapacity; when active, inactivity. When near, make it appear that you are far away. . . . Offer the enemy a bait to lure him; feign disorder and strike him. When he concentrates, prepare against him; where he is strong, avoid him. Pretend inferiority and encourage his arrogance. . . . Attack where he is unprepared; sally out when he does not expect you."[54]

When the counterattack proved successful and U.N. forces fled from the upper half of the peninsula, the CPV commander, Peng Dehuai, reportedly proposed halting at the narrow sector just below Pyongyang, which had fallen without a battle by December 3.[55] According to the military historian cited above, Peng argued that his forces lacked protection from U.S. aircraft and, therefore, he could only move men and matériel at night. He had too few trucks to transport the necessary supplies from northeast China, and Moscow had not provided anti-aircraft weapons sufficient to the need. The enemy had withdrawn intact with most of its equipment and would gain an increasing advantage as CPV communication lines lengthened and U.N. lines shortened. Therefore, Peng counseled stopping at around the 39th parallel until a strong defensive position could be prepared and forward movement resumed. By this account, however, Mao countermanded Peng's position and ordered the CPV to "throw the Americans out of Korea."

The historian explained that Mao's miscalculation in pushing the CPV beyond its limit stemmed from three factors. First, no Chinese Nationalist army had regrouped and returned full force to battle after it had been defeated. Therefore, once routed, the U.N. command should have offered no serious resistance. Second, Mao had never been constrained to maneuver in a narrow peninsula. Mobility on a wide front had always been possible. And third, he had never suffered the concentration of firepower by air, sea, and ground forces amassed by U.N. forces in and around Korea.

Whatever Peking's initial objective, it appears that MacArthur's precipitous abandonment of the territory above Pyongyang and further to below Seoul prompted Mao to violate the political requirement for crisis management of limiting his objective. Mao's action, in effect, ruled out the possibility of a short, limited war that could be ended by negotiation and compromise. As a parallel to Washington's earlier expansion of its goal from repelling aggression to uniting the peninsula, Peking's behavior suggests that military success evokes similar responses, regardless of cultural differences.

Thus, when the Chinese Communist delegation came to the United Nations, it made no effort to signal publicly or indicate privately a desire to forestall major conflict by negotiation. On the contrary, China's assertive posture communicated confidence in its ability to exploit the counterattack already under way. The delegation quickly returned home, having appeared adamant in demanding the removal of U.S. protection from Taiwan and U.N. forces from Korea.

This does not necessarily prove the futility of hypothetical U.S. soundings of a Chinese willingness to halt at the narrow neck in a ceasefire, pending political efforts to negotiate a broader settlement. One cannot rewrite history, least of all when so many interacting factors might impact differently on one another under different circumstances. On the Chinese side, there were sharply divergent views on the costs as well as the risks entailed in intervention. Reconsideration of gains to be achieved by, as opposed to costs and risks of, pushing further down the peninsula might have restrained a CPV advance. On the U.N. side, allied concern over possible escalation, nuclear as well as conventional, might have found retention of two-thirds of the peninsula preferable to holding half of it in prolonged combat. As a final variable, once a compromise settlement seemed possible, Moscow might have sided with those in Peking who favored it rather than bear the costs and risks of prolonged war and possible escalation.

What is known about Chinese decision making in October–December 1950 does not provide definite information on what Peking intended, much less on what alternative course of action the Chinese might have accepted. It does, however, suggest how mutual misperception and miscalculation, compounded by a mirror-imaging of inept crisis management, resulted in inadvertent war.

REFLECTIONS AND CONCLUSIONS

Having examined in some detail the various aspects of decision making in Washington during the critical period of October–November 1950, we can return to our initial inquiry: What relevance does Chinese intervention in the Korean War and the U.S. response thereto have for our construct of crisis management? What idiosyncratic features differentiate this crisis from more generalizable case studies? What modifications in the construct might be explored to allow for their possible recurrence?

I have already shown that the two political requirements of crisis management were absent at the highest level in Washington: a willingness to limit goals and a determination to limit means. We can hypothesize the causes, but, in the absence of definitive evidence, especially on the thinking of Truman and Acheson, they must be offered as speculation, not conclusions. One such cause is a natural reluctance to reverse course once it has been determined publicly. This unwillingness is reinforced on the one hand by the euphoria of quick and easy victory, such as followed the Inchon landing, and on the other by the fear of political opposition, as was experienced in the November 7 election. In the larger global context, compromise with communism was equated with "rewarding aggression" and thereby with encouraging further attempts elsewhere to exploit "weakness."

The promise of gain was also not offset by the certainty or magnitude of risk. An asymmetry of motivation between Peking and Washington prompted the former to accept greater costs than had been estimated, despite its inferior power position, because national security was seen to be at stake. Meanwhile Washington, for its part, did not think Korea was worth a wider war and projected that calculation onto Peking. Thus, the initial U.S. assumption that "they're bluffing" was given new life when the first combat ended with the Chinese disengagement. In short, what was a "rational" deduction based on Washington's image of Peking differed sharply from the calculations made in China. The net result was incompatible goals that did not brook compromise, or so they were seen in the two capitals.

In contrast with the failure on either side to meet the political requirements, the operational requirements of crisis management won varying degrees of compliance. In evaluating how each proposition applied, I will limit my analysis for the most part to the U.S. side, given the limitations of evidence for China.

1. *Each side's political authorities must maintain control over military options— alerts, deployments, and low-level actions as well as the selection and timing of military moves.*

At the most general level, this injunction was adhered to by both President Truman and General MacArthur. The latter's failure to obtain advance clearance for his trip to Taiwan in July, where he publicly embraced Chiang Kai-shek, and his tendency to make public statements politically at variance with Washington cannot be included under the terminology in this proposition. These developments do, however, suggest the need to control all behavior by military commanders insofar as such behavior might become known to the prospective enemy. The reassurances of nonhostile intent communicated by Truman and Acheson were undermined, in Chinese perception, by the threatening image projected by MacArthur and more bellicose members of the administration.

A more serious problem was the definition of "control" and the degree of specificity in the rules of engagement imposed on military commanders. Taken literally, control could mean the tactical direction of forces in the field from Washington. It has been argued that General MacArthur exceeded his directives in allowing some U.S. troops to reach the Yalu instead of restricting that advance to South Koreans. But except for this single instance, he appears to have acted within the discretion thought necessary at that time for a field commander operating with immediately available tactical intelligence and maximum familiarity with the battlefield conditions at hand.

Ironically, MacArthur's initial schedule, communicated to Washington in advance, called for the final offensive on November 15, but logistical problems delayed it to November 24. This afforded more than ample opportunity for halting his advance to allow for political probing of enemy intent. No record exists of any suggestion from Washington that the advance be delayed further, much less indefinitely postponed. As we have seen, nothing emerged in the extra nine days to alter U.S. policy.

2. *The tempo and momentum of military movements may have to be deliberately slowed down and pauses created to provide enough time for the two sides to exchange diplomatic signals and communications and to give each side adequate time to assess the situation, make decisions, respond to proposals, and so forth.*

This course of action, as already noted, was urged by Clubb and Davies but was not even seriously considered at higher levels. Ironically, the pause created by the Chinese disengagement in early and mid-November was not exploited by the United States for any of the purposes embodied in this principle. The U.S. forces continued their piecemeal advance to the Yalu during this time. Although they encountered no enemy resistance, they communicated a signal of maximum intent: control of all Korea to the Yalu River. Their dispositions were more in the nature of preliminary probes rather than a full-scale advance, but this approach probably confirmed Chinese calculations of a determined U.S. policy.

The three week pause provided time for "diplomatic signals and communications" to clarify the objectives of both sides, yet the available record shows no such effort was made by Washington or Peking. If any subtle covert contacts occurred, they are not reflected in the documents at hand nor do specific references therein suggest they might have occurred. On the contrary, intermittent U.S. admonitions to make such an effort imply that they did not take place during this crucial period for reasons we have already offered.

Nor is there any evidence that Peking undertook the pause in order to test Washington's intent and response, either directly by conducting diplomatic probes or indirectly by observing U.N. military behavior. On the contrary, as we have seen, at least one authoritative Chinese source insists the pause was designed to increase CPV strength and to entrap the anticipated U.N. offensive. Yet without full access to Chinese archives, we cannot determine whether this rationale was offered post hoc to credit a Maoist tactic with success or was based on a priori principles of warfare against a materially superior enemy.

It is true that the absence of all direct diplomatic contact between the two nations because of Washington's refusal to recognize Peking is atypical for most situations. But the Chinese regime was not Mongolia, virtually isolated from all normal international contact. Communication could have been made through a third country, a conventional method under such circumstances. The fact that Indian Ambassador M. M. Panikkar was utilized by Mao to convey a warning to the United States before China crossed the Yalu credits Peking diplomacy before combat. However, no comparable effort is known to have been made by either side during the pause.

3. *Movements of military forces must be carefully coordinated with diplomatic actions as part of an integrated strategy for terminating the crisis acceptably without war.*

We have already acknowledged the absence of any U.S. diplomatic actions directed toward Peking during November. In addition, the key phrase here is "acceptably without war." This requirement must be addressed at two levels: the "acceptable" termination, which addresses goals; and "without war," which involves estimating the enemy's strength and its intended use thereof. The failure to reassess goals during the pause has already been discussed, hence an "acceptable" end for Washington did not involve ceding significant North Korean territory while such U.S. withdrawal was a minimal goal for Peking.

At a second level, however, there must be a cost-benefit analysis that posits the risks to be run in pursuit of goals as well as the costs of compromising those goals. This in turn raises the problem of intelligence concerning enemy capabilities and objectives. The Far East Command grossly underestimated the CPV strength in Korea after the initial round of combat but accorded sufficient size to the growing forces across the border to warrant serious attention. General MacArthur's personality and proclivities may have provided a genuinely idiosyncratic element not normally encountered in such situations. However, the underestimation of Viet Cong forces in South Vietnam prior to the 1967 Tet offensive provides a rough analogy, even though Gen. William Westmoreland's personality was the opposite of MacArthur's. Moreover, although an admittedly unique individual, MacArthur cannot by any means be held solely responsible for the failure of higher officials in Washington to estimate the worst case consequences of major Chinese intervention.

In contrast, the November 17 State Department intelligence analysis posited "the most likely Soviet-Chinese course as follows: a. Continuation of Chinese-North Korean holding operations in North Korea until Chinese over-all preparations have been completed and until prospects of securing U.S. withdrawals from Korea through intimidation and diplomatic maneuvers have been exhausted. b. *In case of the failure of these tactics, increasing unofficial Chinese intervention in Korea to, if necessary, the point of large scale military operations*"[56] (italics added).

While the analysis conceded at the outset that "the military activity of Chinese troops in Korea so far is not sufficiently extensive to indicate a plan for major operations," it quickly added that "military preparations . . . in Manchuria and China generally are on a scale that suggests plans for a major operation of prolonged duration." Reinforcing intelligence on "the climate of opinion prevailing in China" and Chinese propaganda underscored this pessimistic point of view.

Battlefield intelligence is always susceptible to error, especially when an enemy wishes to conceal movement and intention, as in the case of Korea. Miscalculation is an inherent danger in forecasting enemy behavior. Yet what is "acceptable" as an alternative to war depends on what costs war entails. This puts a premium on intelligence estimates that allow both for error in calculating capabilities and for cultural gaps in assessing intentions.

It is important to note that after the initial U.S. confrontation with the Chinese in Korea, the most experienced foreign service officers in Hong Kong and Washington consistently cautioned against ascribing engagement and withdrawal to bluff. Whereas the prevailing judgment in Tokyo and Washington argued the illogic of Chinese intervention at this stage of the war and therefore discounted its serious likelihood, the China specialists disagreed on the basis of their awareness of the specific concerns behind Peking's alarms and actions.

This argues for policy makers to hear divergent viewpoints that can be weighed in advance of final decisions. Specifically, this would have brought the China specialists into direct confrontation with other civilian and military officials, in the presence of the president or at least his national security adviser. Instead of basing joint intelligence estimates on bureaucratic bargaining and compromises, possibly further diluted by direct statements from the CIA head (often an amateur outsider), specialists would spell out the rationale for divergent forecasts in personal presentations.

Admittedly, such a meeting would create a greater demand in time and effort on the part of all concerned, particularly the president himself. Yet at most it would entail three to four hours, a small imposition relative to the importance of the decision. There was plenty of time during the November pause for this to have occurred. While the accuracy of the intelligence forecasts from area specialists in both the Korean and the Vietnam wars does not prove their infallibility, it does suggest the importance of airing such views directly and fully at higher levels than is customary in standard procedures.[57]

4. *Movements of military forces and threats of force intended to signal resolve must be consistent with one's limited diplomatic objectives—that is, "noise" must be avoided or minimized.*

This requirement clearly proved inoperative so long as Washington's objectives were not limited to anything less than a unified Korea under U.N. auspices. Only the abandonment of this goal would have permitted any possible diplomatic resolution of the conflict short of the inadvertent war that raged from November 1950 to June 1953. The problem of "noise" was absent on the Chinese side but not on that of the United States While avoidance of internal conflict is ideal but unfeasible in our system, dissonance can be minimized by executive discipline. President Truman's firing of his secretary of defense in September 1950 and of General MacArthur in March 1951 could be considered extreme worst case situations. However, they have had less dramatic analogs in other crisis situations where leaks amplified dissident views so as to inform (and misinform) friend and foe alike.

5. *Military moves and threats should be avoided that give the opponent the impression that one is about to resort to large-scale warfare, thereby forcing the opponent to consider preemption.*

Contrary to this injunction, General MacArthur's disposition of forces and their advancement in probing action between November 7 and November 24 signaled preparation for a final offensive to clear all remaining Korean soil of the enemy, whether North Korean or Chinese. Although Peking elected to counterattack rather than preempt, the situation was mishandled on the U.S. side because it forced the issue that had been left unresolved when the CPV disengaged: Would the main U.N. force stop well short of the border or march to the Yalu River?

Nothing in MacArthur's behavior made President Truman's assurances of November 16 and the parallel Security Council draft resolution credible. The general's public embrace of Chiang Kai-shek in July, his August declaration of Formosa's military value, and his November preparation for resuming the offensive conjured up a genuine worst case contingency. Peking could easily consider that its counterattack was preempting a later "return to the mainland" effort by Chiang's Nationalist army, assisted by MacArthur from Korea and the U.S. Seventh Fleet in the Taiwan

Strait. Clubb's memoranda focused on the plausibility of this fear as motivating Chinese intervention but to no avail so far as MacArthur's directives were concerned. As was noted, his directives left room for discretion only in achieving what he judged to be success in battle without regard for the subsequent consequences.

6. *Diplomatic-military options should be chosen that signal, or are consistent with, a desire to negotiate a way out of the crisis rather than to seek a military solution.*

Once again, both sides failed to follow this dictum. The final deliberations in Washington prior to MacArthur's November 24 offensive consistently show high-level officials, civilian and military, agreeing to negotiations only after the military action attained as much success as possible. Acheson's celebrated "negotiation from strength" maxim is a common calculation that partly explains Washington's un-willingness to withhold the use of force in order to facilitate negotiations. Only when a military solution risks clearly unacceptable costs is negotiation readily accepted before a show of strength. This is not how Washington assessed the situation and the prospects in mid-November. The Sino-Soviet treaty threatened to exact such costs if China were attacked, hence absolute prohibitions on striking across the Yalu restrained MacArthur's hand. But no cost calculation in Korea itself prompted the United States to precede military action with negotiations. Indeed, at Wake Island, MacArthur personally assured Truman that "the greatest slaughter" would result should the Chinese intervene in the war.

7. *Diplomatic proposals and military moves should be selected that leave the opponent a way out of the crisis that is compatible with its fundamental interests.*

Peking's pause left open the opportunity for the United States to redefine its goals, but Washington proved unwilling to do so. Both in public and in private communications, the United States held to a "free, democratic, and united Korea" as a nonnegotiable objective, hence a "fundamental interest." Peking's public statements had focused on three concerns: aggression by the United States against North Korea, the threat to China's national security, and Formosa. It is likely that the Chinese weighed their fundamental interests differently in the three cases, with national security first, survival of the North Korean regime second, and Formosa third in urgency although not in substance. It is possible that had the United States exploited the pause to communicate a specific proposal whereby a temporary ceasefire allowed for sufficient North Korean territory to be left free of U.N. control to serve as a protective buffer for the Chinese border while providing a respectable base for a northern regime, Peking might have accepted it.

Certainly, there was a general reluctance on the part of some Chinese leaders to engage U.S. power, as evidenced by references to a debate Mao resolved by his own insistence that intervention was necessary. The prospect of a prolonged war, given China's desperate economic condition after decades of foreign invasion and civil war, would have provided grounds for weighing the advantages to compromise. It is possible that Mao would still have ordered a major offensive, capitalizing on a surprise attack by the 300,000 troops massed in the Korean mountains and hoping either to force the United States to leave South Korea or to gain better ground for a settlement based on the status quo ante. But no such proposal came from Washington, where the goal remained unchanged as did the estimate of the costs of attaining it.

A final consideration in this regard is the impact of domestic politics on definitions of national or fundamental interest. The intrusion of electoral politics on foreign policy is not unique in democracies. The November 7, 1950, results did not change U.S. policy, but they may have inhibited change, especially given the problematic role General MacArthur played with respect to the question of Formosa and China. His definition of fundamental interests clashed with that of the White House, as manifest in his memorandum on the British proposal for a demilitarized zone along the Yalu River. Yet the conflict was not resolved until his dismissal the following spring.

An opponent who heads an authoritarian system is also not necessarily free of political constraints, both domestic and allied. Consideration of this factor is necessarily tentative in the absence of reliable information indicating the nature and extent of such constraints in Peking. Allied interests may also impose themselves on decision makers, either forcing or restraining choices. Washington assumed it was Moscow that prompted Pyongyang's initial attack and, subsequently, Peking's intervention, although China specialists differed for the most part. They argued that it was in Peking's fundamental interest to intervene, presumably with Moscow's encouragement and support.

These considerations cannot be evaluated for their importance in the absence of better evidence, even in the U.S. case, where official archives and private papers abound. Yet they challenge the concept of "fundamental interests" as objectively definable by one side and discernible by the other. It requires both intelligence analysis and diplomatic efforts to determine how these interests are perceived and to what extent they are susceptible to compromise prior to combat.

In short, the inadvertent war between China and the United States resulted from the failure of both sides, but especially of Washington, to observe the political and operational requirements of crisis management. The United States limited neither goals nor means after its initial combat with the Chinese made unanticipated escalation a real possibility. No diplomatic efforts toward negotiations preceded U.S. military moves. Peking suspended military operations but took no political steps to seek a compromise settlement. Its public posture reiterated maximum goals while its private behavior prepared to use the maximum force at its disposal for fighting in Korea.

The tragedy of misperception and miscalculation cost the lives of at least 300,000 Chinese, 55,000 Americans, and perhaps 2,000,000 Koreans, together with lesser numbers of British, Turkish, and other U.N. troops. Had either Peking or Washington foreseen these consequences, they almost certainly would have managed the crisis of November 1950 differently and avoided a war neither truly wanted.

BIBLIOGRAPHIC NOTE

In 1990, the 40th anniversary of the beginning of the Korean War occasioned conferences in the United States, the Republic of Korea, and elsewhere, the publication of papers from which will undoubtedly enrich our understanding and knowledge. In addition, the interested reader can profit from a growing literature that draws on newly released U.S. and British archives, as well as the first trickle of serious research studies from the People's Republic of

China. Unfortunately, the possibly definitive official history of China's entry into the war was not yet available to the author at the time of writing. Its publication should be watched for, as it will provide likely answers to questions raised in this essay.

In addition to the works cited in the Notes below, several other books on this subject are of interest. An insightful collection of studies is offered by James Cotton and Ian Neary, *The Korean War in History* (Manchester: Manchester University Press, 1989). In particular, Hak-Joon Kim, "China's Non-Involvement in the Origins of the Korean War: A Critical Reassessment," and Peter N. Farrar, "A Pause for Peace Negotiations: The British Buffer Zone Plan of November 1950," are relevant. An earlier symposium also merits attention: Bruce Cumings, ed., *Child of Conflict: The Korean-American Relationship 1943-1953* (Seattle: University of Washington, 1983). An exhaustive search of sources enriches Michael Schaller, *Douglas MacArthur: Far Eastern General* (New York: Oxford University Press, 1989). A much broader perspective is contained in William Stueck, *The Korean War: An International History* (Chapel Hill: University of North Carolina Press, forthcoming). This should supersede an earlier study by Robert R. Simmons, *The Strained Alliance: Peking, Pyongyang, Moscow and the Politics of the Korean Civil War* (New York: Free Press, 1975). A graphic depiction of the formidable circumstances attending Chinese intervention, based on interviews with eyewitnesses, may be found in Russell Spurr, *Enter The Dragon: China's Undeclared War Against the U.S. in Korea, 1950-51* (New York: Newmarket Press, 1988). However, the purported account of high-level deliberations prior to intervention was authoritatively rejected *in toto* by the official PLA military historian in October 1988.

NOTES

1. Alexander L. George, "Crisis Management: The Interaction of Political and Military Considerations," *Survival* (September/October 1984), pp. 223-34.

2. For a detailed account see Allen S. Whiting, *China Crosses The Yalu* (Stanford: Stanford University Press, 1968), chs. 6-7.

3. *Public Papers of the President of the United States, Harry S. Truman, January 1-December 31, 1950* (Washington, D.C.: U.S. Government Printing Office, 1965), p. 711.

4. Ambassador Loy Henderson to Secretary of State Dean Acheson, October 10, 1950, in *Foreign Relations of the United States, 1950, vol. VII, Korea* (Washington, D.C.: U.S. Government Printing Office, 1976), p. 921. (Hereafter cited as FRUS)

5. For assessments by Asian specialists, see O. Edmund Clubb to Assistant Secretary for Far East Dean Rusk, September 27, 1950, "Chinese Communist Intentions in Formosa and Korea," ibid., p. 795; U. Alexis Johnson to Rusk, October 3, 1950, "Threat of Chinese Intervention in Korean Conflict," ibid., p. 849; Clubb to Deputy Assistant Secretary Livingston Merchant, October 4, 1950, "Chinese Communist Threat of Intervention in Korea," ibid., 864-6. For caution against assuming bluff but a less serious assessment of consequences see Deputy Undersecretary of State H. Freeman Matthews to special assistant to secretary of defense for foreign military affairs and assistance, October 19, 1950, ibid., pp. 980-1.

6. Central Intelligence Agency, "Threat of Full Chinese Communist Intervention in Korea," October 12, 1950, ibid., pp. 933-4.

7. Joint Chiefs of Staff to MacArthur, October 9, 1950, ibid., p. 915.

8. Roy E. Appleman, *The U.S. Army in the Korean War: South to the Naktong, North to the Yalu* (Washington, D.C.: U.S. Government Printing Office, 1961), p. 760.

9. FRUS, p. 1101.

10. Appleman, *The U.S. Army*, pp. 762-3.

11. *New York Times*, November 10, 1950.

12. Ambassador Muccio memorandum of conversation, November 17, 1950, received December 4, 1950, FRUS, p. 1175.

13. Ibid., pp. 757–65.

14. Message to Veterans of Foreign Wars, New York Times, August 29, 1950.

15. Appleman, The U.S. Army, p. 764.

16. Ibid., p. 765.

17. Ibid., p. 765.

18. Clubb to Rusk, "Communist Intentions: Korea," November 1, 1950, FRUS, pp. 1023–5.

19. Memorandum from acting officer in charge of political affairs, Office of Chinese Affairs, to Rusk, Merchant, and Clubb, "Possible Measures to Lessen Tension with Communist China," November 3, 1950, ibid., pp. 1029–30.

20. Barrett to Rusk, "Chinese in North Korea," November 3, 1950, ibid., p. 1030.

21. Consul General Wilkinson to secretary of state, November 3, 1950, ibid., pp. 1034–5.

22. Consul General Wilkinson to secretary of state, October 13, 1950, ibid., p. 946. Wilkinson reported Peking's statements on the thirty-eighth parallel crossing had "caused flurry in hypersensitive gold market [but] it did not seem to alter generally-held Hong Kong opinion that Chinese Communists unlikely become militarily involved."

23. Clubb to Rusk, "Chinese Communist Intervention in Korea: Estimate of Objectives," November 4, 1950, ibid., pp. 1038–41.

24. Appleman, The U.S. Army, p. 762.

25. Draft Memorandum by John Paton Davies of the Policy Planning Staff, November 7, 1950, FRUS, pp. 1078–83.

26. Clubb to Rusk, "Chinese Communist Intervention in Korea: Counterstrategy," November 7, 1950, ibid., pp. 1087–93.

27. National Intelligence Estimate, "Chinese Communist Intentions in Korea," November 8, 1950 (based on information available November 6), ibid., pp. 1101–6.

28. NSC Memorandum (draft), November 14, 1950, ibid., p. 1150.

29. Memorandum of conversation by Rusk with Swedish Ambassador Erik Boheman, November 13, 1950, ibid., pp. 1141–2. For the Clubb proposal of November 10 see ibid., pp. 1123–4.

30. The initial Swedish-Chinese contact is undated and apparently was at a low level as indicated by the report of a December 13 meeting between the ambassador and the Chinese Vice Foreign Minister wherein the latter promised a response "in a few days." No further information was given in the memorandum by Undersecretary of State Matthews on his conversation with the Swedish ambassador in Washington, December 14, 1950. Ibid., pp. 1545–56.

31. Jessup to Rusk, November 20, 1950, ibid., p. 1196.

32. Clubb to Rusk, ibid., p. 1040.

33. MacArthur to Joint Chiefs of Staff, November 9, 1950, ibid., p. 1108.

34. Clubb to Rusk, November 7, 1950, ibid., pp. 1088–93.

35. Memorandum by Davies, November 17, 1950, ibid., pp. 1181–2.

36. Jessup to Acheson, "United States Courses of Action With Respect to Chinese Communist Intervention in Korea, Points for Consideration with Secretary Marshall and the Joint Chiefs of Staff," November 20, 1950, ibid., pp. 1193–6.

37. Enclosure to Memorandum from Rusk to Colonel Marshall S. Carter, Executive to the Secretary of Defense, November 21, 1950, ibid., p. 1204.

38. Memorandum of Conversation by Ambassador at Large Jessup: "Situation in Korea," November 21, 1950, ibid., pp. 1204–7.

39. General Collins described the "high ground" as a "line, perhaps beginning with a small river which comes in about ten miles east of the mouth of the Yalu and then following the high ground which runs at a distance from ten to twenty-five miles back of the River. This line would be followed up to the main bend in the frontier which has now been reached by our forces, after which the line would come down more or less directly to the Coast." Memorandum of conversation by Jessup, November 21, 1950, ibid., p. 1206.

40. Acheson to Embassy in U.K., November 21, 1950, ibid., pp. 1212–13.

41. Memorandum by Lucius D. Battle, special assistant to secretary of state, November 21, 1950, ibid., pp. 1201–3.

42. David S. McLellan, "Dean Acheson and the Korean War," *Political Science Quarterly*, March 1968.

43. FRUS, cable from U.S. Chargé Everett F. Drumright to the secretary of state, November 18, 1950, pp. 1184–5.

44. National Intelligence Estimate 2/1, "Chinese Communist Intervention in Korea," November 24, 1950.

45. This understanding was repeatedly communicated to the author during his tenure as Director, Office of Research and Analysis, Far East, in the Bureau of Intelligence and Research, Department of State, 1962–66. While this applied to written materials it did not, of course, preclude oral discussions on the relevance of domestic politics to policy.

46. *New York Times*, November 8, 1950.

47. Ibid., November 9, 1950.

48. Ibid., p. 20.

49. Ibid., p. 32.

50. MacArthur to JCS, November 9, 1950, FRUS, pp. 1108–9.

51. In October 1988 the author interviewed a Chinese official with access to the classified military history of the Korean War and to classified military-political archives. Specific questions focused on discussions and decisions leading to Chinese intervention in the Korean War and deliberations through January 1951. The official requested anonymity; his answers appeared plausible although they could not be independently confirmed.

52. For a graphic account based on interviews with CPV veterans many years later, see Russell Spurr, *Enter The Dragon* (New York: Newmarket Press, 1988).

53. This account challenges the author's interpretation, advanced initially in *China Crosses The Yalu* and recapitulated in *The Chinese Calculus of Deterrence* (Ann Arbor: University of Michigan Press, 1975). Without fuller access to Chinese archives it is impossible to determine Chinese motivations more definitively.

54. Cited in Eliot A. Cohen, " 'Only Half the Battle': American Intelligence and the Chinese Intervention in Korea, 1950," *Intelligence and National Security* 5, 2 (April 1990).

55. Author's interview with Chinese official, cited in fn. 51.

56. "Estimate of the Most Probable Course of Soviet-Chinese Action With Regard to Korea," November 17, 1950, FRUS, p. 1190.

57. The author participated in all intelligence estimates concerning the Vietnam War from 1962 to 1966. The correctness of views expressed by his office in the Department of State can be confirmed by the Government Printing Office version of the Pentagon papers.

CHAPTER 8

The Arab-Israeli War of 1967: Inadvertent War Through Miscalculated Escalation

Janice Gross Stein

The Arab-Israeli War in 1967 was inadvertent. None of the major participants or the superpowers planned or wanted war, yet they found themselves inadvertently trapped in a process of escalation they could not control. Largely in response to domestic imperatives, Syria increased its support of guerrilla raids across Israel's borders. Israel in turn attempted to deter Syria from supporting irregular military action through repeated threats of punishment. Israel's threats provoked Syria to escalate the conflict and its allies to try to deter Israel from punitive military action against Syria. Egypt's use of threats and troop deployments as part of a strategy of extended deterrence took place within a complex pattern of alliances that magnified their impact and fueled the escalation of a limited conflict.

Egyptian deterrence succeeded. The success of extended deterrence, however, set in motion political developments that President Gamal Abdel Nasser could not control. Even though Egyptian troops sent across the Suez Canal into the Sinai peninsula succeeded in deterring Israel, their presence then unleashed a set of demands the president was unable to resist. He faced an aroused domestic public, the taunts of regional adversaries, and pressure from regional allies. His leadership challenged in the Arab world, Nasser moved incrementally through a series of escalatory steps that challenged Israel's deterrent strategy and thereby broadened the scope of the conflict. Under pressure, Nasser was unable to limit his objectives; instead he escalated the stakes for Israel. Although the Egyptian extension of deterrence succeeded in its immediate objective of protecting a weaker ally, its success simultaneously provoked a wider war through its unintended impact on Egypt's domestic public, its Arab allies and adversaries, and the consequent pressures on President Nasser.

The author acknowledges the generous support of the Canadian Institute for International Peace and Security.

In Israel, the failure of its deterrent strategy against Egypt prompted a redefinition of the issues at stake, raised the consequences of concession, facilitated miscalculation of Egyptian intentions, and worked heavily in favor of a decision to use force. This was so whether or not Israel's leaders considered that Egyptian leaders were preparing to strike first. While the logic of force deployments was a component of the process of escalation, it was not the most important part. In the strategic thinking of Israel's leaders, the logic of their deterrent strategy blurred the distinction between preemption and prevention. The failure of Israel's deterrent strategy dictated a military response, sooner or later.

Two competing explanations dispute this interpretation of the path to inadvertent war. The first explains the escalation to war in 1967 in terms of the dictates of military logic, which led to a loss of control that created incentives to preempt. According to this explanation, the characteristics of the force structures of Egypt and Israel—particularly the vulnerability of their air forces; weaknesses in their systems of command, communication, and control; their mobilization procedures; and the pattern of their military deployments—created incentives for one or both sides to preempt. As the crisis escalated, each side was increasingly aware of the incentive to strike first, and each suspected the other of preparing a first strike. In logic similar to that detailed by Thomas Schelling in his analysis of the "reciprocal fear of surprise attack," this mix of incentives and fears ostensibly led Israel to miscalculate and preempt.[1] Consequently, the outbreak of war is explained as "accidental."

A second explanation points to the flawed execution of deterrence by Israel. Analysts argue that Israel failed to reinforce deterrence in time—that is, to warn unambiguously that it would go to war were Egypt to blockade the Straits of Tiran.[2] This failure to warn led President Nasser to miscalculate Israel's resolve and to proceed incrementally to challenge deterrence. By implication, better strategy could have prevented war.

Both these explanations overemphasize the impact of military reasoning and pay inadequate attention to leaders' calculations of the political consequences of their actions. This chapter argues that political rather than military miscalculation was critical to the process of escalation to inadvertent war. The deterrent strategies used by Israel and Egypt provoked a series of miscalculations that led to a war they sought to prevent. Deterrence inadvertently provoked rather than prevented escalation both because of risks inherent in the strategy and because of the conditions under which it was used: domestic political weakness and alliance politics and commitments.[3] The process of miscalculated escalation was then fueled by loss of political as well as military control over crisis developments, the failure of international institutions to exploit available opportunities to control escalation, and flawed strategies of crisis management by the two superpowers.

STEP ONE: ISRAEL'S ATTEMPT TO DETER SYRIA

In February 1966, a faction of the Ba'thist party took power in Damascus. Beset by serious domestic political and social tension and factionalism within the army, the new regime advocated a war of popular liberation against Israel and began to give active support to el-Fatah raids across Israel's border.[4] As tension along the border grew, on November 4, 1966, Egypt—with the strong encouragement of the Soviet Union—signed a defense pact with Syria. Public opinion in Israel, especially in the north, grew increasingly alarmed as the number of attacks escalated, and the public began to press the government for action. In response to the new alliance, the escalating raids, and the weakening of its deterrent reputation, Israel launched a large-scale daytime operation against Es Samu in Jordan. The target of the military action, however, was the Syrian government; el-Fatah operated across the Jordanian border, but its home base was in Syria.

Jordanian officials bitterly criticized the Egyptian president's failure to meet his obligations under the Unified Arab Command established in Cairo in 1964 and come to the assistance of Arab states attacked by Israel.[5] Prime Minister Wasfi al-Tal insisted that under the arrangements established by the Unified Arab Command, Egypt should have provided Jordan with air support, and he urged Egypt to withdraw its forces from Yemen and concentrate on the real enemy in Sinai.[6] King Hussein accused Egypt of sheltering itself behind the "skirts" of the U.N. Emergency Force (UNEF), set up in 1957 in the Sinai as a buffer between Egypt and Israel.[7] In so doing, he challenged Nasser's credibility as leader of the Arabs and champion of the Palestinians. A full-scale propaganda war broke out between Egypt and Jordan that raged for the following six months.

In the face of Arab charges, the Egyptian commander in chief, Field Marshal Abd'ul al-Hakim Amir, recommended to Nasser in December 1966 that Egypt meet the challenge of Arab leaders by asking for the withdrawal of the U.N. force and sending Egyptian forces to Sharm el-Sheikh.[8] Amir did not recommend a blockade of the Straits but merely the withdrawal of the U.N. force "to put an end to the frenzied campaign."[9] The president resisted; he had long argued that careful coordination of Arab capabilities and the diplomatic isolation of Israel were prerequisites to military action.[10]

Israel's strategy did not succeed in deterring raids across its eastern border, and tension continued to escalate. In early April 1967, a routine incident exploded into major violence. Farmers in the north of Israel, as they had done many times before, sent their tractors to work the agricultural land in the contested demilitarized zone. Syria responded by shelling Israel's agricultural settlements in the Hula valley, and, as the firing increased, Syria's and Israel's air forces engaged in a major air battle. Six Syrian MIGs were shot down, and Israel's planes pursued the Syrian fighters to the outskirts of Damascus.[11] Israel used a mixed strategy of deterrence and coercive diplomacy in an attempt to manage the growing crisis. Its leaders expected that the display of Israel's strength would deter Syria from further challenges and compel Damascus to end its support of military action across Israel's border. Israel's chief of staff, Yitzhak Rabin, later recalled "that the air force had proved its strength so persuasively that one could not suppose that the Arab states would seriously contemplate challenging Israel."[12]

Syria reacted to its public humiliation with defiance rather than restraint. The government in Damascus attacked President Nasser bitterly for failing to come to Syria's assistance. In the immediate aftermath of the Israeli attack, Mohamed Heikal, a close adviser of President Nasser, made it clear that Egypt's obligation to Syria extended only to the defense of Arab territory but not to defense against localized raids.[13] In the first instance, Egypt attempted to manage the crisis by limiting its commitment to its ally. President Nasser, however, made no explicit attempt to persuade Syria to limit its action. Neither the limited Egyptian commitment nor the demonstration by Israel's air force of Syrian military weakness deterred Syria. Renewed shelling of the border area and agricultural settlements, and a sharp increase in the mining of roads within Israel further escalated tension.

Israel's leaders, in a series of warnings and threats, again attempted to deter Syrian action along the border. From May 9 to 13, Prime Minister Levi Eshkol, who was also the minister of defense; Foreign Minister Abba Eban; Israel's ambassador to the United Nations, Gideon Rafael; and a "senior military officer" all threatened grave consequences should the attacks continue.[14]

STEP TWO: THE SOVIET AND EGYPTIAN ATTEMPT TO DETER ISRAEL

The Soviet Union warned Egypt both directly and indirectly that Israel was concentrating large forces near the Syrian border in preparation for attack and urged Egypt to take appropriate action to deter Israel. On May 13, Dimitri Pojidaev, the Soviet ambassador to Egypt, delivered a message from Moscow to Ahmad Hassan al-Feki, the Egyptian undersecretary of foreign affairs and acting foreign minister. The note detailed the number and location of Israel's forces.[15] The Soviet deputy foreign minister added a further intelligence detail that Israel might attack between May 16 and 22.[16] The following day, Anwar el-Sadat, who was visiting Moscow enroute home from North Korea, was told by Vladimir Semenov, the deputy foreign minister, as well as by other officials of Israel's preparations for military action. The Soviet Union urged Egypt to deploy a limited number of troops in the south to deter Israeli military action against Syria and assured Egypt of Soviet support should Israel attack.[17]

The evidence suggests conclusively that there were no Israeli troop concentrations on the Syrian frontier. The U.N. Truce Supervision Organization (UNTSO) sent its observers to the front, and they reported that there was no concentration of forces.[18] General Muhammad Fawzi, the Egyptian chief of staff, confirmed the absence of troop concentrations:

On May 14, 1967, Marshal Abd al-Hakim Amir ordered me to go to Damascus to investigate and to learn the truth about the information we had received from Damascus and the Soviet Union about the Israeli concentration of troops on the Syrian border. I went the same day and stayed there twenty-four hours, during which I inspected the Syrian front command and asked questions of responsible officers in the Syrian staff and at the front about the truth of the report. The result was that I did not get any material proof confirming these reports. To the contrary, I saw two aerial photographs of the Israeli front, taken by the Syrians on the 12th and 13th of May which showed no change from the normal military situation.[19]

The Jordanian radar station at Ajloun, which monitored northern Israel, also reported no evidence of Israeli troop movements.[20]

It is unclear whether Soviet leaders believed that Israel was concentrating its forces or knowingly reported false information. Moscow appears to have made little effort to confirm the report directly. It rejected a request from Israel to inspect the front.[21] The Soviet Union also made no attempt to warn Israel directly against military action as it had several times done in the past, nor did it ask the United States to restrain Israel.[22] The Soviet warnings to Egypt of imminent military action by Israel against Syria can only be explained as a deliberate strategy to reinforce the weak, faction-ridden government in Damascus by activating the Egyptian-Syrian Defense Agreement. In so doing, the Soviet Union badly over-estimated its capacity to control Egyptian decisions once a process of military deployment began. Indeed, because Soviet leaders did not communicate to Egypt either their interest in only limited military action by Egypt or the limits of their support should the crisis escalate, they jeopardized the possibility for effective crisis management. The path to inadvertent war began with this serious miscalculation by Moscow of its capacity to craft and calibrate the actions of its allies in the Middle East.

In the first instance, Soviet warnings had their anticipated impact. On May 14, after meetings of the Supreme Executive Council and of senior military commanders at Marshal Amir's headquarters, the Egyptian army was put on full alert, the head of the reserve administration was ordered to mobilize men and equipment, and army units stationed along the canal crossed and began to move into Sinai.[23] No effort was made to camouflage the movement of troops. On the contrary, they were well-publicized: The passage of troops through Cairo's streets was covered by radio and television, and some units detoured past the U.S. embassy.[24] A public display of force was consistent with Egypt's strategy of extended deterrence.

The president of Egypt also drew an analogy to an earlier case of successful deterrence against Israel.[25] In February 1960, after a raid by Israel against Tawfiq, the Soviet Union reported to Egypt that Israel was concentrating forces against Syria, then part of the United Arab Republic. President Nasser deployed three divisions to the Sinai and stationed them near the Israeli border. Israel responded with a limited mobilization, and both sides gradually withdrew their forces. President Nasser subsequently claimed that Israel had been successfully deterred from attacking Syria.[26]

There is some controversy about Egyptian estimates and intentions in May 1967. The general consensus among Egyptian leaders at the time was that President Nasser believed the reports of an imminent attack against Syria and designed his action to deter Israel.[27] Anwar el-Sadat recalled that after his receipt of Soviet information, "President Nasser therefore ordered Field Marshal Amir to concentrate Egyptian forces in Sinai . . . his real aim was to deter Israel."[28]

This interpretation is not consistent with the report President Nasser received from General Fawzi of the absence of Israeli troop concentrations. Even if Nasser knew that Israel had not moved troops to the north, he may still have believed that Israel was planning to attack at the first available opportunity. More likely, the Egyptian president inferred that the Soviet Union knew there were no such concentrations and, therefore, strongly endorsed some military action by Egypt.[29] This estimate of Soviet support would be critical to his subsequent decisions.

Israel's military and political leaders were surprised by the Egyptian action. In issuing their warnings to Syria, they underestimated the risks of deterrence and did not expect Egypt to come to the assistance of Syria. Military analysts in Israel suggested that President Nasser was sensitive to the risk of escalation through miscalculation; unprepared for a large-scale offensive, he did not wish to be dragged into war through escalation from local violence.[30] Israel's political and military leadership consistently overestimated the effectiveness of deterrent threats and underestimated the vulnerability of President Nasser to the taunts of his Arab allies.

Although Israel's leaders were surprised, they were not threatened. Nor did they miscalculate Egyptian intentions. They interpreted the Egyptian troop movements as deterrent rather than as preparation for a limited attack. Israel's chief of staff explained: "In this phase, the Egyptians wanted to deter Israel, to demonstrate the deterrence of Israel before Syria and not to initiate or create conditions that would lead to war."[31] Like their Egyptian counterparts, military leaders in Israel also drew an analogy with the precedent series of deployments and withdrawals in 1960.[32] Nevertheless, on May 16, as a precautionary and deterrent measure, the prime minister and chief of staff decided on a limited mobilization of reserves.[33]

Extended deterrence by Egypt succeeded in its objective. Israel's leaders abandoned any consideration of punitive action against Syria and waited cautiously to see if mutual deterrence would prevail and military forces would gradually withdraw as they had done in 1960. The political context in Egypt and the interplay of Arab politics, however, were substantially different in 1967 than they had been seven years earlier when President Nasser had been at the apex of his power as leader of the Arab world, secure at home and abroad. Both Egyptian and Israeli leaders ignored these critical differences when they generalized from the past.

STEP THREE: THE WITHDRAWAL OF UNEF AND
THE FAILURE OF INTERNATIONAL INSTITUTIONS
AS CRISIS MANAGERS

Israel's leaders did not have long to wait. In an effort to defuse the criticism of Arab leaders, General Fawzi wrote to the commander of the U.N. Emergency Force, General Indar Jit Rikhye, on the evening of May 16, requesting a partial withdrawal of UNEF forces.[34] The request for a partial rather than a total withdrawal was a deliberate attempt to control escalation. General Rikhye explained that he was not authorized to comply and cabled the secretary-general of the United Nations, U Thant, for further instructions. After very brief consultations with the Egyptian ambassador to the United Nations, U Thant informed Rikhye that any request for a partial or temporary withdrawal of UNEF would be considered as a demand for a complete withdrawal of U.N. forces from Gaza and Sinai.[35] On May 18, Mahmoud Riad, the Egyptian foreign minister, replied that Cairo had decided "to terminate the presence of UNEF from the territory of the UAR and the Gaza Strip."[36]

President Nasser was responding to the humiliation he had suffered in April when he failed to come to Syria's aid and to the strident calls from Arab adversaries who challenged him to expel the peacekeeping force. The government of Jordan was the most vocal in its challenge to Egypt, but its strategy, too, was motivated by its political weakness at home and its isolation in the Arab world. As a member of the Royal Hashemite Court in Amman perceptively acknowledged, Jordanian strategy was fraught with contradiction:

> Although this barrage of criticism against Egypt conflicted with King Hussein's desire not to add to the already unstable situation, the Jordanian Government felt it had to defend itself by pointing out that Egypt's actions contradicted its words. Unfortunately, Jordan's criticisms of Egypt pushed a volatile situation even closer to the brink because Jordan was goading Egypt into taking action which would undoubtedly increase the chances of armed conflict with Israel. Thus the Jordanian Government found itself engaged in activities which it felt were ultimately detrimental to the Arab cause but which were essential if it was to maintain its integrity in the eyes of its people.[37]

The Jordanian challenge and the Egyptian response can best be understood as the politics of vulnerability. Nasser's awareness of the risks motivated his request for a partial rather than complete withdrawal of U.N. forces.[38]

The quick response by Secretary-General U Thant was an error of massive proportions. Egypt was legally entitled to request the withdrawal of UNEF, for in 1957 the force was deployed expressly with the consent of the host government. Nevertheless, when he received the request, the secretary-general had considerable scope for an attempt at crisis management by slowing the momentum of events. When UNEF was established, its administration was delegated to the secretary-general, who was assisted by an Advisory Committee created by the General Assembly. Although procedures for withdrawal of the force were not explicit, some guidelines were in place. Secretary-General Dag Hammarskjöld made clear his understanding of the appropriate procedure on February 26, 1957: "An indicated procedure would be for the Secretary-General to inform the Advisory Committee of the United Nations' Emergency Force [of a request by the host government for its withdrawal] which would determine whether the matter should be brought to the attention of the Assembly."[39] At a minimum, withdrawal of the force could not be unilateral but would require multilateral consent by the host government, the secretary-general, and the members of the Advisory Committee if not the General Assembly as a whole.

The importance of UNEF was not in its formal assignment but in its informal function in a limited security regime put in place in 1957 to manage the conflict between Egypt and Israel.[40] The U.N. force was formally charged with patrolling, manning sensitive border positions, and preventing infiltration across the border. UNEF was not so much a fire brigade, however, as a fire alarm: It could not prevent war, but it could give warning of impending military action and provide valuable time for crisis management. Both Egypt and Israel expected that the withdrawal of the force would require time-consuming multilateral procedures. Consequently, Israel anticipated adequate time for military preparation and international consultation if and when a request for its withdrawal signaled an impending crisis; UNEF's presence stabilized an inherently unstable strategic relationship. Equally important, as we have seen, the presence of the international force protected President Nasser from the demands of his own constituency.

If the secretary-general had invoked the available procedures, he would have had considerable time to engage informally in discussion with the Egyptian government in an effort to modify its request, to consult the major powers, and to attempt to put in place alternative arrangements. Indeed, Israel's foreign minister, Abba Eban, proposed that Israel's ambassador to the United Nations suggest an immediate visit by U Thant to Cairo and Jerusalem. Should the secretary-general arrange his departure while UNEF forces were still at their observation posts, President Nasser might refrain from further escalation until U Thant's arrival in Cairo. Ambassador Rafael proposed such a visit to friendly delegations in New York, but he was too late.[41]

The secretary-general used none of the available consultative mechanisms to delay but instead confronted President Nasser with an immediate and irrevocable choice. U Thant not only lost an opportunity to contribute to effective crisis management by slowing down the momentum of events, but, through his actions, he further destabilized the crisis. The secretary-general took the control rods out of an already overheated reactor, removed the valuable warning time Israel needed of an impending Egyptian attack, denied Nasser the excuse he needed to delay, and increased the pressure on Israel and Egypt to take the next step.

As part of its strategy of deterrence, Israel had long specified a series of actions that would constitute a *casus belli*. Prominent among these were a blockade of the Straits of Tiran, the deployment of Arab military forces on the West Bank of the Jordan, and the concentration of military forces against its frontiers.[42] Israel had not, however, identified the withdrawal of UNEF as a cause of war and in the past had not attempted specifically to deter its removal. The Egyptian request consequently generated considerable uncertainty.

Alarmed by the withdrawal of U.N. forces and by the growing concentration of Egyptian troops in the Sinai, Israel's senior military and political leaders met early on the morning of May 19 to review their estimate of Egyptian intentions. General Aharon Yariv, the head of Military Intelligence, suggested that Egypt would continue its military preparations as a prelude to choice among four options: no further action accompanied by a claim that it had deterred Israel from attacking Syria; a strategy of provocation to force Israel to attack; an immediate surprise attack; or a long period of tension culminating in a surprise attack.[43] In view of the uncertainty along with the possibility of a blockade of the Straits of Tiran now that UNEF had been withdrawn, Israel ordered a large-scale mobilization of its reserves and began preliminary preparations for an attack in the Sinai.[44]

STEP FOUR: EGYPT CHALLENGES ISRAEL'S DETERRENCE

After Israel mobilized its reserves, its leaders attempted to control escalation and manage the crisis through a mixed strategy. It tried simultaneously to reinforce deterrence to prevent the occurrence of any action that Israel had specified as a *casus belli* and to reassure Egypt of its limited intentions. When Israel withdrew from the Sinai in 1957, Foreign Minister Golda Meir had warned that a blockade of the Straits of Tiran would be considered a *casus belli*, and the maritime powers had acknowledged Israel's right to use force if the straits were closed to Israel's shipping.[45] Whether Nasser would now institute a blockade became a critical threshold of escalation.

On May 19, the same day that Israel chose to mobilize on a large scale, Prime Minister Eshkol cabled President Charles de Gaulle of France: "Israel on her part will not initiate hostile acts, but she is firmly resolved to defend her territory and her international rights. Our decision is that if Egypt will not attack us, we will not take action against Egyptian forces at Sharm el-Sheikh—until or unless they close the Straits of Tiran to free navigation."[46] At the same time that Israel attempted to manage the conflict by drawing the line, it tried to reassure Egypt of its limited intentions. In discussions with the Soviet ambassador and in a series of written messages to the principal maritime powers, Eban stated explicitly that Israel had no intention of attacking should Egypt refrain from further provocation.[47] The prime minister, in his speech to Israel's parliament on May 22, focused both on the danger of escalation and on Israel's capability and resolve. He was explicit both about Israel's intentions and capabilities: He strongly denied any concentration of forces on the Syrian frontier and reiterated that Israel planned no attack against any Arab country; at the same time, he stressed that the army was prepared and Israel had both the capability and the will to defend itself.[48] The prime minister deliberately tried to avoid provoking Nasser by refraining from a public warning of the consequences of a blockade.[49]

Eshkol and Eban were attempting to accomplish multiple purposes simultaneously. By reinforcing deterrence, they hoped to improve the credibility of their commitment to retaliate. By signaling their intention to refrain from military action if Egypt did not blockade the straits, they hoped to stop the process of escalation and avoid war. Leaders generally tend to assume that the signals they send are unambiguous and are understood by their adversary, and Eshkol and Eban were no exception. If Nasser ignored this clear and precise warning, their uncertainty about Egyptian intent would be reduced significantly. Eban best summarizes this expectation:

> Our intention to regard the closing of the Straits as a *casus belli* was communicated
> . . . to the foreign ministers of those states which had supported international navigation
> in the Straits in 1957 and thereafter. There can be no doubt that these warnings
> reached Cairo. One thing was now clear. If Nasser imposed a blockade, the explosion
> would not ensue from "miscalculation," but from an open-eyed and conscious readiness
> for war.[50]

The foreign minister's analysis, unfortunately, was oversimplified. Neither deterrence nor reassurance worked as expected, in large part because of the intense pressure on President Nasser to escalate.

President Nasser's response was not long in coming. Anwar el-Sadat recalled the meeting on May 22 of the Supreme Executive Committee of the Arab Socialist Union in Cairo, which made the decision:[51] "Nasser said: 'Now with our concentrations in Sinai, the chances of war are fifty-fifty. But if we close the Straits, war will be a one hundred per cent certainty. . . .' We all knew that our armaments were adequate. . . . When Nasser asked us our opinion, we were all agreed that the Strait should be closed."[52] Only the Egyptian prime minister, Sidqi Sulayman, opposed the decision.[53] He pleaded with Nasser to show more patience and to consider the consequences of war on Egypt's deeply troubled economy. As Sadat recalls, "Nasser paid no attention to Sulayman's objections. He was eager to close the Strait . . . [to] maintain his great prestige within the Arab world."[54] On May 22, speaking to the Advanced Airforce Headquarters in the Sinai, President Nasser announced the closure of the Straits of Tiran to all ships of Israeli registry and to all others with "strategic materials" destined for the port of Eilat.[55]

Why did Israel's strategy of deterrence fail? The evidence suggests that Israel's deterrent threat was credible but insufficiently potent. Sadat's report of the discussion of the Supreme Executive Committee suggests that President Nasser did not miscalculate Israel's resolve. Mohamed H. Heikal, writing in *Al-Ahram* a few days later, estimated that Israel would have no choice but to retaliate; the issue at stake, he argued, was not "the Gulf of Aqaba, but something bigger. It is the whole philosophy of Israeli security. Hence I say that Israel must attack."[56] In the days that followed, the president made clear that Egypt did not intend to attack first, yet he estimated the probability of war as 100 percent. Certain of a retaliatory attack by Israel if the straits were blockaded, President Nasser nevertheless chose to challenge deterrence because Egyptian military leaders badly underestimated Israel's military capability.

The evidence is overwhelming that Egyptian political and military leaders overestimated their relative military capability. In the same speech in which President Nasser announced the blockade of the straits, he went on to argue, "There is a great difference between yesterday and today, between 1956 and 1967. . . . At that time we had a few Ilyushin bombers. . . . Today we have many Ilyushins and other aircraft." He added that although Egyptian troops were still in Yemen, this did not matter because "we are capable of carrying out our duties in Yemen and at the same time doing our national duty here in Egypt."[57]

Senior military leaders were more explicit. Air Force Commander Sidqi Mahmoud told President Nasser that the Egyptian air force would lose only 10 percent of its aircraft if Israel struck first.[58] He claimed that the Egyptian "warning system and air defenses are capable of discovering and destroying any air attack by the enemy, no matter how many aircraft were involved, or from what direction they came."[59] Mahmoud Riad, Egypt's foreign minister, reports that the minister of war, Shams al-Din Badran, claimed that Egypt's air force was even capable of handling intervention by the U.S. Sixth Fleet.[60]

With respect to a ground attack, Egyptian officers estimated that Israel's army would reach only as far as El Arish, less than one hundred kilometers into the Sinai, before an Egyptian counterattack captured Eilat and then advanced to Beersheva, well inside Israeli territory.[61] When Egyptian intelligence reported that the Israeli army would likely concentrate five divisions on the Egyptian border, the commander of the ground forces, General Abdul Muhsin Kamil al-Murtagi, replied that Israel had no firm defenses and that Egypt had superiority in tanks and in the air. Moreover, he added, Egyptian missiles protected the whole theater of battle.[62]

The estimates of Egyptian military capability were so favorable that although Egyptian officials generally did not doubt Israel's resolve, occasionally they questioned whether Israel would indeed attack in light of the defeat it would suffer. Shams al-Din Badran, in his testimony at the trials that followed the war, recalled that Egyptian Military Intelligence estimated that given Egyptian superiority in armor, artillery, and air force, "Israel was not about to commit suicide."[63] Insofar as they momentarily questioned Israel's intention to attack, Egyptian leaders did so not because they doubted its resolve but because they massively overestimated Egyptian capabilities.

Why did Egypt's leaders make such a serious miscalculation? A quantitative comparison of the ground and air capabilities of Egypt and Israel at the time demonstrates some Egyptian superiority in fire power.[64] Nevertheless, only a few months earlier, Nasser had been skeptical of Egypt's ability to defeat Israel in battle, and capabilities had not changed dramatically since.[65] Egypt's foreign minister at the time, Mahmoud Riad, speculates that the change in President Nasser's calculations was based in part on the active role of the United States in calling for restraint. On May 23, the U.S. ambassador to Cairo, Richard Nolte, delivered a message from President Johnson to Nasser as well as a note-verbale to Riad. The note concluded with an emphatic statement: "The government of the United States maintains firm opposition to aggression in the area in any form, overt or clandestine, carried out by regular military forces or irregular groups."[66] Riad read the note as a firm injunction to Israel against the use of force and informed President Nasser that, as a result of U.S. restraint, "an outbreak of hostilities was out of the question."[67] Nasser had long maintained that a central prerequisite of a military confrontation with Israel was its diplomatic isolation; Israel had won in 1956 only with the help of the great powers.[68] Nevertheless, the president was not persuaded that Johnson would refrain from assisting Israel.[69] The modest change in his assessment of likely U.S. action cannot explain the dramatic revision of his estimate of the balance of capabilities.

Some of Nasser's close associates speculated after the war that the president was deliberately misled by Marshal Amir, who strongly favored a military confrontation with Israel. The secretary general of the president's office, Abdul Majid Farid, explicitly attributed President Nasser's decision to blockade the straits to the favorable military reports he received from Field Marshal Amir. Amir assured the president that Egyptian "armed forces are not only capable of repulsing Israel but are also capable of moving east to secure a defence line on the Egyptian border, stretching from Beersheba to Gaza."[70] Indeed, after the war, Nasser told Mahmoud Riad that Amir had misled him about the strength of the Egyptian armed forces.[71] Amir exercised strong control over the armed forces through the promotion of officers who were loyal to him personally.[72] Nevertheless, given Nasser's extensive military background, it is unlikely that the president could have been totally misinformed by Marshal Amir.

Far more important was the overwhelming impact of an aroused public opinion in Egypt and the challenge to his leadership from Syria and Jordan. Nasser, Field Marshal Amir, and other senior officers saw no alternative, once UNEF had been withdrawn, but to blockade the straits and demonstrate their championship of the Palestinian and Arab cause. Six months earlier, humiliated by the poor performance of Egyptian troops in the Yemen and by Jordanian taunts after the Israeli raid against Es-Samu, Amir had recommended to the president the withdrawal of UNEF without a blockade. At the time, Shams al-Din Badran had insisted that once the international force was withdrawn, a blockade would be inevitable if "the frenzied campaign [against Nasser were not] to gain momentum."[73] President Nasser did not respond to the earlier proposal. Now, committed to a challenge, Nasser and his senior military advisers engaged in wishful thinking and post hoc bolstering of their decision. Indeed, the wildly exaggerated claims of the minister of war and the commander of the air force can best be understood as motivated error.

In their analysis of decision making, Irving L. Janis and Leon Mann identify patterns of defensive avoidance and bolstering when leaders deny information that evokes anxiety or fear and discount the costs of the option they have chosen.[74] They are especially likely to do so in situations where they are motivated by deeply felt needs. Nasser was a leader under pressure, beset by an economy in crisis and a protracted and stalemated military involvement in the Yemen, his leadership of the Arab world challenged by adversaries and allies. Politically vulnerable at home and abroad, the Egyptian president saw no option but to challenge deterrence.

The miscalculation of capabilities was in large part the consequence rather than the cause of Nasser's decision. Motivated by need at home and abroad, the president and his advisers, through bolstering and wishful thinking, escalated both their objectives and their means. In so doing, they violated a fundamental precept of crisis management and crossed the critical threshold of escalation. Given the pressures they faced, they persuaded themselves that a blockade would succeed. In the unlikely event that Israel did not attack, President Nasser would score a stunning diplomatic victory and restore his leadership of the Arab world. If, as expected, Israel did attack, it would find itself isolated abroad, the Egyptian army would defeat the attack, and Nasser's preeminent position in the Arab world would be reaffirmed. From this point, the emphasis in Cairo would no longer be on crisis management but on whether to await the attack by Israel that the Egyptian action would almost certainly provoke or to strike first.

Deterrence failed not because Israel's leaders did not adequately demonstrate their resolve but rather because senior Egyptian political and military leaders were strongly motivated by the pressures of regional and domestic politics to challenge deterrence. Under these conditions, once a challenger is committed, defenders can do little to correct the miscalculations of an adversary. Efforts by Israel to signal its resolve more clearly would only have further intensified the pressures acting on Egyptian leaders; moreover, as we have seen, Israel's resolve was not seriously in question. Egyptian officials degraded Israel's capabilities in two ways: They exaggerated their own capabilities, and, as we shall see, they estimated that the United States was least likely to intervene if Israel initiated the war. There was little Israel's leaders could have done to correct these Egyptian miscalculations. Deterrence was defeated not by the ineptitude of the defender but rather by the political vulnerability and wishful thinking of the challenger.

Nor was Israel's reassurance of the limits of its intentions effective as a strategy of crisis management under the circumstances. Public declarations by the prime minister of Israel's intention to refrain from military action were not believed, and, more to the point, they were not relevant. As late as May 23, after Prime Minister

Eshkol's speech to the Knesset, Foreign Minister Riad and President Nasser still spoke of the need to eliminate the "Israeli threat."[75] Jordan believed that Israel was deliberately provoking Nasser as part of a broader strategy that had begun with the raid against Es Samu in November of 1966. Jordanian officials rejected Eshkol's reassurances as part of a strategy of deliberate deception.[76]

Even had Nasser believed Israel's statements of its intention to refrain from military action against Syria, it is unlikely that he would have refrained from blockading the straits. By then, U.N. forces had withdrawn, and the demand for closure of the straits was being voiced by radio stations throughout the Arab world. Vulnerable as Nasser was to the taunts of Arab governments and anxious as he was to re-establish his leadership in the Arab world, it is difficult to conceive that he would have been able to resist the pressure.

When Israel's leaders attempted to reinforce deterrence and to provide reassurance, they expected their message to be obvious and easily understood. They misunderstood the context in which their signals were interpreted and ignored the political weakness of their adversary, the pressures on him to take action, and the consequent likelihood of miscalculation.[77] What was obvious in Jerusalem was by then beside the point in Cairo.

CRISIS INSTABILITY AND THE INCENTIVES TO PREEMPT

Analysts have suggested that an escalating series of troop movements, mobilizations, and military preparations, reinforced by vulnerable strike forces and weaknesses in command, communication, and control, created reciprocal fears of surprise attack in both Egypt and Israel, which led ultimately to preemption by Israel and the outbreak of war.[78] The evidence is not consistent with the argument. Proponents of this thesis rely largely on the arguments of military leaders and pay inadequate attention to the consideration of political and diplomatic factors by the civilian leadership. In Israel, military leaders consistently favored the initiation of war to restore the credibility of their deterrent reputation even when they did not anticipate an immediate Egyptian attack, but civilian leaders refused to authorize preemption even when the probability of an Egyptian first strike was greatest. As I will argue, if preemption was primarily a response to a likely Arab attack, Israel should have gone to war by May 27. It did not. In Egypt, despite the large-scale mobilization by Israel and the expectation that Israel would attack, President Nasser decided against preemption. In both cases, military logic was not determining.

There were curious similarities between the calculations of leaders in Jerusalem and in Cairo. President Nasser anticipated an attack by Israel; as his close associate Mohamed Heikal asserted, Israel's whole philosophy of security was at stake.[79] Like his counterparts in Jerusalem, the Egyptian president also emphasized the critical role of the United States in the outcome of the war. On June 2, the president warned his senior officers that Israel would attack within 48 hours, or at the latest on June 5.[80] Nevertheless, confident of Egyptian military capabilities, Nasser considered that the advantages of a preemptive strike were more than offset by the diplomatic benefits of isolating Israel and forcing it to attack without the support of the United States. As Minister of War Badran recalled, Nasser told his senior officers on May 28:

> . . . political considerations dictated that Egypt should not strike the first blow because the Americans would interfere. . . . General Sidqi Mahmoud, the commander of the air force, objected. . . . Marshal Amir asked the air force chief whether he preferred to strike the first blow and face the Americans, or to be hit first and face Israel only. Sidqi Mahmoud immediately agreed that the latter was preferable.[81]

It appears that at least once, Nasser faced concerted pressure from his military officers for approval of an attack. On May 25, the Egyptian air force was ordered by Amir to prepare a strike against Israel for the morning of May 27. The order was cancelled, however, after a 30-minute meeting between Nasser and Amir on May 25.[82] The Egyptian president considered U.S. military assistance to Israel inevitable if Egypt struck first.[83] Foremost in his calculations was his confidence in the Egyptian capability to defeat Israel if it were forced to fight without the active support of the United States.

Preemption was a far more attractive option to Israel's military leaders. It had long been a fundamental component of Israel's strategy of defense. The constraints of a citizen army, the lack of strategic depth, the vulnerability of major population centers, the possibility of a multifront war, the anticipated pressure from the great powers to end the fighting, and a strong desire to minimize casualties among a small population dictated a preemptive strategy.

Since 1956, Israeli military planners had given high priority to the air force as the instrument of preemption. A preemptive air strike at the beginning of a war would remove the threat to Israel's civilian population and ensure air superiority in the subsequent ground fighting where desert conditions offered virtually no protection from attacking aircraft. Reliance on the air force increased the incentive to strike first; when aircraft were aloft, they were relatively safe from destruction, but stationed on the ground, they were vulnerable to a surprise attack launched by an enemy air force. In Israel's broad strategic plan, a first strike was a crucial component that facilitated the achievement of its fundamental objectives: speed and initiative on the ground, and a transfer of the fighting to enemy territory.[84]

Strategic doctrine set the context for the intensive debate that began in Israel on May 23 immediately after Nasser blockaded the straits. As expected, military officers repeatedly stressed the advantages of initiating the war in their meetings with the senior political leadership. They were confident of victory and did not doubt the outcome of a war, but they pressed for authorization to initiate the fighting even though the Egyptian military deployment was not offensive and they did not anticipate defeat even if Egypt struck first.[85] Although preemption of an Arab attack was important, this was not the primary concern throughout most of the discussions immediately following the imposition of the blockade. Rather, the General Staff emphasized the advantages of an early attack: Initiating the war would minimize civilian and military casualties by reducing the threat posed by Arab air forces. As General Rabin explained, "Taking the initiative would be of decisive importance in determining the length of the war, its results, and the number of casualties expected."[86]

At the cabinet meeting on May 23, Eban urged that Israel delay military action and accept a proposal from President Johnson to consult. When pressed by his colleagues, Rabin acknowledged that a 48-hour delay would impose little military cost: The additional time would be used to complete military preparations.[87] The cabinet voted to delay military action and to consult with the United States, in large part because they considered U.S. support crucial both during the war to deter Soviet intervention and in the postwar negotiations to follow. They did not wish to win the war and lose the peace, as they had in 1957.

On May 25, the evaluation of Israel's Military Intelligence changed dramatically. Jordan and Syria had mobilized their forces, troop concentrations in the Sinai were dense, and Egyptian airfields were on alert. Even more important, the Egyptian Fourth Armored Division had begun to cross into the Sinai. Many of the Egyptian positions were also concentrated far enough forward on the frontier to suggest an offensive deployment.[88] Finally, an Egyptian High Command order on May 25 to one of the Egyptian air force units, ordering preparations to execute offensive operations on May 27, was intercepted by Military Intelligence.[89]

Military Intelligence estimated that an attack was likely. Indeed, the Egyptian High Command had ordered preparations for attack but, unbeknownst to Israel's intelligence, had been overruled by President Nasser. General Yariv expressed his concern to the prime minister that if Israel took no action the following day, Egypt might attack.[90] The head of Mossad (Special Services), Meir Amit, warned that "Egypt already had some eight hundred tanks in Sinai and was continuing to secure reinforcements. The attack would be launched very soon."[91]

In the face of these estimates, General Headquarters ordered preparations for a preemptive strike.[92] The prime minister, however, refused to authorize a preemptive attack even when an Egyptian attack was considered likely. Instead, he cabled Israel's urgent concerns to the United States. Military orders were first postponed for 24 hours and then cancelled.[93] If preemption were primarily a response to a likely Arab attack, Israel should have attacked. It did not. Rather, the prime minister delayed military action because of his worry about the adverse consequences for Israel's relationship with the United States.

In a tense meeting with the prime minister at the headquarters of Southern Command late on May 25, military officers expressed their dissatisfaction with the hesitation of the government and pressed for approval of immediate military action. General Ariel Sharon, the principal speaker, argued forcefully that the growing strength of Egyptian forces would increase the cost of Israel's military action: The earlier the attack, the easier it would be to defeat the Egyptian army. Although General Sharon was the spokesman, he expressed the consensus of the assembled military commanders. They considered the restoration of the credibility of Israel's deterrent reputation to be the central issue and urged immediate military action.

As important as the specific advantages that would accrue from an early attack was the definition of the issue at stake. Major General Yariv, head of Military Intelligence, argued, "It is no longer a question of freedom of navigation. If Israel takes no action in response to the blockade of the Straits she will lose her credibility and the IDF [Israel Defense Forces] its deterrent capacity. The Arab states will interpret Israel's weakness as an excellent opportunity to threaten her security and her very existence."[94] The blockade of the Straits of Tiran on May 22 imposed significant economic costs, disrupted Israel's trade through the Mediterranean, and, most important, jeopardized its supply of oil.[95] These costs paled, however, in comparison to the estimated costs of the erosion of Israel's capacity to deter. The blockade was important not only for the intrinsic interests at stake but principally because Israel had explicitly attempted to deter the forcible closure of the straits. Once the credibility of Israel's deterrent reputation became the central issue, a military response was imperative whether or not Egypt was planning to attack. Senior military leaders insisted that the damage to Israel's capacity to deter made an Arab attack inevitable, sooner or later. In the analysis of military leaders, Israel's critical need to protect its capacity to deter blurred the distinction between preemptive and preventive war.

Two weeks later, military leaders had little difficulty in persuading their civilian colleagues to approve an attack. Again, they estimated the Arab intent to attack as high; again, they were mistaken. They pointed first to the forward deployment of Egyptian forces as evidence of Egyptian preparation to attack. Unknown to Military Intelligence, however, the pattern of deployment was due in large part to confusion and loss of control in the Egyptian command. In 1966, the Egyptian General Staff had developed a plan for a mobile in-depth defense of the Sinai. Except for the retention of a few key defensive positions, such as El Arish and Abu Ageila, the Egyptian army would pull back to encourage Israel's army to penetrate deeply into the Sinai to a designated "killing area." A second line of defense, further back, would reinforce Egyptian troops.[96] If it had been implemented, this pattern of deployment could not have been interpreted as preparation for offense.

President Nasser refused to permit the planned deployment when he ordered Egyptian forces east of the canal in May. He was unwilling to abandon, even temporarily, Egyptian control of forward positions. Consequently, Egyptian troops were sent east and stationed directly against the frontier without specific guidance. Ironically, the Egyptian military planned a defensive deployment in preparation for offense, but President Nasser ordered an offensive deployment in preparation for defense. The loss of control and confusion in the Egyptian General Staff made the pattern of military deployment a poor indicator of Egyptian intentions.[97]

Leaders in Israel gave a great deal of weight as well to King Hussein's visit to Cairo on May 30 to sign a joint defense agreement with Egypt and to the dispatch of Gen. Abdul Moneim Riad to Amman as the joint commander of Arab forces on the Jordanian front. Civilian and military leaders in Israel considered Jordanian participation in an Arab joint command as yet another failure of deterrence: They had repeatedly warned that the stationing of Arab military forces in Jordan, particularly on the West Bank, would be treated as a *casus belli*.[98] Consequently, they evaluated King Hussein's action as an important indicator of intention to attack.[99] Again, they were wrong.

King Hussein's analysis was dramatically different. Ever since Israel's raid on Es Samu, he had argued that Israel made no distinction between Jordan and the more aggressive Arab states.[100] The king and his senior military advisers were also convinced that the closure of the Straits of Tiran made war inevitable.[101] They were persuaded that if war broke out between Egypt and Israel, Israel would invade the West Bank no matter what Jordan did, as "Israel views the Arab world as one."[102] Lieut. Gen. Amer Khammash, the chief of staff of the Jordanian armed forces, was explicit: "What was of particular interest to us in the army was Israel's intentions toward the West Bank. We did not need to ask many questions to understand that if Israel waged war against Egypt, Syria, or both, the West Bank was a primary target and would not be spared."[103]

Jordanian policy had become a self-fulfilling prophecy. To limit domestic political dissent and regional isolation, Jordan had repeatedly taunted Egypt to expel U.N. forces. After President Nasser did so, Jordan did not question Israel's resolve. On the contrary, King Hussein regarded Israel's reassurance of its limited intentions as part of a strategy of deliberate deception.[104] He immediately anticipated an imminent Israeli attack, which would inevitably be directed against the West Bank as well as against Egyptian forces. The decision to join with Egypt and Syria in military alliance was a desperate attempt to compensate for Jordanian military weakness.

Without adequate air cover, Jordanian forces would suffer debilitating attacks from the air, which would weaken their maneuverability and cause devastating losses in ground operations. Only the provision of air cover by Egypt, Syria, and Iraq would permit Jordanian ground forces to fight with some effectiveness. At their meeting in Cairo, President Nasser assured King Hussein that the Jordanian army could depend on the protection of the Egyptian air force.[105] The king also agreed to the entry into Jordan of troops from Egypt, Iraq, Syria, and Saudi Arabia. Israel had repeatedly warned in the past that the deployment of Arab forces in Jordan would constitute a *casus belli*.[106] Once King Hussein considered an attack by Israel inevitable, however, Israel's deterrent strategy became irrelevant.[107]

Finally, King Hussein saw no alternative to military alliance because of the enormous pressure of Jordanian public opinion, especially in the large Palestinian community. Sharif Zaid Ben Shaker, a cousin of the king and then commander of the 60th Armored Brigade, stated publicly at the end of May, "If Jordan does not join the war, a civil war will erupt in Jordan."[108] The strategic and domestic costs of inaction in a war the king considered imminent were enormous: civil war, the loss of the West Bank, and isolation in the Arab world. He went to Cairo not to coordinate plans to attack but to reduce Jordanian losses in the war he knew was inevitable. King Hussein felt he had nothing to lose.

Finally, members of Israel's cabinet gave great weight to the strident demands of an aroused Arab public opinion for war against Israel. At their final cabinet meeting on June 4, Israel's most experienced leaders considered that public opinion throughout the Arab world, reinforced by Arab military coordination, significantly increased the likelihood of an attack in the near future. They did not consider the possibility of confusion and loss of control in the Egyptian command, and, when they paid attention to the domestic political context of their Arab adversaries, they inferred a higher probability of attack.[109] Although most did not consider an attack imminent within the next day or so, all considered it inevitable in the very near future.[110]

The miscalculation of Egyptian and Jordanian intentions fueled the process of escalation and made Israel's decision to initiate war easy. It is misleading, however, to conclude that the miscalculation of Arab intentions was either a necessary or a sufficient condition of war. It was not sufficient because, although Military Intelligence in Israel had warned the prime minister of an imminent Arab attack on May 25, he rejected the urgent advice of senior military commanders to preempt. It was not necessary because the high value placed by Israel's leaders on their capacity to deter blurred the distinction between preemption and prevention once Nasser blockaded the straits.[111] Once the blockade was imposed and the failure of Israel's deterrent strategy was clear, Israel no longer tried to manage the crisis to avoid war but, rather, concentrated on creating the international conditions that would permit war. The prime minister and his colleagues felt free to initiate war only when they considered that they had neutralized U.S. opposition.

In neither Cairo nor Jerusalem did military logic determine strategic choices. As the crisis escalated, estimates of likely U.S. behavior were critical to the final calculations of leaders in both Egypt and Israel. President Nasser considered that U.S. behavior would determine the outcome of the war; if the United States did not intervene on behalf of Israel, Egypt would prevail. Israel considered U.S. support essential to deter the Soviet Union from military intervention in the war to come and to the postwar negotiations to follow.

THE UNITED STATES AS CRISIS MANAGER

The United States was unable to translate its importance to both Israel and Egypt into an effective strategy of crisis management. Its lack of institutional memory and its unwillingness to honor its past commitments to Israel regarding a blockade of the Straits of Tiran strengthened those within Israel's cabinet who favored a use of force. The inability of President Johnson and the State Department to craft an alternative to a use of force by Israel also exposed the contradictions in the U.S. strategy of crisis management. By the end of May, the United States spoke with several voices, and Israel's leaders listened to the voice they preferred.

The United States began early and worked actively to control escalation and avoid war. Even before President Nasser blockaded the straits, President Johnson sent urgent messages to Cairo, Damascus, and Moscow, calling for de-escalation of troop movements and respect for free navigation in the Straits of Tiran. As soon as the blockade was announced, Undersecretary of State Eugene Rostow, in an effort to slow down the momentum, urged Israel to make no decision for 48 hours and to consult with the United States in the interim.[112] It was this request that persuaded Israel's leaders on May 23 to delay the use of force and authorize a trip by Foreign Minister Eban to Washington.

In 1957, Britain, France, and the United States had guaranteed the right of free passage through the Straits of Tiran for ships of their own registry and had recognized Israel's right to self-defense to ensure innocent passage for its ships. The U.S. position was stated on February 11, 1957, in an aide-memoire from Secretary of State John Foster Dulles to Eban, who was then Israel's ambassador to the United Nations.[113] When Eban arrived in Washington, however, U.S. officials at first could not recall and then could not find the relevant document. There was no institutional memory of the management of the previous crisis. President Johnson telephoned former President Eisenhower, who confirmed that in 1957 the United

States had recognized that if force were used to close the straits to Israel's shipping, Israel would be within its rights under Article 51 of the U.N. Charter to respond with force.[114] Secretary of State Dean Rusk argued, however, that the United States did not consider Israel free to resort to military action until and unless Egypt went beyond the blockade and resorted to the use of armed force.[115] Foreign Minister Eban rejected that interpretation.

President Johnson pursued a two-track strategy in an effort to control escalation and avoid war. On the advice of the State Department, he endorsed a proposal to organize an international maritime flotilla to open the straits. The president stated candidly, however, that the proposal would require full congressional support and consultation at the United Nations. At the same time, he repeatedly warned Israel of the risks of unilateral action.[116]

While Eban was meeting with officials at the State Department on May 25 to discuss the organization of the flotilla, he received an urgent cable warning of the imminence of an Arab attack and requesting the United States to reinforce deterrence by a commitment to come to Israel's defense if it were attacked.[117] Secretary of State Rusk consulted immediately with President Johnson and the chairman of the Joint Chiefs of Staff, Gen. Earl Wheeler. American intelligence did not share Israel's appraisal of an imminent attack. Nevertheless, Eugene Rostow summoned Egyptian Ambassador Kemal and warned against any offensive action. Moscow was also asked to use its influence with Egypt.[118] The Soviet Union sent its ambassador in Cairo to see Nasser immediately and urge him to refrain from military action.[119]

The following day, Eban met with Secretary of Defense Robert McNamara, General Wheeler, and CIA Director Richard Helms. The tone of the discussion was very different from Eban's consultations at the State Department. Again, U.S. intelligence officials repeated their evaluation that Egyptian forces were not deployed for an early attack; rather, President Nasser intended to provoke Israel to attack in the expectation that his reinforced army in the Sinai could absorb and repel a first strike. Senior officials also reported the results of Pentagon studies prepared for President Johnson, which suggested that, although casualties would be higher if Egypt struck first, Israel would win a military victory whether it preempted or absorbed an Egyptian attack. Both the CIA and the Pentagon estimated that the fighting would last no longer than a week.[120]

More to the point, General Wheeler and Secretary McNamara opposed the organization of a naval task force. They raised such issues as the likely U.S. response should Egypt fire on a U.S. ship, the possible commitment of U.S. ground troops if Egypt used military force, and the likelihood of an open-ended commitment even if Egypt did not challenge the flotilla immediately. In McNamara's words, the multinational fleet was a "military man's nightmare."[121] Like their military counterparts in Israel, they suggested that the issue was not the blockade but the failure of deterrence. The opening of the straits by an international flotilla, they argued, would not restore the credibility of Israel's deterrent; that problem was principally Israel's.[122] Even if tacit, the policy implications were obvious. The United States continued to speak with two voices until Israel attacked on June 5.

In Jerusalem, a deadlocked cabinet debated the two options—an immediate attack or a delay to await the flotilla.[123] As the cabinet recessed for a few hours on

May 28, Prime Minister Eshkol received a note from President Johnson saying that the Soviet Union had told him it had information that Israel planned to attack and had warned that, if Israel started military action, it would come to the assistance of those who were attacked. Again, President Johnson warned Israel against military action and requested a delay of two to three weeks. Secretary of State Rusk added that plans were proceeding quickly for the international naval escort.[124] President Johnson's warning was decisive. In an effort to secure U.S. diplomatic support both during the war he anticipated and in the postwar period, Prime Minister Eshkol recommended to his colleagues that they delay military action.

In the week that followed, President Johnson sent Robert Anderson and Charles Yost as his personal envoys to meet secretly with President Nasser in Cairo. Nasser agreed to an exchange of vice-presidential visits in an effort to negotiate a compromise solution.[125] Reports of these negotiations worried leaders in Israel who feared an agreement that would reopen the straits to all ships but those of Israel.[126] The search for a compromise alarmed rather than reassured Israel and made the use of military force more, rather than less, attractive. Eshkol and Eban decided to send Meir Amit, the head of Mossad, to Washington to assess the prospects of the flotilla and, more important, to explore the likely U.S. attitude should Israel take unilateral military action.[127]

Amit met with Secretary of Defense McNamara and CIA Director Helms, but not with officials at the White House or the State Department. Not surprisingly, he reported that those he had met with in Washington scoffed at the proposed naval task force. He concluded that the United States would do nothing to open the straits and that U.S. support for unilateral action by Israel was increasing: "It was clear that when the time for action came, they [the United States] would not do a thing."[128] This evaluation was not consistent with the report by Israel's ambassador to Washington, Avraham Harmon, of his last conversation with Rusk and Rostow before leaving for Jerusalem on June 2.[129] Rusk had warned that the issue of who fired first would be extremely important and cautioned again against unilateral action by Israel.[130]

On June 3, President Johnson wrote to Prime Minister Eshkol that the United States was continuing its efforts to establish the naval task force, which would include at least six other countries; at the moment, however, only Australia and one Latin American state had agreed to participate. The president added a distinct note of caution: "Our leadership is unanimous that the United States should not move in isolation." In conclusion, Johnson reiterated his warning: "I must emphasize the necessity for Israel not to make itself responsible for the initiation of hostilities. Israel will not be alone unless it decides to go alone."[131]

Israel's leaders were by now explicitly aware of both the contradictions inherent in U.S. strategy and the divisions among U.S. policy makers. They accurately estimated that the likelihood of international naval action was poor, given the unwillingness of the major maritime powers to participate and congressional insistence on a multinational effort.[132] The U.S. efforts to negotiate a solution directly with President Nasser could only compromise Israel's intrinsic interests in the Gulf of Aqaba and, more important, seriously damage Israel's independent capacity to deter. Moreover, they would not address the concentration of Arab forces on all of Israel's frontiers. Finally, Israel's leaders estimated that the cost in U.S. support if Israel initiated war, the only relevant cost since the imposition of the blockade, had diminished. The Pentagon preferred that Israel take military action to end the crisis, and the inability of the president and the State Department to craft a credible alternative to the use of force mitigated their opposition to an attack by Israel. Israel's leaders were correct in all these estimates. President Johnson's repeated injunctions against unilateral military action by Israel were no longer credible; consequently, they were not sufficient to control escalation and prevent war.

CRISIS MANAGEMENT: A RETROSPECTIVE ANALYSIS

This examination of the causes and processes of miscalculated escalation in 1967 is sobering. It demonstrates that none of the major participants planned or wanted war, yet they found themselves inadvertently trapped in a process of escalation that they could not control. More to the point, a retrospective analysis identifies only a few critical turning points early in the process where better crisis management might have prevented miscalculation and avoided war. Once the blockade was imposed, both Egypt and Israel, for quite different reasons, abandoned their attempt to manage the crisis and concentrated on creating the most favorable conditions for war.

Before the blockade was imposed, Israel and Egypt tried deterrence, extended deterrence, and reassurance in an effort to manage the crisis. None of these strategies of crisis management succeeded in avoiding war; they were confounded by Arab alliance politics and commitments and by the domestic political weakness of Syria, Jordan, Egypt, and Israel. Under these circumstances, the use of threat-based strategies such as deterrence to control escalation provoked rather than prevented miscalculation and war. A new and unstable government in Syria began the process through its support of low-intensity violence across Israel's borders. Israel's attempts, under pressure from its public, to deter through threats and punishment succeeded only in alarming Jordan and the Soviet Union and in provoking Egypt and Syria. Although Israel's leaders might have been more tempered in their language, it is hard to identify an alternative strategy that would have done better in controlling violence along its borders. The Syrian challenge was fueled largely by its acute political weakness at home and its isolation in the Arab world.

The Soviet Union miscalculated badly in using Egypt as a proxy to extend deterrence to Syria. It seriously overestimated its capacity to control its ally and failed to delimit the extent of its support. President Nasser's inflated estimate of likely Soviet action should Israel attack was critical to his exaggeration of Egypt's relative capabilities in a confrontation with Israel. The Soviet Union attempted to restrain Egypt from initiating a war only after the blockade was in place; by then, its attempt to manage the crisis was irrelevant, as Nasser did not intend to strike first.[133]

Egypt's strategy of extended deterrence succeeded in its limited objective of deterring Israel from punishing Syria. Although it was an effective strategy on its own terms, it simultaneously unleashed intense domestic and regional demands from both allies and adversaries for additional steps. President Nasser next took only a limited and partial step but was confounded by the ineptitude of U Thant, who missed the opportunity to slow the momentum of the crisis and increased, rather than limited, the pressures on the Egyptian president. The secretary-general removed Nasser's only shield against the demands of his own constituency. This was the critical error that undermined the possibility of managing the crisis short of war.

The evidence suggests overwhelmingly that had President Nasser stopped with the removal of UNEF, Israel would not have gone to war: The credibility of its deterrent reputation had not been challenged. Indeed, Israel tried to manage the crisis at this point through a two-track strategy of privately drawing the line, to avoid a public challenge to Nasser, and public reassurance. A vulnerable president, however, whose leadership of the Arab world was at stake, was unable to stop.

In his blockade of the straits, President Nasser violated a critical political requirement of crisis management: He failed to limit his political objectives. The political context in which he operated, however, made it extraordinarily difficult for him to do so. Critical to Nasser's decision to impose the blockade was his overestimation of Egypt's military capabilities, particularly the power of the air force. Given his conservative estimate of the balance of capabilities only a few weeks earlier, it appears that his miscalculation was motivated by the challenge to his leadership in the Arab world.

Under these conditions, there was little that Israel could have done to correct that miscalculation. Vigorous public reinforcement of deterrence would, in all likelihood, have further inflamed Arab opinion. More to the point, it would have been irrelevant, for neither Egypt nor Jordan questioned Israel's resolve: Israel's deterrent was credible but insufficiently potent. Again, it is difficult to see how Israel could have reduced Egypt's miscalculation of relative capabilities.

Israel's leaders seriously miscalculated both Egyptian and Jordanian intentions. They did so in part because of the offensive deployment of Egyptian military forces, which was the result of confusion and poor command and control in the Egyptian General Staff. Ironically, the Egyptian standing military plan called for defensive deployment in preparation for offense, but, as the crisis escalated, President Nasser ordered an offensive deployment in preparation for defense.[134] Egypt's failure to coordinate its military deployment with its larger strategy was not, however, the critical factor in Israel's decision to go to war.

Israel also miscalculated Jordanian intentions because of Jordan's decision to join with Egypt in military alliance. The Jordanian decision was the result of intense domestic weakness, the fear of civil war, and Jordan's exposed military position in a war it considered inevitable. There was little that Arab governments could have done to correct Israel's miscalculation. Indeed, President Nasser repeatedly signaled his intention not to attack first—to U Thant at a meeting in Cairo on May 25, to President Johnson, and in public speeches.[135] His assurances were not credible to Israel's leaders, despite the confirming estimates of U.S. intelligence.

More to the point, Israel's erroneous estimates of an imminent Arab attack fueled but did not determine the process of escalation. Leaders in Jerusalem considered Israel's deterrent reputation fundamental to their security. They had been long committed to a strategy of deterrence and, in the event of its failure, to the transfer of military action to the territory of their adversaries because of the constraints imposed by the strategic realities of long borders, shallow space, and vulnerable population centers. Once Israel's leaders defined the issue at stake as the capacity to deter, they no longer attempted to manage the crisis but rather attempted to create the appropriate conditions for the use of force. They waited to attack only until they were reasonably confident that they had neutralized U.S. opposition. As the analysis demonstrated, an estimate of an imminent Arab attack was neither necessary nor sufficient. The high value placed by Israel's leaders on their capacity to deter made the distinction between preemption and prevention largely irrelevant.

Once the blockade was in place, only the United States conceivably could have managed the crisis short of war because of its importance to both Egypt and Israel. It is difficult to see, however, how it could have done so in practice. The U.S. attempt to negotiate a compromise with Egypt was precisely what Israel's leaders feared; if anything, it increased rather than decreased Israel's incentives to attack. Constrained by Congress and heavily committed in Vietnam, President Johnson was unwilling to use force unilaterally to challenge the blockade. It is questionable, moreover, whether that would have been an appropriate strategy of crisis management; the Pentagon asserted vigorously that it was not. The futile U.S. attempt to find an alternative to unilateral action by Israel succeeded only in reducing the diplomatic cost to Israel of a decision to attack.[136]

This analysis of escalation warns against optimistic expectations that better strategies of crisis management can always correct miscalculation and avoid war. The evidence suggests, rather, that miscalculated escalation is extraordinarily resistant to control under conditions of domestic political weakness and alliance commitments. At most, the analysis suggests that better crisis management is most likely to be effective early in the process, before leaders are fully committed.[137] A more careful strategy by the Soviet Union, explicitly delimiting the extent of its support, might have restrained President Nasser before he committed himself fully to the blockade. Similarly, delay by U Thant might have given Nasser the pretext he desperately needed for refraining from a blockade of the straits. Once that step was taken, however, escalation was fueled by strategic, institutional, political, and psychological factors that could not be manipulated from the outside.

The path to inadvertent war I have analyzed began with low-level provocation and crossed the critical threshold through the unintended consequences of deterrence. Both when it failed and when it succeeded, deterrence made subsequent military action more, not less, attractive. Once the critical threshold was crossed, escalation proceeded through loss of political as well as military control to a decision to attack. In both Cairo and Jerusalem, however, military logic did not determine strategic choices. Far more important was the inability of leaders to control their political constituencies and manage their political constraints.

On the road to inadvertent war, the opportunities for effective crisis management were few and early. The analysis suggests that crisis managers did not need a better appreciation of the military and technical obstacles to effective crisis management but required a keener understanding of the political as well as the strategic weaknesses that made leaders vulnerable to miscalculation.

NOTES

1. Thomas Schelling, *The Reciprocal Fear of Surprise Attack* (Santa Monica: Rand Corporation, April 16, 1958). Robert Glasser develops this analysis in "Reciprocal Fear of Surprise Attack: The 1967 Arab-Israeli War," unpublished paper. For broader discussion of the risks of deliberate escalation as "bargaining risks" and the risks of escalation due to loss of control which inhere in the threat of force and its institutional and psychological context, see Glenn H. Snyder, "Crisis Bargaining," in Charles F. Hermann, ed., *International Crisis* (New York: Free Press, 1972), Ch. 10. For analysis of the contradictory dictates of military and political logic, see Alexander L. George, "Crisis Management: The Interaction of Political and Military Considerations," *Survival* 26, 5 (September/October, 1984), pp. 223–234, and his Chapter 3 in this volume.

2. Nadav Safran, *From War to War: the Arab-Israeli Confrontation, 1948–1967* (New York: Western Publishing Co., 1969) and John Orme, "Deterrence Failures," *International Security* 11, 3 (Spring, 1987): 96–127. See also Raymond Cohen, "Intercultural Communication between Israel and Egypt: Deterrence Failure before the Six-Day War," *Review of International Studies* 14 (1988): 1–16.

3. For analysis of the risks of deterrence, the conditions of its success and failure, and its relationship to escalation, see Alexander George and Richard Smoke, *Deterrence in American Foreign Policy* (New York: Columbia University Press, 1974); Robert Jervis, Richard Ned Lebow, and Janice Gross Stein, *Psychology and Deterrence* (Baltimore: Johns Hopkins University Press, 1985); Richard Ned Lebow and Janice Gross Stein, "Beyond Deterrence," *Journal of Social Issues* 43, 4(1987): 1–71; Bruce Russett and Paul Huth, "What Makes Deterrence Work? Cases from 1900 to 1980," *World Politics* 36, 4(1984): 496–526, and "Deterrence Failure and Crisis Escalation," *International Studies Quarterly* 32, 1(1988): 29–46; Paul Huth, "Extended Deterrence and the Outbreak of War," *American Political Science Review* 82, 2 (June, 1988): 423–444, and *Deterrence and War* (New Haven: Yale University Press, 1988); Richard Ned Lebow, "Deterrence: A Political and Psychological Critique," in Robert Axelrod, Robert Jervis, Roy Radner, and Paul Stern, eds., *Perspectives on Deterrence* (New York: Oxford University Press, 1989); and Janice Gross Stein, "Deterrence and Reassurance," in Philip E. Tetlok, Jo L. Husbands, Robert Jervis, Paul Stern, and Charles Tilly, eds., *Behavior, Society, and Nuclear War* (New York: Oxford University Press, 1991), pp. 8–72.

4. The neo-Ba'thist regime was intensely unpopular among wide segments of the Syrian public. Its 'Alawi members were acutely resented by the majority Sunni population who also disliked its emphasis on secular socialism. It antagonized urban capitalists and merchants, who opposed its economic policies, and rural landowners who vigorously fought its land reform program.

Religious, social, and economic tensions were overlaid by intense factionalism within the army. Generals al-Asad and Jadid were rivals for control of the state, a rivalry that had both personal and familial dimensions as well as an ideological component. Jadid's supporters dominated the Ba'th party organization and Syrian intelligence, while al-Asad controlled most of the ground forces and the air force. Jadid advocated a radical restructuring of the Syrian economy and a foreign policy of active hostility to Israel as well as to the conservative Arab states. Al-Asad emphasized less stringent social and economic reform and greater cooperation with the Arab world. By 1966, using his position in the party, Jadid dominated Syrian policy. The acute social, economic, and political tension was projected outward in calls for a mass war of liberation against Israel and attacks against Jordan and Saudi Arabia as agents of imperialism.

Lawson argues that the escalation in Syrian policy toward Israel can be traced directly to the acute socioeconomic crisis which engendered intense factional rivalry. This rivalry was managed through the reorganization of the armed forces and an escalation in the level of hostility toward Israel as a way of regaining political control. Fred H. Lawson, "Domestic Social Conflict and Foreign Policy in Contemporary Syria," unpublished paper, 1988.

5. The Unified Arab Command was established at the Arab summit meeting in Cairo in 1964. It drew up a detailed plan which described the measures needed to improve Arab defensive and offensive capabilities against Israel. Egypt and Saudi Arabia agreed to finance the development of military capabilities in the "confrontation" states. Arab states were also asked to avoid providing Israel with a pretext to start a preventive war; included was the instruction that no Arab state bordering Israel should either encourage or tolerate raids into Israel's territory. See Mahmoud Riad, The Struggle for Peace in the Middle East (London: Quartet Books, 1981), p. 12; Wasfi al-Tal, Writings in Arab Affairs (Amman: Dar al-Liwa, 1980, Arabic), p. 326; and Samir A. Mutawi, Jordan in the 1967 War (Cambridge: Cambridge University Press, 1987), p. 58.

6. Wasfi al-Tal, Writings, p. 243.

7. Radio Jordan Bulletin, December 18–19, 1966.

8. "Statement by Shams al-Din Badran on Events Preceding the June War of 1967," Al-Ahram, February 2, 1968. Reprinted in Zuhair Diab, ed., International Documents on Palestine, 1968 (Beirut: The Institute for Palestine Studies, 1971), Doc. 298, pp. 319–322. Israel's military intelligence gained access to the message from Amir, who was then visiting in Pakistan, to President Nasser. See Yitzhak Rabin, Service Ledger (Tel Aviv: Am Oved, 1979, Hebrew), p. 133. Rabin makes no mention of the message in his English-language memoirs.

9. Cited by Badran, in International Documents, p. 319.

10. President Nasser said publicly that "The cause of Palestine requires preparation, development, and power." Arab Political Documents (Beirut: American University of Beirut, 1964), p. 57.

11. Daniel Dishon, ed., Middle East Record, 1967 (Tel Aviv: Israel Universities Press, 1971), pp. 176–177. Raymond Cohen claims that the decision to escalate the clash into a major confrontation in the air was a deliberate choice by Israel. The date was the anniversary of the Syrian Ba'th party and the dog fight in the air took place in full view of festive celebrators in Damascus. Raymond Cohen, "Intercultural Communication," p. 5.

12. Ma'ariv, June 2, 1972.

13. Cited in Dan Schueftan, "Nasser's 1967 Policy Reconsidered," The Jerusalem Quarterly 3 (1977): 132.

14. On May 12, Prime Minister Eshkol in a speech to a closed meeting of Mapai, the dominant party in the governing coalition, said: "In view of the fourteen incidents of sabotage and infiltration perpetrated in the past month alone Israel may have no choice but to adopt suitable countermeasures against the focal points of sabotage. Israel will continue to take action to prevent any and all attempts to perpetrate sabotage within her territory. There will be no immunity for any state which aids or abets such acts." Cited by Abba Eban, Abba Eban, An Autobiography (New York: Random House, 1977), p. 319. More alarming, but less accurate, was a widely circulated dispatch by UPI datelined May 12 which quoted "a high Israeli source" as saying that "Israel would take limited military action designed to topple the Damascus army regime if Syrian terrorists continue sabotage raids inside Israel." New York Times, May 13, 1967.

15. Also present at the meeting were Ashraf Ghorbal, al-Feki's chef de cabinet, and Salah Bassiouni, a counsellor in al-Feki's office. A report of the meeting was sent immediately by telex to Sami Sharaf, Nasser's chef de cabinet. Richard B. Parker, Essays in Miscalculation, unpublished manuscript, Ch. 1, pp. 4–5.

16. Gamal Abdel Nasser, Speech on the Anniversary of the Revolution, 23 July 1967, in Walter Laqueur, The Israel-Arab Reader (New York: Bantam Books, 1970), p. 200, and

Anwar el-Sadat, *In Search of Identity: An Autobiography* (New York: Harper & Row, 1977), pp. 171–172.

17. In his autobiography, Sadat recalled: "I was seen off at Moscow airport by Mr. Semenov, the Soviet Deputy Foreign Minister who was accompanied by the Speaker of the Soviet Parliament. . . . They told me specifically that ten Israeli brigades had been concentrated on the Syrian border. When I arrived back in Cairo, I realized that the Soviet Union had informed Nasser of this." *In Search of Identity*, pp. 171–172.

18. The report of the UNTSO observers was conveyed in a letter on May 17 from the secretary general of the United Nations, U Thant, to the Egyptian permanent representative, Muhammad Awad al-Kony. United Nations Document A/6669, May 18, 1967, p. 6.

19. Muhammad Fawzi, *Harb al-Thalath Sanawat* (Cairo: Dar al Mustaqbal al-Arabi, 1980), Arabic, p. 71.

20. Wasfi al-Tal, *Writings*, p. 330.

21. Prior to the limited deployment of Egyptian troops, the director general of Israel's foreign ministry, A. Levavi, had called the attention of the Soviet ambassador to the escalating tension on Israel's northern border. When Ambassador Chuvakin countered that Israel was concentrating troops on the Syrian frontier, he was invited personally to inspect the front. The ambassador declined the invitation. See Janice Gross Stein and Raymond Tanter, *Rational Decision-Making: Israel's Security Choices, 1967* (Columbus: Ohio State University Press, 1980), p. 139.

22. See Yaacov Bar-Siman-Tov, in this volume, for a more detailed analysis of Soviet strategy.

23. The Director of Military Intelligence, Major-General Muhammad Ahmad Sadiq, briefed the senior military on the concentration of Israel's forces. He identified the sources of the reports as the United Arab Command, the Lebanese army, the Egyptian embassy in Moscow, and the Syrian general staff. General Murtagi, *al-Fariq Murtagi Yarwa al-Haqa'iq* (Cairo: al-Watan al-Arabi, 1976) Arabic, pp. 53–55. The United Arab Command was under the command of an Egyptian general and headquartered in Syria, but it had no effective intelligence capability and the source in the Lebanese army was the Soviet military attaché in Beirut.

24. Cohen, "Intercultural Communication," p. 8.

25. Mohamed Heikal, "The Six Day War," *Sunday Telegraph*, October–November 1967.

26. Dan Schueftan, "Nasser's 1967 Policy," p. 134.

27. In his memoirs, the Egyptian foreign minister, Mahmoud Riad, claimed that Yitzhak Rabin, Israel's chief of staff, had warned that Israel "would carry out a lightning attack on Syria, occupy Damascus, overthrow the regime there and come back." Riad, *The Struggle for Peace*, p. 17.

28. Sadat, *In Search of Identity*, p. 172.

29. Schueftan, "Nasser's 1967 Policy," p. 135.

30. Mizrahan (Official Commentator for the Israel Defense Forces), "Suria La-Aher Ha-Seara" (Syria After the Storm), *Bamahane* 33, April 27, 1967, Hebrew, pp. 5–7.

31. Yitzhak Rabin, "Address on the Fifteenth Anniversary of the Death of Yitzhak Sadeh," Tel Aviv, Mann Auditorium, September 21, 1967. Transcript in Hebrew in National Library of Israel.

32. On May 16, the military spokesman of the Israel Defense Forces briefed military correspondents on the precedent of 1960 "when Egyptian troops had advanced into Sinai to the Israeli border in demonstrative solidarity with Syria, only to be withdrawn a few weeks later." Eban, *An Autobiography*, p. 323.

33. General Weizman remembers that: "Rabin called me aside and said: 'Move such and such forces, just in case there's any trouble.' A typical routine move, dictated by basic

prudence, but resting on the assumption that there wouldn't be any trouble." Ezer Weizman, *On Eagles' Wings* (Jerusalem: Steimatzky's Agency, Ltd., 1976), p. 209.

34. The original request for redeployment of UNEF was in the form of a letter from General Fawzy to General Rikhye: "Commander UNEF (Gaza): To your information, I gave my instructions to all UAR armed forces to be ready for action against Israel, the moment it might carry out an aggressive action against any Arab country. Due to these instructions our troops are already concentrated in Sinai along our eastern border. For the sake of complete security of all UN troops which install OPs along our borders, I request that you give orders to withdraw all these troops immediately. I have given my instructions to our commander of the Eastern Zone concerning the subject. Inform back the fulfilment of this request." The text of the Egyptian request is included in the Report of the Secretary-General on Withdrawal of the Emergency Force, June 26, 1967, United Nations Document A/6730/Add 3.

35. Orally, when the letter was transmitted to General Rikhye, Egyptian Brigadier Mukhtar requested that U.N. forces be withdrawn from the El-Sabha and Sharm el-Sheikh posts since Egyptian forces intended to occupy the two strategic posts that night. The secretary general's report refers to the oral request for a partial withdrawal.

36. See U Thant's Report to the General Assembly, May 18, 1967, United Nations Document A/6669. Mahmoud Riad, then the foreign minister of Egypt, writes that U Thant requested a formal letter from the Ministry of Foreign Affairs: ". . . in my letter to him I did not ask for the withdrawal of UN troops from Gaza and Sharm el-Sheikh; my request was restricted to a withdrawal from our international borders." *Struggle for Peace*, p. 18.

37. Samir A. Mutawi, *Jordan in the 1967 War*, p. 84.

38. Anwar el-Sadat reports that at a meeting of the Supreme Executive Committee, as he was considering the request for a partial withdrawal of U.N. forces, President Nasser estimated that the concentration of Egyptian forces had increased the chances of war to fifty-fifty. Anwar el-Sadat, *In Search of Identity*, p. 172. According to Hussein Al-Shafi'i, who presided over the trial of the military plotters in 1968, Nasser's estimate was even higher: "The president followed this [his announcement of the decision to withdraw UNEF] by saying, in a word, that this operation would increase the expectation of war from 50 percent to 80 percent." *Al Ahram*, February 26, 1968, p. 1.

39. Cited in U Thant, "The Causes of the Present Crisis," Report of the United Nations Secretary General, June 26, 1967, para 37, *UN Monthly Chronicle* IV, 1 (July 1967), pp. 135–170.

40. For a detailed discussion of the limited security regime created after 1956, see Janice Gross Stein, "Detection and Defection: Security Regimes and the Management of International Conflict," *International Journal* XL, 4 (Autumn 1985): 599–627.

41. Stein and Tanter, *Rational Decision-Making*, p. 144. U Thant did not arrive in Cairo until May 23, after the blockade had been declared.

42. Three other acts constituting a *casus belli* were preparation for attack against Israel's air bases, an attack against Israel's atomic installations and scientific institutions, and a quantitative gap in the balance of forces between Israel and neighboring Arab states. See Stein and Tanter, *Rational Decision-Making*, pp. 105–116.

43. Rabin, *Service Ledger*, p. 71.

44. Only when the withdrawal of U.N. forces became certain, did military leaders in Israel seriously consider the possibility of both a blockade and an Egyptian attack and begin military preparations. Eban, *An Autobiography*, p. 326 and Rabin, *Service Ledger*, pp. 70–71.

45. In her speech to the General Assembly of the United Nations on March 1, 1957, Meir was explicit: "Interference, by armed forces, with ships of Israel flag exercising free

and innocent passage in the Gulf of Aqaba and through the Straits of Tiran, will be regarded by Israel as an attack entitling it to exercise its inherent right of self-defence under Article 51 of the United Nations Charter and to take all such measures as are necessary to ensure the free and innocent passage of its ships in the Gulf and in the Straits." Speech to the General Assembly, 1 March 1957, *General Assembly Official Records* (GAOR), 666th Plenary Meeting, pp. 1275–1276. For the text of the aide-memoire negotiated between John Foster Dulles and Abba Eban on February 11, 1957, see note 115 below.

46. Eban, *An Autobiography*, p. 327.

47. Ibid., pp. 325, 327.

48. Statement in the Knesset, May 22. *Divrei Ha-Knesset* 49: 2225–2227.

49. Cohen, "Intercultural Communication," p. 12, suggests that a public declaration that Israel would go to war if Nasser were to blockade the straits was considered and rejected. Both Eshkol and Eban feared that they would "force Nasser's hand by rhetorical defiance." This was a legitimate concern, given the political pressures the Egyptian president faced.

50. Eban, *An Autobiography*, p. 328.

51. There is some dispute as to when the decision to blockade the straits was made. Nasser and Sadat reported the date of decision as May 22, at the meeting of the Supreme Executive Committee. Gen. Fawzi writes that the decision was made on May 17, five days earlier. *Harb al-Thalath Sanawat*, p. 76.

52. Sadat, *In Search of Identity*, p. 172. Hussein al-Shafi'i confirmed the high estimate of the probability of war if the straits were closed: "Nasser said this would increase the expectation of military confrontation from 80 to 100 percent." *Al-Ahram*, February 26, 1968.

53. Participating in the meeting were Field Marshal Amir, Zakaria Mohieddin, Hussein al-Shafi'i, Ali Sabri, Sidqi Sulayman, and Anwar el-Sadat, as well as President Nasser.

54. Sadat, *In Search of Identity*, p. 172.

55. Speech to Advanced Airforce Headquarters, May 22, 1967. Fuad Jabber, ed., *International Documents on Palestine 1967* (Beirut: Institute for Palestine Studies, 1970), Doc. 318, pp. 538–541. Although few Israeli vessels sailed through the straits, tankers used this route to deliver Iranian oil to Israel.

56. Mohamed H. Heikal, "The Inevitable Confrontation," *Al-Ahram*, May 26, 1967.

57. Nasser, Speech to Advanced Airforce Headquarters, May 22, 1967, *International Documents*.

58. Sadat, *In Search of Identity*, p. 174.

59. Interview, *Al-Musawar*, May 18, 1967.

60. Riad, *Struggle for Peace*, p. 23.

61. Ibid.

62. Interview, *Al-Musawar*, May 20, 1967.

63. Badran, *International Documents*, p. 320.

64. Egypt had approximately 400 fighters compared to Israel's 230; 2500 tanks and armored personnel carriers to Israel's 2000; and a fighting force of 200,000 men in comparison to Israel's army, when fully mobilized, of 300,000.

65. In a conversation with Lucius Battle in Cairo on March 4, 1967, Nasser said that the Egyptian armed forces were not ready for war with Israel. Cited by Parker, *Essays in Miscalculation*, Ch. 5, p. 2.

66. Cited by Riad, *Struggle for Peace*, p. 19.

67. Ibid.

68. As recently as 1966, President Nasser argued that "We can annihilate Israel in twelve days were the Arabs to form a united front. Any attack on Israel from the south is not possible from a military point of view. Israel can be attacked only from the territory of

Jordan and Syria." Cited by Theodore Draper, *Israel and World Politics: The Roots of the Third Arab-Israeli War* (New York: Viking Press, 1968), p. 44.

69. Riad quotes President Nasser's reaction to Johnson's note: "I doubt gravely the sincerity of Johnson. For a man who has always sided with Israel, it is inconceivable that, all of a sudden, he would become even-handed." *Struggle for Peace*, p. 20.

70. Cited by Abdul Majeen Farid, "Records, Secrets, and Deliberations of Hussein-Nasser Talks, 1967-1970," *Al-Rai*, June 4, 1983, cited by Samir A. Mutawi, *Jordan in the 1967 War*, p. 96.

71. Mahmoud Riad, Interview by author, Cairo, June 1977.

72. General Fawzi, *Harb al-Thalath Sanawat*, pp. 76-82, describes in detail the rivalry between Nasser and Amir and the strong institutional base of support Amir enjoyed among the senior officers. In 1962, in an effort to circumscribe Amir's power, Nasser formed a Presidential Council whose members would have to relinquish all executive positions they held. Amir refused to relinquish the command of the armed forces and resigned in protest. Senior officers expressed their support for Amir and Nasser backed down. Subsequently, he was reluctant to challenge Amir directly. Salah Nasser, the Director of General Intelligence, was an Amir appointee and loyal to him.

73. Badran, *International Documents*, p. 319.

74. Irving L. Janis and Leon Mann, *Decision Making: A Psychological Analysis of Conflict, Choice, and Commitment* (New York: Free Press, 1977).

75. Riad, *Struggle for Peace*, p. 20.

76. Samir Mutawi, *Jordan in the 1967 War*, pp. 98-99. At the same time, Jordanians also believed that the Soviet Union and Syria had deliberately provoked Nasser to confront Israel so that he would be defeated in battle. They saw no contradiction between these two interpretations.

77. Cohen, in "Intercultural Communication," argues that the radically different cultural contexts of Israel and Egypt facilitated miscalculation. The Arab emphasis on honor and dignity made a response to Israel's threats inevitable. Similarly, Amos concludes: "For a variety of reasons, 'abd al-Nasir could not let these accusations [of Arab leaders] go unchallenged. The basis of his charismatic strategy at home and abroad rested on his ability to project the image of the ever victorious hero. . . . Moreover, his own rural (*baladi*) origins had stamped him with a tremendous sensitivity to insults, either to himself or to any member of his family. Culture, therefore, combined with personality and politics to assure a response: 'Abd al-Nasir's sense of *wahj* (face), his identification with the collective honor (*sharaf*) of the Egyptians, and his calculus of intra-Arab politics all made a response imperative." John W. Amos, *Arab-Israeli Military/Political Relations: Arab Perceptions, and the Politics of Escalation* (New York: Pergamon Press, 1979), p. 49.

78. Glasser, "Reciprocal Fear."

79. Heikal, "The Inevitable Confrontation."

80. Sadat, *In Search of Identity*, p. 174.

81. Badran, *International Documents*, pp. 321-322. See also Sadat, *In Search of Identity*, pp. 172-174.

82. Both Fawzi and Murtagi confirm that Amir ordered an air strike and that it was cancelled by Nasser. Fawzi, *Harb al-Thalath Sanawat*, p. 124, and Murtagi, *Yarwa al-Haqaiq*, p. 81. Murtagi speculates that Israel intercepted the command. Dayan confirms that the order to one of the Egyptian air force units was intercepted by Israel's military intelligence. See Moshe Dayan, *Story of My Life* (New York: William Morrow & Co., 1976), pp. 325-6.

83. Amos, *Arab-Israeli Military-Political Relations*, p. 60.

84. For an analysis of Israel's strategic planning, see Stein and Tanter, *Rational Decision-Making*, pp. 116-129.

85. The chief of staff, Yitzhak Rabin, did not consider that Egyptian troops were deployed for offensive action. Although 80,000 Egyptian troops were now in the Sinai, technical preparations were deficient and the Fourth Armored Division, Egypt's crack troops, were still deployed on the west bank of the Canal. Stein and Tanter, *Rational Decision-Making*, p. 161.

86. Rabin, *Service Ledger*, p. 70.

87. Ibid., p. 78.

88. Michael Howard and Robert Hunter, "Israel and the Arab World: The Crisis of 1967," *Adelphi Papers* 41 (London: International Institute for Strategic Studies, 1967), p. 20.

89. Dayan, *Story of My Life*, pp. 325–6.

90. Rabin, *Service Ledger*, p. 262.

91. Cited by Dayan, *Story of My Life*, p. 262.

92. Ibid., pp. 325–326.

93. Ibid., p. 259.

94. Cited in Rabin, *Service Ledger*, p. 60.

95. Israel received 90 percent of its oil supplies through the Straits of Tiran and the port at Eilat handled more than 500,000 tons of cargo in 1967.

96. The plan, "Operation Kahir," is described in detail by Trevor Dupuy, *Elusive Victory: The Arab-Israeli Wars 1947–1974* (London: MacDonald and Jane's, 1978), pp. 240–241.

97. Dupuy reports, for example, that, "On May 28, the field army commander, General Mohsen, frustrated by conflicting and confusing orders from Cairo, sent his chief of staff, Brigadier Hassan, back to higher headquarters to ask for clarification and guidance. In essence Hassan was to seek a definition of the objective of his field army in the Sinai and guidance as to whether its role was to be offensive (as seemed to be indicated by its current deployment) or defensive, as had originally been planned. . . . Unable to receive any illumination on the question at Ismailia, either from General Mortagi, the front commander, or from his Chief of Staff, Major General Ahmed Ismail Ali, Brigadier Hassan went back to Cairo to consult with Lieutenant General al Khadi, the Chief of Staff of the Armed Forces. After a brief consultation with General Khadi, Brigadier Hassan returned to Bir el Thamada, General Mohsen's command post, with a simple response. The Armed Forces Chief of Staff, not in the confidence of Field Marshal Amir, could not answer any of the specific questions nor could he give any clarification or guidance as requested by the field army commander." *Elusive Victory*, pp. 241–242.

Lt. Gen. Amer Khammash, the Jordanian chief of staff, describes a similar pattern of confusion. He was sent by King Hussein to Cairo on May 21, after Nasser had ordered troops into the Sinai and as he was considering a blockade of the straits. Khammash recalls: "In Cairo, I was received by the UAC's Commander-in-Chief, General Ali Amer, and his deputy, General Abdul Munim Riad, and a liaison officer from the Egyptian High Command. He [the liaison officer] knew nothing and could answer no questions. The Commander-in-Chief and his deputy knew nothing about war plans. . . ." Interview of Amer Khammash, cited by Samir Mutawi, *Jordan in the 1967 War*, p. 105.

98. Prime Minister David Ben Gurion had warned against Arab troop concentrations in Jordan in his statement to the Knesset on October 15, 1956. "Speech to the Knesset," *Divrei Ha-Knesset* 21, Part I, October 15, 1956, pp. 57–65. Yigal Allon argued that a military response by Israel would be necessary "if Jordan should enter into a military pact with another Arab country and permit the concentration of alien military forces on her territory, and especially on the West Bank of the River Jordan." *The Making of Israel's Army* (New York: Universe Books, 1970), pp. 71–72. See also Stein and Tanter, *Rational Decision-Making*, p. 107.

99. For a detailed summary of the discussions within the Cabinet and the General Staff, see Stein and Tanter, *Rational Decision-Making*, pp. 218–251.

100. Samir Mutawi, *Jordan in the 1967 War*, p. 100.

101. King Hussein recalls: "I was in Aqaba when I heard of Egypt's decision to call for the withdrawal of the international police force from Sinai and to place the Egyptian Army in its place and to close the Straits of Tiran. At that particular moment I knew . . . that war was imminent. . . ." Hussein, *My Profession as a King* (Amman: Ghaleb Toukan, 1978), Arabic, pp. 208–209.

102. *New York Times*, 29 May 1967.

103. Interview, cited by Samir Mutawi, *Jordan in the 1967 War*, p. 100.

104. Ibid., p. 99. See also the analysis by Jordan's prime minister, Saad Juma'a, *The Conspiracy and the Battle of Destiny* (Beirut: Dar al-Kateb al-Arabi, 1968), Arabic, p. 174.

105. Interview with Lt. Gen. Amer Khammash, cited by Samir Mutawi, *Jordan in the 1967 War*, p. 109. They also agreed that two Iraqi Hawker Hunter squadrons should be stationed at and operate from H3 base near the Jordan-Iraq border.

106. Ben Gurion warned against the deployment of Arab forces in Jordan in his statement to the Knesset on October 15, 1956, before the Sinai War. (See note 98.) Yigal Allon was even more explicit: "The territories occupied by Jordan on the West Bank of the River Jordan faced the soft underbelly of the Israel defense lines. . . . If she [Jordan] joined a war-like coalition against Israel and permitted other Arab armies to enter her territory, Israel would have no alternative but to turn the West Bank from a potential wedge against herself into a grand trap for the enemy forces." *The Making of Israel's Army* (New York: Universe Books, 1970), p. 72.

107. King Hussein was far more pessimistic about Arab military capabilities than was President Nasser, but even he overestimated the joint capabilities of Arab forces acting together. President Nasser and Field Marshal Amir emphasized to Lt. Gen. Khammash, the chief of staff, and Brigadier Saleh Al-Kurdi, the commander of the Royal Jordanian Air Force, the strength of the Egyptian air force which would have no difficulty in defeating an attack by Israel. Saad Juma'a, Jordan's foreign minister, was reassured: "From what Field Marshal Amir said at the time, it seemed to me that if armed conflict took place . . . winning the battle would be of no difficulty. . . ." Cited by Saad Juma'a, *The Conspiracy*, p. 110. Lt. Gen. Khammash was more reserved, as was King Hussein, but both were persuaded that joint Arab action would be sufficient to contain an offensive by Israel until the great powers intervened to end the war. Samir Mutawi, *Jordan in the 1967 War*, pp. 102, 110.

108. Cited by Hussein, *My Profession*, pp. 102–103. The king summarized the acute dilemma he faced: "The atmosphere that I found in Jordan, particularly in the West Bank, was one where, frankly we had the following choice: either to act at the right time with no illusion of what the results might be but with a chance to do better than we would otherwise, or not to act and to have an eruption occur within, which would cause us to collapse and which would obviously immediately result in an Israeli occupation of probably the West Bank or even more. . . . That was really the reason why I went to Egypt to meet Nasser to his surprise." Interview of King Hussein, cited by Samir Mutawi, *Jordan in the 1967 War*, p. 103.

109. Moshe Dayan, newly appointed minister of defense, was the only member of the Cabinet to consider briefly that Egyptian fear of a first strike by Israel might prompt Egypt to preempt an Israeli preemption. He acknowledged at the final Cabinet meeting on June 4: "The Egyptians might not strike the next morning, but I believed they were anxious to get in the first blow. If they thought that was our intention too, they would not hesitate to beat us to it and launch their attack the day before we did." Dayan, *Story of My Life*, p. 275. This was the only time, however, that a senior military or political leader expressed

concern that Egypt would preempt an anticipated preemption by Israel. Moreover, it was not the dominant theme in Dayan's presentation to the Cabinet that morning.

110. A group of Israel's former chiefs of staff, interviewed in February 1973, acknowledged that they thought that President Nasser would attack in the face of growing Arab and domestic pressure. See *Ma'ariv*, February 16, 1973, for an interview of Haim Bar-Lev, Moshe Dayan, Haim Laskov, Mordechai Makleff, Yitzhak Rabin, Zvi Tsur, and Yigal Yadin.

111. As Schueftan argues: "Nasser . . . pushed Israel into a position in which she had to choose between an immediate and concrete danger from which she thought she could still extricate herself by mobilizing all her resources, and a far graver danger: an inevitable deterioration leading to a test of strength at a later stage in political, military, and psychological conditions which would be intolerable to her." "Nasser's 1967 Policy," p. 138.

112. Eban, *An Autobiography*, p. 334.

113. The aide-memoire read: "With respect to the Gulf of Aqaba and access thereto—the United States believes that the Gulf comprehends international waters and that no nation has the right to prevent free and innocent passage in the Gulf and through the Straits giving access thereto. . . . In the absence of some overriding decision to the contrary, as by the International Court of Justice, the United States on behalf of vessels of United States registry, is prepared to exercise the right of free and innocent passage and to join with others to secure general recognition of this right." See *United States Senate Document*, 1957, No. 14.

114. Lyndon Baines Johnson, *The Vantage Point: Perspectives of the Presidency, 1963–1969* (New York: Holt, Rinehart, and Winston, 1971), p. 291.

115. William Quandt, *Decade of Decisions: American Policy Toward the Arab-Israel Conflict, 1967–1976* (Los Angeles: University of California Press, 1977), pp. 51–52.

116. In his meeting with Eban, Johnson said: "I do not believe that the procedure outlined for building up an international task force is going to take too long. The purpose is to see that Israeli ships go through. I have been into all aspects of Israel's security situation. I am aware of what it is costing . . . but it is less costly than to precipitate the matter while the jury is still out and to have the world against you. . . . Israel will not be alone unless it decides to go alone." Cited by Eban, *An Autobiography*, p. 358. President Johnson repeated this last phrase three times. As Eban noted, it was to become his watchword throughout the crisis.

117. The prime minister cabled Eban in Washington: "Israel faces a grave danger by Egypt and Syria. In this situation, implementation of the American commitment is vital—in declaration and action—immediately, repeat, immediately, meaning a declaration by the U.S. government that any attack on Israel is equivalent to an attack on the United States. The concrete expression of this declaration will be specific orders to U.S. forces in the region that they are to combine operations with the I.D.F. [Israel Defence Forces] against any possible attack on Israel." Cited by Rabin, *Service Ledger*, p. 87.

118. Quandt, *Decade of Decisions*, p. 49.

119. Mohamed Heikal recalls: "At the same time, in Cairo, the Soviet ambassador went to Nasser's house without an appointment. It was three o'clock in the morning of May 26. He asked for the President to be wakened. The Ambassador explained to Nasser that he had received orders from the Soviet leadership to see him immediately. He had to tell Nasser that the Americans had contacted the Kremlin and told the Russians that the Israelis had information that the Egyptians were going to attack at first light. He said that if that was true, the Soviet Union urged the President not to go ahead with his plans because whoever fired the first shot would be in an untenable political position. As friends, they advised Nasser not to fire that shot. Nasser replied that he had issued no orders for an attack, that there were no plans for an attack in the morning." *The Cairo Documents* (New York: Doubleday and Co., 1973), p. 245.

120. Quandt, *Decade of Decisions*, p. 50.

121. Ibid., p. 47.

122. Quandt, *Decade of Decisions*, and Michael Bar-Zohar, *Embassies in Crisis: Diplomats and Demagogues Behind the Six Day War* (Englewood Cliffs, N.J.: Prentice Hall, 1970), pp. 116–118.

123. In the Cabinet meeting, Yigal Allon was particularly pointed in demonstrating the contradiction in a decision to delay. He argued that Israel would improve its power to deter if it acted alone rather than with the help of a great power. Had it done so in 1956, he insisted, it would have avoided some of its postwar difficulties; the wrong lessons were being learnt from history. Not only was the flotilla irrelevant to the central problem, but it could increase Egypt's incentives to preempt: "Even supposing that an international fleet . . . reached the Red Sea, this in itself would have no effect on the land and air fronts. On the contrary, it is not unreasonable to assume that, in anticipation of the arrival of such an international expeditionary fleet, the Arab High Command might . . . put forward the date of its attack on Israel in order to establish a *fait accompli* before the arrival of the fleet. . . ." Allon, *The Making of Israel's Army*, pp. 81–82. Allon suggested that the American strategy of crisis management could escalate the crisis rather than prevent war by increasing Egyptian incentives to preempt.

124. Foreign Ministry sources, cited by Michael Brecher, *Decision in Israel's Foreign Policy* (New Haven: Yale University Press, 1975), p. 398, and Eban, *An Autobiography*, p. 370.

125. Heikal, *The Cairo Documents*, p. 245, describes Anderson's discussions with Nasser. Riad, *Struggle for Peace*, p. 21, summarizes Nasser's formal letter to President Johnson agreeing to an exchange of vice-presidential visits. Yost cabled the results of his meetings in Cairo to Rusk on June 2. He reported that the Egyptian blockade of the straits could not be lifted without the use of military force. He strongly opposed the use of force because of the serious consequences for the United States in the Arab world and recommended that Washington accept the blockade since access to the straits was not "vital to Israel's existence." Cited in Donald Neff, *Warriors for Jerusalem: The Six Days that Changed the Middle East* (New York: Linden Press, 1984), pp. 187–188. See also Charles Yost, "The Arab-Israeli War: How it Began," *Foreign Affairs* 11 (January 1968), pp. 307–310.

126. Quandt, *Decade of Decisions*, confirms that from May 31 on, the State Department was searching for possible compromises to end the crisis.

127. Amit explained: "A second aim of my mission was to make the Americans realize, in direct contact, the seriousness of the situation, to make them see that Israel had been forced into a situation where there was no way out and hear their reactions." Interview of Meir Amit by Benjamin Geist, July 1973.

128. Amit cabled to Jerusalem: "From hints and scattered hints . . . the maritime-force project is running into heavier water every hour. . . . There is a growing chance for American political backing if we act on our own. . . . It became totally clear that they [the United States] are not planning to do a thing. This does not mean that there were no intentions here or there, or at the time, certain things were said that were not true, or that there was full agreement on what to do. But it was clear that when the time for action came, they would not do a thing." Interview of Amit, *Ma'ariv*, June 2, 1973; Dayan, *Story of My Life*, p. 273; and Eban, *An Autobiography*, p. 384.

129. Rusk had assured him that plans for maritime action were proceeding and would be completed within seven to nine days. Although measures to be taken by the maritime powers were still under consideration, "nothing had been firmly decided." Cited by Eban, ibid., p. 394.

130. Quandt, *Decade of Decisions*, p. 59.

131. Foreign Ministry sources, cited by Brecher, *Decisions in Israel's Foreign Policy*, p. 420.

132. Later that day, Senator Mansfield released a report in Washington on the testimony of Vice-President Humphrey and Secretaries Rusk and McNamara before the Senate Foreign Relations Committee. The report distinguished sharply between a declaration, the use of force, and the use of force to guarantee freedom of passage for ships of the United States as distinct from those of Israel. The committee had been promised that "so far as using force is concerned, anything beyond the declaration would be taken up with Congress." *New York Times*, June 5, 1967.

133. When Shams al-Din Badran, the minister of war, visited Moscow at the end of May, the Soviet leadership urged caution now that the straits had been blockaded. At the same time, however, they suggested that if Israel attacked first, they would deter American intervention. Since that was Nasser's principal concern, and he had independently concluded that American intervention was certain if Egypt attacked first, but unlikely if Egypt provoked an attack by Israel, the Soviet attempt to restrain Egypt after the blockade was beside the point. Riad, *Struggle for Peace*, p. 23, and Mohamed Heikal, *The Sphinx and the Commissar: The Rise and Fall of Soviet Influence in the Middle East* (New York: Harper and Row, 1978), pp. 178–179.

134. Technically, it can be argued that the Egyptian "defensive" strategy in preparation for offense would not have been consistent with the larger strategy of provoking an attack by Israel. Even though the "offensive" strategy in preparation for defense was the result of poor command, control, and communication, it was consistent with the larger Egyptian strategy of provocation. However, once the blockade was in place, formal modelling of the Egyptian preference structure suggests that Egypt's most preferred outcome should have been Israeli acquiescence to the blockade, since Nasser would have reaped all the benefits of his challenge to Israel without the costs of a war. The Egyptian military deployment was not consistent with that kind of preference ordering.

135. When U Thant arrived in Cairo on May 23, he proposed to President Nasser that Israel refrain from sending any of its ships through the Gulf of Aqaba, that ships en route to Eilat refrain from carrying strategic material to Israel, and that Egypt refrain from inspecting ships sailing through the Straits of Tiran. Nasser accepted these proposals. In reply to a question from the secretary-general as to whether Egypt intended to attack, Nasser replied: "We have never at any time intimated that we will attack Israel. It was Israel who has formally threatened to invade Syria. What we are attempting now is a defensive measure to prevent such a threat from materializing. You may have my word therefore that we will never begin the attack." Cited by Riad, *Struggle for Peace*, pp. 20–21.

136. As Quandt astutely observes: ". . . in the ensuing days [of May], changes did indeed occur, but Johnson and his advisers stuck to their definition of the situation. In part this was out of wishful thinking, in part for lack of any better alternative. To the Israelis however the lack of a new policy was tantamount to saying 'We've tried all of our alternatives, and have nothing new to offer.' " *Decade of Decisions*, p. 55.

137. Analysis of immediate deterrence failures similarly suggests that reinforcement of deterrence is most likely to be effective before challengers are fully committed. See Richard Ned Lebow and Janice Gross Stein, *When Does Deterrence Succeed and How Do We Know?* (Ottawa: Canadian Institute for International Peace and Security, 1990).

CHAPTER 9

The Suez War of 1956: Communication in Crisis Management

Christer Jönsson

The Suez Crisis of 1956 coincided with, and was occasionally overshadowed by, the uprising in Hungary. The twin crises made both West and East Europeans "fully aware of their subordination to their own Big Brother and the price to be paid for the security ensured them by a power more powerful than themselves."[1] As a result of Suez, Britain and France, which had long been the major external powers in the Middle East, were reduced to the rank of middle powers, regionally as well as globally.

The Suez Crisis damaged relations within NATO. In addition to causing an acute but temporary Anglo-U.S. rift, the crisis had a longer-term effect on France's relations with the United States and Britain. The French were dismayed not only at U.S. hostility but also at the capitulation of the British in the face of U.S. pressure.

Suez marked the beginning of U.S.-Soviet involvement in, and attempts to influence the development of, regional conflicts in the Middle East. It was the first of a series of superpower confrontations in the region and consituted "the first case of Soviet nuclear saber rattling in a crisis."[2] By comparing Suez with later crises, we may find the extent to which learning has occurred in U.S.-Soviet efforts at crisis management in the Middle East and elsewhere.

RESUMÉ OF THE CASE

In July 1954, Britain and Egypt signed an agreement requiring all British forces to withdraw from Egypt by June 1956. This triumph for the Egyptian nationalists, led by Gamal Abdel Nasser, did not herald diminished unrest in the region. Anti-Western propaganda continued unabated. Meanwhile, the Egyptian-supported

The author acknowledges the useful research assistance of Uri Bar-Joseph.

fedayeen and the Israeli military were exchanging raids and attacks with increased frequency.

In September 1955, Egypt revealed that it had concluded an agreement, ostensibly with Czechoslovakia, to buy Soviet arms. This development brought the United States into the evolving drama in earnest. Through intelligence reports, Washington had known of the Soviet-Egyptian contacts since their inception in late May but wrote them off as a bargaining ploy, as another instance of a Third World nation trying to play off one superpower against the other.[3] Secretary of State John Foster Dulles, who had long refused to accept indicators of a possible Soviet-Egyptian arms deal, reacted vehemently to the Soviet entry into the Middle East melee, labeling it "the most serious development since Korea, if not since World War II."[4]

Tensions reached a new level in July 1956, when the United States abruptly withdrew its previous offer to help finance the Aswan High Dam in Egypt. Within a week, Nasser announced his decision to nationalize the Suez Canal Company. Britain and France, the major shareholders in the company, viewed Nasser's challenge as an act of aggression and launched plans for a military response. The United States tried to buy time and managed to bring its allies to the conference table.

When Nasser refused to meet the conditions for a settlement proposed by the Western powers, France and Britain, over U.S. opposition, referred the dispute to the U.N. Security Council. While the U.N. deliberations were still going on, the French shared with the British their plan for a joint Anglo-French-Israeli operation, according to which Israel was to invade Egypt with Britain and France intervening militarily under the pretext of separating the combatants. Britain consented, and joint war preparations were made in utmost secrecy.

On October 29, Israel attacked Egypt, and the following day the British and French governments sent ultimatums to Israel and Egypt pledging Anglo-French armed intervention unless "all warlike action" was stopped within twelve hours. Following Egypt's rejection of the terms, British and French air assaults on Egypt began on October 31.

The Israeli and Anglo-French military action placed both superpowers on the horns of a dilemma. The United States could either support the Anglo-French action, thereby risking a superpower confrontation, endangering its interests in the Arab world, and alienating Third World opinion; or condemn it, which would give a gratuitous victory to the USSR, jeopardize NATO, and strengthen the Soviet presence in the Middle East. For the Soviet Union, the option was between endangering its national security in a possible clash with the Western powers or abandoning Nasser to his fate, which would entail a serious loss of prestige and influence in the Arab world and throughout the Third World. An aggravating factor for the Soviets was the simultaneous upheaval in Hungary.

The U.S. reaction was swift and determined. Unequivocally condemning the Israeli-Anglo-French military action against Egypt, the United States tabled a U.N. resolution calling for a ceasefire, which was vetoed by Britain and France but received Soviet support. At the same time, Washington exerted strong economic pressure on London. On November 5, the same day that Britain and France landed invasion forces in Port Said, the Soviet Union threatened unilateral Soviet intervention and rocket strikes on Britain and France unless hostilities ended. Under pressure domestically as well as internationally, British Prime Minister Anthony Eden gave in the following day. The Anglo-French advance stopped 23 miles down the Suez Canal from Port Said.

RESEARCH OBJECTIVES

All in all, the Suez Crisis stands out as an example of crisis mismanagement in terms of communication failure, in particular between close allies. My analysis of the events of 1956 will therefore focus on the communicative aspects of crisis management, more specifically on the verbal and nonverbal signaling and the interpretation of these signals by the actors involved.

How and why could the actors, especially the United States and its British allies, be so wide of the mark in their communications and perceptions of each other's policies and intentions? This represents a lingering puzzle of the Suez Crisis and was a central question guiding this inquiry. My research strategy was to start by identifying the underlying beliefs and expectations of each of the actors and then to trace step-by-step the series of faulty communications and misperceptions between them.

A second research objective was to identify the strategies chosen by the principal actors and to explain why they were chosen. This chapter will also address a third question: the extent to which the United States and the Soviet Union coordinated their efforts at preventing the outbreak of war.

BELIEFS AND EXPECTATIONS

The principal national actors in the Suez drama were the two superpowers (the United States and the Soviet Union), the regional protagonists (Egypt and Israel), and the traditional extra-regional powers and major shareholders in the Suez Canal Company (Britain and France). As I will show, these actors proceeded from widely divergent beliefs and expectations, which created the basis for poor communication, important misperceptions, and serious miscalculations as the crisis unfolded. Incompatible beliefs, mutual mistrust, and personal dislikes set the stage for problematic communication over Suez.

The United States

President Dwight D. Eisenhower and Secretary of State Dulles were the key U.S. decision makers throughout the Suez Crisis. To Dulles, the main enemy was international communism, embodied by the Soviet Union. In his view, Soviet leaders were rationalistic, calculating chess players in a game for world domination. Dulles perceived Soviet economic weakness to be the major obstacle to its designs, especially in the Third World. The Soviet Union, he believed, was overextended and unable to meet its economic commitments.[5]

Eisenhower and Dulles "shared common assumptions about the nature of the Soviet threat and on the need to stand firm to meet it."[6] But Eisenhower had a more complex view of the U.S. role in the Middle East conflict, which he did not see only through the East-West prism. Throughout the Suez Crisis Eisenhower tried to follow a basic course of remaining friends with both sides in the regional conflict in order to preserve U.S. effectiveness in helping to achieve a peaceful settlement.[7]

Moreover, Dulles's and Eisenhower's views of their European allies differed in emphasis. The basic dilemma Washington faced in the Middle East was that its concern about combating communism often conflicted with its insistence that the remnants of European colonialism be removed. Dulles, obsessed by the perils of communism, stressed the need to maintain Britain and France as the key U.S. allies in Europe. Eisenhower, for his part, held "fundamental and genuine" anticolonialist views and was sensitive to any traces of colonialist behavior on the part of Britain or France. He believed that the United States was the natural leader of the newly independent countries.[8]

Britain

For the British prime minister, Sir Anthony Eden, the year 1954 represented the peak of his renown as an international statesman, during which he was given credit for the success of the Geneva conference on Indochina and the resolution of the political problem of German rearmament. These successes seem to have created a certain amount of overconfidence.[9]

Of vital importance for later misperceptions and miscommunications was the fact that Eden and his colleagues expected the United States to support, or at least condone, any action they might take in the emerging crisis in the Middle East.[10] At a minimum, the British expected the United States to deter Soviet intervention, or as Eden put it, to "take care of the Bear."[11] The United States might have been reluctant at first, but, as historical experience showed, it would eventually come around if Britain took the lead.[12]

Historical analogies with the 1930s held a prominent place in the activated beliefs of British policy makers. Most members of the cabinet were of the prewar generation that had been scarred by Britain's initial efforts at appeasing Hitler. The Munich analogy permeated British thought about the Suez Crisis, not only in the cabinet but in the opposition and the press as well.[13] The only shade of difference among British policy makers seemed to be whether Nasser was to be regarded as a "new Hitler" or as a "new Mussolini." Eden, for his part, favored the Mussolini analogy, considering Nasser to be "effectively in Russian hands, just as Mussolini was in Hitler's."[14]

Paradoxically, Eden, was, at heart, friendly toward the Arab world, of which he had expert knowledge, and his sympathies in the Arab-Israel conflict had consistently lain with the Arabs.[15] Thus, his hatred for Nasser did not necessarily entail warm feelings for Israel.

Nor did British decision makers have any favorable image of their other partner-to-be, France, which they "classed with Egypt, Israel and Saudi Arabia in the mixed ranks of the enemies of the Baghdad Pact, which was becoming the core of British policy." In 1955, Eden had commented on "their obstructive attitude" and French "double-crossing."[16]

France

The Munich syndrome loomed large in the perceptions of French policy makers as well. Prime Minister Guy Mollet labeled Nasser an "apprentice dictator" who, like Hitler, used "the policy of blackmail alternating with flagrant violations of international agreements."[17]

But there was another predominant and unique element in French perceptions of the Suez Crisis: linkage with the bitter war in Algeria. The French believed the rebels of the Front de Libération Nationale (FLN) were encouraged and supported by Nasser. French officials suspected that Radio Cairo's constant appeals to Arabs everywhere to unite behind the Algerian rebels were only the tip of a large covert supply operation of arms and money to the FLN.[18]

The Algerian problem also directed the attention of French policy makers to Israel. After the Algerian rebellion started in 1954, the Jewish state came to be seen as a counterbalance to the Arab insurgents; as a result, French arms transfers to Israel were stepped up dramatically.

As for their NATO allies, the United States and Britain, the French were traditionally suspicious of British interests in the Middle East and feared a possible British-U.S. collusion.[19] A strong wave of anti-Americanism began building up in France, as Washington's opposition to colonialism was applied to the Algerian war.[20] Among French policy makers the suspicion grew that the U.S. anticolonial stance reflected a hope of replacing the French presence in North Africa rather than genuine idealism; they saw it as part of a long-term U.S. strategy of eliminating British and French influence around the world.[21] Yet the French seem to have shared the British expectation of U.S. benevolence or noninterference if and when forceful actions were taken. At the least, the United States was expected to deter the Soviets from intervening.[22]

Israel

Basic to the belief system of Israeli decision makers in the 1950s was a fundamental sense of insecurity. They consistently perceived the Arabs as hostile, threatening, unwilling to recognize Israel's right to exist, and certain to exploit every sign of weakness to destroy the Jewish state.[23] The Israeli leaders were firmly convinced that Nasser organized the escalating fedayeen raids into Israel.[24]

The Israelis did not view the evolving conflict from an East-West perspective. Israel felt a kinship for, and assumed friendliness from, the United States while mistrusting and expecting hosility from the Soviet Union.[25] However, the negative U.S. reaction to Israeli probes for a military alliance or treaty of guarantee during 1955 and its consistent refusal to grant or sell arms to Israel contributed to an increasing sense of desperation.[26]

The Israeli leaders, David Ben-Gurion in particular, also harbored a deep mistrust of Britain, based on long years of bitter experience and acquaintance with the pro-Arab tradition of the Foreign Office. Anthony Eden's Guildhall speech in November 1955, in which he alluded to the need for adjustments in Israel's frontiers, caused great resentment in Israel and added to Eden's reputation for sympathy toward the Arab world.[27]

To complete this image of a hostile environment regionally as well as globally, the Israeli leaders mistrusted the United Nations, especially Secretary-General Dag Hammarskjöld, because of perceived pro-Arab bias.[28] France, on the other hand, was perceived as an island of understanding and sympathy in this sea of hostility. The material basis of this affection was France's willingness to supply Israel with arms when others refused.

Egypt

In May 1953, Dulles had a telling conversation in Cairo with Nasser, in which he tried to convince the Egyptian strongman and president-to-be that the Soviet Union constituted the main threat against Egypt. Nasser answered that he could not see the Soviets attacking the Middle East except in the event of a global war and that communism represented an internal threat that had to be fought with reforms and by Egypt's keeping its distance from the West.[29]

If the British were identified as the main enemy by Nasser in 1953, Israel was soon to vie for that position. In February 1955, Israel launched a fierce attack on a small Egyptian army camp in the Gaza Strip. It was the bloodiest incident between Egypt and Israel since the 1948 war. The Gaza raid had a profound effect on the Egyptian leader, who had previously showed scant interest in the usual Arab expressions of hatred for Israel.[30] At the same time, Nasser's anti-Western sentiment gradually carried over to the United States as well.

Another aspect of Nasser's mind-set that several observers have commented on was his conspiratorial bias. For instance, Cyrus Sulzberger noted that Nasser "tends to look beneath and behind even the most simple proposition for invidious meanings," attributing this to "his heritage of conspiracy and of deep resentment against colonialism and imperialism."[31]

The Soviet Union

Soviet leaders evidently looked at the Suez Crisis from a simplified East-West perspective. Nikita Khrushchev admits in his memoirs to initial doubts about Nasser, who was seen to be leading a "bourgeois government." The Soviets decided to support the Egyptian leader only when it became clear that he "promised to weaken the influence of English colonialism in the Near East—and that was in the interest of the Soviet Union."[32]

The Soviet two-camp view entailed exaggerated expectations of Western unity. Soviet press commentaries consistently dismissed allegations about a growing rift between the United States and its allies.[33] There was a considerable element of self-interest, and probably a shade of wishful thinking, in the Soviet projection of an image of Western unity. By attacking the Western powers for their "neocolonialism," the Soviet Union could present itself as the best and most reliable friend of the newly independent nations of Asia and Africa.[34]

Summary

This brief overview of relevant beliefs and expectations shows that the main actors in the Suez drama viewed one another and unfolding events from markedly different vantage points. First, their images of the enemy diverged. The two superpowers were alone in defining the conflict primarily in East-West terms, with "international communism" and "the West" as the principal villains. For Egypt, Britain and Israel were the main enemies; for Israel, the Arabs. Britain and France zeroed in on the person of Nasser. Thus, the Suez Crisis was placed in different contexts by the participating national actors. To the United States and the Soviet Union, it represented another episode in the Cold War; to Egypt, it was the convergence of colonialism and Israeli aggression; to Israel, the crisis was one more eruption of the Arab-Israeli conflict; to Britain and France, it represented a serious threat to their status as world powers.

Another observation emerging from the preceding overview of differing images concerns the obvious lack of trust between the protagonists, including allies. The fact that some of the individuals involved disliked and distrusted one another compounded these national images. John Foster Dulles was not well-liked by his European allies, who often agreed with Winston Churchill's portrayal of the U.S. secretary of state as "the only case of a bull I know who carries his china closet with him."[35] Of special significance were Eden's and Dulles's mutual aversion and lack of sympathy.[36]

SENDING AND INTERPRETING SIGNALS

In the following section, I shall concentrate on key phases of the Suez Crisis in which signaling was of particular significance: (1) the withdrawal of the Aswan Dam loan, (2) Egypt's nationalization of the Suez Canal Company, (3) the ensuing efforts to solve the conflict through conference diplomacy, (4) the British-French-Israeli collusion, and (5) the belated Soviet threats of intervention.

Withdrawal of the Aswan Dam Loan

Plans to build a new dam higher up the Nile to replace the existing Aswan Dam figured high on Nasser's domestic agenda. The World Bank seemed to have come close to an agreement with Egypt on Western financing by the end of January 1956, although Nasser remained suspicious of British and U.S. loan conditions. British and U.S. policy makers supported the Aswan Dam project for political reasons. By financing it, the West would get a major stake in the Egyptian economy, the Soviets would be kept out, and tensions between Egypt and the West would be reduced.[37]

To the United States and Britain, the Aswan High Dam not only represented a political opportunity but also entailed political risks. Within the United States, the project faced strong opposition from pro-Israel groups, cotton producers who worried about increased Egyptian cotton production, and conservative opponents of any kind of foreign aid.[38] Nasser's machinations in other Middle Eastern countries and anti-British propaganda eroded Eden's original enthusiasm and political support for the dam.[39] According to Selwyn Lloyd, the British learned for the first time of U.S. doubts about the Aswan Dam loan in connection with the Eisenhower-Eden summit in Washington in February 1956. By May 1956, the British and Americans had agreed to let the project "wither on the vine."[40]

Yet Anglo-U.S. discussions on financing the dam continued throughout June. During that month U.S. decision makers appear to have made a reassessment of Nasser and the Aswan Dam project.[41] In mid-July, Dulles made several personnel changes in his Middle East team in the Department of State to give it a stronger anti-Nasser cast. Most important, Ambassador Hank Byroade, who was close to Nasser, was replaced by Raymond Arthur Hare, who had participated in a work group studying ways to cooperate with Britain in its covert actions to destabilize regimes in the Middle East. This signal was not lost on Nasser.[42]

By July, the Egyptian president reportedly had come to the conclusion that Washington would not go ahead with support for the Aswan Dam. Ambassador Ahmed Hussein, on leave from Washington, was authorized to go to Dulles and tell him that the Egyptians would not insist on their conditions relating to the Aswan Dam loan.[43]

At his meeting with Dulles on July 19, Ambassador Hussein made a remark about a Soviet offer to finance the dam if the West refused. An irritated Dulles told Hussein in brusque terms that the United States would not submit to blackmail and that the U.S. offer of aid was withdrawn. While the decision to renege had been taken prior to the meeting, the ambassador's gaffe served as a cue for Dulles's indignation and abruptness.

Dulles's decision to summarily withdraw the U.S. loan offer was taken with little prior consultation: "[I]n perhaps no other decision during his tenure at the State Department did he play so lone a hand."[44] He did not seek the advice of either the State Department or the World Bank.[45] At a short meeting hours before his meeting with Hussein, Dulles showed a draft of a press release announcing Washington's withdrawal to the president, who made no objections.[46] Yet, Eisenhower afterward expressed his concern to Dulles "that we might have been undiplomatic in the way the cancellation was handled."[47] The British, as Eden later expressed it, "were informed but not consulted and so had no prior opportunity for criticism or comment."[48] Like Eisenhower, the British reacted against the style rather than the substance of Dulles's action.

Similarly, it was the manner in which the U.S. acted that Nasser perceived as a deliberate humiliation to himself and his country. Several years later, he admitted that he was surprised "not by the refusal itself" but "by the insulting attitude with which the refusal was declared."[49] An official U.S. government statement issued after the loan withdrawal[50] bore an uncanny similarity to the way the Eisenhower administration had denied aid to Iran's Mohammed Mossadegh just prior to his CIA-sponsored ouster. Seen in combination with the shakeup of the State Department's Middle East team a few days earlier, the statement's assertion that "the United States remains deeply interested in the welfare of the Egyptian people" could be read by Nasser as an appeal to Egyptians to get a new leader.[51]

Nasser's own signaling, on the other hand, played a major role in shaping the U.S. decision. Constant rumors from Cairo about Soviet offers to finance the Aswan High Dam, obviously intended to enhance Egypt's leverage in its negotiations with the West, proved counterproductive by arousing Washington's—especially Dulles's— anticommunist sensitivity. While initially interpreted as blackmail, Egypt's signaling was deemed more credible after the Soviet-Egyptian arms deal.[52] As it turned out, however, no Soviet commitment had been made or was made in the wake of the U.S. withdrawal.[53]

For Dulles the Aswan issue, above all, suggested an opportunity to call the bluff on Soviet economic aid. Based on his conviction that the Soviet Union was economically weak and his belief in the efficacy of brinkmanship to defeat Soviet tactics, Dulles decided to use the Aswan issue as a means of meeting the Soviet "economic counteroffensive." Dulles firmly believed the Soviets were in no position to deliver on their economic offers. By calling their hand, Dulles would expose the hollowness of Soviet pretensions and humiliate regimes in countries that had staked their own futures on Soviet promises. If, on the other hand, the Soviets tried to fulfill a possible Aswan offer, their economy would bleed.[54]

To summarize, the Aswan loan episode displayed an unfortunate failure in U.S. and Egyptian communication insofar as the signals that were sent touched raw nerves among the recipients and conveyed messages other than those intended. Egyptian rumors of Soviet offers, read against the background of the Soviet-Egyptian arms deal and Nasser's recognition of Communist China, confirmed U.S. beliefs that the Middle East was an arena of East-West confrontation. The heavy-handed and humiliating manner in which the United States reneged, read against the "body language" of State Department personnel changes, confirmed Nasser's beliefs about U.S. "neocolonialist" plots.

Nasser's Nationalization of the Suez Canal Company

On July 26, a week after Dulles's withdrawal of the loan and two weeks after the last British troops had left Egypt, Nasser made an impassioned speech to a huge and enthusiastic crowd in Alexandria in which he announced the nationalization of the canal company. Widely perceived as Nasser's reply to Dulles, the dramatic Egyptian action apparently "came as a complete surprise to the American Government."[55] Available warnings had not been taken seriously.[56] Nor was Nasser's move met with undue alarm in Washington.[57]

If the mood was sedate in Washington, the reaction in London "bordered on panic and hysteria."[58] These differences reflected disparate interests. Less than 3 percent of the ships using the canal were American, the U.S. government had no financial interest in the canal company, and the United States was self-sufficient in meeting its oil needs. Britain, by contrast, was the largest single shareholder in the canal company, one-third of all ships passing through the canal were British, and two-thirds of its oil came through the canal.[59] In London, therefore, Nasser's move was generally viewed as an act of aggression against Britain, and, following Eden's lead, the British cabinet unanimously agreed to subject Egypt to "maximum political pressure" in order to restore international control over the canal, including "the threat—and, if need be, the use of force." As a consequence, preparations for military action were to be initiated.[60] In these planning sessions, Eden repeatedly declared that his objective was to get rid of Nasser and his regime. Nasser could not be allowed, in Eden's phrase, "to have his hand on our windpipe."[61]

Eden immediately informed Eisenhower of the British position. Pointing out that "we are unlikely to attain our objective by economic pressures alone," Eden declared Britain's readiness "in the last resort, to use force to bring Nasser to his senses."[62]

That same day Eisenhower received cables from Paris reporting that the French government's reaction was even more heated than the British.[63] The feeling that Nasser had to be brought down, by force if necessary, was shared by every shade of political opinion in France.[64]

Eisenhower, however, felt "there is no reason to panic."[65] He dispatched Deputy Undersecretary Robert Murphy to London (another signal of the lack of urgency) with instructions to "just go over and hold the fort."[66]

On the evening of July 30, Murphy was invited to dine informally with his old wartime associate Harold Macmillan. The dinner conversation left Murphy "in no doubt that the British Government believed that Suez was a test which could be met only by the use of force." Macmillan intimated that "military moves might start in August." Though the venture would be risky, "Nasser has to be chased out of Egypt."[67] Macmillan "succeeded in thoroughly alarming Murphy,"[68] who immediately reported the conversation to Eisenhower.

On July 31, Eisenhower wrote a long and blunt letter to Eden, sending Dulles, who had returned from Latin America, to deliver it personally. Eisenhower emphasized "the unwisdom even of contemplating the use of military force at this moment" and recommended a conference of maritime nations. Yet Eden's interpretation of the letter was that "the President did not rule out the use of force."[69] He could come to that conclusion through a selective reading of Eisenhower's letter, which contained the following passages:

> We recognize the transcendent worth of the Canal to the free world and the possibility that eventually the use of force might become necessary in order to protect international rights. . . .
>   If unfortunately the situation can finally be resolved only by drastic means, . . .
>   As you realize, employment of United States forces is possible only through positive action on the part of Congress, which is now adjourned but can be reconvened on my call for special reasons. If those reasons should involve the issue of employing United States military strength abroad, . . . [70]

Dulles reiterated that "force was the last method to be tried, but the United States did not exclude the use of force if all other methods failed." What stuck in Eden's mind was a remark Dulles made at their meeting: "A way had to be found to make Nasser disgorge what he was attempting to swallow." "These were forthright words," Eden recollected. "They rang in my ears for months."[71]

Thus started a confusing exchange of ambiguous signals between Washington and London in the months to come. The U.S. signals to France were no less ambiguous. "While I recognize that events may ultimately make forceful action necessary," Eisenhower wrote to Guy Mollet on July 31, "I feel that the present situation demands that we act moderately, but firmly, to bring about a dependable administration of the Canal."[72]

Efforts at Conference Diplomacy

Dulles persuaded Britain and France to agree to the idea of a conference of the maritime nations interested in the status and operation of the Suez Canal. But behind this semblance of consensus were divergent expectations. The conference was designed by Dulles primarily to gain time and to cool British and French passions; in Dulles's own words, "to avoid resort to military force against Egypt at least until such time as world public opinion had been mobilized and tested."[73] Therefore, Dulles favored several weeks of preparation, whereas Britain and France would have preferred the conference to be convened as soon as possible. August 16 was agreed upon as a compromise.[74] If U.S. policy makers saw the conference as a means to avoid violence and a starting point for a negotiated settlement, Britain and France viewed it as a convenient smokescreen behind which preparations for an intervention could be, and were, made.

The British Egypt Committee—a smaller group of ministers acting as a kind of inner cabinet on the Suez issue—had, in fact, agreed on July 30 that "while our ultimate purpose was to place the Canal under international control, our immediate goal was to bring about the downfall of the present Egyptian Government." If there were to be a conference, as the U.S. urged, Britain should seek "to limit the function of the conference to the approval of a declaration of policy . . . [that] would form the basis of a Note to the Egyptian Government which . . . would be a virtual ultimatum. If Colonel Nasser refused to accept it, military operations could then proceed."[75] It was against this background that British policy makers read subsequent signaling. From the United States, the British, along with the French, were looking for a green—or even a yellow—light to go ahead with their military plans; from Nasser, they were looking for a *casus belli*.

The London conference produced an eighteen-nation proposal, initiated by the United States, for an international "non-political" body to administer the Suez Canal. Of the twenty-two participant nations, the Soviet Union, India, Indonesia, and Ceylon refused to support the proposal. A group of conference representatives, under the leadership of Australia's Prime Minister Robert Menzies, was dispatched to Cairo to present the majority view to Nasser. The Menzies mission failed: Nasser categorically rejected the eighteen-nation proposal.

The United States during this phase of the crisis engaged in highly ambiguous signaling vis-à-vis its allies concerning the possible use of military force. In part, this seemed to stem from differences between the president and the secretary of state. Dulles appeared to be ambivalent on the subject, while Eisenhower seemed more categorical in his refusal to consider the use of force as an alternative. Immediately after learning about Nasser's nationalization, Eisenhower remarked that he "doubted if we would use force unless they attacked our people."[76] He told Dulles that if Nasser were to prove that he could operate the canal and maintain it as a world waterway, "then it would be nearly impossible for the United States ever to find real justification, legally or morally, for use of force."[77] This, in Eisenhower's opinion, applied to Britain and France as well. "In my telephonic and other communications with Prime Minister Eden," he wrote in his memoirs, "I frequently expressed the opinion that the case as it stood did not warrant resort to military force."[78] In reality, at the time Eisenhower was far from unequivocal in communicating this message; it was expressed "with more courtesy than clarity."[79] His clearest signal was a letter to Eden dated September 2:

> I am afraid Anthony, that from this point onward our views on this situation diverge. As to the use of force or the threat of force at this juncture, I continue to feel as I expressed myself in the letter Foster carried to you some weeks ago. . . . I must tell you frankly that American public opinion flatly rejects the thought of using force, particularly when it does not seem that every possible peaceful means of protecting our vital interests has been exhausted without result. Moreover, I gravely doubt we could secure Congressional authority even for the lesser support measures for which you might have to look to us. I really do not see how a successful result could be achieved by forcible means.[80]

Eden found this letter "most disturbing."[81] A few days later, Eisenhower went public with his rejection of military force. Questioned at a press conference about the possible use of force, he answered, "We are committed to a peaceful settlement of this dispute, nothing else." Foreign Secretary Selwyn Lloyd retrospectively considered this signal "Tragedy No. 1," coming as it did when Menzies was still in Cairo. In Lloyd's opinion, Eisenhower's statement destroyed any chance the Menzies mission might have had of success.[82]

Yet the effect of Eisenhower's seemingly clear message was offset by subsequent signaling. After receiving Eden's reply to his September 2 letter, in which the prime minister dwelt on parallels with the experience of the 1930s, Eisenhower wrote back on September 8. This time his letter contained mixed signals. On the one hand, Eisenhower repeated his previous rejection of the use of force: "The use of military force against Egypt *under present circumstances* might have consequences even more serious than causing the Arabs to support Nasser. It might cause a serious misunderstanding between our two countries because I must say frankly that there is *as yet* no public opinion in this country which is prepared to support such a move."[83]

The qualifiers in this passage were amplified by statements later in the letter, such as "[a]t the same time, we do not want any capitulation to Nasser" and "I assure you we are not blind to the fact that eventually there may be no escape from the use of force."[84] Moreover, asked about the U.S. reaction to the eventual resort to force by Britain and France, Eisenhower, in a press conference on September 11, answered cryptically that "if after all peaceful means are exhausted, there is some kind of aggression on the part of Egypt against a peaceful use of the Canal, you might say that we would recognize that Britain and France had no other recourse than to continue to use it even if they had to be more forceful than merely sailing through it."[85]

Meanwhile, Dulles consistently sent mixed and ambiguous signals. In meetings with the British during the London conference, Dulles left Eden with the impression that he "seemed not to exclude [the] possibility of *joint* use of force."[86] And Macmillan concluded, "I cannot help feeling that he really wants us to 'go it alone', and has been trying to help us by creating the right atmosphere."[87]

After the failure of the Menzies mission, Dulles made yet another attempt to avoid war when he introduced the idea of a Suez Canal Users' Association (SCUA) to Britain and France. The user states were to club together, employ their own pilots, pay their own dues to themselves, and make their own way through the Suez Canal. If Egypt refused to cooperate with the association, the members would reroute their oil traffic around the cape and the United States would offer loans to cover the financial losses. The plan was accepted reluctantly by Britain and with even greater misgivings by France. A second London conference was convened on September 19, attended by the eighteen "majority" states.

A joint U.S.-British-French formulation, used by Dulles in his press conference and by Eden in his speech before the House of Commons, held that Egyptian interference with the operations of the SCUA would be a breach of the 1888 convention, in which event the parties concerned would be "free to take steps to assure their rights through the United Nations or through other actions appropriate to the circumstances."[88] Both Dulles and Eden were asked to explain the meaning of these words; both declined to do so, as the agreed purpose was to leave the course of future action deliberately vague so as to maximize pressure on Egypt.[89] Yet Dulles, at a press conference, emphasized that the United States did not intend to "shoot its way through" if met by force, adding that he understood Eden to share this position.[90]

This was a blow to Eden. Dulles "had not only said that America would turn the other cheek to Nasser, but also suggested that Britain might do likewise." Furthermore, "to make matters worse, he had said all this in the middle of a difficult two-day emergency debate in the House of Commons."[91] Eden's exasperation is palpable in his retrospective comment:

> It would be hard to imagine a statement more likely to cause the maximum allied disunity and disarray. . . . The words were an advertisement to Nasser that he could reject the project with impunity. We had never been told that a statement of this kind was to accompany the announcement of the Users' Club. Had we known that they were to be used as an accompaniment to the American announcement, we would have never endorsed it.[92]

At the second London conference, Dulles again spoke "with emotion, apparent conviction and sincerity" about the need to use force under certain circumstances, resurrecting British expectations of an eventual green light.[93] However, Dulles undermined such hopes by his comments in an October 2 press conference: "There is talk about teeth being pulled out of the plan, but I know of no teeth. There were no teeth in it, so far as I am aware."[94] Anthony Nutting characterized Dulles's renewed rebuff as Eden's "final let-down" and a "breaking-point" as far as Britain was concerned.[95] Yet when confronted by Lloyd and French Foreign Minister Christian Pineau a few days later, Dulles repeated his objections to the actual use of force but accepted its "potential" use if a real effort to reach a peaceful settlement were made and failed.[96]

The United States, in addition, appeared to vacillate on the other type of leverage envisaged under the SCUA plan, economic sanctions. Dulles had recommended that the users make a concerted rerouting of their ships if Egypt failed to cooperate, thereby making a "dry ditch" of the Suez Canal.[97] Eisenhower, however, in his press conference said, "A program of economic sanctions has never been placed before me as of this moment, never."[98] And Dulles himself asserted that "it is not our purpose to try to bring about a concerted boycotting of the Canal," but "each country would have to decide for itself what it wanted its vessels to do."[99]

With such ambiguity and obvious lack of compatibility between Eisenhower's and Dulles's messages, Washington's signaling appeared "hopelessly and fatally mixed" to its allies.[100]

British-French-Israeli Collusion

If the signaling reviewed thus far was highly ambiguous, the process culminating in the Israeli attack on Egypt and the Anglo-French ultimatum involved mistrust, concealment, and outright deception on several planes. The joint British and French military planning was problematic from the outset. British planners were wary of the risks involved in sharing secrets with the French,[101] while the French were incensed by the constant British revisions of the Operation Musketeer plans and apparent foot-dragging.[102] The French-Israeli military collaboration, which predated the Anglo-French plans for joint action, was kept secret from the British. When in mid-October British decision makers were finally brought into France's plan for collusion with Israel, they made it clear that Britain would never join with Israel to attack Egypt and that the British attack would come as a consequence of, not in cooperation with, the Israeli action. Open collusion with Israel would sever Britain's ties with the Arab world. The advantage of the plan from the British point of view was that it provided a long sought-for *casus belli*.[103] An Anglo-French-Israeli accord was eventually reached, but the atmosphere of distrust prevailed.

The parties agreed not to inform their U.S. allies of their accord. In order to avoid disclosure of the plan, everything would be done to reinforce the impression that Israel was about to attack Jordan, including planting rumors of Iraqi forces entering Jordan.[104] The deception was successful. American expectations of an Israeli attack on Jordan were not lowered by a virtual blackout of communication between the United States, on the one hand, and its British and French allies, on the other, at the same time that U.S. interceptors were picking up heavy radio traffic between Paris and London as well as Paris and Tel Aviv, and information about large French arms shipments to Israel was reaching Washington. Eisenhower apparently believed that Israel would attack Jordan, supplied by the French and with covert British sanction, and that Britain and France might take advantage of the ensuing imbroglio to occupy the canal.[105]

On October 27 and 28, Eisenhower sent messages to Ben-Gurion expressing his anxiety over the Israeli mobilization and urging the Israelis to refrain from any action that would endanger the peace. From both his messages it was apparent that Eisenhower believed that imminent conflict was likely to erupt between Israel and Jordan. He explained that, according to U.S. information, no Iraqi units had entered Jordan. His signals revealed to the Israelis that their deception had been effective and that Eisenhower remained uninformed of the actual situation.[106]

Immediately after Israel's Sinai attack on October 29 and the Anglo-French ultimatum the next day, Eisenhower let it be known through his press secretary that he had obtained "his first knowledge" of the ultimatum "through press reports." In a radio and television address the next day, Eisenhower denied any advance consultation or information concerning any phase of these actions.[107] Adding to the feeling of betrayal was the communication U.S. decision makers believed they had received earlier from Lloyd, in private conversation at the United Nations, to the effect that Washington would be consulted before the British moved.[108]

Both then and later, CIA Director Allen Dulles objected to any implication of intelligence failure over Suez, maintaining that the intelligence community "estimated the approximate time and place of the Israeli attack well before the attack was made"[109] and "was well alerted as to what Israel and then Britain and France were likely to do."[110] To this day, the degree of U.S. foreknowledge of the British-French-Israeli collusion remains a matter of controversy.[111]

What is clear from the available record is that the newly operational U-2 reconaissance planes were used to monitor the crisis. By mid-October, U-2 flights had revealed heavy British and French military concentrations in Malta and Cyprus as well as the Israeli mobilization and armament with French Mystère jets.[112]

It is also evident that, in the weeks preceding the outbreak of violence, Washington received contradictory intelligence reports—some predicting an impending invasion, others discounting its probability.[113] In short, uncertainty reigned. While material information about war preparations accumulated, the intentions and motives of the main protagonists remained a puzzle to U.S. decision makers. One major intelligence estimate dated September 19 had concluded that "UK-French resort to military action is likely only in the event of some new and violent provocation."[114] And as late as October 21, John Foster Dulles told Eisenhower that he "was really baffled to know the real purposes of the British and the French," adding that "perhaps they did not know themselves."[115]

Without foreknowledge of the Anglo-French-Israeli collusion, the Israeli attack must have appeared mystifying. Egyptian decision makers were reportedly unable to infer the Israeli objective. The Israelis neither made use of their air force nor attacked the Egyptian air force, which contributed to suspicions that the attack in Sinai might be a feint or diversionary maneuver.[116] The available records indicate similar confusion in Washington. At a White House meeting on the evening of October 29, Allen Dulles suggested that "the Israelis might still be planning to withdraw—that the operations thus far have been in the nature of probing action" (which belies his later claims that the intelligence community had firm advance knowledge of the conspiracy). John Foster Dulles, for his part, voiced the suspicion that the British and French "may in fact have concerted their action with the Israelis," but he believed "there was still a bare chance to 'unhook' the British from the French."[117]

The Anglo-French ultimatum met with "astonishment bordering on disbelief" in Cairo.[118] In Washington, it added indignation to confusion. Eisenhower confessed in a cable to Eden that "we here felt very much in the dark as to your attitude and intentions with respect to the Mid East situation."[119] At a White House meeting, Eisenhower said he was "extremely angry with both the British and the French" who were "planning to present us with a fait accompli, then expecting us to foot the bill."[120]

Perhaps the simplest answer to the question of why U.S. decision makers were taken by surprise despite seemingly ample warning is the one proffered by Stephen Ambrose:

As a general rule, the easiest way to achieve complete strategic surprise is to commit an act that makes no sense, or is even self-destructive. . . . To Eisenhower in 1956, it made no sense—indeed was self-destructive—for the British and the French to attempt to seize and hold the canal, or for the Israelis to act aggressively when they were surrounded by a sea of Arabs, and it especially made no sense to him for Britain and France to attempt to act independently of the United States, much less against the expressed policy of the Eisenhower Administration.[121]

If U.S. decision makers miscalculated Anglo-French-Israeli intentions, the U.S. response to their concerted action came as no less a surprise to British, French, and Israeli policy makers. To their consternation, the United States submitted a draft resolution to the U.N. Security Council calling upon Israel to withdraw its forces and urging all U.N. members to "refrain from the use of force or threat of force in the area in any manner inconsistent with the purposes of the United Nations."[122]

The U.S. initiative was "warmly welcomed" and given an affirmative vote by the Soviet U.N. representative. After the U.S. draft resolution was vetoed by France and Britain, the Soviet Union tabled a strikingly similar resolution that encountered the same fate.[123] On November 1, the Uniting for Peace procedure was invoked with U.S. and Soviet support, and an emergency session of the General Assembly was held the following day. A resolution proposed by the United States, the gist of which was similar to that of the resolutions vetoed by France and Britain in the Security Council, received Soviet support and was adopted by the General Assembly. It was a rare manifestation of superpower consensus in the United Nations.

Concomitantly, Washington exerted strong economic pressure on Britain. A run on the pound, long expected by the British treasury, had developed, and standby support from the International Monetary Fund was blocked by the U.S. The Eisenhower administration explicitly made financial support conditional on a political settlement of the Suez imbroglio.[124] In addition, word reached London that the United States was contemplating oil sanctions against its allies.[125]

Neither member of the conspiracy had foreseen a development like this. The greatest disillusionment was probably felt by British decision makers. Macmillan later confessed to "a profound miscalculation as to the likely reaction in Washington to the Franco-British intervention" on the part of the British cabinet, and he accepted for himself "a heavy responsibility": "I believed that the Americans would issue a protest, even a violent protest in public; but that they would in their hearts be glad to see the matter brought to a conclusion. They would therefore content themselves with overt disapproval, while feeling covert sympathy."[126]

This "deadly assumption that the Americans would lament publicly and do nothing"[127] was shared by key British policy makers, who tended to rely on wartime bonds with Eisenhower. Macmillan came away from a brief personal meeting with Eisenhower in Washington in late September with the conviction that "Ike will lie doggo" until the election.[128] "Perhaps we were all personally on too good terms, influenced too much by our previous close and friendly relations with Eisenhower," Selwyn Lloyd later admitted. "We felt that we might argue away like members of a family but at the end of the day would never seriously fall out."[129]

To summarize, in the same way that Israeli-Anglo-French behavior ran counter to U.S. expectations, so U.S. behavior was unanticipated by its allies. Expectations were so firmly held that signals to the contrary were ignored or discounted in the communication process preceding the outbreak of violence.

Soviet Threats of Intervention

One major consideration behind the prompt and unequivocal U.S. reaction was the fear of Soviet efforts to capitalize on the new situation. At a meeting of the National Security Council on November 1, John Foster Dulles "warned with emphasis that if we were not now prepared to assert our leadership in this cause, leadership would certainly be seized by the Soviet Union." As a result, the newly independent countries in the Third World would turn from the United States to the Soviet Union.[130]

In reality, the Soviet Union showed considerable caution and restraint at this stage. The concurrent Soviet armed intervention in Hungary undoubtedly contributed to this caution. The Soviets made no threats to take action on behalf of the assaulted Egyptians and announced no commitments to the active defense of Cairo. Moreover, immediately after the Israeli attack and the Anglo-French bombardment of Egypt, Soviet technicians and advisers as well as recently delivered IL-28 jet bombers were withdrawn from Egypt, thus signaling Soviet interest in avoiding direct participation in hostilities.[131]

To the Egyptians, Soviet leaders privately confessed their helplessness. Syria's president, Shukri Quwatli, who was in Moscow on October 31, asked Khrushchev and Marshal Georgi Zhukov what the Soviets were going to do to help Egypt. Zhukov pointed out that if the Soviet Union were to intervene, the Red army would have to pass through Iran, Iraq, and Israel, as well as Syria—an unrealistic proposition. And at a diplomatic reception on November 2, Khrushchev told the Egyptian ambassador that there was unfortunately no way which the Soviet Union could help Egypt militarily. All he could promise was "to mobilize world opinion."[132]

Only on November 5, one week after the outbreak of hostilities, did the Soviet Union seize the initiative. By then the British and French had already neutralized the Egyptian air force and landed invasion forces in Port Said, while the Israelis had occupied all of Sinai and opened the Straits of Tiran. In messages from Premier Nikolai Bulganin to the leaders of Britain, France, Israel, and the United States, and in a letter from Foreign Minister Dmitri Shepilov to the U.N. Security Council, the Soviet Union communicated warnings and threats of varying severity and explicitness, spelling out the possible consequences of the failure of Anglo-French and Israeli forces to cease fire and withdraw from Egypt. There was an inverse relationship between the severity of these commitments and their explicitness. In order of decreasing severity and increasing explicitness, four conditional commitments may be distinguished: (1) a warning of global war as a result of the Suez crisis; (2) implicit threats of Soviet strategic rocket strikes on Britain and France; (3) a threat of unilateral Soviet intervention in the Middle East; and (4) an "offer" of joint Soviet-U.S. intervention under U.N. auspices.[133]

The vague warning that the fighting in Egypt might "spread to other countries and develop into a third world war" appeared in all of Bulganin's messages except the one to Ben-Gurion, which merely stated that the Israeli government, by "acting as an instrument of outside imperialist forces," had put "in jeopardy the very existence of Israel as a state."[134]

Israel was also exempted from the specific threats of Soviet rocket strikes, which were issued in the letters to Eden and Mollet. These letters were "extremely vivid but at the same time quite imprecise."[135] To both Eden and Mollet, the threat of rocket strikes was made in the noncommittal form of a conditional question. In his letter to Mollet, Bulganin merely asked rhetorically: "In what situation would France find herself were she attacked by other states that have formidable means of destruction?"[136] The threat was, however, made more specific in the communication to Eden. Britain was reminded that it might be attacked by "stronger states, possessing all types of modern destructive weapons," including "rocket weapons."[137] It is noteworthy that the Soviet notes nowhere actually stated that Britain and France *would* come under Soviet attack if they did not obey the ceasefire, only that they *could*.[138]

The threat of unilateral Soviet intervention, too, was "so cautiously phrased, and the proposed action so carefully justified, that the appearance of a threat was technically avoided."[139] Shepilov's note to the Security Council proposed intervention by either the United Nations or by the USSR and the United States acting together, in the event that Britain, France, and Israel failed to accept a ceasefire and withdraw. Shepilov added, "The Soviet government, on its part, declares its readiness to make its contribution to curbing the aggressors, to defending the victims of aggression and restoring peace, by dispatching to Egypt the necessary air and naval forces."[140] In a similar vein, Bulganin in his letters to Eden and Mollet expressed the determination of the Soviet Union to "crush the aggressors by the use of force."[141]

To back these threats of unilateral intervention, Moscow spread rumors about Soviet "volunteers" being on their way to, or already present in, Egypt. The possibility of Soviet volunteers in Eygpt had been hinted at by Khrushchev as early as August in an exchange with the British ambassador in Moscow,[142] was implied in Shepilov's note to the Security Council,[143] and was made public in a TASS statement of November 10. Along with rumors of Soviet aircraft overflying Turkey, Soviet submarines arriving in Alexandria, and Soviet troops taking up positions in Syria, the volunteer theme appears to have been part of a disinformation campaign directed from Moscow.[144]

The idea of joint superpower military action to defend Egypt, which was hinted at in Shepilov's note, was spelled out in quite explicit terms in Bulganin's message to Eisenhower:

> The Soviet Union and the United States of America are both permanent members of the Security Council and great powers possessing all modern types of weapons, including atomic and hydrogen weapons. We bear a special responsibility for stopping the war and restoring peace and tranquility in the area of the Near and Middle East. We are convinced that if the governments of the U.S.S.R. and the United States firmly declare their determination to ensure peace, and come out against aggression, then aggression will be ended and there will be no war.[145]

The proposal for joint Soviet-U.S. intervention gave the impression of being made in order to derive from its rejection a justification for unilateral Soviet intervention in Egypt.[146]

The vague Soviet threats had low credibility. The USSR in 1956 possessed limited capabilities to engage in a strategic rocket attack. There was confidence in the West of overwhelming strategic superiority over the Soviet Union and of U.S. readiness to retaliate if the USSR were to attack Britain and France.[147] Moreover, the vague character of these threats and the lack of any time stipulation within which Britain and France were to comply with the Soviet demands reduced the credibility of the threats.

Although British policy makers in retrospect have tended to downgrade the impact of the Soviet threats,[148] the cabinet minutes of November 6 give a different impression. Selwyn Lloyd is recorded as urging that "we must not appear to be yielding in the face of Soviet threats" yet admonishing that if the Anglo-French occupation is continued, "we must reckon with the possibility of a Soviet invasion of Syria or some other area in the Middle East, and possibly a direct Soviet attack on the Anglo-French forces in the Canal area." Apparently the Soviet threat of unilateral intervention in the Middle East, but not the threat of rocket attacks on British cities, was given serious consideration.[149]

The Soviet threats seem to have been taken seriously by most Israeli and French policy makers as well. Ben-Gurion was infuriated by Bulganin's message to Tel Aviv, which, unlike those to London and Paris, breathed contempt and scorn and threatened the very existence of Israel as a state.[150] He sent his foreign and defense ministers to Paris for advice. They found their French counterparts "divided in their opinions about the significance of the Russian threat—but far from tranquil." Pineau pointed out that France was defenseless against missiles and suggested that the Israelis not belittle Bulganin's threat. Defense Minister Maurice Bourgès-Maunoury, on the other hand, considered the Soviet threat "nothing but a bluff."[151] While Ben-Gurion leaned toward the latter view, other leading Israeli policy makers took the Soviet threat seriously.[152]

In Washington, as in London, the Soviet threat of unilateral intervention in the Middle East was perceived as the most credible and disturbing threat. Eisenhower believed that the Soviets' failure in Hungary might make them more prone to undertake unilateral action elsewhere. He saw them as "scared and furious, and there is nothing more dangerous than a dictatorship in this state of mind."[153] From Moscow, Ambassador Charles Bohlen cabled that "events here have gone beyond simple proposition of cover for Soviet action in Hungary."[154] And the intelligence community concluded that Moscow was indeed ready to send arms and volunteers to Egypt and had told Nasser that "the USSR in its support of Egypt is prepared to 'go all the way' even if it risks World War III."[155]

Washington reacted swiftly to the veiled Soviet threats. Within a few hours, the White House issued a statement categorically rejecting Bulganin's proposal for joint U.S.-Soviet action as "unthinkable." A counterthreat was issued to the implied Soviet threat of unilateral intervention: If new forces were introduced in the Middle East without a U.N. mandate, the statement said, "it would be the duty of all United Nations members, including the United States, to oppose any such effort."[156]

The threats to Britain and France were ignored in the statement, but Eisenhower authorized his press secretary to state that if the Soviets attacked U.S. allies, the United States would oppose them.[157] Concomitantly, Washington pressed Israel to accept a ceasefire. The Israelis took the U.S. position to be that, unless they accepted, the United States would not protect Israel against a Soviet attack. In telephone conversations, Eisenhower urged Eden and Mollet to accept an early ceasefire, arguing that ending the war would remove the temptation and the excuse for Soviet military intervention.[158]

The president also ordered U-2 reconnaissance flights over Syria and Israel, which did not discover any Soviet airplanes on Syrian airfields or any moving into Egypt, as rumored.[159] All the same, Eisenhower ordered low-profile increases in military preparedness and cancelled some military leaves.[160] These measures were not well publicized but were designed to signal resolve as well as restraint to the Soviets. In Eisenhower's own words:

> though many of the measures were simply precautionary, I believed that we should progressively achieve an advanced state of readiness, starting the next morning. Many precautionary items would escape notice but I suggested that the military services might soon call back personnel from leave, an action impossible to conceal which would let the Russians know—without being provocative—that we could not be taken by surprise.[161]

The United States also sent signals to Israel that underscored the severity of the new situation created by the Soviet threats. The CIA leaked a report to Paris that the Soviets intended to "flatten" Israel the next day. The French passed it on to Tel Aviv. A similar threat was communicated to the Israeli ambassador in Rome by his Soviet counterpart. Israeli decision makers had also taken note of the conspicuous omission of Israel in U.S. assurances to France that a Soviet missile attack on Britain or France would lead to U.S. retaliation. Furthermore, the United States threatened economic sanctions against Israel if it refused to abide by a ceasefire and withdraw. American Jews, too, pressed for withdrawal.[162] Under this combination of pressures, Ben-Gurion and his colleagues decided on a conditional withdrawal in accordance with a formula suggested by Abba Eban: Israel would withdraw "when satisfactory arrangements are made with the international force that is about to enter the Canal Zone."[163] It was the combination of U.S. and Soviet threats that made the Israelis change course, as expressed by one of the policy makers: "If the US had been more sympathetic, we would have seen the Soviet threat as not too serious. Just as the US and Russian conjunction of policy led to the creation of the State, so on this occasion their conjunction led to our decision to withdraw."[164]

Similarly, a combination of pressures forced Eden to take the lead in calling off the Anglo-French military action. In addition to U.S. diplomatic prodding and economic pressure and the Soviet threat, Eden faced a run on the pound, dwindling petroleum reserves, and vociferous internal opposition. Even his own ministers had turned against continued military operations. The most hawkish minister, Macmillan, warned his colleagues that Britain could not afford to alienate the United States, upon whom Britain might have to rely for economic assistance. In this situation, the prospect of a U.N. force became increasingly attractive as a reasonable formula that could end the nightmare.[165]

Eden called Mollet to inform him of his decision to bring hostilities to an end. Foreign Minister Pineau and Defense Minister Bourgès-Maunoury were for the French continuing the military operation alone, but Mollet, supported by the majority, refused.[166] The U.N. General Assembly established an emergency force (UNEF) under the administration of Secretary-General Hammarskjöld to supervise the ceasefire and troop withdrawal. After almost four tumultuous months, the crisis was moving toward resolution.

CONCLUSIONS AND LESSONS

Returning to the research questions posited initially, we can conclude, first, that communication among participants in the Suez Crisis was hampered by divergent beliefs and expectations. Resistant to change, these expectations sensitized the actors to certain signals while desensitizing them to others. In retrospect, the crisis is almost reminiscent of a classic Greek tragedy with all the actors blindly proceeding toward their inevitable fate.

Divergent expectations entailed recurrent misreading of signals. The greatest communication failure occurred within the Western alliance, where crisis behavior displayed a pattern of "muddled perceptions, stifled communications, disappointed expectations, paranoid reactions."[167]

The basic policy dilemma of crisis management—how to protect one's interest while not triggering unwanted escalation to war[168]—was keenly felt by U.S. decision makers but ineptly communicated to their British allies. In Herman Finer's words, Washington "negligently left them guessing with far too much room for miscalculation. This is not a wise practice for the strongest party in an alliance."[169]

The firm belief of Eden and his colleagues in U.S. support or at least tacit acceptance caused them to misread U.S. signaling and to look for green lights in messages that were not intended as such. These expectations also contributed to Britain's secrecy and deception at a decisive stage of the crisis, which was no less disastrous for crisis management than the U.S. ambiguity. Explaining why London left Washington in the dark, Macmillan, in 1971, referred to his "instinct that the Americans didn't wish to be informed when he took the final action . . . because that would embarrass them . . . but would support us when action was taken. My judgement was wrong," Macmillan admitted.[170]

Key actors on both sides of the Atlantic suffered from tunnel vision during the crisis. Dulles's preoccupation with the Soviet Union predisposed him to treat Nasser's Egypt as "an undifferentiated pawn in a larger game."[171] Eden's reliance on the Munich analogy alerted him to behavior on Nasser's part that reminded him of the dictators of the 1930s while blinding him to other aspects of Nasser's conduct. His frequent allusions to lessons of the 1930s obviously represented genuine beliefs rather than rhetorical or tactical devices. Around Christmas 1956, after the Suez Crisis was over, Eden complained in a private letter to a close friend and supporter:

I find it strange that so few, if any, have compared these events to 1936—yet it is so like. Of course, Egypt is no Germany, but Russia is, and Egypt just her pawn. If we had let events drift until the spring I have little doubt that by then, or about then, Russia and Egypt would have been ready to pounce, with Israel as the apparent target and western interests as the real one. . . . Yet so many seem to fail to see this and give Nasser almost as much trust as others gave Hitler years ago.[172]

Divergent expectations cannot fully explain why close allies could fail so utterly in communicating with each other. Another contibuting factor was the tendency to use a limited set of communication channels. Specifically, there were few face-to-face meetings between key actors, and no attempts were made to use backchannels to validate the official communication between the involved states—devices that proved useful in later crises. Stephen Ambrose's observation on U.S. decision making is to the point: "Eisenhower had close friends in Eden's Cabinet and in the British military, as well as in the French government and military. But there is no evidence he made any attempt to get in touch, secretly, with his friends (Macmillan, for example, or Mountbatten, both of whom opposed Eden's adventurism) in order to find out what was going on. As a result, he was surprised."[173]

On the British side, several observers have lamented the absence of summitry:

Macmillan's successor, Alec Douglas-Home, felt things might have ended differently 'if Anthony had gone to see Ike in person, to get things absolutely clear'. This was a view shared by Macmillan, who, in retrospect, felt that discussion should never have been allowed to remain at the Foreign Secretary level—Dulles to Selwyn Lloyd—and that if Eden had gone to see Eisenhower earlier, the issue would have been brought to a head in September.[174]

Nor were diplomatic channels fully utilized. The U.S. embassy in London and the British embassy in Washington were largely out of the picture. Britain's ambassador, Sir Roger Makins, had shown so much sympathy for Washington and was so close to Dulles that his superiors thought he had "gone native" and thus discounted his warnings during the summer of 1956. Early in the fall, Makins left his post, and his successor, Sir Harold Caccia, arriving at the height of the November crisis, was made to wait six weeks before he could present his credentials. The U.S. ambassador to Britain, Winthrop Aldrich, provided little useful input to the crisis management process. Dulles and Eisenhower apparently paid little attention to his reports; British ministers, perceiving that Aldrich carried little weight in Washington, were not prone to share any secrets with him.[175]

In addition to underutilizing available communication channels, decision makers in Washington and London experienced strong domestic pressures that complicated crisis communication between the allies. Eisenhower was campaigning for re-election in November on the twin themes of "prosperity" and "peace." Eden, who had resigned from the cabinet in 1938 as a protest against Chamberlain's appeasement policy, was the architect of the 1954 troop withdrawal treaty with Egypt. As a result, he had become vulnerable and extremely sensitive to criticism from the conservative Suez Group for preferring appeasement to confrontation vis-à-vis Egypt.

These internal pressures were not fully and correctly perceived by the other ally. The U.S. policy makers seem to have believed that the rising press and parliamentary opposition against Eden would reinforce their own calls for restraint. Yet the main threat to Eden came from the right, not from the left; from hard-liners, not soft-liners. Rather than slow him down, opposition thus spurred him on. Similarly, British policy makers expected that concern for the Jewish vote would keep Eisenhower from punishing Israel before the presidential election. They also believed the U.S. could not help but draw a parallel between the Suez Canal and the Panama Canal. They were wrong on both counts.[176]

Finally, the lack of communication in critical stages of the crisis had to do with the "special relationship" between London and Washington:

> In an alliance such as this the membrane between sovereign states is paper-thin and porous. Transatlantic reticence is of a piece with reticence at home. For any word to friends across the ocean may come back to other ears at home. As well, a word to friends at home may skip across the water. The relationship is reciprocal. Either way the motive is the same; prudence counsels reticence.[177]

Turning from perceptions and communication difficulties to strategies for crisis management, we find the following pattern. Egypt, the original challenger, chose a strategy of controlled pressure in nationalizing the canal company. Nasser knew that Britain, France, and, to a lesser degree, the United States were committed to defend the status quo but believed it would be possible to erode or bypass their commitments. Through intelligence reports from Cyprus and Malta, Nasser knew that Britain was ill-prepared militarily for a quick invasion. Nasser's decision calculus has been described by Mohamed Heikal:

> He decided that however angry Dulles and the Americans might be they could not resort to force because that would show them as vindictive bullies, and in any case the Saudis would restrain them. The French were bogged down in Algeria and he did not think they would act unless the British did. He thought Israel would stay quiet because he knew that Ben-Gurion, though no doubt tempted to take some dramatic action, was still keen to be accepted as part of the Afro-Asian world—the role that had been denied him at Bandung—and would not wish to appear as the tool of Western imperialism. He calculated that Britain and France would certainly keep their distance from Israel for fear of fatally compromising their reputations in the Arab world.[178]

Nasser considered the first few weeks after the nationalization to be the most dangerous period. Thereafter, the risk of an armed attack on Egypt would steadily decline. By late October, he had every reason to believe that events were moving in accordance with his initial calculus.[179]

The Israeli-Anglo-French military operation, though masquerading as a defensive action to restore the status quo, was seen as most outside observers as an attempt to use an offensive *fait accompli* strrategy. The ultimate goal of the intervention was not to recapture the canal but to get rid of Nasser. Discussing alternative courses of action on October 24, the British cabinet spelled out the drawbacks of negotiations:

They could frame their demands is such a way as to make it impossible for the Egyptians to accept them—being resolved, on an Egyptian refusal, to take military action designed to overthrow Colonel Nasser's regime. Alternatively, they could seek the sort of settlement of the Canal issue which might be reached by negotiation—recognising that, by accepting such a settlement, they would abandon their second objective of reducing Colonel Nasser's influence throughout the Middle East.[180]

The cabinet recognized that a military operation "must be quick and successful." Otherwise, "international pressures . . . would develop against our continuance of the operation." Also, "its effect in other Arab countries would be serious unless it led to the early collapse of Colonel Nasser's regime."[181] The *fait accompli* strategy failed in all these respects: The eventual military action was anything but swift, Nasser was not overthrown, and the ensuing international pressures were led by the United States.

British decision makers apparently never gave serious consideration to the possible consequences of active U.S. opposition to the British military action.[182] The feeling of Anglo-Saxon affinity proved to be more burdensome than beneficial, reducing incentives to probe and ask searching questions.[183]

Having initially followed the strategy of buying time to explore a negotiated settlement, the United States now engaged in successful coercive diplomacy vis-à-vis its allies. Britain's vulnerability economically and in terms of public opinion contributed to the success of this strategy, as did the fact that the Anglo-French military operation was too sluggish and inefficient to accomplish a genuine *fait accompli*.

The belated Soviet intervention in the Suez Crisis was interpreted at the time as blackmail: Moscow demanded that the adversaries give up the invasion on pain of suffering serious punishment. In retrospect, the vague and imprecise nature of the threats makes the possible Soviet intervention look more like a limited reversible probe. At any rate, the Soviet bluff was never called. All the same, it had an indirect yet far from negligible effect, insofar as it was useful to the United States for putting pressure on Britain, France, and Israel.

The Suez pattern of strategies has recurred in other crises as well, especially in the Middle East: A *fait accompli*, created by U.S. clients, triggers Washington's use of coercive diplomacy; the effort to persuade U.S. clients to stop is aided by Soviet threats of questionable credibility.

Representing a rare incident of U.S.-Soviet collusion, the Suez Crisis was interpreted by many observers at the time as a first indication of nascent superpower condominium.[184] U.S.-Soviet collusion, however, was accidental rather than premediated. The Soviet bid for condominium—the call for joint U.S.-Soviet military intervention to defend Egypt—was categorically rejected by the United States.

Direct communication between the superpowers was rare throughout the crisis. Moreover, the "body language" of the two superpowers was still underdeveloped in 1956. In short, both were still novices at signaling.

Neither superpower was able to control the course of events leading up to the acute crisis. The eventual outbreak of hostilities took both by surprise. To both superpowers Suez brought home the need to control the regional actors, at the same time that it gave an early indication of their less than complete ability to do so.

As in the Arab-Israeli conflict of 1967, U.S. efforts to prevent escalation of the crisis to war failed because Washington's efforts to find a peaceful solution to the grievances of its allies proved unsuccessful. In 1967, some officials in Washington finally gave Israel an informal green light to resort to force; no such signals were sent in 1956, although British and French leaders, as a result of poor communication and wishful thinking, convinced themselves that the United States would condone their military action against Egypt.

U.S.-Soviet interaction was characterized by considerable caution and restraint after the outbreak of hostilities in 1956. The Soviet threats, for example, came only after Moscow was assured of the U.S. attitudes toward both the Hungarian and Suez crises.[185] The fact that the strategic doctrines of both superpowers at the time of the Suez Crisis were couched in terms of massive retaliation obviously narrowed the range of available instruments for crisis management. The United States and the Soviet Union alike were unprepared, intellectually as well as materially, for the limited employment of force. Fear of escalation prevailed, and the provocation threshold was still lower than that to which we have since become accustomed.

In short, considerable learning has occurred since the rather unsophisticated attempts at crisis management in 1956. The importance of signaling has gradually been recognized, the superpowers have learned to back their words by deeds, their repertoire of signaling instruments has progressively widened, and there has been a gradual improvement in the ability of each side to signal its own intentions and to understand the other's signals.

NOTES

1. Raymond Aron, *The Imperial Republic: The United States and the World 1945–1973* (Englewood Cliffs: Prentice-Hall, 1974), pp. 54–55.

2. Richard K. Betts, *Nuclear Blackmail and Nuclear Balance* (Washington, DC: Brookings Institution, 1987), p. 62.

3. Cf. Dwight D. Eisenhower, *Waging Peace 1956–1961* (Garden City, NY: Doubleday, 1965), p. 24; OIR Memorandum, Soviet Arms Offer to Egypt, September 6, 1955, p. 6 (*Declassified Documents*, 1976, No. 182E).

4. As quoted in Herman Finer, *Dulles over Suez* (Chicago: Quadrangle, 1964), p. 28.

5. Ole R. Holsti, "The Belief System and National Images: John Foster Dulles and the Soviet Union" (Ph.D. diss., Stanford University, 1962), pp. 89–90, 146.

6. Stephen E. Ambrose, *Eisenhower: The President* (New York: Simon & Schuster, 1984), p. 525.

7. Ibid., p. 317.

8. Robert Rhodes James, *Anthony Eden* (London: Weidenfeld & Nicolson, 1986), pp. 464–65.

9. Keith Kyle, "Britain and the Crisis, 1955–1956," in William Roger Louis and Roger Owen, eds., *Suez 1956: The Crisis and its Consequences* (Oxford: Oxford University Press, 1989), p. 103.

10. Cf. Sir Anthony Eden, *Full Circle* (London: Cassell, 1960), p. 138; Harold Macmillan, *Riding the Storm 1956–1959* (London: Macmillan, 1971), p. 104; Selwyn Lloyd, *Suez 1956: A Personal Account* (London: Jonathan Cape, 1978), p. 42.

11. Eden to U.S. envoy Robert Murphy, July 29, 1956, quoted in Robert Murphy, *Diplomat Among Warriors* (Garden City, NY: Doubleday, 1964), p. 381.

12. Lloyd, *Suez 1956*, p. 90.

13. Cf. Donald Neff, *Warriors at Suez* (New York: Simon & Schuster, 1981), pp. 204, 276-77; Lloyd, *Suez 1956*, p. 191; Eden, *Full Circle*, pp. 440-41.

14. As quoted in James, *Anthony Eden*, p. 525.

15. See, e.g., Anthony Nutting, *No End of a Lesson: The Story of Suez* (New York: Clarkson N. Potter, 1967), p. 22.

16. Kyle, "Britain and the Crisis," p. 111.

17. As quoted in Neff, *Warriors at Suez*, p. 280.

18. Cf. ibid., p. 161; Terence Robertson, *Crisis: The Inside Story of the Suez Conspiracy* (New York: Atheneum, 1965), p. 23.

19. Maurice Vaïsse, "France and the Suez Crisis," in William Roger Louis and Roger Owen, eds., *Suez 1956: The Crisis and its Consequences* (Oxford: Oxford University Press, 1989), pp. 138-39.

20. Neff, *Warriors at Suez*, p. 192.

21. See ibid., p. 190; Christian Pineau, *1956 Suez* (Paris: Robert Lamont, 1976), p. 93.

22. Vaïsse, "France and the Suez Crisis," p. 140.

23. Michael Brecher, *Decisions in Israel's Foreign Policy* (London: Oxford University Press, 1974), p. 244; cf. Neff, *Warriors at Suez*, p. 120.

24. See Moshe Dayan, *Diary of the Sinai Campaign* (New York: Harper & Row, 1966), pp. 5-6, 19. Israeli intelligence reports indicating that the Egyptian government did not support the fedayeen raids but did its best to curb infiltration were disregarded; see Raymond Cohen, "Israeli Military Intelligence before the 1956 Sinai Campaign," *Intelligence and National Security* 3, 1 (Jan. 1988).

25. Brecher, *Decisions in Israel's Foreign Policy*, p. 239.

26. Ibid., p. 258; Yaacov Bar-Siman-Tov, "Ben-Gurion and Sharett: Conflict Management and Great-Power Constraints in Israeli Foreign Policy," *Middle Eastern Studies* 24, 3 (July 1988).

27. Dayan, *Diary of the Sinai Campaign*, p. 53; Nutting, *No End of a Lesson*, pp. 86-87.

28. Brecher, *Decisions in Israel's Foreign Policy*, p. 235.

29. Mohamed H. Heikal, *Cutting the Lion's Tail: Suez Through Egyptian Eyes* (London: André Deutsch, 1986), p. 39.

30. Neff, *Wariors at Suez*, p. 33. Nasser told Cyrus Sulzberger: "Once I thought we could live in peace. I said to my troops and officers in Palestine that we must do our best to have peace in this area. But after the bloody Gaza incident, I felt responsible for the deaths of those men." (Quoted in ibid., p. 82.)

31. As quoted in Neff, *Warriors at Suez*, pp. 82-83.

32. Nikita S. Khrushchev, *Khrushchev Remembers* (Boston: Little, Brown, 1970), pp. 431, 432.

33. O. M. Smolansky, "Moscow and the Suez Crisis, 1956: A Reappraisal," *Political Science Quarterly* 80, 4 (Dec. 1965): 586.

34. Cf. ibid., p. 584.

35. Neff, *Warriors at Suez*, p. 39; Townsend Hoopes, *The Devil and John Foster Dulles* (London: André Deutsch, 1973), p. 221.

36. Cf. Neff, *Warriors at Suez*, pp. 142-48; Lloyd, *Suez 1956*, p. 257; Nutting, *No End of a Lesson*, pp. 52-53.

37. James, *Anthony Eden*, p. 446.

38. Ambrose, *Eisenhower*, p. 329; Hoopes, *The Devil and John Foster Dulles*, p. 331.

39. Eden, *Full Circle*, p. 421.

40. Lloyd, *Suez 1956*, pp. 41, 68–69.

41. Eisenhower, *Waging Peace*, p. 31; Finer, *Dulles over Suez*, p. 43.

42. Neff, *Warriors at Suez*, p. 258.

43. Mohamed H. Heikal, *The Rise and Fall of Soviet Influence in the Middle East* (New York: Harper & Row, 1978), p. 67; Heikal, *Cutting the Lion's Tail*, pp. 110–11.

44. Hoopes, *The Devil and John Foster Dulles*, p. 340.

45. Murphy, *Diplomat Among Warriors*, p. 377.

46. Neff, *Warriors at Suez*, p. 260; Hoopes, *The Devil and John Foster Dulles*, p. 340.

47. Eisenhower, *Waging Peace*, p. 33.

48. Eden, *Full Circle*, p. 422; cf. Lloyd, *Suez 1956*, pp. 69–71.

49. James, *Anthony Eden*, p. 452.

50. *Documents on International Affairs 1956* (London: Oxford University Press, 1959), pp. 69–70.

51. Neff, *Warriors at Suez*, p. 262.

52. Cf., e.g, Eisenhower, *Waging Peace*, pp. 31–32.

53. Robertson, *Crisis*, pp. 69–70.

54. Cf. Hoopes, *The Devil and John Foster Dulles*, pp. 341–42; Finer, *Dulles over Suez*, p. 52; Holsti, "The Belief System," pp. 169–70.

55. Murphy, *Diplomat Among Warriors*, p. 378.

56. Cf. Finer, *Dulles over Suez*, p. 47.

57. Murphy, *Diplomat Among Warriors*, p. 379; cf. Memorandum of Conference with the President, 8:30 AM, July 27, 1956 (*Declassified Documents*, 1981, No. 254B).

58. Nutting, *No End of a Lesson*, p. 11.

59. Neff, *Warriors at Suez*, pp. 281–82.

60. British Cabinet Minutes, 27 July, 1956, reprinted in David Carlton, *Britain and the Suez Crisis* (Oxford: Basil Blackwell, 1988), pp. 132–35. See also James, *Anthony Eden*, pp. 459–62.

61. Anthony Gorst and W. Scott Lucas, "Suez 1956: Strategy and Diplomatic Process," *Journal of Strategic Studies* 11, 4, (December 1988), pp. 399, 401.

62. Eden, *Full Circle*, p. 428.

63. Department of State, Incoming Telegram from Paris, 2:51 PM, July 27, 1956 (*Declassified Documents*, 1987, No. 1476).

64. James, *Anthony Eden*, p. 455.

65. Eisenhower, *Waging Peace*, p. 37.

66. Murphy, *Diplomat Among Warriors*, p. 379.

67. Ibid., p. 380; cf. Macmillan, *Riding the Storm*, pp. 104–5.

68. Macmillan, *Riding the Storm*, p. 105.

69. Eden, *Full Circle*, p. 436; cf. Lloyd, *Suez 1956*, p. 116.

70. Eisenhower, *Waging Peace*, pp. 664–65; James, *Anthony Eden*, pp. 471–73.

71. Eden, *Full Circle*, p. 437.

72. Eisenhower letter to Mollet, July 31, 1956 (*Declassified Documents*, 1981, No. 254C).

73. Memorandum, Discussion at the 295th Meeting of the National Security Council, Thursday, August 30, 1956, p. 1 (*Declassified Documents*, 1980, No. 381C).

74. Eden, *Full Circle*, p. 438.

75. James, *Anthony Eden*, p. 469.

76. Memorandum of Conference with the President, 5 PM, July 27, 1956 (*Declassified Documents*, 1981, No. 384B).

77. Eisenhower, *Waging Peace*, p. 44.

78. Ibid., p. 39.

79. Richard E. Neustadt, *Alliance Politics* (New York: Columbia University Press, 1970), p. 156, note 6.

80. Eisenhower, *Waging Peace*, p. 667.

81. Eden, *Full Circle*, p. 464.

82. Lloyd, *Suez 1956*, p. 76.

83. Eisenhower, *Waging Peace*, pp. 669–70, emphasis added.

84. Ibid., p. 670. Selwyn Lloyd (*Suez 1956*, p. 124) confirms that these statements were carefully noted by British policy makers.

85. *Documents on International Affairs 1956*, p. 203.

86. Eden's diary, as quoted in James, *Anthony Eden*, p. 501, emphasis added.

87. Macmillan's diary, as quoted in Alistair Horne, *Macmillan, 1894–1956* (London: Macmillan, 1988), p. 409.

88. *Documents on International Affairs 1956*, p. 214; cf. Eden, *Full Circle*, p. 482.

89. Eden, *Full Circle*, p. 484.

90. Ibid., p. 483; *Documents on International Affairs 1956*, pp. 215, 217; Nutting, *No End of a Lesson*, p. 62.

91. Nutting, *No End of a Lesson*, p. 62.

92. Eden, *Full Circle*, pp. 483–84.

93. See Lloyd, *Suez 1956*, p. 144.

94. Ibid., p. 152; Neff, *Warriors at Suez*, p. 320; Nutting, *No End of a Lesson*, p. 69.

95. Nutting, *No End of a Lesson*, p. 70.

96. Lloyd, *Suez 1956*, p. 154.

97. Finer, *Dulles over Suez*, p. 235.

98. *Documents on International Affairs 1956*, p. 203.

99. Ibid., p. 212.

100. James, *Anthony Eden*, p. 538.

101. Kyle, "Britain and the Crisis," p. 116.

102. Cf. Robertson, *Crisis*, p. 148; Nutting, *No End of a Lesson*, pp. 134–35, 140; Dayan, *Diary of the Sinai Campaign*, p. 160; James, *Anthony Eden*, pp. 507–9.

103. Lloyd, *Suez 1956*, pp. 184–87; Neff, *Warriors at Suez*, pp. 345–46.

104. Dayan, *Diary of the Sinai Campaign*, pp. 67, 70–71; Cohen, "Israeli Military Intelligence," p. 135.

105. Ambrose, *Eisenhower*, p. 353.

106. Dayan, *Diary of the Sinai Campaign*, pp. 71, 74; Neff, *Warriors at Suez*, pp. 355–56.

107. *Documents on International Affairs 1956*, pp. 263, 268.

108. Neustadt, *Alliance Politics*, pp. 23, 121.

109. Status Report on the Near East given by the CIA Director at the White House to a bipartisan Congressional group, November 9, 1956, p. 5 (*Declassified Documents*, 1978, No. 18A).

110. Allen Dulles, *The Craft of Intelligence* (New York: Signet, 1965), p. 157.

111. At one extreme, the claim has been made that the Anglo-French-Israeli plan "never was revealed to any American, privately or otherwise" (Murphy, *Diplomat Among Warriors*, p. 389). Others argue that the Americans were "privately informed of their general plans but not of any details" (John Ranelagh, *The Agency: The Rise and Decline of the CIA* [New York: Touchstone, 1987], pp. 299–300).

112. Ranelagh, *The Agency*, p. 300; Ambrose, *Eisenhower*, pp. 351, 356, 367; Neff, *Warriors at Suez*, pp. 333, 353.

113. Walter Laqueur, *A World of Secrets: The Uses and Limits of Intelligence* (New York: Hill & Wang, 1985), p. 123; Neff, *Warriors at Suez*, pp. 352–53.

114. Special National Intelligence Estimate, Number 30-5-56: "The Likelihood of a British-French Resort to Military Action against Egypt in the Suez Crisis," September 19, 1956, p. 1 (*Declassified Documents*, 1978, No. 9D).

115. Department of State, Memorandum of Dulles conversation with the President, October 21, 1956 (*Declassified Documents*, 1985, No. 277).

116. Heikal, *Cutting the Lion's Tail*, pp. 177–78.

117. Memorandum of Conference with the President, 7:15 PM, October 29, 1956, pp. 2, 5 (*Declassified Documents*, 1981, No. 385B).

118. Heikal, *Cutting the Lion's Tail*, p. 179.

119. Department of State, Outgoing Telegram to London, 12:09 PM, October 30, 1956 (*Declassified Documents*, 1984, No. 2556).

120. Memorandum of Conference with the President, October 30, 1956 (*Declassified Documents*, 1978, No. 450C).

121. Ambrose, *Eisenhower*, p. 354.

122. *Documents on International Affairs 1956*, p. 264.

123. Ibid., pp. 254–65.

124. See Diane B. Kunz, "The Importance of Having Money: The Economic Diplomacy of the Suez Crisis," in William Roger Louis and Roger Owen, eds., *Suez 1956: The Crisis and its Consequences* (Oxford: Oxford University Press, 1989), pp. 228–31; Carlton, *Britain and the Suez Crisis*, p. 76.

125. Horne, *Macmillan*, p. 439.

126. Macmillan, *Riding the Storm*, p. 157.

127. James, *Anthony Eden*, p. 544.

128. Neustadt, *Alliance Politics*, p. 21; Horne, *Macmillan*, pp. 420–22.

129. Lloyd, *Suez 1956*, p. 42.

130. Memorandum, Discussions at the 302nd Meeting of the National Security Council, Thursday, November 1, 1956, p. 5 (*Declassified Documents*, 1980, No. 384A).

131. Smolansky, "Moscow and the Suez Crisis," p. 603; Jon D. Glassman, *Arms for the Arabs: The Soviet Union and War in the Middle East* (Baltimore: Johns Hopkins University Press, 1975), pp. 19–20; Uri Bar-Joseph, "Soviet Intervention Threats in Short Arab-Israeli Wars: 1956, 1967, 1973 and 1982" (mimeo, Stanford University, 1987), p. 29.

132. Heikal, *The Rise and Fall of Soviet Influence*, pp. 70–71; Heikal, *Cutting the Lion's Tail*, pp. 192–93.

133. Cf. Hans Speier, "Soviet Atomic Blackmail and the North Atlantic Alliance," *World Politics* 9, 3 (April 1957), p. 318.

134. *Documents on International Affairs 1956*, pp. 291–92.

135. Francis Fukuyama, "Nuclear Shadowboxing: Soviet Intervention Threats in the Middle East," *Orbis* 25, 3 (Fall 1981), p. 582.

136. *Documents on International Affairs 1956*, p. 290.

137. Ibid., p. 289.

138. Fukuyama, "Nuclear Shadowboxing," p. 582.

139. Speier, "Soviet Atomic Blackmail," p. 320.

140. *Documents on International Affairs 1956*, p. 287.

141. Ibid., pp. 289, 291.

142. Heikal, *The Rise and Fall of Soviet Influence*, p. 69.

143. *Documents on International Affairs 1956*, p. 287.

144. Bar-Joseph, "Soviet Intervention Threats," p. 37.

145. *Documents on International Affairs 1956*, p. 293.

146. Cf. Speier, "Soviet Atomic Blackmail," p. 322.

147. Glassman, *Arms for the Arabs*, p. 16.

148. Cf. Eden, *Full Circle*, p. 555; Macmillan, *Riding the Storm*, p. 161; Lloyd, *Suez 1956*, p. 261.

149. Carlton, *Britain and the Suez Crisis*, pp. 78, 153–55.

150. Dayan, *Diary of the Sinai Campaign*, pp. 185–86.

151. Brecher, *Decisions in Israel's Foreign Policy*, pp. 284–85.

152. Ibid., p. 290.

153. Memorandum of Conference with the President, 5 PM, November 5, 1956 (*Declassified Documents*, 1987, No. 551); cf. Eisenhower, *Waging Peace*, p. 90.

154. Department of State, Incoming Telegram from Moscow, 10:44 AM, November 6, 1956 (*Declassified Documents*, 1987, No. 269).

155. Status Report on the Near East given by the CIA Director at the White House to a bipartisan congressional group, November 9, 1956, p. 7; cf. Department of the Navy, Office of the Chief of Naval Operations, Memorandum for the Joint Chiefs of Staff, November 13, 1956, p. 2 (*Declassified Documents*, 1978, No. 18A).

156. *Documents on International Affairs 1956*, p. 294.

157. Betts, *Nuclear Blackmail and Nuclear Balance*, p. 63.

158. John C. Campbell, "The Soviet Union, the United States, and the Twin Crises of Hungary and Suez," in William Roger Louis and Roger Owen, eds., *Suez 1956: The Crisis and its Consequences* (Oxford: Oxford University Press, 1989), pp. 248–49.

159. Ambrose, *Eisenhower*, pp. 268–69.

160. Cf. Betts, *Nuclear Blackmail and Nuclear Balance*, p. 64; Neff, *Warriors at Suez*, p. 413.

161. Eisenhower, *Waging Peace*, p. 91.

162. Brecher, *Decisions in Israel's Foreign Policy*, pp. 285–87.

163. Ibid., pp. 287–88.

164. As quoted in ibid., p. 290.

165. James, *Anthony Eden*, pp. 574–75.

166. James, *Anthony Eden*, p. 575; Robertson, *Crisis*, pp. 264–65.

167. Neustadt, *Alliance Politics*, p. 56.

168. See Alexander L. George, Chapter 4, in this volume.

169. Finer, *Dulles over Suez*, p. 494.

170. Horne, *Macmillan*, pp. 444–45.

171. Hoopes, *The Devil and John Foster Dulles*, p. 344.

172. As quoted in James, *Anthony Eden*, p. 593.

173. Ambrose, *Eisenhower*, p. 353.

174. Horne, *Macmillan*, p. 446.

175. Neustadt, *Alliance Politics*, pp. 130–31.

176. Ibid., pp. 21–22, 81–85.

177. Ibid., p. 65.

178. Heikal, *Cutting the Lion's Tail*, pp. 121–22.

179. Ibid., pp. 119, 175.

180. British Cabinet Minutes, 24 October 1956 (Confidential Annex), reprinted in Carlton, *Britain and the Suez Crisis*, pp. 145–46.

181. Ibid., p. 145.

182. Cf. Horne, *Macmillan*, p. 414; Carlton, *Britain and the Suez Crisis*, pp. 38–39.

183. Cf. Neustadt, *Alliance Politics*, p. 73.

184. See, e.g., Carsten Holbraad, *Superpowers and International Conflict* (London: Macmillan, 1979), p. 20. Such images of the crisis have lingered. For instance, Oran Young

(*The Politics of Force: Bargaining During International Crises* [Princeton: Princeton University Press, 1968, p. 55]) excludes Suez from his study of coercive crisis bargaining on the grounds that it was "characterized by effective, though tacit, Soviet-American coordination to guarantee the stability of the international system."

185. Smolansky, "Moscow and the Suez Crisis," p. 591.

CRISIS MANAGEMENT WITHOUT WAR

Introduction to Part Three

Alexander L. George

Three cases of war-threatening crises that did not result in war are examined in Part Three. Other serious diplomatic crises in which war was avoided include the Quemoy-Matsu Crisis of 1958 and the Berlin Crisis of 1961, but the three presented here suffice to provide evidence of the relevance of crisis management precepts under quite diverse circumstances.

The Sino-Soviet Crisis of 1969 is of particular interest in that it demonstrates very careful adherence to crisis management principles by both communist states. As Arthur A. Cohen notes, Mao Zedong employed a strategy of protracted attrition on the border, carefully circumscribing both its geographical scope and the means employed. The Soviets initially responded with a strategy of double doses of tit-for-tat; when this policy of limited retaliation did not suffice to persuade Mao Zedong to call off his challenge, Moscow resorted to a strategy of coercive diplomacy. It threatened a strike against China's nuclear weapons facility, and this seems to have persuaded Mao to desist.

Very strong incentives to avoid war present in all three cases undoubtedly motivated the two sides involved to actively seek opportunities for crisis management and to hone their skills for dealing with the confrontation without plunging into war. Clearly neither Mao nor Nikita Khrushchev wanted the border clash to escalate to a major war. In the Berlin Blockade case, M. Steven Fish notes that despite their deep-seated conflict of interests, both sides clearly wished to avoid a shooting war of any kind. The shared incentive to avoid war was particularly powerful in the Cuban Missile Crisis. The antipathy to war in this case, as we noted in the Introduction to Part Two, was much more powerful than it had been during the six-week crisis that culminated in World War I or in any of the other cases of inadvertent war we have examined. The *image of war* held in 1914 was that although war would be painful, it would certainly not be catastrophic. In contrast, the image of war in the 1962 crisis was that of a horrible thermonuclear holocaust.

In all three cases, opportunities for crisis management were available; they were highly valued and were not wasted but carefully cultivated. In the Cuban Missile Crisis, the United States conducted the blockade of Cuba to deliberately create pauses in the momentum of events in order to allow time for careful reflection and communication between John F. Kennedy and Khrushchev. In the Berlin Blockade

Crisis, the United States may have missed an early opportunity for a favorable settlement, and the two sides' mutual misperceptions did pose threats to crisis management. Several such threats also emerged in the Cuban Missile Crisis.

In general, however, in all three cases crisis bargaining between the two sides was conducted with considerable sensitivity to the importance of adhering to crisis management considerations. The risk of war inherent in Stalin's pursuit of ambitious objectives in the 1948 crisis was alleviated by considerable restraint in the means he employed. For its part, Washington rejected more forceful measures to break the Soviet blockade of ground access to West Berlin and improvised an unconventional strategy—the airlift—for supplying West Berlin.

Analysis of the behavior of the actors in all three cases reveals their considerable skill in adapting the operational requirements of crisis management to the specific geographical and political configuration of the crisis.

CHAPTER 10

The Berlin Blockade Crisis of 1948–1949

M. Steven Fish

The Soviet blockade of ground access to the Western sectors of Berlin in June 1948 marked the beginning of the first postwar crisis that carried a high risk of war between the superpowers. In Berlin, unlike earlier crises in Iran, Greece, and Turkey, the two sides clashed over control of territory to which each attached supreme importance, and Soviet and U.S. military forces stood face to face.

Examination of the case from the standpoint of crisis management and war avoidance raises several difficult questions. First, how did the two powers stumble into a hazardous situation that entailed a risk of war that neither side desired? Second, how did the United States recover from the miscalculations and perceptual errors of the period preceding the onset of the crisis and go on to formulate a novel strategy that led to an effective response to the Soviet challenge in Berlin? Finally, during the tense early months of the confrontation, how did the two sides overcome a number of serious impediments to effective crisis management and avoid the outbreak of armed hostilities?

OVERVIEW OF THE CRISIS

The breakup of the London Conference of Foreign Ministers in December 1947 signaled the demise of Allied cooperation in Germany. After the conference failed to produce agreement on Germany's future, Western leaders in London accelerated their plans for the creation of a West German state. In early 1948, Western military governors and German leaders began discussions on the unification of the Western zones and the establishment of a federal system of government. Predictably, the Soviet government strongly opposed Western policy, which it regarded as a violation of the existing agreement for a quadripartite system of control in Germany.

Tension between the Western powers and the Soviet Union over policy toward Germany had been building throughout 1947. The intensification of the Cold War, manifested in the Marshall Plan, the Truman Doctrine, and the creation of the Cominform, ensured that the administration of conquered territory would become a competitive rather than a cooperative venture. By the time of the abortive London conference, U.S. policy makers had come to view an economically revived West Germany, allied with the Western powers, as crucial to the economic revitalization and security of Western Europe. The Soviet Union regarded the creation of a West German state, free from quadripartite control, as entirely inimical to Soviet security interests.

In late February 1948, Soviet-backed forces seized power in Czechoslovakia. In London, Western officials redoubled their efforts toward the formation of a West German government and the inclusion of the new state in the European Recovery Program. In Berlin, Soviet authorities began demanding the right to board and inspect military trains traveling from the Western zones of Germany. On March 20, tensions came to a head in the Allied Control Council in Germany, when the head of the Soviet delegation, Marshal V. D. Sokolovsky, walked out of a meeting after asserting that the actions of the Western powers in their zones of occupation had rendered the council inoperative.[1] On March 31, the Soviet government announced that the activities of "subversive and terrorist elements" necessitated tighter regulation of traffic between Berlin and the Western zones and imposed a set of restrictions that reduced highway traffic into the city and cut off the movement of military trains between the city and the Western zones. When the U.S. military governor in Germany, Gen. Lucius Clay, sent several trains with armed guards toward Berlin with orders not to submit to inspection, the Soviets blocked their passage into the city. Clay responded, on his own initiative, by ordering a small-scale airlift to supply the needs of U.S. personnel in the capital and by halting all deliveries from the Western zones to the Soviet zone and other satellite countries. But the measures soon became unnecessary, as the Soviets lifted most restrictions on surface transport on April 12.[2]

During the next several months, U.S. policy makers pondered the significance of what has come to be referred to as the "baby blockade." Some officials, notably General Clay and his political advisor, Robert Murphy, believed that the Soviets intended to drive the Western powers out of Berlin. They argued vigorously against abandoning the city and urged Washington to devise a plan for the use of force in the event of future Soviet encroachments. In Washington, however, although Soviet action spurred a debate over the tenability of the Western position in Berlin, it failed to prompt a systematic reappraisal of alternative policies. The White House and the State Department gave little thought to the need for strategic planning and did not formulate an explicit commitment to West Berlin.[3]

The U.S. government was, therefore, scarcely prepared for the suspension of all rail passenger and freight traffic into Berlin that Soviet authorities put into effect on June 24. The immediate cause of the Soviet action was the decision of the Western powers to introduce currency reform into their own zones of occupation, including the Western sectors of Berlin. The deeper cause of the Soviet move was a hope that pressure on West Berlin might induce the Western powers to call off or modify their plans for unification and economic revitalization of the Western zones of occupied Germany. If this objective could not be achieved, the blockade might at least weaken or eliminate the Western position in Berlin.[4]

The blockade confronted the United States with an unattractive set of options. One was to withdraw from Berlin. A second option was to compromise with the Soviets on the London program and on currency reform. A third involved the use of an armed convoy to break the blockade. Clay and Murphy favored this option. The use of an airlift to circumvent the blockade of ground access represented a fourth alternative. Clay, on his own initiative, actually ordered an airlift on June 25 to supply the city with food and other critical supplies. Yet, Clay regarded this measure as a stopgap, time-buying response, not as a substitute for a decision on how the Western powers would ultimately deal with the blockade.[5]

During the first week of the crisis, President Harry S. Truman turned down Clay's call for an armed convoy and rejected the options of early withdrawal from Berlin or compromise on the London program. He endorsed the airlift, although like all policy makers in Washington, he shared Clay's skepticism regarding its long-term capacity for countering the blockade.[6] As the first step in an inchoate strategy of deterrence, Truman also ordered the transfer of two groups of B-29s—aircraft ostensibly capable of delivering atomic bombs—from North America to Britain on July 15.

During the fourth week of July, the U.S. commitment to Berlin began to solidify. At the National Security Council meeting of July 22, Clay, who returned to Washington in order to attend the meeting, reported that the airlift was now potentially capable of sustaining the Berlin population indefinitely. Truman endorsed Clay's request for an expansion of the airlift but rejected his idea of supplying Berlin by armed convoy. The meeting formalized what had been operational policy since the onset of the crisis in late June: to stand pat in Berlin and to supply the city entirely by means of an airlift.[7]

The next several months were filled with futile attempts by the Western powers to alter Soviet policy, first by means of direct approaches to Stalin and Soviet Foreign Minister Vyacheslav Molotov, and then in the forum of the United Nations. But the success of the airlift reduced time pressure and allowed the Truman administration to pursue its primary objective in Germany—the expeditious implementation of the London program—at the expense of an early settlement of the crisis in Berlin. The effectiveness of the counterblockade of the Soviet zone, which the Western powers had placed into effect following the imposition of the Soviet blockade in late June, contributed to the success of U.S. strategy. By the end of February 1949, it had cut off manufactured goods, chemicals, steel, and other essential products from Western Germany and had significantly reduced trade between Western Europe and Eastern Germany.[8]

The success of the airlift, the effects of the counterblockade, and the West's refusal to compromise on the formation of a West German state caused the Soviets to reconsider the utility of their policy in early 1949. In late January, after months of diplomatic impasse, Stalin indicated in an interview with a U.S. journalist a willingness to consider the removal of restrictions on access to Berlin, provided that the counterblockade was also lifted. Secret discussions between the U.S. and Soviet ambassadors to the United Nations ensued. On May 4, the two sides agreed to a mutual lifting of restrictions, and the Berlin Blockade Crisis came to a close.[9]

THE MAKING OF THE CRISIS: MISPERCEPTIONS, MISCALCULATIONS, AND MISSED OPPORTUNITIES

How did the United States and the Soviet Union stumble into a crisis that brought them to the brink of a war that neither desired? The conflict over Berlin and Germany as a whole was to some extent the product of deep-seated conflicts of interest between East and West. But it arose partly out of misperceptions and flawed policies. Why did earlier Soviet actions in Berlin, including the baby blockade of April 1948, fail to elicit a vigorous response on the part of U.S. policy makers? Rather than follow what amounted to a wait-and-see policy in Berlin during the first half of 1948, why did the United States not adopt and announce a formal commitment to West Berlin and then mount a strong effort to deter future Soviet pressure against the city or, alternatively, prepare for a negotiated, face-saving withdrawal on the best terms possible?

The failure to respond forcefully and imaginatively to Soviet encroachments prior to late June did not result from a lack of warning or from ambiguity in Soviet signaling. The baby blockade of early April by no means represented the first or the sole incident involving Soviet harassment of Western transport and communications; the Soviets had begun interfering occasionally with these at the beginning of the year.[10] After the baby blockade, the Soviets pursued a clear, deliberate, and graduated policy of pressure on Berlin. Some Soviet moves were explicitly timed as responses to Western actions. In the weeks preceding the imposition of the full blockade, for example, the Soviets imposed partial traffic restrictions immediately after the announcement by the Western powers of plans for currency reform in the Western zones of occupation.[11] Soviet behavior in the four-power Allied Kommandatura in Berlin during the first half of 1948 provided additional evidence of growing hostility. In early March, Murphy reported to Secretary of State George C. Marshall that the atmosphere of the quadripartite meetings of the Allied Control Council in Berlin had begun to deteriorate in mid-January, and that the Kommandatura had now reached the point where "agreement is impossible on even the most routine questions." The Soviet delegation now seized upon "every question on the agenda and every statement by any other delegation no matter how simple, how friendly, or how innocent, to launch violent propaganda attacks on the other three delegations."[12]

A significant change in Soviet tactics portending major Soviet action against Berlin might not by itself have prompted a vigorous U.S. response. The manner in which this information flowed upward and was interpreted by those who gathered it was also of crucial importance. Yet, examination of documentary evidence reveals no shortage of admonitions regarding Soviet intentions. As early as mid-December 1947, the CIA warned President Truman that the Soviets would likely use "every means short of war" to push the Western powers out of Berlin.[13] In early May, after the baby blockade, U.S. Army Intelligence reported that according to one of its sources, the Soviets intended to drive the Western powers out of Berlin by August, even at the risk of war, and that this would be accomplished by cutting off food supplies to the Western sectors.[14] Communications from Clay and Murphy to the Departments of State and the Army were replete with warnings. Immediately following the imposition of the baby blockade in early April, Clay told Gen. Omar

Bradley, army chief of staff, and Gen. Kenneth Royall, secretary of the army, that he considered the recent Soviet action only an early step in a determined campaign to drive the Western powers from Berlin. Both he and Murphy warned of the need for strategic planning and the potentially devastating consequences of forced withdrawal.[15]

Not all intelligence flowing to decision makers in Washington contained such caveats and predictions. Much of it showed little understanding of the significance of Soviet actions and little sensitivity to Soviet strategic calculations. Some reports from Moscow or from intelligence sources working in Berlin overestimated considerably the extent to which Soviet policy was motivated by a desire to gain a petty propaganda advantage or simply to irritate the Western powers. They neglected the possibility that the Soviets were pursuing a far more serious strategy: namely, a gradual, cautious, calculated probe intended to test the Western commitment to Berlin and to its larger German policy. This tendency was particularly pronounced in the information and estimates of Soviet intentions flowing to the State Department from Bedell Smith, the U.S. ambassador in Moscow.[16] Some intelligence estimates tended to minimize Soviet apprehensions over the formation of a West German state. As late as June 9—more than two months after the imposition of the baby blockade and the Soviet walkout from the Allied Kommandatura, and just two weeks before the imposition of the full blockade of ground access—the director of the CIA, Roscoe Hillenkoetter, informed Truman that the Kremlin was likely to delay any "countermoves" in Berlin or elsewhere in Germany "until [it] is convinced that the Western German organization is becoming a threat to Soviet foreign policy." He asserted that the Soviets would take "careful note" of the many difficulties the West would face in securing the necessary German cooperation and in "furnishing the new regime with proper political guidance and adequate and timely economic assistance."[17]

Ironically, while the CIA underestimated the extent to which the Soviet leadership regarded U.S. policy in Germany as a fundamental, immediate challenge to its supreme security interests, the agency may have overestimated the extent to which U.S. firmness, even in the absence of an explicit U.S. commitment to Berlin, was responsible for Soviet restraint. In mid-March, for example, two weeks before the imposition of the baby blockade, the CIA told Truman that "delay in the formation of a separate Eastern German Government and in Soviet attempts to force the Western Powers from Berlin has probably been caused in large measure by the firm attitude of US officials in Berlin." The CIA did not ignore the possibility that the Soviets might eventually take some action against Berlin. But its high estimation of the influence of U.S. officials in Berlin on Soviet calculations, coupled with its underestimation of the sense of threat that Soviet leaders may have experienced over Western plans for Germany, led it to produce analyses and predictions that encouraged complacency and inaction in Washington.[18]

The U.S. actions during the precrisis period suggest that decision makers in Washington accepted the latter, more sanguine assessments more readily than analyses, such as those issued by Clay's office, that offered graver and more urgent estimates of Soviet intentions. Records of conversations among top-level State Department officials, as well as the minutes of cabinet meetings, reveal that policy makers downplayed the significance of Soviet encroachments and failed to formulate contingency plans for a possible Soviet move against Berlin. Some assumed that if a major Soviet challenge to Western interests came in the near future, it would come in the Middle East or in Greece. The U.S. leaders tended to believe that the Soviets would regard bold actions in Europe as carrying an unacceptably high risk of war.[19]

Given some intelligence information that warned of possible Soviet moves against Berlin and urged a policy of bolstering deterrence, and other, more optimistic reports that encouraged complacency, why did officials in Washington opt for the latter? A number of baneful cognitive phenomena may have contributed to the failure to formulate an effective policy. The first is a type of wishful thinking that has been called "possibilistic thinking."[20] Here, U.S. leaders based their policies on an exaggerated estimation of the *probability* that the Soviets would respect their position in Berlin and recognize their commitment, though such an outcome was, at best, only a *possibility*. A propensity to overestimate one's own effectiveness may have also been at work in U.S. thinking.[21] CIA estimates that attributed Soviet restraint in the precrisis period to factors such as the "firm attitudes" of U.S. officials in Berlin may have found a receptive audience in President Truman, who throughout his presidency often regarded Soviet retreats or instances of restraint as the direct results of U.S. fortitude. He may have believed that Joseph Stalin was, at least for the time being, sufficiently impressed by U.S. "firmness" that a formal assertion of a commitment to Berlin was unnecessary. Truman may have assumed that the Soviets were well aware of the strong U.S. commitment to Berlin—even if most U.S. leaders were not. The recentness of Soviet retreats in Southern Europe and the Middle East in the face of U.S. resistance may have reinforced his views in this regard.[22]

Yet, one would expect such cognitive phenomena to operate only if U.S. leaders perceived the formulation of a firmer commitment as difficult and potentially costly. This indeed appears to have been the case. Even leaders who were inclined to resist Soviet challenges wherever they occurred feared that U.S. public opinion would not countenance risking conflict with the Soviet Union over Berlin. Secretary of State Marshall appeared to have been particularly concerned with the difficulties of securing public support for a commitment to Berlin and with the potential consequences of investing U.S. prestige in the city without strong public backing.[23] Army Chief of Staff Bradley shared Marshall's concerns. In mid-April, he told Clay that he doubted that the American people considered Berlin to be worth the risk of war and suggested that "we might ourselves announce withdrawal and minimize loss of prestige rather than being forced out by threat." Like Secretary of the Army Royall and other high military officials, Bradley was deeply skeptical of the military defensibility of West Berlin.[24] The positions of U.S. alliance partners also discouraged strong action. In mid-April, the U.S. embassy in London reported that British leaders believed it was only a matter of time before Western powers would have to leave Berlin and favored concentrating on developing Frankfurt as the future capital of a new West Germany. The French reportedly believed that the loss of Berlin would not represent a tragedy and opposed any actions or statements that might further invest Western prestige in the city.[25]

In sum, Washington's failure to respond effectively to Soviet actions in Berlin during the precrisis phase appears to have resulted from its overestimation of Soviet respect for, and awareness of, the U.S. commitment to Berlin, and its underestimation of the ability of the U.S. to form and sustain a genuine, defensible commitment. This inauspicious combination of overconfidence and insecurity begat a sluggish, ineffective policy that neither anticipated nor deterred the Soviet action of late June.

The Soviet decision to impose the full blockade of ground access to Berlin in June has been widely perceived as a tremendous blunder and miscalculation on the part of Stalin.[26] The outcome and aftermath of the crisis indeed demonstrated that Soviet policy hastened precisely what it sought to avert. Yet, from the perspective of Moscow in the spring of 1948, one might ask how Stalin might have better pursued his objective of checking the early formation of a West German state. That an attempt of *some* kind had to be made to block or slow Western plans was probably not a point of dispute among Soviet decision makers. The prospect of an economically revitalized West Germany, closely allied with Western imperialism, represented the least desirable of all possible developments; indeed, it threatened to annul the gains purchased with enormous sacrifices during the war against Hitler. The blockade—a limited, reversible action that did not necessitate the use of force— probably appeared to be a controllable, relatively low-risk strategy for providing leverage to pressure the West to abandon its new German policy. It doubtless appeared all the more attractive given the lack of an effective, concerted response by the Western powers to earlier probes. As Thomas C. Schelling has pointed out, if a commitment is ill-defined and ambiguous, a challenger will expect its opponent "to be under strong temptation to make a graceful exit (or even a somewhat graceless one) and he may be right."[27] The failure of Soviet leaders to anticipate the effectiveness of the airlift, moreover, was hardly surprising, as few if any Western policy makers envisaged the potential of the airlift prior to the onset of the crisis.

Yet, Stalin's decision to impose the full blockade of ground access was not necessarily made on the basis of a full and wholly accurate picture of his own capabilities or those of his German allies. In fact, some evidence suggests that the Soviets significantly underestimated the difficulties that the economy of the Eastern zone would encounter after being cut off from the West. According to a CIA memorandum to the president, dated June 30, 1948, and based on a "very reliable" source, Soviet occupation authorities in Germany had expressed shock after being informed by East German authorities of the probable consequences of a Western counterblockade of the Eastern zone. The memorandum stated that in a meeting on June 28 (four days after the imposition of the blockade), Soviet and East German officials had met to discuss the economic effects of the severance of transportation links with the West. The Soviet military governor reportedly showed "great consternation" at being informed of the likely devastating effects of the blockade on Eastern industry, stating that he had been led to believe that the Eastern economy could function normally without the West. The memorandum quoted the Soviet general in charge of trade and supply as stating that his government "would not have gone so far" had it realized the likely effects of a Western counterblockade.[28]

Did Sokolovsky inform Moscow of this discussion? Perhaps he did, and Stalin decided to press ahead with the blockade anyway. Western positions in Berlin were, after all, ostensibly more vulnerable to the effects of blockade than were industries in East Berlin, even if the East Germans were correct in their grim estimates. But the possibility remains that Stalin was not informed of proceedings of the conference, or at least did not receive fully candid and accurate reports. Hannes Adomeit has noted that in Stalin's Soviet Union, bad news was dispatched with fear and assessed with reservation.[29] Soviet officials in Germany may well have feared that they would be held responsible for failure to inform Moscow, before the blockade was imposed, of its probable economic consequences, and their (understandable) apprehensions might have affected the quality of intelligence flowing from Berlin to Moscow. The fearsome authority that Stalin exercised over his subordinates may have enhanced the ability of political authorities to maintain tight control over military options. But it also may have undermined the quality of information he received from the field and thus impeded rational decision making and reduced the flexibility and adaptiveness of Soviet policy.

THE ONSET OF CRISIS AND THE SELECTION OF STRATEGIES

The blockade in June forced U.S. leaders finally to face a number of acute policy dilemmas and gave rise to two debates within U.S. leadership. The first debate was over whether the United States should remain in Berlin and accept the risks involved in a policy of defiance. The second was concerned with how the United States could best protect its position in Berlin while minimizing the threat of war.

The first struggle pitted those who took a predominantly military view of the decision on whether to stay in Berlin against those who held a mainly political view of the crisis. The former held that the Western position in Berlin was so unfavorable that international political considerations would have to adjust to military and logistical reality. While aware of the possible political consequences of backing down in the face of aggression, they favored an early withdrawal from Berlin, or at least the formulation of a plan for withdrawal. They feared that a strong commitment would force the United States to risk and squander precious military resources in Europe, while raising the possibility of an unwinnable war over a small and extremely vulnerable piece of territory. This position was summarized succinctly by Adm. William Leahy, Truman's chief of staff, who noted in his diary during the first week of the crisis: "American military position in Berlin is hopeless because sufficient force is not available. . . . It would be advantageous to United States prospects to withdraw from Berlin." Many military planners in Washington, including Secretary of the Army Royall as well as some of General Clay's advisors, shared Leahy's pessimism.[30]

Officials who took a mainly political view of the crisis held that the United States could not quit Berlin without suffering an unacceptable loss of prestige. Clay and Murphy represented the strongest advocates of this position. According to Clay, Berlin had already become "a test of U.S. ability in Europe"; no military disadvantage could justify voluntary withdrawal. According to Murphy, such action "would be the Munich of 1948" and would "raise justifiable doubts in the minds of Europeans as to the firmness of our European policy and of our ability to resist the spread of Communism, especially in central Europe."[31]

The second debate occurred among leaders who took this second, predominantly political view of the need to resist the Soviet challenge. It was here that the tension often experienced in crisis management between "military logic" and the requirements of diplomacy, discussed in Chapter 3, appeared most clearly and acutely. The first tendency, which was dominated by a concern for military logic, sought above all to assert Western rights in Berlin as forcefully and expeditiously as possible; to resupply Berlin quickly and open reliable transport channels from the Western zones to the Western sectors of Berlin; and to test Soviet resolve and—if possible— force the Soviet Union to abandon its policy of pressure. Opposed to this was a second set of concerns, stemming from sensitivity to the requirements of diplomacy, which sought to avoid any movement of forces that might bring them into conflict with Soviet forces, thus leading to war; to leave open an avenue for negotiated settlement, or possibly a face-saving retreat by the adversary; and to avoid actions that might strain relations with allies by exposing them to undue dangers of war.

The first position was held by the top U.S. officials in Germany, Clay and Murphy. In accord with the military logic that predominantly influenced their selection of strategies (though both men held intensely political rather than military conceptions of the crisis itself), Clay and Murphy advocated breaking the blockade with the movement of an armed convoy from Western Germany to the western sectors of Berlin. During the early weeks of the crisis, Clay repeatedly urged Washington to authorize the planning of this action and to inform the Soviets that it would be carried out at an early date.[32] Furthermore, he sought to obtain standing orders that would allow him to control personally the organization and timing of the movement of the convoy.[33] While awaiting authorization from Washington, Clay ordered his staff to draw up plans for the convoy. By mid-July, Clay's military staff had drawn up an elaborate plan for breaking the blockade by force, which included not only the movement of a convoy but also a contingency option for bombing Soviet airfields in East Germany and Soviet troops engaged in enforcing the blockade.[34]

The requirements of diplomacy figured more prominently in the thinking of other policy makers and analysts. Ambassador Smith warned that the movement of an armed convoy would be a challenge to Soviet prestige. It could, therefore, easily lead to "a little shooting," which might escalate to war.[35] Many military planners in Washington shared Smith's fears.[36] Moreover, even before a final decision had been reached on Clay's proposal for an armed convoy, his superiors in Washington displayed a preference for rules of engagement characterized by "positive command" rather than "command by negation" when dealing with the impatient, strong-minded military governor. During the first week of the crisis, Clay was forbidden to make any statements referring to the possibility of war over Berlin, and, in mid-July, General Bradley reminded him that any decision to use armed convoys "can obviously be taken only at the highest level."[37]

The debates discussed above were not settled definitively during the first few weeks after the imposition of the blockade, but the major decisions taken during this crucial early stage did determine to a large extent the course of U.S. policy for the remainder of the crisis. Truman's decision to stay in Berlin, which was announced by Marshall on June 30 and confirmed publicly by the president two days later, represented a victory for those who viewed the crisis through political rather than military lenses.[38] The announcement did not represent an irrevocable pledge to remain in the city at any cost, but it did begin a process of formal commitment that would solidify over the coming weeks.[39] In fact, despite the lack of a genuine commitment to Berlin before the onset of the crisis, a consensus emerged among top civilian policy makers during its early days that an early withdrawal would carry an unacceptable political cost. Truman, who later noted that he had regarded the Soviet move on Berlin as an integral part of Moscow's plan to extend its control over all of Germany, and eventually all of Europe, never seems to have seriously entertained the idea of withdrawal, despite the tenuousness of the U.S. military position.[40]

Yet, Truman and Marshall heeded scrupulously the requirements of diplomacy and war avoidance in their selection of crisis management strategy and in their implementation of policy. They rejected Clay's call for an armed convoy and insisted on maintaining control over any military movements that carried the risk of armed hostilities. In a note of June 27 to the U.S. ambassador to Great Britain, Marshall insisted that U.S. strategy would be "unprovocative" as well as "firm," and the administration's early, critical decisions seemed to verify the sincerity of Marshall's intentions.[41]

The decision to supply the city by air served as the centerpiece of the administration's firm but unprovocative policy. During the early weeks of the crisis, however, the airlift was not regarded as a long-term strategy capable of achieving Western objectives but rather as a scheme that would buy time for strategic planning and for a diplomatic approach to the Soviet Union. No one believed that the airlift would prove capable of supplying all of Berlin's inhabitants indefinitely.[42] In a National Security Council (NSC) meeting of July 15, air force officials termed the operation a "failure"; Undersecretary of State Robert Lovett described it as an "unsatisfactory expedient" and maintained that the Soviets were well aware of this fact.[43] Only after the NSC meeting of July 22, as noted above, at which Clay offered an optimistic estimate of the ability of the airlift to supply West Berlin, and Truman authorized its expansion and rejected the use of an armed convoy, did some U.S. leaders begin to conceive of the operation as part of a viable strategy for breaking the blockade.[44]

Truman's endorsement of the airlift and rejection of an armed convoy were not based solely on what he perceived as the diplomatic exigencies of the crisis. Truman also regarded a movement of convoys as militarily unsound. After the NSC meeting of July 22, he told Clay privately that his military chiefs had convinced him that the convoy idea was a bad one.[45] General Bradley later recalled that he had advised against the movement of an armed convoy not only because it "might be opposed by armed force, which of course would be war," but also because "they could stop you in so many ways short of armed resistance. . . . A bridge could go out just ahead of you and then another bridge behind you, and you'd be in a hell of a fix. . . . The Russians could have embarrassed us on the airlift too, but it would be harder to do, short of war, than with a convoy, we thought."[46] Indeed, two disparate and competing military logics appear to have been at work during the early weeks of the crisis, one of which guided the thinking of the military governor in Germany and a second that influenced his superiors in Washington. The second, of course, was far more acceptable to those whose selection of a strategy was predominantly based on the diplomatic requirements for war avoidance.

Yet, while he shunned action that could lead to combat between U.S. and Soviet forces, Truman endorsed two major noncombat actions by U.S. military forces. The first was the transfer of B-29 bombers from North America to Great Britain in mid-July. The action moved the atomic bomb to the center of U.S. military policy well before the administration had integrated it into a coherent strategy of deterrence. Evidence now available reveals that none of the planes carried atomic weapons or was even equipped to do so.[47] Which U.S. officials were aware of this fact is still not known. But the transfer of the B-29s signaled to both the Soviets and to Europeans the U.S. willingness to exploit its nuclear monopoly for the purpose of deterring Soviet escalation of the crisis. The extent to which U.S. strategic power moderated Soviet behavior, or even whether or not the Soviets were aware of the bombers' lack of capability, must be left to question. But the Soviets clearly were sensitive to the U.S. nuclear monopoly, and the transfer of bombers may have helped discourage Stalin from exploiting his conventional superiority in a manner that could have led to escalation of the conflict.[48]

Effective management of the bomb meant striking a balance between several objectives. First, the United States sought to demonstrate resolve, deter escalation, and neutralize the coercive power inherent in the Soviet blockade of the Western sectors. Against these strategic objectives, it had to balance a fundamental require-ment of crisis management—namely, to avoid military threats and moves that give the opponent the impression that one is about to resort to large-scale warfare, thereby forcing him to consider preemption. If the B-29 transfer had caused Stalin to believe the United States was planning a strike against the Soviet Union—or even the threat of such a strike—in order to break the blockade, he might have moved forces quickly into Berlin and mobilized for war. Sensitivity to the require-ments of effective crisis management may have contributed to the nonprovocative manner in which the bombers were transferred to Britain. Rather than execute the transfer with fanfare or threats, the administration described it publicly as a routine training mission.[49] The bombers' actual lack of atomic capability may also have heightened the administration's desire to carry out the operation in a manner that would draw some attention, but not too much. Finally, considerations of public opinion may have influenced U.S. policy. The desire to impress the Soviets had to be balanced against the need to avoid action that public opinion—U.S. as well as British—might construe as provocative.[50]

In sum, Truman employed the bomb as a deterrent but not as an instrument of coercive diplomacy. This strategy enhanced the credibility of U.S. commitments in Germany while heeding the requirements for effective crisis management. Yet, by shunning any military action designed to compel a Soviet retreat, Truman tacitly accepted a protracted, nonviolent war of attrition in Berlin. The counterblockade, in fact, served as the only element of U.S. strategy that included a coercive component, and it eventually forced upon the Soviets an element of time pressure that the airlift and the B-29 transfer alone were incapable of exerting. It was entirely consistent with both diplomatic requirements for crisis stability and the need to build some coercive counterpressures. But the counterblockade was essentially a defensive measure, and its effects were felt only gradually. At no time did it function as a genuine compellant, with the potential effectiveness—and dangers—involved therein.

Explaining the bases for disparities in the positions of U.S. decision makers on the selection of strategies poses a difficult task. Divisions did not occur clearly along civilian-military lines. Both Clay, the general, and Murphy, the diplomat, held intensely political views of the nature of the crisis, yet both prescribed policies that were dominated by a military logic. Military planners in Washington, including the Joint Chiefs of Staff, held a more military perspective of the nature of the crisis. Like Clay and Murphy, their policy prescriptions were driven by a military logic, but it was a military logic of a very different kind: While Clay urged the use of military forces to exert coercive pressure on the adversary and break the blockade, and planned offensive operations to achieve these political ends, military planners in Washington stressed the need to reduce the vulnerability of U.S. forces and avoid commitments that might weaken U.S. defensive capabilities in the event of war with the Soviet Union.[51] Like Clay and Murphy, Truman and Marshall—the key civilian policy makers (although the secretary of state was, of course, also a general)—viewed the crisis in political terms, but they rejected aspects of the military logic that informed Clay's choice of strategies. In fact, the reactions of leaders to the Soviet challenge probably derived more from their basic belief systems and cognitive dispositions than from "where they sat."

J. Philip Rogers's "crisis bargaining codes," discussed by him in Chapter 18, may help provide a richer understanding of the debates over selection of strategies. Rogers includes in his codes decision makers' beliefs regarding the optimal mixture and timing of coercive and accommodative strategies. He groups his codes into four types. Two of these, Types A and B, are particularly relevant to how U.S. officials perceived and coped with the Soviet challenge in Berlin. Both Type A and Type B policy makers perceive the adversary as aggressive in its objectives, and neither is likely to view the opponent's actions as the products of legitimate defensive concerns. Yet, crucial differences exist in how policy makers of these two types regard crisis dynamics. Type As believe that crisis escalation is easily controlled and reject the concept of inadvertent war. They usually shun bargaining and prefer dramatic coercive action as the best means for resolving crises. Type B policy makers have less faith in their own abilities to prevent dangerous escalation. They fear that interaction with the adversary may lead to a spiral over which they might, after a certain point, lose control. Type B policy makers, therefore, are particularly concerned to avoid moves that might lead to inadvertent escalation. Some type Bs, however, hold that bluffs and nuclear threats may be employed with little risk of escalation, provided these are taken early enough in the crisis. They believe that a nuclear war is less likely to occur as a result of a nuclear alert—a measure over which leaders can maintain tight control—than through unintended conventional conflict.[52]

Clay and Murphy provide nearly perfect examples of Type As. They held that the movement of an armed convoy—a bold stroke that risked conventional combat with Soviet forces—did not necessarily carry a risk of dangerous escalation. Truman and Marshall, on the other hand, were Type B policy makers. Their rejection of Clay's advice reflected beliefs that any attempt to break the blockade by force carried an unacceptable risk of war. Yet, their decision to transfer the B-29s to Britain shortly after imposition of the blockade indicated to the Soviets the willingness of the United States to consider the use of atomic weapons to deter a Soviet military takeover of Berlin. Truman held the beliefs, which Rogers says are typical for many Type Bs, that it may be dangerous to appear unwilling to use nuclear weapons and that sometimes one can effectively threaten action one has no intention of carrying out.[53] An NSC paper, approved by Truman in September 1948, asserted that the Soviets should "never be given the slightest reason to believe that the U.S. would even consider not to use atomic weapons against them if necessary." Demonstration of reluctance might "provoke exactly that Soviet aggression which it is fundamentally U.S. policy to avert."[54] In Truman's mind, the bomber transfer, coupled with the airlift strategy, allowed the United States to exploit its nuclear monopoly for deterrence purposes while minimizing the threat of escalation.

Discussion of strategic choices to this point has focused on the U.S. side. The Soviet Union, of course, also undertook a process of selecting a strategy, although its decision to impose a full blockade of ground access in late June in some respects represented only the logical culmination of a policy that had been developing for several months. The imposition of the full blockade did, however, provoke the onset of a full-blown superpower crisis and did signal some shift in Soviet strategy. Until late June, the Soviets engaged in a controlled, reversible probe in their approach to Berlin. Their policy was motivated by three basic objectives: to ascertain and force some clarification of the West's commitment to Berlin; to signal their displeasure with the organization of a West German state; and to weaken the Western powers' strategic positions in Berlin. As a CIA report of early June noted, Soviet restrictions to date had greatly reduced the strategic value of the city to the United States, particularly its utility as a center for the gathering of intelligence and dissemination of Western propaganda, and as a sanctuary and transfer point for anticommunist refugees and Soviet army deserters, although the U.S. logistic position had not been seriously impaired.[55]

The imposition of the full blockade, however, signaled a shift in goals and an alteration of strategy. Now, rather than merely registering its opposition to the London program, the Soviet Union employed a strategy of coercive diplomacy in order to pressure the West into abandoning or deferring it. Rather than challenging the U.S. strategic position and forcing it to clarify its commitment to the city, the Soviets now attempted to undermine its logistic position and drive the U.S. out. As the U.S. commitment to remaining in Berlin took shape and solidified during the early weeks of the crisis, what Moscow had begun as a tentative, limited probe assumed the character of a strategy of controlled pressure against the Western position in Berlin. The Soviet Union now exploited fully its overwhelming logistical and geographical advantages in Berlin, although it continued to eschew forceful, high-risk actions in favor of reversible, nonmilitary impingements.

STRATEGIC INTERACTION:
THE DYNAMICS OF WAR AVOIDANCE

Oran Young has noted that the problem of balancing considerations of prudence and demonstration of resolve was simplified in the Berlin case by the fact that the basic tactical patterns of the crisis were established early on and, for the most part, were allowed to run their course.[56] Yet, the process of strategic interaction did carry a significant risk of war, and a number of obstacles to effective crisis management and resolution surfaced during the long months of the protracted crisis.

Several of the factors that threatened to complicate peaceful resolution of the crisis grew directly out of the strategies chosen by the two sides during the initial weeks of the confrontation. The Soviet decision to impose a full blockade of ground access and to demand that the Western powers reconsider their plans for a West German state or face an erosion of their positions in Berlin appeared to leave the West with no peaceful way out of the crisis that was compatible with its fundamental interests—a highly risky strategy on the Soviets' part from the standpoint of effective crisis management. Only when the airlift began to prove its capacity for circumventing the blockade without resort to force did the immediate threat of war begin to subside.[57]

The airlift strategy eventually enabled the Western powers to transfer back to the Soviet Union the decision of whether to escalate or accept defeat.[58] But the very effectiveness of the airlift, combined with the B-29 bomber transfer, also carried potential costs and hazards of its own. Most significantly, it contributed to the development of a highly intransigent U.S. negotiating position. By the time the West began negotiations with Stalin and Molotov at the end of July, the airlift had demonstrated its surprising capacity for supplying Berlin's inhabitants (although some policy makers remained skeptical of its long-term viability), and the B-29 transfer had been executed successfully. In negotiations with the Soviets, the United States, although willing to consider some compromise on minor issues relating to currency reform, demonstrated complete inflexibility on the broader issue of the organization of a West German state. On August 3, in discussions between Stalin and representatives of the three Western governments, Stalin actually offered to back away from his original condition that the Allies defer a decision on implementation of the London accords. In his account of the meeting, Ambassador Smith noted that Stalin admitted that this requirement had put the Western governments in a "difficult position." The Soviet leader therefore stated that he was prepared to lift the blockade if the Western powers would agree to a communiqué that would record opposition to the London decisions as "the insistent wish of the Soviet Government." Stalin's remarks actually led Smith to conclude that Stalin and Molotov were "undoubtedly anxious for a settlement."[59] The United States, however, was unwilling to consider even this offer: In their proposed joint announcement, communicated to the Soviets on August 6, the Western powers omitted reference to Stalin's "insistent wish," causing Molotov to claim that the proposal was completely different than the "agreed decision" produced three days before.[60] The episode recurred several weeks later, when Stalin attempted to secure the incorporation of his objection to the London agreements in a joint proposal, and the Western powers refused the inclusion of such an item.[61]

Was Stalin sincerely prepared to lift the blockade in early August in exchange for mere Western recognition of his opposition to the formation of a West German state? Did he realize the potential of the airlift, feel his options constrained by the B-29 transfer, and therefore seek an early end to the crisis, roughly on Western terms? Perhaps not: His negotiating strategy throughout August was characterized by inconsistency and oscillation, leading many U.S. policy makers and, later, scholars to the conclusion that he was confident in the eventual effectiveness of the blockade and was merely trying to wear down and confuse Western leaders. Some speculated that Stalin toughened his stance after encountering opposition in the Politburo to an agreement to lift the blockade without obtaining substantial Western concessions. The hardening of the Soviet position, and Stalin's apparent loss of interest in a negotiated settlement in September, reinforced U.S. policy makers' beliefs in the accuracy of their assessments.[62] But it is noteworthy that Stalin did not seem to lose interest in a negotiated settlement until after the West on several occasions rejected his requests that his opposition to the London program be acknowledged and after the German Constituent Assembly began its work in Bonn on September 1.

Whether or not a more accommodating Western response to Stalin's offer would have led to an early, favorable (from the Western view) cessation of the crisis must be left to question. The point here is that the Western powers never attempted to find out, precisely because they could afford not to. By the time the United States referred the case to the United Nations in late September, U.S. leaders were resolved to avoid any compromise whatever in Berlin—provided, of course, that the airlift proved able to sustain the Berlin population through the winter. In January 1949, after the operation overcame decisively a number of serious obstacles created by bad weather conditions, the U.S. government decided to proceed with currency reform in the Western zones, although the British and the French feared that such a move would slam the door on ever reaching a final settlement in Berlin.[63] By late January, the Americans were discussing their policy in the United Nations in terms of creating an "impression of reasonableness" without giving an inch on matters of substance.[64] In sum, although the spectacular success of the U.S. strategy of supplying Berlin by air and reinforcing deterrence by means of the B-29 transfer enabled the United States to avoid both war and concessions, it also reduced U.S. flexibility and enabled the United States to ignore opportunities that may have— although this is by no means certain—made possible an early, favorable settlement of the crisis.

The U.S. intransigence may, in fact, have been rooted in a perception that the United States had to "win" the battle for Berlin, not just bring it to a close at the earliest possible date. For even if they could have achieved a lifting of travel restrictions without granting substantial concessions as early as August 1948, U.S. leaders were well aware that Stalin could simply reimpose the blockade at a time of his own choosing, possibly after finalization of plans for implementation of the London accords.[65] They may have been correct in assuming that the Soviets had to be convinced that reimposing the blockade entailed substantial economic and political costs. Only by outlasting Stalin—by supplying the Western sectors by air while waiting patiently for the counterblockade to squeeze the economy of the Eastern zone—could the United States feel certain that it had achieved its primary objective in the crisis.

In addition to these factors that grew out of the two sides' selections of strategies, a number of mutual misperceptions and counterproductive cognitive tendencies threatened the successful management of the crisis. One such problem concerned U.S. estimations of Soviet risk-taking strategy. Clay and Murphy in particular assumed that Soviet leaders had decided before they imposed the blockade whether or not they intended to go to war. Their understanding of Soviet strategy led them to assume, as Murphy asserted in a note of July 13, that the sending of an armed convoy involved no more risk than the mere decision to stay in Berlin.[66] If the Soviets had decided on war, it would come regardless of whether or not the United States challenged the blockade by force; if they had decided against war, it would not break out in any case. Clay provided a particularly bald statement of this view in a note of July 10 to General Bradley: "If the USSR does intend war, it is because of a fixed plan. Hostilities will not result because of action on our part to relieve the blockade unless there is such a fixed plan."[67]

Such reasoning may have represented a particularly clear example of a failure by U.S. leaders to understand Soviet styles of risk-taking—in particular, they tended to interpret Soviet behavior according to their own approach to risk calculation, and they failed to appreciate the Soviet tendency to distinguish between long- and short-term risks.[68] The U.S. approach may have also resulted from a common cognitive tendency to regard one's adversary as more unified, deliberate, and purposive than may actually be the case. Rather than regard an opponent's actions as contingent or improvised, actors may view them as invariably the product of well-laid plans.[69] Whatever the bases for the thinking of the top U.S. officials in Germany, their policy recommendations in retrospect were imprudent from the standpoint of effective crisis management. The assumption that the consequences of one's actions are out of one's own hands, but are preordained by the adversary's plans, is not always a strong basis for responsible policy making. Yet, since calls by Clay and Murphy for an armed convoy were rejected by decision makers in Washington, their policy prescriptions never posed more than a potential threat to effective crisis management. Had Truman and Marshall opted for a relationship with them based purely on "command by negation"—that is, command based on looser control, in which Washington allowed Clay the freedom to pursue his own strategy and intervened only after the fact—the outcome of the crisis may have been quite different.

In addition to misunderstanding Soviet risk management strategy, some U.S. leaders may have erred seriously in their estimates of the motivations that underlay Soviet policy. They appear to have projected some of their own motivations onto the adversary and analyzed Soviet behavior from the perspective of their own concerns. The tendency to assume that the Soviets were as strongly motivated as were the Americans by considerations of prestige and reputation was particularly evident throughout the crisis. The U.S. decision to remain in Berlin following the onset of the crisis was motivated primarily by prestige considerations, specifically by a desire to avoid the political and psychological damage that might result from leaving the city under pressure. Few U.S. policy makers regarded the Western portion of Berlin, a small piece of territory buried deep inside territory occupied by the adversary, as in itself worth the risk of war. Early in the crisis, the Soviets suggested informally that they might be willing to trade territory in Thuringia or Saxony for West Berlin. From a strictly geopolitical standpoint, such a deal might have offered the United States a number of advantages. But U.S. leaders feared that such an arrangement would undermine U.S. prestige in the eyes of Germany and all of Western Europe—a price they were not willing to pay.[70] As the State Department's Policy Planning staff noted in November 1948, U.S. policy was not, and could not be, based on immediate, practical strategic considerations but rather on maintaining Europeans' confidence in the United States. The situation illustrated "one of the great imponderables of foreign policy: an emotional factor which may bear little logical relation to practical considerations involved but which is of major, and unanswerable, importance."[71]

The U.S. sensitivity to subjective, emotional, and symbolic concerns of prestige and reputation did not, in itself, hinder effective management of the crisis. But U.S. leaders tended to assume that Soviet policy was also motivated primarily by such considerations. At a number of points during and before the crisis, U.S. officials' decisions were influenced strongly by how they believed their actions would affect Soviet prestige interests. In late July, Marshall rejected a public campaign against Soviet policy, arguing that a direct approach should be made to Stalin prior to the dispatch of a formal note in order to avoid "elevat[ing] the matter further into the realm of prestige considerations." He told Lewis Douglas, U.S. ambassador to the United Kingdom, that "we do not feel, up to the present, that the Soviet Government has committed itself so irretrievably to maintain the blockade to preclude the possibility of some face-saving retreat on their part." Marshall argued that the Soviets' action in Berlin was motivated by the recent loss of face they had suffered in Italy, France, Finland, and Yugoslavia; if a face-saving revocation of the blockade could be arranged, an early end to the crisis might even be possible.[72]

But subjective factors, such as a concern for prestige interests, may have played a less central role in Soviet policy than U.S. leaders tended to assume. The Soviets did impose the blockade under the pretext that traffic restrictions were due to "technical difficulties," which seemed to imply a desire to leave open the possibility of retreat without loss of face. But Soviet policy may have also been aimed at dividing or confusing the Western powers or minimizing the risks of Western overreaction to Soviet pressure. Even if prestige considerations influenced the manner in which the Soviets imposed the blockade, their calculations of their own prestige interests may have differed greatly from the way the United States calculated its own. Most analyses of the motivations that underlay Soviet foreign policy during the Stalin period must rest on conjecture. Yet, some evidence suggests that Stalin, and indeed most Soviet leaders, often seemed to believe that the superpowers and their allies were quite capable of deducing capabilities and probable behavior from the military balance. Demonstration of resolve for the purpose of impressing the adversary and third countries might have been, in Soviet eyes, neither necessary nor particularly effective.[73]

Disparities in alliance structures and in foreign policy priorities may have helped create differences in the ways in which the superpowers calculated their prestige interests. The Truman administration's policy during the crisis was strongly influenced by a desire to maintain the U.S. standing in the eyes of Germans and

Europeans in general. On the other hand, it is doubtful that Soviet policy was greatly affected by concerns for how the Germans, Poles, or Italians would view the outcome of the crisis. The U.S. policy makers and analysts may not have been aware of this possibility. A week after the onset of the crisis, a CIA report to the president cautioned that the Soviets would not likely revoke the blockade at an early date, for "it is difficult to see how they could back down without a maximum loss of face even in their own camp."[74] One may question, however, whether the Soviets were as concerned as the United States, or needed to be as concerned, with earning prestige and good will in "their own camp" and in Germany.

The U.S. tendency to assume that the Soviets calculated their prestige interests in much the same way as the United States may have blurred U.S. officials' understanding of Soviet policy. Their hypersensitivity to Soviet prestige concerns and tendency to regard every Soviet move in terms of Soviet concerns with appearances, "face," and propaganda advantage, were accompanied by a disinclination to consider the possibility that the adversary may have been motivated primarily by the simple, strategic, objective goal of checking the revival of German economic and military power. Indeed, U.S. decision makers seemed at times utterly incapable of grasping this possibility. As late as September 9, for example, after weeks of negotiations in which the Soviets stated clearly and repeatedly the basis for their decision to blockade Berlin—that is, their objection to the London agreements on the organization of a West German state free from quadripartite control—Undersecretary of State Lovett noted with frustration in a National Security Council meeting that the United States had to "find out what [the Soviet Union's] real intentions are." Truman, according to the minutes of the meeting, concurred.[75] The misperception that may have arisen from such incomprehension helped foreclose an early resolution of the crisis by reducing the quality of communication between the two sides and hindering the search by U.S. policy makers for mutually acceptable terms for settlement.

Like the Americans, the Soviets may also have projected their own attitudes toward prestige and reputation on the adversary. By late August, Stalin seemed willing to let the blockade run its course, despite the proven capability of the airlift and growing Western determination. He may have been late to realize the airlift's potential; his patience and lack of eagerness to settle may have been based on U.S. intransigence and an assumption that the airlift could not sustain Berlin's population through the winter. Yet perhaps by late August, Stalin did appreciate the airlift's potential but believed that the United States would not be willing to continue the operation indefinitely just to save a small and strategically vulnerable piece of territory. His own position in Poland, Czechoslovakia, and Eastern Germany rested on force and the loyalty of dominant fraternal parties, not on how leaders in these countries regarded the credibility of Soviet commitments. He may not have appreciated the belief, held by many U.S. policy makers, that the U.S. reputation for resolve might decisively influence the outcome of future political struggles in France, Italy, and Germany. Greater sensitivity on the part of Stalin to the Truman administration's preoccupation with prestige interests might have enabled him to anticipate strong, sustained U.S. intransigence, even in the face of great difficulties, and led him to an earlier re-evaluation of the blockade's long-term utility.

Discussion of strategic interaction to this point has focused on threats and impediments to effective management and resolution of the crisis. A number of factors, of course, facilitated its peaceful resolution. Prominent among them was the tight—but not rigid—control that political authorities maintained over military options. Leaders in Washington on several occasions exhibited an auspicious penchant for "positive command" in their dealings with their military governor in Berlin. Yet, while political leaders maintained control over important military decisions, and while General Clay certainly chafed at the restrictions that Washington placed on his plans for an armed convoy, political leaders avoided the pitfalls of micromanagement. They allowed Clay to retain extensive authority over day-to-day operations, and his periodic requests for expansion of the airlift were in every case honored by Truman—sometimes over the objections of military planners in Washington. The presence of military men in high places in the political leadership—most notably Secretary of State Marshall, himself a general with considerable European experience—may have facilitated effective relations between civilian and military command.

Absence of documentary evidence makes it difficult to appraise the relationship between political and local military authorities on the Soviet side during the crisis. Marshal Sokolovsky presumably was well aware of the consequences of precipitate or unauthorized action under Stalin's command. Clearly, whatever the difficulties involved in commanding the forces in charge of the blockade, aiding communist demonstrations in Berlin, and managing the massive Soviet military presence in Berlin, at no time did Moscow lose effective control over military options.

Perhaps the most important factor facilitating peaceful resolution of the crisis was the restraint both sides exercised in the means they employed, even while pursuing ambitious ends. Although it pursued an uncompromising policy, the United States also abstained from the use of force, ultimatums, or coercive threats and accepted a protracted attrition contest in Berlin. The Soviet Union, while attempting to force a Western reappraisal of the London decisions, showed similar restraint in the means it employed.

I have noted earlier that the blockade strategy seemed inconsistent with requirements for prudent action during the crisis, for it did not—at least until the airlift proved its potential—leave the West a peaceful way out of the crisis that was compatible with its fundamental interests. Did Soviet strategy include a type of blackmail? In a sense, it did: The Soviets did seem to be issuing notice that if the Western powers did not alter their plans for a West German state, they would lose their positions in Berlin. But close examination of Soviet behavior in the crisis reveals that if the Soviets adopted a blackmail strategy, it was a limited one. It amounted to a warning that "you must reconsider the London accords or face a continuation of the blockade, which will probably force you to leave Berlin eventually." But at no time—and this distinction is crucial—did Soviet strategy entail the threat that "you must reconsider the London accords or we will drive you out of Berlin, by means of the blockade if possible and by other means if necessary." Indeed, Stalin let the blockade run its course, and accepted the outcome of the struggle rather than escalating to a higher level of threats and actions once the scheme failed. Although the Soviets did on occasion harass aircraft involved in airlift operations and did sponsor some disruptive mass actions in Berlin, these incidents did not create major difficulties for the Western powers in their efforts to maintain a presence in the city. To a significant degree, the peaceful outcome of the confrontation over Berlin resulted from the Soviet decision to forego new options, such as serious interference with the airlift or the use of force against West Berlin, after its aims were frustrated completely by Western counteractions.

A number of special factors that were highly specific to the crisis under discussion also promoted effective management of risk. One was the looseness of time constraints. Once the airlift strategy began to prove its capability, both sides gained a release from time pressures known in few, if any, other postwar superpower crises. A second factor was the smallness and restrictiveness of the site of the conflict, which facilitated effective control over military forces. Management of ground forces posed a far less complex and hazardous problem in the Berlin case than in, say, Korea in 1950 or Europe in 1914. A third factor that may have promoted crisis stability was the U.S. monopoly on atomic weapons. From the Soviet standpoint, this condition certainly did not facilitate a favorable outcome. It did, however, rule out the possibility of escalation to nuclear exchange and general nuclear war—a specter that has hung over every subsequent superpower crisis.

CONCLUSION

The Berlin Blockade Crisis of 1948–1949 illustrates how adversaries may recover from misjudgments and overcome major threats to crisis stability, even while clashing over issues of fundamental importance to both sides. While the event has sometimes been treated as a masterpiece of smooth and effective crisis management, here I have shown that the crisis was itself the product of serious miscalculations and missed opportunities and that the very strategies that helped the two sides terminate the confrontation without war also carried their own risks and disadvantages. Furthermore, although the U.S. strategy proved remarkably capable of deflecting and eventually defeating the Soviet challenge, the success of the strategy was due at least as much to mutual restraint as to the ingenuity of U.S. planning. The U.S. strategy, moreover, was itself the product of intensive debate among civilian and military leaders, whose positions on strategy selection appeared to be determined more by their basic political beliefs and personal temperaments than by their competences and professional responsibilities. The tension between requirements of diplomacy and military logic was experienced acutely by policy makers during the crisis, particularly at the stage of strategy selection. Yet, the case illustrates that diplomatic requirements and military logic need not appear as unitary, mutually exclusive categories. Indeed, one could identify several competing military logics: Which logic a leader found most compelling depended to some degree on his beliefs regarding the relative necessity and desirability of various noncombat military actions and on whether he viewed the crisis primarily in political or military terms. Finally, the case leaves considerable cause for optimism on questions of superpower crisis management and war avoidance. It illustrates how policies of restraint can enable the two sides to avoid inadvertent war, even while operating in an extremely fluid, uncertain, and tense international environment and while laboring under serious mutual misperceptions and misunderstandings.

BIBLIOGRAPHIC NOTE

The best account and analysis of the Berlin Blockade Crisis, particularly from the standpoint of U.S. decision making, is the book by Avi Shlaim. Though dated, the books by Davison, Windsor, and Young contain useful analyses. Adomeit's book furnishes valuable analysis of Soviet decision making. Collier, Morris, and the Tusas provide interesting, if less scholarly, accounts. The memoirs of Truman, Clay, and Murphy provide useful information on U.S. decision making. Clay's papers, the *Foreign Relations of the United States* volumes, and documents available at the Harry S. Truman Library Institute in Independence, Missouri, contain essential materials for study of U.S. decision making and policy during the crisis.

Adomeit, Hannes. *Soviet Risk-Taking and Crisis Behavior.* London: George Allen and Unwin, 1982.

Auriol, Vincent. *Journal du Septennat, 1947–54,* vol. 2. Paris: Armand Colin, 1974.

Bohlen, Charles. *Witness to History.* New York: Norton, 1973.

Clay, Lucius D. *Decision in Germany.* Garden City, NY: Doubleday, 1950.

Collier, Richard. *Bridge Across the Sky.* New York: McGraw-Hill, 1978.

Davison, W. Phillips. *The Berlin Blockade: A Study in Cold War Politics.* Princeton: Princeton University Press, 1958.

Divine, Robert. "The Cold War and the Elections of 1948." *Journal of American History,* 59 (June 1972).

Gaddis, John L. *The Long Peace: Inquiries into the History of the Cold War.* New York: Oxford University Press, 1987.

George, Alexander L. "The 'Operational Code': A Neglected Approach to the Study of Political Leaders and Decision-making." *International Studies Quarterly,* 13, 2 (June 1969).

George, Alexander L., and Richard Smoke. *Deterrence in American Foreign Policy: Theory and Practice.* New York: Columbia University Press, 1987.

Gottlieb, Manuel. *The German Peace Settlement and the Berlin Crisis.* New York: Paine-Whitman, 1960.

Guhin, Michael A. *John Foster Dulles: A Statesman and His Times.* New York: Columbia University Press, 1972.

Harrington, Daniel. *American Policy in the Berlin Crisis of 1948–49.* Ph.D. dissertation, Indiana University, 1979.

Howley, Frank. *Berlin Command.* New York: Putnam, 1950.

Jervis, Robert. *Perception and Misperception in International Politics.* Princeton: Princeton University Press, 1976.

LeMay, Curtis, and MacKinlay Kantor. *Mission with LeMay.* New York: Doubleday, 1965.

Millis, Walter, ed. *The Forrestal Diaries.* New York: Viking, 1951.

Morgan, Patrick. "Saving Face for the Sake of Deterrence." In Robert Jervis, Richard Ned Lebow, and Janice Gross Stein, *Psychology and Deterrence.* Baltimore: Johns Hopkins University Press, 1985.

Morris, Eric. *Blockade: Berlin and the Cold War.* London: H. Hamilton, 1973.

Murphy, Robert. *Diplomat Among Warriors.* Garden City, NY: Doubleday, 1964.

Public Opinion Quarterly, 14, 4 (Winter 1950–51).

Robson, Charles, ed. *Berlin: Pivot of German Destiny.* Chapel Hill: University of North Carolina Press, 1960.

Rosenberg, Jerry P. *Berlin and Israel, 1948: Foreign Policy Decisionmaking During the Truman Administration.* Ph.D. dissertation, University of Illinois, 1977.

Schelling, Thomas. *Arms and Influence.* New Haven: Yale University Press, 1966.

Selden, Elizabeth. *Papers, 1946–48.* Hoover Institution Archives, Stanford, CA.

Shlaim, Avi. "Britain, the Berlin Blockade, and the Cold War." *International Affairs*, 60, 1 (Winter 1983–84).

———. *The United States and the Berlin Blockade: A Study of Crisis Decisionmaking.* Berkeley: University of California Press, 1983.

Shulman, Marshall D. *Stalin's Foreign Policy Reappraised*. New York: Atheneum, 1965.

Smith, Gaddis. "The Berlin Blockade through the Filter of History." *The New York Times*, April 29, 1973.

Smith, Jean Edward, ed. *The Papers of General Lucius D. Clay: Germany, 1945–49*, vols. 1 and 2. Bloomington: Indiana University Press, 1974.

Smith, Walter Bedell. *My Three Years in Moscow*. New York: Lippincott, 1950.

Tanter, Raymond. *Modelling and Managing International Conflicts: The Berlin Crises.* Beverly Hills: Sage, 1974.

Taubman, William. *Stalin's American Policy: From Entente to Detente to Cold War*. New York: Norton, 1982.

Truman, Harry S. *Memoirs*, vols. 1 and 2. London: Hodder and Stoughton, 1956.

Truman, Margaret. *Harry S. Truman*. New York: Morrow, 1973.

Tusa, Ann and John. *The Berlin Airlift*. New York: Atheneum, 1988.

U.S. Department of State. *Foreign Relations of the United States, 1948*, vols. 1 and 2. Washington: U.S. GPO, 1973.

Vandenberg, Arthur. *The Private Papers of Senator Vandenberg*. Boston: Houghton Mifflin, 1952.

Williamson, Samuel, and Steven Rearden. "The View from Above: High-Level Decisions and the Soviet-American Strategic Arms Competition, 1945–50," mss.

Windsor, Philip. *City on Leave*. New York: Praeger, 1963.

Young, Oran. *The Politics of Force: Bargaining During International Crises*. Princeton: Princeton University Press, 1968.

NOTES

1. Robert Murphy, *Diplomat Among Warriors* (Garden City, NY: Doubleday, 1964), p. 313; Letter of March 23, 1948, Horst Mendershausen (assistant chief of price control, Office of the Military Government of the United States in Germany) to Karl Mundt (member of U.S. Congress), *Elizabeth S. Selden Papers*, Box 2, Hoover Institution Archives, Stanford, CA; Murphy to Marshall, March 20, 1948, in Foreign Relations of the United States, 1948, vol. 2 (Washington, D.C.: U.S. GPO, 1973), pp. 883–84. (Hereafter cited as *FRUS*.)

2. Murphy to Marshall, April 6, 1948, in *FRUS*, 1948, vol. 2, pp. 890–91; Avi Shlaim, *The United States and the Berlin Blockade: A Study in Crisis Decisionmaking* (Berkeley: University of California Press, 1983), pp. 110–35; W. Phillips Davison, *The Berlin Blockade: A Study in Cold War Politics* (Princeton: Princeton University Press, 1958), pp. 65–66; Jean Edward Smith, ed., *The Papers of General Lucius D. Clay: Germany, 1945–49*, vol. 2 (Bloomington: Indiana University Press, 1974), pp. 617–18. (Hereafter cited as *Clay Papers*.)

3. Department of State Brief, June 14, Naval Aide Files, Box 21, Harry S. Truman Library; Alexander L. George and Richard Smoke, *Deterrence in American Foreign Policy: Theory and Practice* (New York: Columbia University Press, 1974), pp. 124–32; *Clay Papers*, pp. 614–15, 622–23.

4. Hannes Adomeit, *Soviet Risk-Taking and Crisis Behavior: A Theoretical and Empirical Analysis* (London: George Allen and Unwin, 1982), pp. 93–94; George and Smoke, pp. 117–18.

5. Clay to Department of the Army, June 25, 1948, in *FRUS*, 1948, vol. 2, pp. 917-18; Murphy to Marshall, June 26, 1948, in *FRUS*, 1948, vol. 2, pp. 919-21; Royall to Clay, June 28, 1948, in *FRUS*, 1948, vol. 2, pp. 929-30; *Clay Papers*, pp. 697, 699-704.

6. Harry S. Truman, *Memoirs*, vol. 2: *Years of Trial and Hope, 1946-53* (London: Hodder and Stoughton, 1956), p. 130.

7. Minutes of the 16th National Security Council Meeting, July 22, 1948, President's Secretary's Files, Box 204, Harry S. Truman Library; Truman, *Memoirs*, vol. 2, pp. 131-33; Charles E. Bohlen, *Witness to History, 1929-69* (New York: Norton, 1973), pp. 277-78.

8. Davison, pp. 250-51, 264-65; Elizabeth Seldon Papers, Box 2.

9. Marshall D. Shulman, *Stalin's Foreign Policy Reappraised* (New York: Atheneum, 1965), pp. 69-70; Shlaim, pp. 380-87.

10. Jerry Philipp Rosenberg, "Berlin and Israel, 1948: Foreign Policy Decisionmaking During the Truman Administration," Ph.D. dissertation, University of Illinois, 1977, pp. 41-43.

11. Murphy to Marshall, June 17, 1948, and "Editorial Note," in *FRUS*, 1948, vol. 2, pp. 908-09.

12. Murphy to Marshall, March 3, 1948, in *FRUS*, 1948, vol. 2, pp. 878-79; Murphy to Marshall, February 21, 1948, in *FRUS*, 1948, vol. 2, pp. 876-77.

13. Memorandum for the President from R. H. Hillenkoetter (Director of Central Intelligence), December 22, 1947, President's Secretary's File, Intelligence File, Box 249, Harry S. Truman Library.

14. Rosenberg, p. 132.

15. Teleconference between Royall and Bradley (Washington), and Clay (Berlin), April 2, 1948, President's Secretary's Files, Box 171, Harry S. Truman Library; Murphy to Marshall, April 1, 1948, in *FRUS*, 1948, vol. 2, pp. 885-86.

16. Smith to Marshall, March 31, 1948, and April 23, 1948, Naval Aide Files, State Department Briefs, Box 21, Harry S. Truman Library; Smith to Marshall, May 10, 1948, President's Secretary's File, Subject File, Box 187, Harry S. Truman Library.

17. Memorandum for the President from Hillenkoetter, June 9, 1948, President's Secretary's Files, Intelligence File, Box 249, Harry S. Truman Library.

18. Memorandum for the President from Hillenkoetter, March 16, 1948, President's Secretary's File, Intelligence File, Box 249, Harry S. Truman Library; CIA ORE Report, April 28, 1948, "Possible Program of Future Soviet Moves in Germany," President's Secretary's File, Intelligence File, Box 255, Harry S. Truman Library. The tendency to attribute Soviet restraint to American firmness during the months preceding the imposition of the full blockade was also evident in Ambassador Smith's analyses. In a note of April 23, 1948, Smith reported to the State Department that he detected a shift in Soviet propaganda, possibly toward a more peaceful line. "If this shift is confirmed," Smith wrote, "it will be the first concrete result of our firm policy during the past year." Naval Aide Files, State Department Briefs, Box 21, Harry S. Truman Library.

19. Although accounts of cabinet meetings held during the first half of 1948 betray American leaders' concerns with "tensions in Europe" and with relatively minor questions such as how trade restrictions might be applied against the Soviet Union in response to Soviet policy in Germany and Czechoslovakia, they reveal no awareness of the possible need for strategic planning in Berlin. Papers of Matthew J. Connelly, Notes on Cabinet Meetings, 1948, Box 1, Harry S. Truman Library. Even experienced State Department officials tended to underestimate Soviet willingness to challenge American interests in Western Europe. In a note written just over one month before the onset of the blockade crisis, Robert Lovett, after consultation with Charles Bohlen and George Kennan, told Ambassador Smith in Moscow that the State Department feared "unwise actions" by the Soviet Union in

Greece or Iran—countries in which the Soviet Union had already challenged Western positions—more than in Western Europe, where the "risk of actual hostilities" would be higher. State Department to U.S. Embassy, Moscow (undated, but written between May 10 and 25, 1948), President's Secretary's File, Subject File, Box 187, Harry S. Truman Library.

20. George and Smoke use this phenomenon as part of their explanation for the failure of the United States to bolster deterrence during the precrisis period. The other main factor to which they attribute American policy was the ambiguity of Soviet tactics. They warn against oversimplifying the task Allied leaders faced and against an "overfacile interpretation of the lost opportunities to deter the Soviets from imposing the full blockade." While I recognize that much of the intelligence flowing to Washington reflected a lack of understanding of Soviet policy and promoted complacency, my analysis suggests that Washington was exposed to a great deal of evidence suggesting the possibility of a Soviet move against Berlin. I disagree with George and Smoke's argument that the baby blockade of early June "constituted only an equivocal warning of what was to come in late June." On the contrary, the early blockade, in combination with the numerous other interferences and harassments, including the downing of a British transport plane by a Soviet fighter plane over Berlin on April 5, the intermittent interference with the movement of barge traffic between sectors, abusive Soviet behavior in the Allied Control Commission and the walkout from the Kommandatura, and declarations that the West had forfeited its juridical rights in the city, hardly constituted a case of "ambiguous" signaling. One would not have expected American officials to have known the precise nature and timing of Soviet actions against Berlin in advance. But their unpreparedness for any Soviet move against the city, after months of what amounted to a clear and sustained campaign against Western positions in Berlin and Western policy in Germany as a whole, can only be regarded as the product of negligence and miscalculation. See George and Smoke, pp. 107–36.

21. See Robert Jervis, *Perception and Misperception in International Politics* (Princeton: Princeton University Press, 1976), pp. 343–48.

22. Truman, *Memoirs*, vol. 2, pp. 130–39; Adomeit, p. 84.

23. Notes on Cabinet Meetings, March 12, 1948, Matthew Connelly Papers, Post-Presidential File, Box 1, Harry S. Truman Library.

24. *Clay Papers*, pp. 614–15, 622–23.

25. Summary of Telegrams, April 16, 1948, Naval Aide Files, State Department Briefs, Box 21, Harry S. Truman Library; Caffery to Marshall, June 24, 1948, in *FRUS, 1948*, vol. 2, pp. 916–17.

26. See Adomeit, pp. 179–80; Gaddis Smith, "The Berlin Blockade through the Filter of History," *New York Times*, April 29, 1973.

27. Thomas C. Schelling, *Arms and Influence* (New Haven: Yale University Press, 1966), pp. 47–48.

28. Memorandum for the President from R. H. Hillenkoetter, June 30, 1948, President's Secretary's File, Box 249, Harry S. Truman Library.

29. Adomeit, p. 152.

30. See Shlaim, pp. 218–24. Leahy quoted in Shlaim, p. 224.

31. Murphy to Marshall, June 26, 1948, in *FRUS, 1948*, vol. 2, pp. 919–21.

32. Clay to Royall, June 25, 1948, in *FRUS, 1948*, vol. 2, pp. 917–18; Clay to Bradley, July 10, 1948, in *FRUS, 1948*, vol. 2, pp. 956–58.

33. Clay to Bradley, July 15, 1948, in *Clay Papers*, pp. 739–40.

34. Lt. General Arthur Trudeau, "Aborting of Task Force Trudeau," *Washington Star*, May 12, 1978; Curtis LeMay and MacKinlay Kantor, *Mission with LeMay* (New York: Doubleday, 1965), pp. 411–12.

35. Naval Aide Files, State Department Briefs, July 20, 1948, Harry S. Truman Library.

36. Record of Conversation with General Omar Bradley, March 29–30, 1955, Harry S. Truman Library; Rosenberg dissertation, pp. 141–44; Shlaim, pp. 242–43.

37. Memorandum of Conversation between Truman, Lovett, Forrestal, and Royall by Jacob D. Beam (Chief of the Division of Central European Affairs), in *FRUS*, 1948, vol. 2, pp. 928–29; Bradley to Clay, July 15, 1948, in *Clay Papers*, vol. 2, p. 740.

38. A clear and informative statement on this conflict appears in an interview with Clay conducted 25 years after the crisis. According to Clay, most military planners, including the Joint Chiefs of Staff, "visualized [the crisis] as a military operation." But Clay held that Truman, like himself, "realized that the Berlin crisis was a political, not a military war." Oral History Interview with Lucius D. Clay, July 16, 1974, President's Secretary's File, Box 171, Harry S. Truman Library.

39. For a detailed and nuanced account of the making of this decision, see Shlaim, pp. 219–53.

40. Truman, *Memoirs*, vol. 2, pp. 130–39; see also Margaret Truman, *Harry S. Truman* (New York: William Morrow, 1973), pp. 359–60.

41. Marshall to Douglas, June 27, 1948, in *FRUS*, 1948, vol. 2, p. 926.

42. Douglas to Marshall, June 26, 1948, in *FRUS*, 1948, vol. 2, pp. 921–26; Truman, *Memoirs*, vol. 2, p. 130.

43. Minutes of the 15th Meeting of the NSC, July 15, 1948, President's Secretary's File, Box 204, Harry S. Truman Library.

44. Minutes of the 16th Meeting of the NSC, July 22, 1948, ibid.

45. Clay interview, Harry S. Truman Library.

46. Conversation with Bradley, Harry S. Truman Library.

47. John Lewis Gaddis, *The Long Peace: Inquiries into the History of the Cold War* (New York: Oxford University Press, 1987), p. 110.

48. See Adomeit, pp. 133–37, 143–44; and Daniel F. Harrington, *American Policy in the Berlin Crisis of 1948–49* (Ph.D. dissertation, University of Indiana, 1979), p. 112.

49. *New York Times*, July 16, 1948.

50. Marshall was particularly concerned with the appearance of the transfer, and the possibility that the American people might regard it as a provocative action. Interestingly, in the NSC meeting of July 15, Marshall stated that while the action would have the advantage of demonstrating American firmness to the Soviets, that an even greater advantage would be gained from the effect of offsetting any tendency toward appeasement on the part of the British or French. According to Marshall, the United States had already demonstrated its own determination to the adversary; bolstering the Allies' commitments to Berlin now appeared as an even more urgent objective. Marshall feared that any deterioration of the Western position in Berlin might lead to unfavorable changes in British opinion that would make the transfer impossible; thus, the earlier the operation could be carried out, the better. British Foreign Minister Ernest Bevin, who strongly favored the action, appears to have shared Marshall's views in this regard. He agreed, moreover, that the transfer should be described as a "routine training mission," and should be executed without fanfare. Whether the operation was motivated primarily by a desire to deter Soviet aggression or to encourage fortitude on the part of the European allies, an early, nonprovocative operation appeared as the most attractive option to American policy makers. Minutes of the 15th Meeting of the NSC, July 15, 1948, President's Secretary's Files, Box 204, Harry S. Truman Library; Shlaim, p. 236; Message from Bevin to Department of State, as transmitted by British Ambassador (Franks), July 14, 1948, in *FRUS*, 1948, vol. 2, p. 966; Walter Millis, ed., *The Forrestal Diaries* (New York: Viking, 1951), pp. 457–58; Samuel R. Williamson, Jr. and Steven L. Rearden, "The View from Above: High-Level Decisions and the Soviet-American Strategic Arms Competition, 1945–50" (unpublished manuscript, 1975), p. 106. Marshall's anxieties over American public opinion and Britain's commitment to a firm policy

both proved to be unjustified: American opinion never wavered in its support for staying the course in Berlin, even at the risk of war, and the British government tended to be more, rather than less hawkish than the American. See Avi Shlaim, "Britain, the Berlin Blockade, and the Cold War," *International Affairs*, 60, 1 (Winter 1983-84); National Opinion Research Center poll, August and October 1948, in *Public Opinion Quarterly*, 14, 4 (Winter 1950-51): 809.

51. At several points during the crisis, Clay clashed openly with military chiefs in Washington over the use of aircraft for airlift operations. During the July 22 NSC meeting, for example, General Hoyt Vandenberg, the Air Force chief of staff, urged Truman to deny Clay's request for additional C-54s and C-47s on the grounds that their use in the airlift effort would increase their vulnerability. In the event of general war in Europe, he argued, many such airplanes might be destroyed, reducing the nation's ability to supply U.S. forces and hold outlying bases, and thus undermining its capacity for waging strategic warfare. Similar debates occurred in later months, as the crisis wore on and the airlift expanded. In every event, Truman, over the objections of his military chiefs, honored Clay's requests for more airplanes. Minutes of 16th Meeting of the NSC, July 22, 1948, President's Secretary's File, Box 204, Harry S. Truman Library; Clay interview, Harry S. Truman Library.

52. Philip Rogers, "Crisis Bargaining Codes: Potential Obstacles to Effective Crisis Management," in this volume.

53. Ibid.

54. *FRUS*, 1948, vol. 1, p. 626.

55. "Effect of Soviet Restrictions on the US Position in Berlin" (based on information as of June 1, 1948), CIA Report ORE 41-48, President's Secretary's File, Intelligence File, Box 255, Harry S. Truman Library.

56. Oran Young, *The Politics of Force* (Princeton: Princeton University Press, 1968), p. 182.

57. General William Draper, undersecretary of the Army, who was closely involved in the organization of the airlift, later recalled that during the initial weeks of the crisis: "In Berlin the war clouds were everywhere. It was a question of what hour or day the war might break out." Oral History Interview with General William H. Draper, Jr., Oral History Collection, Box 145, Harry S. Truman Library.

58. In Chapter 16 of this volume, this strategy is referred to as the acceptance by the defender of a "test of capabilities within very restrictive ground rules" that initially favored the adversary.

59. Smith to Marshall (two telegrams), August 3, 1948, in *FRUS*, 1948, vol. 2, pp. 1005, 1006.

60. Smith to Marshall, August 6, 1948, in ibid., p. 1018.

61. Smith to Marshall, August 24, 1948 (two telegrams); Marshall to Smith, August 24, 1948 (two telegrams); Smith to Marshall, August 27, 1948; Marshall to Smith, August 28, 1948, in ibid., pp. 1072-77, 1088-92.

62. Shlaim, p. 344; William Taubman, *Stalin's American Policy: From Entente to Détente to Cold War* (New York: Norton, 1982), pp. 190-91; Adomeit, pp. 98-100; *Washington Post*, October 8, 1948.

63. Naval Aide Files, January 13, 1949, State Department Briefs, Box 21, Harry S. Truman Library; Draper interview, Harry S. Truman Library. Currency reform posed a complicated, if not crucial, problem throughout the crisis period. In January 1949, the United States rejected a proposal, formulated by a committee of experts at the United Nations, that would have made the Soviet mark the sole currency in Berlin and withdrawn the Western "B" mark from circulation. Both Western and Soviet currencies were circulating in the city at the time. In addition to rejecting the U.N. committee's proposal, the United States decided to press for a reform in which the West mark would become the sole currency in the

Western sectors. The British and French, who initially were receptive to the U.N. committee's recommendations, voiced their fears that the American plan would increase Soviet intransigence in Berlin. The United States therefore backed away from its insistence that the Soviet mark be withdrawn from circulation, but insisted that West mark also continue in circulation until a unified city administration could be restored. Britain and France concurred, thus tacitly rejecting the U.N. committee's proposal. See Shlaim, pp. 374–77.

64. Naval Aide Files, January 28, 1949, State Department Briefs, Box 21, Harry S. Truman Library.

65. Smith to Marshall, August 4, 1948, in *FRUS*, 1948, vol. 2, pp. 1010–11.

66. Naval Aide Files, State Department Briefs, Box 21, Harry S. Truman Library.

67. Clay to Bradley, July 10, 1948, in *FRUS*, 1948, vol. 2, p. 958.

68. According to Alexander George, Soviet leaders often differentiate keenly between short-term risks of war, which necessitate prudence and extreme caution, and long-term risks, which Soviet leaders believe they can manage quite effectively even while pursuing an ambitious "optimizing" strategy. See Alexander L. George, "The 'Operational Code': A Neglected Approach to the Study of Political Leaders and Decisionmaking," *International Studies Quarterly*, 13, 2 (June 1969): 190–222.

69. See Jervis, pp. 319–29.

70. Murphy to Marshall, June 23, 1948, in *FRUS*, 1948, vol. 2, p. 915; memorandum by Chief of the Division of Central European Affairs (Beam), June 28, 1948, in *FRUS*, 1948, vol. 2, pp. 928–29; *Clay Papers*, pp. 614–15, 622–23.

71. Report by the Policy Planning Staff, November 2, 1948, in *FRUS*, 1948, vol. 2, p. 1241.

72. Marshall to Douglas, July 20, 1948, in *FRUS*, 1948, vol. 2, pp. 971–73; Notes on Cabinet Meetings, July 23, 1948, Matthew Connelly Papers, Post-Presidential File, Box 1, Harry S. Truman Library. See also Smith to Marshall, April 15, 1948, in *FRUS*, 1948, vol. 2, pp. 894–95. Interestingly, John Foster Dulles, who served as foreign policy advisor to Republican candidate Thomas Dewey during the 1948 presidential campaign, also favored an approach that was solicitous of Soviet prestige concerns, and communicated his views on this score to State Department officials. See Shlaim, pp. 248–49; and Michael A. Guhin, *John Foster Dulles: A Statesman and His Times* (New York: Columbia University Press, 1972), pp. 153–55.

73. See Adomeit, pp. 324–25; and Patrick Morgan, "Saving Face for the Sake of Deterrence," in Robert Jervis, Richard Ned Lebow, and Janice Gross Stein, *Psychology and Deterrence* (Baltimore: Johns Hopkins University Press, 1985), pp. 142–43.

74. Memorandum to the President from Hillenkoetter, June 30, 1948, President's Secretary's File, Intelligence File, Box 249, Harry S. Truman Library.

75. Minutes of 20th Meeting of the NSC, September 9, 1948, President's Secretary's File, Box 204. Hannes Adomeit has attributed American confusion in part to Soviet failure to convey a clear sense of its objectives to the West. He argues that Russia "maneuvered itself into the position of a blackmailer refusing to state the exact amount of money to be paid, while at the same time retaining the innocuous and polite manners of a gentleman." Adomeit, p. 168. Yet documentary evidence on the negotiations that took place in August between Soviet leaders and Western representatives demonstrate that the Soviets could hardly have stated more clearly and repeatedly the basis for their policy and their terms for settlement.

CHAPTER 11

The Cuban Missile Crisis

Alexander L. George

The Soviet attempt to deploy some 42 medium- and 24 to 32 intermediate-range ballistic missiles (IRBMs) into Cuba during the late summer and early fall of 1962 triggered the most dangerous crisis of the Cold War. Unforeseen and unwanted by either side, this war-threatening confrontation was eventually resolved peacefully through careful crisis management by both Washington and Moscow. In a hastily arranged quid pro quo that Nikita Khrushchev initially proposed, the Soviet leader agreed to remove the missiles in return for a pledge by President John F. Kennedy not to invade Cuba in the future and certain assurances regarding the removal of U.S. Jupiter missiles from Turkey.

This case provides a sobering example of how two leaders can stumble into a war-threatening crisis; it calls attention to the importance of the views and person-alities of top-level leaders; it provides a striking example of the fundamental policy dilemma of crisis management; and, most important, it demonstrates the critical importance of adhering to the political and operational "requirements" of crisis management in order to avoid war. At the same time, ironically, the crisis was resolved in part *because* it became difficult to meet some of these requirements and the process of managing the crisis began to break down during the last day of the confrontation, strengthening the incentives of both Kennedy and Khrushchev to end it immediately before it escalated.

To gain his objectives, Khrushchev chose a *fait accompli* strategy for achieving a covert deployment of missiles into Cuba. Before Kennedy discovered that strategic missiles were being deployed into Cuba, and at a time when he regarded such a bold action by Khrushchev as unlikely, the president employed the familiar strategy of "drawing a line." He distinguished between the deployment of "defensive" weapons (after U.S. intelligence reported the presence of Soviet air defense missiles in Cuba), which he regarded as acceptable, and "offensive" weapons that could hit

The author is indebted to Scott Sagan and David Welch for many incisive comments that have helped to sharpen and clarify the analysis presented in this chapter. Stimulating discussions with Barton Bernstein over the years and his own publications on the Cuban Missile Crisis have forced me to address relevant issues and to clarify and revise some of my interpretations.

the United States, which the president warned would be unacceptable. After the belated discovery by U.S. intelligence that a large number of strategic missiles were already in Cuba, Kennedy chose a variant of the strategy of coercive diplomacy as a means of persuading Khrushchev to remove them rather than resorting either to military options or a purely diplomatic approach.

Kennedy's initiation of the blockade as the initial move in his strategy of coercive diplomacy triggered a period of intense crisis bargaining between the president and Khrushchev. Both sides improvised tactics that juxtaposed efforts at rational persuasion, threats, and—eventually—offers of accommodation. The risk of escalation cast an ominous pall over the crisis bargaining and played an equivocal role that deserves close scrutiny. Without engaging in a reckless competition in risk-taking, each side attempted to some extent to play upon the other's fear of escalation, but, at the same time, both also acted cautiously to avoid escalation and generally adhered to crisis management principles.

One of the striking characteristics of the crisis is that several of the requirements for a robust variant of coercive diplomacy conflicted with some important requirements of crisis management. At first, Kennedy gave priority to prudent crisis management, and, as a result, the pressure he put on Khrushchev initially resembled the somewhat weaker "try-and-see" variant of coercive diplomacy.[1] He continued in this vein until, paradoxically, the threatened breakdown of crisis management on the last day of the crisis forced Kennedy to move toward a stronger form of coercive diplomacy resembling an ultimatum. However, the president coupled this threat with concessions, in order to bring the confrontation to an end before it reached the stage of possible escalation to a shooting war.

Given that so dangerous a crisis was unforeseen and unwanted by both sides, it is important to understand how it came about. We shall briefly examine each leader's motivations and objectives and the sources of misperceptions and miscalculations that plunged them into the war-threatening confrontation. The major focus of the chapter, however, will be on the crisis bargaining between the two sides, the important role that psychological variables played in the crisis bargaining, the threats posed to effective crisis management, and the circumstances that led to the resolution of the crisis.

KHRUSHCHEV'S MOTIVATIONS, OBJECTIVES, AND STRATEGY

For many years after the Cuban Missile Crisis, Western analysts were forced to infer the motivations and calculations that led Khrushchev to decide upon the missile deployment as best they could without benefit of useful data from well-informed Soviet sources. More recently, several conferences and interviews with Soviet personnel and, later, with Cuban officials, organized since October 1987 by Harvard University's Center for Science and International Affairs of the Kennedy School, and a number of articles by Soviet and Cuban officials, have thrown important new light on various aspects of the Cuban Missile Crisis. However, only limited information has been made available from the Soviet archives, and the recollections and opinions of Soviet participants in these meetings have not settled the question of Khrushchev's motives and objectives. At the same time, these more recent accounts strongly suggest that Khrushchev's motivation included a complex emotional dimension that sprang from frustration at the exposure by the United States of Soviet strategic inferiority and the collapse of his Berlin policy, resentment of the U.S. deployment of Jupiter missiles in Turkey, and concern over mounting foreign policy problems.

While some Soviet participants in these dialogues have argued that fear of a U.S. invasion of Cuba was uppermost in Khrushchev's mind in deciding on the missile deployment, they have not been able to document this claim or to provide a wholly persuasive argument on its behalf.[2] At the same time, other Soviet participants have stated as firmly that the major (or only) purpose of the missile deployment was to redress the strategic imbalance. Given the paucity of hard evidence on this matter and the inherent difficulty of sorting out and assigning weights to different motivations, the question of whether Khrushchev was more interested in deterring a U.S invasion of Cuba or in redressing the strategic imbalance cannot be resolved. Certainly, Khrushchev did use concern about U.S. intentions to persuade some of his colleagues, and in particular the reluctant Cubans, that installation of Soviet nuclear missiles, and not lesser means, would be necessary to deter a U.S. attack. And, after the crisis, that indeed became the official Soviet rationale for the deployment.

In his memoirs, on the other hand, Khrushchev admitted that his objective in deploying the missiles was not limited to deterring an attack on Cuba but was also aimed at achieving a significant improvement in the strategic nuclear balance.[3] It remains entirely plausible that Khrushchev seized upon the possibility of a threat to Cuba as an opportunity for securing a quick fix of the strategic nuclear imbalance, which the slowly developing Soviet ICBM program could not achieve for a number of years, by deploying medium-range missiles into Cuba.[4] Certainly, no source disagrees that Khrushchev's motivation for finding a way to redress the imbalance was extremely strong following the collapse in late 1961 of his assertive foreign policy of the late 1950s and early 1960s. During these years, it may be recalled, the Soviet leader had attempted to nourish and exploit U.S. fears of a missile gap by repeatedly making dramatic and chilling boasts of a rapid and substantial growth of the Soviet ICBM force. In the autumn of 1961, Khrushchev's boasts were exposed by the Kennedy administration as wholly unfounded.[5]

If the question of Khrushchev's motivation and objectives cannot be fully resolved, what can be said about his calculation of the risks of the missile deployment? Information and opinions offered by Soviet officials in recent years have encouraged U.S. analysts of the crisis to attempt to reconstruct the calculations and reasoning that led Khrushchev to believe that the secret missile deployment was an acceptable risk. Soviet officials as well as U.S. analysts have advanced plausible interpretations of considerable complexity that probe the Soviet leader's personality and decision-making style as well as his estimates of the situation and his operative assumptions.[6] There is considerable agreement among Soviet officials and U.S. analysts that the policy-making procedure Khrushchev employed in this case was seriously flawed and that important components of the decision were so questionable as to raise the possibility that a strong element of wishful thinking on the Soviet leader's part was at work. Still, although the attempt to achieve the missile deployment by means of a covert *fait accompli* was not a well-calculated risk—indeed, it was much more of a gamble than Khrushchev and his supporters believed—the irony is that it almost worked.

That Khrushchev badly miscalculated is evident. It is not clear on what grounds Khrushchev based his confidence that the missile deployment could be completed before the United States became aware of it. Several of his advisers have claimed that they conveyed their doubts on this score to Khrushchev at the time. The risk that the missile deployment would be discovered and trigger a strong U.S. reaction also worried Cuban leaders. Another critical miscalculation was Khrushchev's confident assumption that once Kennedy learned there were missiles in Cuba, he would accept the *fait accompli* without creating a dangerous, war-threatening crisis.[7]

The available record makes amply clear that Khrushchev and some of his key advisers convinced themselves that there was an excellent chance of achieving the *fait accompli* via secrecy and deception. They gave surprisingly little thought to what would happen if the deployment were discovered before it was completed. The available record gives no indication of advance contingency planning for that possibility. It would appear that Khrushchev and his advisers assumed that in the unlikely event the deployment was discovered before it was completed, the initial U.S. response would be at the diplomatic level rather than one of a military character. The graver risk of a shooting war would develop, if at all, only at a later point in the crisis, which would allow Moscow to introduce crisis control measures before a military clash occurred. As Roger Hilsman put it: "This is not to say that the Soviets thought the Cuban venture was without risk. But it does indicate that they thought of it as an easily manageable risk. As it turned out, the risk was manageable; the error was thinking that it would be easy."[8]

KENNEDY'S MOTIVATIONS, OBJECTIVES, AND STRATEGY

Upon learning of Khrushchev's bold move, President Kennedy quickly perceived multiple dangers and high stakes. Complex motivations were aroused in the president. If the deployment of so many missiles into Cuba, carried out secretly and coupled with deception, were allowed to succeed, he believed it would have a variety of damaging consequences for the U.S. position in the world, for Kennedy's foreign and domestic policies, for his ability to provide leadership during the rest of his term in office, and for his chances for a second term. Not merely his personal prestige and political future but also the prestige and interests of the United States were considered to be at stake.

It is idle to attempt to sort out and weigh separately, as some critics have tried to do, these various dimensions of the president's motivation. A leader's view of his own personal and political stakes does often influence in some way his judgment of his country's interests. And, indeed, Khrushchev could hardly have thought of a better way to arouse Kennedy's personal and political concerns or to ensure that they became so fused with calculations of national interest as to become virtually inseparable from them. It is highly doubtful that Kennedy, however hard he might have tried, could have found a way to accept damage to his personal political stakes without also accepting severe damage to major U.S. interests. One wonders whether the kind of political damage that the covert deployment of missiles would inflict upon the president could have escaped Khrushchev's attention when he decided to undertake it. Indeed, a plausible although necessarily speculative case can be made that the aim of damaging Kennedy's personal and political stature was part of the overall motivation of the Soviet leader, a person noted for his tendency to take the measure of his opponents and to bully them.

The president's domestic political stakes were indeed substantial. Particularly after Soviet military assistance to Cuba began in July 1962, his administration was placed under increasingly severe domestic pressure to take stronger action against Fidel Castro. The Republicans announced that Cuba would be the dominant issue in the midterm Congressional elections in November. The administration mobilized itself to reassure the public that the dangers of the Soviet military buildup in Cuba were being exaggerated and that there was no reason to respond with war-like measures such as a blockade. The administration disclosed considerable intelligence information concerning the character of the Soviet military supplies and personnel flowing into Cuba, hoping thereby to assure the public that it was well-informed as to what the Soviets were and were not doing.

An important development was the discovery in late August of Soviet SA-2 surface-to-air defense missiles in Cuba. Perhaps as much to calm the war psychosis being encouraged by critics such as Senators Kenneth Keating and Barry Goldwater as to deter the Soviets,[9] the president decided to draw the line. On September 4 and again on September 13, Kennedy explicitly warned the Soviets that his administration would not tolerate the introduction of offensive weapons into Cuba. Thereby, it should be noted, the president had publicly committed himself to act if strategic missiles were introduced into Cuba. Such a pledge was relatively easy to make, as Kennedy thought it most unlikely that the Soviets would undertake such a move, a belief buttressed by National Intelligence Estimates. But once he had taken his stand on this issue in the heated domestic political environment, the public pledge to act if challenged was virtually irrevocable. When the missiles were discovered in mid-October, therefore, "The United States might not be in mortal danger but the Administration most certainly was."[10] For the president to have retracted his recent public commitment not to tolerate offensive missiles in Cuba risked eroding other U.S. commitments and inviting Khrushchev and others to question Kennedy's future credibility in ways that could prove to be painful and dangerous.

Even without the impetus of Kennedy's personal and political stakes, Washington considered the need to find a way to remove the missiles compelling, but not because their placement in Cuba would shift the strategic nuclear balance in the Soviet Union's favor. Even now, with additional time and the benefit of hindsight, efforts to assess the real military significance of the 42 MRBMs that were already in Cuba or on the way and the additional 24 to 32 IRBMs that were to follow lead to intricate technical calculations. We forego discussion of this aspect of the issue here, not because it is irrelevant or unimportant but because the president and most of his advisers were swayed less by the military threat posed by the missiles than by the important political-diplomatic advantages they saw accruing to Khrushchev if the missiles remained in Cuba. Administration specialists on the Soviet Union foresaw that Khrushchev would be able to reinvigorate his assertive foreign policy not only to renew pressure on Berlin but in dealing with a variety of other issues as well.[11]

The president's motivation was indeed strong insofar as it was focused on the limited objective of securing the removal of the missiles. His motivation and willingness to accept risks were much more limited, however, for the objective of going beyond removal of the missiles to getting rid of Castro or eliminating Soviet influence from Cuba, as some of his advisers urged. These objectives were significantly more ambitious, and their costs and risks were perceived by Kennedy to be excessive. Even with respect to removal of the missiles, it is uncertain, to say the least, whether the value the president attached to this objective would have been compelling and durable enough to lead him to order an air strike if the pressure he exerted on Khrushchev, coupled with the quid pro quo offer on Saturday, October 27, failed to secure their removal. As we shall note later, Kennedy was not yet committed to the air strike or invasion options when the crisis ended. In fact, Dean Rusk's recent disclosure of new information indicates a propensity on Kennedy's part to make an additional last-minute concession, if his quid pro quo offer did not suffice, to obtain Khrushchev's agreement to remove the missiles.

KENNEDY'S LIMITATION OF OBJECTIVES AND MEANS

Kennedy followed prudent crisis management principles in dealing with the situation created by Khrushchev's gambit. The president adhered to the two political requirements for dealing with the policy dilemma of crisis management: He limited both his objectives and the means employed on their behalf. One of the first decisions Kennedy made soon after the discovery of the missiles was to firmly reject the view that the administration should set as its objective in the crisis the overthrow of Castro or, at least, the elimination of all Soviet influence in Cuba. Instinctively grasping that the pursuit of such ambitious objectives would substantially increase the risk of war, the president made it clear at the outset that his objective would be limited to removal of the missiles, no more and no less, and he held firmly to this throughout the crisis.

Although leaning toward an air strike at first, Kennedy soon saw the merits of limiting not only his objective but also the means to achieve it. The president's interest in the blockade option was caught by the possibility that it might rescue him from the policy dilemma confronting him: how to get the missiles out without possibly triggering escalation of the crisis to war. From the beginning, he had rejected acquiescence to the missile deployment; to do nothing seemed to him the worst of all options. A purely diplomatic overture to Khrushchev—that is, words without action—which several of his advisers favored as the opening U.S. move, might be not only ineffectual but dangerous. It could precipitate a crash effort by Khrushchev to capitalize on the situation created by the missile deployment. Further, a purely diplomatic response might have been interpreted by Khrushchev as demonstrating irresolution and could have encouraged the Soviet leader to regard any subsequent threats by the president as mere bluff. An air strike or invasion, on the other hand, would result in heavy casualties; moreover, these military options could trigger a strong Soviet response and lead to war.

The blockade would prevent additional missiles from reaching Cuba, but its inadequacy as a means for obtaining the *withdrawal* of missiles already in Cuba was self-evident. This was argued very cogently by those members of the National Security Council who advocated an air strike. Adherents of the blockade acknowledged its limitations and conceded, in addition, that they had no specific plan or concept for utilizing the blockade in order to obtain removal of the missiles. Thus, when on October 22 the president disclosed knowledge of the missile deployment and announced a naval quarantine of Cuba, the administration entered the overt phase of the crisis without having resolved critical ambiguities in its strategy. In the end, Kennedy chose the blockade option because it enabled him to postpone and control the risk of a major war better than an air strike would have. In this respect, the blockade offered advantages that an air strike lacked altogether: It enabled the president to initiate a showdown with Khrushchev without immediate resort to force, and, most important, it offered time for an effort to persuade Khrushchev to remove the missiles voluntarily. The president, however, would have to find a way of utilizing the blockade for this purpose, and, as we shall see, this was not an easy matter.

In the interests of crisis management, the president limited both his objective and the means to be employed on its behalf. Limiting the means employed to a blockade required the administration to strengthen its coercive impact on Khrushchev by making sufficiently credible and sufficiently potent threats of further action should he refuse to comply with the demand to remove the missiles. Therefore, the nature of the confrontation, as it was defined by Kennedy's choice of coercive diplomacy, emphasized the critical importance of an essentially psychological variable—the relative motivation of the two sides. The United States clearly enjoyed an asymmetry of power capabilities in the Caribbean as well as a distinct advantage in strategic nuclear weapons. Khrushchev understood this from the beginning, but it had not deterred him from undertaking the deployment. What was more questionable and what Khrushchev doubted was whether the United States—and, in particular President Kennedy—could summon the motivation and will to utilize its assets to prevent Khrushchev from succeeding.

The basic question, of course, was whether Khrushchev could be persuaded to remove the missiles by means other than actual use of force. No one among Kennedy's circle of advisers—even those who favored beginning with a quiet diplomatic effort to persuade the Soviet leader to do so—believed that Khrushchev would lightly forego the considerable advantages he expected to obtain from the missile deployment or that he would easily accept the considerable domestic costs and, if his retreat became public, the loss of international prestige associated with a conspicuous retreat. Pressure of some kind would be necessary. But what kind of pressure? And would even strong pressure be effective? These questions were of fundamental importance, and the answers that Kennedy and his advisers gave were at the root of the decision to try coercive diplomacy rather than resort immediately to force. Were Khrushchev and his associates coercible on this matter? Were they capable of retreating under pressure, as the old Bolshevik doctrine enjoined Soviet leaders to do when faced with overwhelming danger?[12] Or, had the deployment proceeded so far and were Soviet leaders so committed to the daring venture on which they had embarked that, for them, there could be no turning back?

This was indeed a critical question, but available accounts of policy discussions held by Kennedy and his advisers hardly refer to it. An affirmative, hopeful answer was implicit in their assessment of the calculations that may have led to the Soviet decision to deploy the missiles. The dominant view was that Khrushchev had miscalculated the risks of his initiative and that if made fully aware of these risks, he would be capable, at least in principle, of retreating and withdrawing them without the necessity of bloodshed. In the end, we are told by Robert Kennedy, the president's image of Khrushchev was decisive: "The President believed from the start that the Soviet Chairman was a rational, intelligent man who, if given sufficient time and shown determination, would alter his position."[13]

What this suggests, of course—and what is amplified in Philip Rogers's chapter on crisis bargaining codes—is that the image of the opponent plays an important role in crisis management. Just as Khrushchev's defective image of Kennedy—a young, inexperienced, weak leader who could be pushed around and, at the same time, a rational person who would not risk war to get the missiles out—is widely believed, even by some Soviet analysts,[14] to have played a role in his miscalculation of the risks of the missile gambit, so too did Kennedy's correct image of the Soviet leader play a role in his choice of coercive persuasion rather than military means to secure the removal of the missiles.

THE CRITICAL ROLE OF INTELLIGENCE

We need to pause and reflect on the critical and equivocal role that intelligence played in the development of the crisis and, in particular, in Kennedy's choices. "If we had to act on Wednesday in the first twenty-four hours" of the crisis, the president said later, "I don't think we would have chosen as prudently as we finally did."[15] It was indeed fortunate that the administration finally decided to resume overflights of western Cuba, permitting the U-2 photo reconnaissance flight of Sunday, October 14, which discovered the secret Soviet preparation of missile sites. In response to Kennedy's question as to how much time there would be before the missiles were ready for firing, intelligence specialists estimated about ten days.

Given the breathing space that the U-2 flight provided, one of the president's first decisions was that he would not be hurried into action but would take full advantage of the available time for a careful consideration of the situation. This decision was possibly momentous. At first, most members of the group of advisers Kennedy assembled, which came to be known as the ExComm (Executive Committee of the National Security Council), thought the president would have to resort to an air strike in order to remove the missiles. "A so-called 'surgical' strike," Theodore C. Sorensen reports, appealed "to almost everyone first considering the matter, including President Kennedy."[16]

However, if timely discovery of the missiles gave the president an opportunity to consider options other than direct military action, the failure of intelligence to discover the missile deployment at an earlier stage severely aggravated the crisis and probably made the task of managing it more difficult for both sides. We will not review here the reasons why the deployment was not discovered, as perhaps it might have been, much earlier.[17]

Had the deployment been spotted at an early stage, it probably would have been easier for Kennedy to have persuaded Khrushchev to call it off. The option of taking the matter up with Moscow in private diplomatic channels would then have appeared to the administration more promising and worth trying before it engaged in a massive mobilization of U.S. military power. The president would probably still have had to employ some variant of the strategy of coercive diplomacy to pressure Khrushchev into halting the deployment and removing the few missiles that may have already arrived in Cuba. Kennedy might have had to threaten a blockade and undertake preparations to initiate it, and perhaps threats of military action against the construction of missile sites would also have been necessary.

Even as of this day, we do not know whether Khrushchev had contingency plans for calling off the deployment had it been discovered at a quite early stage and firmly opposed by the United States. Certainly, even in this alternative scenario of the crisis, Kennedy would have had to impress Khrushchev with his resolution and with the credibility of his threat to take action if necessary. And Khrushchev may well have engaged in counterthreats and tough bargaining to see what he could get in return for calling off the operation. But with few, if any, missiles in Cuba, Khrushchev's crisis bargaining position would have been weaker; besides, discovery at an early stage of the deployment would have made it easier for him to retreat, although he would still have had to contend with domestic critics of his abortive initiative. Had the attempt to deploy the missiles been discovered early enough and a blockade threatened, it is even possible that Khrushchev could have saved face by denying that missiles were being shipped to Cuba. (We will note later that Khrushchev turned back the ships carrying military equipment to Cuba shortly after Kennedy announced the blockade on October 22.)

KENNEDY'S PROBLEM: HOW TO DEMONSTRATE RESOLUTION WITHOUT TRIGGERING WAR

The question of Kennedy's capacity to act in a resolute manner in dealing with Khrushchev was a central element in the origins of the crisis as well as in its resolution. One would like to believe that fateful questions of war or peace are not influenced by subjective, psychological variables of this kind. However, a fully adequate understanding of the Cuban Missile Crisis is not possible without taking into account the personal aspects of the interaction between the two leaders. There is reason to believe, although it is arguable, that Khrushchev's image of Kennedy as an inexperienced, weak opponent may have played a role in his calculation that the missile deployment was an acceptable, easily controllable risk. (A somewhat different rendition of Khrushchev's image of Kennedy attributed to him by some Soviet officials is that he believed the president to be too rational and prudent to risk war in order to get the missiles out.)

As for Kennedy, from the beginning of the crisis he was deeply concerned— indeed, perhaps haunted—by the feeling that Khrushchev's missile gambit could be adequately understood only in terms of a long-standing problem that had plagued him. Almost from the day he entered office, the president had wrestled with the problem of how to convey his determination to the Soviet leader in order to discourage him from attempting dangerous encroachments on the world position of the United States and, more particularly and urgently, with respect to the unresolved crisis in Berlin. The Bay of Pigs disaster and Khrushchev's behavior at their summit meeting in Vienna severely exacerbated Kennedy's problem and his concern.

As the tension over Berlin mounted once again in the summer of 1961, the president unburdened himself to James Wechsler of the *New York Post*:

> What worried [Kennedy] was that Khrushchev might interpret his reluctance to wage nuclear war as a symptom of an American loss of nerve. Some day, he said, the time might come when he would have to run the supreme risk to convince Khrushchev that conciliation did not mean humiliation. "If Khrushchev wants to rub my nose in the dirt," he told Wechsler, "it's all over." But how to convince Khrushchev short of a showdown? "That son of a bitch won't pay attention to words," the President said bitterly on another occasion. "He has to see you move."[18]

As the prolonged negotiations over Berlin ground to an inconclusive halt during the summer of 1962, the administration readied itself for new Soviet pressure against West Berlin. Many indications pointed to the likelihood that Khrushchev was preparing another major challenge. Some of them were imbedded in his curiously juxtaposed assurances in September and October that Soviet military assistance to Cuba was for purely "defensive" purposes and that he would not embarrass the president by raising the Berlin issue again until after the forthcoming congressional elections in November.[19] In other ways, too, Khrushchev was suggesting a linkage between Cuba and Berlin. This was not lost on the administration, but Kennedy and his advisers failed to penetrate the deception and to guess the linkage—and the trap—that Khrushchev was preparing. Even in September, Sorensen reports, Kennedy was concerned over the possibility that Khrushchev was giving increasing military assistance to Cuba in order to provoke Washington into another invasion of Cuba that would make a martyr out of Castro and wreck U.S. relations with Latin America, while the Soviets moved in on West Berlin. This suspicion was revived briefly after the missiles were discovered and is contained in one of the early theories, the Diverting Trap theory, that ExComm entertained when mulling over the motives behind the missile deployment.[20] This, then, was the president's mental set when he learned on October 16 that Khrushchev had been secretly putting missiles into Cuba, even while systematically deceiving him with false assurances.[21]

Some commentators, extremely critical of Kennedy for taking the world to the brink of nuclear war in response to the missile deployment, have attributed the president's desire to demonstrate resolution to personality shortcomings.[22] There is much more reason to support the interpretation that Kennedy's emphasis on the need to demonstrate resolution was a requirement of the situation and that he correctly perceived it as a necessary prerequisite, although certainly not a sufficient one, for the success of his strategy to secure the removal of the missiles without having to resort to an air strike or invasion. Further, we may suppose that this perceived requirement contributed to Kennedy's decision, for which he has also been criticized, not to disclose his knowledge of the missile deployment until he was ready to act and to seize the initiative.

THE CRISIS AS A BARGAINING CONTEST

Kennedy's decision to utilize the blockade as a tool of coercive diplomacy initiated a contest in bargaining. The phenomenon of "bargaining" is usefully analyzed in terms of its three components: persuasion, coercive actions and threats, and accommodative gestures and promises. A "bargaining strategy," in turn, is fashioned by employing some mixture of these three elements and determining the sequence of their use over time. Hence, a variety of bargaining strategies is possible depending upon the relative importance given to these three elements and the sequence in which they are employed.[23]

The issue confronting Kennedy was not merely whether he could persuade Khrushchev to remove the missiles but also what price the Soviet leader could exact in return for doing so. Khrushchev had a well-deserved reputation for being a tough bargainer. According to the imperatives of their old operational doctrine, Soviet leaders were expected to strive for optimal gains when embarked on an initiative to advance Soviet interests or when engaged in negotiation. Only through struggle for maximum gains in such situations could it be determined what was objectively possible. One should push to the limit to extract as much as possible, subject only to the caveat of "knowing when to stop" if the risks of continuing seem to be getting out of hand.[24]

There was no basis for assuming that Khrushchev would back off in the event that Kennedy, foregoing mobilization of military forces, confined his response to a stern diplomatic protest, even if it were backed by a verbal threat of action.[25] Had Kennedy chosen this diplomatic option, which several of his advisers favored, the crisis would have entered its bargaining phase under conditions highly favorable to the Soviet leader and severely disadvantageous for Kennedy. When the deployment was discovered, a large number of medium-range missiles were already in Cuba. These provided important bargaining assets for Khrushchev, and his negotiating leverage would increase with every passing day, as preparations for making the missiles operational, already well advanced, were continuing and a large number of additional missiles, including longer-range intermediate missiles, and possibly nuclear warheads were on the way.[26]

It is conceivable that in this disadvantageous bargaining position, the president, foregoing even a blockade, might have bought his way out of the crisis. But in this event, Khrushchev's price tag for removing the missiles, if indeed he would agree to remove all of them, would probably have been extremely high and might well have included demands for a substantial change in the status of West Berlin. In short, in this alternative scenario of the crisis, Khrushchev would have had Kennedy over a barrel.

Almost intuitively, the president saw that in the dangerous situation created by Khrushchev's miscalculation, the only chance of getting the missiles out without war lay in finding a way of impressing the Soviet leader, as never before, with his determination. Kennedy perceived that if he tried to bargain with Khrushchev before correcting the Soviet leader's mistaken view of his resolution, Khrushchev's appetite and expectation of gains to be extracted would remain excessive and unrealistic. In that event, either Kennedy would have to pay too high a price to secure removal of the missiles—a deal that could have had devastating domestic political consequences at home and for the world position of the United States— or else the negotiations would break down and the president in the end would have to take forceful action.

Indeed, this alternative scenario of the crisis—a negotiation without a military buildup and blockade—could have led to a rapidly deteriorating, possibly prolonged bargaining situation for Kennedy in which he could be eventually pressed to employ the air strike or invasion options. That the risk of war might well have become much greater had Kennedy pursued the purely diplomatic option has been ignored by those who have criticized Kennedy for not trying the quiet diplomatic track first before initiating the blockade and the military buildup.

What Kennedy believed he badly needed was action that would counteract Khrushchev's bargaining advantages as much as possible and give the United States the enhanced leverage it would need in order to negotiate an acceptable deal for withdrawal of the missiles. The blockade would not only prevent Khrushchev from deriving additional bargaining leverage from a continuation of the missile deployment, it would also indicate to the Soviet leader that he had miscalculated and, hopefully, signal Kennedy's resolution to secure the removal of the missiles.[27] And backed by the implicit threat of military action against Cuba, Kennedy's demand for removal of the missiles *might* generate sufficient coercive pressure and bargaining leverage to induce Khrushchev to agree to a formula for withdrawing the missiles.

Kennedy's Bargaining Strategy and Tactics

Coercive action embodied in the blockade and the additional coercive threats conveyed by the military buildup of U.S. forces, which lent credibility to the implicit threat of action against Cuba, were one component—and arguably the most important component—of Kennedy's bargaining strategy. As noted earlier, the most useful way to approach the task of devising a bargaining strategy is to view it as a particular mixture, and some pattern or sequencing, of three elements: persuasion, coercion, and accommodation. Kennedy employed all three elements, but he deliberately withheld indicating willingness to accommodate Khrushchev until he felt that the coercion and persuasion components of his bargaining strategy had made an impression on him.

It may come as a surprise even to those who have followed closely the literature on the Cuban Missile Crisis if we assert that from an early stage, the president believed he would probably have to pay a price to get the missiles out. Not only the president himself but others within the ExComm—including his brother and Robert McNamara as well as Adlai Stevenson—believed this.[28]

At an early stage in the deliberations of the ExComm, the president indicated that a delay in offering a quid pro quo was all-important. In the ExComm planning session on the day after Stevenson outlined his thoughts regarding the need for concessions, the president expressed the belief that such talk of negotiating formulas was "premature." Rather, the president wanted to concentrate in his signaling and communications to Khrushchev "on a single issue—the enormity of the introduction of the missiles and the absolute necessity for their removal."[29]

The president's awareness of the eventual necessity of concessions was conveyed more explicitly by his brother. Arthur Schlesinger reports that after the president, Robert Kennedy, Dean Rusk, and others had finished going over the draft of the initial speech on the crisis that Ambassador Stevenson would deliver before the United Nations, "The Attorney General drew me aside to say, 'we're counting on you to watch things in New York. . . . *We will have to make a deal in the end, but we must stand absolutely firm now. Concessions must come at the end of negotiations not at the beginning.*' "[30]

The need to avoid being drawn into serious bargaining until he had impressed Khrushchev with his determination and developed important bargaining assets remained with the president as the crisis unfolded. We see this consideration at work when he and a few advisers were going over a draft of the television address to the nation that the president delivered on October 22. Discussion turned to the question of what the president should say about negotiation in the speech. President Kennedy's answer, Sorensen reports, was in effect, "Nothing that would tie our hands, anything that would strengthen our stand." Furthermore, "*the President deleted from my* [Sorensen's] *original draft a call for a summit meeting,*" preferring to state simply, in the words of the speech as given, that "this nation is prepared to present its case against the Soviet threat to peace, and our own proposals for a peaceful world, at any time and in any forum . . . *without limiting our freedom of action.*"[31]

Later on, when he became depressed and worried by signs that the Russians were about to challenge the quarantine, the president controlled his impulse to rush into negotiations prematurely. On Tuesday evening, October 23, his brother relayed a private conversation with the Soviet ambassador, Anatoly Dobrynin, in which Dobrynin said he knew of no change in instructions to Soviet vessels nearing the blockade line and expected that they would attempt to go through to Cuba. The president, evidently agitated at hearing this, spoke at once about the possibility of arranging an immediate summit with Khrushchev, "but finally dismissed the idea, concluding that *such a meeting would be useless until Khrushchev first accepted, as a result of our deeds as well as our statements, the U.S. determination in this matter.* Before a summit took place, and it should, the president wanted to have some cards in his own hands."[32]

Clearly, then, while envisaging a bargaining strategy that would eventually include accommodation, the president believed that he must give priority in time as well as in emphasis to the coercion and persuasion components of his strategy. The president was relying on coercion to reduce substantially his part in a quid pro quo, the precise terms of which would have to be worked out later.

Legitimate questions can be raised concerning the wisdom of Kennedy's decision to withhold any indication of a willingness to offer concessions until late on Friday, October 26. Such a bargaining strategy risks conveying to the opponent that one is unalterably opposed to any modification of one's negotiating position and that escalation of the crisis can be avoided only through unilateral concessions by the opponent. Thus, this tactic violates the seventh operational requirement of crisis management, which emphasizes the desirability of leaving open to the opponent a face-saving way out of the crisis compatible with his basic interests and prestige. Failure to do so may result in an unwanted, unexpected hardening of the opponent's determination. It is possible that Kennedy's bargaining strategy did have this effect for a while on Khrushchev. To be sure, from the beginning of the overt phase of the crisis, the president also relied on efforts to persuade the Soviet leader—both in public as well as in the private letters they exchanged—that he sought a peaceful resolution of the crisis. It is also true that we do not know whether early hints of a willingness to make concessions on Kennedy's part would have been interpreted by Khrushchev, as the president feared, as an indication of weakness and irresolution that would have strengthened the Soviet leader's determination to persist. But in this connection, it has to be noted that Khrushchev also withheld hints of a willingness to negotiate a compromise until he did so on Friday, October 26.

The fact is that for almost four days—from late Monday, October 22, to late Friday, October 26—both sides gave priority to the coercive component of bargaining strategy. Although neither leader initiated a reckless competition in risk-taking, nevertheless the crisis bargaining during these tense days did assume some of the chilling characteristics of the game of "chicken." However, to control and reduce the risks, both sides employed techniques of crisis management that will be discussed later.

Khrushchev's Bargaining Strategy and Tactics

Confronted by the unexpected discovery of his missile deployment and surprised by Kennedy's announcement of a blockade, Khrushchev had to improvise a bargaining strategy under unfavorable conditions. Had the Soviet leader anticipated Kennedy's action, he would have had an opportunity to seize the initiative himself. Thus, Khrushchev could have publicly (or privately) disclosed that a missile deployment was in progress, justified it, and asserted a tough negotiating position.

Kennedy's announcement that his crisis objective was the removal of missiles secretly introduced into Cuba and that his opening tactic was a blockade aimed at persuading the Soviet leader to reconsider his move clearly placed Khrushchev on the defensive, as it was indeed intended to do. The important parameters of the initial crisis bargaining having been set for the time being by the United States, Khrushchev now had some difficult policy questions to address. First, he was immediately confronted by the need to decide whether and when he should admit that a missile deployment was underway and how he should attempt to justify it. Second, the Soviet leader had to consider what objectives he should pursue in the crisis bargaining now set into motion and what strategy to adopt.

What, in other words, should Khrushchev bargain for—completion of the missile deployment in defiance of the blockade? Retention of missiles already in Cuba? Maximal concessions from the United States in return for removal of the missiles? Very little information is available to clarify whether these policy choices were clearly identified in Moscow and, if so, how they were evaluated and on what basis they were settled. As already noted, Soviet sources have not revealed whether any contingency plans existed for responding to a premature discovery of the missiles by the United States and, if so, what use, if any, was made of them by Khrushchev. We are forced to rely on what Khrushchev did and did not do, and what he said and did not say, to infer how he addressed difficult policy choices as to objectives and strategy in the following days.

One of the first decisions Khrushchev made after Kennedy's announcement of the blockade—and he made it sooner than U.S. policy makers at the time were aware of and sooner than most analysts of the crisis have noted—was to give orders to Soviet vessels carrying the missiles to immediately turn back.[33] (Other ships carrying nonmilitary cargo en route to Cuba halted but then were allowed by Moscow to continue, and they eventually reached the blockade line.) This order was evidently given sometime late Monday or early Tuesday, appreciably less than 24 hours after Kennedy's announcement of the blockade.[34] Temporarily but perhaps only temporarily, in order to gain more time to assess the situation and to gauge Kennedy's resolution, Khrushchev retreated from the objective of completing the deployment of missiles.[35] At the same time, however, the Soviet leader decided to test and weaken, if possible, Kennedy's resolution to implement the blockade by sending ships carrying nonmilitary cargo into the restricted zone.

Khrushchev relied more on coercive threats and persuasion than on actions to enhance his bargaining leverage. Thus, just as Kennedy had, the Soviet leader operated on the premise that if a retreat and concessions were necessary to terminate the crisis, they should come later, not at the outset, and that he should rely on whatever coercive threats he could prudently muster to convey his own resolution and to weaken Kennedy's. Hence, he would oppose the blockade but in ways that would not risk escalation to a military clash on the high seas or the capture of missiles and warheads intended for Cuba. In addition, Khrushchev placed heavy reliance on efforts to persuade the president and others of the legitimacy of his military assistance to Cuba and his claims that the weapons moved into Cuba were defensive—that is, had no offensive purpose.

Even before Kennedy announced the blockade and, indeed, before he learned of the secret missile deployment, important domestic critics of his policy of allowing the Soviet military buildup of Castro's forces had been calling publicly for a naval blockade of Cuba. No doubt aware of this, Khrushchev attempted to preemptively deter such a move by labeling it a violation of international law that would amount to an act of war, which he would resist by military means.[36] After Kennedy announced the blockade, Khrushchev continued to denounce it as a violation of international law and threatened to defy it at the risk of war. In his private letter to Kennedy on Tuesday evening, Khrushchev objected to the "ultimatum" given him to remove the missiles, and he denounced the blockade as an act of aggression that was in violation of international law. The Soviet leader ended his letter with an ominous threat:

> Our instructions to Soviet mariners are to observe strictly the universally accepted norms of navigation in international waters and not to retreat one step from them. And if the American side violates these rules, it must realize that responsibility will rest upon it in that case. Naturally we will not simply be bystanders with regard to piratical acts by American ships on the high seas. We will then be forced to take the

measures we consider necessary and adequate to protect our rights. We have everything necessary to do so.[37]

On the same day, in an interview with U.S. businessman William Knox, Khrushchev was even more explicit: Soviet submarines, he warned, would sink any U.S. naval ship that tried to force a Soviet vessel to stop.[38] In private conversations on October 22 through 24, several Soviet ambassadors, including Dobrynin, soberly predicted that Soviet ships would challenge the blockade.[39]

The coercive component of Khrushchev's bargaining strategy, however, was confined to rhetorical threats. His threat to challenge and to resist the blockade by force, if necessary, was not carried out, and, in fact, in a subsequent letter to Kennedy in the late afternoon of October 26, the Soviet leader assured him "that the vessels which are now headed for Cuba are carrying the most innocuous peacetime cargoes. . . . I assure you that the ships bound for Cuba are carrying no armaments at all."[40] Khrushchev added that there had been shipments of armaments earlier and that Cuba already had the armaments needed for defense. And, indeed, Soviet ships that did approach the blockade line were not carrying military supplies, and they were allowed to pass on to Cuba.

Other ways of exerting coercive pressure on behalf of Khrushchev's objectives in Cuba were conspicuously limited. There was talk but no evidence of Soviet strategic forces being alerted, and there were no threats of counterpressure against Berlin or Turkey, but U.S. intelligence did report that Soviet military leaves and discharges were cancelled and Warsaw Pact forces placed on some degree of alert.

Khrushchev's use of persuasion as part of his bargaining strategy required him to convey a credible, acceptable justification for the missile deployment. But the fact that it was carried out secretly conflicted with his effort to claim legitimacy for the action.[41] Khrushchev's failure to publicly acknowledge the deployment as soon as it was discovered, and denials of it by Soviet officials in the next few days made the argument that it was legitimate ring hollow. The Soviet position had been further weakened on October 23 when the Organization of American States voted unanimously to condemn the missile deployment.

What remained open for Khrushchev as a means of increasing his bargaining leverage was to rush the missiles already in Cuba to operational status. And this he did, evidently in the hope that he could manage somehow to neutralize U.S. pressure to remove them and to stabilize and terminate the crisis without having to withdraw the missiles. Certainly, it was as obvious to the Soviet leader as it was to Kennedy that while the blockade could prevent additional missiles from reaching Cuba, it could not in itself bring about the removal of missiles already there. If Soviet missiles remained in Cuba, such an outcome of the crisis would be a substantial success for Khrushchev and a substantial defeat for Kennedy.

In the last analysis, however, keeping the missiles in Cuba was not worth the risk of provoking U.S. military action—either a massive air strike against the missile sites or an invasion of Cuba. Khrushchev had to watch closely for signs that U.S. plans for military action were proceeding to the point of action. In the meantime, he made use of several efforts, which proved abortive, to neutralize the emerging U.S. military threat via a hastily contrived diplomatic formula designed to draw Kennedy into either negotiations or a summit meeting.

THE ABORTIVE U.N. INITIATIVES

The most serious of these initiatives was U Thant's proposal of Wednesday, October 24, calling for a "voluntary suspension of all arms shipments to Cuba" coupled with "the voluntary suspension of the quarantine measures involving the searching of ships bound for Cuba." That this proposal was quickly accepted by Khrushchev is not surprising. He had already suspended shipment of missile systems to Cuba, and the proposal, if accepted by Kennedy, would offer assurance that other Soviet vessels carrying nonmilitary supplies would not be stopped and searched—an action that, in fact, Kennedy had not yet implemented. The origins of U Thant's proposal are not clear; the possibility cannot be excluded that the proposal was inspired, perhaps through third parties, by the Soviet Union.

The U.N. secretary-general's proposal was quickly turned down by Kennedy. Admittedly, it would have avoided the possibility of a confrontation on the high seas but in a way that would have proven disadvantageous to important elements of the president's evolving bargaining strategy. For one thing, he had not yet demonstrated his resolution by enforcing the blockade against ships bound for Cuba. (The *Bucharest*, a tanker, had been allowed to pass the quarantine line without being boarded and inspected. And later, an East German passenger ship was allowed to go through.) U Thant's proposal was also disadvantageous because it did not state a time limit for its operation. Hence, it would have made it difficult for Kennedy to step up pressure by adding additional items such as petroleum, as was already contemplated by some of his advisors, to the list of materials banned from transit to Cuba.[42]

U Thant's proposal to Khrushchev and Kennedy made no reference at all to the importance of stopping work on the missile sites. Instead, for some reason, the secretary-general directed such an appeal to Castro. Khrushchev's reply accepting the first proposal made no reference to the secretary-general's appeal to Castro, nor did it hint that the Soviet Union might be willing to discontinue work on the missile sites under certain conditions. In the absence of a reply from Castro, U Thant renewed his appeal to him on Friday, October 26, and requested an affirmative reply "very urgently." Castro replied the following day, indicating he "would be prepared to accept the compromises you request as efforts in favor of peace, provided that at the same time, while negotiations are in progress, the United States Government desists from threats and aggressive actions against Cuba, including the naval blockade of our country."[43] But by then, Khrushchev had already set into motion his feelers regarding a quid pro quo for removal of the missiles.

KHRUSHCHEV'S MISSED OPPORTUNITY

The secretary-general's well-intentioned initiative, then, came to naught. More surprising is that Khrushchev himself did not introduce into the bargaining an offer that might well have enabled him to obtain a more favorable resolution of the crisis. The Soviet leader could have offered to freeze any further work on the missile sites (many of which were thought by U.S. intelligence at the time to have achieved operational status, although it was not known whether nuclear warheads for them were present) without agreeing to dismantle them, and to couple this offer with a requirement that Kennedy agree to immediate U.N.-sponsored negotiations. Then, after waiting for the steam behind Kennedy's coercive pressure to dissipate, as it surely would have under such an agreement, the Soviet leader could have renewed the bargaining in a more leisurely fashion in order to extract as high a price as possible for removal of the missiles. By employing this alternative bargaining strategy, the Soviet leader might even have succeeded in obtaining an agreement to leave some of the missiles in Cuba.[44]

Had Khrushchev made such an offer early in the crisis before the blockade went into effect or before it was seriously enforced, he could have coupled it with the declaration of a "voluntary" halting of the movement of Soviet vessels toward Cuba (an action that, in any case, he ordered on Tuesday, October 23, but did not publicize). Kennedy might well have found it difficult to justify turning down such a prosposal. Whether Khrushchev considered such an option remains entirely uncertain. What is clear is that Kennedy and some of his advisers were seriously concerned that the United States might be drawn into negotiations prematurely under arrangements that would be disadvantageous. It is also possible that Khrushchev hesitated to offer or to accept any proposal requiring cessation of work on the missile sites in the belief that the more missiles that achieved operational status, the greater his leverage would be for extracting concessions from Kennedy for removing them, should that become necessary.

In any case, Khrushchev's delay in settling for what he could get in return for removing the missiles is consistent with some of the fundamental beliefs of earlier Bolshevik leaders regarding correct strategy in the struggle against stronger opponents. In situations of the kind that characterized the Cuban crisis, which "objectively" offered the possibility of substantial gains, a good Bolshevik was supposed to pursue an optimizing strategy—that is, to "push to the limit" to achieve maximal gains and not settle too quickly for lesser ones. Moreover, a good Bolshevik should not retreat until it becomes necessary in order to avoid a catastrophic defeat, at which point then—and only then—should the leader be ready to do so.[45]

KENNEDY'S ADHERENCE TO THE OPERATIONAL REQUIREMENTS OF CRISIS MANAGEMENT

We noted earlier the president's decision to limit both the objectives he would pursue in the crisis and the means he would employ on their behalf. The efficacy of crisis management often depends not only on satisfying these political requirements to some degree but also on governing one's behavior in ways that are sensitive to a number of operational desiderata. The seven operational requirements identified in Chapter 4 deal with different aspects of the need to integrate the military and diplomatic measures that top policy makers choose to employ in managing a crisis. In this respect the president and his advisers were remarkably successful. Although an explicit theory of crisis management was lacking at the outset of the crisis, Kennedy and his advisers displayed an intuitive, common-sense appreciation of the relevance of these operational desiderata and were often guided by them in their choice of what they did and what they said. Let us consider each of these seven operational requirements in turn.

Engaging in remarkably little direct micromanagement of military operations, the president maintained indirect control over most of the military alerts, deployments, and low-level actions that were taken, as well as over the selection and timing of measures to implement the blockade. This first of the operational requirements on our list was achieved largely by Secretary of Defense McNamara's approval of appropriate rules of engagement and consultation with the military chiefs. Contrary to a widespread belief, the president and his top advisers worked through a well-defined chain of command and did not communicate directly with officers commanding the navy ships engaged in blockade operations.[46] Through the chain of command—from midday Wednesday morning, October 24, onward—the president and Secretary of Defense McNamara indicated which ships were to be stopped and boarded.

The president was especially sensitive to the second operational principle. He felt it essential to slow down the tempo and momentum of the implementation of the blockade. Pauses in blockade operations were deliberately introduced in order to give time for Khrushchev to deliberate and for exchange of diplomatic communications. We will provide a more detailed account of Kennedy's adherence to this requirement after completing this brief account of his efforts to adhere to the various operational desiderata.

The third, fourth, and fifth operational criteria emphasize that military moves must be carefully selected, coordinated with, and made consistent with political objectives and diplomatic actions. There is much evidence in reports of the crisis of efforts to develop and apply an integrated diplomatic-military strategy for reaching an acceptable termination of the confrontation that would avoid war. Movements of U.S. military forces and efforts to signal resolve were generally consistent, with some exceptions,[47] with the way in which the president attempted to manage the crisis. "Noise" was largely avoided and minimized. Thorough preparations were undertaken for a possible invasion of Cuba and strikes against the missile sites. These preparations were highly visible, but Washington made it clear that their *immediate* purpose was to provide a credible threat to back up the president's strategy of trying to achieve removal of the missiles peacefully through coercive diplomacy rather than through military action. Toward the end of the week, however, preparations for an invasion reached the stage at which Soviet and Cuban intelligence became concerned that an invasion might be imminent.[48]

The alert of U.S. strategic forces to DefCon-2 did perhaps risk alarming Soviet leaders that the United States was contemplating initiation of nuclear war and, if so, perhaps forcing Moscow to consider preemption. Whether Soviet leaders were inclined to place this interpretation on the U.S. alert is unlikely; nothing at the time and none of the recent Soviet disclosures have indicated that Soviet leaders misperceived the action. Certainly, the strategic alert had some coercive intent, but its objectives were—as Kennedy indicated in his address of October 22—to deter use of the Cuban-based missiles against the United States or any countries in the Western hemisphere, to discourage escalation by the Soviets, and to provide extended deterrence of possible Soviet moves elsewhere—such as Berlin.

Kennedy's handling of the crisis was also consistent in the main with the sixth operational requirement. Both his choice of diplomatic signals and his restraint in the choice and application of military actions conveyed a strong preference on his part for a peaceful resolution of the crisis rather than a military solution to the problem of the Soviet missiles.

Finally, turning to the very important seventh operational principle, with the exception already noted of his initial unwillingness to offer concessions, Kennedy chose his military actions carefully and eventually coupled them with diplomatic proposals that were intended to leave Khrushchev with a way out of the crisis that would be compatible with his fundamental interests.

Let us take a closer look at how adherence to these operational principles of crisis management permeated the implementation of the blockade.

THE CONDUCT OF THE BLOCKADE[49]

In discussion of the blockade option, it was assumed that if stopping Soviet ships bound for Cuba did not suffice to persuade Khrushchev to remove the missiles already there, other steps would be necessary. However, when Kennedy turned his attention to implementing the blockade option, he began his actions many rungs of the ladder below enforcement of the blockade. Why he did so reflects his sensitivity to the second operational requirement of crisis management. The president foresaw that the critical and most dangerous point in the blockade scenario would be reached when U.S. naval vessels were called upon to stop and inspect a Soviet vessel or a Soviet submarine. Unless one or the other side backed away from confrontation, or unless Soviet vessels bound for Cuba submitted to the U.S. navy's procedure for boarding and inspecting, the confrontation could result in a dangerous military clash.

While such a confrontation would indeed display determination, Kennedy was mindful of its risks and shied away from it. All accounts indicate that he feared that Khrushchev might feel himself obliged to retaliate, most likely by some action against West Berlin. Accordingly, the president felt it necessary to give Khrushchev time to consider what he would do and time to issue new orders to the captains of the vessels bound for Cuba. And he hoped that something short of actually boarding and inspecting a Soviet vessel would signal his determination sufficiently to persuade Khrushchev not to attempt to force the blockade. What that lesser action might be, and even whether a lesser action would suffice, remained to be seen.

Kennedy, then, inserted several discrete steps into his implementation of the blockade in order to delay a direct, possibly fateful confrontation on the high seas. As Albert and Roberta Wohlstetter have observed, Kennedy's behavior in this respect shows that "where the alternative is to be ruled by events with such enormous consequences, the head of a great state is likely to examine his acts of choice in crisis and during it to subdivide these possible acts in ways that make it feasible to continue exercising choice."[50]

The logic of Kennedy's tactic of subdividing the blockade option, we may add, grew out of his recognition that the possibility for careful presidential control of the conflict would decline rapidly once a military incident occurred. He was concerned throughout the crisis that it would reach the dangerous point of no return toward war; he spoke movingly of his fear that, as had happened at the outset of World War I, the momentum of events would at some point sweep aside efforts to maintain control of the conflict. Accordingly, the president jealously safeguarded his options and withheld use of them as long as possible to avoid reaching that dangerous threshold too soon and perhaps unnecessarily. At the same time, he was imaginative in subdividing one option into several smaller ones so as to slow down the momentum of the unfolding crisis and retain control of it. Ironically, it was a desperate feeling at the end of the week that he was about to lose control over the momentum of events that forced him to pass from the careful "try-and-see" approach to something approximating an ultimatum. Let us review quickly the way in which Kennedy introduced the blockade in a deliberately slow, piecemeal fashion.

In his speech of Monday, October 22, Kennedy announced his intention to impose a quarantine. He waited until after obtaining approval from the Organization of American States on Tuesday to issue the official proclamation of the quarantine. In turn, the proclamation stated that the interdiction of vessels bound for Cuba would begin on the following day, at 10:00 A.M. (2 P.M. Greenwich time) Wednesday, October 24.

In the evening of Tuesday, October 23, the president and his advisers were informed by intelligence that an extraordinary number of coded messages had been sent by Moscow to all Soviet ships on their way to Cuba. "What they said," Robert Kennedy has written, "we did not know then, nor do we know now."[51] In fact, as noted earlier, we do now know that these coded messages, sent much earlier on Tuesday or perhaps even late Monday, instructed Soviet vessels carrying weapons to Cuba to turn back. However, intelligence reports that Soviet vessels approaching the blockade line had halted would not reach the president until mid- and late morning of Wednesday.[52] In the meantime, lacking up-to-date information on the movements of Soviet vessels, Kennedy and his advisers were operating on the assumption that the Soviets were about to challenge the blockade. Washington's concern—indeed anxiety—was magnified by the threat contained in Khrushchev's private letter to Kennedy of Tuesday evening (cited above).

Although Khrushchev had already ordered Soviet vessels to move away from the blockade area, it is obvious that for the time being he had decided to exert counterpressure to test the depth and scope of the president's determination to enforce the blockade. To this end, the Soviet leader attempted to mobilize world opinion by playing on the danger of war and to undermine and soften the U.S. position. It became clear rather quickly, therefore, that the mere announcement of a blockade would not suffice and that its implementation would have to play an important role in Kennedy's strategy.

Upon receiving Khrushchev's letter Tuesday evening, Kennedy immediately composed a reply asking the Soviet leader to observe the quarantine and making it clear that the United States did not want to fire on Soviet vessels. Other decisions taken that evening reveal the president's heightening concern to find ways of reducing and controlling the risks of an untoward incident on the high seas. If a confrontation took place with a vessel that refused to cooperate with the interdiction procedures, the U.S. navy was to shoot only at rudders and propellers of the vessel in order to avoid loss of life or the sinking of the ship.[53] Kennedy's advisory group also considered ways and means whereby vessels clearly not carrying military equipment might be let through without being boarded and searched.

At the close of the Tuesday evening meeting with his advisers, the president sent his brother to see Soviet Ambassador Dobrynin, among other reasons to find out the import of the coded messages of a few hours earlier from Moscow to the Russian vessels en route to Cuba. At the end of their conversation, Robert Kennedy asked Dobrynin if the Soviet vessels were going to go through to Cuba. Dobrynin replied that this had been their instructions and he knew of no changes.[54] According to another account, Robert Kennedy reported back to the president late that evening that Dobrynin had "seemed very shaken, out of the picture and unaware of any instructions" and that "this meant the imposition of the quarantine the next day might well bring a clash."[55]

Before the blockade was to go into effect, tension mounted on Wednesday morning as, according to Robert Kennedy's account,[56] reports (by now out of date) continued to come in that Soviet vessels were approaching the blockade line. However, news finally arrived in the late morning (belatedly, as we now know) that Soviet vessels had stopped dead in the water or turned back. The significance of this action was not immediately evident. Some of Kennedy's advisers thought the Soviet ships were changing course or were waiting to join up with Soviet submarines before challenging the blockade. Later on Wednesday, it finally emerged that all sixteen of the Soviet freighters suspected of carrying military cargoes had turned back. Most of those continuing were tankers.[57] One of them—the *Bucharest*—was allowed to pass, upon identifying itself, without being boarded or inspected. This evidently followed from an instruction issued hurriedly by the president when he learned that some Soviet vessels were turning back. The president's decision was sharply challenged by some of his advisers who felt that the *Bucharest* should be stopped and boarded so that Khrushchev would not be misled as to the administration's intent and will.[58]

In the following days, an East German passenger ship was allowed to go through, again after strong argument against allowing it to do so within the administration; and finally, on Friday morning, October 26, the first vessel was stopped and boarded. This vessel, the *Marcula*, was carefully selected by the president for this purpose. Since it was not a Soviet vessel but a Panamanian-owned, Lebanese-registered vessel under Soviet charter, it could be stopped without offering a direct affront to the Soviets. At the same time, by stopping and searching a vessel carrying Soviet cargo, the president hoped to demonstrate to Khrushchev that he was going to enforce the quarantine.

But by the morning of Friday, October 26, when the *Marcula* was boarded, it had become somewhat less urgent and certainly far less risky to stage such a confrontation. For evidently Khrushchev had already been sufficiently impressed with Kennedy's determination. Khrushchev had not carried out the threat made in his October 24 letter to Kennedy to challenge the blockade. It was evident that vessels carrying weapons to Cuba, which earlier had been ordered to turn back, were not resuming movement toward the blockade line. Instead, it was becoming clear that Khrushchev was seeking to find a way of stabilizing the crisis by freezing the existing situation—hence, his ready acceptance of U Thant's first proposal of

Wednesday, to which we have already referred, and his acceptance on Friday of U Thant's second proposal.

The Navy's Antisubmarine Operations

If the boarding and inspection of the *Marcula* on Friday morning were not the decisive turning point of the confrontation—if, indeed, there were any clearly identifiable turning point—let us consider whether earlier developments may have convinced the Soviet leader that his counterpressure would not succeed in weakening Kennedy's determination to press the blockade and softening his demand for removal of the missiles. It is possible, although speculative in the absence of confirmation from Soviet sources, that the U.S. navy's actions against Soviet submarines in the Caribbean and in the Atlantic had already convinced Khrushchev of the strength of Kennedy's motivation and determination. Despite the account provided in Robert Kennedy's *Thirteen Days* and more important recent disclosures regarding the antisubmarine operations of the U.S. navy during the crisis, important details are still lacking.[59]

On Tuesday evening, October 23, according to Robert Kennedy's account, when the president learned that Soviet submarines were beginning to move into the Caribbean, he ordered the navy "to give the highest priority to tracking the submarines and to put into effect the greatest possible safety measures to protect our own aircraft carriers and other vessels." It should be noted that the rules of engagement given the U.S. navy included permission to initiate military action in self-defense against Soviet submarines if they acted in a manner that could be reasonably interpreted as the inception of hostile action against U.S. ships. Concern over the role that Soviet submarines might play in the crisis had already emerged some days earlier when the president and other officials took note of the possibility that submarines might be used to bring nuclear warheads into Cuba for the missiles. Accordingly, submarines had been included in the general order for quarantine operations; they could be stopped and searched if proceeding to Cuba.

On the evening of October 23, McNamara and the navy had to devise a special set of signals to be used to signal Soviet submarines to surface. Since this was a more aggressive measure than navy ships were normally authorized to take in peacetime, there was no accepted method for signaling such a request. Sonar signals accompanied or followed by nonlethal depth charges and an international code signal IDKCA, meaning "rise to the surface," were now authorized for this purpose. If a submarine refused to cooperate, warning shots and minimal use of force could be employed to warn it to do so. Since IDKCA was not contained in the *International Code of Signals*, which did not include a signal for submarines to surface, these special instructions for antisub operations issued to the U.S. navy were broadcast publicly on October 25 and may have been provided privately to Moscow on the 24th. By doing so, Washington hoped to ensure that Moscow had advance warning that antisubmarine operations were to be undertaken and could so inform its submarine commanders.

These special measures to require Soviet submarines to surface were employed many times, apparently on at least two of the five confirmed Soviet submarines and possibly on two others as well. All five of the Soviet submarines were of the

Foxtrot-class diesel-electric attack submarines. (Separate contacts with one of them led to the mistaken belief that two different submarines were identified, which accounts for previous reports that six Soviet submarines were involved.) When the crisis erupted, two of these submarines were already operating in the Caribbean, perhaps on routine missions but possibly in readiness to support the missile deployment in some way. The three others were detected moving from the Atlantic to the Caribbean before the blockade went into effect. Contrary to some accounts, none of these submarines was escorting Soviet merchant ships carrying offensive arms to Cuba, but their mission remains unclear.

Both the Morse code IDKCA signal and the nonlethal explosive charge signal (which consisted of four or five practice depth charges dropped by antisubmarine warfare [ASW] aircraft, and hand grenades by surface ships) were employed. According to Bouchard, the first positive contact by the navy's ASW forces with a Soviet submarine did not occur until 3:29 P.M. Wednesday, October 24. The result of the ASW operations, Bouchard reports, were mixed:

> Submerged Soviet submarines essentially ignored the sonar and explosive charge signals. There were no reported instances of a Soviet submarine immediately surfacing upon hearing the signals—the Navy did not literally "force" any Soviet submarines to surface. Soviet submarines surfaced because they needed to replenish air and batteries, or because they had some kind of mechanical problem that had to be repaired on the surface. . . . The Soviet submarines did not react to the signals with other than their normal efforts at evasion.

Nonetheless, since the Soviet submarines were pursued until they eventually had to surface, "the Navy can claim, however, that it forced Soviet submarines to surface in the presence of U.S. ships—a humiliation for a submarine captain."[60]

At the same time, there is indirect evidence that the Soviet government directed its submarines to accommodate the U.S. navy's desire that they come to the surface. Normally this type of submarine need only expose its snorkel in order to recharge its batteries and replenish its air. It was unusual, therefore, that all of the Soviet submarines "fully surfaced, sometimes repeatedly, rather than just snorkeling. This led some Navy officers to conclude that the submarines *were* ordered [by Moscow] to surface and identify themselves if challenged by the U.S. Navy."[61]

Particularly noteworthy, and contrary to the impression conveyed in previous accounts, the data obtained by Bouchard indicate that the three Soviet submarines previously identified as heading from the Atlantic to the Caribbean "had all reversed course and were headed home by the time U.S. Navy ASW forces were able to locate them and prosecute them." It appears, therefore, that the Soviet government decided to recall these three submarines on October 24, and possibly as early as October 23—the same day the merchant ships carrying missiles and other military equipment were ordered to halt or turn back. The other two Soviet submarines in the Caribbean attempted, "with little success, to maintain surveillance of the two U.S. attack carriers operating south of Cuba."[62]

It is noteworthy that the navy certainly did not place a conservative interpretation on its authorization to conduct ASW operations to protect the fleet engaged in the blockade and to prevent Soviet submarines from passing through to Cuba. Rather, as noted, it not only sought out three of the five Soviet submarines before they reached the blockade line but also aggressively pursued them after they turned and attempted to return to the Atlantic. In other words, the ASW forces not only monitored the movement of the submarines to ensure that they would continue to move away, they also put into effect the authorized rules of engagement designed to force them to the surface even though they were well outside the designated blockade zone.

As it turned out, with the exception of the possible crippling by U.S. action of one of the Soviet submarines, there were no significant incidents between the ASW forces and the Soviet submarines: there were no near collisions with submerged or surfaced submarines. When Soviet submarines surfaced, they were asked, in accordance with peacetime procedures, whether they required assistance. None was ordered to stop for boarding. It seems clear, from Bouchard's search of available navy records and his questioning of officers involved in the ASW operations, that no torpedoes or full-size (lethal) depth charges were directed against the submarines. As both Sagan and Bouchard note, however, the possibility cannot be excluded that one of the Soviet submarines that surfaced for repairs may have been damaged by nonlethal depth charges.[63]

Two questions arise: First, did the president know of and approve the vigor and scope of the navy's ASW operations? Second, did the assertive prosecution of the Soviet submarines contribute to Khrushchev's decision to forego further efforts to exert counterpressure on Kennedy; in other words, did the ASW operations constitute a possibly decisive turning point in the crisis bargaining? Neither of these questions can be answered with certainty. It is quite possible, as Sagan argues and as Bouchard acknowledges, that the president and the secretary of defense may not have fully understood the operational implications of their authorization of ASW operations.[64] That is, they may not have anticipated that the navy would interpret the rules of engagement given it for ASW operations as broadly and as assertively as it did. Moreover, as Bouchard notes, "ASW was not one of President Kennedy's top priorities during the crisis. Available ExComm records do not reveal navy ASW operations to be a frequent topic of conversation. The White House did not attempt to exercise the same kind of control over the implementation of ASW operations as it did over the enforcement of the blockade on individual Soviet surface vessels approaching the blockade zone. Operational reports on ASW activity were available at the White House, but it is not clear how closely they were monitored. Had close monitoring been undertaken, the president and the secretary of defense, as well as the chief of naval operations, could seemingly have intervened if prosecution of a submarine appeared to be excessive or seemed to be getting out of hand.[65]

Thus, we are left with a conflict between two interpretations that cannot be resolved. It is possible that a better informed, more alert White House might have intervened to curtail ASW operations against the three Soviet submarines that had turned back. But it is also possible, although the evidence is slim, that there was a measure of approval for the assertive ASW actions on the grounds that this might increase coercive pressure on Khrushchev.[66]

The second question—did the navy's assertive prosecution of Soviet submarines influence Khrushchev's decision to forego further counterpressure to test U.S.

resolve—can be dealt with more briefly. Only Sergei Mikoyan's conjecture that this was the case[67] and circumstantial evidence are available at this time, so that in the absence of authoritative Soviet accounts, only a highly speculative answer is possible. The Soviet leader's efforts to stabilize the crisis on advantageous terms began with his acceptance of U Thant's first proposal on Wednesday, October 24. By Friday, Khrushchev was ready to accept the more even-handed second proposal made by the U.N. secretary-general. More significantly, the Soviet leader did not repeat his earlier threats to resist implementation of the blockade by force, if necessary. Rather, as already noted, in his letter of October 26, Khrushchev took a more conciliatory tone, assuring the president that ships now headed for Cuba were not carrying any armaments even while admitting that such shipments had occurred earlier. We conclude that Moscow was no doubt impressed by the willingness of the United States to vigorously demonstrate its naval superiority in the Caribbean, but we cannot determine how important an impact this had in persuading Khrushchev to alter his bargaining strategy and objectives.

Stepping Up the Pressure

The successful boarding of the *Marcula* notwithstanding, a feeling of gloom began to settle over Kennedy's advisers on Friday morning, and for good reason. Soviet acquiescence to the blockade did indeed cut off the flow of missiles and related weapons to Cuba, but U.S. intelligence reported that at least 30 MRBMs were already in Cuba. (In fact, as was learned later, 42 had already arrived.) The determination that Kennedy had conveyed and the successful imposition of the blockade did not provide the leverage needed to secure the president's irreducible objective: the removal of the missiles. Intelligence reports indicated that work on the missile sites was continuing at a rapid pace.

As seen by the president and his advisers, therefore, the situation on Friday morning was still a most difficult one and could rapidly get worse. Khrushchev was in a position to gain the upper hand in the bargaining without having to directly challenge the blockade. For three-and-a-half days, Kennedy had adhered faithfully to his conviction that he must slow down events leading to a confrontation in order to give Khrushchev time to reflect, time to reconsider and alter his policy, and time to issue new directives to his vessels approaching the blockade line. He had thereby avoided a possibly dangerous confrontation on the high seas. But the time given Khrushchev for this purpose had also enabled the Russians to rush the missiles already in Cuba to completion and to improvise a counterstrategy for salvaging as many gains as possible.

Thus, the president had paid a price—how large and how serious it would turn out to be no one yet knew—for his adherence so far to prudent crisis management principles. He had knowingly decided to abide by these principles a week earlier when in the ExComm planning sessions he had listened carefully to the arguments against the blockade option, accepted their validity, and decided nonetheless that the blockade was preferable to the air strike. Since then, he and other members of the ExComm had seen the predicted limitations of the blockade option begin to materialize. Indeed, sober forecasts by ExComm members of the blockade's chief limitations and risks had been remarkably prescient.[68]

When he announced his choice of the blockade to the ExComm, the president, striving to pull together the badly divided group, had said half jokingly that those whose advice on what to do had been rejected were the truly fortunate ones, as they would be able later to say they had been right.[69] That time was at hand on Friday, October 26, and even more so the following day. Now the fact that even a successful blockade would not remove the missiles from Cuba, and the additional fact that the Russians were completing the operational readiness of the missiles, reactivated the powerful voices of the air strike advocates. Their arguments took on new force and relevance that could not be turned aside so easily as before. Their pressure on Kennedy mounted with every passing hour, with every new disturbing development that Friday and especially Saturday brought.

During these two days, two distinct phases can be detected in Kennedy's response to the situation. On Friday morning, when he began to tighten the screws, he distinctly confined his actions to a "gradual increase in pressure."[70] There is no indication that at this stage the president was thinking of moving beyond a gradual increase in pressure to an ultimatum. He ordered more low-level flights and, significantly, as evidence of the gradual escalation he had in mind at this stage, he asked the State and Defense Departments to prepare to add petroleum and lubricants to the embargo list.

"But privately," his brother reports, "the President was not sanguine about the results of even these efforts. Each hour the situation grew steadily more serious."[71] Recognizing this and looking ahead to actions he might be forced to take, the president also ordered the State Department to proceed with preparations for a crash program on civil government in Cuba after a U.S. invasion.

On Friday, even while stepping up the pressure, the president was still trying to retain some of his earlier allegiance to ultraprudent crisis management principles. Lincoln White, the State Department press officer, went somewhat beyond his instructions in threatening additional action by calling attention to the sentence in the president's speech of October 22 which stated that "further action will be justified" if work on the missile sites did not stop. This triggered headlines that an invasion was imminent. Kennedy immediately rebuked White and also made his displeasure known to Rusk and others, although later the president acknowledged that White's unauthorized statement may have helped impress the Soviets.[72] The president's major interest at this time was to communicate, which he did in various ways, the U.S. sense of urgency that work on the missile sites must stop very soon. But added to the signal that emerged, whether or not the president fully intended it, was the widespread interpretation that the United States could hold off its next step for no more than a few days. While members of the administration may have fostered rumors and leaks to this effect, the president was not officially committed to an early deadline, even though he may have instigated or approved some of these reports himself.

An unexpected opportunity to impress upon the Soviets that the president might soon have to employ military force to remove the missiles emerged on early Friday afternoon. John Scali, a State Department correspondent, received a telephone call from Aleksandr Fomin, a member of the KGB serving as "counselor" at the Soviet embassy, requesting an immediate meeting. Fomin urged Scali to find out whether the administration would be interested in a solution to the crisis whereby the Soviet government would remove the missiles, with U.N. inspection, in return for a public pledge by the United States not to invade Cuba. Secretary of State Rusk, after discussion with other members of the ExComm including the president, authorized Scali to reply that the United States was interested, but that it was his (Scali's) "impression" that "time is very urgent."[73]

Khrushchev now resolved an important question the president had not yet faced. Kennedy had refused, as we observed earlier, to begin serious bargaining with Khrushchev over the terms of a quid pro quo for ending the crisis until he had succeeded in impressing the Soviet leader with his determination and accumulated some bargaining assets. So far as can be established from available materials, Kennedy had not developed a formula of his own for a quid pro quo that he was holding back to introduce at the right moment. The subject had not been discussed much in the ExComm—indeed, the president had actively discouraged discussion of whether the United States should pay a price to secure voluntary removal of the missiles.[74] Lack of preparation on the subject is evidenced in accounts of the ExComm's last-minute efforts on Saturday to consider whether and how the Jupiters in Turkey might be offered up as part of the quid pro quo.

Very conveniently for Kennedy, Khrushchev took the initiative in signaling on Friday, October 26, that the time for serious bargaining to resolve the crisis was at hand.[75] The Soviet leader had evidently decided that it was time to begin serious exploration of how to bring the crisis to an end and to find out how much he could hope to salvage out of it.

Crisis Management Begins to Break Down

Before we turn to the often confused bargaining that occurred, particularly on Saturday, we should make several additional observations. Earlier in the week, tacit cooperation in careful crisis management had developed between Kennedy and Khrushchev. Even while the Soviet leader blustered and exerted pressure of his own in order to undermine Kennedy's resolve and his ability to implement a coercive strategy, Khrushchev nonetheless also went to great lengths to guarantee the avoidance of a clash at sea.

Once the danger of a confrontation on the high seas was safely managed, however, U.S. and Soviet cooperation in managing the crisis began to break down. The tempo of events speeded up on Saturday, and a startling lack of synchronization began to characterize the interaction between the two sides. The context and meaning of certain possibly critical moves and communications that one side was making became confusing to the other. For each side, deciphering the intentions and calculations behind the specific moves of the opponent became difficult. We know that Kennedy experienced this problem acutely and that his adversary felt the same unsettling phenomenon in Moscow. There was real danger in this, but the disturbing sensation that things were getting out of control and the mounting fear that one side or the other might miscalculate were probably not without value in helping to bring the crisis to a sudden halt on early Sunday morning.[76]

United States policy makers and those writing about the crisis thereafter found it difficult to explain the discrepancy between Khrushchev's more personal and more emotional private letter of Friday evening, in which he suggested removal of the missiles in return for Kennedy's pledge not to invade Cuba, and the more formal and composed letter he issued publicly on Saturday morning demanding that the United States remove its missiles from Turkey as well. Members of Kennedy's advisory group speculated that the hawks in the Kremlin, learning of and disapproving Khrushchev's personal initiative of Friday night, overruled him and wrote a new letter that demanded more. This possibility was an additional source of confusion and anxiety among U.S. policy makers on Saturday.[77]

Was it so unlikely that the president would agree to throw in removal of the obsolescent Jupiter bases in Turkey? There was, after all, Walter Lippmann's article of Thursday, October 25, suggesting that the president do so. Soviet leaders might well have thought this was a trial balloon inspired by the more dovish members of the administration, and, additionally, they might have noticed that the administration did not disassociate itself from Lippmann's position.

Even before Lippmann's article appeared, the Soviet government had been preparing the ground for a demand for a "symmetrical" trade of U.S. and Soviet overseas bases. Thus, although the Soviet government had carefully refrained from threatening action in Berlin in response to the blockade, it had been exerting counterpressure with regard to U.S. bases in Turkey.[78] Removal of the Jupiter missiles from Turkey would not constitute the large gain Khrushchev had expected when he deployed missiles into Cuba, but his problem now was to salvage as much as he could. Besides, to force Kennedy into agreeing to remove the bases in Turkey would by no means constitute an insignificant prize—not so much because of the military significance of the Jupiters to either the United States or the Soviet Union but because such a concession would provide Khrushchev political and psychological benefits at home and inflict political-diplomatic consequences for the U.S. position in NATO. We shall note later President Kennedy's attitude toward trading the Jupiters and the role it played in the formula for settling the crisis.

Other disturbing actions took place on Saturday. A U.S. reconnaissance plane wandered over Siberia; a U-2 was shot down over Cuba in midmorning; two other reconnaissance planes were shot at as they swooped low over the missile sites Saturday morning; it was reported that a single Soviet ship outside the quarantine line detached itself from the others and headed for the blockade line. In Washington, these actions were interpreted, not surprisingly, as grim indications that the Soviets had perhaps decided to test U.S. determination. Some ExComm members reasoned that since the Soviets must have realized that shooting down the U-2 would force the United States to take direct action against the surface-to-air missiles (SAMs), "their action seemed to mean that they had decided on a showdown."[79] There was speculation as to whether Khrushchev was still in charge in the Kremlin and contradictory speculation that Khrushchev was trying to extract a higher price. The president would have to decide what to do next under the burden of considerable uncertainty and confusion as to what was going on in the Kremlin.

It now seems reasonable to conclude that the U-2 shoot-down was *not* a calculated part of Khrushchev's bargaining strategy, as had been feared at the time by some of Kennedy's advisers.[80] What impressed itself on the president and his advisers was that a possibly momentous turning point in the crisis had been reached. Contingency plans called for a retaliatory air strike against one of the SAM sites in Cuba. To do so, however, would be to cross a major threshold in the level of violence, which, even if justified by political as well as military considerations, could trigger additional escalation. Kennedy withstood pressure from his advisers to put into effect the contingency plan for retaliation, adding to the mounting internal strains within the advisory group.

But it was clear that the reconnaissance flights over Cuba would have to continue in order to monitor the status of the missile sites and that if another U-2 were shot down, which had to be expected, the president could not easily hold off approving a reprisal attack against the SAM sites. What would happen thereafter, he feared, could lead to uncontrollable escalation.[81]

A new sense of urgency to end the crisis emerged, as it could be only a matter of a few days before another U-2 was shot down. An immediate effort to end the crisis before it went out of control was necessary. Motivated as never before—not merely by a desire to get the missiles removed but by a desperate need to try to end the crisis before it resulted in war—Kennedy was finally ready to exert additional pressure on Khrushchev; at the same time, however, he also saw the need to couple the pressure with concessions to make it easier for Khrushchev to agree to remove the missiles. In other words, the president now improvised a carrot and stick strategy in an effort to bring the crisis to a close before it escalated. Let us consider first the coercive component of his strategy.

Kennedy accepted his advisers' suggestion that he reply to the two contradictory letters from Khrushchev by ignoring the Saturday morning demand for exchange of missile bases and accepting the suggestion contained in Khrushchev's first letter for a quid pro quo linking removal of the missiles from Cuba with a U.S. pledge not to invade Cuba. (As we shall see, the president decided to deal with the issue of the Jupiters in private discussions his brother would have with Dobrynin.) Kennedy's formal reply to Khrushchev did not hint at an ultimatum, although it did convey a sense of urgency. The equivalent of an ultimatum was conveyed by Robert Kennedy in a private meeting with Dobrynin in the early evening of October 27, although this has recently been denied by the former Soviet ambassador.

According to the summary provided in Robert Kennedy's posthumous account in *Thirteen Days*, he told Dobrynin, "we had to have a commitment by tomorrow that those bases [missiles in Cuba] would be removed. I was not giving them an ultimatum but a statement of fact. He should understand that if they did not remove those bases, we would remove them. . . . Time was running out. We had only a few more hours—we needed an answer immediately from the Soviet Union. I said we must have it the next day."[82] If Robert Kennedy's account can be taken at face value, it meant that President Kennedy had finally decided to add to his long-standing demand that the missiles be removed the two missing elements of a full-blown ultimatum—a time limit for compliance with the demand and a credible threat of potent punishment for noncompliance—even though, as Robert Kennedy puts it, this was conveyed not as an explicit ultimatum but as "a statement of fact."[83]

Robert Kennedy's account of his conversation with Dobrynin appears to have been contradicted by the former Soviet ambassador at the Harvard-sponsored

Moscow conference on the Cuban crisis. Dobrynin at first denied that any ultimatum was conveyed or, indeed, that any threats were made. Rather, his recollection was that Robert Kennedy had soft-pedaled the danger of imminent U.S. action and that his cable to Moscow summarizing the meeting with the president's brother was similarly low-key on this point. Later in the Moscow conference, however, Dobrynin acknowledged that Robert Kennedy had indeed conveyed acute time pressure for a response; he "persistently asked, it is true, to convey the president's request that if possible he wanted to receive an answer on Sunday. So I conveyed this to Moscow." Continuing, Dobrynin added that he himself had experienced time urgency for a reply and made the telling comment that "[a]ccording to the evidence we had available [in the Soviet embassy], an air strike was considered very likely, perhaps in the coming days. There might have been also an invasion."[84] The former Soviet ambassador to the United States did not disclose or quote from his cable to Moscow, nor did he say he had recently reread it to refresh his memory.[85] If Dobrynin's cable is declassified, it might well help to clarify what Robert Kennedy told him on that occasion.[86]

The possibility that an ultimatum may have been conveyed by another American is suggested and given some weight by Allyn, Blight, and Welch. At the Moscow conference, Aleksandr Fomin recalled that in his meeting with John Scali on Saturday, October 27, the U.S. newsman angrily threatened that if the missiles were not removed within hours, a U.S. attack would be mounted.[87]

Finally, it should be recognized that the substance of an ultimatum can sometimes be effectively conveyed to an adversary without being fully transmitted in verbal terms. Particularly, the sense of urgency for compliance and the threat of punishment for noncompliance can be effectively conveyed by actions taken that either themselves convey such time-urgent pressure or suggest that the threatener may not be able to maintain control over his side's actions much longer. Thus, before the end of the day on Saturday, October 27, preparations for an invasion of Cuba had reached an advanced stage, and Soviet and Cuban intelligence appears to have reported to Moscow the possibility of imminent U.S. military action.[88] It is possible, therefore, whether or not something like an ultimatum was conveyed by Robert Kennedy, that Khrushchev concluded for other reasons that time was running out and that he had better terminate the crisis immediately.

Including the removal of Jupiters from Turkish bases in the quid pro quo, as we have noted, was a delicate political matter for the president. However, disclosure of new information in recent years establishes that Kennedy felt strongly that the political costs for the U.S. position in NATO should be accepted if including the Jupiters in the deal were necessary for a quick settlement of the crisis. The president's attitude emerges most clearly in his meeting with his advisory group on Saturday, October 27, when he put forward and pressed this view. He was finally persuaded by his Soviet expert, Llewellyn Thompson, to try first to resolve the crisis without including the Jupiters in the quid pro quo.[89] And, as noted earlier, the president made no reference to Khrushchev's demand for removal of the Jupiters in his formal reply to the Soviet leader. But then, as few if any other members of the advisory circle were to know, the president evidently authorized his brother to make a secret deal that explicitly included removal of the Jupiters in the private conversation he had with Dobrynin later that day. The earlier account in *Thirteen Days* of Robert Kennedy's discussion of the Jupiters with Dobrynin on this occasion is incorrect. At the Moscow conference, Theodore Sorensen disclosed that in editing the manuscript of the book, which was based on Robert Kennedy's diaries, he had altered the facts of the secret missile deal to convey erroneously that Robert Kennedy had told Dobrynin that although the Jupiters were in any case to be removed from Turkey, they could not be made a part of the formal settlement terms.[90]

However, these recent disclosures do not challenge the fact that an understanding was reached with the Soviets to keep the missile swap secret. We are now told, too, that the president's determination not to let the matter of the Jupiters prevent a quick settlement of the crisis went further than his authorization of the secret deal for a missile swap. Dean Rusk disclosed at the Hawks Cay Conference in March 1987 that the president quickly followed up the concession for a secret deal his brother made on Saturday evening by creating a fallback option. If the secret deal on the missiles did not suffice, the U.N. secretary-general might then be asked to propose an open missile swap as part of the terms for settling the crisis.[91]

We noted earlier that crisis management began to break down on Saturday, October 27, and that the disturbing sensation that things were getting out of control had a significant impact on Kennedy's policy. These developments had an unsettling effect in Moscow as well and motivated Khrushchev to accept within a matter of hours the formula for settling the crisis that the president proposed toward the end of that day. A few months later, on December 12, 1962, Khrushchev defended his conduct of the Cuban venture in a major speech to the Supreme Soviet. Khrushchev did not allude to having received an ultimatum; however, he did say that he had been placed under urgent pressure to settle the crisis immediately by information that an attack on Cuba would shortly take place: "We received information from our Cuban comrades and from other sources on the morning of October 27 directly stating that this attack would be carried out in the next two or three days. We interpreted these cables as an extremely alarming warning signal. And the alarm was justified. Immediate action was necessary to prevent the attack on Cuba and to preserve the peace."[92] Soviet and Cuban sources have recently added useful details on some of the reasons for Khrushchev's sense of urgency.[93] And we have already alluded to the role played by the shoot-down of the U-2, Scali's statement to Fomin, the advanced military preparations for an invasion of Cuba, the possibility that Cuban air defenses might succeed in their efforts to shoot down U.S. reconnaissance planes, and Robert Kennedy's warning to Dobrynin that time was running out, in heightening Moscow's sense of urgency for ending the crisis.

WHAT IF?

What would Kennedy have done had Khrushchev not accepted the formula he proposed on Saturday for ending the crisis? Would the president have then ordered an air strike or an invasion, or would he have tried to find still other ways of persuading Khrushchev to remove the missiles? While an answer to this question is necessarily speculative, the available evidence—even before Dean Rusk revealed the fallback option of an open missile swap that the president asked him to prepare—

strongly suggests that Kennedy would not have resorted immediately to an air strike or an invasion.

It is useful to recall that during the days when the ExComm was meeting to plan a response to the discovery of the missiles, its members were badly divided on how the general concept of graduated escalation ought to be employed. Some advisers felt that there should be relatively few, if any, steps between the blockade and an air strike (or invasion). Others thought in terms of a series of intervening steps that would permit the president to increase pressure more gradually in the hope that Khrushchev would agree to remove the missiles before either an air strike or invasion became necessary.

Disagreement on this critical issue had not been resolved during the planning sessions. The issue came to the fore again, however, when it became clear that despite the success of the blockade, more pressure would have to be applied to persuade Khrushchev to remove the missiles. On Saturday afternoon, October 27, Sorensen reports, "the Executive Committee was somewhat heatedly discussing plans for the next step. . . . The POL [petroleum products] blockade, air strike and invasion advocates differed over what to do.[94] Consistent with his earlier advocacy of gradual step-by-step escalation McNamara was now in favor of tightening the blockade rather than going immediately to the air strike. The next morning, Sunday, before news arrived of Khrushchev's acceptance of Kennedy's proposal for ending the crisis, McNamara rose early to draw up a list of steps to take short of invasion."[95] At the same time, the Joint Chiefs of Staff and other advisers were pressing the case for an air strike with renewed vigor.

Given the circumstance of a badly divided advisory group and fearing that he was losing control over crisis developments, it is not surprising that the president should bypass the ExComm as a decision-making body and resort to his brother's back-channel meetings with Dobrynin to make additional concessions regarding the Jupiters in order to bring the crisis to a close. Nor is it surprising that he would also secretly prepare the way for an ostensible U.N.-initiated proposal for an open missile swap, should the version of a secret missile swap that his brother had proposed to Dobrynin fail to end the crisis. By portraying himself as having no choice but to accept the U.N. secretary-general's proposal—even though it had been privately and indirectly instigated by the president—Kennedy could hope to reduce the political costs of doing so, both among the hawks in his advisory group and in the U.S. public as well as among his NATO allies.[96]

Even though the president had not decided as yet, for he did not have to, whether he would trigger the U.N. initiative, his preparation of this option for possible use later reflects his strong determination not to let the question of the Jupiters stand in the way of a settlement. He was equally determined to end the crisis peacefully, if possible, before additional U-2 shoot-downs might force him to retaliate against the SAM sites, thereby possibly setting into motion further escalation of the crisis.

ANALYTICAL CONCLUSIONS

As in the four cases of inadvertent war discussed earlier, at the outset of this crisis, too, neither side wanted or expected war. Unlike those four cases, however, in this case all of the various paths to war were avoided. During the course of the missile crisis, neither Kennedy nor Khrushchev came to regard initiation of war as an attractive step, one that offered an opportunity to make important gains. Nor did they come to regard initiation of war as necessary in order to avoid unacceptable damage to their interests.

Also absent in this crisis was the occurrence of miscalculated escalation of the kind that helped trigger war in several of the cases of inadvertent war. It is additionally significant that although both Kennedy and Khrushchev became alarmed that crisis management was breaking down on the last Saturday of their confrontation, neither believed that war was inevitable and that there was nothing more he could do to prevent it.

In brief, war was avoided because the *incentive* to avoid it remained powerful throughout the crisis; because *opportunities* for avoiding escalation were available, were recognized, and were not frittered away; and because the two leaders operated with sufficient *skill* in managing the crisis so as to bring it to a close without being drawn into a shooting war.

The incentive to avoid war was much more powerful in this case than it had been during the six-week crisis that ended in World War I or in any of the other cases of inadvertent war we have examined. The image of war held by most leaders and peoples in 1914 was that war might be painful but certainly not catastrophic. Few in 1914 foresaw that it would develop into a total war with the carnage that followed; many, in fact, tended to glorify war as a noble experience. In contrast, the image of war in 1962 was that of a horrible thermonuclear holocaust, an unimaginable catastrophe; and this image created powerful incentives to manage and terminate the confrontation before it began to escalate.

Whereas there were few good opportunities for effective crisis management in the 1914 and 1967 crises, as Levy and Stein have noted, there were such opportunities in the missile case and these were not pushed aside and wasted. Opportunities for crisis management in the Cuban missile confrontation were highly valued: They were sought out, preserved, and even deliberately created.

Finally, absent in the missile crisis was the ineptness in crisis management so painfully evident in retrospect in the Crimean War case and at various points in the other cases of inadvertent war. Rather, both Khrushchev and Kennedy behaved with sober prudence and reasonable skill to extricate themselves from the war-threatening confrontation in which, quite unexpectedly, they found themselves. Although they did seek to gain advantage through crisis bargaining and their behavior during the blockade evoked concern that they might be about to embark on the dangerous game of chicken, in fact neither Kennedy nor Khrushchev engaged in a reckless competition in risk-taking. In this connection, Kennedy's adherence to the political and operational requirements of crisis management was of critical importance. Unlike Truman and Acheson in 1950, who imprudently escalated the U.S. objective in Korea to unification of the two Koreas by force of arms after the North Korean army was routed and who, after Chinese forces entered North Korea, permitted General MacArthur to resume his provocative march to the Yalu, Kennedy limited both his objectives and the means employed on their behalf.

Similarly, however ambitious Khrushchev's appetite may have been when he decided to place missiles into Cuba, he quickly saw the need to pull back his missile-carrying ships and his submarines and to settle for whatever he could safely gain once confronted by the president's unexpectedly tough response. And in his crisis bargaining with Kennedy, the Soviet leader limited himself to efforts at persuasion and rhetorical threats, foregoing coercive actions. One must agree with McGeorge Bundy's observation that each leader was "determined not to let matters spin out of control through any decision of his own."[97] Each was highly sensitive to the possibility that what he did could force the hand of the other and lead to unwanted escalation.

Therefore, while it is true that in some sense Kennedy went to the brink and that Khrushchev stayed with him for a few days, both were determined not to cross the brink or stumble over it. Moreover, they conveyed this to each other and found a way to cooperate in safely stepping back. The strategy of coercive diplomacy that Kennedy improvised worked in the end, but it is fair to say that his carrot and stick version of it relied heavily on accommodation and not just on coercive threats.

We will not enter into the long-standing debate as to just how close the two sides came to nuclear war. However, it is indisputable, as we have already noted, that several important threats to crisis management emerged during the confrontation that might have triggered escalation to some form of a shooting war. It is important to recognize that threats of this kind, even though surmounted in one crisis, could easily recur in a new crisis, where they would become latent triggers of inadvertent war that challenge the ability of leaders to manage the crisis effectively.

A worrisome threat to crisis management was the Soviet shoot-down of a U-2 on Saturday morning, October 27, which might have triggered a U.S. decision to retaliate against one or more of the Soviet air defense sites, a development that would have shifted the burden of decision to Khrushchev. Equally worrisome was the possibility of military incidents between the U.S. navy and the Soviet submarines that it was prosecuting so energetically. The rules of engagement (ROE) under which the navy operated during the blockade included the right to initiate appropriate military action in self-defense if threatened by hostile action. Such ROEs always carry with them the risk of a *Vincennes*-type incident based on the mistaken perception that one is about to be subjected to hostile fire. The danger of a military clash during blockade operations would be heightened, of course, if the ROE issued by Moscow to the Soviet submarines permitted them similar discretion to initiate hostile action in self-defense. We do not know under what ROE the Soviet submarines were operating; certainly their behavior under the vigorous prosecution to which they were subjected by the U.S. navy indicates great caution and unwillingness to be provoked into retaliatory action. Unlike the commanders of the Soviet SAM sites in Cuba who interpreted their standing orders as permitting them to shoot down the U-2, the commanders of the Soviet submarines were more circumspect. But it easily could be otherwise in a new crisis and in different circumstances in the contemporary era.

Finally, while leaders and their advisers on both sides experienced considerable psychological stress and cumulative fatigue during the intense Cuban Missile Crisis, there is no evidence that the well-known dysfunctional effects of stress, fatigue, and sleep deprivation seriously distorted the decisions and actions of the two sides.[98]

BIBLIOGRAPHICAL NOTE

This chapter draws heavily on the author's earlier analysis of the missile crisis in *Limits of Coercive Diplomacy* (Boston: Little, Brown, 1971, pp. 86–143). It has been updated and revised, as necessary, on the basis of new primary source materials and a number of excellent secondary analyses, but much of the earlier analysis has withstood the passage of time. Particularly useful for this purpose have been the publications cited in the footnotes by James Blight, David Welch, and Bruce Allyn; Joseph Bouchard; Scott Sagan; Raymond Garthoff; and McGeorge Bundy. All students of the missile crisis remain indebted to the seminal study by Graham Allison, *Essence of Decision* (Boston: Little, Brown, 1971). The author expresses appreciation also to Richard Ned Lebow for permitting him to see parts of an important new study of the missile crisis he is preparing.

NOTES

1. For the distinction between the weaker "try-and-see" and the stronger "ultimatum" variants of coercive diplomacy and a fuller discussion of this strategy, see A. L. George, D. K. Hall, and W. E. Simons, *The Limits of Coercive Diplomacy* (Boston: Little, Brown, 1971), pp. 27–28, 26–27, 214–215.

2. An accumulation of declassified U.S. government documents, some that have become available only in recent years, indicates that contingency plans for possible direct U.S. military intervention in Cuba, as a possible back-up for covert operations associated with "Operation Mongoose," were initiated in late 1961. If Soviet leaders had knowledge of this early contingency planning, it could have stimulated fear of U.S. intentions and thus encouraged Khrushchev to consider putting missiles into Cuba. In addition, Soviet suspicions regarding U.S. intentions might well have been fed by various indications of increased U.S. diplomatic pressure against Castro and a series of U.S. military exercises in the Caribbean, beginning in early April. However, the more serious U.S. contingency plans came later and were in good part a result of Washington's mounting concern over the substantial buildup of Soviet military assistance to Cuba that began in July. That a considerable step-up in U.S. military preparations occurred in late September and early October, before the discovery of the missiles, is not surprising given Kennedy's warning on September 4 and again on the 13th that he would not tolerate introduction of offensive weapons. And it should be noted that the most serious and urgent planning of military options prior to the actual discovery of the missiles via photo reconnaissance on October 16 was initiated on October 2 on the basis of disturbing, but as yet not conclusive evidence, that missiles were entering Cuba. For a useful compilation and interesting interpretation of U.S. contingency planning and political-military pressure on Cuba see James G. Hershberg, "Before 'The Missiles of October': Did Kennedy Plan a Military Strike Against Cuba?" Occasional Paper #89-1, Nuclear Age History and Humanities Center, Tufts University, October 1989.

3. "In addition to protecting Cuba, our missiles would have equalized what the West likes to call 'the balance of power,' " Nikita Khrushchev, *Khrushchev Remembers* (Boston: Little, Brown, 1970), p. 494. It should be noted that Khrushchev's talk of extending nuclear deterrence to protect Cuba from the United States goes back to June 1960, as do U.S. charges that missiles bases were being installed in Cuba. On that and subsequent occasions Khrushchev stated that the Soviet Union did not need bases for missiles in Cuba since it had the capability of launching missiles from the Soviet Union. At the same time, on this and subsequent occasions he was careful not to commit the Soviet Union to launch its missiles in defense of Cuba. Khrushchev repeated his threat to intervene on behalf of Cuba on April 18, 1961, at the outset of the Bay of Pigs invasion before the extent of U.S. support for the invasion was known. Cf. Herbert S. Dinerstein, *The Making of a Missile Crisis:*

October 1962 (Baltimore: Johns Hopkins University Press, 1976), pp. 80–98, 101–111, 115, 125, 129–131, 133.

4. For detailed discussions, which generally support the interpretation offered here see, for example, Raymond L. Garthoff, *Reflections on the Cuban Missile Crisis*, revised edition (Washington, D.C.: Brookings Institution, 1989), pp. 21–24; and the forthcoming study by Richard Ned Lebow.

5. For a detailed description and analysis of Khrushchev's boasts and threats, see Arnold Horelick and Myron Rush, *Strategic Power and Soviet Foreign Policy* (Chicago: University of Chicago Press, 1965).

6. See particularly Garthoff, *Reflections*, pp. 6–42; James G. Blight and David A. Welch, *On the Brink* (New York: Hill and Wang, 1989), pp. 291–301; Bruce J. Allyn, James G. Blight, and David A. Welch, "Essence of Revision," *International Security* 14, 3 (Winter 1989/90): 138–149; and the important forthcoming study by Richard Ned Lebow.

7. As Khrushchev described it in his memoirs, his plan was to install "missiles with nuclear warheads in Cuba without letting the United States find out they were there until it was too late to do anything about them. . . . My thinking went like this: If we installed the missiles secretly and then the United States discovered the missiles were there after they were already poised and ready to strike, the Americans would think twice before trying to liquidate our installations by military means."

8. Roger Hilsman, *To Move a Nation* (New York: Doubleday, 1967), p. 182. For a fuller description of Soviet risk calculations and the basis for Khrushchev's miscalculation, see A. L. George and R. Smoke, *Deterrence in American Foreign Policy: Theory and Practice* (New York: Columbia University Press, 1974), pp. 459–466.

9. McGeorge Bundy recalls that the president's September 4 statement "was more an assurance to his countrymen than a direct warning to Khrushchev." *Danger and Survival* (New York: Random House, 1988), pp. 393, 413. See also Hilsman, *To Move a Nation*, pp. 196–197. On the other hand, as Arthur Schlesinger reports, Robert Kennedy, who took the lead in urging the president to issue the warning, did so because he was concerned that the deployment of the SA-2 air defense missiles to Cuba might be followed by surface-to-surface nuclear missiles. Schlesinger, *Robert Kennedy and His Times* (New York: Ballantine Books, 1978), pp. 544–545.

10. Hilsman, *To Move a Nation*, pp. 196–198. Two historians, Thomas G. Paterson and William T. Brophy, have recently examined charges that Kennedy was driven "as much by political motives as by considerations of national security or prestige." While acknowledging that a definitive answer to this question is not possible and that presidents "necessarily make decisions that derive from a complex of private thoughts and public pressures that the historians cannot easily disentangle," they conclude as follows: "Kennedy did not engage Cuba and the Soviet Union in the missile crisis in October in order to silence his noisy Republican critics or to attract votes for Democrats in November. As Kennedy knew before October 16, the Democrats already enjoyed a formidable position in the elections. . . . The Democrats had no political need for manufacturing a war scare, and Kennedy did not welcome a new Cuban crisis. From October 16 to October 22, Kennedy's choice of the quarantine was not dictated by politics, though the tactic of the television address may have been. From the alarmist speech to the fading of the crisis on October 28, Kennedy ruminated about the political effects of the imbroglio, but, again, his decisions did not reflect a partisan stance. . . ." "October Missiles and November Elections: The Cuban Missile Crisis and American Politics, 1962," *Journal of American History* 73, 1 (June 1989): 87–119.

On the importance of domestic political constraints on President Kennedy see also Bundy, *Danger and Survival*, pp. 410–413, and Fen Osler Hampson, "The Divided Decision-Maker: American Domestic Politics and the Cuban Crises," *International Security* 9 (Winter 1984/5): 130–165.

11. Hilsman, *To Move a Nation*, pp. 161, 164. The fact that Khrushchev did not threaten pressure against Berlin *after* the crisis got under way, in order thereby to deter Kennedy from implementing the blockade, which the president and his advisers feared, should not obscure the fact that on several occasions *before* the missiles were discovered Soviet sources had indicated that the Berlin issue would be raised again after the U.S. midterm elections.

12. See, for example, Nathan Leites, *A Study of Bolshevism* (New York: Free Press, 1953).

13. Robert F. Kennedy, *Thirteen Days* (New York: Norton, 1969), pp. 126–127.

14. Cf., e.g., Blight and Welch, *On the Brink*, pp. 236, 298. Garthoff (*Reflections*, p. 22), however, argues that while Khrushchev may have misjudged Kennedy's mettle after the Vienna meeting such a judgment "would have been superceded by the tough and effective Western stand over Berlin. . . ."

15. Schlesinger, *A Thousand Days: John Kennedy in the White House* (Boston: Houghton Mifflin, 1965), p. 803.

16. Theodore C. Sorensen, *Kennedy* (New York: Harper & Row, 1965), p. 684. Later in the discussions of the ExComm it emerged that the type of air strike against the missile sites contemplated at that time by no means fit the conception of a "surgical" strike but would have entailed considerable collateral damage and casualties.

17. For an account of the reasons for cancellation of direct U-2 overflights of western Cuba on September 10 see A. L. George and R. Smoke, *Deterrence*, pp. 474–477. By as early as October 1, intelligence of a possible missile deployment—particularly photo reconnaissance that indicated the preparation of a launch site for offensive missiles in the San Cristobal area—was taken seriously enough to lead Secretary of Defense McNamara to order military readiness and preparations for various possible military actions, including particularly a *possible* U.S. invasion of Cuba, geared to an October 20 date. Had the October 1 intelligence interpretations been regarded by the president as a clear indication that a missile deployment was underway, he might have fashioned a strategy for nipping it in the bud. But Kennedy evidently believed he needed hard evidence—such as the U-2 eventually provided on October 14—before he could take firm action. For a fuller discussion, see Joseph F. Bouchard, "Use of Naval Force in Crises: A Theory of Stratified Crisis Interaction," Ph.D. dissertation, Department of Political Science, Stanford University, September 1988, pp. 527–533. (An abbreviated version of the dissertation will be published in 1991 by Columbia University Press under the title *Command in Crisis: Four Case Studies*.)

18. Arthur Schlesinger, Jr., *A Thousand Days*, p. 391.

19. Garthoff, *Reflections*, pp. 29, 48. For summary of Soviet statements indicating that the issue of Berlin would be raised again after the U.S. midterm congressional elections, see James Marc Goldgeier, "Soviet Leaders and International Crises," Ph.D. dissertation, Department of Political Science, University of California at Berkeley, 1990, pp. 146, 148, 151.

20. Sorensen, *Kennedy*, pp. 671, 677, 681.

21. Joseph Bouchard, "Use of Naval Force," p. 506, notes that between September 2 (at the end of Che Guevara's visit to Moscow) and October 18 (Gromyko's meeting with President Kennedy) the Soviets on at least eight occasions stated that they were sending only defensive weapons to Cuba. On Soviet deception see also Hilsman, *To Move a Nation*, pp. 165–167; Schlesinger, *A Thousand Days*, pp. 798–799, 805; and Garthoff, *Reflections*, pp. 47–48. Bundy, *Danger and Survival*, 414, offers an interesting speculation that Khrushchev's deceptive statements may have also been clumsy efforts to offer assurances that the purpose of the missile deployment was "defensive."

22. One variant of this thesis alleges that Kennedy had an aggressive, competitive "macho" personality that typically expressed itself in a desire to dominate others and to win.

A somewhat different variant of this thesis alleges that Kennedy overreacted to the missile deployment because he was afflicted with a neurotic sense of personal weakness and lack of self-confidence and needed to "prove himself." Still another variant of the thesis deemphasizes the idea of a personality defect and suggests, instead, that Kennedy acted impulsively; having been humiliated by Khrushchev's behavior towards him, Kennedy gave vent to aggressive impulses to inflict humiliation on the Soviet leader.

None of these personality explanations is persuasive. They rest heavily on conjecture; I find no evidence in available materials that the president's judgment was distorted by an emotional response to being deceived by Khrushchev. Moreover, to assign critical importance to Kennedy's "macho" personality fails to recognize that his judgment that it was necessary to display resolution was shared by many of his advisers.

See, for example, I. F. Stone, "The Brink," a review of Elie Abel's *Missile Crisis* (Philadelphia: J. B. Lippincott, 1966) in the *New York Review of Books*, April 13, 1966; R. J. Walton, *Cold War and Counterrevolution* (New York: Viking Press, 1972), pp. 103, 116; Louise FitzSimons, *The Kennedy Doctrine* (New York: Random House, 1972), chapter 5; David Horowitz, *The Free World Colossus* (New York: Hill and Wang, 1965); Thomas M. Mongar, "Personality and Decisionmaking: John F. Kennedy in Four Crisis Decisions," *Canadian Journal of Political Science*, II (1964): 200–225; Ronald Steel, "Endgame," a review of Robert F. Kennedy's *Thirteen Days*, in *New York Review of Books*, March 13, 1969; Nancy Gager Clinch, *The Kennedy Neurosis* (New York: Grossett & Dunlap, 1973); Barton J. Bernstein, " 'Courage and Commitment': The Missiles of October," *Foreign Service Journal*, December 1975, and "The Cuban Missile Crisis" in *Reflections on the Cold War*, L. H. Miller and R. W. Pruessen, eds. (Philadelphia: Temple University Press, 1974), pp. 108–142. For critical assessments of the "macho" interpretation see Schlesinger, *Robert Kennedy*, pp. 551–554; and Graham Allison, "Cuban Missiles and Kennedy Macho: New Evidence to Dispel the Myth," *Washington Monthly* (October 1972), pp. 14–19.

23. In conceptualizing bargaining strategy here I have drawn on the excellent discussion in Glenn H. Snyder and Paul Diesing, *Conflict Among Nations* (Princeton, N.J.: Princeton University Press, 1977), chapter 3, "Crisis Bargaining: Strategies and Tactics." See also the further development of these ideas in Philip Rogers's chapter on crisis bargaining codes in this book.

24. See Nathan Leites, *Bolshevism*, and Alexander L. George, "The 'Operational Code': A Neglected Approach to the Study of Political Leaders and Decision-making," *International Studies Quarterly* 13, 2 (June 1969).

25. Bundy, *Danger and Survival*, pp. 393–395, 397, 408–411, and Schlesinger, *Robert Kennedy*, pp. 552–553, 555, 557, 572, present arguments against the purely diplomatic option similar to those advanced here. See also Graham T. Allison, *Essence of Decision*, pp. 58, 201–202.

26. An important question that has not been satisfactorily clarified concerns the operational status of the missiles—when they achieved this status and what it means. Members of Kennedy's advisory group attached a great deal of weight to whether the missiles were reaching operational status, but as the Hawks Cay conference indicated, there was lack of clarity and agreement among them as to what this meant. Blight and Welch, *On the Brink*, pp. 54–57, 125–126.

CIA intelligence estimates early in the crisis indicated that many of the missiles had achieved operational status. And yet work on the missile sites continued and Kennedy's advisers seemed genuinely concerned that they would soon be fully operational or, if not removed soon, would come to be regarded as part of a new status quo.

It should be added that U.S. policy makers did not know whether there were any nuclear warheads in Cuba. In the Moscow conference of January 27–28, 1989, organized by the Kennedy School, General Dimitry Volkagonov, head of the Institute of Military History,

Soviet Ministry of Defense, disclosed that twenty nuclear warheads had arrived in Cuba in late September or early October, and that twenty more were in transit aboard the *Poltava* when the blockade went into effect. Allyn, Blight, and Welch, "Essence of Revision," pp. 153–155.

27. Overstating to make this point, Hugh Sidey asserts that Kennedy ordered the blockade of Cuba "not to stop ships from bringing in missiles—that did not matter in the time which the U.S. had to act—but as a device to send the message of our determination through clearly to Nikita Khrushchev." *Life Magazine*, November 22, 1968.

28. The president's rejection of Adlai Stevenson's more explicit and more extreme views regarding what the United States ought to be prepared to contribute to a quid pro quo and the notoriety that Stevenson's views achieved thereafter have obscured the fact that the president and other close advisers—including his brother and McNamara—also believed that the United States might have to, and ought to be willing to, make concessions in return for the removal of the missiles. See Schlesinger, *Robert Kennedy*, pp. 554–560. Even before Stevenson joined the late afternoon meeting of the ExComm on Friday, October 18, "someone observed that the United States would have to pay a price to get them out: perhaps we should throw in our now obsolescent and vulnerable Jupiter missile bases in Turkey and Italy, whose removal the Joint Congressional Committee on Atomic Energy as well as the Secretary of Defense had recommended in 1961." Schlesinger, A *Thousand Days*, p. 807.

29. Ibid., p. 810.

30. Ibid., p. 811 (emphasis added).

31. Sorensen, *Kennedy*, p. 699 (emphasis added).

32. Kennedy, *Thirteen Days*, pp. 66–67 (emphasis added).

33. Bouchard, drawing on a number of declassified sources, reports that the U.S. Navy had "mounted intensive surveillance of Soviet bloc shipping to Cuba since early August. When the President announced the quarantine on October 22, the Navy already had a complete list of the Soviet bloc ships en route to Cuba, including those suspected of carrying offensive missiles. The Soviet bloc ships were being tracked by the Navy's Univac Sea Surveillance Computer System, which projected their position based on their last known course and speed. On October 23 there were twenty-five Soviet and two other Soviet bloc ships en route to Cuba, including nineteen Soviet freighters (dry cargo ships) and two Soviet tankers. Of the nineteen Soviet freighters, three (*Okhotsk, Orenburg,* and *Poltava*) were large hatch ships suspected of carrying offensive missiles, two were carrying suspected missiles or missile-related equipment on deck, and eleven others were suspected of carrying other military equipment (for a total of sixteen freighters suspected of carrying military cargoes). Additionally, there were eighteen Soviet bloc ships in Cuban ports when the quarantine was announced.

Of the nineteen Soviet freighters en route to Cuba when the quarantine was announced, all sixteen suspected of carrying military cargoes turned back, and the other three proceeded on to Cuba. . . ." Bouchard, "Use of Naval Force," pp. 628–629.

34. Bouchard (p. 633) reports that Moscow had HF radio links with all its merchant fleet and used them to control the ships en route to Cuba. He notes that all sixteen ships suspected by the United States of carrying missiles and other military equipment were immediately ordered to reverse course and return to the Soviet Union. Bouchard cites the October 25 daily CIA report ("Crisis USSR/Cuba," p. II-1): "The course changes of those ships which have turned back were executed around noon EDT [Eastern Daylight Time] on 23 October. . . . The ships turned around well before President Kennedy signed the proclamation establishing a quarantine zone around Cuba."

35. Khrushchev, it may be noted, did not notify the United States that he had done so until his letter to Kennedy late in the afternoon of October 26 (Moscow time). This gives

indirect support for the interpretation offered here that the order to turn back may have been a time-buying tactic to see whether the U.S. naval blockade would be implemented, and that the possibility of resuming the missile deployment later was not at this time excluded.

36. Garthoff, *Reflections*, p. 27.

37. Cited in Ronald R. Pope, ed., *Soviet Views on the Cuban Missile Crisis* (Washington, D.C.: University Press of America, Inc., 1982), pp. 32–36.

38. The substance of Knox's conversation with Khrushchev was relayed to Washington. See Hilsman, *To Move a Nation*, p. 214; Sorensen, *Kennedy*, p. 710; Abel, *Missile Crisis*, p. 151. Knox himself later published a full account: "Close-up of Khrushchev During a Crisis," *New York Times Magazine*, November 18, 1962. In the interview with Knox the Soviet leader admitted the presence of missiles in Cuba (which was still being publicly denied) and said that the United States would have to learn to live with the new situation just as the Soviets had with U.S. missiles in Turkey. Khrushchev also stated that nuclear warheads were in Cuba but under strict Soviet control, and suggested a summit meeting to resolve the crisis. For additional details of Khrushchev's efforts to persuade and/or coerce Kennedy see James Marc Goldgeier, "Soviet Leaders," pp. 153–159, 166–167.

39. Garthoff, *Reflections*, p. 79.

40. Cited in Pope, *Soviet Views*, p. 42.

41. On the importance of legitimacy in crisis bargaining see Snyder and Diesing, *Conflict Among Nations*, pp. 498–499; and Paul C. Stern, et al., eds., *Perspectives on Deterrence* (New York: Oxford University Press, 1989), pp. 298–304.

42. Through diplomatic channels the State Department succeeded in persuading U Thant to modify his proposal by restricting its application to but a few days in order to make it more acceptable to Kennedy. On Thursday morning, October 25, the U.N. secretary-general called upon Khrushchev "to instruct the Soviet ships already on their way to Cuba to stay away from the interception area *for a limited time only.*" In return, Kennedy was "to do everything possible to avoid direct confrontation with the Soviet ships *in the next few days* in order to minimize the risk of any untoward incident." David L. Larson, ed., *"The Cuban Crisis" of 1962: Selected Documents and Chronology* (Boston: Houghton Mifflin, 1963) (emphasis added). U Thant's second proposal was immediately accepted by the president on the same day it was made. And Khrushchev accepted it the following day, Friday, October 26. But by then the crisis had evolved into a new phase.

43. The relevant documents are reproduced in Henry M. Pachter, *Collision Course* (New York: Praeger, 1963), and also in David L. Larson, ed., *Selected Documents*.

44. A briefer version of this interpretation of Khrushchev's "missed opportunity" was presented in A. L. George, et al., *Coercive Diplomacy*, p. 119. A similar interpretation with interesting nuances appeared in Goldgeier, "Soviet Leaders," pp. 272–274.

Some indirect evidence indicates that the Soviet government finally decided to call off work on the missile sites but without agreeing as yet to dismantle and remove them. Khrushchev's letter of Sunday morning, October 28, which accepted Kennedy's formula for removing the missiles, contained a cryptic reference to "previously issued instructions on the cessation of further work at the weapons construction sites." Pope, *Soviet Views*, p. 58.

Available materials do not indicate whether Khrushchev had attempted to bring such an earlier order to Kennedy's attention. Indeed, none of the commentaries and analyses of the crisis that I am familiar with have taken note of this passage in Khrushchev's letter. If the Soviet government finally resorted to this option because it was suddenly impressed with the danger of an American attack, then it had waited too long to put into effect the attractive bargaining strategy described in the preceding paragraphs. We note, finally, without being able to clarify or document it, the possible link between Castro's belated reply to U Thant earlier on Saturday in which he conditionally agreed to a cessation of work on the missiles, and Khrushchev's reference to such an order as having been given in his letter to Kennedy.

Khrushchev may have considered it necessary to obtain Castro's acquiescence before ordering work to stop on the missile sites; but this in itself does not clarify the other components of the Soviet decision.

45. Cf. Leites, *Bolshevism*, pp. 30–34, 52, 57–60. Goldgeier, "Soviet Leaders," disagrees with the interpretation offered here and offers a different one based on a deductive model that emphasizes the importance of the domestic political experience of each Soviet leader.

46. Bouchard, "Use of Naval Force," pp. 636–638. Bouchard observes that Allison, *Essence of Decision*, p. 128, errs in reporting that the White House circumvented the chain of command and gave orders directly to local commanders. The heated exchange at one point between McNamara and Admiral George Anderson over the Navy's procedures for intercepting ships is described in Abel, *Missile Crisis*, p. 155; see also Allison, *Essence of Decision*, pp. 131–132.

47. Some military actions did take place that were either not authorized by the president or were inconsistent with his efforts to control events. These included SAC Commander General Thomas S. Power's unauthorized sending of the DefCon 2 alert in open channels, the extent of U.S. covert operations in and around Cuba of which the president may not have been aware, the straying of a U-2 over Siberia, and the possibility that the Navy's antisubmarine operations were more vigorous than the president was aware of and to which he might not have given approval, which is discussed later in this chapter.

48. Allyn, Blight, and Welch, *Essence of Revision*, pp. 166–167.

49. A controversy has arisen among scholars on the Cuban crisis as to the distance from Cuba at which the blockade line was established and whether it was moved closer to Cuba by the president in order to give Khrushchev more time before the first interception of Soviet ships would occur. The latest evidence from U.S. naval records, as obtained and interpreted by Bouchard (see also Scott A. Sagan, "Nuclear Alerts and Crisis Management," *International Security* 9 [Spring 1985]: 110), now establishes rather conclusively that the blockade line was established on October 24 (the decision to do so having been taken on October 20) on an arc 500 nautical miles from Cape Maisi and that it was not moved closer to Cuba until October 30. Hence Robert Kennedy, (*Thirteen Days*, p. 67) and others who recall that the line was initially established at 800 nautical miles are mistaken. Similarly, Graham Allison (*Essence of Decision*, pp. 129–130) and others are mistaken in holding that the navy did not carry out Kennedy's order to pull the blockade line closer to Cuba. See the detailed account in Bouchard, "Use of Naval Force," pp. 618–28, which also notes several errors in Dan Caldwell's interpretation, "A Research Note on the Quarantine of Cuba, October 1962," *International Studies Quarterly* 22 (December 1978): 625–633.

50. Albert Wohlstetter and Roberta Wohlstetter, "Controlling the Risks of Cuba," Adelphi Papers, No. 17, Institute of Strategic Studies, London, p. 19.

51. Kennedy, *Thirteen Days*, pp. 79–80.

52. Ibid., p. 74; Bouchard, "Use of Naval Force," p. 634.

53. For a detailed discussion of the rules of engagement given to the U.S. Navy, see Bouchard, "Use of Naval Force," pp. 597–606, 630–631.

54. Kennedy, *Thirteen Days*, p. 66.

55. Schlesinger, *A Thousand Days*, p. 817.

56. Kennedy, *Thirteen Days*, p. 74.

57. Bouchard, "Use of Naval Force," pp. 629, 633–634.

58. Kennedy, *Thirteen Days*, pp. 51, 52, 54, 102.

59. The following summary account draws primarily from Bouchard, "Use of Naval Force," pp. 643–675; important material and interpretation is contained also in Scott A. Sagan, "Nuclear Alerts," pp. 112–117.

60. Bouchard, "Use of Naval Force," pp. 659–660.

61. Ibid., pp. 660–661.

62. Ibid., p. 678, also p. 684 and pp. 662–663. Bouchard's source is the report by the Commander in Chief Atlantic, CINCLANT Historical Account of the Cuban Crisis 1962, April 29, 1963 (Operational Archives, Naval Historical Center, Washington, D.C.), p. 11.

63. Bouchard, "Use of Naval Force," pp. 664–668. See also Sagan, "Nuclear Alerts," p. 117.

64. Sagan, "Nuclear Alerts," p. 113; Bouchard, "Use of Naval Force," p. 669. At the same time it should be noted that the data now available renders questionable views expressed by previous writers that the navy initiated ASW operations without prior authorization. Allison, Essence of Decision, p. 138.

65. Bouchard, "Use of Naval Force," pp. 669, 657–658. Bouchard also notes that in his oral history Vice Admiral Alfred G. Ward, Commander U.S. Second Fleet, which conducted the blockade, recalls reporting a submarine contact to the White House and being told not to take offensive action against it. See also Sagan, "Nuclear Alerts," p. 115.

66. This was implied in Robert Kennedy's account which suggests that the president "increased the pressure" on Khrushchev among other things by ordering the navy to harass the Soviet submarines. Thirteen Days, p. 55. See also George, Coercive Diplomacy, pp. 112–113. Several statements by Chief of Naval Operations Admiral George Anderson, in 1973 and 1987, as noted by Bouchard, give indirect support for the view that the assertive ASW actions were intended—at least by the navy, if not also the president—to put pressure on Khrushchev by demonstrating U.S. naval superiority. Bouchard, "Use of Naval Force," pp. 654–656; see also Allison, Essence of Decision, p. 138.

67. In an interview with German correspondent Bernd Greiner on October 13, 1987, Sergei Mikoyan stated that after being initially surprised by Kennedy's announcement of the blockade Soviet leaders "wanted to find out how far he would go. See, we knew that despite the blockade some ships had been allowed to pass. Therefore, we wanted to find out where Kennedy's limits were. . . . When some of our submarines in the Caribbean were forced to surface, we knew: this is a sign that war might be at hand. Perhaps this was the episode when we understood that the blockade was a very serious thing." Bernd Greiner, "The Soviet View: An Interview with Sergo Mikoyan," Diplomatic History 14, 2 (Spring 1990). I am indebted to Marc Trachtenberg and Barton Bernstein for calling this to my attention.

68. "At first there had been very little support of a blockade," Sorensen recalls, for "it appeared almost irrelevant to the problem of missiles. . . . The greatest single drawback to the blockade was time. Instead of presenting Khrushchev and the world with a fait accompli, it offered a prolonged and agonizing approach, uncertain in its effect, indefinite in its duration, enabling the missiles to become operational, subjecting us to counter-threats from Khrushchev . . . and in all these ways making more difficult a subsequent air strike if the missiles remained." Sorensen, Kennedy, pp. 687–688.

69. Ibid., p. 694.

70. Kennedy, Thirteen Days, p. 83; see also Hilsman, To Move a Nation, pp. 213–214; Abel, The Missile Crisis, p. 173; and Sorensen, Kennedy, p. 711.

71. Kennedy, Thirteen Days, p. 83.

72. An interesting indication that even at this stage in the crisis the president envisaged the possibility that it might drag on for a considerable period is contained in his rebuke to the State Department for White's press conference. According to Sorensen (Kennedy, p. 712), the president argued that "this was going to be a prolonged struggle . . . requiring caution, patience and as little public pressure on him as possible." But in the next twenty-four hours the president joked about White's unauthorized statement saying that it may have helped the Soviets realize how urgent the situation really was. Hilsman, To Move a Nation, p. 214.

73. This quotation is taken from Hilsman's record of what Rusk wrote on a piece of paper for Scali to say. However, Rusk was evidently more specific in his verbal instructions

to Scali; according to Hilsman, Rusk told Scali to say that *"no more than two days"* remained. Hilsman, *To Move a Nation*, p. 218 (emphasis added). We have no independent account of what formulation of the sense of urgency Scali actually transmitted to Fomin when they met again at 7:35 P.M. Detailed accounts of the Scali-Fomin meetings, which continued into November, appear also in Abel, *Missile Crisis*, pp. 175–177; and particularly in Pierre Salinger, *With Kennedy* (New York: Doubleday, 1966), pp. 341–348.

New information from Fomin himself and other Soviet sources called into question whether his approach to Scali was ordered by Moscow or taken on his own initiative, but it has also been stated that he operated under general guidance from Soviet Ambassador Dobrynin to sound out possible American positions. Garthoff, *Reflections*, p. 80; see also Moscow conference transcript, pp. 71–73, 74. Goldgeier, "Soviet Leaders," p. 177ff, effectively challenges the assertion that Fomin acted "independently" in deciding to approach Scali.

74. By October 25, however, the president was beginning to think of some kind of international guarantee for Cuba against an invasion in return for removal of the missiles, and on the 26th in an ExComm meeting he asked whether the United States should make such a commitment. Rusk's reply was that the United States had already made such a commitment under the U.N. Charter and the Rio Treaty of 1947. Garthoff, *Reflections*, pp. 72–73.

75. The Soviets employed multiple channels for this purpose. At about the same time that Fomin was talking to Scali, Schlesinger (A *Thousand Days*, p. 827) reports, "in New York . . . we heard that Zorin had advanced the same proposal to U Thant, and that the Cubans at the United Nations were beginning to hint to unaligned delegates that the bases might be dismantled and removed if the United States would guarantee the territorial integrity of Cuba." Garthoff (*Reflections*, p. 81) reports that on the 26th U Thant made a similar suggestion to U.N. Ambassador Adlai Stevenson and John McCloy.

76. For a useful discussion of external and subjective pressures contributing to a sense of urgency to resolve the crisis, see Blight and Welch, *On the Brink*, pp. 128–131, 310–312; also James G. Blight, *The Shattered Crystal Ball: Fear and Learning in the Cuban Missile Crisis* (Savage, Md.: Rowman and Littlefield, 1990); and Bundy, *Danger and Survival*, pp. 423–427.

77. Hilsman, *To Move a Nation*, pp. 220–221; Abel, *Missile Crisis*, pp. 188–189.

78. As early as Tuesday, October 23, Soviet Defense Minister Rodion Malinosky, in a conversation with a Western diplomat, had compared Cuba and Turkey. In the middle of the week, according to unconfirmed sources, the Soviet ambassador in Ankara had threatened annihilation of Turkish cities in case the American bases there were not soon dismantled. On Friday the Red Army paper, *Red Star*, referred to the idea of a trade of the Cuban and Turkish bases. Henry M. Pachter, *Collision Course* (New York: Praeger, 1963), pp. 49–52. The idea of such a base swap had received sympathetic mention in the British press early in the week and attracted widespread support in the United Nations where it appeared to many representatives to be a natural and reasonable way to end the dreadful danger of war.

79. Hilsman, *To Move a Nation*, p. 220.

80. The various interpretations that have been offered since the crisis to explain the U-2 shootdown are summarized and evaluated by Allyn, Blight, and Welch in their article, "Essence of Revision." New details concerning the incident made available at the Harvard-sponsored Moscow conference confirm that the action against the U-2 was undertaken by local Soviet commanders, not by the Cuban military as some earlier accounts have alleged. However, the information and views provided by Soviet participants in the conference suggest that it is likely that Soviet commanders in Cuba believed that they had authority under the "standing orders" or "rules of engagement" given them by Moscow under certain circumstances to undertake hostile action against the U-2 and that they did not believe they were exceeding their orders and undertaking an unauthorized act.

Allyn, Blight, and Welch, "Essence of Revision," p. 60, place a different interpretation on the new information on the U-2 incident than the one presented here; they regard the new information as "confirming" that the U-2 shoot-down was indeed an unauthorized act by Soviet air defense forces." However, on closer analysis the information these authors provide lends greater support to the alternative interpretation that the standing orders to local Soviet commanders were phrased in ways that allowed these local commanders discretion under certain circumstances to act as they did. Thus, former Soviet ambassador to Cuba Aleksandr Alekseev stated at the Moscow conference that "There was no instruction [to shoot down the U-2] from Moscow, the right had been given to our command to make such decisions—to General Pliyev in particular. . . . They decided that they had the full right to give such an order. The two [Soviet] generals [in Cuba] decided and called Pliyev, who was out, and so they launched the missiles." *Proceedings of the Moscow Conference on the Cuban Missile Crisis*, January 27, 28, 1989. Edited by Bruce J. Allyn, James G. Blight, and David A. Welch (Cambridge, MA: Center for Science and International Affairs, Harvard University, December 1989), p. 19. (In a private communication of May 27, 1990, David Welch agreed with the alternative interpretation advanced here, indicating that what he and his co-authors meant to convey was that the shootdown of the U-2 was not deliberately ordered by Khrushchev at the time as a test of the United States.) An interpretation similar to that offered here is also favored by Goldgeier, "Soviet Leaders," p. 180. Significantly, Soviet participants in the Moscow conference did not disclose the standing orders under which local Soviet commanders were operating. Thus, it is entirely plausible that although top-level political and military leaders in Moscow were indeed upset to learn of the U-2 shootdown, the fault might lie with their failure to review standing orders given Soviet air defense forces in Cuba prior to the shootdown. This interpretation is in fact strengthened by evidence, to which Allyn, Blight, and Welch call attention, that top-level Soviet military leaders may have attempted to avoid responsibility for the action. For a somewhat different interpretation see Garthoff, *Reflections*, pp. 82–85.

81. The dilemma the U-2 shootdown created for Kennedy is clearly identified in earlier accounts of the crisis by his advisers (Hilsman, *To Move a Nation*, p. 220; Kennedy, *Thirteen Days*, p. 98; Sorensen, *Kennedy*, p. 713) and was emphasized by George, *Coercive Diplomacy*, pp. 124–125. Important details that depict the gravity with which this policy dilemma was experienced have emerged in the transcript of the meetings of the advisory group on Saturday, October 27, reproduced in McGeorge Bundy and James G. Blight, "October 27, 1962: Transcripts of the Meetings of the ExComm," *International Security* 12, 3 (Winter 1987–88).

82. Kennedy, *Thirteen Days*, p. 169. A similar version of what Robert Kennedy told Dobrynin was included in a written account of the meeting he provided Rusk three days later. Cited by Schlesinger, *Robert Kennedy*, p. 561. That Robert Kennedy gave Dobrynin the equivalent of an ultimatum is indirectly supported by Bundy (*Danger and Survival*, pp. 432, 438) who was present when the president instructed his brother what to convey to the Soviet ambassador. On p. 441 Bundy refers to it as an "ultimatum." As for Sergei Mikoyan, in his interview with Bernd Greiner ("The Soviet View," pp. 27–28) he states that Robert Kennedy "delivered an urgent message, and we got it."

83. Some analysts, struck by the president's emphasis during the ExComm meeting of Saturday October 27 on the need to conciliate Khrushchev by offering the removal of the Jupiters as part of a quid pro quo to end the crisis may find it surprising—and therefore perhaps implausible—that the president would so soon thereafter resort to an increase in coercive pressure via the equivalent of an ultimatum. What this overlooks, however, is that the president not only *combined* the increased pressure with accommodation but, as we shall note later, the offer conveyed by his brother making removal of the Jupiters part of the *formal* quid pro quo went further than what the ExComm had agreed to just a few hours

before. Nor would this have been the first time the president used his brother to convey an informal ultimatum to Khrushchev. See Arthur Schlesinger's account of the message Robert Kennedy conveyed through one of his back-channel Soviet contacts during the tense U.S.-Soviet tank confrontation at the Brandenburg Gate during the last days of the Berlin 1961 crisis. *Robert Kennedy,* p. 538.

84. *Proceedings of the Moscow conference,* pp. 54, 93.

85. Allyn, Blight, and Welch, "Essence of Revision," p. 163. Dobrynin also contradicted the account of his conversation with Robert Kennedy contained in Khrushchev's memoirs (Cf. *Khrushchev Remembers,* pp. 497–498) which stated that the president's brother had spoken alarmingly of the danger of an imminent coup against his brother or the loss of civilian control over the U.S. military.

86. It is perhaps relevant to note, also, that *Thirteen Days* was not the first occasion on which Robert Kennedy spoke of having conveyed an ultimatum-type warning to Dobrynin. Several of Kennedy's advisers have also referred to a deadline for compliance or an ultimatum in their accounts of the crisis. Robert Kennedy initially disclosed his role in the ultimatum six months after the crisis in a speech prepared for delivery in Columbia, South Carolina, on April 25, 1963. *New York Times,* April 26, 1963. This account of it was less detailed than that which he gave later and there are some discrepancies. Another statement about the ultimatum was given by Robert Kennedy for quotation in a memorial volume for his brother. As quoted on this occasion, he erroneously indicated that the deadline for compliance was contained in the president's letter to Khrushchev. See Goddard Lieberson, ed., *John Fitzgerald Kennedy, As We Remember Him* (New York: Atheneum, 1963).

In an interview with Daniel Ellsberg in 1964, Robert Kennedy repeated his account of an ultimatum, adding to it that he had also warned that any further shootdown of U-2s would trigger retaliation against all SAM sites and probably the missile sites as well. Cited by Allyn, Blight, and Welch, "Essence of Revision," p. 163.

87. Ibid., p. 166. They add, by way of reinforcing the interpretation of the significance of Scali's threat, that after the Cuban crisis was settled Fomin communicated to Scali a personal message from Khrushchev saying that his outburst had been very valuable. See also John Scali, "I was the Secret Go-Between in the Cuban Crisis," *Family Weekly* (October 25, 1964), p. 14. The possible importance of Scali's "ultimatum" to Fomin was stressed also by Bundy, *Danger and Survival,* pp. 438–439. See also Garthoff, *Reflections,* pp. 80–81, 90, 103, 158.

88. New information supporting this interpretation, gained from Soviet and Cuban sources, reinforces what was known earlier regarding the sense of urgency with which Khrushchev acted to terminate the crisis on Saturday night and early Sunday morning. See Allyn, Blight, and Welch, "Essence of Revision," pp. 166–168. These authors report, without giving a source, that President Kennedy (perhaps in response to an official recommendation by the Joint Chiefs) issued instructions on Saturday morning, October 27, to prepare for a possible attack on Cuba on the morning of October 30, and suggest that this may have become known to Soviet and/or Cuban intelligence.

89. Bundy and Blight, "October 27, 1962." The president's willingness to include the Jupiters in the negotiations may have been conveyed by his brother to Dobrynin in a private meeting on the preceding evening, Friday. This observation rests solely on Dobrynin's recollection at the Moscow conference. (Cf. Allyn, Blight, and Welch, "Essence of Revision," p. 158.)

90. Additional pressure by the president in mid-November abetted the Soviet effort to persuade Castro to accept the withdrawal of the IL-28 bombers that had been sent to Cuba together with the missiles. (Allyn, Blight, and Welch, "Essence of Revision," p. 164.) Sorensen's explanation for the change he made in *Thirteen Days* was that the missile swap was still a secret at the time, known only to six members of the president's advisory group.

Information on the meeting of this smaller group after the ExComm meeting is contained in Bundy, *Danger and Survival*, pp. 432–435. What these other advisers knew as to the *exact* nature of the quid pro quo regarding the removal of the Jupiters from Turkey, however, remains uncertain. Thus, in his written report to Rusk three days after his meeting with Dobrynin Robert Kennedy evidently concealed the fact that the Jupiters were part of the *formal* quid pro quo; instead, he stated that he had told Dobrynin " 'that there could be no quid pro quo—no deal of this kind could be made. . . . It was up to NATO to make the decision. . . .' " Schlesinger, *Robert Kennedy*, p. 562.

For an account of the abortive effort Khrushchev made several days later to make the quid pro quo part of the formal diplomatic record see Schlesinger, *Robert Kennedy*, pp. 563–564.

91. Blight and Welch, *On the Brink*, pp. 83–84; also pp. 171–174.

92. *Pravda* and *Izvestia*, December 13, 1962. Translation in *Current Digest of the Soviet Press*, and quoted in Pope, *Soviet Views*, pp. 87–88.

93. Allyn, Blight, and Welch, "Essence of Revision," pp. 166–168.

94. Sorensen, *Kennedy*, p. 715.

95. Ibid., p. 716.

96. Bundy provides a detailed analysis of how the president might have reduced the political and diplomatic costs of an open missile swap. *Danger and Survival*, pp. 436–437.

97. Ibid., p. 453.

98. For additional discussion, see the chapter in this volume by Dr. Jerrold Post, and also Alexander L. George, "The Impact of Crisis-induced Stress on Decisionmaking," in *Medical Implications of Nuclear War*, National Academy of Sciences (Washington, D.C.: National Academy Press, 1986), pp. 529–552.

CHAPTER 12

The Sino-Soviet Border Crisis of 1969

Arthur A. Cohen

The Sino-Soviet border crisis of March–September 1969 is a case of two hostile powers managing a military confrontation with sufficient skill to avoid escalation into war. War was avoided despite a basic miscalculation by the Chinese.

Mao Zedong, trying to change the long-standing border status quo and, at the same time, to indicate that his border guards were not to be bullied on their own territory, was willing to risk escalation. But he calculated that the risk was small. He believed, correctly, that the Soviet leaders feared war with China, a vast country of nearly a billion in population. Moreover, Mao kept the risk small by drastically limiting the extent and degree of provocation at the border. In other words, in limiting both his immediate objectives and the means employed on their behalf, Mao met reasonably well the political and operational requirements of crisis management that were discussed in Chapter 4.

For six months the Soviet leaders responded to sporadic probing of small sections of Soviet-claimed border territory with a defensive strategy marked by tit-for-tat reprisals using conventional forces. Subsequently, they established escalation dominance and then intensified their threats to go beyond the border to attack China— to escalate to full-scale war. Mao had believed, wrongly, that the Soviets would remain restrained indefinitely. His miscalculation resulted in a Soviet military buildup on the USSR's border with the People's Republic of China (PRC) that placed China under a long-term threat from Soviet troops on its northern and western borders.

This study will discuss Mao's escalation of the diplomatic dispute over the border to a military confrontation, management of the crisis by both sides at the border, and Soviet efforts to compel Mao to desist and accept negotiations. It was up to Mao to abandon his offensive strategy of attrition and return to the precrisis status quo. It was up to the Soviets to make him desist by increasing the credibility of their coercive threats.

This study will show the following:

269

- Moscow's ability and willingness to apply crisis management principles in disputes with states other than the United States
- Moscow's ability and willingness to make careful, effective use of coercive diplomacy as a strategy for crisis management
- Moscow's ability to use its military capabilities to establish credible escalation dominance in a low-level confrontation
- Moscow's and Beijing's sophistication in strategies employing careful risk control

Crisis management proved effective enough so that an inadvertent war—in this case, a major war—was avoided.

EVOLUTION OF THE CRISIS

Mao Acquiesces in Border Status Quo (1949–1959)

Cooperation with the Soviet Union and acceptance of the status quo on the Sino-Soviet border marked China's policy following the establishment of the PRC in 1949. Mao did not assert Beijing's claims but, rather, adopted the passive attitude of the Chinese Nationalists by leaving disputed sectors of border marked on Chinese maps as "unestablished" (or "undefined"). Russian and Japanese troops had clashed over islands in the border rivers (the Amur and Ussuri) before the end of World War II, but after Japan surrendered the Russians established complete control of the islands and waterways up to the Chinese bank. The border—approximately 4,150 miles long—remained peaceful for many years.[1]

The Chinese apparently made no effort to challenge Soviet control when they signed the Border Rivers Navigation Agreement in 1951. They agreed to establish a mixed Soviet-Chinese commission, which was to meet annually to discuss methods for keeping the rivers navigable, such as fixing and maintaining navigation markers, dredging, and charting newly created islands. Control was asserted by armed Soviet border guards patrolling up to the Chinese bank when the rivers were icebound (November–April) and by armed Soviet patrol boats when the rivers became navigable. In addition, the Chinese accepted Soviet frontier regulations requiring them to obtain Soviet permission to use the islands or rivers. Although more than six hundred islands are on the Chinese side of the main channel, Chinese peasants and fishermen were required to gain Soviet consent to come out and cut timber or hay on the islands or to fish in the rivers. Local disagreements, whether on the border rivers or in Xinjiang, where Chinese herdsmen wishing to graze cattle in better pastures just across the border required the permission of Soviet border guards to do so, were managed by Soviet and Chinese border guards without direct consultation with central authorities. In effect, the border rivers were Soviet rivers, and actual control derived not from earlier treaties but rather from long-established practice.

Mao Challenges Soviet Control, Phase I (1959–1966)

When the overall Sino-Soviet relationship deteriorated seriously toward the end of the 1950s, Mao changed the territorial border issue from a latent disagreement about claims on maps to claims on the ground. It was one thing to accept Soviet *diktat* when the overall relationship was beneficial to China but another thing to accept it when the relationship was, in Mao's view, worthless. He decided to assert China's claims gradually and without resort to shooting, intending thereby to limit the degree of provocation in the interests of a controlled crisis. As early as 1959, the Chinese began border intrusions into Soviet-claimed territory on the Xinjiang border.[2] More intrusions occurred "in the early 1960s."[3] Khrushchev was in this manner confronted with the choice of accepting a prolonged period of no-shooting challenges to Soviet control or accepting, in negotiations, China's territorial claims.

Mao had begun a process of negotiating border disputes with other countries. Armed clashes had occurred on China's border with India and Burma.[4] His policy was to try to persuade India, the most urgent case, and the Soviet Union, the less urgent but more difficult case, to agree to negotiate new, overall, and final treaties delimiting their borders with China. Zhou Enlai may have been trying to gain Khrushchev's agreement to begin negotiations as early as January 1957, when they discussed various matters. If so, Zhou failed. In an effort to depict India, publicly, and the Soviet Union, by implication, as the recalcitrant countries, Zhou in 1960 persuaded Burma and Nepal to conclude overall boundary settlements with China. He continued to work openly to persuade Prime Minister Jawaharlal Nehru to accept an overall boundary agreement. Nehru was willing to negotiate but not to accept China's claims. Khrushchev was willing to accept neither talks nor claims.

However, by tacit agreement, the Sino-Soviet border dispute was still kept in secret channels. Zhou publicly depicted the extent of the territorial disagreement as small.[5] In secret channels, Beijing proposed to Moscow in August and September 1960 that "negotiations be held to settle the Sino-Soviet boundary question."[6] Khrushchev refused to negotiate about areas already under Soviet control: The border was fixed permanently, he maintained, and aside from small sections, there was no "boundary question."

However, by 1963 he was impelled to change his no-negotiations policy. Chinese military activity in 1961–1962 suggested that Beijing might move forcefully to assert its border claims against the Soviet Union. Chinese defenses in Xinjiang had been strengthened.[7] In China's southwest, the Chinese attacked deep into Indian territory to force Nehru to stop challenging Beijing's version of the border. Nehru's acceptance of Defense Minister Krishna Menon's decision to send Indian troops up to and around Chinese border posts provoked Mao to order an attack (in two phases, beginning October 20 and November 15, 1962, respectively). Khrushchev almost certainly was impressed by the boldness of Mao's decision, the extent southward of the People's Liberation Army (PLA) attacks, and China's striking display of military preparation and execution in routing veteran Indian troops. Also in 1962, unarmed Chinese military personnel and civilians in China's northeast were "systematically violating the Soviet border and attempting, without authorization, to 'absorb' individual sections of Soviet territory."[8]

This unarmed probing, employing the strategy of salami tactics, continued in 1963. For example, along the Amur River:

- Chinese personnel landed from boats on several small islands and remained for several weeks before complying with demands of Soviet border guards to leave.
- Chinese officials refused to allow Soviet navigation workers to construct water fences on the Chinese side of the river.
- Chinese civilians had to be taken by the Soviets as prisoners from river islands.[9]

Moreover, on the political level, Sino-Soviet polemics intensified in 1962 after Khrushchev's retreat during the Cuban Missile Crisis. Mao's propaganda department attacked him for deploying the missiles in Cuba in the first place ("adventurism") and for removing them to avert a possible nuclear war with the United States ("capitulationism").[10] Khrushchev responded in December 1962 that the Soviet Union acted from simple common sense, as had China when it refrained from seizing Hong Kong and Macao—it was a policy of restraint, he said, not "capitulationism."[11] Then, the Chinese riposte of early March 1963 finally brought the territorial issue to the surface. Beijing warned ominously that China would seek a "general settlement" of "unequal treaties" imposed on China "when conditions are ripe."[12]

Khrushchev now abandoned his no-negotiations policy. The Cuban missile debacle had taken the Soviet Union close to war. He now acted to avoid war with China. On May 17, 1963, Moscow secretly proposed "consultations" (the Soviet-preferred word, implying talks less extensive than those required for the overall settlement Mao demanded).[13] He was later to put forth this initiative more emphatically.

On November 29, 1963, Khrushchev sent a secret Soviet party letter to Mao personally over his own signature, proposing consultations "to define accurately the boundary in different sections of the border." He implicitly rejected the Chinese position that a new, overall border agreement should be negotiated, stating that a historically formed boundary already existed. He warned Mao against challenging long-existing Soviet dominance at the border: "Any attempt to ignore this [border status quo] can become the source of misunderstandings and conflicts. . . It would be simply unreasonable to create territorial problems artificially at the present time." He urged Mao to turn events away from "the zone of danger" toward normalization of Sino-Soviet relations. Khrushchev's letter was, therefore, both an appeal to eliminate border tensions and a warning against further probing.[14]

Mao accepted negotiations (started in Beijing on February 25, 1964), but he was to insist on a new border agreement.[15] The most important part of his demand was that prior to an overall settlement, Soviet troops "must not cross the central line of the main channel in border rivers."[16] Khrushchev was willing to accept the central line of the main channel as the border.[17] However, his acceptance probably was linked to Beijing's relinquishing claims to certain big and strategically important islands. The key demand that the Soviets must keep their troops from crossing the central line of the main channel was clearly unacceptable prior to a final agreement. It would have required a unilateral Soviet withdrawal from all islands and a cessation of patrolling. The secred border negotiations remained at an impasse for six months.

Mao was unwilling to sustain the talks and thereby remain tied to Khrushchev's political strategy. He broke secrecy and personally publicized the dispute. He emphasized the extent of earlier Russian landgrabbing. On July 10, 1964, he criticized Russian acquisition of territory in Europe and Asia and went on to complain of Moscow's control over Vladivostok, Khabarovsk, and the Kamchatka Peninsula (among other areas), the implication being that Russian imperialism had illegally seized China's territory.[18] This breach of secrecy impelled Khrushchev to withdraw the Soviet delegation to the talks. Mao was not suggesting that China would try to regain these areas or even start trouble within them. His rhetoric was intended to depict Moscow as the new imperialist. This breach of secrecy and Chinese probes at the border provoked a warning of nuclear retaliation from Khrushchev.[19] Nevertheless, he was to propose a renewal of "consultations," and his successors were to continue the effort for five years.

Mao also had complained publicly that "the Soviet Union is concentrating troops along its border." (The tacit rule—keep news of the border incidents out of the media—already had been broken by Moscow in 1963.)[20] Actually, the increase in Soviet forces near the border in the early 1960s, to a total of some seventeen to twenty divisions, was a small effort compared to force increases that would be made later by Khrushchev's successors.[21]

Within the first year of Khrushchev's expulsion, Leonid Brezhnev and his lieutenants made a decision to begin long-term strengthening of their military position in the Far East.[22] The Soviets established new border posts, especially near the border rivers—the area of greatest Chinese activity. For example, on the Soviet side of Zhenbao/Damanskiy Island in the Ussuri—site of the first firefight in 1969—a border guard post was established in 1965.[23] In other ways as well, the Soviets reinforced their effort to deter Chinese escalation of the border dispute and to pose the possibility of Soviet escalation. An agreement between Brezhnev and Yumjaagiyn Tsedenbal (January 1966) for a joint defense of Mongolia opened the way for a Soviet troop presence in Mongolia. The Chinese later complained that these troops were stationed near China's border.[24] A U.S. newspaper reporter was permitted to visit the Soviet Far East, including secluded Vladivostok, and to report on the buildup of "Soviet military muscle," which was particularly evident "in regions close to the frontier."[25] Therefore, by the time Mao issued an appeal for vigilance ("an instruction") to the PLA in January 1967—"There are more air activities along the Xinjiang border, and [Soviet] ground forces are on the move"— he had received a whole range of warnings from Moscow to desist.[26]

Thus, Khrushchev's successors had moved beyond political polemics, beyond what Mao had referred to as "war on paper," to a real and substantial buildup that could lead to war with bullets.[27] However, Mao did not retreat; indeed, he soon moved to a new and riskier stage of asserting territorial claims. He did so despite indications that some officials of the Chinese Communist Party (CCP) had disapproved of provoking the Soviets at even the lower level of risk involved in sending Chinese citizens to the islands without requesting Soviet permission. For example, PLA Chief of Staff Luo Ruiqing is said to have demurred from the policy in place in the early 1960s: "[Luo] slanderously charged that we 'created artificial tension' on the Sino-Soviet borders. He cleared the Soviet revisionists of criminal responsibility for the disputes on the Sino-Soviet borders, saying: 'It cannot be said that most of the disputes were stirred up by them. A concrete analysis must be made.' "[28] "Created artificial tension" is a phrase that suggests incidents initiated by the Chinese. Two officials in Heilongjiang, the province of the border rivers, are said to have preferred a policy of " 'no frontier defense' and of 'retreating, yielding, and tolerance' to meet the needs of Soviet revisionism."[29] This fragmentary evidence of dissent probably reflected only the tip of the iceberg; it may be stated as a general analytical principle of Chinese politics that for every important official denounced in the media for opposition to CCP policy, there are many throughout the party apparatus with similar views. However, Mao was not, as various other CCP officials were, sufficiently impressed by Soviet conventional military superiority (in armor, mobility, and firepower) to accept a policy of "retreating, yielding, and tolerance."

Mao Challenges Soviet Control, Phase II (1966–1968)

In late 1966, Mao changed from a policy of sending soldiers (frequently in civilian clothing), Red Guards, and civilians onto Soviet-claimed islands (for an hour, a day, or several weeks) with orders to avoid fighting. The new policy was one of sending such composite groups with orders to fight if necessary when "normal patrol routes" were blocked by Soviet border guards. The controlling idea was to assert China's claim more forcefully but without shooting. The Chinese restricted (1) the activity of the composite groups and (2) the location of the confrontation sites.

The activity of the composite groups was to be nonmilitary in nature. Group members generally were to be unarmed (carrying, if anything, a club or a stick), and in civilian clothing (although soldiers were occasionally in uniform). On most occasions when soldiers were in civilian clothing, they professed to be local fishermen. For example, on December 17, 1967, the Chinese challenged Soviet control of Chilichin/Kirkinskiy, an island near Zhenbao/Damanskiy Island, with civilians and "fishermen."

> The Chinese concentrated about 1,000 civilians on their bank, and they came out to the center of the river. The Ussuri was frozen over. The head of our border post, Senior Lieutenant Strelnikov, went out to meet them. There were talks. In this photograph, a group of so-called fishermen has separated—they are *military men in civilian clothing* including many we know who serve at the Gongsi border post. *They carry sticks*, and they make the same demands—that the Ussuri River be made a boundary along the deep-water channel [emphasis added].[30]

The Zhenbao/Damanskiy area was to be the scene of several stick-swinging fights between armed Soviet border guards and Chinese "fishermen" before the first firefight occurred.

The Chinese selected confrontation sites in isolated areas. They challenged Soviet border guards only:

- on the Chinese side of the main channel and on islands close to the Chinese bank (where the Soviet claim was weakest)
- on almost barren unoccupied islands (where the Soviets could not complain of economic loss)

- on a small number of islands (avoiding the appearance of reconnaissance for a general attack all along the border)
- in areas far from Soviet cities and military bases (avoiding any appearance of threatening the security of population centers and military depots)

Mao and his lieutenants calculated correctly that Soviet border guards were under orders not to use their weapons—certainly not to shoot unarmed men. That is, within an increasingly provocative policy, the degree of provocation was kept limited.

A striking example of Beijing's caution was its avoidance of patrolling onto Heixiazi/Big Ussuri Island, the big island opposite Khabarovsk at the confluence of the Amur and the Ussuri. It is strategically important, as it defends the western approaches to the city. Although it is on the Chinese side of the main channel and, as the Chinese complained, "occupied" by Soviet troops, Beijing has not challenged Soviet control by civilian harassment or border guard patrolling.[31]

The Chinese especially avoided challenging border guards near the big river cities of Khabarovsk and Blagoveshchensk. There are no reported incidents on islands near these cities. There are many small islands near Blagoveshchensk on the Chinese side of the Amur's main channel. However, authorities in Heihe (Aigun), the Chinese city directly across the river, sent a convoy of PLA soldiers, Red Guards, and civilians to Mohe, a town more than three hundred miles from Blagoveshchensk, to assert claims and confront Soviet border guards on a small island there.[32] Unlike the Blagoveshchensk area, Mohe is an isolated area, and the nearest Soviet town of substantial size is more than sixty miles away. Moreover, the first firefight (1969) was to occur on a Chinese-side island in a desolate, isolated area approximately thirty miles from the nearest Soviet city.

Mao's decision to move to a policy of fighting if necessary apparently was made in 1966 at the start of the Cultural Revolution—his euphemism for bringing down the pragmatic leadership of the CCP and imposing on intellectuals a reign of terror. By 1967, the party apparatus of senior party Vice Chairman Liu Shaoqi had been destroyed, and the PLA was carrying out the functions of administration and control on the regional and local levels. Mao put in place radical (antipragmatic) leaders to carry out extreme left policies, including a foreign policy that in part violated normal diplomatic practice. The controlling idea of this foreign policy was to "dare to struggle," not only against the United States but also against the Soviet "revisionists."

Mao and his lieutenants reduced the frequency of official communications with the Soviet leaders to an occasional protest note. The level of official contacts was reduced following a probable exchange of recriminations in February 1965 when Mao met with Premier Aleksei Kosygin in Beijing. Thereafter, charge d'affaires and border guard post commanders carried the burden of communication. Mao broke party relations in 1966 and refused to send a Chinese delegation to the annual session of the Border River Navigation Commission in 1968. Signals from the Soviet Union became increasingly ominous, and Moscow conveyed them indirectly by sustaining the buildup of forces in the Far East and occasionally sending reconnaissance aircraft on shallow-penetration overflights of Chinese territory.

After 1965, Soviet forces in the Far East gradually expanded from the base of some seventeen to twenty divisions to about forty in the early 1970s.[33] Brezhnev and his aides were increasingly uncertain about Mao's intentions, and the force expansion reflected a policy of having a military deterrent in place.[34] Mao's basic assumption was that Brezhnev feared even a small war with China. But if the Chinese leader ever accepted the idea that forward patrolling by the PRC encouraged the Soviets to increase their forces, that idea was kept subordinate to the desire to assert territorial claims.

The Soviet invasion of Czechoslovakia in August 1968 strengthened Mao's determination not to retreat, not to be intimidated. He would warn the Soviets, on the one hand, and portray them as unprovoked aggressors (the new imperialists), on the other hand. China would not be cowed by Soviet military power.

When, therefore, the Chinese publicized a protest note to Moscow in September 1968 regarding Soviet overflights of Chinese territory, they directed "a stern warning" to the Soviet government that the 700 million Chinese people "are not to be bullied."[35] Zhou Enlai, using the occasion of a visit by the virulently anti-Soviet Albanians, declared that "we solemnly warn" the Soviets that their "threats and war blackmail" will have "no effect" on China and Albania.[36] The Chinese did not commit themselves to anything more than verbal support of their only European ally. But the implication of their statements for China was clear: The invasion of Czechoslovakia would increase rather than reduce Beijing's resolve to concede nothing at the border. Indeed, Mao in early 1969 was to make an even more militant challenge there.

To sum up, during his Cultural Revolution, Mao changed from a policy of sending composite groups (soldiers, Red Guards, and civilians) to challenge but *avoid fighting* with Soviet border guards, to a policy of *fighting if necessary*. In these new fight if necessary confrontations, the Chinese carefully limited their actions so as to avoid shooting clashes. At the same time, they sought to impose restraints on Soviet border guards by establishing tacit "rules of confrontation" whereby both sides were to refrain from shooting, carrying weapons, crossing the main channel in the rivers, and publicizing the confrontations in official media. The Soviets tacitly agreed not to shoot and not to publicize the confrontations, but they would not accept the Chinese effort to keep Soviet border guards from carrying weapons and from crossing the main channel. To have accepted the restraint on crossing the main channel would have been a territorial retreat for the USSR. From Brezhnev's viewpoint, Mao's policy was provocative, as it was directed at reducing Soviet control. From Mao's viewpoint, it was nonprovocative, even defensive, as Chinese were under instructions not to cross the central line of the main channel.

THE SINO-SOVIET BORDER CRISIS OF 1969

Following the Soviet invasion of Czechoslovakia, Mao apparently decided to adopt a clear, unambiguous military policy. More precisely, composite groups were discarded and forward patrolling was to start. Patrolling would be carried out by border guards (not "fishermen") *in uniform and with weapons*. The border guards, now carrying automatic weapons, were to stand their ground, confront the Soviets, and shoot only if necessary. Brezhnev had bullied the Czechs; he would not be permitted to bully the Chinese.

Zhenbao/Damanskiy Island: No-Shooting Confrontations (January–February 1969)

The new policy was carried out in the winter of 1968–1969, most vigorously on Zhenbao/Damanskiy Island in the Ussuri. The island is about nine-tenths by three-tenths of a mile in size. A nearby island—Chilichin/Kirkinskiy—on the Chinese side of the main channel and the site of club-swinging fights between Chinese "fishermen" and Soviet border guards since 1967, was not chosen as a site for firefights, probably because it was farther from the Chinese bank than Zhenbao/Damanskiy and provided fewer tactical military advantages.

The Chinese almost certainly selected the island as the site for prospective armed clashes because it was at least 30 miles from a Soviet city, had no significant strategic or economic value (becoming a marsh during the spring thaw), was closer to a nearby Chinese border post than the nearest Soviet border post, and was close to the Chinese bank.[37] Another tactical advantage was its easy accessibility to Chinese troops from the bank.[38] Finally, the high terrain on the Chinese shore provided excellent visibility for PLA heavy machine gun, mortar, and artillery crews. Fully armed border guards from each side came face to face in a no-shooting fight on January 23, 1969, when the Soviets crossed the main channel in armored vehicles to demand that a 25-man Chinese patrol return to the Chinese shore.

In hand-to-hand fighting that occurred, both sides used the butts of carbines and submachine guns as clubs, and several Chinese and Soviets were injured. The Soviets claimed that Senior Lieutenant Ivan Strelnikov, the officer in command of the nearby post, was made a special target of the Chinese.[39] He was to survive this and other confrontations prior to the first firefight. For example, he was a central figure in the no-fighting argument of February 7, when he and about 30 armed Soviet border guards in two command cars and two armored personnel carriers (APCs) came out to turn back a Chinese patrol. The Chinese stated that after "reasoning with" the Soviets, most of the border guards returned to their vehicles. "However, a petty officer of the Soviet revisionist frontier troops (5th from left) keeps on making trouble."[40] Within a month, Strelnikov, the Chinese-designated troublemaker, was the first to be killed on the island.

Zhenbao/Damanskiy Island: The Firefights of March 1969

Before the start of shooting in March, the Chinese apparently conveyed a warning to the Soviets at every meeting, demanding that they keep off the island. For example, they claim to have warned the Soviets during the confrontation of February 7: "Fully armed Soviet revisionist frontier troops in armored vehicles and cars brazenly intrude into China's Chenpao Island. Chinese frontier guards on normal patrol duty immediately warn them, ordering them to halt their provocation and preventing them from intruding further."[41] Direct warnings to the Soviet leadership may not have been sent by Beijing. The Chinese may have assumed that their on-site warnings quickly would be sent to KGB Border Guard Headquarters and on to the Soviet leaders. There were no warnings in the Chinese media, as both sides continued to honor for the time being the tacit agreement to avoid publicizing the confrontations.

When, on the morning of March 2, Strelnikov and six border guards crossed the frozen river to the island, again to demand that the Chinese leave, the Chinese opened fire—point blank—with submachine guns, killing him and six patrol members. In the shooting and subsequent firefight, the Soviets lost 31 killed and 14 wounded.[42] The Chinese claim that the Soviets fired first with "cannon and gun fire," killing and wounding "many" border guards.[43]

Moscow and Beijing provided different versions in the media, especially as to which side broke the first and most important tacit rule of confrontation—that is, no shooting. The Soviets made their protest five hours before the Chinese responded with a protest note of their own. Moscow was the first to publicize its note, breaking the second tacit rule of confrontation—no media discussion of border guard confrontations. The Soviets provided greater detail than did the Chinese. More than four years after the event, in July 1973, the Chinese gave their version to a Western observer, but it was not published in the Chinese media.[44] Beijing's first editorial comment on the event implied that the Chinese action had been justified: "Our frontier guard units had warned the Soviet revisionist frontier guards on many occasions, but the Soviet frontier guards paid no attention."[45]

The Soviets claim that Strelnikov and six border guards, walking "with their weapons strapped to slings on their chests," were gunned down point blank when they approached the Chinese. According to a Soviet survivor of the firefight, the Chinese carried out an ambush using the elements of surprise and close-range firing to kill the post commander: "The Chinese approached our commander in rows. Those in the front line had no weapons in hand. When only three meters were left between them and the Soviet border guards, the first row of Chinese scattered. It turned out that they were followed by soldiers of the CPR with submachine guns at the ready, and they fired point blank into our friends."[46] When a Soviet support group opened fire on the Chinese on the island, a bigger unit of Chinese lying hidden in ambush in foxholes and trenches on the nearby shore opened fire with mortars, grenade-launchers, and large-caliber machine guns. Their fire probably had been preadjusted.[47] The Soviets responded by sending in men on armored personnel carriers from two border posts other than Strelnikov's. After a battle lasting two hours in which the Chinese used "more than a battalion" (more than three hundred soldiers),[48] both sides disengaged.

The Chinese had deployed in two groups on the night before the firefight. One group was deployed to the island under cover of darkness and lay in ambush beyond an elevation of the terrain. Another group had dug in on the Chinese bank with preadjusted mortars, grenade-launchers, and heavy machine guns. Field telephone lines had been laid between the group on the island and the group on the bank. An additional 30 Chinese later crossed to the island to confront Strelnikov. After Strelnikov and six other border guards had been gunned down, Soviet reinforcements were moved up, only to come under fire from the Chinese bank.[49]

The version provided by Beijing in July 1973 to a Western observer (Neville Maxwell) depicts the Soviets as firing first. This version also claims that after January 1969, Chinese border guards were under instructions to avoid, even to run away from, the Soviets. However, this post-facto version conflicts with statements made by the Chinese at the time of the events.

For example, the post-facto version states that after the no-shooting fight in January 1969, Chinese border guards "were under orders not to fight back," and in February, they had "orders to 'keep their distance' from the Russians—that is, to run away if they had to."[50] This depiction of Chinese policy as devoid of any challenge to Soviet claims to Chinese territory directly conflicts with the thrust of Mao's policy at the time. It also conflicts with Beijing's own earlier statements. In 1969, Beijing published a photograph with a caption indicating that in February the Chinese in fact stood their ground and confronted Soviet border guards, "warning them" against intruding. The caption to a second photograph described Chinese forces as confronting Strelnikov and others and "reasoning with" them.[51] That is, according to the official 1969 version, Chinese border guards challenged the Soviets in February and did not run away. In fact, the caption to a third photograph of Soviet armored vehicles leaving the island states that the Soviets "flee" after a Chinese rebuff.

During a 12-day pause in the military contest for the island, mutual warnings escalated in the media, and each side temporarily besieged the other side's embassy and manhandled several of its officials.[52] Official communications were temporarily broken at the charge d'affaires level.[53] However, more important communications were established between border guard officers.

Mao did not retreat from the prospect of a second firefight, inasmuch as to retreat was to relinquish China's claim to Zhenbao/Damanskiy and all other China-side islands. A warning from Mao personally was sent to Soviet border guards, according to Maj. Gen. V. F. Lobanov, chief of troops of the Red-Banner Pacific Military District: "On March 12, an officer of the Chinese border post at Hutou came to hold talks with our border guards. Citing Mao Tse-tung's instructions, the Chinese officer threatened to use armed force against Soviet border guards protecting Damanskiy Island."[54] The Soviets, who never occupied the island but rather came out to intercept the Chinese, rejected the warning and prepared to retaliate for the March 2 ambush. They moved in more troops and APCs and prepared to use tanks and artillery. Before the attack, the Chinese sent a vehicle with a loudspeaker onto the ice, warning the Soviets "for several hours" against attacking.[55]

Beginning early in the morning of March 15, the Soviets attacked the Chinese border guards on the island, using "large numbers of armored vehicles, tanks, and armed troops."[56] The Soviets made three attacks with tanks and APCs and opened artillery fire on the Chinese, who later complained that the Soviets "went so far as to use heavy artillery from the rear areas of the Soviet side" and that "the shelling reached as far as seven kilometers inside Chinese territory."[57] The Chinese also used artillery.[58] However, they apparently did not use tanks or other armored vehicles. Beijing did not at the time claim that the Soviets had used aircraft. Each side operated with a fighting force of at least one regiment (about 1,500 soldiers). After seven hours, both sides disengaged.

The intention of the Soviet leaders was to indicate to the Chinese leaders that Moscow would retaliate by giving back double what its border guards had received. Wherever along the border their men were attacked, counteraction would be taken on roughly the same ground and at roughly the same level of conventional arms. However, they would use their superior mobility (tanks and APCs) and weaponry (more and heavier artillery) to strike at the Chinese in more than equal measure.

The Soviets heavily shelled the Chinese positions. "Soviet artillery had joined the battle. The Maoist positions were pulverized."[59] On the other hand, the Soviets suffered some losses, including the colonel in command of the retaliatory strike.[60] The Chinese had the tactical advantage of terrain, and the mobility of the APCs apparently was restricted.[61] They also had the advantage of firing as defenders from well-prepared positions and with weapons corrected for field of fire. They knocked out at least one tank and one APC.[62] The Soviets did not use aircraft to bomb or strafe, denying their troops what almost certainly would have been a highly effective weapon against the Chinese. This restraint was remarkable.

Despite their superiority in armor and weaponry, the Soviets were eventually forced to stop coming out to the island, in effect conceding Mao's claim to it.[63] They preferred to fight where the terrain and location did not provide the Chinese with tactical advantages. They did not concede bigger and more important islands on the Chinese side of the main channel. Mao's policy was still to limit the degree of risk by claiming but not contesting these larger islands.

The two firefights of March 1969 went beyond the earlier tacit rules of confrontation but were fought under tacit rules of engagement that reflected the determination of both sides to avoid a war. That is, they cooperated in escalation control. These rules of engagement required that firefights must be kept:

- relatively small in size, involving not more than a regiment (1,500 troops)
- short in duration (less than one day)
- infrequent (not daily, not incessant)
- at one site (not extended to many border sites)
- at the border (excluding deep probes)
- at the level of conventional forces (excluding strafing by ground-support aircraft)

The Soviets used tanks, APCs, and heavy artillery in the March 15 clash; they fired against targets on the Chinese shore and used helicopters for reconnaissance and evacuation of the wounded. The Chinese did not get near the Soviet shore. Moreover, they did not use tanks and APCs, probably because they intended to limit the degree of provocation (risk control) and denigrate the views of pragmatists in the CCP and PLA who had argued that modernization of the PLA required mechanization.

The domestic constraints on Mao were to avoid war. On April 28, Mao defended his policy in a speech to party officials at a plenary session of the CCP's new Central Committee. He tried to assure them that his policy was defensive, as he intended to keep the PLA inside China's borders. Even if attacked, he said, China would not strike outward at the attacking country. "I say we will not be provoked." That is, in contrast to his decision to attack India (at small risk) during an earlier border war, in the current border dispute Mao would not risk advancing inside the territory of the USSR. On the other hand, if attacked and a "big" or "small" war occurred, China could be defeated. A small war would be fought at the border.

A big war—presumably started by a Soviet invasion—would require relinquishing some territory to buy time, but eventually the invader would suffer defeat from "encirclement" by China's millions of people. He did not refer to a possible Soviet attack with nuclear weapons (Lin Biao had referred to the possibility on April 1), but he went on to disparage by implication Soviet superiority in conventional weapons: "As to airplanes, tanks, and armored cars and so on, experience has proven that they can be dealt with." Although he emphasized the need to be prepared against war, he probably continued to believe that Brezhnev's fear of war with big China would significantly reduce the prospect of a Soviet attack, either conventional or nuclear.[64]

Soviet conduct in the March 15 firefight may have confirmed Mao's conviction. The Soviets had kept their action down to the conventional level and limited it to only one site, and to less than one day of fighting. Moreover, they had conceded the island—a small tactical success for Mao. Soviet troops apparently did not come out to the island following the March 15 firefight but retreated to a policy of firing at it with light and heavy machine guns and artillery from the Soviet side of the Ussuri. On April 3, a Soviet border guard representative in effect confirmed the USSR's loss of the island and its unwillingness to return and fight for it when he stated at a meeting with his Chinese counterparts that the Soviets would continue to fire at Chinese on the island. According to Beijing, the Soviet representative said that "The Soviet Union will not cease fire unless the Chinese Government holds negotiations with the Soviet Government, nor will it cease fire unless *the Chinese withdraw* from Damanskiy Island" [emphasis added].[65] This position confirmed to Mao Soviet reluctance to escalate to a battle of greater numbers and duration or even to fight again for the island. Finally, he probably believed that the Soviet leaders' fear of an extension of fighting into a general border war was reflected in their urgent requests to defuse the crisis by starting negotiations without delay. (A defused border crisis, from Moscow's viewpoint, would have the additional effect of depriving the United States of the obvious political-psychological leverage it was deriving from the Sino-Soviet dispute.)[66]

Mao Rejects Leadership-Level Contacts and Negotiations

Within a week after the March 15 firefight, Moscow tried to raise the level of communications from that of charge d'affaires and border guard post commander to contacts between leaders. At the same time, the Soviets believed the dispute could be demilitarized if Mao were willing to resume border negotiations broken off in 1964. Mao refused.

This refusal reflected his belief that the Soviet leaders would not go beyond retaliation at the border despite challenges by Chinese border guards. Mao's unwillingness to negotiate also reflected the intensity of his anti-Soviet feeling. The Soviet leaders were searching for a way out of a tense and, in their view, uncertain and dangerous situation. Mao refused to provide them a way out. Chinese statements erected a wall against leadership contacts and chided the Soviets for their display of alarm and anxiety.

Mao's chosen successor and defense minister, Lin Biao, boasted to Communist party officials that Moscow's appeal had been rejected:

Kosygin asked on March 21 to communicate with our leaders by telephone. Immediately, on March 22, our government replied with a memorandum, in which it was made clear that, "In view of the present relations between China and the Soviet Union, it is unsuitable to communicate by telephone. If the Soviet government has anything to say, it is asked to put it forward officially to the Chinese Government through diplomatic channels."[67]

Within a week after this rejection, the Soviet leaders asked for a meeting of negotiators to start consultations on the border dispute.[68] In less than two weeks, they repeated the request for border talks, and the Chinese finally responded, chiding them for their apparent sense of alarm:

On April 11, the Soviet Government further addressed a note to the Chinese side, pressing the latter to arrive in Moscow within four days for "consultations" with it on the Sino-Soviet boundary question and, without waiting for a reply from the Chinese Government, it made public the note on April 12. On April 14, the Chinese Government told the Soviet Government in explicit terms: "We will give you a reply; please calm down a little and do not get excited."[69]

The effect of these statements was to deprive the Soviet leaders of any reprieve from the prospect of indefinite Chinese probes along a border of 4,150 miles. Opportunities to attain any change of policy from possible disagreements among Mao, Lin Biao, and Zhou Enlai were closed to them. Zhou, then the third most important leader and a relative moderate, apparently was complying with Mao's policy. For example, he publicly depicted the Soviet leaders as being a small "revisionist clique" governing a landgrabbing country.[70]

At the annual meeting of the Border River Navigation Commission, which convened on June 18, it was clear that Mao had agreed only to talks between low-level officials regarding navigation procedures. His acceptance of Moscow's proposal to send a Chinese representative to meet in Khabarovsk when it was China's turn to meet in a Soviet city was not an indication that he was willing to defuse the border dispute. On the contrary, Foreign Minister Andrei Gromyko was later to complain that the Chinese representative, at the start and in the course of the meeting, had made "certain statements" that made Chinese intentions suspect.[71] The statements may have been intended to go beyond Moscow's position, which Gromyko said was that discussions should focus "on a narrow question: the settlement of river navigation in some border areas." Beijing apparently wanted the discussion to deal with the question of *ownership* of the islands. Gromyko also complained about "the recent new provocation carried out by the Chinese side on the Amur River." This was a reference to the ambush of Soviet river transport workers on the Chinese-claimed island, Bacha/Goldinskiy. (One Soviet was killed, and three were wounded.) In sum, Moscow faced the task of beating back Mao's offensive policy of attrition.

Brezhnev's Policy of Intimidation

Together with the search for a political way out (through negotiations), Brezhnev and his aides put in place after mid-March 1969 a defensive military policy of tit-for-tat, whereby the Soviets would respond in double measure to try to compel Mao to desist. There were two aspects to the policy.

First, direct military force was to be used on-site to punish and intimidate the Chinese. More precisely, the Soviets would respond immediately to every Chinese probe (whether by Chinese border guards, or civilians, or both) and with superior armor and firepower. The intruders were to be intercepted and then beaten up, expelled, fired upon, or kidnapped at any sector of the border. Zhenbao/Damanskiy was the only exception when it came to responding in double measure, as Soviet forces there were confronted by important disadvantages.

Second, Moscow would threaten Beijing openly in the media and, later, both in the media and privately through third parties, with the prospect of a nuclear weapons attack.

Intensified Conventional Forces Intimidation. The decision by Soviet leaders to strike the Chinese forcefully at every challenged sector was reflected, in early May, in *Pravda* (among other places). The Soviets were determined that challenges at the border would not go unpunished, no matter where or when they occurred or whether they were carried out by border guards or "civilians." The Chinese were to recognize that there would be a punitive response to every probe.

Can you imagine that on a border of 7,000 kilometers long one side can keep the other in its sights for a long time with impunity and without harm to itself?[72]

When, before our very eyes, a dangerous force comes into being, one which is prepared—if given the chance—to confer on mankind not tens or hundreds but tens and hundreds of millions of graves, then a bitter but iron logic comes into play: This force must be made to feel that not a single one of its actions will go unpunished.[73]

The Soviets extended their policy beyond the border rivers in the east to the border with Xinjiang in the west, and the Chinese began to complain about "a series" of Soviet "armed provocations."[74] For example, they complained publicly that:

"Large numbers of troops, together with several hundred tanks, armored cars and vehicles" intruded into Yumin County, Xinjiang, penetrating as deep as "seven kilometers" into Chinese territory and intercepting Chinese herdsmen and their flocks; the Soviets aimed their guns at Chinese border guards there and told them to withdraw or they would be wiped out "by force of arms"; the Chinese withdrew (May 2);

Soviet troops fired at Chinese border guards who were patrolling on a China-side island in the Amur River, "killing one of them" (May 15);

Supported by a patrol boat, a transportation boat, and a gunboat, and led by a Soviet officer, "15 fully armed soldiers" landed on a China-side island in the Amur River, beat with rifle butts "nine Chinese civilians engaged in productive labor on the island," took four of them into Soviet territory, detained them for "eight days," and were compelled to send them back "only after repeated protests from the Chinese frontier representative" (May 14);

"Large numbers of Soviet troops" crossed into Chinese territory in Tacheng County, Xinjiang, "beat up three civilians engaged in production there and two Chinese frontier guards, carried them away by force, seized arms and ammunition of the Chinese frontier guards, and have thus far refused to send them back" (May 20);

Soviet troops near Heihe on the Amur River sent "a gunboat and three patrol boats to carry by force to the Soviet side three Chinese civilians together with their boat, and have thus far refused to send them back" (May 25); and

"Supported by a helicopter, Soviet troops in three gunboats" landed on a China-side island in the Amur River; "over 40 fully armed" troops "carried away 10 Chinese fishermen engaged in production on the island and seized their four fishing boats and one motor boat, and have thus far refused to send them back" (May 28).[75]

Beijing demanded the immediate return of the sixteen kidnapped "civilians" and two border guards as well as the cessation of all Soviet military action.

Particularly striking in this Chinese protest is the absence of any reference to Chinese troops shooting to prevent their personnel from being taken prisoner. The Soviets did not claim that the Chinese had opened fire in this period (mid-March to late May). This suggests that Mao temporarily—that is, during the Ninth Party Congress in April and throughout May as well—retreated from the policy of shooting if necessary to the pre-March 1969 policy of challenging Soviet claims without shooting. His intention was probably to signal Brezhnev to comply with the pre-March tacit rule against shooting.[76]

Brezhnev refused to comply. He and his aides intended to sustain pressure on Mao to desist from provocation and to negotiate. Brezhnev in early June again indicated a desire to direct the dispute into the political channel. Referring to Beijing's May 24 Government Statement, which professed a desire to negotiate but did not state a time or place, Brezhnev declared that the future would show whether the Chinese leaders "are really eager to negotiate." He continued, "However, we cannot afford to overlook the fact that the provocations by Chinese military personnel on the Soviet border have not stopped."[77] Chinese activities—that is, the movement of "herdsmen" and "fishermen" supported by border guards into Soviet-claimed territory at various sections of the border—indeed had not stopped. Shooting incidents occurred subsequently in June, July, and August, signaling Mao's return to the policy of shooting if necessary, and from prepared ambush.

On June 10, for the first time since mid-March, Chinese border guards fired at Soviet border guards. Soviet border guards intercepted three Chinese "herdsmen" who were supported by Chinese border guards as they moved cattle or sheep into Soviet-claimed territory from the Barluk Mountains area of Yumin County, Xinjiang. (Moscow referred to it as the Tasta River area, Semipalatinsk Region.) The Soviets killed one "herdsman" (one "herdswoman," according to Beijing) and took another prisoner. The Chinese exchanged fire with "dozens" of Soviet troops. Subsequently, the Soviets "sent large numbers of tanks and armored cars" (which Moscow denied) into the firefight. The Chinese claimed that the Soviets, in sending in armor, were trying to provoke "still larger conflicts."[78] This complaint suggests that the Soviets, who probably did use tanks and APCs, also attacked the Chinese with superior numbers of men. It also suggests a new anxiety on the part of the Chinese about the prospect of expanded ("still larger") Soviet retaliation.

The Soviets on July 8 responded with superior force following a Chinese ambush on Bacha/Goldinskiy Island on the Chinese side of the Amur River. Chinese militiamen ambushed four unarmed Soviet river transport workers who had landed on the island to repair a navigation marker they routinely serviced. One Soviet worker was killed and three were wounded from submachine gun fire and grenades. The Soviets sent in gunboats and troops together with observation aircraft and set fire to a civilian house and a forest on the island. The Chinese militiamen left the island before the Soviets arrived in force to rescue the navigation workers.[79]

In late July, the Chinese may have become less confident that Brezhnev would not decide to launch a large-scale conventional or nuclear weapons attack on China. Chinese officials probably received information or rumors concerning letters sent in the summer of 1969 by Moscow to several communist parties in the West suggesting the possibility of a Soviet attack against Chinese nuclear installations.[80] Moreover, they clearly were aware of the threats made by Soviet military leaders in Soviet media. The Chinese apparently decided to make a new statement to stress the presumed defensive aspect of Mao's policy and his desire to avoid war. Using the occasion of the 42nd anniversary of the founding of the PLA, Chief of the General Staff Huang Yongsheng declared, "As far as our own desire is concerned, we do not wish to fight for even a single day."[81] This sentence, unique at the time in Chinese media, had also appeared one day earlier in the anniversary editorial of three of China's most authoritative publications.[82] It may well have been intended as a signal to Moscow that Mao did not desire any expansion of the sporadic and relatively small-scale clashes and certainly did not want a big war.

However, Huang's statement did not signal a change in the policy of conducting small probes. Nor was such a change indicated by the signing of a protocol in Khabarovsk where on August 8 the Sino-Soviet commission had concluded discussions on facilitating river navigation for 1969. The Chinese continued to select sections of the border where they believed they had a good legal claim and where the Soviets continued to reject that claim.

An area along the border in Xinjiang that had been increasingly disputed since 1967 was to be the site of the biggest firefight since March 15. The clash occurred six miles east of a small settlement, Zhalanashkol, in Semipalantinsk Oblast, Kazakhstan (or, according to Beijing, in the Tieliekedi area of Yumin County, Xinjiang). A sheepraising, mountainous area, it had been the site in May of a Chinese effort to send men, disguised as shepherds, into Soviet-claimed territory.[83] The Chinese claimed (and Moscow denied) that the Soviets had moved about 1.8 miles into Xinjiang, built a highway and military works there, and laid boundary markers on their territory.[84] The Chinese subsequently prepared to contest what they said was a Soviet seizure of a strip of hilly land.

During a one-hour firefight on August 13, Soviet border guards in APCs (and tanks, according to the Chinese) supported by two helicopters for observation attacked three groups of Chinese soldiers (about thirty men who had dug in across the Soviet-claimed border on the previous night), killing and wounding an unspecified number, losing an unspecified number, and taking two prisoners.[85] Although the Chinese had the initial advantage, firing from hill positions, the Soviets apparently prevailed partly because of their advantage in armor, which provided superior mobility and firepower. The Chinese were hit in double measure and complained that Moscow was "trying to provoke larger-scale armed conflicts."[86]

The Chinese accusation that the Soviets were trying to provoke still larger armed conflicts had been made earlier (in Beijing's protest note of June 11 on a Xinjiang border clash). The accusation was intended to counteract the widespread belief that Beijing was the instigator of the firefights.[87] It was also intended as a complaint to Moscow that the Soviets were trying to break the tacit rules of engagement, which called for clashes of short duration and small numbers of troops. The Chinese seemed to show more anxiety about Soviet retaliation in August than they had shown in March.

The Chinese were using a double standard. On the one hand, they continued to challenge the Soviets at preselected sections of the border, shooting if necessary. On the other hand, they insisted that the Soviets must not escalate the small clashes—that is, must not strike at Chinese troops in double measure in an effort to impose a crushing defeat on them. In contrast to the Chinese response to the first firefight (March 2)—a virulently anti-Soviet demonstration in front of the Soviet embassy in Beijing—there was no such activity following the final firefight (August 13). Beijing was calm, and the only organized protest came from steel workers inside their factory.[88]

However, despite this relative moderation, the Soviet leaders would not accept China's dual tactics of shooting and then demanding an immediate halt to Soviet two-fold retaliation. They desired a halt to all border challenges rather than less intense clashes and the absence of demonstrations against their embassy.

Brezhnev's policy of striking back at the Chinese by giving tit-for-tat in double measure with conventional forces at every site of challenge had not dissuaded Mao from continuing with his offensive strategy of attrition, of sporadic probing. Mao apparently believed that Moscow's policy had not put China's security at risk. If Brezhnev were to continue to accept the tacit rules of engagement, there would be no general war threatening China. The Chinese would continue to take relatively small personnel losses indefinitely in a protracted war of small, short, isolated skirmishes. Mao had to be convinced that the prospect of a general war was real— a war in which China could not hope to prevail. Mao also had to be convinced that he was on the brink of war, that he was facing a Soviet attack using either conventional or nuclear weapons.

The Threat of a Soviet Attack on China. Brezhnev's chief difficulty in confronting the Chinese was to attain credibility. Soviet threats, both implicit and direct, to use nuclear weapons had been publicized in the media as early as March 8 and 17 and had been repeated sporadically into August.[89] Invariably, the Chinese disparaged such nuclear threats as being "nuclear blackmail" and ineffective; Beijing would not be frightened into changing its policy.[90] The Chinese did not desist, as is shown by the firefight of August 13.

The Soviet leaders turned to using the testimony of third parties to convince Mao and his lieutenants that the possibility of a Soviet attack on China was real. In the summer of 1969, they apparently sent letters to several communist parties in the West that suggested the possibility of a Soviet attack on Chinese nuclear installations in Xinjiang. Following the August 13 firefight, a Soviet official implied in remarks to a U.S. Department of State official that such an attack was an option under consideration. On August 27, the director of the Central Intelligence Agency (CIA) informed diplomatic correspondents that Moscow had discussed with foreign communists a possible attack on China, and he indicated genuine concern about the matter.[91]

On the following day, the view of some intelligence analysts and academics on the increased likelihood of a Soviet attack was publicized in Washington. An article in the *Washington Post* also cited the view of a key official, presumably the director of the CIA, on the prospect of a Sino-Soviet war: "One key official who only a month earlier had rated the chances of a major Chinese-Soviet fight at about 10 percent recently said that the chances are now only slightly less than 50–50."[92] The article, "Russia Reported Eyeing Strikes at China A-Sites," was printed under a map depicting, among other things, the locations of some of the known Chinese nuclear plants and test sites. The possibility of a Sino-Soviet war was said to be the subject of "a National Security Council study."

For Chinese officials, the estimates publicized in this article were probably the most alarming information thus far received on Soviet intentions. The Chinese probably also detected in late August a standdown of the Soviet airforce in the Far East—a possible indication that air units were being prepared for operations.[93] Chinese leaders would undoubtedly consider the information in the *Washington Post* article to be far more reliable in estimating Soviet intentions than the continuing threats in Soviet media. The standdown, if detected—and the Chinese almost certainly were monitoring Soviet flights—would have significantly increased their concern. The cumulative effect of these indicators probably convinced Chinese officials that the possibility of a Soviet attack on Chinese nuclear facilities, whether with nuclear or conventional weapons, was real.

We do not know, of course, whether the Soviet threat of launching an attack was a bluff, but it was evidently credible enough to persuade Mao and his aides to curtail their actions and cool off the crisis.

Mao Desists and Accepts Negotiations

Anxiety about a possible attack on China's nuclear facilities was probably felt by all important leaders, including Mao. Zhou Enlai, in particular—a relative moderate—almost certainly viewed the threat as real. The perceived danger of war provided him with the opportunity to convince Mao of the need to change course, reduce the degree of hostility at the border, and desist from further challenges there. Lin Biao, a radical and a less imaginative and constructive leader than Zhou, was less likely to have advised restraint.

Zhou may well have persuaded Mao that to stop border patrolling and to accept negotiations could be depicted internationally as a policy of restraint. Brezhnev would attain no territorial concessions on disputed sectors of the border because negotiations could safely be kept at a deadlock indefinitely.

Zhou was given the task of defusing the crisis without conceding territorial claims. He made it clear to the Soviets that negotiations would not be the first step toward a rapprochement but rather a move to avert war.

Contacts between leaders were reluctantly and discourteously restored by the Chinese. Kosygin, in Hanoi on September 8 for Ho Chi Minh's funeral, reportedly tried to speak with Deputy Premier Li Xiannian, but Li refused.[94] Information that Zhou would be willing to meet with Kosygin apparently was received only after Kosygin left Hanoi for Moscow, and it was from Soviet Central Asia that he was summoned to Beijing Airport on September 11. Zhou and Kosygin apparently discussed (in the airport lounge) the matter of starting border negotiations.[95] Confining the meeting to the airport reflected Mao's unmitigated disdain for the "revisionist" Soviet leaders. This was the first time in four-and-a-half years that Mao had permitted a Chinese leader to meet with a Soviet leader.

The crisis had been defused. There were no further reports of firefights at the border. The next step was to set forth a negotiating position in advance of negotiations. The Chinese probably carried this out in private official letters sent to Moscow. More than a month before negotiations started (in Beijing), the Soviet leaders probably believed it to be prudent to sustain some political-psychological pressure on the Chinese. For this they used the Western press. Victor Louis, a Soviet agent who posed as a free-lance journalist, wrote in an article published in the London Evening News on September 16, 1969, that "Russian nuclear installations stand aimed at the Chinese nuclear facilities," that "the Soviet Union prefers using rockets to man-power" in responding to border attacks, that the USSR "has a variety of rockets to choose from," and that the Soviets have a "plan to launch an air attack on Lop Nor" (the Chinese nuclear testing site in Xinjiang).[96] As the Chinese moved toward negotiations, which started on October 20, Chinese media indicated leadership awareness of the Soviet threat. Beijing warned on October 7 that there would be war if "a handful of war maniacs dare to raid China's strategic sites." This was the first reference in the Chinese media to the possibility of such an attack.[97]

However Zhou Enlai may have portrayed the need to desist to Mao, the change to negotiations was a policy defeat. The Chinese leader was compelled to accept customary Soviet control of the islands (except for Zhenbao/Damanskiy and Chilichin/Kirkinskiy in the Ussuri) and to abstain from resuming any military challenge to that control.

In terms of China's security interests, challenging the Soviets at the border had been a bad policy. Although Mao had been correct in calculating that Brezhnev feared a general war with China, he had been wrong in believing that Brezhnev's attitude would prevent him from making threats that eventually had to be considered credible. Moreover, Mao was wrong in calculating that the Soviet leader would tolerate indefinitely a policy of limited provocation, even though only small numbers of Soviet troop losses were involved. Finally, although Mao had limited the degree of provocation in each firefight, the overall policy of disputing territorial claims with force was a provocation by definition. The policy led to the development of a permanent threat to China's security from the north: a major buildup of Soviet troops near the border.

MANAGING THE CRISIS

Despite Mao's temerity in challenging the USSR militarily, the Soviet leaders demonstrated remarkable restraint by not striking back with a large-scale conventional force attack or with nuclear weapons. Whether some high-level Soviet military officers preferred such a course is conjectural. But it seems clear that the political leaders considered the costs prohibitive.[98] They tolerated Mao's offensive strategy for the better part of six months. They were successful in managing the crisis without going to war. They not only did not use bombers or missiles against strategic targets in China, but they also held back from using even tactical aircraft to support their troops in the border firefights.

Brezhnev and his lieutenants opted instead, as has been indicated, for a mix of diplomatic and military activity. They adopted a strategy of defensive tit-for-tat retaliation at the border. They used this strategy to counter the Chinese offensive strategy of a protracted war of attrition (see Chapter 16). Simultaneously, they used diplomacy in an effort to persuade the Chinese to negotiate, first using political appeals and then using the threat of an attack on China's nuclear installations. A way out was always kept open for the Chinese. Moscow's rejection of the large-scale attack option provided the Chinese with sufficient latitude eventually to negotiate. Having avoided war with China, the Soviets saw the way clear after Mao's death to reduce tensions at the border and work with his successors, who were pragmatists rather than ideologues.

Most Soviet and Chinese actions would seem to fit well with the seven principles of crisis management set forth in Chapter 4. Let us now briefly consider how the two sides behaved in ways consistent with these principles.

1. *The need for top-level political control of military options.* There probably was politburo-level control from Moscow of army/border forces small-unit actions against the Chinese following the initial Chinese ambush on March 2, 1969. On the Chinese side, Lin Biao and Zhou Enlai probably controlled Chinese actions day to day, with Mao being briefed regularly. However, the decisive and ultimate voice in decision making was apparently Mao's.[99]

2. *Pauses in military operations.* The Soviets used pauses to indicate to the Chinese that they preferred to resolve the crisis through negotiations. Pauses were used by the Chinese to indicate that although they refused to negotiate, they nevertheless wanted to avoid a big war. The Chinese tried to establish ground rules for quite limited military engagements, keeping their probes against Soviet-held territory sporadic rather than constant in time. And for more than a month, during and after their CCP congress, the Chinese may have been trying to use a pause to signal a desire to return to the pre-March no-shooting rule of engagement.

3. *Military action coordinated with political-diplomatic action.* The Soviets coordinated military with diplomatic action before and after almost every tit-for-tat retaliation, with Moscow reiterating its genuine preference for negotiations. Soviet diplomatic action included an attempt to persuade the United States to restrain the Chinese when Ambassador Anatoly Dobrynin, in Washington on March 11, 1969, briefed Kissinger on the Chinese ambush in emotional language and stated that the China problem was also Washington's problem.[100] Mao, on the other hand, avoided diplomatic action, thus creating uncertainty in Moscow regarding his intentions. He remained obstinate about negotiations until Soviet threats became credible.

4. *Threats of force consistent with limited diplomatic objectives.* The Soviets used clear signals to threaten the Chinese with an attack on their nuclear facilities

if they did not desist at the border. But throughout this period, the Soviets indicated that negotiation was the preferred course. Their problem was to make the threat credible. The standdown of the Soviet air force in the Far East and warnings issued through third parties gave their threats credibility by late August 1969. For their part, the Chinese, in Foreign Ministry notes, suggested that they did not want any firefight to develop into a major battle; nor did they want any battle that lasted more than a day. They did not make changes in the disposition of their forces, tacitly assuring the Soviets that large-scale combat was not in their strategy.

5. *Avoidance of impression of resort to large-scale warfare.* Both sides engaged in only limited, carefully controlled firefights. This was particularly evident in the behavior of the militarily superior Soviets. After each engagement with Chinese forces, they could have plunged deep into Chinese border territory near the firefight, but they did not adopt such a strategy.

Only when the Soviets decided for purposes of coercive diplomacy to introduce the threat of a strike at China's nuclear facilities did Moscow create the prospect of significant escalation.

For their part, the Chinese, as indicated above, did not change the disposition of their forces. Furthermore, they did not increase the size of their probes, never going beyond deployment of one regiment.

6. *Diplomatic-military options consistent with a desire to negotiate.* The Soviets attained escalation dominance only in mobility and weaponry. Although they used APCs, tanks, and heavy artillery, they retaliated only at the conventional weapons level. They were even careful to avoid using aircraft for strafing and bombing despite their greatly superior air force. On the political-diplomatic level, they kept open the negotiating option even as they denied the Chinese any reason for calculating that they could continue their probes indefinitely. For their part, the Chinese kept their probes sufficiently small to avoid provoking major Soviet escalation. They were well aware that Moscow on almost a moment's notice would accept a clear sign from them of a willingness to begin negotiations. In that event, Kosygin would be rushed by Moscow to the Beijing airport on only short notice.

7. *A way out compatible with the opponent's fundamental interests.* The Soviets did not seek to acquire more Chinese territory than they held when the crisis started. Their military retaliation was confined to clearly defined geographic limits, meeting each probe on the same ground. For their part, the Chinese carefully confined their probes to the China side of the border to demonstrate the strict geographical limits of their strategy. Their probes were launched at sites of no economic or military value.

In addition to these seven principles, Chapter 4 sets forth two requirements of crisis management. These were also met by both sides. The political requirement was met when Moscow and Beijing limited their objectives. Mao also claimed only China-side islands in the border rivers. He kept his border guards away from Soviet-side islands. The Soviet leaders sought only to meet each attack at the border. They had no more ambitious military objective than this.

The operational requirement was met when both sides carefully limited the means employed on behalf of the objectives. Conventional level Chinese attack provoked only conventional level Soviet retaliation with relatively small numbers of men. The only meaningful escalation carried out by the Soviets was in the area of psychological warfare when Moscow threatened China's nuclear installations with destruction.

BIBLIOGRAPHICAL NOTE

Primary sources from unclassified Soviet and Chinese publications and broadcasts were sufficiently good to support the reconstruction, in some detail, of the border crisis.

For secondary sources, the author used Harry Gelman, "The Soviet Far East Buildup and Soviet Risk-Taking Against China" (RAND R-2943-AF, August 1982); Dennis J. Doolin, *Territorial Claims in the Sino-Soviet Conflict* (Stanford: Hoover Institution Studies 7, 1965); Henry Kissinger, *White House Years* (Boston: Little, Brown, 1979); Neville Maxwell, "The Chinese Account of the 1969 Fighting at Chenpao," *The China Quarterly* 56 (October/December 1973); Thomas Robinson, "The Sino-Soviet Border Conflict," in Steven Kaplan, ed., *Diplomacy of Power: Soviet Armed Forces as a Political Instrument* (Washington, D.C.: Brookings Institution, 1981); and various articles in English language newspapers.

NOTES

1. Moscow later emphasized Beijing's acceptance of the most visible indication of Soviet control, i.e., unilateral Soviet patrolling. For example, along the rivers, "the border line was patrolled by Soviet guards prior to . . . 1949 and in the years following the founding of the PRC." Moscow broadcast in Mandarin to China, March 6, 1969. Foreign Broadcast Information Service Daily Report (hereafter FBIS DR) USSR, March 11, 1969.

2. In the Tian Shan Mountains where China's Xinjiang borders on the Kirghiz S.S.R., there occurred in 1959 "the first intrusions across our frontiers, quite crude but still bloodless." Article by K. Simonov, *Pravda*, May 3, 1969.

3. "It was then that the situation on the fronter began to worsen. At first there were minor, insignificant violations of the existing frontier regulations which were committed, as a rule, by civilians, or, in any case, by people not wearing military uniform. In certain sections, Chinese servicemen tried pointedly to violate the state frontier of the Soviet Union. At the same time the PRC started to construct airfields, roads, barracks, and military depots in districts bordering on the Soviet Union." Soviet Government Statement, March 29, 1969. FBIS DR USSR, April 1, 1969.

4. Regarding Burma, there were "clashes on the border between the two countries while the two sides were seeking a friendly solution to the boundary question." Zhou Enlai, speech in Rangoon, April 16, 1960, on the signing of the Sino-Burmese Boundary Agreement. *Beijing Review*, April 19, 1960.

5. Zhou, when asked at his press conference in Kathmandu on April 28, 1960, whether there was a section of the Sino-Soviet border which was "not delimited," replied that, "There is a very small discrepancy on maps and it is very easy to settle." *Beijing Review*, May 3, 1960.

6. Lin Biao, Report to the Ninth National Congress of the Chinese Communist Party (CCP), April 1, 1969. *Beijing Review*, April 30, 1969.

7. The Chinese party's Military Affairs Committee had issued a directive in January 1961 to ensure security of the borders of the southwest (opposite India) and the northwest (opposite the Soviet Union). *Gongzhuo Tongxun* (Bulletin of Activities), Beijing, February 1, 1961.

8. *Trud*, March 16, 1969.

9. Ibid.

10. Khrushchev was taunted by implication for putting "trust in empty promises" of Kennedy; the "so-called assurances given by the US that it will not attack Cuba are nothing but a hoax." Beijing, *Renmin Ribao*, editorial, October 31, 1962. The Cuban people will not be "duped by any honeyed words." Beijing, *Renmin Ribao*, editorial, November 5, 1962.

Dennis J. Doolin, *Territorial Claims in the Sino-Soviet Conflict* (Stanford: Hoover Institution Studies: 7, 1965), pp. 19–20, has a good analysis of mutual recriminations during the Cuban missile crisis.

11. Khrushchev's speech to the Supreme Soviet, *Pravda*, December 13, 1962.

12. Beijing, *Renmin Ribao*, March 8, 1963.

13. Soviet Government Statement, March 29, 1969.

14. Letter of November 29, 1963, made public by Beijing on May 8, 1964. *Beijing Review*, May 8, 1964.

15. He desired nothing less than a new treaty, "a general settlement" of all China's territorial claims against Moscow—the phrase used in the *Renmin Ribao* editorial of March 8, 1963.

16. Chinese Government Statement, May 24, 1969. FBIS DR Communist China, May 26, 1969.

17. Ibid. At the 1964 negotiations, the Soviet representative "could not but agree that the central line of the main channel should be taken for determining the boundary line on the rivers and ownership of islands."

18. For Mao's interview with Japanese visitors see Doolin, *Territorial Claims*, pp. 42–44.

19. "Now, given today's weapons of annihilation, it is especially dangerous, I might even say criminal, to seek wealth through the expansion of 'lebensraum'. . . . The sole acceptable means of changing borders is negotiations. A different path as a rule leads to war . . . if we are attacked we will defend our borders with all the means at our disposal." September 15, 1964 Khrushchev interview with Japanese visitors. *Pravda*, September 20, 1964.

20. The Chinese had "systematically" violated Soviet borders since 1960. *Pravda*, September 21, 1963.

21. Harry Gelman, "The Soviet Far East Buildup and Soviet Risk-Taking Against China," RAND R-2943-AF, August 1982, p. 13.

22. Ibid., pp. 17–18.

23. *Sovetskaya Rossia*, May 7, 1969.

24. These deployments in Mongolia not only secured the flank of the Transbaykal Military District, but also became a potential threat to China's defense of the north China plain and the approaches to Beijing. Gelman, "Soviet Far East Buildup," pp. 19–20.

25. Harrison E. Salisbury, *New York Times*, August 17, 1966.

26. Mao Zedong's "Instruction to the PLA," as conveyed by Marshal Ye Jianying on January 27, 1967. American Consulate General, Hong Kong, *Current Background*, October 21, 1969.

27. Mao, in rejecting Khrushchev's appeal for a cessation of polemics, had stated (July 10, 1964): "As regards war on paper, there are no dead in such a war." Doolin, *Territorial Claims*, p. 43.

28. "Down With Luo Ruiqing, Usurper of the Army Power," pamphlet. American Consulate General, Hong Kong, *Selections from China Mainland Magazines*, January 20, 1969.

29. They were denounced in Harbin on September 1, 1969, as "agents" of senior party Vice Chairman Liu Shaoqi. FBIS DR Communist China, September 3, 1969.

30. Cited from a comment on a Soviet documentary film of border incidents. Moscow domestic service in Russian, May 12, 1969. Broadcast for soldiers entitled: "How it Began." FBIS DR USSR, May 22, 1969.

31. The Soviets sent "fully armed troops to occupy by force the Chinese territory Heixiazi Island. . . ." New China News Agency (hereafter NCNA), April 18, 1969. FBIS DR Communist China, April 21, 1969. Soviet control of Heixiazi is a sensitive matter and the island is infrequently referred to in Chinese media.

32. In December 1966, Chinese authorities in Heihe sent a convoy of six trucks and two passenger cars carrying a composite group of "25 PLA fighters, 15 young Red Guard fighters, and 23 passengers" to support Chinese border guards. Confronted by armed Soviet border guards, who blocked their route to the small island, the Chinese demanded access, but the border guards hit, kicked, and shoved them in "fierce struggles." The Chinese camped nearby "for two days and a night," having been well prepared because "we have brought along big quantities of supplies in a determined effort to confront them for a prolonged period." The Soviets called in a helicopter, an armored car, and five motor vehicles carrying "10 army officers and 19 soldiers," but eventually they went away according to Red Guards of the composite group. *Red Flag Bulletin* (Guangdong), May 26, 1968. American Consulate General, Hong Kong, *Survey of the China Mainland Press*, June 20, 1968.

33. Gelman, "Soviet Far East Buildup," pp. 13–14.

34. The Soviets also put in place "nuclear-tipped surface-to-surface rockets." Henry Kissinger, *White House Years* (Boston: Little, Brown, 1979), p. 167.

35. Foreign Ministry note of September 16, 1968. NCNA, September 16, 1968. FBIS DR Communist China, September 16, 1968.

36. Speech of September 29, 1968. FBIS DR Communist China, October 1, 1968.

37. To reach the island from the nearest Soviet border posts, Soviet troops had to be transported "about 4 kilometers along the frozen Ussuri—easy targets from the high Chinese shore." *Literaturnaya Gazeta*, May 21, 1969.

38. Regarding accessibility, only "a narrow channel of 60 or 70 meters separates the island from the Chinese bank." *Sovetskaya Rossia*, May 8, 1969. Indeed, the island "connects with the Chinese bank at low water." PRC Government Statement, May 24, 1969. FBIS DR Communist China, May 26, 1969.

39. *Pravda*, March 12, 1969.

40. Photograph and caption, *Beijing Review*, March 21, 1969.

41. Second photograph and caption, ibid.

42. Soviet Foreign Ministry press conference, *Pravda*, March 8, 1969.

43. Chinese Foreign Ministry note of March 2, 1969. NCNA March 3, 1969. FBIS DR Communist China, March 3, 1969.

44. Neville Maxwell, "The Chinese Account of the 1969 Fighting at Chenpao," *The China Quarterly*, 56 (October/December 1973), pp. 730–739.

45. Joint Beijing *Renmin Ribao-Jiefang Junbao* editorial, March 4, 1969.

46. TASS, March 9, 1969. FBIS DR USSR, March 11, 1969.

47. *Sovetskaya Rossia*, March 19, 1969. Interview with Major General A. N. Anikushin, Border Guards.

48. *Izvestia*, March 8, 1969.

49. Soviet Foreign Ministry press conference, *Pravda*, March 8, 1969.

50. Maxwell, "The Chinese Account," pp. 733–734.

51. *Beijing Review*, March 21, 1969.

52. The Chinese besieged the Soviet embassy for several hours, and roughed up an embassy driver and two TASS correspondents. FBIS DR Communist China, March 4 and 7, 1969; FBIS DR USSR, March 10, 1969. The Soviets then besieged the Chinese embassy

and smashed windows and gates of its consular department. FBIS DR Communist China, March 11, 1969.

53. For example, Chinese Foreign Ministry officials refused to receive Soviet embassy officials "despite their numerous requests." FBIS DR USSR, March 10, 1969. Soviet Foreign Ministry officials "refused again and again" to meet with the Chinese charge on March 7. It is not clear whether subsequently they accepted directly from him Beijing's notes of protest (March 11 and 12) regarding "destructive activities" against the Chinese embassy and the punching of Chinese personnel who went out to meet with foreign journalists. FBIS DR Communist China, March 14, 1969.

54. *Pravda*, March 17, 1969.

55. A Moscow domestic service broadcast in Russian on March 17, 1969, concedes that Soviet troops had been warned in this manner. FBIS DR USSR, March 18, 1969.

56. Chinese Foreign Ministry note, March 15, 1969. FBIS DR Communist China, March 17, 1969.

57. NCNA, March 16, 1969. FBIS DR Communist China, March 17, 1969.

58. *Pravda*, March 17, 1969. NCNA, August 15, 1969, refers to Chinese fighters of an artillery unit who fought at Zhenbao/Damanskiy. FBIS DR Communist China, August 18, 1969.

59. *Sovetskaya Rossia*, May 16, 1969.

60. Ibid.

61. On the island, "The mound-covered terrain, overgrown with bushes, restricted the maneuverability of APCs. At short-range, the Chinese could set the vehicles on fire. . . ." *Krasnaya Zvezda*, March 20, 1969.

62. A photograph taken by the Chinese after the battle shows a damaged tank. *Beijing Review*, May 5, 1969. The Soviets concede that one of their APCs "was set on fire." *Krasnaya Zvezda*, March 20, 1969.

63. A Yugoslav, reporting from Moscow and citing a *Pravda* article of March 28, 1969, conjectured that the island "is deserted and that not even the permanent [sic] Soviet crew is there." Belgrade, TANYUG (March 1970), p. 96.

64. "Mao Tse-tung's Speech to the 1st Plenary Session of the CCP's 9th Central Committee," April 28, 1969. Taipei, *Issues and Studies*, Vol. VI, No. 6 (March 1970), p. 96. Beijing media disparaged Soviet armor as being unable to ensure success in battle. For example, Chinese border guards were depicted as pointing to the damaged Soviet tank after the March 15 skirmish and saying: "You fight your 'mechanized' war and we will fight our revolutionized war. The outcome is foregone; our revolutionization will always beat the reactionaries' mechanization." NCNA, May 14, 1969. FBIS DR Communist China, May 15, 1969.

65. PRC Government Statement of May 24, 1969. FBIS DR Communist China, May 26, 1969.

66. *Pravda* on March 14, 1969 published Moscow's complaint that media in the West approved of Mao's current foreign policy which, among other things, prevented the establishment of a Sino-Soviet united front against the West.

67. Lin Biao, "Report to the Ninth National Congress of the CCP," April 1, 1969. *Beijing Review*, April 30, 1969.

68. Soviet Government Statement of March 29, 1969. FBIS DR USSR, April 1, 1969. The statement almost begged for practical steps to normalize the border situation "without delay," and it "urged" the Chinese to resume consultations "in the near future."

69. NCNA Note of May 24, 1969. FBIS DR Communist China, May 26, 1969. The patronizing sentence in quotations may well have been Mao's.

70. Zhou Enlai's Statement to Japanese visitors, April 6, 1969. FBIS DR Communist China, April 15, 1969.

71. Speech to the Supreme Soviet, July 10, 1969. FBIS DR USSR, July 11, 1969. The low-level discussions, which were held from June 18 to August 8, did not signal a Chinese retreat. During this Commission session the Chinese carried out the July 8 ambush on Bacha/Goldinskiy Island.

72. *Pravda*, May 3, 1969.

73. *Pravda*, May 4, 1969.

74. Chinese Foreign Ministry note of June 6, 1969. FBIS DR Communist China, June 6, 1969.

75. Ibid. The Chinese also complained of overflights by Soviet military aircraft, several having flown as deep as 36 miles into Chinese territory. These overflights almost certainly were intended partly as intimidation and partly as reconnaissance.

The Chinese were aware that the Soviets had not used their vastly superior airforce to bomb or strafe in the firefights. They intended to hold the Soviets to the tacit "rule of engagement" prohibiting the use of aircraft for ground-support strafing or bombing. Thus they are not known to have tried to shoot down any overflying Soviet planes.

76. Mao's apparent effort to persuade the Soviets to accept the pre-March no-shooting tacit rule is suggested by a phrase in the PRC Government Statement of May 24, 1969; "Each side ensures that it shall avert conflicts and that under no circumstances shall the frontier guards of its side fire at the other side. . . ." FBIS DR Communist China, May 26, 1969.

Moreover, the Chinese did not shoot even on May 28, when 10 "fishermen" in the eastern section of the Amur River were taken prisoner in Soviet gunboats, beaten up, conveyed in two helicopters to a Soviet prison, interrogated, and released only after three weeks. Broadcast to Taiwan by PLA Fukien Front Radio, July 21, 1969. FBIS DR Communist China, July 23, 1969.

77. Speech at the International Meeting of Communist Parties in Moscow, June 7, 1969. FBIS DR USSR, June 9, 1969.

78. Chinese Foreign Ministry note, June 11, 1969. FBIS DR Communist China, June 11, 1969.

79. NCNA, July 8, 1969. FBIS DR Communist China, July 9, 1969. TASS, July 8, 1969. FBIS DR USSR, July 9, 1969. See also FBIS DR USSR, July 14, 1969.

80. Gelman, "Soviet Far East Buildup," p. 38.

81. Speech of August, 1969. FBIS DR Communist China, August 4, 1969.

82. *Renmin Ribao, Hongqi*, and *Jiefang Junbao* joint editorial, July 31, 1969.

83. *Literaturnaya Gazeta*, August 20, 1969.

84. NCNA, August 13, 1969. FBIS DR Communist China, August 14, 1969.

85. Chinese Foreign Ministry note of August 13, 1969. FBIS DR Communist China, August 13, 1969. *Izvestia*, August 15, 1969.

86. Beijing's August 13 note suggested that the Chinese did not want an expanded firefight, but Moscow did: "At present, the Soviet side is continuing to mass large numbers of troops and tanks in an attempt to provoke larger-scale armed conflicts. The incident is still developing."

87. In order further to portray the Soviets as the aggressor, the Chinese note complained that the Soviets had used tanks. This was denied (*Pravda*, August 15). The Soviets insisted that they used only APCs. Soviet media throughout the crisis did not concede the use of tanks—a position contradicted by Chinese photographs showing at least four Soviet tanks in combat at Zhenbao/Damanskiy and one disabled Soviet tank, which the Soviets had tried, unsuccessfully, to retrieve following the March 15 firefight.

88. Report from Beijing of the French correspondent on August 16, 1969. FBIS DR Communist China, August 18, 1969.

89. *Krasnaya Zvezda*, March 8, 1969, and Moscow Radio Peace and Progress in Mandarin to China, March 17, 1969. FBIS DR USSR, March 29, 1969.

90. For example, Beijing complained that Moscow, having "brandished nuclear weapons at China" will have "completely miscalculated" if it believed that China was "weak and could be bullied, thinking that the Chinese people can be cowed by its policy of nuclear blackmail. . . ." PRC Government Statement of May 24, 1969, FBIS DR Communist China, May 26, 1969.

On occasion, Beijing also publicized the key phrases of Soviet media threats. For example, Moscow "has kept on clamoring that 'the main weapon of the Soviet forces is the infinitely destructive ballistic missiles with nuclear warheads,' and that the nuclear ballistic missile units stationed at lower Lake Baykal and along the Sino-Mongolian border have 'made good preparations' and are 'ready at any time' to launch 'all-out destructive nuclear counterattacks' against China." NCNA domestic service in Chinese, June 2, 1969. FBIS DR Communist China, June 3, 1969.

91. Gelman "Soviet Far East Buildup," pp. 38–39.

92. *Washington Post*, August 28, 1969.

93. Kissinger, *White House Years*, p. 183. Regarding the standdown, Kissinger states that: "Such a move, which permits all aircraft to be brought to a high state of readiness simultaneously, is often a sign of a possible attack; at a minimum it is a brutal warning in an intensified war of nerves. The standdown continued through September." A standdown of one month's duration (late August through September) almost certainly would have been detected by the Chinese.

94. Report from Beijing of the French correspondent on September 12, 1969. FBIS DR Communist China, September 15, 1969.

95. Beijing's report of the airport meeting included the terse, cold comment that "They had a frank conversation." NCNA, September 11, 1969. FBIS DR Communist China, September 12, 1969.

96. Gelman, "Soviet Far East Buildup," pp. 39–40.

97. PRC Government Statement of October 7, 1969. FBIS DR Communist China, October 8, 1969.

98. The Soviet defector, Shevchenko, claims that during the border crisis Marshal Grechko advocated attacking China with nuclear weapons, but not many military men shared his view, and the view that prevailed was Brezhnev's: not to attack. Arkady N. Shevchenko, *Breaking with Moscow* (New York: Knopf, 1985), pp. 165–66.

99. Moscow's view of Mao as the ultimate decision-maker was suggested by K. Simonov in *Pravda* (May 3, 1969) when, discussing the Chinese ambush of March 2, he stated that: "I am absolutely certain that this order to kill was not given by the commander of the Chinese frontier regiment, nor by the chief of their frontier guards, nor even by the commander of their military district. I am absolutely certain that this order to kill was given by a higher authority. So high that it is impossible to get any higher."

100. Kissinger, *White House Years*, p. 172.

SUPERPOWER INVOLVEMENT IN MIDDLE EAST CONFLICTS

Introduction to Part Four

Alexander L. George

The three case studies presented in this part of the volume focus on the role of the superpowers in regional conflicts in the Middle East. Special attention is given to the policy dilemmas Moscow and Washington experience as a result of their involvement in the continuing Arab-Israeli conflict. These dilemmas arise both when the superpowers attempt to prevent a crisis between their regional allies from escalating to war and after war breaks out when they try to balance support for the ally's war effort with efforts to avoid a dangerous superpower confrontation.[1]

Both the United States and the Soviet Union have important security interests of their own in the Middle East. However, from an early stage in the Cold War, concern over their respective interests in that region was much magnified by their global rivalry. While each superpower acknowledges that the other also has important interests in the Middle East, each has found it particularly difficult to sort out and delimit its respective interests for several reasons. Unlike the division of Europe during the Cold War that helped to stabilize East-West rivalry in that region, it has not been possible for Moscow and Washington to draw a clear geographical line in the Middle East to separate each side's area of predominant interests and provide reasonably stable quasi-spheres of influence. Instead, proclaimed interests in the Middle East have overlapped and intermingled geographically, giving the political landscape the character of a confusing and changeable chessboard. Aggravating efforts to define and delimit their interests has been the pronounced instability within the region, which made it difficult for either superpower to be content with the measure of influence it managed to achieve for the time being with one or another of the Arab states. Although the first Eisenhower administration was reluctant to commit itself to Israel, the United States moved in that direction after the Suez War of 1956, largely out of concern over growing Soviet influence in the Middle East.

The volatility and geographically open-ended character of superpower competition in the Middle East have served, in turn, to exacerbate the tendency for global, geopolitical, and ideological considerations to magnify each superpower's conception of its purely regional interests and to heighten mutual distrust. In brief, the circumstances under which Moscow and Washington have interacted in the Middle East have deepened the basic security dilemma that is deeply imbedded in

299

any set of adversarial relations in the anarchic international system. That is, what one side does to enhance its security interests, the other side often perceives as an increased threat to its own interests that requires it, in turn, to undertake additional moves to buttress its position. But this response, in turn, plays back and has a similar effect on the other side, and so there evolves a dynamic to the competition that takes on the character of a vicious action-reaction cycle. Thus, the early U.S. effort to implement containment in the Middle East by creating a military base structure and a network of alliances in response to what was perceived to be Soviet expansionist aims was interpreted in Moscow as part of a plan for hostile encirclement motivated by offensive, not defensive, objectives. Similarly, Moscow's efforts to develop friendly relations and to increase influence with Middle East countries in order to counter what was perceived as a U.S. effort to involve countries in that region in anti-Soviet plans reinforced U.S. suspicions as to Soviet expansionist intentions.

As a result, much of the superpower competition for influence in the Middle East lacked self-imposed or mutually agreed-upon restraints of a clear or consistent character derived from a careful delimitation of interests. The U.S.-Soviet rivalry in the region, therefore, took on characteristics of a zero-sum game. Each superpower tended to view any increase in influence in the area by the other as a setback for itself, one that could lead to further destabilization of the region and further weakening of its own overall regional position, which, if not halted, would eventually result in a serious erosion of its global position as well.

These concerns and attitudes of Moscow and Washington are very much in evidence in their involvement in the long history of the Arab-Israeli conflict and, more particularly, in the Arab-Israeli wars of 1967, 1970, and 1973 that Yaacov Bar-Siman-Tov analyzes. As he notes, each superpower has not merely offered assistance to its client states but has repeatedly taken advantage of the Arab-Israeli conflict to increase its own influence at the expense of the other superpower.

Nonetheless, the two superpowers do have an important residue of common interests in the Middle East, which on occasion has led them to operate with restraint and to try to cooperate with each other. These occasions have arisen particularly in the context of war-threatening crises and actual wars between Israel and Arab states. Both Moscow and Washington have genuinely feared that their regional allies might drag them into a war with each other. The three Arab-Israeli wars under scrutiny here give striking evidence of acute policy dilemmas that Washington and Moscow have found it difficult to manage while backing rival regional actors. In each of these three conflicts, each superpower had interests of its own that converged with the interests of its regional client, and, therefore, it was motivated to support its client up to a point. At the same time, Moscow and Washington also had other interests that were threatened by the prospect of an Arab-Israeli war and that, during the course of each of these wars, led them to try to limit the costs and risks they would accept on behalf of a regional ally.

The basic policy dilemma for each superpower in these three conflicts arose from a tension between the desire—indeed, at times the necessity—to lend meaningful support to its regional ally and the determination not to allow itself to be drawn into a dangerous, war-threatening confrontation with the other superpower.

The general policy dilemma of crisis management discussed in Chapter 4—namely, the tension between doing what is necessary to further one's most important interests while at the same time avoiding actions that might trigger unwanted escalation to war—was in important respects more difficult for Moscow and Washington to manage in these regional conflicts than in their direct confrontations in other crises because of their limited leverage and control over the behavior of their regional clients.

As Bar-Siman-Tov's case studies indicate, Moscow and Washington did attempt to persuade their regional allies not to initiate war. Their efforts were unsuccessful in all three cases for reasons that are extremely sobering and counterintuitive, in that they challenge the assumption that a strong patron should be able to impose its will on a client state. Our case studies clearly demonstrate that, in fact, client states themselves have considerable leverage over their superpower patrons. It is only a small exaggeration to say that, at times, the client state can exercise a type of tacit blackmail against its patron.

In all three cases, only a political-diplomatic resolution of the issues threatening to generate another Arab-Israeli war could have prevented it. This was recognized by Moscow and Washington, but their efforts to use diplomacy to prevent crises between their client states from escalating to war failed repeatedly. In 1967, the United States did persuade Israel to hold off in the face of Arab provocations for a considerable period of time while it attempted to arrange a peaceful resolution that would satisfy Israel. Failing to achieve such a resolution, however, Washington officials felt they had no choice but to condone the initiation of war by Israel. Similarly, the Soviet Union failed to find a diplomatic solution to satisfy Egypt in 1970 and again in 1973, and reluctantly accepted Egypt's resort to the war option.

Even when the superpowers cooperated in an attempt to find diplomatic solutions for at least some of the deep issues dividing the Arab states and Israel, they encountered insurmountable difficulties. Arab and Israeli positions were too far apart and too rigid to permit easy construction of a compromise settlement. Besides, it was difficult for Moscow and Washington to agree on what would constitute reciprocal concessions by their regional allies in the interest of a political solution. In several instances, Moscow stopped short of exerting maximum pressure on its regional allies for fear of endangering its relationship with them. The United States did eventually exert strong pressure on Israel in all three wars, but only when it seemed necessary to do so to prevent a war-threatening confrontation between the two superpowers or, as in 1973, when a more sweeping Israeli military success was not considered to be in the overall U.S. interest.

If their efforts at preventing these Arab-Israeli wars were ineffectual in the last analysis, the superpowers did only somewhat better in managing the crisis after war broke out and in attempting to bring it to a speedy conclusion. Both Moscow and Washington responded to the outbreak of war with an uneasy mixture of a desire to gain advantages for themselves and their allies, coupled with real concern that the regional conflict might develop into a dangerous confrontation between themselves. Each superpower felt obliged to provide its ally with military supplies to enable it to achieve a measure of success and, certainly, to avoid defeat. Ceasefires were difficult to arrange, as a ceasefire in place would favor the side that had gained an advantage on the battlefield, while a ceasefire based on the principle of returning to the status quo ante would deprive it of that advantage. At different points in the 1973 war, each superpower was bemused by the expectation that the outcome of negotiations to terminate the war would be dependent on the relative success or failure of its client(s) on the battlefield. Although surprised by the outbreak of war in October 1973, U.S. leaders quickly saw in it an opportunity to gain their long-standing objective of bringing about a reversal of Egypt's ties to the Soviet Union. This objective, which guided Washington's policy and actions throughout the crisis, was in fact achieved, but not before a somewhat dangerous confrontation brought about by the Soviet threat of military intervention.

Our case studies indicate that efforts by the United States and the Soviet Union to manage crises between their allies are likely to be much more difficult than crises in which the superpowers directly face each other. Given the acute nature of the Arab-Israeli conflict, neither of these regional actors has much use for the political requirement of limiting one's objectives or the means employed on their behalf in the interest of avoiding escalation. In fact, in 1967 Nasser deliberately escalated his objectives after his initial successes, and, during the War of Attrition in 1970, both sides escalated their objectives in ways that made it difficult to bring the confrontation to a close. Other important operational requirements of crisis management also seemed barely relevant to the regional actors. During the crises of 1967, 1970, and 1973, neither the Arab states nor Israel displayed much interest in slowing down the momentum of events in the interest of preserving peace. (In fact, on several occasions they seemed more interested in speeding up their efforts to gain territory and to inflict damage on the opposing force.) Similarly, neither side found much relevance in the crisis management principle that calls for leaving the adversary a way out compatible with its fundamental interests and honor.

Although the superpowers did not succeed in preventing these wars, they at least managed to develop a tacit norm for regulating and limiting their own involvement. As Bar-Siman-Tov and other writers have shown, a pattern of restraint—perhaps even a tacit understanding—emerged as to what a superpower is and is not entitled to do in support of its regional ally. Each superpower evidently recognized the likelihood that the other superpower would itself intervene militarily in some way if this became necessary to prevent its regional ally from suffering a catastrophic defeat. Conversely, to avoid such an intervention, the superpower backing the winning local actor had to recognize the necessity of pressuring its ally to stop short of inflicting an overwhelming defeat on the opponent. At critical points in the 1967, 1970, and 1973 wars, the Soviet Union made it clear—that is, credible enough to U.S. leaders—that it could not allow Israel to threaten the existence of Arab regimes allied to Moscow. Accepting the credibility of such Soviet threats of intervention, the United States immediately exerted strong pressure on Israel to desist in 1967 and perhaps again in 1973. (Washington's failure to do so in 1970 was followed by Soviet military intervention.) Similarly, in the Syrian-Jordan crisis of September 1970, a case not included in this book, the United States activated a threat of Israeli military intervention in an effort to induce the Soviet Union to pressure its ally, Syria, to call off the tank invasion of Jordan that was threatening to topple King Hussein's regime.

Variations of this tacit ground rule can be seen in all three Arab-Israeli wars. It comes into play only when the regional ally is threatened with an imminent, shattering defeat. In this circumstance, the balance of interests clearly shifts in favor of the superpower backing the regional actor that is in jeopardy. This makes it both legitimate and credible for the patron of the beleaguered regional actor to intervene, if necessary, to save its local ally from defeat. But this tacit norm does not come into play automatically. Rather, it must be activated by a credible threat of intervention. For obvious reasons, this tacit ground rule cannot be regarded as a stable, reliable basis for enabling the superpowers to back regional client states without being drawn into war with each other.

NOTES

1. There are a number of useful overall assessments of superpower efforts over the years to prevent crises between Arab states and Israel and to regulate their involvement in Arab-Israeli wars. See, for example, Yaacov Bar-Siman-Tov, *Israel, The Superpowers, and the War in the Middle East* (New York: Praeger, 1987); Gabriel Ben-Dor and David B. Dewitt, eds., *Conflict Management in the Middle East* (Lexington, MA: Lexington Books, 1987); Alexander L. George, "Mechanisms for U.S.-Soviet Cooperation in Crisis Avoidance," American Enterprise Institute, *Defense and Foreign Policy Review* 6, 1 (1986): 5–13; Benjamin Miller, "Perspectives on Superpower Crisis Management and Conflict Resolution in the Arab-Israeli Conflict," in George W. Breslauer, et al., *Soviet Strategy in the Middle East* (Boston: Unwin Hyman, 1990); pp. 247–284; Harold H. Saunders, "Regulating Soviet-U.S. Competition and Cooperation in the Arab-Israeli Arena, 1967–86," in A. L. George, P. J. Farley and A. Dallin, eds., *U.S.-Soviet Security Cooperation: Achievements, Failures, Prospects* (New York: Oxford University Press, 1988), pp. 540–582; Janice Gross Stein, "The Managed and the Managers: Crisis Prevention in the Middle East," in Gilbert R. Winham, ed., *New Issues in International Crisis Management* (Boulder, CO: Westview Press, 1988), pp. 171–198.

CHAPTER 13

The Arab-Israeli War of 1967

Yaacov Bar-Siman-Tov

In Chapter 8, Janice Gross Stein showed how the Arab-Israeli crisis in May 1967 developed into a war that neither side had wanted or expected at the outset. Her analysis traced the process of miscalculated escalation on Egypt's part that provoked Israel to initiate war. Stein noted that the possibility of effective crisis management in this case was severely limited by several critical factors: the intense domestic and regional pressures on President Gamal Abdel Nasser, the strong commitment of Israel to deterrence, and the limited and missed opportunities for effective crisis management by the superpowers and the United Nations.

The 1967 war also needs to be studied from the standpoint of the policy dilemmas Moscow and Washington experienced in backing rival regional actors and the extent to which they cooperated to prevent the crisis from escalating to war. While each superpower had some interests of its own that converged with the interests of its regional client and was therefore motivated to support the client up to a point, each superpower also had other interests that led it to try to limit the costs and risks it would accept on behalf of its regional ally. The basic policy dilemma for each superpower in this crisis, as well as in subsequent ones in 1970 and 1973, therefore, arose from a tension between the desire to support the regional ally and the necessity to avoid being drawn thereby into a dangerous, war-threatening confrontation with the other superpower.

The policy dilemma the superpowers experience in these regional conflicts mirrors the type of policy dilemma that has been inherent in efforts at crisis management when Moscow and Washington have directly confronted each other in Berlin and Cuba. As noted in Chapter 4, the dilemma arises from the tension between doing what is necessary to further one's most important interests at stake in a crisis and avoiding actions that can trigger unwanted escalation of the crisis. This policy dilemma is, if anything, more difficult for the superpowers to manage in regional conflicts because, as we shall see in this case, they have limited leverage and control over the behavior of their regional clients.

This chapter is a much abbreviated version of an unpublished study that contains fuller documentation.

BACKGROUND TO THE CRISIS

It is important to recall some of the historical developments leading to the 1967 crisis that help clarify the superpowers' involvement in the Arab-Israeli conflict. Washington and Moscow had pursued highly divergent and competitive policies in the Middle East since the early 1950s. The United States undertook to implement a containment policy in the area in response to what it perceived to be Soviet expansionist aims. However, U.S. efforts to develop an anti-Soviet regional alliance to block Soviet military-political expansion and to create a military base structure in the area were interpreted in Moscow as hostile encirclement motivated by offensive aims. Each superpower attempted to take advantage of regional developments to increase its own influence at the expense of the other, both in order to strengthen its overall global position and to protect specific security interests in the Middle East. Rivalry between the two superpowers in the Middle East quickly took on the characteristics of a zero-sum game. Each superpower tended to view any increase in influence in the area by the other superpower as a setback for itself that it feared would further destabilize the region and contribute to an additional weakening of its overall position. Although both Moscow and Washington might acknowledge that in principle the other did indeed have important, legitimate interests in the Middle East, in practice this recognition was dimmed and rendered largely irrelevant as a result of the impact of the ideological and geopolitical rivalry of the Cold War.

After a new government came into power in Syria in early 1966, the Soviet Union saw opportunities for enhancing its interests in the Middle East by bringing Egypt, with which it already had a strong position, into a closer relationship with Damascus. Seizing the opportunity for encouraging Egyptian-Syrian reconciliation, Moscow helped to bring about an Egyptian-Syrian defense pact in November 1966.[1]

In early May, Israel responded to an increasing number of raids against its territory initiated by Syria with a warning that it might be forced to take strong action unless Syria acted to curb these activities. There is no evidence that Israel was planning a large-scale operation against Syria, although there were some indications that it was considering a punitive raid; in any case, the series of public and private warnings the Israeli government issued aroused concern over Israeli intentions in Syria, Egypt, and the Soviet Union as well as in Western and U.N. quarters. Israeli leaders themselves appeared to become alarmed by the possible misinterpretation of their warnings and made efforts to reduce this concern.[2] Nonetheless, Moscow circulated and gave credence to allegations of huge Israeli troop concentrations and an imminent attack on Syria. Its purpose evidently was to activate the Egyptian-Syrian defense pact and to induce Nasser to act in support of Syria. It is not clear what actions the Soviets asked or expected Egypt to take. Knowing that Nasser was opposed to the use of force against Israel, Moscow probably wanted and expected no more than a limited demonstration of force by Egypt to deter Israel from undertaking a heavy retaliatory raid against Syria.[3] Deterrence of such an Israeli action (whether deterrence was necessary or not) brought about via Soviet-inspired Arab unity was probably Moscow's main objective, which, if accomplished, would strengthen the Soviet position in the Middle East.

CONSTRAINTS ON SUPERPOWER ABILITY
TO AVOID CRISIS ESCALATION

However, Moscow's expectation that the crisis could be kept safely limited proved to be a gross miscalculation. As Stein noted in Chapter 8, Soviet leaders did not anticipate that Nasser would escalate his objectives and perhaps did not foresee the limits of their ability to control Nasser's actions. Although it appears that Soviet leaders were not consulted by Nasser regarding removal of the United Nations Emergency Force (UNEF) from Sinai, they supported Egypt's right to do so in part because they had no choice but to back their ally but also in part because, not anticipating Nasser's subsequent moves, they did not expect the removal to lead to a further, more dangerous escalation of Nasser's objectives and actions.[4]

Within a few days, Israel's concerns mounted as the concentration of Egyptian forces in the Sinai increased. Beginning to fear an Egyptian blockade of the Straits of Tiran and a possible Egyptian attack, Israel ordered a large-scale mobilization of reserves and initiated a diplomatic campaign to bring pressure on Nasser to refrain from a blockade of the Straits, an action that many years earlier Israel had defined as a casus belli. The United States encouraged U Thant to step up efforts to avoid war. Washington was reluctant, however, to take strong diplomatic initiatives of its own to deter Nasser from closing the Tiran straits. Instead, the Johnson administration reacted with caution and hesitancy, warning Israel not to use force against Egypt and not to take unilateral action even if Nasser closed the straits.

Even before U Thant arrived in Cairo, the virulent demands from within Egypt and from other Arab nations for further action against Israel (described in Stein's chapter) finally pushed Nasser into proclaiming a blockade of the Tiran straits on May 22. Thus far, Nasser had taken no action to close the straits, apparently waiting to see how Israel and the United States would react to UNEF's removal. Nasser no doubt took note of the fact that Washington failed to make any public statement confirming its long-standing commitment to Israel to uphold freedom of navigation in the Tiran straits. Nor did the administration respond to Israel's request for an immediate public declaration of U.S. commitment to Israel's security, preferring to wait until U Thant's return from Cairo and to initiate diplomatic contact of its own directly with Nasser. Washington's reluctance to take strong unilateral actions to deter further moves by Nasser was underlined when President Johnson sent a message to Premier Aleksei Kosygin suggesting a joint effort to calm the situation. The absence of any forceful U.S. effort to deter Nasser from closing the Tiran straits no doubt made it more difficult for him to resist pressures from his own domestic opinion and from the Arab world to step up action against Israel.

The United States did not offer Israel any concrete means of resolving the crisis and refused to actively restrain Nasser, while at the same time it was pressuring Israel to refrain from taking unilateral military action of its own. President Johnson wanted the main thrust of U.S. diplomacy to be channeled through the United Nations, although he was prepared to use U.S. influence to avoid war through contacts with Moscow, Cairo, and Jerusalem. Johnson was unwilling to allow Israel to act unilaterally with military force to maintain freedom of navigation, contrary to the commitment President Eisenhower had given Israel in 1957. In addition,

Johnson was unwilling from the onset of the crisis to take unilateral U.S. action for this purpose. Instead, the president tried—without success—to gain the support of France and Britain for an invocation of the old and by now obsolete Tripartite Declaration on this matter, which the three powers had undertaken in 1950.

Whether the Soviets were consulted by Nasser or were told beforehand of his intention to close the Tiran straits, they evidently did little to discourage him from doing so. After the action was taken, they endorsed it. But at that point, Moscow began to urge Nasser to act with restraint, now that he had achieved his objectives by peaceful means, in order to avoid war. At the same time, Moscow evidently carefully limited its commitment to Nasser, in case war broke out, to deterring active U.S. involvement on behalf of Israel.

Indeed, having secured the removal of UNEF and proclaimed a blockade of Israel's use of the Tiran straits, Nasser had succeeded in returning the situation to its pre-Suez war status. Israel, on the other hand, seeing its deterrence policy and security interests severely challenged by Nasser, was now strongly motivated to initiate war unless, with the help of superpower diplomacy, Egypt could be induced to call off the blockade and to de-escalate its threatening military buildup in Sinai.

CONSTRAINTS ON SUPERPOWER COOPERATION TO AVOID WAR

In this situation, both Moscow and Washington perceived a common interest to act in order to avoid the outbreak of war between Israel and the Arab states. Each enjoined its regional ally not to initiate war, but this limited degree of superpower cooperation in crisis management could not suffice to prevent war. Only a political-diplomatic solution to the crisis that was acceptable to both Egypt and Israel could have prevented war, and this could have been accomplished—if at all—only by a joint superpower effort. But while the United States acted to find such a diplomatic solution, the Soviet Union refused to cooperate, for this would have required a diplomatic retreat on Nasser's part. It was relatively easy to persuade him, if indeed such persuasion were needed, not to initiate war himself—and that was as far as the Soviets would go—for such restraint would leave him in a highly advantageous position.

Thus, U.S.-Soviet cooperation to prevent war was fundamentally flawed by virtue of the fact that the two countries had different outcomes of the crisis in mind. The superpowers were indeed working together to prevent the outbreak of hostilities. But, as Theodore Draper correctly points out, they "were also working at cross-purposes politically."[5] Thus, Moscow wanted to prevent Nasser from suffering the consequences—either war or a diplomatic retreat—of the moves he had made. Moscow's willingness to try to restrain Nasser from initiating war, which he was in any case not disposed to do, was secondary to its commitment to prevent a change of the situation he had imposed in the Sinai and in the Tiran straits. Washington's success in restraining Israel for the time being was of a different order altogether, for at bottom it rested on the ability of the United States to deliver on its commitment to Israel to find a way to keep the Tiran straits open. Given Soviet unwillingness to pressure Nasser to modify actions that had brought the crisis to the point of war, the burden for working out a peaceful resolution of the crisis was thrown exclusively on the United States.

In the end, Washington failed to persuade Nasser to cancel his threat of a blockade. Its stern warnings to Israel not to initiate war, repeated frequently during the crisis, were heeded in Jerusalem for several weeks. Thus, the United States did achieve the important crisis management requirement of slowing down the momentum of events to give time for diplomatic efforts. Unwilling to take unilateral action to challenge the blockade, Washington launched a concerted effort to organize a broad multilateral initiative for this purpose, with, however, meager results. Anticipating the failure of this effort, Washington gave increased emphasis to diplomatic efforts to persuade Nasser to back down or to accept a compromise. The prospects for success, however, were never encouraging.

In the first place, any substantial retreat by Nasser from a major diplomatic victory already achieved—one, moreover, that seemed to promise additional success against Israel and additional glory—would have been extremely difficult for him, if, indeed, not impossible. He preferred to accept the possibility of war. Bellicose domestic Egyptian and Arab opinion had pressured him into escalating his objective and undertaking the blockade after his success in deterring Israel from strong action against Syria. As Stein has noted, Nasser's boldness and risky behavior in the crisis were in important respects imposed on him by his political weakness and vulnerability, both at home and in the Arab world. Indeed, he was being pressed to provide energetic leadership of the Arab world in order to mount additional action against Israel.

In the second place, with U.S. military forces already heavily engaged in a prolonged and increasingly controversial war in Vietnam, President Johnson was reluctant from the very beginning of the crisis to act in ways that might lead to U.S. military involvement in the Middle East and new political troubles at home. As a result, the administration operated with quite limited leverage for achieving the difficult task of persuading Nasser to be reasonable. Wielding neither a potent stick nor an enticing carrot of its own, and deprived of Soviet cooperation in pressuring Nasser, Washington approached the task from a position of weakness that was plainly evident in Cairo.

Two special envoys, Charles Yost (a retired diplomat) and Robert Anderson (a former secretary of the treasury), both experienced in Middle East affairs, were dispatched to Cairo to try to elicit a compromise from Nasser. Their mission was to obtain, if possible, a suspension of the blockade of the Tiran straits or at least some sort of mitigation of it. Nasser assured Anderson on June 1 that he would not launch a preemptive war but made it clear that he was determined to initiate the blockade against Israeli shipping. Any effort to open the straits, Nasser stated, would be viewed as an act of aggression, but he offered to continue talks to try to work out a settlement. In his personal report to Johnson, Anderson recommended that Washington avoid actions that "could be construed as favoring Israel's cause."[6]

As for Yost, his report to Secretary of State Dean Rusk offered little hope that the United States could arrange a diplomatic resolution of the crisis. There was no possibility of changing Nasser's position on the closure of the straits "except as a result of overwhelming application of military force," an option Yost opposed because of the serious consequences it would have for U.S. relations with the Arab world. Yost's recommendation was that Washington should "concentrate on limiting damage," and this included acquiescence with a blockade of the straits. Significantly, Yost recognized that this would mean a victory for Nasser but justified his recommendation on the ground that keeping the straits open to Israeli shipping was not "vital to Israel's existence."[7] Yost's views succinctly expressed an important divergence of interests at stake in the crisis between the United States and Israel and the fact that the U.S. commitment to Israel was narrower than Israel's own view of its overall security requirements.

Although Anderson's and Yost's reports made it clear that Nasser would not abandon a blockade, U.S. officials, including Johnson and Rusk, still hoped that through personal diplomacy with Egypt an alternative to war could eventually be found. The administration's leaning toward a compromise with Nasser was mainly the result of its failure to arrange either a multination declaration opposing interference with the international right of passage through the straits or sufficient support for a multilateral naval force to challenge the blockade.

Actually, Washington itself was divided on the question of a multilateral force. Not only was there little enthusiasm for it within the administration, but military and civilian officials in the Pentagon had strong reservations. Because of the heavy U.S. involvement in Vietnam, the Pentagon sought to avoid another military intervention. The proposed multilateral force seemed to it both ineffectual and provocative. Some State Department officials also opposed such a force because of the consequences it would have for U.S. relations with the Arab world.[8] As a result, no serious planning for the multilateral force option was made. The Pentagon not only stated on several occasions that there was no plan to test the blockade but signaled that the United States would not become involved. No measures were taken to reinforce the Sixth Fleet or to call up reserves, and the fleet's dispositions clearly indicated Washington's desire to avoid a military involvement.[9]

Not surprisingly, the Anderson and Yost missions to Cairo prompted concern in Jerusalem that the United States had embarked on a course that would result in demands for significant concessions on Israel's part. Israeli diplomats reported from Washington that key U.S. officials had indicated, in effect, that the United States was unable to fulfill its commitment to lift the blockade, either via multilateral action or through the unilateral use of force, and that some U.S. officials had clearly intimated that they would understand if Israel felt obliged to resort to military action itself.

Israel's earlier assurance to Washington that it would not initiate war was further undermined by new developments in the crisis. On May 28 and 29, Nasser asserted that "Israel's existence in itself is an aggression" and that Egypt had an interest "to restore the situation to what it was in 1948."[10] This was followed by the announcement of a mutual defense pact between Jordan and Egypt on May 30 and a defense pact between Egypt and Iraq on the following day.

These ominous developments made the resort to war a virtual certainty for Israel. What remained was to ascertain the U.S. position in that event. Through various channels, Israeli leaders satisfied themselves that although U.S. leaders were not giving Israel an explicit green light to initiate war, Washington could be counted upon not to take a hostile position if it did so. The fact that Israel had made a supreme effort to comply with U.S. restraints made Israel more confident of U.S. support. Israeli leaders also counted on their ability to achieve a quick military success to ensure them of U.S. political support. Accordingly, they launched a blitzkrieg air and ground assault on June 5.

As for Nasser, he had prepared militarily and psychologically for war; he expected that Israel would attack, although at times he seems to have thought U.S. pressure on Israel might prevent it from doing so. Nasser ruled out initiating war, expecting the Soviet Union to deter U.S. involvement if Israel attacked and anticipating a lower likelihood of U.S. military involvement if Israel, rather than Egypt, initiated war. As the danger of war increased, in large part because of his own actions, Nasser and his generals found ways of convincing themselves that they would do well militarily even if Israel seized the military initiative, thus adding the final wrinkle to the process of miscalculated escalation in which Nasser had been engaged.

In retrospect, it is clear that neither superpower was able to resolve the fundamental policy dilemma of crisis management—namely, to find a balance between giving a regional ally the support it needed to achieve its most important crisis objectives and restraining it from acting in ways that risked escalation of the crisis to war. As the crisis developed, each superpower also experienced an acute tension between its own interests and those of its regional client. The superpowers did have a shared interest in preventing an Arab-Israeli war, as they were fully aware that a war would place them in the difficult position of having to decide how much support to give their regional allies and, worse, create the possibility of a dangerous superpower confrontation. But the shared superpower incentive to cooperate to avoid war was not strong enough to enable them to cope with the forces that fed the process of crisis escalation. Both superpowers were inhibited from doing what was required to avoid war. To avoid war, the Soviets would have had to restrain Nasser from escalating the crisis and, after he did so, induce him to give up some of his gains; this they were unwilling or unable to do, in part because the diplomatic success he had achieved strengthened the Soviet position in the Middle East. Besides, to have exerted pressure strong enough to induce Nasser to stop or to retreat not only would have jeopardized this important Soviet gain but, indeed, could have resulted in a collapse of the Soviet position in the area. Conversely, to avoid war the United States would have had to find a way of restoring to Israel a security position that had been severely eroded and threatened by the Arab moves, and this the United States was unwilling or unable to do for the reasons already indicated.

Thus, during the course of the crisis, both superpowers experienced important limits on the leverage they could bring to bear on their regional allies as well as the limits of the interests they held in common with their regional clients. Having failed to prevent the unwanted Arab-Israeli war, the superpowers now faced the task of finding a way to end the conflict on terms as favorable as possible for their regional allies and for themselves but without allowing themselves to be drawn into the war.

SUPERPOWER EFFORTS TO END THE WAR

The outbreak of war on June 5 evidently surprised both Washington and Moscow. Having failed to cooperate to prevent the outbreak of war, they were now suddenly confronted with the necessity to decide how to avoid direct military confrontation with each other. The policy dilemma of crisis management experienced in the prewar phase of rising Arab-Israeli tensions persisted, but in a new and more dangerous context. Each superpower now had to decide how much support it could safely give to its regional ally's war effort without risking a clash with the other superpower. And both U.S. and Soviet leaders had to ascertain as quickly and reliably as possible what commitments, if any, the other had already given or might give to its local ally in support of its war effort. Finally, Moscow and Washington would have to clarify each other's readiness to seek an immediate or early termination of the war and to ascertain the conditions for a ceasefire the other side favored or would insist upon.

The initiative to establish superpower communication to clarify some of these questions and to ascertain the possibility for cooperation in seeking a ceasefire was taken by President Johnson. Within a few hours of receiving news of the Israeli attack on the morning of June 5, he communicated through normal diplomatic channels—via Secretary of State Rusk to Soviet Foreign Minister Andrei Gromyko—his urgent desire that the Security Council act quickly to bring the fighting to an end, adding that he was ready "to cooperate with all members of the Council to that end."[11] The Soviet reply came with remarkable speed, not from Gromyko but from Soviet Premier Kosygin, and it was not sent through normal diplomatic channels but over the hotline—the first use of this channel in a crisis situation. Kosygin indicated that the Soviet Union intended to work for a ceasefire and expressed the hope that the United States would use its influence with Israel to that end. Moscow's upgrading of the political level at which it replied and its resort to the hotline were unmistakable signals of serious concern that it might become embroiled militarily with the United States and of its desire to avoid any misunderstanding as to its intentions. Johnson's reply, in turn, conveyed similar assurances regarding U.S. intentions.

The dramatic early success of the Israeli air force and the advance of its army in the Sinai created an asymmetry on the battlefield that would temporarily constrain the ability of the two superpowers to cooperate effectively in seeking a ceasefire. Whereas during the earlier prewar phase of the crisis Washington's incentive to find a peaceful resolution of the crisis was stronger than that of the Soviet Union, the success of Israeli military arms reversed the balance of incentives and left Moscow more eager than Washington to bring about a speedy termination of the war. Johnson had worried that Israeli preemption would embroil the United States in the war. Israel's quick battlefield success made it clear that it was in no danger of defeat, and, given the Soviet Union's unwillingness to intervene on behalf of its allies,[12] Washington could allow itself to approve for the time being Israel's effort to achieve maximal gains. The prewar Israeli assessment that rapid military success by its armed forces would produce U.S. support was vindicated. Constraints on Israel by the United States during the first few days of the war were virtually nonexistent; for the time being Israel enjoyed staunch U.S. support, for, indeed,

Washington's regional and global interests were being served by Israel's military success. Washington did indeed work toward obtaining a ceasefire, but it was not under the same time pressure to do so as was Moscow.

Both superpowers agreed on June 5 to support a Security Council resolution calling for an immediate ceasefire. But Moscow and Washington differed as to whether the ceasefire should be linked to a withdrawal of Israeli forces from territory they had occupied. The United States wanted any such withdrawal to be contingent upon abandoning plans to blockade the Tiran straits and the withdrawal of Egyptian forces that had been introduced into the Sinai. The Soviet Union, predictably, called only for an immediate ceasefire and Israeli withdrawal, which would have left Nasser with the gains he had made before Israel initiated the war. Consequently, the Security Council adjourned without agreement on a ceasefire resolution.

Why Moscow delayed its acceptance of a simple ceasefire in place is not clear. An immediate ceasefire could have prevented Israeli occupation of the entire Sinai, the subsequent defeat of Egypt, and the Israeli move into Jordan and Syria. Possibly Moscow delayed at first because it was uncertain as to the direction of the fighting. Although the air war was decided in the first hours, there were land battles near Israel's border. It is possible that Moscow, influenced by Egyptian estimates, hoped that the Egyptian army could block an Israeli advance and even carry out its battle plan for a counteroffensive to cut across the Israel border. But even after Moscow realized the hopelessness of the Egyptian position, it could not bring itself for several days, until the afternoon of June 7, to embrace a simple ceasefire in place without Egypt's acceptance.[13] Finally, on the next day, Egypt's stubbornness gave way, and it too accepted the U.N.'s simple ceasefire resolution, which made no mention of an Israeli withdrawal.

While the Israeli-Egyptian war was now over, fighting continued between Syria and Israel. (Jordan had accepted a ceasefire on June 7.) The United States was aware that the Soviet Union was extremely sensitive to any significant threat to Syria, which it appeared to regard as a rather special client. Washington suspected that, in addition to large supplies of Soviet weapons in Syria, there were substantial numbers of Soviet advisers. When the administration learned of an intensified Israeli air and artillery bombardment of Syrian positions on June 8, apparently a prelude to a large-scale attack to seize the Golan Heights, Rusk dispatched an urgent message to Jerusalem urging that it desist. Nevertheless, Israel launched its offensive early the next morning, June 9. Israel justified its offensive to the Security Council by claiming that sixteen Israeli villages had been shelled by Syrian artillery attacks. The United States made no further efforts to restrain the Israeli advance into Syrian territory until the Soviet threat of intervention the following day.

The Soviet Union treated the Israeli advance on the Golan Heights with the utmost gravity. The perception that its client was on the verge of disaster caused Moscow to adopt a much more threatening stance toward Israel than at any time during the entire crisis. An urgent meeting of the leaders of the communist states was called in Moscow to contemplate joint action. A statement was released from the conference containing an explicit threat to act if Israel did not cease its attack. Although both Israel and Syria agreed to a ceasefire shortly after 3 P.M. on June 9, the fighting continued to spread on the Israeli-Syrian front.

The Syrian government charged that Israel was bombing Damascus and that its ground forces were heading for the city. These charges were aired at a special session of the Security Council on the next day and were denied by Israel. U.N. observers at the front lines reported that three separate air attacks had taken place around, but outside, the city of Damascus and that Israeli forces were advancing.

Around this time, in the early morning of June 10, Moscow broke off diplomatic relations with Israel and issued a blunt threat. Shortly thereafter, Kosygin activated the hotline again and expressed the Kremlin's determination to halt the fighting. Kosygin said a "very crucial moment" had arrived and referred to the possibility of an "independent decision" by Moscow. If Israel did not stop fighting within the next few hours, the Soviet Union would take "necessary actions, including military."[14]

Although Washington thought Moscow would find it difficult to intervene directly in the war, it regarded the threat of intervention as credible and not to be ignored. This supposition was supported by intelligence reports that Soviet paratroop divisions had been placed on alert.

Faced with a virtual ultimatum by the Soviet Union to Israel, Johnson decided on and quickly implemented three courses of action. First, he signaled the determination of the United States to confront any Soviet intervention by ordering the Sixth Fleet to sail toward the Syrian coast.[15] Second, the president exerted strong pressure on Israel to terminate military action against Syria. In fact, that morning Israel had already conveyed through Gen. Odd Bull, chief of staff of the U.N. Truce Supervision Organization, near the zone of combat, that it would agree to cease hostilities if Syria complied, and, accordingly, a ceasefire was scheduled for 12:30 P.M.

Third, Johnson assured the Soviets that the Israelis would stop the war and that he had received assurances that this would be done. Nonetheless, throughout the morning the hotline was repeatedly activated by the Soviets, Kosygin complaining that the fighting was continuing and Johnson trying to reassure him that it was stopping.

Whether and in what way the Soviet Union would have intervened had the fighting not stopped cannot be established. For Johnson, it made no real difference that Moscow might not carry out its threat to intervene; once the threat was made, the United States had to act firmly to deter possible Soviet intervention. Washington indeed wanted a prompt termination of the war, but it could not allow the impression to be gained that the war ended because the Israelis and the United States had knuckled under to Soviet pressure. The movement of the Sixth Fleet was intended not merely to deter a possible Soviet military intervention but also to demonstrate that the United States could not be coerced by the Soviet Union.

It must be noted, however, that the Soviet threat did accomplish what Moscow had sought—namely, U.S. pressure on Israel to secure a prompt termination of the war before Syria suffered a shattering defeat. As a result, the Soviets could now claim that their threat had constrained Israel. Indeed, in his statement at the special session of the U.N. General Assembly, convened one week after the termination of the war, Kosygin stated that Israeli forces had intended to break Syrian lines to Damascus and that Soviet warnings had prevented them from doing so.[16]

ANALYSIS: PROBLEMS OF CRISIS MANAGEMENT

A number of events during this tense, fast-paced six-day war could easily have embroiled the two superpowers in a dangerous confrontation and, possibly, led to a military clash between their forces. These threats to crisis management were, in fact, met through a combination of effective communication between Washington and Moscow, restrained behavior on both sides, timely and accurate intelligence, and good sense. (There was also, as often is true in matters of this kind, an element of good luck.)[17] As was noted in Chapter 2, one of the objectives of the present study is to identify the variety of threats to effective superpower crisis management that have been experienced in past crises. In conflicts between their regional client states, efforts by the superpowers to cope with the crisis can be hampered as a result of interactions between the local actors, interactions between a superpower and the regional combatants, and interactions between the superpowers themselves. Some of the threats that arise are fortuitous, while others, as we shall see, stem from the deliberate efforts of a regional actor to influence or to manipulate its superpower patron into giving it greater support.

In the case of the 1967 war, the first of these threats occurred on the second day, June 6. Nasser and King Hussein of Jordan, in a telephone conversation monitored by Israeli intelligence, agreed to circulate an accusation that U.S. and British planes had participated in the Israeli attack by defending Israel's airspace and aiding in the destruction on the preceding day of the Arab air forces.[18] It is not clear whether this story was based on incorrect intelligence or fabricated by Nasser—perhaps to cover up the debacle his air force had suffered or to trigger Soviet intervention. In any case, Nasser is reported to have conveyed this accusation to the Soviet ambassador, complaining at the same time that Moscow had not extended aid to the Arab states.[19]

Johnson quickly took up the matter that same morning in a hotline conversation with Kosygin; the president firmly denied the accusation and reminded Kosygin that Soviet intelligence knew where the U.S. aircraft carriers were deployed in the Mediterranean and had the intelligence capability for keeping track of the activities of U.S. naval aircraft in the area. The U.S. ambassador to the United Nations, Arthur Goldberg, invited U.N. observers to "interview air crews" and "look at logs" on the U.S. aircraft carriers. In any case, Soviet leaders evidently quickly ascertained that there was no basis to Nasser's allegations and, operating with prudent restraint, did not attempt to exploit the matter. However, as U.S. leaders had feared, Nasser's charges did trigger breaking of relations with the United States by Algeria, Iraq, Sudan, and Yemen as well as Egypt and Syria.

On the next day, June 7, another threat to crisis management occurred when Israeli forces threatened a major escalation of the fighting. Upon learning that Israeli units, having swept through the West Bank, were now crossing the Jordan River to the East Bank, Rusk promptly demanded that Israel cease any further advance, lest it constitute a threat to Hussein's regime. In addition, Rusk demanded that Israel immediately accept a ceasefire with Jordan. Israel quickly complied.[20]

The section Analysis: Problems of Crisis Management is co-authored with Alexander L. George.

Early the next morning, June 8, the U.S. intelligence gathering vessel, the *Liberty*, operating in close proximity to the zone of hostilities, was subjected to a damaging attack by Israel. In the Pentagon, it was throught that the Soviets had perpetrated the attack. Fortunately, the commander of the U.S. Sixth Fleet had reason to believe that this was unlikely. However, he did launch naval aircraft to defend the *Liberty* against further attacks.[21] In Washington, at least 70 minutes elapsed between the first reports of the attack to the Pentagon and the time when Secretary of Defense Robert McNamara and the Joint Chiefs concluded that it was unlikely that the Soviets were responsible.[22] While still not certain as to who was responsible, the president ordered U.S. aircraft to search for survivors. In order to prevent any misunderstanding on the part of the Soviets as to the intentions behind the movement of the Sixth Fleet and the mission of the U.S. planes, Johnson rushed a message over the hotline to Kosygin.[23]

Shortly thereafter, Israel admitted responsibility for the attack on the *Liberty*, and Johnson then sent a fuller report to Kosygin.[24] Quite obviously, timely intelligence that pointed responsibility for the attack away from the Soviet Union and prompt communication between U.S. and Soviet leaders contributed greatly to reducing the risk of a clash over the incident between U.S. and Soviet naval forces in the Mediterranean. If the Sixth Fleet commander had immediately launched a retaliatory strike against Soviet naval forces or engaged in provocative actions threatening elements of the Soviet fleet, a dangerous situation could have developed.

Another threat to effective crisis management arose on June 7 as a result of interactions between tightly coupled elements of the U.S. and Soviet fleets in the Mediterranean. The 1967 crisis was the occasion for the first significant employment of the Soviet navy in a crisis. Soviet surveillance ships adopted aggressive shadowing tactics, maneuvering dangerously close at times to U.S. ships. The U.S. Sixth Fleet had earlier sent these Soviet vessels warnings to keep clear of U.S. naval formations. On the 7th, a suspected Soviet submarine operating near the U.S. aircraft carrier *America* was tracked by U.S. destroyers, antisubmarine warfare (ASW) helicopters, and patrol planes, evidently to force the submarine either to surface or to snorkel. This appears to have sparked in return the most severe Soviet harassment of the Sixth Fleet during the crisis. A Soviet ship trailing the *America* task group threatened to collide with a U.S. destroyer in a nautical version of the game of "chicken." In response, the Sixth Fleet commander sent a message to the Soviet destroyer, warning it to stay clear of the *America* task group. The Soviet ship withdrew, but the next morning it returned with a Soviet corvette and they maneuvered dangerously close to the *America* in an apparent attempt to force the aircraft carrier to change its course while it was conducting flight operations. However, a collision was avoided, and no shots were fired.

Because U.S. and Soviet naval forces were in close proximity throughout the crisis, there was a strong possibility of inadvertent or intended incidents. However, the activity of these Soviet ships during the June 7–8 incident was not typical of the cautious and circumspect behavior of the Soviet navy during the crisis as a whole.[25]

Perhaps the most severe threat of escalation to military involvement by the superpowers occurred on June 10 when Israeli leaders decided to expand military operations against Syria—a decision made after Egypt had accepted the ceasefire on the preceding day. It is not clear how far Israel wished to push into Syrian territory. In any case, this threat was contained through clear and timely communications between Moscow and Washington and through Washington's acceptance of its responsibility for persuading Israel to stop its advance into Syria and to accept an immediate ceasefire with Damascus.

The Israeli offensive into Syrian territory and, particularly, the development of a possible threat to Damascus gave the appearance of a major escalation in Israel's war objectives. We saw how the escalation of Nasser's objectives and actions against Israel during the prewar phase of the crisis had set into motion a train of events that led to the Arab-Israeli war. This time it was Israel's escalation of its objectives and actions that threatened to embroil the superpowers in the war. But faced with this even graver danger, the superpowers were able to cooperate to avoid becoming militarily involved in their clients' war. Obviously, their incentives to avoid a superpower military confrontation were greater than their incentives had been earlier to avoid the outbreak of war between their regional allies.

The superpowers' incentives to avoid a direct military confrontation may have been a necessary condition but certainly not a sufficient one to bring about the termination of the 1967 war. Their success in avoiding embroilment in the conflict required sensitivity to the requirements of crisis management and an ability to meet those requirements when confronted by developments that threatened unwanted escalation. The importance of clear, responsible, and timely communications between the superpowers in this case cannot be overemphasized; such communications were probably essential for enabling Moscow and Washington to manage and terminate the war before being dragged into it themselves. The all-important shared desire to cooperate to this end, the limited objectives and the restraint with which both superpowers operated, their unwillingness to provide their regional allies with support that could have contributed to escalation—all of these factors were also of critical importance. But without the opportunity the hotline provided for clear, timely, and responsible communication at the highest levels of the governments, it is extremely doubtful that Moscow and Washington would have succeeded. Certainly, their efforts at crisis management would have been much more difficult.

The contribution of the hotline, used repeatedly throughout the crisis, was of particular importance because events moved so rapidly. One of the difficulties experienced in crisis management in regional crises such as the present one is that typically it is the regional actors, not the superpowers, who control the momentum of events. Given Israel's blitzkrieg military strategy and its success in implementing it, it was not possible to meet the important crisis management requirement of deliberately slowing down the momentum of events in order to give adequate time for the processes of diplomacy to work. The availability and effective use of the hotline in this case compensated in a sense for the unwillingness and inability of the combatants to slow down the momentum of military operations.

BIBLIOGRAPHICAL NOTE

The literature on the 1967 crisis and war is very rich. A useful account of developments that led to the crisis is Daniel Dishon, ed., *Middle East Record 1967* (Jerusalem: Israel

Universities Press, 1971). Important studies of the Egyptian role are provided in Janice Gross Stein's chapter in this volume and in Dan Schueftan, "Nasser's 1967 Policy Reconsidered," *The Jerusalem Quarterly* 3 (1977): 124–144.

Other useful accounts are Mohamed Heikal, *The Cairo Documents* (New York: Doubleday and Company, 1973) and *The Sphinx and the Commissar: The Rise and Fall of Soviet Influence in the Middle East* (New York: Harper and Row, 1978); and Mahmud Riad, *The Struggle for Peace in the Middle East* (London: Quartet Books, 1981). On Israeli decision making, see Yaacov Bar-Siman-Tov, *Israel, the Superpowers and the War in the Middle East* (New York: Praeger, 1987); and Michael Brecher, *Decisions in Israel's Foreign Policy* (London: Oxford University Press, 1974) and *Decisions in Crises: Israel, 1967 and 1973* (Berkeley: University of California Press, 1980).

Among the few studies that discuss the Soviet role in 1967, the most important are Jon D. Glassman, *Arms for the Arabs: The Soviet Union and War in the Middle East* (Baltimore: The Johns Hopkins University Press, 1975); and Theodore Draper, *Israel and World Politics: Roots of the Third Arab-Israel War* (New York: The Viking Press, 1968). For the U.S. position, see Lyndon B. Johnson, *The Vantage Point: Perspectives of the Presidency 1963–1969* (New York: Holt, Rinehart and Winston, 1974); Jonathan T. Howe, *Multicrises: Sea Power and Global Politics in the Missile Age* (Cambridge: MIT Press, 1971); Donald Neff, *Warriors for Jerusalem: The Six Days That Changed the Middle East* (New York: Lindon Press, 1984); William B. Quandt, *Decade of Decisions: American Policy Toward the Arab-Israeli Conflict 1967–1976* (Berkeley: University of California Press, 1977); and Steven L. Spiegel, *The Other Arab-Israeli Conflict: Making America's Middle East Policy from Truman to Reagan* (Chicago: Chicago University Press, 1985). On discussions at the U.N. Security Council, see Arthur Lall, *The UN and the Middle East Crisis, 1967* (New York: Columbia University Press, 1968).

NOTES

1. The Egyptian-Syrian defense pact was signed on November 4, 1966, as a result of Soviet mediation. The pact stated that an attack against either state would be regarded as an attack on the other. The Egyptian-Syrian reconciliation was regarded by the Soviet Union as an important positive manifestation of growing "anti-imperialist" unity in the Middle East. See Jon D. Glassman, *Arms for the Arabs: The Soviet Union and War in the Middle East* (Baltimore: The Johns Hopkins University Press, 1975), p. 37.

2. The prime minister's office asked the Israeli press to tone down Rabin's statements in its reports. Rabin's statement that could have been interpreted by the Arabs as having implied an intention to overthrow the Syrian regime was criticized by most of the ministers—Rabin was rebuked by the prime minister. Eshkol even demanded that Rabin ask his permission before any interviews and show him the content of any declaration to the press. See Eitan Haber, *Today War Will Break Out: Reminiscences of Brigadier General Israel Lior, Aide-de-Camp to Prime Ministers Levi Eshkol and Golda Meir* (Tel Aviv: Edanim, 1987) (Hebrew), pp. 146–147.

3. Anwar el-Sadat, *In Search of Identity: An Autobiography* (New York: Harper and Row, 1977), pp. 171–172. According to Dayan, on May 12 an intelligence officer in the Soviet embassy in Cairo transmitted to Egyptian intelligence "confirmation" of the Syrian report that Israel was massing troops on the Syrian border. Moshe Dayan, *Story of My Life* (New York: William Morrow and Company, 1976), p. 291.

4. Arthur Lall, *The UN and the Middle East Crisis, 1967* (New York: Columbia University Press, 1968), p. 30.

5. Theodore Draper, *Israel and World Politics: Roots of the Third Arab-Israeli War* (New York: Viking Press, 1968), p. 94.

6. Donald Neff, *Warriors for Jerusalem: The Six Days that Changed the Middle East* (New York: Lindon Press, 1984), p. 179.

7. Ibid., pp. 187–188. According to Burdett, during Yost's conversations in Cairo, there were hints on the Egyptian side that Nasser might agree to arrangements similar to those of the U.S. Battle Act, permitting trade in certain goods between belligerent countries, possibly including oil—but always in non-Israeli ships. Winston Burdett, *Encounter with the Middle East: An Intimate Report on What Lies Behind the Arab-Israel Conflict* (New York: Atheneum, 1969), p. 305.

8. Steven L. Spiegel, *The Other Arab-Israeli Conflict: Making America's Middle East Policy from Truman to Reagan* (Chicago: Chicago University Press, 1985), pp. 143–144, 146–147; William B. Quandt, *Decade of Decisions: American Policy Toward the Arab-Israeli Conflict, 1967–1976* (Berkeley: University of California Press, 1977), pp. 56–57.

9. Jonathan T. Howe, *Multicrises: Sea Power and Global Politics in the Missile Age* (Cambridge: MIT Press, 1971), pp. 57–58, 67, and 70–71.

10. Draper, *Israel and World Politics*, p. 230, Walter Laqueur, ed., *The Israel-Arab Reader* (New York: Bantam Books, 1970), p. 186.

11. Lyndon B. Johnson, *The Vantage Point: Perspectives of the Presidency 1963–1969* (New York: Holt, Rinehart and Winston, 1974), p. 297.

12. Indeed, Moscow did attempt to exert some pressure on Israel to stop its advance. But its threats were notably moderate, particularly in private diplomatic communications to Jerusalem, and its more bombastic public threats, designed to create an aura of staunch support of its allies, did not commit the Soviet Union to take specific action. Later, on June 7, Moscow did threaten to break diplomatic relations with Israel and did so on the 10th. It was only when the Israeli army, having defeated the Egyptian forces in the Sinai turned its attention to Syria that, as we shall see, Moscow generated more credible and more potent threats against Israel.

13. Howe, *Multicrises*, p. 115.

14. Johnson, *The Vantage Point*, p. 302.

15. In his communications to Kosygin, Johnson evidently made no mention of the Sixth Fleet nor did Kosygin in his Hotline messages. Around 1 P.M. the movement of the Sixth Fleet towards Syria stopped. Ibid.; Howe, *Multicrises*, p. 108; Neff, *Warriors for Jerusalem*, p. 284.

16. Glassman, *Arms for the Arabs*, p. 58.

17. It should be noted, at the same time, that a number of potential threats to crisis management did *not* occur during this crisis—e.g., no serious loss of control over their forces by the regional actors or the superpowers, no serious misperceptions, little "noise" in communication, no serious tension between "military logic" and the requirements of diplomacy.

18. The telephone conversation was monitored by Israeli intelligence. There are several possible explanations for the fabrication. While it may have been an attempt by Nasser to cover up his debacle, it might also have been devised to trigger Soviet intervention. It seems, as Rabin mentions in his memoirs, that Nasser was incredulous of Israel's capability to achieve such an overwhelming victory in the absence of external assistance. Yitzhak Rabin, *Rabin Memoirs* (Boston: Little, Brown, 1979), p. 107; see also Mahmud Riad, *The Struggle for Peace in the Middle East* (London: Quartet Books, 1981), p. 25.

19. According to Heikal, in the afternoon of June 6, Nasser summoned the Soviet ambassador, complaining that the United States had taken part in the destruction of the Egyptian Air Force, while the Soviet Union had not extended aid of any sort, including providing an accurate picture of the disposition of Israeli troops. Mohamed Heikal, *The Sphinx and the Commissar: The Rise and Fall of Soviet Influence in the Middle East* (New York: Harper and Row, 1978), p. 181.

20. Neff, *Warriors for Jerusalem*, pp. 239–240.

21. The actions ordered by the Sixth Fleet commander were strictly limited to defending the *Liberty*, and the rules of engagement he issued were carefully designed to avoid further incidents. See Joseph F. Bouchard, "Use of Naval Force in Crises: A Theory of Stratified Crisis Interaction," Ph.D. dissertation, Stanford University, 1988, pp. 888–905.

22. Howe, *Multicrises*, pp. 102–103; Johnson, *The Vantage Point*, p. 300.

23. Howe, *Multicrises*, p. 103; Neff, *Warriors for Jerusalem*, p. 258. Actually the commander of the Sixth Fleet did order carrier aircraft to go to the *Liberty's* rescue within minutes after receiving the initial report.

24. Johnson, *The Vantage Point*, p. 301.

25. This brief description of the June 7–8 incident draws on the detailed account in Bouchard, "Use of Naval Force in Crises," pp. 708–755 passim.

CHAPTER 14

The War of Attrition, 1969–1970

Yaacov Bar-Siman-Tov

The disastrous outcome of the Six Day War weakened the Soviet position in the Middle East and left it with new challenges and new dilemmas. Having suffered a shattering military defeat, Egypt had to contend with the fact that Israel now occupied both the Sinai and the Gaza Strip. The Soviet Union had failed to couple a ceasefire with withdrawal of Israeli forces from these territories. Moscow had been more successful in its efforts to spare its Syrian ally from suffering a more severe setback, but the war left Israeli forces in occupation of the strategic Golan Heights. In the aftermath of the Six Day War, both Egypt and Syria would want Soviet assistance in rebuilding their shattered military forces and would demand meaningful Soviet support of their efforts to evict Israel from the territories it occupied during the war.

Faced with this new situation, Moscow acted to secure its position in the Arab world by rearming and rebuilding the Egyptian and Syrian armed forces. At the same time, fearing another defeat, Soviet leaders were determined not to allow their Arab clients to launch a new war. Accordingly, Moscow limited arms supplies to Egypt to an amount that would enable President Gamal Abdel Nasser to re-establish a defense capability but would not enable him to initiate a new war aimed at recovering Egyptian territory. Soviet leaders tried to convince Nasser that he should rely on Soviet diplomatic efforts, especially through discussions with the United States, to regain the lost territory.

Ironically, the Soviet Union was now in a position vis-à-vis its regional client similar to that of the United States during the 1967 crisis. As noted in the preceding chapter, in order to restrain Israel from initiating war on that occasion, the United States had to commit itself to finding a way to persuade Egypt not to blockade the Tiran straits. When Washington's diplomacy failed to do so, Israel then initiated war. Now, it was the Soviet Union that offered its regional client a commitment to

---

This chapter is a much abbreviated version of an unpublished study that contains fuller documentation.

achieve its goals through diplomacy, and, as we shall see, its inability to deliver led Nasser to initiate what came to be known as the War of Attrition in March 1969. Once again, the strong incentives of a superpower to avoid war in the Middle East did not suffice. Although Moscow and Washington engaged in serious, sustained diplomatic efforts in 1968–1969 to resolve the Arab-Israeli conflict, their cooperative efforts failed. Once again, as in 1967, a diplomatic solution was not possible because the Arab and Israeli positions were too far apart and too rigid to permit a compromise solution. Not only did the Soviet Union fail to restrain Nasser from initiating war, but the situation became more serious later when the United States did not restrain Israel from escalating the war in a way that was highly threatening to Egypt.

Poor communication between the superpowers led to a further, even more serious aggravation of the crisis. In response to Washington's failure to prevent Israeli escalation of the fighting, the Soviet Union threatened to intervene militarily unless the United States forced Israel to call off its deep penetration air attacks against Egypt. Misreading the Soviet message, Washington did not regard Moscow's threat as credible, and, accordingly, it failed to act quickly enough to deter Soviet military intervention on behalf of Egypt or to make it unnecessary by restraining Israel's military actions. The movement of Soviet air defense forces into Egypt led to combat between Soviets and the Israeli air force and posed the threat of another superpower confrontation. The crisis was eventually resolved through U.S. diplomatic initiatives.

SOVIET FAILURE TO RESTRAIN EGYPT

Moscow's policy toward Egypt following the Six Day War was based on the assumption that Nasser's complete dependence on the Soviet Union for military assistance and protection would enable the Soviets to prevent him from initiating war while they were pursuing a diplomatic solution to the conflict. As time passed, however, the vulnerabilities of Moscow's well-intentioned policy became increasingly evident. In fact, the Soviet Union's massive aid and political backing put Egypt in a position to refuse the kind of compromise settlement that the Soviet Union itself might have been prepared to accept. Ironically, the more Moscow reprovisioned the Egyptian army, the less able it was to influence Egypt to continue with the negotiating process and to restrain it from starting a war.

Nasser, completely dependent on the Soviet Union for military assistance, went along for the time being with Moscow's preference for ruling out military means. Actually, Nasser's compliance was not a great sacrifice on his part, as he needed more time to rebuild his army and to prepare it for a new military round. Moreover, once Moscow was committed to a restoration of Egypt's defensive capability, it lost whatever interest it had in an arms control proposal for the Middle East. The Soviet Union rejected Washington's suggestion that the two superpowers cooperate to limit the arms race in the Middle East.

By late fall 1967, the Soviet Union had replaced 80 percent of the aircraft, tanks, and artillery that Egypt had lost in June. At the same time, the number of Soviet military experts had increased considerably. From approximately five hundred Soviet military advisers before the 1967 war, the number rose to two thousand. Soviet advisers moved into all phases of training, planning, and air defense.[1]

Nasser, who had no hope of a peaceful solution, understood that the only way to start a war was to convince the Russians that there was no diplomatic solution. This was why Mahmoud Riad, Egypt's foreign minister, visited Moscow in April 1968. At the meeting with Riad, the Soviet leader Leonid Brezhnev insisted once again on the importance of pursuing a peaceful solution. Riad replied that Egypt believed a political solution remained a remote possibility. Therefore, military action to recover the territories had now become inevitable. Brezhnev, who understood that Nasser planned to resort to force, stated that Egypt not only had to rebuild its army first, a matter that would take at least two years, but it also had to make sure of a unified home front as well as the support of the other Arab states before starting a war. Moscow continued to believe that war could be avoided because of Egypt's military weakness and its refusal to provide Nasser with the sophisticated weapons he would need for offensive operations.[2]

During 1968, Nasser became impatient regarding the prospects of a political solution and the delay of arms deliveries from the Soviet Union. He believed there could be no hope of any political solution unless Israel realized that Egypt would start a new war. However, this strategy demanded coordination of policy with the Soviet Union, for without Moscow's arms deliveries Egypt could not resort to force. With this in mind, Nasser visited Moscow in July 1968. He argued that a limited war was a necessary element for achieving a political solution and that, to this end, Egypt must be supplied with new offensive arms. Soviet leaders agreed to an increase in military assistance but continued to refuse to supply offensive weapons or to support Nasser's view that initiation of a limited war would be necessary. Once again, they emphasized that their highest priority was to avoid a direct clash with the United States in the Middle East and that Egypt was not capable of starting a new war. They insisted that Egypt should give the search for a political solution a chance and called upon Nasser to moderate his demands in the bargaining process. Nasser agreed to continue on the diplomatic path but refused to make any concession regarding a political settlement. His position was that not an inch of the occupied Arab territory could be given up, and he refused to negotiate with Israel, to sign a peace treaty with it, or to recognize it.[3]

Although the Soviets believed they had succeeded in convincing Nasser to defer initiation of war, they evidently did not fully appreciate that Nasser's political vulnerability at home and in the Arab world made it impossible for him to continue a policy of inaction much longer. Indeed, in September 1968, Nasser decided to start the War of Attrition against the advice and judgment of the Soviet Union. His decision to do so rested upon a military appraisal that Egypt's defense capability was now sufficient to wage a static war along the Suez Canal front. On September 8 and on October 26, the Egyptians initiated the heaviest artillery exchanges across the canal since June 1967. The Soviet Union reacted by reducing its military supplies, especially vehicles, troop carriers, and other equipment, including ammunition. When an Israeli ground raid deep inside Egypt on November 1 revealed serious shortcomings in Egypt's military readiness, Nasser decided to postpone further military activity in order to improve the effectiveness of the Egyptian army in utilizing the attrition option.[4]

Egypt's initiation of a limited war in the canal area had political-diplomatic objectives. Nasser hoped that it would enhance Egypt's bargaining power not only vis-à-vis Israel and the United States but the Soviet Union as well. Indeed, Egypt's abortive military effort in September and October did stimulate new diplomatic activity. In December, Soviet Foreign Minister Andrei Gromyko visited Cairo with a Soviet proposal for a peace settlement, containing a timetable for the implementation of U.N. Resolution 242. Gromyko urged Nasser not to resort to war but instead to enable the Soviet Union to negotiate directly with the United States as a substitute for the U.N.-sponsored Jarring Mission. Gromyko stated that he expected the Nixon administration to be more positive regarding a political solution and that Washington would be more ready to pressure Israel to withdraw from all the Arab territories. Nasser agreed that the Soviet proposal should be submitted to the United States so as to continue the dialogue between the two superpowers, although he himself did not believe that a political solution would emerge. Nasser agreed to refrain from launching any major attack along the canal for three months, but he warned Gromyko, "If I do not do something soon the people will hang me."[5] In December 1968, Nasser decided that a military operation against Israel would be launched within weeks.[6]

The last formal attempt by Moscow to restrain Egypt from resuming hostilities was made at the end of January 1969 when Politburo member Alexander N. Shelepin visited Cairo and submitted an important letter from Brezhnev to Nasser urging him not to initiate a war. Nasser refused to comply.[7] Despite the fundamental divergence between Egypt and the Soviet Union, however, new arms were supplied by the Soviet Union in February 1969.[8] Shortly thereafter, on March 8, Nasser launched a war of attrition along the canal front.

The Soviet Union's failure to restrain Nasser cannot be attributed to weak Soviet incentives to prevent war. The Soviets did not realize how intolerable his situation in Egypt and in the Arab world had become due to the consequences of the Six Day War and the humiliating stalemate that followed the war. Nasser considered inaction to be an even greater risk than those involved in initiating a war. Although the Soviet Union tried to convince Nasser not to initiate a new war, it did not use its full muscle against Egypt. Aware that its supply of arms would enable Egypt to initiate a limited war, the Soviet Union nonetheless continued to supply arms so as not to endanger relations with its regional ally. As it turned out, the only way the Soviets could have convinced Egypt not to initiate war was to have achieved through diplomacy the recovery of the occupied territories, but this proved to be impossible because Israel and the United States would not meet Egypt's demands.

In sum, the Soviet Union was deeply interested in a peaceful solution and in preventing war but, when the chips were down, not at the price of losing its influence in Egypt and in the Arab world.

SUPERPOWER FAILURE TO PREVENT ESCALATION OF THE WAR

Unlike the 1967 war when the Soviet Union and the United States acted immediately to try to obtain a ceasefire, the slow-moving War of Attrition in March 1969 created no great sense of urgency to do so in either Moscow or Washington. Instead, for a number of months—indeed, until December—the superpowers undertook intensive diplomatic activities in the hope of achieving a formula for a political solution to the Arab-Israeli conflict and, more particularly, to the Egyptian-Israeli conflict. Soviet and U.S. leaders recognized that the course of the fighting along the canal could have an indirect impact on the success of their diplomatic efforts; but, as the war was quite limited and localized and as long as it remained so, neither Egypt nor Israel would be in danger of suffering a catastrophic defeat that might, as in 1967, require its superpower patron to intervene on its behalf. The nature of the fighting itself, therefore, provided a slowdown in the momentum of events—an important requirement for crisis management—that gave ample time to the search for a political solution.

What could not be easily foreseen, however, was the possibility that Nasser's controlled attrition strategy would succeed in bleeding Israel's manpower sufficiently to force its leaders to decide upon a major escalation of the war. That is, indeed, what eventually occurred at the end of 1969. With this development in the war, the superpowers' search for a political solution to the Egyptian-Israeli conflict gave way to an effort to avoid, if possible, a confrontation between Washington and Moscow. It now became more urgent to bring about a termination of the war, but, as we shall see, this was not accomplished until almost six months after Soviet military intervention took place.

We will not describe in any detail the superpowers' diplomatic efforts to find a political solution to the Egyptian-Israeli conflict. Even after Moscow and Washington agreed in principle on some elements of a political formula, each refused to pressure its Middle East client beyond a certain point into making the necessary political concessions. Egypt and Israel remained too far apart in their conception of acceptable terms for a political settlement of the territorial issues. And, in general, neither superpower was disposed to risk serious damage to its own position in the Middle East by alienating its regional client. Moreover, it was difficult for the superpowers to agree on what would constitute reciprocal concessions by Egypt and Israel in the interest of a political solution.

How far one could go in pressing one's regional client for concessions was also a matter of internal disagreement, at least in the U.S. government. Thus, when some State Department officials were prepared to try to impose a solution on Israel, President Richard Nixon and National Security Adviser Henry Kissinger refused to do so because of Moscow's unwillingness to commit itself to placing similar pressure on its own client.[9] Thus, when Egypt refused in mid-June 1969 to accept a U.S. compromise proposal that had already been endorsed by the Soviet Union, the latter then declared its unequivocal support for the Egyptian position and refused to pressure Nasser to change his position.[10]

On other occasions during this long period, similar policy dilemmas for the superpowers occurred when they tried unsuccessfully to deal with the tension between their desire to find a political solution or to terminate the war and their perceived need not to press their regional clients too hard.

One such failed attempt was the Rogers Plan, presented by the United States to the Soviet Union on October 28, 1969, after both superpowers agreed to renew their efforts to settle the Arab-Israeli conflict. It was a compromise proposal, ostensibly sponsored by both superpowers and framed to solve the main components of the Egyptian-Israeli conflict.[11] On November 10, 1969, Egypt was presented with the plan by both the United States and the Soviet Union. The proposal was made public by Secretary of State William Rogers on December 9, 1969, after nearly a month had passed without any definitive Egyptian or Soviet reply.[12] In fact, it was the Egyptian rejection of the plan that led to the subsequent Soviet rejection. This was apparently due to Egyptian pressure, as Nasser did not want to negotiate from an inferior position.[13] On December 23, the Soviet Union informed the United States of its formal rejection.

The Rogers Plan took Israel's decision makers by surprise. The United States had not consulted Israel concerning the plan, which was diametrically opposed to Israeli policy. On December 10, a day after its official proclamation, the Rogers Plan was categorically rejected by the Israeli cabinet.[14] Once Egypt and the Soviet Union rejected the plan, it became impossible for the United States to impose it on Israel.[15]

The failure of the Rogers Plan indicated the end of superpower cooperation to resolve the Arab-Israeli conflict. Two lessons can be drawn from this failure: (1) Only if there is symmetry and reciprocity in the superpowers' willingness to put strong pressure on their clients is there a prospect for sustained superpower cooperation; and (2) due to the wide gulf that divided the Israeli and Egyptian positions, the time was not ripe for an overall settlement, and there was a need for a more modest approach to ending the conflict.[16]

During the course of this prolonged search for a settlement, both superpowers became bemused by the possibility that the outcome of the negotiations might be dependent on the relative success or failure of their clients on the battlefield. If one's own client managed to achieve an advantage in the fighting, it might weaken the other regional actor's will and force it into making concessions. From this it was a small step for the superpowers to shift their policies away from attempting to restrain their clients' military activity to lending them greater support to enable them to gain an advantage in the fighting or at least to avoid suffering a disadvantage.

In the first phase of the war, the Soviet Union had made various attempts to curb Egyptian belligerency and even to halt the war. By limiting its arms supply to defensive weapons, the Soviet Union hoped to prevent Egypt from escalating the war, a step that would be likely to trigger an escalatory response from Israel.[17] Nasser refused to comply and insisted on carrying out his plan to cross the canal and secure footholds on the eastern shore of the canal. Only the activation of the Israeli air force prevented Nasser from carrying out his plan. Having failed to restrain Nasser from expanding the scope of the fighting, the Soviet Union now faced a new challenge—how to prevent an Egyptian defeat. As long as the war remained a ground war, Egypt could hope to, and indeed did, succeed in exploiting the advantages that stemmed from the difference in the deployment of Israeli and Egyptian forces along the canal. Once the war became an air war, however, Israeli air superiority altered the balance. The Soviets correctly judged that Egypt could not endure an air war of attrition for any length of time, and therefore, in the second half of 1969, they stepped up arms deliveries. Moreover, Moscow gradually moved toward assuming responsibility for Egypt's air defense and increasing its own military presence in that country.[18]

In October 1969, the Kremlin began to deliberate whether to send pilots to Egypt in order to counter Israel's air superiority.[19] On December 9, Nasser dispatched a delegation, headed by Vice-President Anwar el-Sadat, to Moscow with the aim of obtaining sophisticated arms. The Soviet leaders "were very worried at the escalating military operation on both sides of the Suez Canal" and "were apprehensive" that "Egypt would undertake a premature military action to cross the waterway." Brezhnev emphasized that Egypt must refrain from battle until it had completed its military preparations and that it should "never allow the enemy to drag" Egypt "into battle prematurely." Brezhnev refused to supply Egypt with long-range aircraft, despite Sadat's promise that Egypt would not undertake any offensive action before consulting with the Soviet Union. Indeed, the Soviet leader agreed only to strengthen Egypt's defensive capabilities. According to Riad, Brezhnev promised the Egyptian delegation that over 60 Soviet pilots would be sent to Egypt within a month as "military advisors." The Soviet Union also decided to dispatch a large number of SAM-3s manned by Soviet crews and to train Egyptian soldiers in their operation. Furthermore, Brezhnev promised additional missiles for the defense of Egypt's major cities, to be accompanied by approximately a thousand Soviet military personnel who would operate the missiles during the first phase of action.[20]

It is interesting to note that although Moscow recognized Egypt's military vulnerability, it did not as yet warn Israel to stop its military activity or pressure the United States to restrain its client.[21] Although it is not clear that a Soviet warning to Israel or pressure on the United States to restrain its client at this stage would have prevented Israel from a further escalation of the air war, there is no doubt that its absence encouraged Israel to regard as an acceptable risk its initiation of in-depth air raids into Egypt.[22]

During the first months of the war, the United States did not make much of an effort to restrain Israel, as Israel on its own refrained from escalating the war. Beginning in July 1969, the United States tacitly acquiesced in the Israeli employment of its air force along the canal. It appears that the United States accepted the legitimacy of Israel's basic grievance and its need to employ its air power, for it was suffering serious casualties. Yitzhak Rabin, the Israeli ambassador to Washington, for example, inferred from his talks with U.S. officials that the United States had found itself forced to adopt a conciliatory position in its negotiations with the Soviets, as its client, Israel, was incapable thus far of putting an end to the War of Attrition. Indeed, Rabin thought that the United States expected Israel to take vigorous action to terminate the war and thereby deprive the Soviets of a major advantage in their discussion of a possible settlement.[23] The delivery of the first of 50 Phantom jets to Israel in September 1969 was a direct indication that the United States supported the Israeli effort to destroy the Egyptian air defense system along the canal and to carry out punishing air raids deep inside Egypt.[24]

THE FAILURE TO PREVENT
SOVIET MILITARY INTERVENTION

On January 7, 1970, Israel commenced bombing military targets deep in Egyptian territory in an ambitious effort to end the war by threatening to weaken or overthrow

Nasser's regime and to prevent the imposition of a political solution unfavorable to Israel. Israel and U.S. leaders did not believe this action would provoke Soviet military intervention. This was a dangerous miscalculation. After eight raids by the Israeli air force, Nasser realized that Egypt had no other recourse than to appeal for Soviet assistance. He embarked on a secret trip to Moscow on January 22, during which he desperately pressed for the deployment to Egypt of a more sophisticated anti-aircraft system to be manned by Soviet crews. The Egyptian leader argued that the risks posed by Soviet military intervention had to be weighed against the danger that his regime would be overthrown, with all that this would imply for Soviet regional interests. Nasser even threatened to submit his resignation should the Soviets choose to deny his request.[25]

Aware of the danger of provoking a superpower crisis, the Soviet Union nonetheless decided that it must give priority to maintaining its relationship with its client and its overall regional interests. First, however, Moscow tried to persuade the United States to restrain its ally. No doubt Soviet leaders recalled that a similar gambit on their part when Syria had been under threat in the 1967 war had been effective. Should this effort fail to result in Israeli compliance, it would at least provide an element of justification for movement of Soviet air defense equipment and personnel into Egypt.

On January 31, 1970, Ambassador Anatoly Dobrynin delivered a letter from Soviet Premier Aleksei Kosygin to Nixon. Similar communications were sent to British Prime Minister Harold Wilson and French President Georges Pompidou. Kosygin warned that if Israel's attacks continued, "The Soviet Union will be forced to see to it that the Arab states have means at their disposal." Kosygin called on the four powers to "compel Israel to cease its attacks and to establish a lasting peace beginning with the 'speediest withdrawal of Israeli forces from all the occupied Arab territories.'"[26]

Kosygin's letter did not threaten any specific action. In retrospect, it is not clear whether Moscow intended to press the United States to restrain its client or to test Washington's reaction to possible Soviet intervention. The vagueness of Kosygin's threat, however, weakened the attempt to convince the United States that it must curb Israeli military activity, and it contributed to Washington's misreading of Soviet willingness to enforce its demand.[27]

From Kissinger's memoirs it is clear that he did not initially view Kosygin's note as a threat of military intervention. Instead, he saw it as another Soviet effort to induce the United States to restrain Israel and to pressure it to withdraw from all the Arab occupied territories. Kissinger's initial misinterpretation of Kosygin's letter went further. He viewed it somewhat jubilantly as another indication that the U.S. policy of holding firm, which he had advocated, was creating a dilemma for the Soviets and the Egyptians that would work to the advantage of the United States: "If they *do not* agree to our proposals they get nothing."[28]

The administration decided upon a firm reply. In his February 4 letter to Kosygin, Nixon dismissed the Soviet allegation that Israel bore sole responsibility for the fighting and called for a restoration of the ceasefire and an agreement on the limitation of arms deliveries to the area. He warned that if the Soviet Union rejected this proposal, the United States would be obliged to continue supplying arms to Israel.[29] Evidently Washington was trying to exploit the success of Israel's strategic bombing to induce the Soviet Union into renewing superpower negotiations on the restoration of the ceasefire and limitation of arms deliveries to the Middle East.[30] Further, instead of calling upon Israel to halt its deep penetration bombings, the United States even tacitly encouraged Israel to continue its attacks. In a meeting with Rabin on February 2, Assistant Secretary of State Joseph Sisco informed Rabin of Kosygin's letter and Nixon's firm reply, indicating that the administration was skeptical as to the credibility of the Soviet threat. Rabin was impressed that the United States was not perturbed by the Soviet communication and that it recommended that Israel not be concerned by it either. Although Sisco did not explicitly say so, Rabin was convinced that the firm attitude Washington was taking toward the Soviets was due to Israeli air raids. As a result, he cabled Jerusalem: "We have achieved a marked improvement in the United States' position. Continuation of that improvement depends first and foremost on keeping up our air raids in the heart of Egypt."[31]

Both the United States and Israel were aware that Nasser had traveled secretly to Moscow with an urgent plea for immediate assistance in strengthening Egypt's anti-aircraft defense, but neither Washington nor Israel correctly evaluated the extent to which the Soviet Union believed important interests to be at stake that required it to come to Egypt's assistance.[32] Nixon's reaction to Kosygin's letter was probably perceived in Moscow as irrefutable evidence that the United States was unwilling to impose constraints upon Israel and that it desired to capitalize on Israel's strategic superiority in order to dictate a political settlement. Consequently, the Soviets felt they had no other alternative but to take unilateral action to restrain Israel.[33]

Upon further analysis of Kosygin's note, Kissinger began to have second thoughts. He now suspected that Kosygin's letter was perhaps more a smoke screen to cover Soviet intervention than an operative warning to the United States: "Its vagueness might be explained by the desire to discourage a response that might interfere with decisions [the Soviet Union had] already made."[34] He now believed that the Soviets had already committed themselves to direct military intervention, in part because of the inability of the Egyptians to operate the sophisticated Soviet military equipment. Nixon instructed Kissinger "to talk directly with the Soviets on this,"[35] apparently in an effort to discourage possible intervention. Consequently, Kissinger instructed Ambassador Jacob Beam in Moscow to tell Gromyko that the United States was prepared to work on restoring the ceasefire and a mutual limitation of arms supplies. Kissinger again did not mention any possibility of restraining Israel. Gromyko responded on February 11 that the USSR "could not consider a ceasefire unless Israel first stopped its deep penetration raids."[36] But even before receiving Gromyko's response, Kissinger met with Dobrynin on February 10 and "on behalf of the President" warned Dobrynin that "we want the Soviet leaders to know that the introduction of Soviet combat personnel in the Middle East would be viewed with the gravest concern."[37]

Neither of these deterrence statements conveyed any specific indication of how the United States would respond to the introduction of Soviet air defense forces into Egypt. No other actions were undertaken to reinforce the U.S. warning. Therefore, Soviet leaders, who carefully assessed the risks of their plan, probably did not view the U.S. warning as a credible or potent deterrent. Moreover, in the absence of any signal that the United States intended to curb Israeli military activities, Soviet leaders remained firm in their motivation to carry out their plan.

Curiously, the absence of a Soviet reply to Nixon's warning for almost a month was not interpreted by the administration as either a success or a failure. There was no clear picture regarding the Soviets' next step. In his memoirs, Kissinger emphasizes his attempts, albeit unsuccessful, to persuade the president and other administration officials that the United States had no choice but to resist if the Soviets introduced military personnel. He states that he called for contingency plans "in case the Soviets threatened Israel with retaliation" and for "measures to prevent the attrition of the Israeli air force should the Soviets introduce sophisticated equipment manned by their own personnel."[38] However, officials in the Pentagon and in the Department of State "were less than enthusiastic." Interestingly, they regarded Israel's strategic bombing as responsible for causing the problem and opposed any large-scale aid to Israel at this juncture. As for contingency plans, Kissinger claims there was massive opposition within the administration to considering a military counter to any major Soviet move. Although Nixon agreed with Kissinger's geopolitical analysis, he accepted the view that Israel's policies were the basic cause of the difficulty. It appears, according to Kissinger, that Nixon preferred "to wait for a need for decision to arise," that is, until it was clear that Moscow had introduced combat forces into Egypt.[39]

Nevertheless, in the beginning of March, Nixon decided to defer consideration of the pending Israeli arms package indefinitely. This decision, which could be interpreted as an attempt to restrain Israel, was in fact to a great extent linked to Nixon's displeasure at the way in which the U.S. Jewish community had treated French President Pompidou during his visit in late February.[40] Indeed, even the Israeli cabinet did not consider Nixon's decision as an effort to constrain it.[41]

On February 22, according to Riad, Donald Bergus, head of the U.S. Interest Section in Cairo, delivered a message to Egypt in which the United States proposed an immediate ceasefire. He warned that if Egypt refused, Israel's air raids would continue, perhaps becoming more intensive and widening to include economic targets.[42] This was the first time the United States appealed directly to Egypt and attempted to exploit the Israeli air raids in order to secure an immediate ceasefire. It remains unclear, however, why the United States appealed directly to Egypt and whether this was due to the absence of a Soviet response. At any rate, although Riad does not mention the Egyptian response, the U.S. appeal could not have had any positive influence on Egypt, not only because it was a threat but because Egypt was expecting Soviet military assistance.

On March 10, Dobrynin finally submitted the Soviet response to Kissinger's warning of February 10. He did not mention the U.S. warning against the introduction of Soviet combat personnel into the war; in fact, they had already been sent to Egypt. Dobrynin brought a proposal for an informal ceasefire: "If the Israelis stop their bombings of the UAR [Egypt] the UAR on its part will display restraints in its actions, without, of course, any official statements to that effect." In a further effort to control and limit the risks of the Soviet intervention, Dobryin also announced that the Soviet Union had agreed to the resumption of the two-power talks. Furthermore, Dobrynin stated that the Soviet Union was prepared to make important concessions.[43]

Enthusiastic over Dobrynin's conciliatory reference regarding the resumption of the ceasefire and U.S.-Soviet bilateral talks, Kissinger ignored the facts—namely, that not only had the Soviet Union not responded to his warning but that it was on its way to direct intervention. Kissinger once again fell prey to wishful thinking; he reported immediately to the president that the Soviets had made "significant concessions" and that the U.S. policy "of relative firmness has paid off on contested issues."[44] Kissinger and Nixon failed to comprehend the significance of the latest Soviet message and, instead, reacted to it positively. One day later (March 11), Ambassador Dobrynin told Secretary of State William Rogers, no doubt in order to cushion the impact of the Soviet intervention, that the Soviet Union had obtained Egyptian political concessions in return for the new arms shipments that were fast arriving in Egypt.[45] This was the first time the Soviet Union notified the United States about its shipment of new arms to Egypt; however, no details were made available regarding the SA-3 missile system and the introduction of Soviet combat personnel into Egypt.

On March 12, in an abrupt about-face, the United States attempted to impose a ceasefire on Israel, the terms of which were essentially favorable to Egypt. Kissinger informed Rabin of the U.S. acceptance of the Soviet ceasefire proposal and advised him of its terms. Israel was to accept an undeclared 60-day ceasefire and would be required to cease all aerial operations west of the Suez Canal as long as Egypt desisted from air assaults against targets on Israeli-held territory. This meant the suspension not only of the in-depth raids but also of the use of Israeli planes against Egyptian artillery stationed on the canal bank. Moreover, Israel would have to refrain from responding to Egyptian artillery fire for a limited period of time. As an inducement, Kissinger promised that the United States would replace Israeli aircraft losses with up to eight Phantoms and twenty Skyhawks.[46]

On March 17, Rabin returned to Washington from a quick trip to Jerusalem with his government's reply. According to Rabin, Israel's Prime Minister Golda Meir urged the administration to reject the Soviet proposal for an undeclared ceasefire on the grounds that Egypt would exploit it to deploy the SA-3 missiles. However, Israel agreed to a ceasefire of unlimited duration. While Israel would not commit itself to refraining from employing the air force as "flying artillery" on the canal front, it would be willing to halt its in-depth air raids for three to five days if the Egyptians would also respect such a ceasefire.[47]

According to Kissinger, Rabin indicated that Israel would agree to an undeclared ceasefire subject to the following conditions: simultaneous cessation of both Egyptian and Israeli military activity, doubling of the aircraft replacement figure, and a public announcement by Nixon to the effect that the United States was committing itself to the maintenance of Israeli air strength and the regional military balance.[48]

On March 18, one day after Rabin submitted Israel's conditions for a ceasefire, he received a cable from Jerusalem informing him that the Soviet Union had dispatched a large number of personnel to Egypt to man the SA-3 missile systems (information already known to U.S. intelligence). Rabin submitted this information to Kissinger, stating that this development nullified Israel's willingness to accept the ceasefire proposal.[49]

Although the administration had been aware of the possibility that Soviet military personnel might be introduced into Egypt, it was surprised by the Soviet act, especially by the large number of Soviet military personnel involved. The Soviet proposal of March 10 for an undeclared ceasefire, regarded by Kissinger as a conciliatory move, had strengthened his perception that the U.S. policy framework was working well. Only now was it perceived that the administration had not correctly read that Soviet message.

The first reaction of the United States to the Soviet move was conveyed in Kissinger's conversation with Dobrynin on March 20, but this was two days after he was informed of the move by Rabin. It is not clear from Kissinger's memoirs why it took the administration such a long time to react. Kissinger states that he called in Dobrynin for "a tough dressing down." However, it appears from his memoirs that it was more of an attempt to express U.S. dissatisfaction over the Soviet act and to complain about the Soviets having misled the administration than an attempt to pressure the Soviet Union to withdraw its forces from Egypt. Kissinger complains that "the troops had been sent despite my explicit warning of the dangers of such a step." The weakness of the U.S. response to Soviet intervention, however, belied the "dangers" of such a step. Other than calling off further efforts for a ceasefire, the United States did not take any other action to punish the Soviets for having ignored the U.S. warning.[50] This soft U.S. reaction to its intervention no doubt facilitated the Soviet decision later in the crisis to escalate its military intervention.

Why did the United States fail to prevent Soviet military intervention? Although we cannot be certain that Soviet military involvement could have been avoided, it was at least possible had the administration acted differently. But this would have required the administration to take the threat of Soviet intervention more seriously, and this it did not do as a result of the combination of the somewhat vague nature of the Soviet threat and Washington's wishful thinking that its policy of firmness was working. In consequence, the administration did not respond to the threat of Soviet intervention on this occasion as it had in 1967. More specifically, it did not press Israel to call off its air attacks immediately after receiving Kosygin's note of January 31, and it did not take strong steps to effectively deter the Soviet move. Not only did the administration make no attempt to halt the Israeli attacks, but, as we have noted, it tacitly encouraged them. Even if Rabin dramatized to some degree the amount of direct encouragement he had been given, it seems that his reports to Jerusalem reflected the views of Kissinger and even Nixon. The administration viewed the Israeli air attacks as a means of demonstrating to Nasser that Moscow could not help him recover the territory lost in 1967 and that he must eventually turn to the United States.

This was indeed the mind set of U.S. policy, as Kissinger avows in his memoirs, and it served as a prism by means of which Soviet statements regarding intervention were evaluated and their significance misinterpreted. Kissinger and Nixon did not regard the Soviet threat of intervention as credible until it was too late. The warnings they did issue to Moscow against intervention were nonspecific and perfunctory. They were not accompanied, as in the 1967 case, with a movement of the Sixth Fleet or other alerts.

Besides, as Kissinger admits, the administration was not in a position to mount stronger threats due to its involvement in crises in Vietnam, Cambodia, Laos, and the domestic sector as well. The administration simply did not wish to become embroiled in a new crisis. Moreover, after the Soviets intervened, many officials in the administration argued that Israeli belligerence had provoked the Soviet move, and they viewed the limited Soviet military intervention as an understandable and legitimate move to prevent the collapse of its Egyptian client. In retrospect, it is clear that if U.S. policy makers did not want to take measures strong enough to deter Soviet intervention, they had to conclude that the only alternative was to exert sufficient pressure on the Israelis to make them call off their air attacks. However, by the time U.S. decision makers realized that the only viable means of preventing Soviet military intervention was halting Israeli air attacks, it was too late. The United States had therefore missed the opportunity to do its best to avoid Soviet intervention.

SOVIET MILITARY INTERVENTION AND SUPERPOWER CRISIS MANAGEMENT

Soviet military intervention in the War of Attrition was an important departure from superpower crisis management of past Arab-Israeli wars. For the first time, a superpower intervened militarily in such a war. However, the Soviet move did not carry an immediate danger of confrontation between the superpowers, as the United States conveyed no serious concern so long as the intervention remained limited to the defensive aim of shielding Nasser's regime from Israeli deep penetration air raids. For the time being, Washington's policy was based on the belief that Soviet intervention was of a purely defensive nature and did not constitute a grave danger to either U.S. or Israeli interests.[51]

Thus, on March 23, Rogers announced that Nixon had decided to hold Israel's request for additional aircraft in abeyance, pending further developments in the area. This statement implied that the United States did not perceive the presence of sophisticated Soviet weapons and combat personnel in Egypt as a threat to the regional military balance. The announcement was devised as a means of compelling Israel to demonstrate self-restraint and as a signal to the Soviets that the United States was prepared to curb its ally, if necessary. This delay of arms shipments to Israel was also intended to indicate to Nasser that the United States was contemplating a new approach toward Egypt.[52]

The U.S. decision to delay further aircraft deliveries to Israel and the deployment of Soviet air defense into Egypt caused Israel to terminate its in-depth raids at the beginning of April. However, Washington's effort to stabilize the military situation proved to be an inappropriate signal to the Soviets. The United States had not perceived Soviet intervention as jeopardizing either U.S. or Israeli interests as long as it was confined to the installment of SA-3 missiles in the vicinity of Egyptian urban centers. But on April 24, Rabin informed Kissinger that Soviet pilots were flying defense missions over Egypt's interior. Only then, on April 29, did Nixon order a reappraisal of the political and military situation. The need for the re-evaluation of U.S. policy was especially recommended by Sisco (following his visit to the Middle East) and Kissinger. However, U.S. officials, including members of the intelligence community, had not altered their basic analysis that the Soviet intervention was of a purely defensive nature. Nixon was still hoping to get Moscow to agree to a summit meeting and was also heavily preoccupied with the domestic and international backlash triggered by the invasion of Cambodia by U.S. troops. The president was not ready to offer a firm challenge to the Soviet intervention. Instead, he opted for the State Department's proposal for a new diplomatic initiative to bring about an immediate termination of the war as the only way of evading the danger of a superpower confrontation.

In the absence of a real U.S. challenge, the Soviets began, in early May 1970, to implement a second phase in their intervention.[53] They apparently judged that unless Israel was deprived of its air superiority on the canal, there was no possibility of bringing the war to an acceptable end. By installing an advanced anti-aircraft system on the western bank of the canal, they hoped to neutralize Israel's air superiority, thus enabling Egypt to conduct an effective war of attrition on the ground.[54]

The Soviet Union's effort to neutralize Israel's air superiority in the Canal Zone, coupled with Israel's resolve to retain it, produced a discernible change in the U.S. stance. Once the Soviet Union actively began to strive toward achievement of a strategic balance on the canal front, apprehension grew in Washington regarding the possibility that the United States would become embroiled in a superpower confrontation. Concern for the balance of interests now shifted to the U.S. side, as the Soviets tried to achieve an outcome more favorable to its side at the expense of Israel and the United States. It now became necessary to impress upon the Soviet Union that it would not be allowed to impose a solution favorable to its own interests.[55]

During May and June, the United States sought simultaneously to limit the magnitude of the Soviet intervention and to seek an end to the war. On June 2, after initial Soviet attempts to install the SA-3 missiles in the Canal Zone failed, Rogers (without informing Kissinger and Nixon) told Dobrynin that the United States did not perceive the Soviet military intervention in Egypt as defensive. He warned that the "introduction of Soviet military personnel into the delicate Suez Canal combat zone [within 30 kilometers of the canal] could lead to serious escalation with unpredictable consequences to which the U.S. could not remain indifferent."[56] The U.S. warning was not strong enough to deter the Soviets. Indeed, Washington's warnings lacked sufficient credibility because, without a serious fear of confrontation with the United States, there was little to deter the Soviet Union.[57]

In order to prevent further deterioration and to avoid a confrontation with the Soviet Union, Rogers suggested a swift diplomatic initiative. He maintained that the only hope of containing the increasing Soviet intervention was by advancing a political proposal acceptable to both Egypt and the Soviet Union. On June 10, in a meeting of the National Security Council, Rogers submitted a proposal designed "to get the parties 'to stop shouting and start talking.'" The belligerents would be asked to accept a 90-day standstill ceasefire in the course of which indirect negotiations would be conducted by U.N. official Gunnar Jarring. Rogers's initiative, however, made no reference to a withdrawal of Soviet troops already in Egypt.[58]

Kissinger opposed Rogers's proposal, arguing that it ignored the issue of the Soviet presence in Egypt and would benefit only the Soviets and the Egyptians. He suggested instead that the United States explicitly inform Nasser that only Washington was capable of bringing about an Israeli air withdrawal; in return, Egypt would have to negotiate detailed conditions of peace with Israel. Despite Kissinger's objection, however, Nixon accepted Rogers's initiative on June 18.

The U.S. proposal for a ceasefire and negotiations was transmitted to Israel, Egypt, Jordan, and the Soviet Union on June 19 and was announced publicly on June 25. The proposal was rejected outright by Israel, which regarded it as damaging to its security. Egypt did not comment at all. On June 23, in a meeting with Kissinger, Dobrynin reacted coolly to the U.S. initiative. Faced with Soviet intransigence, Washington decided, as Kissinger notes in his memoirs, "to make clear that the President was not acting from weakness and that Soviet troops were a serious issue." On June 26, Kissinger authorized the release of a background briefing in which he stated that the Soviet military presence in Egypt represented a strategic threat to U.S. interests and that the United States was seeking to expel Soviet combat pilots and personnel.[59] Nonetheless, in disregard of the U.S. warnings, the Soviets finally successfully installed the missile network in the Canal Zone during the night of June 29.

On July 1, Nixon warned in a televised interview that the two superpowers could be drawn into confrontation over the Middle East and that the United States would not tolerate the upsetting of the military balance in the region.[60] However, the Soviets continued to ignore these U.S. warnings. In two meetings with Kissinger on July 7 and 9, Dobrynin made no reference to the warnings. The Soviet military intervention, which had started as a defensive move against Israeli deep penetration raids, was now on the verge of altering the regional balance and the entire strategic equation between the superpowers in the Middle East. The United States seemed incapable of deterring the Soviet Union from achieving these aims.

On July 1, Meir wrote a bitter letter to Nixon in which she protested the U.S. claim that the military balance was being maintained when, in fact, it had been clearly upset by the installation of the missile network. She warned that Israel would have no choice but to bomb the sites despite the risk of military confrontation with the Soviet Union.[61] Indeed, a confrontation between Israeli planes and Soviet missile crews had already begun on June 30, and it escalated to a clash between Israeli and Soviet pilots. In this situation, only an immediate termination of the war could prevent further Israeli-Soviet military clashes and the consequent danger of a superpower confrontation. However, the Israelis continued to object to the ceasefire proposal, and the Soviet Union's attitude remained negative as well.

Ironically, it was Egypt that suddenly accepted the U.S. proposal for a ceasefire and negotiations on July 23. According to Mohamed Heikal, then minister of information, Nasser accepted the Rogers initiative while he was still in Libya before he went on to Moscow on June 29. Furthermore, his decision came as a surprise to the Soviet leadership.[62] The purpose of Nasser's visit to Moscow was to report the Egyptian decision to the Soviet leaders and to shape a common strategy with them vis-à-vis the U.S. initiative. According to Heikal and Riad, who had joined Nasser in Moscow, the Egyptian acceptance of the U.S. initiative was not received positively by the Soviets, and they even tried to discourage Nasser from accepting it. The Soviet leadership was concerned that Egypt's acceptance would give credit to the United States and that the "settlement would then appear tied to them alone, while the Soviets would find themselves relegated to the role of spectators."[63]

Nasser's reasons for accepting the U.S. ceasefire proposal are not entirely clear. He does not seem to have done so due to a fear of a U.S. military intervention. Moscow's continued refusal to supply Egypt with deterrent weapons may have been an important factor.[64] No less important a reason for accepting the ceasefire was that it gave Egypt an opportunity to build a missile wall along the canal after the ceasefire took place, with immunity from risk of attack. Nasser emphasized this aim in his talk with the Soviet leadership, and it appears that he received Soviet support.[65]

Egypt's acceptance of the U.S. initiative for a ceasefire was followed by Soviet acceptance of it. On July 23, Dobrynin separately informed Kissinger and Rogers that the Soviet attitude toward a temporary ceasefire was positive and that the Soviet Union also favored the resumption of the Jarring Mission. The Soviets also agreed to include a military standstill as part of the ceasefire but refused to link this acceptance of the U.S. initiative with a commitment to terminate their military presence in Egypt.

The Soviet acceptance left Israel as the only party that still refused to accept the ceasefire initiative. The Nixon administration heightened efforts to persuade Israel to change its attitude. To this end, the United States primarily employed inducements, extending commitments to Israel's security and survival in the form of increased military and economic aid. It also promised to prevent the imposition of a political settlement.[66] The need to convince Israel to comply became even more urgent following clashes between Israeli and Soviet pilots. On July 25, two Soviet-piloted MiG-21s attacked two Israeli Skyhawks that were on their way to bomb SA-3 missiles. In retaliation, Israeli pilots laid an ambush for Soviet pilots in the air space over the Suez Gulf on July 30. In the fighting that ensued, the Soviets lost five planes. On July 31, aware of the danger of a continued confrontation with the Soviets and unable to extract further commitments from the United States, the Israeli government accepted the U.S. initiative.

On August 7, the ceasefire went into effect. However, a new crisis soon erupted due to the introduction of missiles into the standstill zone by the Egyptians and the Soviets. Washington made a major effort to restrain Israel from reacting militarily while sending a very strong protest to both Cairo and Moscow. Israel insisted that the Egyptians and the Soviets would first have to withdraw the missiles from the standstill zone. However, both Egypt and the Soviet Union refused to comply. Only Washington's commitment of massive military support to Israel convinced it to participate in the settlement talks. The crisis ended without a solution to the violations of the ceasefire and the change in the military balance in the area.

Washington's willingness to terminate the war immediately, without exacting a Soviet commitment to remove its forces from Egypt, reflected the weakness of the administration's posture throughout the crisis. The Soviet military intervention became "a precedent that enhanced the credibility of Brezhnev's threat two years later to intervene in the Arab-Israeli War of October 1973. And the successful intervention of 1970 no doubt encouraged Soviet leaders to believe that the growing global reach of their military forces would provide new opportunities for their foreign policy in the future."[67]

ANALYSIS: PROBLEMS OF CRISIS MANAGEMENT

Despite Moscow's strong desire and persistent efforts to avoid another war in the Middle East, it was not able in the end to restrain Nasser from initiating one. Contrary to Moscow's expectations, limiting Egypt to a defensive military capability did not provide sufficient leverage to prevent Nasser from launching a war of attrition when it became clear to him that his Soviet ally could not achieve the return of the territory Egypt lost in 1967.

The major threats to crisis management arose through two miscalculated escalations: the Israeli decision (supported by the United States) to mount highly damaging deep penetration air raids into Egypt; and Moscow's escalation of its intervention from the initial defensive objective of protecting Egypt from Israeli air attacks to the offensive aim of neutralizing Israeli superiority in the Suez Canal area, a development that brought the two superpowers close to a confrontation.

Unlike the 1967 crisis, in which effective and timely superpower communication did much to prevent a more dangerous confrontation between Moscow and Washington, in the present case poor communication between the superpowers at several critical junctures as well as their unwillingness to cooperate in the immediate termination of the war contributed to escalation of the crisis. As already noted, Kosygin's warning of possible Soviet intervention was sufficiently ambiguous to permit Kissinger and Nixon initially to misjudge its credibility and significance. As a result, the United States lost an opportunity to deter Soviet intervention or, more prudently for crisis management purposes, to make it unnecessary by pressuring Israel to call off its air raids against Egypt. Washington clearly underestimated the seriousness of the Soviet commitment to prevent the Israelis from inflicting a catastrophic defeat on Nasser. This critical misperception was abetted by the mindset underlying the administration's Middle East strategy at the time. Kissinger, particularly, had for some time believed that Moscow's inability to help Nasser regain territory lost to Israel in the 1967 war would eventually lead the Egyptian leader to recognize that only the United States could mediate on Egypt's behalf. Although this strategic insight was indeed prescient, it did contribute to Kissinger's misreading of Kosygin's threat as constituting a further indication of Soviet impotence.

These miscalculated escalations were made possible by the failure of the superpowers to realize that they should have acted promptly to bring about an early ceasefire in the War of Attrition. Instead, Moscow and Washington pursued the more ambitious goal of searching for a political solution to the Israeli-Egyptian conflict as a way of terminating the war. They mistakenly assumed that the fighting along the Suez Canal area would remain localized and inconclusive or that it would somehow allow them time to seek a negotiated political settlement of the issues

---

The section Analysis: Problems of Crisis Management is co-authored with Alexander L. George.

dividing Egypt and Israel. Not surprisingly, this objective proved to be much too difficult to achieve. Egypt and Israel remained far apart on the terms of a political solution, and neither superpower could or would press its regional ally beyond a certain limited point into making the necessary concessions.

Perhaps the most significant contribution to superpower management of the Middle East conflicts that emerged from the War of Attrition was a tacit rule recognizing the legitimacy of military intervention by a superpower to prevent a catastrophic defeat of its regional client that threatened its political survival. This crisis management norm had been foreshadowed at the end of the Six Day War, when the Soviets had threatened intervention to forestall a possible move by Israeli forces against Damascus unless the United States acted to restrain its ally. On that occasion, Washington did not want to test the credibility of the Soviet threat and immediately exerted pressure, which in fact may not have been needed, on Israel to stop its advance into Syria. However, the pattern of superpower interaction on that occasion, which in effect constituted a form of cooperation to avoid a direct confrontation between them, had evidently not been internalized by Washington into a norm or tacit rule that would constrain its crisis behavior in 1970. The fact that the Six Day War had ended after the Soviet threat of intervention activated U.S. pressure on Israel was forgotten or regarded as irrelevant by U.S. leaders when, in early February of 1970, Moscow made a similar conditional threat, coupled with a demand that Washington restrain Israel. It was only after the United States first encouraged Israel's deep penetration air attacks on Egypt and then later failed to press Israel to halt them and only after the Soviets intervened, that many U.S. officials recognized the legitimacy of the Soviet action on behalf of its beleaguered client.

One can regard this aspect of the War of Attrition as a learning experience that helped to define a tacit, but nonetheless important, norm for regulating superpower involvement in regional conflicts between their rival local clients. A similar situation arose, as we shall see, in the Arab-Israeli War of 1973 when the Soviet Union found it necessary once again to employ the threat of intervention—this time successfully—in order to induce the United States to restrain Israel from inflicting a shattering defeat on Egypt.

BIBLIOGRAPHICAL NOTE

There are few detailed studies of the War of Attrition. The most important ones on Soviet policy are Alvin Z. Rubinstein, *Red Star on the Nile* (Princeton: Princeton University Press, 1977) and Jon D. Glassman, *Arms for the Arabs: The Soviet Union and War in the Middle East* (Baltimore: Johns Hopkins University Press, 1975). On the U.S. role, most interesting are Henry A. Kissinger, *White House Years* (Boston: Little, Brown, 1979) and William B. Quandt, *Decade of Decisions: American Policy Toward the Arab-Israeli Conflict 1967– 1976* (Berkeley: University of California Press, 1977.) On Israel's policy the following are useful: Yitzhak Rabin, *The Rabin Memoirs* (Boston: Little, Brown, 1979); Yaacov Bar-Siman-Tov, *The Israeli-Egyptian War of Attrition 1969–1970: A Case Study of Limited Local War* (New York: Columbia University Press, 1980). On Egypt's role, useful material is to be found in the memoirs of Mohamed Heikal, *The Road to Ramadan* (New York: Ballantine Books, 1975) and Mahmoud Riad, *The Struggle for Peace in the Middle East* (London: Quartet Books, 1981).

NOTES

1. Alvin Z. Rubinstein, *Red Star on the Nile* (Princeton, N.J.: Princeton University Press, 1977), pp. 29–30; Yaacov Ro'i and Ilana Diamant-Kass, *The Soviet Military Involvement in Egypt, January 1970–July 1972* (Jerusalem: The Hebrew University of Jerusalem, 1972), pp. 4–5.

2. Mahmoud Riad, *The Struggle for Peace in the Middle East* (London: Quartet Books, 1981), pp. 84–86.

3. Heikal, *Al-Ahram*, July 12 and 25, 1968; *Guardian*, July 5, 1968; *Daily Telegraph*, July 10, 1968; see also Rubinstein, *Red Star on the Nile*, pp. 59–65; Ilana Kass, *Soviet Involvement in the Middle East; Policy Formulation, 1966–1973* (Boulder, CO: Westview Press, 1978), pp. 65–67; Yaacov Ro'i, *From Encroachment to Involvement* (New York: John Wiley, 1974), p. 484; George W. Breslauer, "Soviet Policy in the Middle East, 1967–1972: Unalterable Antagonism or Collaborative Competition?" in Alexander L. George, ed., *Managing U.S.-Soviet Rivalry: Problems of Crisis Prevention* (Boulder, CO.: Westview Press, 1983), pp. 71–72.

4. Anwar el-Sadat. *In Search of Identity* (New York: Harper and Row, 1977), p. 196; Yaacov Bar-Siman-Tov, *The Israeli-Egyptian War of Attrition 1969–1970: A Case Study of Limited Local War* (New York: Columbia University Press, 1980), p. 45; Daniel Dishon, ed., *Middle East Record* (Jerusalem: Israeli-Universities Press, 1973), pp. 358–363.

5. *New York Times*, December 29, 1968; Rubinstein, *Red Star on the Nile*, p. 75.

6. Riad, *The Struggle for Peace*, p. 96.

7. Rubinstein, *Red Star on the Nile*, pp. 78–79.

8. Janice G. Stein, "The Managed and the Managers, Crisis Prevention in the Middle East," in Gilbert R. Winham, ed., *New Issues in International Crisis Management* (Boulder, CO.: Westview Press, 1988), p. 175.

9. Henry A. Kissinger, *White House Years* (Boston: Little, Brown, 1979), p. 367; William B. Quandt, *Decade of Decisions: American Policy Toward the Arab-Israeli Conflict 1967–1976* (Berkeley: University of California Press, 1977), p. 86.

10. Quandt, *Decade of Decisions*, p. 87; Bar-Siman-Tov, *The Israeli-Egyptian War of Attrition*, pp. 77–78; Rubinstein, *Red Star on the Nile*, pp. 85–86.

11. Kissinger, *White House Years*, pp. 372–379; Quandt, *Decade of Decisions*, pp. 89–90; Riad, *The Struggle for Peace*, pp. 109–110.

12. Quandt, *Decade of Decisions*, pp. 90–91. The plan was made public on Nixon's instructions; he was disappointed by the Soviet rejection. Marvin Kalb and Bernard Kalb, *Kissinger* (New York: A Dell Book, 1974), p. 218. According to Hersh, Rogers decided to publicize the initiative in the wake of the continuous criticism of his diplomacy from the Israeli embassy and the American Jewish community. Seymour M. Hersh, *The Price of Power: Kissinger in the Nixon White House* (New York: Summit Books, 1983), p. 219. According to Riad, he had replied to Rogers on November 16. Egypt did not reject Rogers's proposals, but made their acceptance conditional on the position of the United States regarding delineation of Israel's borders with Jordan and Syria. Riad, *The Struggle for Peace*, pp. 110–111.

13. Riad, *The Struggle for Peace*, p. 114.

14. Michael Brecher, *Decisions in Israel's Foreign Policy* (London: Oxford University Press, 1974), pp. 479–483.

15. On December 17, after Nixon authorized the submission of the Yost document, a plan aimed at resolving the Israeli-Jordanian conflict, to the four-power talks, he instructed his aide, Leonard Garment, to assure Meir privately that he would not affix his full backing to the State Department's new initiative, and would not impose its provisions. This was

conveyed to American Jewish leaders as well. Kissinger, *White House Years*, p. 376; Hersh, *The Price of Power*, p. 220.

16. Kissinger, *White House Years*, pp. 378–379; Quandt, *Decade of Decisions*, p. 93.

17. More than once, close Soviet control led to clashes between Soviet experts in Egypt and the Egyptian military, and also between the experts and Nasser himself. For details, see Edgar O'Ballance, *The Electronic War in the Middle East 1968–1970* (London: Faber, 1974), pp. 64, 73, 91, 93.

18. Ro'i, *From Encroachment to Involvement*, p. 514; Ze'ev Schiff, *Phantom Over the Nile: The Story of the Israeli Air Corps* (Haifa: Shikmona, 1970) (Hebrew), pp. 208–209; O'Ballance, *Electronic War*, pp. 89, 92; Jon D. Glassman, *Arms for the Arabs: The Soviet Union and War in the Middle East* (Baltimore: The Johns Hopkins University Press, 1975), pp. 73–74; Ezer Weizman, *On Eagles' Wings* (Tel Aviv: Steimatzky's Ltd., 1979), p. 261; Riad, *The Struggle for Peace*, p. 109.

19. Ro'i, *From Encroachment to Involvement*, pp. 514–515; Rubinstein, *Red Star on the Nile*, p. 105.

20. Riad, *The Struggle for Peace*, pp. 112–113; see also Glassman, *Arms for the Arabs*, pp. 73–74; Rubinstein, *Red Star on the Nile*. pp. 99–100.

21. The only time during the period between July 20 and the end of December 1969 that the Soviets warned Israel to limit its air strikes was after an Israeli assault on two Soviet warships during a raid on the area of Port Said. The Soviet Union delivered a stern note of protest via Finland, which represented its interest in Israel. Punitive measures were threatened in the event of any future recurrence. Israel replied through the United States and the Finnish Embassy that its forces had orders to confine their attacks to Egyptian targets; see Yitzhak Rabin, *Pinkas Sherut* (Tel Aviv: Ma'ariv, 1979) (Hebrew), pp. 250–251; Gideon Rafael, *Destination Peace: Three Decades of Israeli Foreign Policy: A Personal Memoir* (New York: Stein and Day, 1981), p. 204.

22. For Israeli evaluation of the Soviet factor in the decision for in-depth strategic bombing of Egypt, see Bar-Siman-Tov, *The Israeli-Egyptian War of Attrition*, pp. 126–130; and Yaacov Bar-Siman-Tov, *Israel, the Superpowers and the War in the Middle East* (New York: Praeger, 1987), pp. 163–165.

23. Rabin, *Rabin Memoirs*, p. 150; Rabin, *Pinkas Sherut*, p. 252.

24. Rabin's views on the lack of U.S. opposition to in-depth raids, which he expounded to the government, influenced tremendously the decision to carry out the raids. Bar-Siman-Tov, *The Israeli-Egyptian War of Attrition*, pp. 130–132; Bar-Siman-Tov, *Israel, the Superpowers and the War*, pp. 161–162.

25. Heikal, *The Road to Ramadan*, pp. 79–84; Mohamed Heikal, *The Sphinx and the Commissar: The Rise and Fall of Soviet Influence in the Middle East* (New York: Harper and Row, 1978), p. 197; Riad, *The Struggle for Peace*, p. 119.

26. Kissinger, *White House Years*, p. 560; Riad, *The Struggle for Peace*, pp. 121–122.

27. Alexander L. George suggests the following possible reasons why Kosygin did not refer to, or imply more clearly, the possibility of direct Soviet military intervention: (1) an explicit threat might be considered too provocative by the United States; (2) Soviet unwillingness to be committed to an intervention; (3) for security reasons, that is, to enable the covert delivery of Soviet military equipment and personnel. Alexander L. George, "Missed Opportunities for Crisis Prevention: the War of Attrition and Angola," in *Managing U.S.-Soviet Rivalry*, pp. 191–192.

28. Kissinger, *White House Years*, pp. 560–561 (emphasis in original).

29. Ibid., p. 561; Quandt, *Decade of Decisions*, p. 96; Rabin, *Pinkas Sherut*, p. 276.

30. Evidence of this inclination was provided by Nixon's announcement on January 30 that he would publicize his decision on Israel's outstanding arms requests within thirty days. This was a public reply to the "shopping list" presented to Nixon by Meir during her visit

to Washington in September 1969. This list included twenty-five Phantoms, one hundred Skyhawks, and a substantial number of tanks and armored personnel carriers. Quandt, *Decade of Decisions*, p. 95; *Rabin Memoirs*, p. 167.

31. Rabin, *Rabin Memoirs*, p. 166–167; Rabin, *Pinkas Sherut*, pp. 275–276.

32. Rabin mentions in his memoirs that both U.S. and Israeli intelligence knew about Nasser's trip to Moscow. Rabin, *Rabin Memoirs*, p. 166; Rabin, *Pinkas Sherut*, p. 273.

33. It seems that the straw that broke the camel's back for the Kremlin was the unintentional Israel raid of February 12 on the factory of Abu Zabal, which killed some seventy to eighty workers and injured one hundred. Soviet leaders concluded that Nasser's demand for the immediate delivery of SA-3s was valid. Sadat, *In Search of Identity*, p. 197; Riad, *The Struggle for Peace*, p. 122; Glassman, *Arms for the Arabs*, p. 76; Lawrence L. Whetten, *The Canal War: Four Power Conflict in the Middle East* (Cambridge, Mass.: The MIT Press, 1974), pp. 93–94.

34. Kissinger, *White House Years*, p. 561.

35. Ibid., p. 562.

36. Ibid.

37. Ibid.

38. Ibid., p. 563.

39. Ibid., pp. 563–564.

40. Ibid., p. 565; Quandt, *Decade of Decisions*, p. 97; Steven L. Spiegel, *The Other Arab-Israeli Conflict: Making America's Middle East Policy from Truman to Reagan* (Chicago: University of Chicago Press, 1985), p. 190.

41. Bar-Siman-Tov, *Israel, the Superpowers and the War*, p. 169.

42. Riad, *The Struggle for Peace*, p. 121 (unconfirmed by other sources).

43. Kissinger, *White House Years*, p. 567.

44. Ibid., p. 568.

45. Quandt, *Decade of Decisions*, p. 97.

46. Rabin, *Rabin Memoirs*, pp. 169–170. Kissinger, however, maintains in *White House Years* (p. 568) that he had asked only that Israel cease its deep penetration raids and agree to an undeclared ceasefire.

47. Rabin, *Pinkas Sherut*, pp. 281–282.

48. Kissinger, *White House Years*, pp. 568–569.

49. Ibid., p. 569; Rabin, *Pinkas Sherut*, pp. 282–283.

50. Kissinger, *White House Years*, p. 570.

51. Ibid., pp. 570–571.

52. Quandt, *Decade of Decisions*, p. 98; Glassman, *Arms for the Arabs*, p. 77.

53. It is not clear whether the expansion of Soviet intervention signified a new decision or whether it was a further step in the implementation of the original decision to intervene in the war. Glassman, *Arms for the Arabs*, p. 78.

54. Ibid., p. 79.

55. Kissinger, *White House Years*, p. 574.

56. Ibid.

57. Ibid., pp. 574–575.

58. Ibid., pp. 575–576.

59. Ibid., pp. 579–580.

60. *Department of State Bulletin*, July 17, 1970; pp. 112–113.

61. Kissinger, *White House Years*, pp. 581–582.

62. Heikal, *The Road to Ramadan*, pp. 89, 91; Heikal, *The Sphinx and the Commissar*, p. 201.

63. Riad, *The Struggle for Peace*, p. 141, see also, pp. 137–148; Heikal, *The Road to Ramadan*, pp. 89–91; Heikal, *The Sphinx and the Commissar*, pp. 201–202; Sadat, *In Search of Identity*, p. 198.

64. Kissinger, *White House Years*, p. 582; Sadat, *In Search of Identity*, p. 198; Riad, *The Struggle for Peace*, pp. 127–150.

65. Heikal, *The Sphinx and the Commissar*, p. 201; Heikal, *The Road to Ramadan*, p. 89.

66. Bar-Siman-Tov, *Israel, the Superpowers and the War*, pp. 180–184.

67. George, "Missed Opportunities," p. 198.

CHAPTER 15

The Arab-Israeli War of October 1973

Yaacov Bar-Siman-Tov

The outcome of the War of Attrition did little to alter the basic configuration of the intractable Arab-Israeli conflict or to give Moscow and Washington fresh perspectives on how to moderate their own competition for influence in the Middle East in order to prevent another war and another confrontation. Nor did the emergence of the Nixon-Brezhnev détente of 1972 sufficiently moderate the momentum of events that led to the war. But despite the seemingly unreconcilable differences between Israel and the Arab states, the United Nations continued to make efforts to break the deadlock. Superpower incentives and willingness to work together to bring about a settlement were weakened by their continuing reluctance to impose any political solution on their clients and by their preference, in the last analysis, for policies that might yield unilateral advantages for themselves as well as their regional allies. A unilateral proposal by the United States for a limited interim agreement that would reopen the Suez Canal was opposed by the Soviet Union; it feared a U.S.-Egyptian agreement to which it was not a partner. Indeed, to short-circuit any step toward a U.S.-Egyptian rapprochement, Moscow signed a Friendship and Cooperation Treaty with Egypt in May 1971.

Soviet concern over the possibility of a U.S.-Egyptian rapprochement was in fact well founded. President Richard Nixon and especially Henry Kissinger continued to prefer a prolonged stalemate in the Middle East as a means for heightening the Soviet Union's diplomatic difficulties with its Arab clients. By demonstrating to Egypt that the Soviet Union was unable to help it to recover territory lost to Israel as a result of the Six Day War in 1967, Nixon and Kissinger hoped to markedly weaken Moscow's influence and, if not to totally expel it from the Middle East, to bring about a reversal of alliances whereby the United States would replace the Soviet Union as Egypt's friend. Thereby, the United States would be able to advance its own approach to moderating, if not resolving, the Arab-Israel conflict. As long

---

This chapter is a much abbreviated version of an unpublished manuscript that contains fuller documentation.

as Egypt remained a Soviet client, as Kissinger stated in his memoirs, the United States preferred a no war–no peace situation in the Middle East.[1]

The outbreak of the war on October 6, 1973, far from undermining Washington's confidence in the correctness of its Middle East policy, was seen as an opportunity to achieve its long-standing objective. The October war did indeed enable the United States to achieve the objectives of its Middle East policy, but questions remain as to whether a war-threatening confrontation with the Soviet Union was necessary to achieve those objectives.

LIMITED SUPERPOWER COOPERATION TO ACHIEVE A SETTLEMENT

Continued superpower competition in the Middle East following the War of Attrition did not keep the two powers from exploring the possibility of cooperation in trying to develop at least a framework or a set of general principles for resolving the Arab-Israeli deadlock. Whether or not a joint effort of this kind could possibly break the impasse between the Arab states and Israel, the attempt served other purposes for Washington and Moscow. In July 1971, Nixon authorized Kissinger to explore this possibility with Moscow, in part to avoid a new crisis in the Middle East during the forthcoming presidential election campaign.

Indeed, Kissinger and Soviet Foreign Minister Andrei Gromyko were able to make progress in developing general principles for a joint U.S.-Soviet approach in the Middle East. At the very least, Kissinger thought such a development might provide the Soviets with an incentive for behaving with restraint in the area.[2] For their part, the Soviets agreed to cooperate in developing a joint approach even though they could not realistically expect that it would pave the way to a political solution of the Arab-Israeli conflict. Moscow may have hoped that its participation in a cooperative superpower approach might serve at least to constrain Washington's unilateral diplomacy in the Middle East and provide its Arab clients with some evidence that it was trying to achieve an acceptable political solution.

In fact, the Soviet Union did not want another war in the region for the same reasons it had tried to restrain Nasser in 1967 and in 1969. In addition, there was now another incentive for the two superpowers to cooperate in an effort to prevent the Middle East situation from exploding again. Both Moscow and Washington wished, for similar reasons as well as divergent ones, to bring about a détente in their relationship. Keeping the Arab-Israeli conflict quiescent was in their mutual interest as preparations went forward for a summit meeting between Nixon and Brezhnev. The two leaders were preoccupied with other important issues to be taken up at the Moscow summit of May 1972 and, indeed, reached important agreements on arms control and other matters at that meeting. But they also felt it necessary to issue a supplementary communiqué on the Middle East situation, one that urged a peaceful settlement but contained no concrete guidelines for negotiations. The communiqué clearly implied that the Soviets preferred détente with the United States to undertaking serious and risky efforts on behalf of Egypt.

THE SOVIET FAILURE TO RESTRAIN EGYPT
FROM INITIATING WAR

As they did in the period before the War of Attrition, Soviet leaders also tried after 1970 to dissuade Egypt's President Anwar el-Sadat from resorting to force. Moscow counseled him to seek his objectives through diplomacy, but, in fact, its perfunctory diplomatic efforts in effect froze the situation. The bland communiqué on the Middle East situation issued by Soviet leader Leonid Brezhnev and Nixon at the end of their Moscow summit came as a "violent shock" to Sadat, and it led him in less than two months to expel Soviet military advisers from Egypt. It also reinforced the Egyptian leader's conviction that another war was the only viable option for recovering the Sinai.[3]

The Soviet acceptance of the deadlock in the Middle East and the expulsion of their military advisers could be regarded as a victory for Kissinger's strategy. But Kissinger failed to exploit this opportunity to move into a closer relationship with Egypt. Evidently, Kissinger felt it was not urgent to move quickly to assure Sadat that Washington would work expeditiously on Egypt's behalf. Israel's military supremacy would deter a new Arab attack, and, since Sadat did not have a realistic military option, "Egypt had no choice but to await the American diplomatic initiative."[4] Kissinger deliberately delayed initiating serious contacts with Egypt until late February 1973, by which time Sadat had already decided to repair his rupture with Moscow and had obtained promises of significant new military shipments.

Until early 1973, the Soviets indeed had withheld the arms deemed necessary by Sadat for a new war. The Soviet opposition to war was not accompanied by a flat refusal to supply Egypt with any arms, but Moscow did refuse to supply Sadat with offensive arms, especially long-range bombers that would enable Egypt to open a full-scale military offensive against Israel.[5] If Moscow believed that it could retain its relationship with Egypt under these circumstances, it was rudely shocked by Sadat's expulsion of its military advisers and must have been deeply apprehensive that the United States would seize the opportunity for a rapprochement with Egypt. Washington's failure to offer Sadat adequate assurance of support led him to turn again to the Soviet Union in October 1972. This time, given an opportunity to recoup its position with Cairo, Moscow was more forthcoming. Egypt and the Soviet Union began to develop a new set of conditions for renewing military relations and political cooperation. The new understanding was facilitated by Sadat's decision to opt for a limited war rather than an all-out war against Israel and his renewal of the five-year agreement granting the Soviets naval facilities in Egypt.[6]

Still clinging to the hope that a new war could somehow be avoided, Moscow reluctantly accepted the fact that its resumption of increased military aid to Egypt, which now included medium bombers and medium-range missiles, would make a war possible. Sadat not only declared his satisfaction with the flow of military supplies[7] but is reported to have exclaimed on one occasion, "It looks as if they want to push me into a battle."[8]

It seems, therefore, that when the Soviets realized that Sadat was determined to resume hostilities, they preferred to supply the weapons needed for a limited war rather than to endanger once again their assets in the Middle East.

A complicating factor for the Soviets was how to square their support for Sadat's new war with some of the agreements they had only recently concluded with the United States. At their Moscow summit in May 1972, Brezhnev and Nixon had signed the Basic Principles Agreement. Several of its provisions clearly implied agreement to cooperate in preventing crises that were "capable of causing a dangerous exacerbation of their relations" and, further, to forego "efforts to obtain unilateral advantages at the expense of the other."[9] At their second summit in Washington in June 1973, Nixon and Brezhnev signed the Agreement on Prevention of Nuclear War, which explicitly obliged the two sides to engage in "urgent consultations" if situations developed anywhere in the world that raised the risk of nuclear war.[10] Nonetheless, such an obligation lacked precision when applied to crises such as a new Arab attack would generate. In any case, the Basic Principles Agreement also contained a provision stating that it did not affect any obligations that Moscow and Washington had undertaken toward allies.

Developments leading to the Arab-Israeli War of October 1973 provided the first test of this nascent crisis prevention agreement. The Soviets were faced with the dilemma of having to decide whether and how to fulfill the cloudy obligation to consult with the United States to head off the crisis that would be created by Sadat's initiation of war, an action by their regional client they felt they had to support.

According to Nixon's own account, at their second summit in the United States in June 1973, Brezhnev hammered at him about the danger of a new war in the Middle East and the need for U.S. diplomatic pressure on Israel in the interest of a Middle East settlement.[11] Brezhnev's warnings, however, were of a general character; he did not state that Sadat had definitely decided upon and planned a new war. And it is not surprising that Nixon and Kissinger dismissed the Soviet leader's warnings as scare tactics designed to pressure the United States to change its Middle East policy. In fact, it appears that Moscow itself received definite information about the forthcoming Arab attack from Sadat and the Syrian President Hafez el-Assad only a few days before it occurred, whereupon Moscow immediately evacuated Soviet civilian personnel from Egypt and Syria. It is not clear whether the evacuation was intended as an indirect signal to the United States of the imminent Arab attack; certainly, the United States and Israel did not regard the evacuation of Soviet personnel as an indicator of possible war.

Quite obviously, Soviet leaders had been caught in a situation in which honoring more fully the new crisis prevention principles imbedded in the Basic Principles Agreement and in the Agreement on Prevention of Nuclear War would have drastically conflicted with their responsibilities to their Arab allies. For Moscow to have given the United States unequivocal warning of the forthcoming attack would have betrayed its Arab allies and deprived its military attack of the surprise on which any chance of success depended.

INITIAL SUPERPOWER REACTIONS TO THE WAR

The Egyptian-Syrian strategy in the war was to inflict a defeat on the Israeli standing army before Israel could mobilize its reserves; this would enable Arab armies to quickly seize strategic positions in the Sinai and the Golan Heights and then set up defensive positions to ward off Israeli counterattacks. They hoped that the conflict would then move quickly into active diplomacy that would force Israel to withdraw from the occupied territories.

From the outset of the war, both superpowers responded with, on the one hand, a real concern to avoid the danger of a war-threatening confrontation between themselves and, on the other hand, a desire to exploit the war to achieve unilateral advantages. Moscow and Washington were aware that the war threatened to severely damage their own relationship and the détente process so recently set into motion. At the same time, developments in the war soon revealed that, contrary to the language of the Basic Principles Agreement of 1972, neither superpower was really ready to give up the pursuit of "unilateral advantage" at the other's expense.

Although the war caught Washington by surprise, it was almost immediately perceived as providing an opportunity to further the long-range goal of U.S. policy making—to bring the Arab states to abandon the patronage of the Soviet Union for that of the United States.[12] Another quickly emerging U.S. objective was to use the war to start an advantageous peace process thereafter. To this end, U.S. policy makers preferred that the war should end without a decisive victory for either side, an outcome that would enable the United States to mediate the negotiation process that followed. Nixon recalls: "I believed that only a battlefield stalemate would provide the foundation on which fruitful negotiation might begin. Any equilibrium—even if only an equilibrium of mutual exhaustion—would make it easier to reach an enforceable settlement."[13] Nevertheless, Washington clearly preferred that, before such a stalemate developed, Israel should achieve sufficient military success over Egypt to expose Moscow's inability to protect Egypt's interests.

THE DISAGREEMENT OVER A CEASEFIRE FORMULA

Two policies were immediately adopted by Washington. The first was to promote a ceasefire favorable to Israel—that is, one that called for a return to the status quo ante. Such a ceasefire based on a return of combat forces to their prewar lines would serve Israel's interests, prevent Soviet intervention, and, Washington hoped, together with other measures also preserve U.S. relations with the Arab states. The other policy was to restrain the resupply of military materiel to Israel, a policy based on the expectation that Israel would be successful and the war would be over in a short time; therefore, there was no need to antagonize the Arab states by shipment of military supplies to Israel. Moreover, U.S. policy makers hoped that the withholding of supplies to Israel would encourage the Soviets to observe a similar restraint toward its regional clients.[14]

The United States did not succeed in obtaining Soviet support for an immediate ceasefire of the kind it favored. But Moscow indeed experienced an acute dilemma: Prolongation of the war could result in a reversal of the initial Arab military successes; on the other hand, to accept the U.S. proposal would hazard Arab friendship. Therefore, Moscow openly opposed a ceasefire tied to a return of military forces to the status quo ante, but privately it attempted without success to persuade Sadat to accept a ceasefire in place that would have allowed the Arab forces to remain in the territory gained by their attack. From Cairo's standpoint, however, Moscow's proposed ceasefire would not provide sufficient success for Arab arms, for such a ceasefire would not be tied to an assurance of the return of all of the territory acquired by Israel in the 1967 war. At one point, Kissinger tried to persuade Egypt to accept a simple ceasefire in place, warning that Israel's expected counterattack would reverse the battlefield situation; at the same time, he offered Sadat encouragement by assuring him that the United States would not allow Israel to occupy more Arab territory. As for Israel, it was not interested in a ceasefire before it could demonstrate that its armed forces were capable of reversing the military situation in Israel's favor.

On October 8, having failed to cooperate effectively on behalf of an immediate ceasefire, Moscow and Washington now concentrated on pursuing unilateral policies. While the Soviet Union had to be seriously concerned lest the tide of battle turn against its clients, the United States hoped that Israeli military successes would soon put it in a better position to pursue its political objective. At the same time, Nixon and Kissinger were concerned that if Israeli forces went beyond prewar lines and penetrated deep into Arab territory, the possibility for achieving a termination of the war that accorded with U.S. diplomatic objectives would be endangered. Kissinger therefore warned Israeli Ambassador Simcha Dinitz that in the end, Israel would in any event have to withdraw to the lines it had maintained prior to the outbreak of the war. As an inducement for Israeli restraint, he held out the prospect of accelerated delivery of a number of Phantom fighter aircraft that had been approved in the prewar schedule and promised that Israel's request for special equipment would be fulfilled.[15]

On October 8, the Soviets moved toward escalation of the war by directly appealing to various Arab countries to help Egypt and Syria.[16] At the same time, the Soviets increased the risk of a superpower confrontation by initiating a massive airlift of arms to Egypt and Syria. It was clear that Moscow was now acting to enable its Arab allies to maintain or extend their gains or at least to prevent their eventual defeat.

Early on October 9, it appeared that Israel's southern offensive of October 8 had failed. Kissinger was informed by Dinitz and Mordechai Gur, the Israeli military attaché in Washington, that Israel had suffered heavy losses in manpower (a thousand casualties) and equipment (49 planes and 500 tanks). Golda Meir, Israel's prime minister, even considered flying to the United States in order to express to Nixon Israel's urgent need for more arms. Kissinger realized that his earlier optimistic expectation of Israeli military success had been badly mistaken. He understood that Israel now "stood on the threshold of a bitter war of attrition that it could not possibly win given the disparity of manpower." Kissinger concluded that the United States "had to do something decisive."[17] Accordingly, Washington now decided to replace all Israeli losses to enable it to continue fighting and to recoup the military situation. This was to be implemented via "a low profile in the method of resupply" in order "to preserve Arab self respect" and to avoid Soviet massive arms supply to the Arabs.[18]

It was evident, therefore, that although the superpowers seemed to be moving in the direction of cooperating to end the war, in fact they still regarded their *both powers seem to be attacking to stop the war while keeping the conflagration going so as*

clients' gains on the battleground as the factor that would determine the final decision regarding termination of the war.

not to have one side win or lose

THE SOVIET AIR- AND SEALIFT TO SYRIA AND EGYPT

A massive Soviet airlift and sealift of supplies to Syria and Egypt began on October 10. It appears that Soviet leaders decided on the airlift after the first signs of Arab retreat on the Syrian front on October 8 and 9 in order to prevent a serious defeat of their allies. The magnitude of this undertaking indicates that preparations had been underway for some time, but its implementation was almost certainly a consequence of the Israeli air strikes on Damascus on October 9. By October 11, the magnitude of the Soviet airlift had greatly increased. It now included flights to Syria, Egypt, and Iraq. Three Soviet airborne divisions had been placed on alert (this number increased to seven on the following day).[19] This alert was probably intended to deter any serious Israeli interference with the Soviet resupply operation as well as possible Israeli moves into Syria.[20] In addition, the Soviet Union warned the United States and Israel not to push for the defeat of Syria. In a luncheon meeting with Kissinger, Dobrynin cautioned that "the Soviet Union could not be indifferent to threats to Damascus. If Israel continued its advance, matters might get out of hand." In return, Kissinger warned Dobrynin that "any Soviet military intervention would be resisted and would wreck the entire fabric of U.S.-Soviet relations."[21]

Dobrynin delivered a further threat to Kissinger during the evening, the essence of which, according to Kissinger, was that "Israeli population centers would not remain immune indefinitely." The message included a warning to Israel to refrain from further attacks on Soviet vessels. (A Soviet ship had been sunk during an Israeli air raid on the Syrian port of Tartus.) Kissinger cautioned Dobrynin that "any Soviet military intervention—regardless of pretext—would be met by American force," adding that the United States would do its best to discourage assaults on purely civilian targets.[22]

Israel's decision makers reacted immediately to these Soviet warnings, especially to the Soviet Union's mobilization of three airborne divisions to fly to the aid of the Arabs.[23] They decided that if a proposal for a separate ceasefire on the Syrian front was introduced, Israel would accept it. Kissinger, however, was concerned that such sudden acquiescence would invite aggravated pressures, and he preferred to delay the submittal of the ceasefire resolution.[24] Kissinger, who advised Dinitz of the Soviet threats, stated that, while he had not yet consulted with Nixon, it was his view that "we would intervene if 'any Soviet personnel, planes or ground personnel appear in the area,'" As evidence of his intention, an additional U.S. aircraft carrier was ordered to move into the Mediterranean.[25] In effect, therefore, Kissinger assured the Israelis that the United States would act to deter Soviet intervention so that Israel could continue military operations against Egypt.

These assurances helped to alleviate Israel's immediate anxiety regarding Soviet intervention, but more to the point, Israel thought it best to halt its northern offensive against Syria. The Israelis were convinced that any further advance toward

Damascus would trigger a strong Soviet response. However, Israel decided to initiate a new military offensive on the southern front against Egyptian forces to change the military situation there in its favor.

The Soviet air- and sealift had a tremendous political and military impact. According to various observers, without resupply the Egyptians possessed stocks to continue fighting for only five days after the beginning of the war. With a resupply of certain key items, Egypt could prolong the war two more weeks beyond the five-day period. The Syrians were in an even worse military position.[26]

THE U.S. RESPONSE TO THE SOVIET AIRLIFT
AND SEALIFT: COMPETITION IN RISK-TAKING

The Soviet airlift was a major factor in changing the U.S. view of Soviet behavior in the war. The original inclination in Washington had been to take an understanding, nonalarmist view of Soviet actions and intentions. Even the initiation of the Soviet airlift on October 10 did not cause an immediate change in this attitude. The airlift was at first interpreted as a response to the military setback suffered by Syria on October 8 and 9 rather than a change in basic Soviet policy toward the war.

By the end of the week, however, the United States had changed its interpretation of Soviet behavior. Not only had the Soviet airlift increased in magnitude and been extended to Egypt and Iraq, but it was accompanied by a large-scale sealift. The sealift, which obviously had been set in motion before the war or immediately after it began, was of greater scope and more significant militarily than the airlift. Washington policy makers were in fact more impressed by the sealift than by the airlift.[27]

In addition, Washington was increasingly concerned that U.S. restraint was encouraging further Soviet moves. The step-up in the Soviet airlift reinforced this concern. On October 13, 67 new flights were detected, the bulk of them to Egypt. This was interpreted by U.S. policy makers as indicating that the Soviet Union had decided to stiffen Sadat's refusal to accept a ceasefire.[28] The Soviet Union's behavior was now seen as a violation of the spirit and tacit norms of détente.

Convinced that it had to stiffen U.S. policy, the administration decided to show that the United States could match the Soviets and prevent them from dominating developments in the military situation. There could be no ceasefire and no diplomatic process until it was made clear to the Soviets and the Arabs that they could achieve nothing more on the battlefield and that their initial gains were in jeopardy. This would require a decisive Israeli counterattack, but Israel was in no position to do so unless the U.S. resupplied it massively. This was the rationale behind Washington's decision on October 13 to airlift arms to Israel.

The superpowers were now pursuing similar but incompatible strategies, each seeking to enable its client to gain the upper hand on the battlefield or at least to prevent its defeat. Each side believed that the outcome of the war would be heavily influenced by the client's military position and by the patron's readiness to risk a superpower crisis. The lines were drawn for a superpower competition in risk-taking.

Although it is difficult to ascertain the degree to which the U.S. airlift contributed to Israel's emerging victory on the southern front, there is no doubt that it had a significant psychological impact on Israel, the Arabs, and the Soviets. To the Arabs and the Soviets, it symbolized the determination of the United States not merely to support Israel generally but also to support an Israeli offensive west of the canal into Egypt. Resupply enabled Israel to proceed without regard to the rate of depletion of its weaponry. Meir and Moshe Dayan emphasized that without the airlift, the war would have been tougher and Israel's casualty rate could have been far higher.[29] Egypt eventually rationalized its acceptance of the ceasefire as having been necessitated by the impact of the U.S. airlift.[30]

The United States hoped and expected that a controlled and limited Israeli military victory would help to persuade the Arabs and the Soviets to terminate the war.[31] Indeed, the new strategy seemed to give evidence of success almost immediately. By the time the first C-5 plane set down in Israel on the afternoon of October 14, an armored battle Egypt had initiated on the same day ended with a major Israeli victory. On the following day, Israeli forces crossed the Suez Canal and started an offensive into Egypt. These developments had an immediate impact on Soviet policy. Dobrynin informed Kissinger on October 14 that the Soviet Union was studying the U.S. proposal to link a ceasefire not to an Israeli withdrawal to the 1967 borders but to a general reaffirmation of U.N. Resolution 242. The following day, the Soviets indicated that they were actively trying to persuade the Arabs to accept a ceasefire. Kissinger was told that Soviet Premier Aleksei Kosygin would go to Cairo the next day for that reason.[32] No less important was a message from Sadat's national security adviser, Hafez Ismail, to Washington late on October 15 saying that Egypt, despite the U.S. airlift to Israel, was determined to keep open its "special channel of contact" with the United States. Ismail also urged Kissinger to redouble his efforts to link a political to a military solution and even invited him to visit Egypt.[33]

On October 16, Kosygin flew secretly to Cairo; his presence was not officially announced until October 18. He came to convince Sadat to accept an immediate ceasefire in place. Kosygin's trip was in response to the deterioration in Egypt's military position as a result of the crossing of the canal by Israeli forces, and the beginning of the U.S. airlift, which indicated that Washington was determined to prevent an Arab victory. During his three-day visit to Egypt, Kosygin tried to convince Sadat to agree to an immediate ceasefire on the existing lines. Sadat, who was not fully aware of his deteriorating military situation, refused to comply until he was convinced, probably by the aerial photographs of the battle that were introduced by Kosygin. The Soviets were informed of Sadat's agreement to a ceasefire at 1 A.M. on October 19.[34]

SUPERPOWER COOPERATION TO END THE WAR

Superpower cooperation in terminating the war may be said to have gotten seriously underway on the morning of the 19th when Washington received an urgent message from Brezhnev referring to the escalating danger of the Middle East war and warning of possible ramifications for superpower relations. Brezhnev proposed that

Kissinger make an immediate trip to the Soviet Union (or alternately to receive Gromyko in Washington) for urgent consultations on the Middle East.[35] Presumably the reason for the urgent Soviet appeal was the successful crossing of the Suez Canal by Israeli forces, which raised the prospect of catastrophic Egyptian defeat.[36]

Nixon and Kissinger accepted the Soviet invitation almost immediately. Kissinger stated two conditions that proved acceptable to the Soviets—that the negotiations would not start before Sunday morning October 21, and that there would be no discussion of any final settlement or any issue except the ceasefire. Kissinger regarded acceptance of the Soviet invitation under these conditions as favorable to his strategy: "It would keep the issue out of the United Nations until we had shaped an acceptable outcome. It would discourage Soviet bluster while I was in transit and negotiating. It would gain at least another seventy-two hours for [Israeli] military pressures to build."[37]

Before leaving for Moscow, Kissinger attempted to assuage Israel's fears by explaining that the United States had accepted the Soviet invitation in order to allow Israel the time necessary for it to achieve its war objectives and in order to preclude the possibility of direct Soviet intervention. Kissinger committed himself to consult Israel prior to the adoption of any proposal and to permit the Israeli government to preview the joint U.S.-Soviet statement that would inevitably be issued at the close of his visit.[38]

Kissinger arrived in Moscow at 7:30 P.M. Moscow time on Saturday, October 20. In the course of the flight, Kissinger received notification of Saudi Arabia's decision to declare an embargo of oil shipments to the United States and a message from Nixon granting him full and absolute authority to negotiate the terms of the ceasefire agreement. Moreover, in a letter to Brezhnev on October 20, Nixon implied that the United States was prepared to cooperate with the Soviet Union in order to impose a comprehensive settlement of the Arab-Israeli conflict, adding that Kissinger was empowered to discuss that.[39] The president repeated this offer in a verbal message he asked Kissinger to convey to Brezhnev. As quoted by Kissinger in his memoirs, Nixon's message to the Soviet leader was as follows: "The Israelis and Arabs will never be able to approach this subject by themselves in a rational manner. That is why Nixon and Brezhnev, looking at the problem more dispassionately, must step in, determine the proper course of action to a just settlement, and then bring the necessary pressure on our respective friends for a settlement which will at last bring peace to this troubled area."

Kissinger regarded Nixon's intended message to Brezhnev as a major error that contradicted U.S. strategy as he perceived it. Kissinger strongly preferred that a ceasefire be kept separate from the question of a postwar settlement, and he insisted that the Soviet Union's role in such negotiations be kept at a minimum. Kissinger states that he decided to ignore the president's instruction to convey this message to the Soviet leader. And Brezhnev, who was preoccupied with arranging an immediate ceasefire, never inquired of Kissinger what instructions he had received from Nixon.[40]

In his discussions with Kissinger, Brezhnev quickly conceded the essential points—a simple ceasefire in place linked to a call for direct talks. But at the Moscow talks, the two sides unaccountably failed to make arrangements for supervision of the ceasefire. No provision was made for enforcing it or even for returning U.N. observers to the canal area to oversee possible violations. The reason for this oversight is not clear; Steven L. Spiegel regards it as Kissinger's "gravest diplomatic mistake of the crisis, an omission that resulted two days later in a nasty U.S.-Soviet confrontation."[41]

Even before meeting with Brezhnev, Kissinger had received word of Egypt's inclination to agree to a ceasefire divorced from an overall settlement. This made Israel's agreement the only remaining obstacle to termination of the war. Kissinger, who failed to honor his commitment to consult with the Israelis with regard to the ceasefire proposal worked out in Moscow, was apprehensive over Israel's reaction to the proposal despite his confidence that it would ultimately comply.[42] Nonetheless, under pressure from Washington, the Israeli government decided to accept the ceasefire proposal. Golda Meir asked that Kissinger stop in Israel on his way back from Moscow for the purpose of U.S.-Israeli consultations prior to the formulation of the final resolution and its submission to a vote in the U.N. Security Council.[43]

Kissinger arrived in Israel at 12:40 P.M. on October 22. He sought to assuage Israeli fears, emphasizing that no secret deals had been concluded in Moscow and recommending that Israel view the ceasefire proposal as a substantial gain. But Israel was interested in achieving a more decisive war outcome. Kissinger was informed that Israel needed another two or three days to fully encircle the Third Army or even to destroy it.[44] According to several unsubstantiated accounts, Kissinger hinted that Israel would not be held to strict observance of the ceasefire; it could continue fighting for an additional two or three days.[45] While there is no reliable testimony on this point, it is clear that, at the very least, Kissinger was willing to tolerate minor Israeli advances in response to presumed Arab transgressions of the ceasefire and that he did not press strongly enough the urgency of an immediate ceasefire. As he later admitted: "I might have emboldened them; in Israel, to gain their support, I had indicated that I would understand if there were a few hours' 'slippage' in the ceasefire deadline while I was flying home, to compensate for the four hours lost through communications breakdown in Moscow."[46] It appears that Kissinger did not anticipate the possibility that the "slippage" to which he referred would lead ultimately to dangerous escalation of the crisis.

BREAKDOWN OF THE CEASEFIRE AGREEMENT

The ceasefire did not go into effect on October 22 at 6:52 as planned. There are conflicting views as to who was responsible for continued fighting on the Egyptian front. To be sure, the military positions of the two sides were confusing and highly conducive to flare-ups.[47] Israel immediately exploited what it regarded as an Egyptian violation to encircle the Third Army. Cairo promptly submitted a formal complaint of Israel's ceasefire violations to the United Nations. The Egyptians also sent messages to the United States and to the Soviet Union calling for action to enforce Israel's observance of the ceasefire. Kissinger tended to credit the Egyptian allegations but did not perceive the situation as an imminent crisis.[48] And only now did he begin to discuss the methods of policing the ceasefire. This followed after U.N. Secretary-General Kurt Waldheim suggested that an international force be introduced for that purpose. At 7:50 A.M., Kissinger called the Soviet chargé, Yuli M. Vorontsov, and suggested that the Security Council instruct Waldheim to call on the parties to observe the ceasefire immediately and to send U.N. observers or a U.N. force.

Soviet efforts to get the United States to restrain Israel proved ineffectual; Washington remained unwilling for the time being to exert maximum pressure on its ally. Accordingly, Moscow began to step up its own pressure on Washington. At 12:36 P.M. on October 23, Nixon received on the hotline an urgent message from Brezhnev, who called on the United States to take jointly with the Soviet Union "the most decisive measures" and "without delay" to impose the ceasefire. Although it is not clear what Brezhnev meant by "jointly," the Soviet leader probably wanted each superpower to pressure its ally to accept the ceasefire. Brezhnev implied that the United States had colluded with Israel to violate the ceasefire.[49] In his response to Brezhnev within the hour, Nixon assured the Soviet Union that the United States would "assume full responsibility to bring about a complete end of hostilities on the part of Israel." In return, he urged the Soviets to assume a similar commitment regarding Egypt. It is interesting to note that the U.S. response claimed that "responsibility for the violation of the ceasefire belongs to the Egyptian side."[50]

Within a few hours, at 2:26 P.M., Brezhnev sent another urgent message to Nixon. Although Kissinger does not say what Brezhnev's new message contained, this exchange of messages with the Soviets brought him to realize the delicate situation of the Egyptian army.

The arrival of an urgent message to Nixon from Sadat an hour later at 3:15 P.M. proved the gravity of Egypt's plight. Sadat now requested that the United States intervene, even by force, in order to guarantee the full implementation of the ceasefire resolution. Failure to do so would induce the termination of the budding U.S.-Egyptian relationship.[51] Kissinger now took a more sober view of the fact that Israel was interested not only in encircling but also in destroying the Third Army and undertook to prevent its annihilation.[52] An acerbic dispute ensued between Kissinger and the Israeli cabinet throughout the remainder of the afternoon of October 23. Kissinger emphasized that the United States had no interest in the collapse of Sadat's regime, the humiliation of Egypt, or a confrontation with the Soviet Union. It was Israel's duty to aid its patron in the enhancement of its regional position. It must understand that the United States would endeavor to wean Egypt away from the Soviet Union. Kissinger persisted in his demand that Israel accept a new ceasefire and provide an indication of its willingness to return to the lines of October 22. It should at least pull back its forces a few hundred meters for symbolic effect. However, Kissinger still stopped short of threatening sanctions if Israel did not comply. Israel refused. Any withdrawal, even symbolic, would loosen the siege of the Third Army and thus hinder a total Israeli victory.

Kissinger decided to stop the fighting immediately and encourage a negotiation over the location of the ceasefire lines. In a message to Brezhnev, he mentioned that the United States agreed with the Soviets regarding a new Security Council resolution. Thus, by late in the day on October 23, a new Resolution 339 was passed that reaffirmed the October 22 ceasefire and urged (not demanded, due to

Kissinger's insistence) the parties to return to the previous lines. Israel and Egypt agreed to observe it effective at 7 A.M. on October 24. In addition, Syria finally announced its formal acceptance of the ceasefire.[53] But the crisis was to intensify and to threaten to embroil the superpowers before it was finally resolved.

TOWARD A SUPERPOWER CONFRONTATION

The new ceasefire did not go into effect because Egypt continued efforts to lift the siege of the Third Army. Israeli forces responded by capturing Suez City. Sadat rushed urgent demands to Nixon and Brezhnev that Israel be forcibly compelled to respect the ceasefire. In an ominous development, the Egyptian leader called upon the superpowers "to intervene, even on the ground, to force Israel to comply with the ceasefire."[54]

Kissinger realized that if he did not act immediately, a confrontation with the Soviets would be inevitable, and Washington's hopes for a new relationship with Egypt would have been in vain. He decided not only to warn Israel but to threaten to leave it to face the Soviets alone if it refused to comply. In order to avoid a personal confrontation with the Israeli cabinet, he asked Alexander Haig, the White House chief of staff, to warn Dinitz on behalf of the president that Israel must immediately halt all military activity, adding that if the fighting did not stop at once, he might "disassociate himself" from Israel.[55] That was a threat Israel could not ignore. Israel responded that it would refrain from attacking Egyptian forces on the west bank of the canal.[56]

While Kissinger was assuaged by the Israeli reply and forwarded it to the Soviets and the Egyptians, Sadat claimed at 3 P.M. that Israel once again had initiated offensive activity. He demanded that U.S. and Soviet forces be sent to the area for the purpose of implementing the ceasefire on the Egyptian side. In addition, Egypt announced publicly that it was calling for a Security Council meeting to ask that U.S. and Soviet forces be sent to the Middle East. The administration also picked up reports that Soviet airborne divisions were on alert, that augmentation of the Soviet Mediterranean fleet had intensified, and, most ominously, that the Soviets were urging nonaligned nations to sponsor and support the sending of a joint U.S.-Soviet force.[57]

At 7:05 P.M., Dobrynin announced to Kissinger that the Soviet Union had decided to support a U.N. Security Council resolution calling for the dispatch of U.S. and Soviet troops to the Middle East. Kissinger said that the United States would veto it. Kissinger instructed the U.S. ambassador to the United Nations to veto any measure to send a peacekeeping force that included the superpowers and also to veto any condemnation of Israel, as this might serve as a pretext for Soviet intervention. As an alternative, the United States suggested an augmentation of the U.N. observer force already called for in Resolution 339.[58]

In other calls to Dobrynin that evening, Kissinger urged him "not to push to an extreme." He suggested that the two superpowers cooperate in sending more U.N. observers but refused to accept any Soviet troops. However, Dobrynin replied that in Moscow, "they have become so angry they want troops." He blamed the United States for allowing "the Israelis to do what they wanted." Kissinger maintained that, according to his information, no fighting was now going on and therefore "there was still time to avoid a confrontation."[59]

Dobrynin's statement increased U.S. apprehensions, especially as intelligence sources had spotted Soviet military moves indicating preparations for possible Soviet military intervention. The CIA reported that the Soviet airlift to the Middle East had stopped early on the 24th, which suggested that an air fleet was being assembled to move Soviet troops into Egypt to enforce the ceasefire. In addition, seven airborne divisions were on alert, Soviet transport planes were ready at embarkation points, and an airborne command was established in the southern part of the Soviet Union. The staff of one airborne division was reportedly already deployed in Syria. The number of Soviet ships in the Mediterranean had increased to eighty-five.[60]

At 9:35 P.M., a new message from Brezhnev triggered the intense crisis between the superpowers that their efforts at crisis management had attempted to avoid. Brezhnev proposed that joint Soviet and U.S. military forces be introduced to ensure the implementation not only of the ceasefire but also "of our understanding with you on the guarantee of the implementation of the decisions of the Security Council," namely, "the imposition of a comprehensive peace." Brezhnev emphasized that "it is necessary to adhere without delay. I will say it straight that if you find it impossible to act jointly with us in this matter, we should be faced with the necessity urgently to consider the question of taking appropriate steps unilaterally."[61]

Kissinger perceived the Soviet message as an ultimatum and "one of the most serious challenges to an American President." Nixon later defined it as the "most serious threat to U.S.-Soviet relations since the Cuban missile crisis."[62] There was no question in Nixon's and Kissinger's minds that the United States had to reject the Soviet proposal in a manner that "shocked the Soviets into abandoning the unilateral move they were threatening." Kissinger recalls that Nixon even mentioned the "shock of military alert."[63]

Kissinger again assembled the Washington Special Action Group (WSAG). The questions for discussion were: What motivated the Soviets, did they really intend to intervene, and, if so, did they have the capability to intervene? Kissinger and those around him were inclined to believe that the Soviets had decided on such action as a consequence of the Arab defeat. The Soviets could not tolerate another decisive Israeli victory over Egypt, and they were indeed capable of desperate action to prevent the total collapse of Egypt. This motivation was especially augmented by their perception that Israel and the United States had tricked them by violating the ceasefire to strangle the Third Army. Kissinger and others believed that the Soviets had the capability to intervene. This had been shown by their intervention in Egypt in 1970. Although a massive Soviet intervention was not perceived to be necessary, it was plausible that the Soviets would undertake a limited intervention that would suffice for the purpose at hand.[64]

Kissinger and the other participants in the meeting reached two conclusions. The Soviets had not taken previous U.S. statements and warnings against the introduction of their forces seriously and were not convinced that the United States had the will and the ability to react to any move they might make. The U.S. reply had to be conciliatory in tone but strong in substance in order to slow down the Soviets' timetable and draw them into talks. However, the tough U.S. response should be noted in Moscow before a written reply reached there, and it should reflect the U.S. determination to resist unilateral moves.[65] To this end, the U.S. military forces were to be placed on a DefCon 3 alert at midnight. It was decided to alert the 82nd Airborne Division for possible movement, and another aircraft carrier was ordered to move rapidly to the eastern Mediterranean. These later moves were made due to new information that had arrived indicating that eight Soviet An-22 transport planes were due to fly from Budapest to Egypt in the next few hours and that elements of the East German armed forces had been put on alert.[66]

Around 5:40 A.M. on October 25, following the alert of U.S. forces, Nixon's reply to Brezhnev was delivered. Nixon warned that Soviet intervention would produce "incalculable consequences." At the same time, the president also made a conciliatory gesture, agreeing to the addition of a limited number of U.S. and Soviet personnel to the U.N. contingent to serve as observers. Nixon's message did not refer to the alert of U.S. military forces. That was not considered necessary. The alert was a clear signal that the Soviets would get through their electronic intelligence.[67]

Kissinger also acted immediately to persuade Egypt that it should withdraw its invitation to the Soviets to send troops and to warn Israel to stop without delay its advances on the Egyptian front. Kissinger warned Sadat that should Soviet forces appear, the United States would have to resist them on Egyptian soil, and, in these circumstances, his plan to visit Cairo to start the peace process would have to be cancelled.[68]

In several conversations with Israeli Ambassador Dinitz, Kissinger used the threat of Soviet intervention to demand that Israel stabilize the ceasefire and lift the siege of the Egyptian Third Army. Neglect of the Soviet threat could provoke the landing of Soviet airborne divisions in the vicinity of Cairo, which would undoubtedly link up with the Egyptian army in a drive to repel the Israeli defense forces (IDF) from the west bank of the canal. Kissinger was adamant that the United States would not allow the destruction of the Third Army. "An endless exchange of telephone calls between Washington and Jerusalem" in the early morning of October 25 ended with a U.S. demand that Israel grant a one-time permit to allow an Egyptian convoy of nonmilitary supplies through to the Third Army. If Israel did not acquiesce, it would find itself in "a crisis situation with the United States." The Israeli cabinet unanimously decided around 5 P.M. (Washington time) to permit the passage of one hundred supply trucks. Israel limited its compliance to allowing the passage of a single convoy, which necessitated a partial lifting of the siege.[69]

While pressing Israel, Kissinger promised that the United States would resist Soviet intervention by force, if necessary. He did not rule out the dispatch of a U.S. military contingent to Sinai and asked Dinitz "how long it would take Israel to destroy the Third Army if a showdown became unavoidable."[70] These remarks indicated that in a case of confrontation, Kissinger hoped to limit it to Sinai.

Now the United States waited for the Soviet reaction. All indications in the early morning of October 25 seemed to be that the Soviets were moving to confrontation.[71] The publicity the U.S. alert unexpectedly received made Kissinger concerned that it would be very difficult for the Soviets to retreat because it "would inevitably turn the event into an issue of prestige for Moscow."[72] However, an important development around 8 A.M. moderated the crisis. Messages from Ismail and Sadat to Kissinger and Nixon indicated that Egypt was withdrawing the request for a joint U.S.-Soviet force that had triggered the crisis and was ready for an international force that excluded the superpowers. This made it much easier for the United States to resist a Soviet attempt to send troops unilaterally. Kissinger felt the United States was now on the verge of winning the game. Sadat had decided to lean on the United States rather than on Soviet military pressure.[73]

At 10:15 A.M., Kissinger convened the WSAG once again; he was worried that the Soviets did not seem to be interested in resolving the crisis. The meeting concluded with Kissinger's request for a contingency plan for sending U.S. forces to the Middle East.[74] Shortly after noon, Kissinger appeared before the press. After reviewing the diplomatic efforts of the first two weeks, Kissinger spoke of the immediate crisis. He reiterated Washington's objection to the sending of U.S.-Soviet forces to the Middle East and opposed even more strongly a unilateral Soviet move into the area. Kissinger carefully suggested to the Soviets a way out without loss of prestige. He declared that the Soviet Union had not yet taken any irrevocable action and that the United States was not asking it to pull back from anything it had done: "We are not yet prepared to say that they have gone beyond their limits." He offered the Soviets cooperation in passing a resolution that permitted the introduction of U.N. forces with the exception of units from the permanent members of the Security Council.[75]

A few hours later, at 2:40 P.M., Dobrynin passed along a new message from Brezhnev. "It was written," Kissinger observes, "as if the crisis of the night before had never occurred." Brezhnev maintained that he had dispatched 70 Soviet "representatives," apparently not military personnel, to observe implementation of the ceasefire, as the United States had decided to send U.S. observers to Egypt with the same task. Brezhnev's message indicated that the Soviets had backed off, apparently satisfied with the way the crisis was being terminated. It is possible that Soviet leaders concluded that their threat of intervention had succeeded in persuading Nixon and Kissinger to get the Israelis to halt their efforts to destroy the Egyptian Third Army.[76]

On the afternoon of October 25, the Security Council passed Resolution 340, calling for an immediate ceasefire, a return to the lines of the original ceasefire of October 22, and the dispatch of an international observer force that would include no U.S. or Soviet units. This resolution represented the end of the crisis between the superpowers.

Specialists on the Soviet Union have advanced the view that the Soviets did not intend to intervene militarily. They only threatened to intervene and made their threat credible by maintaining several alerts of military forces as signals to persuade the United States to pressure Israel to stop the war before totally defeating Egypt.[77] One can attribute to Soviet leaders a strong belief, coupled with anger, that Nixon and Kissinger had not fulfilled their obligation to ensure that the Israelis observed the ceasefire that Brezhnev and Kissinger had agreed to in Moscow. Without doubt the Soviets were concerned over the consequences of Egypt's defeat, and they probably felt tricked by Israel and the United States as the Israelis exploited the real or alleged violations of the ceasefire to destroy the Third Army.

With the benefit of hindsight and comparison with earlier cases, one can regard the Soviet threat to intervene militarily in October 1973 as a legitimate and perhaps necessary step to prevent its client from suffering an even more catastrophic defeat. Compared to the earlier Middle East crises, the Soviets now had a much better military capability for intervening, which was demonstrated by their intervention in the War of Attrition. Perhaps the U.S. failure to prevent Soviet military intervention in the War of Attrition contributed to the perception in Washington that the Soviets would be willing to intervene this time, if necessary.

Kissinger appears to have considered Soviet military action a possibility, especially because he thought Moscow could not tolerate another decisive Israeli victory. For Nixon and Kissinger, as for Johnson in 1967, it did not matter in a sense whether the Soviet threat was real or not; the United States had to react firmly once it was made. But Washington certainly could not limit itself to pressuring Israel to stop its action against the Egyptian Third Army in response to Brezhnev's threat, for this would portray the United States as bowing to Soviet pressure.

The U.S. alert, therefore, was intended not merely—and perhaps not primarily—to deter a possible Soviet intervention but also to demonstrate that the United States could not be coerced by the Soviet threats into pressuring Israel to stop.[78] The Soviets probably did not expect the United States to alert its nuclear forces. After all, Washington had not done so in previous Middle East crises. Possibly, too, Moscow thought that détente would prevent the United States from reacting so firmly. Nevertheless, notwithstanding the U.S. strategic alert and the subsequent superpower confrontation, the Soviet threat did accomplish what the Soviet Union had sought—a termination of the war before Egypt suffered a more shattering defeat.

THE ROLE OF DÉTENTE IN THE CRISIS

A new factor in this latest Middle East crisis was the U.S.-Soviet détente that had been formalized at the Moscow summit of May 1972. Four observations can be made regarding the impact of détente in this new crisis. First, by placing a hold on the unresolved Arab-Israeli conflict, the détente agreements at the Moscow summit in May 1972 severely exacerbated Sadat's impatience and desperation. Second, the improvement of U.S.-Soviet relations and their effort to create a crisis prevention procedure as part of the détente process did not suffice to prevent the war. Third, détente did not restrain either of the superpowers, once the war started, from trying to make gains for their clients and for themselves until developments led to a superpower confrontation. Finally, although the détente process did survive the October war, it was definitely weakened. Laid bare were some of the ambiguities and limitations of the détente undertaking, in particular the inadequacies of the poorly conceptualized and inadequately implemented crisis prevention regime that had been set forth in parts of the Basic Principles Agreement at the first summit and the Agreement on Prevention of Nuclear War signed at the second summit of June 1973 in the United States. The October War began the process of disabusing both superpowers of some of the hopes and expectations they had attached to détente and, certainly in the United States, seriously weakened public support for a continuation of the détente process.

It is interesting to note that in order to limit the damage to détente, Nixon and Kissinger quickly made public statements to the effect that détente had proven itself because it had helped the superpowers to terminate the war and to avoid a more serious confrontation. At a press conference on October 26, 1973, Nixon stated that "without détente, we might have had a major conflict in the Middle East. With détente we avoided it."[79] Similarly, Kissinger stated in his press conference on November 21, 1973: "The relationship that had developed between the two governments and between the two leaders played a role in settling the crisis even though it had not yet been firm enough to prevent the crisis."[80] In his memoirs, Kissinger writes: "Détente had not prevented a crisis. . . . But I believe détente mitigated the succession of crises that differences in ideology and geopolitical interests had made nearly inevitable."[81]

ANALYSIS: PROBLEMS OF CRISIS MANAGEMENT

As in the 1967 and 1970 crises, the irreconcilable conflict of interests between Israel and the Arab states was the fundamental obstacle to avoiding another war. Arab-Israeli enmity imposed major constraints on the ability and willingness of their superpower patrons to cooperate in crisis prevention and in crisis management. Moscow and Washington each had complex interests in the Middle East, several of which conflicted with one another. At various points in the crisis, each superpower was confronted with the challenging task of balancing its competing interests. Each superpower attempted to promote its client's interests as well as its own so long as it was possible to do so simultaneously. When this was no longer possible, the task was to try to restrain the regional ally from pursuing its own objectives in ways that jeopardized important interests of its superpower patron.

The divergence of interests imbedded in each superpower-patron relationship was compounded by the tension between the several objectives each superpower pursued in its relationship with the other superpower. Thus, a superpower's desire to advance its own and its patron's interests came into conflict with its need to avoid plunging into a war-threatening confrontation with the other superpower. Similarly, both superpowers were restrained to some extent in 1973 by a desire not to damage too severely the détente relationship they had only recently achieved.

It required extremely fine tuning of its crisis behavior by each superpower to avoid undue damage to any of its conflicting interests. The detailed history of the 1973 crisis that has been presented richly illustrates the playing out by each superpower of the trade-offs between its competing objectives, the persistent struggle each superpower had with its stubborn client, and the difficult challenges Moscow and Washington experienced in dealing with each other. Their efforts to fine-tune their actions in order to advance some of their objectives while, at the same time, trying to manage and terminate the war before other major interests were severely damaged were reasonably successful in the end; but the efforts can hardly be regarded as a model of virtuosity in crisis management.

The section Analysis: Problems of Crisis Management is co-authored with Alexander L. George.

The United States was more successful in this respect than the Soviet Union, for Moscow did lose its position of influence with Egypt to the United States. More important, both superpowers were successful in crisis management in that, after much fumbling, they finally succeeded in ending their increasingly tense confrontation without being drawn into a shooting war with each other. However, the crisis did inflict serious damage to their overall relationship and contributed to the erosion of the détente process they had only recently established.

Several threats and obstacles to crisis management deserve more specific attention. Superpower cooperation to obtain an early termination of the war was half-hearted and perfunctory, thereby allowing the fast-moving war to develop in a more dangerous direction. While ostensibly trying to cooperate in order to bring about a quick ceasefire, in fact each superpower attempted to obtain the type of ceasefire that would favor its regional client. The Soviets wanted a ceasefire in place, which would allow Egyptian and Syrian forces to remain in the territories gained by their initial attack. Washington spoke of a ceasefire linked to a return of forces to their original line, but actually it hoped to delay a ceasefire until the expected counterattack by Israeli forces could yield a substantial military success. Initial disagreement on the type and timing of a ceasefire led to a decision by each superpower to wait either until its regional ally improved its battlefield situation or until its regional client was threatened by a major defeat.

This threat to crisis management was compounded when first the Soviets and then the United States rushed military supplies to its client to enable it to improve its performance on the battlefield. The superpowers' objective in so doing, however, was not to bring about a stalemate that, once recognized by the belligerents, would facilitate efforts to achieve a ceasefire. Rather, each superpower's resupply of its client was aimed at enabling it to achieve a substantial battlefield success that would yield political payoffs to the superpower as well as to its client.

Hence, instead of doing what they could to slow down the momentum of events—often a critically important requirement for crisis management—in order to give diplomacy an opportunity to end the conflict, the superpowers competed in rapid resupply of their clients to facilitate and speed up efforts to achieve battlefield success.

At the same time, as noted earlier, the superpowers attempted to fine-tune their efforts to control the risks of the enterprise. Not surprisingly, the effort to promote some of these interests without jeopardizing others proved too ambitious a crisis management task for several reasons. In the first place, it was difficult for policy makers in Washington and Moscow to obtain prompt, reliable intelligence on the rapid, confusing course of the battle. What is more, there were striking differences in the information on battlefield developments available in Moscow and Washington that severely complicated their efforts to synchronize efforts to bring about a stable ceasefire during the tense days that followed initial Israeli military successes on the Egyptian front. The difficulty the United States experienced in this respect was compounded by Israel's reluctance or inability to supply Washington with up-to-date and accurate information as to the activity and intentions of its military forces after they crossed the canal and began to cut off the Egyptian Third Army. (It is not certain that the top-level Israeli political authorities were able to exercise tight control over military commanders in the field or that they had up-to-date, reliable information themselves on all battlefield developments.)

Effective crisis management depended upon the workings of an intricate network of communications between each superpower and its regional client, between the superpowers themselves, between top political authorities in Egypt and Israel and their respective military forces on the battlefront, and, in the case of the United States, between it and Egypt. The flow of communications in this network could not keep up very well with the rapidly changing, at times confusing, situation. Eventually, the necessary communications were made, correctly understood, and acted upon in time by all parties concerned, but this occurred only after several days of flawed communications and judgments that raised tensions to very high levels. The war was brought to an end when the Soviet Union, out of desperation, threatened unilateral intervention if the United States did not finally restrain Israel.

One may properly ask whether the war could have been ended earlier, before the Soviet threat of intervention and the strategic DefCon 3 alert by the United States. Could some of the flaws and obstacles to crisis management that contributed to this tense superpower confrontation have been avoided? With the benefit of hindsight, to be sure, it is clear that crisis management was made much more difficult insofar as both superpowers attempted to derive important gains from the war for themselves and for their clients. While neither superpower had wanted another Arab-Israeli war, once it occurred both Moscow and especially Washington saw in it opportunities for gain. Both pursued objectives that were sufficiently ambitious as to make a quick termination of the conflict virtually impossible. In addition to violating an important political requirement of crisis management— namely, the limitation of objectives—the superpowers were surprisingly inept when they finally saw the need to cooperate in good faith to bring about a ceasefire. We have reference to the failure of Brezhnev and Kissinger, when working out the terms of a ceasefire in Moscow, to add a provision for monitoring it, the absence of which soon contributed to its breakdown.

The possibility of achieving an effective, stable ceasefire several days earlier than it was finally concluded was lost when the United States failed to ensure Israel's compliance. Admittedly, there was the formidable obstacle of Israel's determination to go as far as possible in destroying the Egyptian Third Army, which only very determined, timely pressure from Washington might have forestalled. But, as we have seen, such an effort was not forthcoming. The problem of obtaining timely, reliable intelligence on the battlefield situation contributed to this failure, but it does not carry the full burden of explanation. The available facts suggest also that Kissinger's perception of the situation and his way of dealing with it hindered the translation of his agreement with Brezhnev into a stable ceasefire. There is not only the likelihood that, on his stopover in Jerusalem, he gave some encouragement to Israeli leaders to press their military success. In addition, Kissinger seems himself to have wanted a full and unmistakable setback for Egypt and the Soviets before the war terminated. When the right moment arrived, he would intervene to prevent the Israeli army from crushing the Egyptian forces, thereby fully demonstrating to Sadat the Soviet Union's impotence, emerging as Egypt's savior, and replacing the Soviet Union as Egypt's friend.

There was perhaps a touch of overconfidence and miscalculation in Kissinger's belief that he could orchestrate developments leading to the termination of the war on his own terms and according to his own scenario. Certainly, he did not expect that Sadat, increasingly desperate over the fate of the Third Army, would suddenly request joint U.S.-Soviet intervention, a development Kissinger had to work hard to undo. He did not succeed in doing so before the Soviets were encouraged to advance a similar suggestion. The Israelis, in the meantime, not yet placed under significant pressure from Kissinger, continued to press the Egyptian Third Army until Brezhnev made his threat of a unilateral Soviet intervention, again a development Kissinger had not expected. Hence, through a combination of overconfidence, miscalculation, ineptness, and bad luck, Kissinger inadvertently contributed to the development of the superpower confrontation.

The lesson in this crisis, as well as in several others, appears to be that an effort to optimize the gains that a crisis seems to offer is laden with risks that cannot be easily foreseen or controlled. Hence, the temptation to exploit opportunities for gain in a crisis must be disciplined and either avoided altogether or moderated.

Finally, we should take note of a threat to crisis management that fortunately did not materialize.[82] Both the United States and the Soviet Union used their naval forces in the Mediterranean for political signaling throughout the crisis. The Soviet Mediterranean squadron, substantially augmented since the earlier Middle East wars of 1967 and 1970, conducted operations on a much larger scale than previously. Moreover, Soviet ships were deployed and operated in ways that clearly conveyed that their objective was to deter the U.S. Sixth Fleet from participating in the war. It was, indeed, the first U.S.-Soviet confrontation in which Soviet naval forces posed a significant and unmistakable threat to the U.S. navy.

In a crisis situation of this type, the possibility of clashes between the naval forces of the two sides is ever present. Such incidents can serve as triggers for escalation whether they result from accidents of one kind or another, whether they take place through the unauthorized actions of a local commander, or whether— as in the *Vincennes* incident in the Persian Gulf—they are authorized by rules of engagement that give a local commander discretion to launch preemptive military action when he determines there is a threat of an attack by hostile forces.

The possibility of one or another type of incident between U.S. and Soviet naval forces was clearly present during the 1973 war. Tactical-level interactions between their ships were intense: Soviet "tattletale"[83] ships and land-based aircraft closely monitored the Sixth Fleet. Armed with antiship cruise missiles, they kept U.S. aircraft carriers that ventured into the eastern Mediterranean constantly within range. This threat, in turn, was countered by preparations by the Sixth Fleet to immediately fire upon the Soviet vessels on indication of a Soviet attack. During much of the crisis, U.S. and Soviet naval vessels "were constantly maneuvering for tactical advantage, attempting to be in a favorable position to instantly strike the first blow in the event of hostilities."

Tensions were particularly acute during the October 26–31 period when, after U.S. strategic forces were placed on a DefCon 3 alert on October 25, Soviet ships engaged in highly threatening, provocative exercises against the U.S. aircraft carriers. Bouchard reports, "It is not clear how quickly the [U.S.] Navy discerned that the

Soviet anti-carrier activities were on an exercise rather than an actual attack." Quite clearly, in this type of situation, prompt and reliable tactical intelligence and cool judgment are essential factors if military incidents are to be avoided.

It should be noted that the White House imposed political constraints on the Sixth Fleet, in the interest of crisis management, that were clearly at odds with sound military logic. Thus, the Sixth Fleet was ordered to remain in small, fixed operating areas to avoid movements that might have proven to be inconsistent with Washington's efforts to provide Moscow with reassuring signals. In consequence, the Sixth Fleet commander was deprived of some freedom of maneuver needed to reduce the vulnerability of his ships to a Soviet preemptive strike. Soviet naval commanders must have experienced similar concerns due to the targeting of their vessels by the Sixth Fleet.

Despite the intense tactical-level interactions between the two naval forces, no dangerous incidents or collisions at sea occurred. In the main, both sides observed the provisions of the Incidents at Sea Agreement concluded by the United States and the Soviet Union in 1972. Noteworthy, too, is the fact that Soviet ships did not engage in highly provocative maneuvers to harass units of the Sixth Fleet as they had during the 1967 war.

BIBLIOGRAPHICAL NOTE

Important material on U.S. policy is contained in Henry A. Kissinger, *Years of Upheaval* (Boston: Little, Brown, 1982). Also important are Richard M. Nixon, *Memoirs* (London: Sidgewick and Jackson, 1978); Alan Dowty, *Middle East Crisis: U.S. Decision-Making in 1958, 1970 and 1973* (Berkeley: University of California Press, 1984); and Steven L. Spiegel, *The Other Arab-Israeli Conflict: Making America's Middle East Policy from Truman to Reagan* (Chicago: University of Chicago Press, 1985). Analysis of Soviet policy is provided by Galia Golan, *The Yom Kippur War and After* (Cambridge: Cambridge University Press, 1977). Important for understanding Israeli policy are the accounts in Moshe Dayan, *Story of My Life* (London: Weidenfeld and Nicolson, 1976); Hanoch Bartov, *Dado: 48 Years and 20 More Days* (Tel Aviv: Ma'ariv Book Guild, 1981); and Shlomo Nakdimon, *Low Probability* (Tel Aviv: Revivim, 1982) (Hebrew). Egypt's policy and decision making are documented in Anwar el-Sadat, *In Search of Identity* (New York: Harper & Row, 1978); Mohamed Heikal, *The Sphinx and the Commissar: The Rise and Fall of Soviet Influence in the Middle East* (London: Collins, 1978).

For an analysis of relations between the superpowers and their regional allies during the 1973 war that employs an explicit theoretical framework, see also Yaacov Bar-Siman-Tov, *Israel, the Superpowers and the War in the Middle East* (New York: Praeger, 1987); and Christopher C. Shoemaker and John Spanier, *Patron-Client State Relationships* (New York: Praeger, 1984).

A systematic comparative analysis of Soviet threats in a number of Arab-Israeli conflicts is provided in Uri Bar-Joseph and John P. Hannah, "Intervention Threats in Short Arab-Israeli Wars: An Analysis of Soviet Crisis Behavior," *Journal of Strategic Studies* 11, 4 (December 1988): 437–67.

NOTES

1. Henry A. Kissinger, *White House Years* (Boston: Little, Brown, 1979), p. 1279.
2. Ibid., pp. 1288–1289.

3. Anwar Sadat, *In Search of Identity* (New York: Harper and Row, 1978), p. 229.

4. Henry A. Kissinger, *Years of Upheaval* (Boston: Little, Brown, 1982), p. 206.

5. Jon D. Glassman, *Arms for the Arabs: The Soviet Union and War in the Middle East* (Baltimore: Johns Hopkins University Press, 1975), pp. 88–89.

6. Ibid., p. 98.

7. Ibid., p. 99; Sadat, *In Search of Identity*, p. 238.

8. Mohamed Heikal, *The Sphinx and The Commissar: The Rise and Fall of Soviet Influence in the Middle East* (London: Collins, 1978), p. 254.

9. The text of the Basic Principles Agreement is reproduced in *Department of State Bulletin*, June 26, 1972, pp. 898–899. For discussion see Alexander L. George, "The Basic Principles Agreement of 1972: Origins and Expectations," in *Managing U.S.–Soviet Rivalry*, (Boulder, CO.: Westview Press, 1979), pp. 107–118.

10. The text of the Agreement on Prevention of Nuclear War is reproduced in Kissinger, *Years of Upheaval*, pp. 1234–1236.

11. Richard M. Nixon, *Memoirs* (New York: Grosset & Dunlap, 1978), p. 885; see also p. 1031. Kissinger, too, recalls that Brezhnev and Gromyko warned of the danger of war both in Moscow in early May of 1972 and at the second summit in June 1973. "But we dismissed this," he adds, "as psychological warfare because we did not see any rational military option that would not worsen the Soviet and Arab positions." *Years of Upheaval*, p. 461. Kissinger's account contains important new information about intelligence warnings of the Arab attacks and the American response to them. Ibid., pp. 461–465.

12. Kissinger, *Years of Upheaval*, pp. 467–468; Alan Dowty, *Middle East Crisis: U.S. Decision-Making in 1958, 1970 and 1973* (Berkeley: University of California Press, 1984), pp. 226–227; Nixon, *Memoirs*, pp. 921–922.

13. Nixon, *Memoirs*, p. 921; Kissinger, *Years of Upheaval*, p. 468.

14. Kissinger, *Years of Upheaval*, pp. 471–472, 478; Dowty, *Middle East Crisis*, p. 227.

15. Kissinger, *Years of Upheaval*, pp. 489–490.

16. Galia Golan, *The Yom Kippur War and After* (Cambridge: Cambridge University Press, 1977), p. 81; Golan, "Soviet Decisionmaking in the Yom Kippur War, 1973," in Jiri Valenta and William Porter, eds., *Soviet Decisionmaking for National Security* (London: George Allen & Unwin, 1985), p. 201; Alvin Z. Rubinstein, *Red Star on the Nile* (Princeton: Princeton University Press, 1977), pp. 266–267.

17. Kissinger, *Years of Upheaval*, p. 492; Golda Meir, *My Life* (New York: Dell, 1975), p. 415; Shlomo Nakdimon, *Low Probability* (Tel Aviv: Revivim, 1982) (Hebrew), pp. 168–169; Matti Golan, *The Secret Conversations of Henry Kissinger* (New York: Quadrangle, 1976), p. 48.

18. Kissinger, *Years of Upheaval*, pp. 495–496; William B. Quandt, *Decade of Decisions: American Policy Toward the Arab-Israeli Conflict 1967–1976* (Berkeley: University of California Press, 1977), p. 176; Nixon, *Memoirs*, p. 992; Mordechai Gazit, *Maariv*, 7 October 1981.

19. Kissinger, *Years of Upheaval*, pp. 504 and 507.

20. Golan, "Soviet Decisionmaking in the Yom Kippur War," p. 202.

21. Kissinger, *Years of Upheaval*, p. 508.

22. Ibid., p. 510.

23. Moshe Dayan, *Story of My Life* (London: Weidenfeld and Nicolson, 1976), pp. 527–528; Hanoch Bartov, *Dado: 48 Years and 20 More Days* (Tel Aviv: Ma'ariv Book Guild, 1981), p. 444.

24. Kissinger, *Years of Upheaval*, p. 509; Hanoch Bartov, *Dado*, p. 444. Abba Eban, *An Autobiography* (New York: Random House, 1977), p. 515; Nakdimon, *Low Probability*, pp. 200–201.

25. Kissinger, *Years of Upheaval*, pp. 510–511.

26. Glassman, *Arms for the Arabs*, pp. 130–131.

27. Dowty, *Middle East Crisis*, p. 246.

28. Kissinger, *Years of Upheaval*, p. 512.

29. Yaacov Bar-Siman-Tov, *Israel, the Superpowers, and the War in the Middle East* (New York: Praeger, 1987), pp. 210–213.

30. Sadat, *In Search of Identity*, p. 261; Ismail Fahmy, *Negotiating for Peace in the Middle East* (Baltimore: The Johns Hopkins University Press, 1983), p. 31.

31. Quandt, *Decade of Decisions*, p. 184.

32. Kissinger, *Years of Upheaval*, p. 525; Quandt, *Decade of Decisions*, p. 186.

33. Kissinger, *Years of Upheaval*, p. 527.

34. It is not clear whether Sadat's acceptance of the ceasefire preceded or followed Kosygin's departure from Cairo. Sadat has explicitly stated that he made up his mind only after Kosygin's departure. Heikal mentions that Kosygin left Cairo convinced that Egypt was ready for a ceasefire. Sadat, *In Search of Identity*, pp. 259, 264; Mohamed Heikal, *The Road to Ramadan* (New York: Ballantine Books, 1975), p. 241.

35. Kissinger, *Years of Upheaval*, p. 542; Nixon, *Memoirs*, p. 931; Quandt, *Decade of Decisions*, p. 190.

36. Golan, "Soviet Decisionmaking in the Yom Kippur War," p. 207. The Soviets had a Cosmos over the battlefield during October 17–20 which supplied clear pictures of the Israeli crossing.

37. Kissinger, *Years of Upheaval*, p. 542.

38. Kissinger, *Years of Upheaval*, pp. 542–543; Golan, *Secret Conversations*, pp. 75–76; Nakdimon, *Low Probability*, pp. 213–215.

39. Kissinger, *Years of Upheaval*, pp. 547–551; Marvin Kalb and Bernard Kalb, *Kissinger* (New York: A Dell Book, 1975), p. 547.

40. Kissinger, *Years of Upheaval*, pp. 551–552; see also Raymond L. Garthoff, *Detente and Confrontation: American-Soviet Relations from Nixon to Reagan* (Washington: Brookings Institution, 1985), p. 371.

41. Steven L. Spiegel, *The Other Arab-Israeli Conflict: Making America's Middle East Policy from Truman to Reagan* (Chicago: University of Chicago Press, 1985), p. 262.

42. The formal justification for this breach of promise was a "technical hitch" in the transferral of news from Moscow and the lack of time at Kissinger's disposal. Nixon, *Memoirs*, p. 936; Nakdimon, *Low Probability*, p. 216. It appears quite evident that Kissinger had no real intention of consulting Israel, especially given his conviction that he had elicited the best possible agreement under the circumstances.

43. Bartov, *Dado*, pp. 543 and 545; Kissinger, *Years of Upheaval*, p. 559.

44. Kissinger, *Years of Upheaval*, pp. 561–565, 569; Bartov, *Dado*, pp. 550–551.

45. Scott D. Sagan, "Lessons of the Yom Kippur Alert," *Foreign Policy*, 36 (1974), p. 176; Golan, *Secret Conversations*, p. 86. Sagan and Golan do not provide sources for their argument. Dowty, *Middle East Crisis*, p. 254; Quandt, *Decade of Decisions*, p. 193.

46. Kissinger, *Years of Upheaval*, p. 569. According to Eban, Kissinger told him during his meetings in Jerusalem that the ceasefire could come into effect "within a day or two." Eban, *An Autobiography*, p. 532.

47. Bartov, *Dado*, pp. 551–553; Sadat, however, claimed that Israeli forces violated the ceasefire two hours after it had gone into effect. *In Search of Identity*, pp. 265–266.

48. Kissinger, *Years of Upheaval*, pp. 568–569.

49. Ibid., 572; Nixon, *Memoirs*, p. 936.

50. Kissinger, *Years of Upheaval*, p. 572; Nixon, *Memoirs*, pp. 936–937.

51. Kissinger, *Years of Upheaval*, pp. 573–574.

52. Ibid., p. 573.

53. Ibid., p. 575.

54. Ibid., pp. 575-576; Heikal, *The Road to Ramadan*, p. 257.

55. Kissinger, *Years of Upheaval*, p. 578; Bartov, *Dado*, p. 569; Nakdimon, *Low Probability*, p. 225.

56. Kissinger, *Years of Upheaval*, p. 579.

57. Ibid., pp. 579-580; Heikal, *The Road to Ramadan*, p. 257. Also see Quandt, *Decade of Decisions*, p. 195; Nixon, *Memoirs*, pp. 937-938; Kalb and Kalb, *Kissinger*, p. 552.

58. Kissinger, *Years of Upheaval*, p. 582.

59. Ibid.

60. Ibid., p. 584; Nixon, *Memoirs*, p. 957; Dowty, *Middle East Crisis*, p. 256.

61. Kissinger, *Years of Upheaval*, p. 583.

62. Ibid., Nixon, *Memoirs*, p. 938.

63. Kissinger, *Years of Upheaval*, p. 584; Nixon, *Memoirs*, p. 938.

64. Kissinger, *Years of Upheaval*, p. 587; Kalb and Kalb, *Kissinger*, p. 553; Dowty, *Middle East Crisis*, p. 256; Quandt, *Decade of Decisions*, pp. 196-197.

65. Quandt, *Decade of Decisions*, p. 197; Kissinger, *Years of Upheaval*, p. 587.

66. Kissinger, *Years of Upheaval*, p. 589.

67. Ibid., p. 591; Nixon, *Memoirs*, p. 939; Kalb and Kalb, *Kissinger*, pp. 555-556.

68. Nixon, *Memoirs*, pp. 938-939; Kissinger, *Years of Upheaval*, p. 588.

69. Bartov, *Dado*, pp. 572-575; Nakdimon, *Low Probability*, pp. 226-230; Dayan, *Story of My Life*, pp. 551-552; Eban, *An Autobiography*, pp. 535-537; Kissinger, *Years of Upheaval*, pp. 588-590; Quandt, *Decade of Decisions*, pp. 197-198.
In a forthcoming study, which the author has kindly made available to us, Janice Gross Stein cites interview sources which challenge Eban's version that these important telephone calls between Washington and Jerusalem took place in the early morning of October 25, thereby strengthening the alternative interpretation which she and some of her sources favor, namely that Kissinger deliberately delayed pressure on Israel until after the Soviet threat of intervention subsided.

70. Kissinger, *Years of Upheaval*, p. 590; Nakdimon, *Low Probability*, p. 226. According to Nakdimon, Kissinger told Dinitz that Israel should immediately demolish the Third Army in the event of Soviet intervention; see also Sadat, *In Search of Identity*, p. 269.

71. Quandt, *Decade of Decisions*, p. 198.

72. Kissinger, *Years of Upheaval*, p. 591.

73. Ibid., pp. 591-592.

74. Quandt, *Decade of Decisions*, p. 199; Kissinger, *Years of Upheaval*, p. 593.

75. Secretary Kissinger's News Conference of October 25, 1973, *Department of State Bulletin*, November 12, 1973, pp. 585-590; see also Kissinger, *Years of Upheaval*, pp. 594-596.

76. Kissinger, *Years of Upheaval*, p. 597.

77. Golan, "Soviet Decisionmaking in the Yom Kippur War," p. 210; Glassman, *Arms for the Arabs*, p. 164.

78. In her forthcoming study Janice Gross Stein disagrees with the interpretation offered here that Kissinger put immediate pressure on the Israelis at the same time the U.S. alert was undertaken. Her sources support an alternative interpretation, namely that Kissinger deliberately did *not* pressure the Israelis until after the Soviet threat of intervention subsided. In our view, the available data do not resolve the question of which divergent interpretation is correct. (See also footnote 69.)

79. President Nixon's News Conference of October 26, 1973, *Department of State Bulletin*, October 29, 1973, pp. 532-541.

80. Secretary Kissinger's News Conference of November 21, 1973, *Department of State Bulletin*, December 10, 1973, pp. 701–710.

81. Kissinger, *Years of Upheaval*, p. 600.

82. This brief account draws upon the detailed study by Joseph F. Bouchard which incorporates new data obtained from U.S. Navy sources. "Use of Naval Force in Crises: A Theory of Stratified Crisis Interaction," Ph.D. dissertation in Political Science, Stanford University, September 1988.

83. The term "tattletale" is employed by the U.S. Navy to refer to Soviet ships that trail U.S. warships not merely to monitor their movements but also to provide near real-time targeting data to Soviet commanders of ships, aircraft, and submarines that possess capabilities for taking quick hostile action against these U.S. vessels. The presence of a Soviet "tattletale" puts the U.S. naval commander under notice that his ships are constantly targeted for preemptive attack.

FACTORS INFLUENCING CRISIS MANAGEMENT

Introduction to Part Five

Alexander L. George

In preceding sections of this book, we have examined problems and modalities of crisis management in eleven historical cases. Case studies of past crises have several unique advantages for research on this topic. The investigator has an opportunity to ascertain how crisis management developments were experienced by participants in the crisis. Insofar as available data permit, the writer of a case study tries to develop an understanding of how and why each side behaved as it did and to trace the interaction between the participants that led to the outcome. In developing a case study of a historical crisis, the investigator deals with all relevant dimensions of crisis management and attempts to integrate them into a single coherent account.

Research on crisis management is also needed that compares the experiences of different crises and focuses attention on some of the specific problems that are experienced in many crises. At this point in the study, we single out for more detailed examination five of these recurrent problems. One of these is the choice of strategies for crisis management. It will be recalled that Chapter 4 emphasized that strategy of some kind is needed for dealing with the fundamental policy dilemma decision makers experience in attempting to manage a crisis.

Another major problem concerns the critical role of intelligence in anticipating crises and monitoring their development.

A third issue has to do with how policy makers' image of the opponent and their general beliefs about bargaining strategy and the danger of escalation influence their decisions.

A fourth issue arises from the necessity, to which attention was directed in Chapter 3, for top-level policy makers to integrate as best they can military desiderata with the requirements of diplomacy, a task that is dealt with in part by devising and issuing appropriate rules of engagement to military forces.

Finally, a problem that did not receive much attention in our case studies—in good part because relevant data on such matters are difficult to obtain—concerns the effects of crisis-induced stress and fatigue on the performance of decision makers and their advisers.

Efforts to develop international relations theory have highlighted the need to pay more attention to studying the strategic interaction between states. In order to do this well, we need to devote more systematic attention to the strategies by which states seek to influence each other. As used here, the concept of "strategy" is not synonymous with military strategy, the scope of which is too narrow for what we want to address. Rather, as Thomas Schelling emphasized many years ago in his seminal work *The Strategy of Conflict*, strategy needs to be thought of more broadly in terms of how one actor attempts to get another actor to do something it might not otherwise do.[1] Thus conceptualized, strategy provides a link between each side's decision making in a crisis and the "strategic interaction" that takes place as the sides attempt to influence each other toward a preferred outcome of their dispute.

The interaction between strategies the two sides pursue in a crisis strongly influences the nature of the bargaining and negotiation that take place. The strategy each side chooses is, or should be, highly sensitive to the strategy and course of action the other side is pursuing or might adopt. Crises are among the many situations in international politics in which the best course of action for each side depends on what the other side does or is expected to do. The outcomes of crises are also strongly influenced by the interaction between the strategies chosen by the two sides. Developments in game theory have usefully identified a variety of conflict situations in which such strategic choices must be made.

This perspective argues that the outcomes of competitive or conflictual inter-actions between states are not simply determined or reliably predicted by the relative distribution of power between them. The structural variable of relative power is not without importance, as it may well constrain and channel behavior of the two sides to some extent; but the relative power capabilities of the two sides do not strictly determine either their specific choices of action or the outcomes of their interaction. There is considerable room for variation in outcomes depending on a number of other variables: choices of strategy, skill in applying strategy, the values and interests of the two sides, the relative motivation of the two sides aroused by what they perceive to be at stake, and the quality of the knowledge and information relevant to effective crisis management the two sides bring to bear. Additional complexity arises insofar as, as is often the case, all of these variables can change during the course of the crisis.

Each of the chapters in Part Five draws upon a larger body of historical experience and relevant scholarly writing as well as on the findings of the eleven case studies presented earlier in this book. The material in these case studies, although quite relevant to the five topics addressed in Part Five, by no means exhausts the relevant historical experience and the analytical writings already available on these aspects of crisis management.

In Chapter 16, Alexander L. George focuses on the ways in which strategy attempts to deal with the fundamental policy dilemma of crisis management. Policy makers must decide what particular strategy to employ in order to cope with the task of trying to achieve their objectives in the crisis without triggering unwanted escalation. He finds that a surprisingly large number of strategies are available for this purpose and have been used on past occasions. He emphasizes that there is no superior strategy that can be expected to do well in every crisis. Rather, optimal strategy for crisis management is heavily context-dependent. Drawing upon what is known about the successes and failures of different strategies in the past, George offers a provisional assessment of the conditions that favor each strategy as well as some of its major vulnerabilities. He finds it useful to distinguish between strategies designed for pursuing *offensive* goals in a crisis—for example, when a state deliberately initiates a crisis or decides to utilize an existing crisis in order to obtain favorable changes in a status quo situation—and *defensive* strategies that are intended to prevent an adversary from changing the status quo. George discusses five offensive and seven defensive strategies in his effort to develop a comprehensive typology of crisis management strategies.

Chapter 17 by Stan A. Taylor and Theodore J. Ralston addresses the enormously important problem of improving the quality and timeliness of intelligence and its effective use by policy makers in all stages of a crisis. Included among these problems is the well-known one of providing warning of an impending crisis. In addition, there are the problems of producing quick and reliable diagnoses of a crisis at the beginning and as it develops over time and making timely and correct estimates of the adversary's intentions and likely responses to one's own moves. The tasks of intelligence in crisis management are numerous, often critically important, usually difficult, and likely to encounter severe obstacles in their implementation.

Taylor and Ralston analyze the impediments to good crisis intelligence that stem from communication problems between intelligence specialists and policy makers; from bureaucratic problems and compartmentation of intelligence within different parts of the intelligence community; from various well-known but difficult to correct psychological impediments in processing intelligence and gaining a hearing for its findings; and from ideological and political constraints that often impinge on the tasks of producing intelligence and gaining policy makers' receptivity to it. Finally, the authors of this chapter offer a number of suggestions for enhancing the role of intelligence in crisis management.

We emphasized in Chapter 3 the importance of the rules of engagement (ROEs) that top-level political leaders provide their military forces. The use of force and threats of force—indeed, all actions taken by different military units—should be coordinated with and made to serve the crisis objectives and the strategy for achieving them chosen by central political decision makers. Chapter 3 listed and briefly discussed eight different options for employing military forces as an instrument of crisis management policy. ROEs provide instructions and guidance to military forces regarding the circumstances and ways in which different military options may be undertaken. The purpose of ROEs is to make force a controllable as well as a relevant instrument of policy.

In Chapter 19, Scott D. Sagan examines how rules of engagement have been utilized to balance the need for top-down guidance on the use of force with the need for enough flexibility to enable field commanders to take appropriate action. He identifies two general types of ROE failures. One of these occurs when military forces erroneously exercise the discretionary authority given them by the ROE to take hostile action in self-defense on the basis of what turns out to be an incorrect perception of threat to themselves. The opposite type of ROE failure occurs when the defending military force is indeed threatened by an actual attack that is in process but does not exercise the right to self-defense in a timely manner and, as a result, becomes the victim of hostile action. The shoot-down of an Iranian commercial plane by the *USS Vincennes* is an illustration of the first type of ROE failure. An earlier incident in which the USS *Stark* suffered a damaging attack from an Iraqi military plane illustrates the second type of ROE failure. Differences in the provisions for self-defense in the ROEs on these two occasions may have contributed to each failure.

Sagan provides a detailed discussion of several issues that must be addressed in devising ROEs that govern the way in which force may be used. He draws upon the Bay of Pigs invasion and the Cuban Missile Crisis to identify other difficulties that can arise from the ways in which ROEs are formulated and implemented.

Sagan's conclusion is a sobering one: There is no perfect solution to ROE problems. As in any complex organization, "there is an inevitable trade-off between centralized and decentralized decision making." Different ROEs balance in different ways the competing requirements of centralized control and decentralized application of initiative and judgment. Sagan observes that even if ROEs are relatively well chosen and well drafted, "they can nevertheless fail to produce the desired military action in the fog of the crisis." He concludes with several recommendations for reducing the likelihood of ROE problems.

In Chapter 18, J. Philip Rogers addresses an important puzzle: Why do different members of a policy-making group, such as the ExComm in the Cuban Missile Crisis, often disagree so sharply on the relative merits of different strategies and options? Related to this is an additional question: Why do different policy makers apply so differently the general principles and requirements of crisis management identified in this study? One familiar answer to these questions that has emerged and enjoys widespread use is that some policy makers are "hawks" and others are "doves." The essence of this distinction appears to be that hawks, more so than cautious doves, generally wish to pursue more ambitious objectives in a crisis, favor tougher actions, and discount the risk that this will trigger unwanted escalation.

As Rogers persuasively argues, the dichotomy between hawks and doves is not a wholly adequate answer to these questions because it fails to incorporate all of the relevant variables that underlie disagreements over crisis policy. Rogers argues that analysis of three general issues on which policy makers hold different beliefs will provide a better explanation—and, incidentally, a basis for prediction—of their disagreement on specific choices of strategy and action in a crisis. These three beliefs are (1) the policy maker's image of the opponent; (2) his beliefs about escalation dynamics—that is, what will and will not trigger escalation; and (3) his beliefs about what constitutes optimal crisis bargaining strategy. Rogers calls the particular combination of an individual policy maker's beliefs on these three questions a "crisis bargaining code." Employing this analytical framework as a starting point, Rogers studies the policy preferences and the views expressed in support of them by a number of high-ranking U.S. policy makers in several crises. From these empirical data, he identifies four basic types of crisis bargaining codes (several of which have variants). Rogers then shows how individual U.S. leaders holding different crisis bargaining codes differed in evaluating the utility and risks of different options in several crises.

Extending his analysis into the realm of cognitive psychology, Rogers argues that crisis bargaining codes act as cognitive prisms that influence an individual's receptivity to and evaluation of information about crisis developments. Such beliefs also shape an individual's expectations as well as his preferences for different strategies. Another contribution of this pioneering study is the analysis of how crisis bargaining codes can lead to misperceptions, miscalculations, and faulty cost-benefit calculations. Rogers offers a trenchant analysis of the function performed by such belief systems in situations in which the amount and quality of available information vary. Thus, in a situation of information overload, a policy maker will be inclined to use his beliefs as a "cognitive shortcut." In a situation of information deficits, these beliefs perform a "gap-filler" function for the policy maker. And in a situation dominated by contradictory information and competing interpretations, a policy maker's crisis bargaining code may serve the function of "arbiter," encouraging him to select information and favor analyses that are congruent with his beliefs.

To illustrate his analysis, Rogers recalls how Dean Acheson drew upon his crisis bargaining code to judge whether Soviet objectives in the Berlin Crisis of 1961 were of an ambitious, offensive nature or were limited, as other advisers argued, to defensive objectives. Similar examples are presented of the role played by such beliefs held by Richard Nixon, Gen. Lucius Clay, Dean Rusk, and Robert McNamara in other crises. In brief, Rogers's study reinforces a sense of caution, indeed sobriety, as to the difficulty of making effective use of general crisis management requirements when members of a policy-making group differ in the beliefs they bring to bear.

Still another threat to effective crisis management arises from the possibly harmful effects of psychological stress and fatigue experienced by policy makers during a tense crisis. The literature on decision making during the Cuban Missile Crisis offers glimpses of the quite varied effects of stress on members of President Kennedy's policy-making group. One of them, Theodore Sorensen, subsequently made the cryptic statement that he had seen at firsthand, "during the long days and nights of the Cuban crisis, how brutally physical and mental fatigue can numb the good sense as well as the senses of normally articulate men."[2] A similar observation was made by Robert Kennedy in his memoir of the Cuban crisis: "That kind of crisis-induced pressure does strange things to a human being, even to brilliant, self-confident, mature, experienced men. *For some it brings out characteristics and strengths that perhaps even they never knew they had, and for others the pressure is too over-whelming.*"[3] Details of what lay behind Sorensen's and Kennedy's observations were lacking for many years; the facts are difficult to ascertain and still remain obscure and disputed. In 1984, Alexander George was told by a high-ranking official in the Kennedy administration that two important members of the president's advisory group (whose names were not revealed) had been unable to cope with the stress, becoming quite passive and unable to fulfill their responsibilities. Their condition was noticeable, however, and others took over their duties.

In these and other cases that have been reported, the dysfunctional effects of stress on a policy maker were highly visible and could be easily recognized by others, thus providing opportunities for timely intervention and compensatory action. But as is well known, undue stress can also have less visible but nonetheless insidious effects on the performance of decision makers.

A great deal is known in general about the ways in which acute psychological stress, fatigue, and sleep deprivation degrade performance of cognitive and judgmental tasks of the kind policy makers must discharge in a crisis. In addition to summarizing this general knowledge, Dr. Jerrold M. Posts's chapter breaks important new ground. Heretofore, the literature on the effects of crisis-induced stress has not distinguished the effects of stress on different personalities. Post emphasizes that different personality types will react differently to stress. He addresses three personality types—compulsive, paranoid, and narcissistic. Two of these personality types, the narcissist and the compulsive, are frequently found in highly successful individuals. The paranoid type is less common but, when present, can have important influences on the decision-making process. The behavioral characteristics of each personality type, Post observes, tend to become accentuated, sometimes severely magnified, under conditions of severe stress. His chapter provides rich descriptions of the transformations that can occur. Dr. Post also addresses the complex interactions between individuals of different personality dispositions in a decision group where power and influence are differentially distributed and points to the flawed decision making and inhibitions on free exchange of information that can result from such interactions.

Dr. Post also calls attention to other psychophysiologic phenomena that can appear in highly stressed individuals. He highlights the dangers inherent in pronounced sleep deprivation; the misuse and abuse of sleeping pills, alcohol, and stimulants such as amphetamines; and the manner in which judgment and decision making can be adversely affected by these physiological and pharmacological effects.

NOTES

1. Thomas Schelling, *The Strategy of Conflict* (Cambridge, MA: Harvard University Press, 1960).
2. Theodore Sorensen, *Decision-Making in the White House* (New York: Columbia University Press, 1964), p. 76.
3. Robert F. Kennedy, *Thirteen Days* (New York: W. W. Norton, 1969), p. 22 (emphasis added).

CHAPTER 16

Strategies for Crisis Management

Alexander L. George

Some months after the Cuban Missile Crisis, Secretary of Defense Robert McNamara observed in testimony before a congressional committee that "[t]oday there is no longer any such thing as strategy; there is only crisis management." In this striking statement, McNamara conveyed one of the major lessons of the missile crisis—namely, that the requirements for prudent crisis management may indeed seriously conflict with and, in the interest of avoiding war, have to be given priority over some of the standard requirements of conventional military strategy.

Contrary to McNamara's injunction, strategy of some kind is necessary for managing and terminating crises without warfare. To understand why this is so requires us to recognize, as noted in Chapter 3, the basic policy dilemma experienced by leaders in war-threatening diplomatic confrontations. Of course, there need be no war-threatening crisis if either side is willing to back off and accept damage to the interests at stake. The policy dilemma arises when neither side is willing to do so—when both sides feel it is necessary to take actions to protect their most important interests at stake *but*, at the same time, avoid actions that may result in a military clash. Some way of coping with this dilemma is essential if inadvertent war is to be avoided. The accomplishment of this task requires a sense of strategy. Policy makers need to devise a strategy appropriate to the specific configuration of a crisis that promises to protect the essential interests at stake without inadvertently triggering war.

Accordingly, we must reject the sharp antithesis that McNamara drew in his testimony between strategy and crisis management. It may be true—and this is what McNamara probably had in mind—that a strategy based solely on standard concepts of military logic will not offer adequate insurance against the risk of unwanted escalation of the crisis to warfare. What will be needed is a strategy that takes into account and balances both military and diplomatic desiderata in order to reconcile, however imperfectly, the two objectives of crisis management.

As stressed in Chapter 3, although military preparations and threats of force are often indispensable for supporting diplomatic efforts in a crisis situation, the logic of military operations—even logic derived from sound military doctrine—can seriously conflict with the logic and requirements of diplomacy. Therefore, the effective management of war-threatening crises requires policy makers to develop and employ strategies and tactics that are sensitive to both diplomatic and military considerations. In such crises, threats of force and movements of military forces must be carefully employed as instruments of diplomacy, not as substitutes for diplomacy.

Optimal strategy for crisis management is extremely context-dependent. While all crises share some characteristics in common, the precise configuration of each crisis varies in ways that have different implications for the selection of an appropriate strategy. In consequence, there is no single dominant strategy that is equally suitable for managing every crisis. Rather, strategy needs to be carefully formulated and sometimes carefully adapted to meet the distinctive configuration of the crisis.

When a crisis erupts, it generally displays features that were not anticipated. Hence, even the best of contingency plans needs prompt reconsideration and adaptation before action is taken, and often such plans need to be set aside and a new strategy for responding has to be improvised. Moreover, since the adversary may respond in unexpected ways, policy makers have to be prepared to make quick changes of strategy during the course of a crisis. Indeed, as we have seen in some of our case studies, some crises offer such difficult dilemmas and unpleasant choices for policy makers that they are forced to exercise considerable ingenuity to improvise an unconventional strategy for meeting the needs of the situation. Finally, as for example in the Cuban Missile Crisis, considerable disagreement within the policy-making group can be expected over the choice of a strategy for managing a crisis. How such policy disagreements are resolved may have as much to do with the relative influence of different advisers and with domestic and alliance constraints as with an analytical resolution of the dispute.

Some strategies for crisis management have riskier escalation potential than others. On the other hand, in certain situations, low-risk strategies may bend so far in the direction of minimizing the risk of escalation that they prove to be less effective or ineffective in protecting the interests at stake in the crisis. It is also possible that a low-risk strategy will inadvertently encourage the adversary to act in a bolder fashion, which then leads to greater escalation that might have been avoided. Thus, unwanted escalation may occur because one side leaned over backward to avoid it.

Of some assistance to policy makers faced with these difficult choices will be an understanding of the variety of strategies available for managing crises. In this chapter, we shall list, discuss, and illustrate these strategies and say something about the conditions under which each strategy is likely to be effective, ineffectual, or highly dangerous. We shall also distinguish between crisis management strategies that are intended to alter an existing situation at the expense of an adversary ("offensive" strategies) and strategies that attempt to prevent or reverse such gains ("defensive" strategies). However, we should keep in mind that there are also highly fluid, unstable situations in which there exists no clearly defined or mutually acknowledged status quo.[1] In order to develop as comprehensive a treatment of these strategies as possible, this chapter will draw not only upon eleven case studies presented in this book but also on a larger body of relevant empirical research and writing that has accumulated over the years.

OFFENSIVE CRISIS MANAGEMENT STRATEGIES

A number of different strategies can be employed for attempting to change an existing status quo at the expense of an adversary. At least five different strategies for dealing with the situation can be identified: (1) blackmail, (2) limited probe, (3) controlled pressure, (4) *fait accompli*, and (5) slow attrition. Some of these strategies only threaten harmful actions (blackmail, for example), while the others involve actions that vary in the type of encroachment or degree of force employed or threatened.

Each of these offensive strategies may be accompanied by reassurances of various kinds to encourage compliance and to reduce risks of escalation by the adversary: Thus, the challenger may convey that its objectives in the crisis are quite limited; that the action taken does not imply a deeper, more pervasive hostility toward the adversary that will express itself in additional challenges in the future; or that the challenger wishes to develop more positive relations with the adversary and is willing to move in that direction after the present crisis is resolved.[2]

1. Blackmail

This familiar strategy has a number of variants. It consists essentially of demanding that the adversary give up something on pain of suffering serious punishment or damage if he refuses to do so. In other words, the challenger uses the blackmail strategy to generate a crisis from which he hopes to benefit. The strategy is attractive insofar as it offers the blackmailer the possibility of achieving a gain without having to use force; when it succeeds, blackmail avoids the risk of unwanted escalation. It is in this peculiar sense that blackmail can qualify as a crisis management strategy.

Blackmail strategy offers the possibility (although not the certainty) that even if the defender calls the blackmailer's bluff and refuses to give what is demanded, he will not necessarily initiate counteraction against the blackmailer. If his bluff is called, the blackmailer hopes he will be free to decide whether to take the punitive action he has threatened (or some more modest version of it) or to drop his demand. But in many situations, the blackmailer must reckon with the possibility that his use of this strategy will provoke his intended victim to seize the initiative himself and take some forceful action of his own. The intended victim, in refusing the blackmailer's demand, also has the option of making a counterthreat to deter the blackmailer from carrying out his threat.

From what has been said, it is clear that blackmail strategy not only is uncertain of success but, also, that it is not a risk-free strategy for generating a manageable crisis. If the blackmail strategy fails, the blackmailer may find himself in a quite different kind of crisis than he expected or wanted. If so, then the blackmailer may find it necessary to back down completely, to reduce his demands to something the intended victim may be willing to provide (thereby defusing the crisis and avoiding escalation), or to resort to another of the offensive strategies to be discussed.

What are some of the factors that affect the efficacy of the blackmail strategy in different contexts? First, and quite obviously, the credibility of the blackmail threat is of critical importance. Also relevant is what may be called the reasonableness or "legitimacy" of the blackmailer's demand. If he can link his demand for a change in the status quo with norms of the international system, the blackmailer can justify his resort to this strategy as a method for rectifying a historical injustice, for meeting a political necessity, or for achieving a security need.

Second, the outcome of a blackmail effort is likely to be influenced by the relative motivation of the two sides in the matter at issue. If what is at stake is much more important to the side employing a blackmail strategy than to its adversary (and, moreover, if the blackmailer's demand benefits from some claim to legitimacy), not only will the blackmail effort be more credible but the adversary will have to decide whether the little that is at stake for him is worth resisting the blackmailer's demand. Anticipating this, the blackmailer may deliberately make only a strategically modest demand, one he hopes will set into motion a sequence of developments that will eventually result in a major gain for himself but, because it calls for a seemingly modest change in the status quo, will be harder for the adversary to reject. If, however, the target of blackmail believes that to accede to the demand will not genuinely appease the blackmailer but only encourage him to make additional demands in the future, he may be reluctant to accede to even a modest demand.

A third factor that can influence the outcome exists when the defender proves to be unwilling to accede to even a modest demand for fear of the reputational costs and the domestic and international costs of knuckling under to a blackmailer. Knowing this, the blackmailer may attempt to make it easier for the victim to save face by offering to follow certain respectable diplomatic procedures, to accept verbal formulations in an agreement that moderate the impression of surrender to blackmail, or even to offer minor concessions of his own. These are, in fact, well-known nuances in the diplomacy of conflict. And, as has been suggested, there are ways in which a blackmailer can try to reduce the risks of his strategy and to increase the likelihood of its succeeding.

This brief analysis of the blackmail strategy suffices to indicate that it has a number of variants. It need not be a crude, vulgar hold-up of the victim; it can be a nuanced strategy that represents itself with considerable plausibility as being an acceptable means of bringing about "necessary" change in a complex situation, a change that can contribute to greater stability and, indeed, even to an improvement in overall relations between the two sides. And, in fact, on occasion diplomatic crises and confrontations initiated through some variant of the blackmail strategy do perform a constructive catalytic function by encouraging a fresh consideration of disputes with high conflict potential. Such crises may, if successfully managed, result in changes in policy that contribute to reduction of tension if not conflict resolution. Thus, while the blackmail strategy has highly unpleasant features and is sometimes employed on behalf of a dangerously expansionist foreign policy, in other contexts the strategy may have a role to play in facilitating peaceful change in interstate relations.

Variants of the blackmail strategy have been utilized on two occasions by the Soviet Union in pressing for changes in Western policy on Berlin and, more generally, on Germany. These are the Berlin "Deadline" Crisis of 1958–1959 and Khrushchev's renewal of the Berlin Crisis with his ultimatum to Kennedy at their meeting in Vienna in June 1961.[3]

2. The Limited, Reversible Probe[4]

In certain situations, the challenger attempts to deal with the policy dilemma of crisis management by initiating a probing action that begins the process of bringing about a favorable change in the status quo but, in the interest of avoiding unwanted escalation, does so by means of an action that can be quickly and easily called off. In this strategy, the action taken to initiate a challenge to the status quo is intended to be both limited and reversible.

This strategy recommends itself particularly when the challenger is uncertain as to whether the adversary is committed to oppose an effort to change the status quo. The probe, then, is intended to force the defender to clarify the ambiguity of his commitment. If the defender's response does not demonstrate an intention to defend the status quo, then the challenger may conclude that he can pursue his effort to change the situation without fear of a response that will trigger unwanted escalation. If, on the other hand, the defender responds to the probe by conveying that he is committed and will act to oppose a challenge to the status quo, then the challenger can either call off the probing action or, at least, not intensify his effort to achieve change. The challenger avoids unwanted escalation by acting in a way that offers an opportunity for monitoring and controlling the risk of escalation.

Although this strategy is a cautious way of seeking to change the status quo, it is not free of the possibility of critical miscommunication, misperception, and miscalculation. The strategy requires that the probing action be sufficiently clear and, indeed, threatening enough so as to force the adversary to signal his commitment in a clear and timely way. But the defender may fail to recognize that the challenger's action is intended as a probe, and, although committed to defend the status quo, the defender may see no need to convey this. The defender's lack of response, in turn, may be misinterpreted by the challenger as indicating that he is not committed to defend the status quo. Or the defender, although in fact committed to do so, may dilute or delay his response in ways that encourage the challenger to mistakenly believe that it is safe to proceed. A third possibility is that even if the defender responds with a sincere effort to convey resolution to defend the status quo, the challenger may find reason to dismiss it as an empty bluff.

Hence the strategy rests upon the challenger's confidence that the risks of his probing action can be correctly monitored and are calculable and controllable. This assumption is not always justified; the challenger may miscalculate and take further action that finally triggers a strong response by the defender. The challenger is then unexpectedly caught up in a situation where he must either back off or engage in possibly risky escalation.

3. The Strategy of Controlled Pressure[5]

This strategy differs from the limited, reversible probe in that the challenger recognizes that the defender is committed to defend the status quo. Nonetheless, the challenger initiates a campaign to alter the status quo by employing low-level options that he believes may erode or bypass the defender's commitment. A strongly motivated, resourceful challenger may contrive small actions that exert pressure against continuation of the status quo that the defender finds it difficult to counter, either because he does not possess appropriate capabilities or options for doing so or because he is reluctant to use them.

Controlled pressure may be exerted by various nonmilitary encroachments on a status quo position, such as interference with or blockade of a defender's access to disputed territory; piecemeal "salami tactics" that encroach on the defender's rights in a series of modest actions; and warnings that the defender's response to such minor provocations will trigger uncontrollable escalation.

This strategy is an attractive one when the structure of the disputed situation contains asymmetries that favor the challenger and handicap the defender. Such asymmetries were present and exploited by the Soviet Union in the Berlin crises of 1948–1949, 1958–1959, and 1961. The outpost of West Berlin the allies were committed to hold was vulnerable because of its geographical isolation. Moscow could hope that its controlled pressure would arouse disagreements among the Western allies and their publics regarding the value of maintaining their position in West Berlin and the level of risk that should be incurred in defending it. Confronted by the controlled pressure exerted by the challenger in a case of this kind, the defender might find it difficult to implement his commitment to defend a vulnerable status quo position. The defender's dilemma is accentuated insofar as the challenger has carefully refrained from initiating any military hostilities and engages only in a variety of nonmilitary encroachments. Subjected to a clever strategy of controlled pressure, the defender is faced with the onerous decision of whether, when, where, and how to initiate use of limited force himself in order to put an end to the nonmilitary encroachments. Caught in this predicament, if the defender is unable to draw a line against continuation of the minor, but cumulative, provocations, he may be forced to accept the gradual erosion of his position. Or he may decide to undertake one of the defensive strategies discussed later in this chapter. The strategy of controlled pressure, as Christer Jönsson indicates in his chapter on the Suez Crisis of 1956, was employed by Gamal Abdel Nasser in nationalizing the Suez Canal Company. The Egyptian leader knew that Britain, France, and, to a lesser degree, the United States were committed to defend the status quo but hoped that his strategy might erode their commitment.

4. The *Fait Accompli* Strategy[6]

We noted earlier that strategy for crisis management is highly context-dependent. We have identified the special conditions under which a challenger may come to regard each of three offensive strategies as an appropriate way of dealing with the fundamental policy dilemma of finding a way to alter a situation in his own favor without triggering unwanted escalation. Under a different set of conditions the *fait accompli* strategy may recommend itself as a suitable means for doing so. When the challenger is confident that the adversary is not committed to defend the position under dispute, that he has for all practical purposes written it off, then the challenger may decide that quick, decisive action is not only the most efficient way to change the status quo but is also risk-free insofar as the likelihood of unwanted escalation is concerned. (Other risks of a *fait accompli* attempt, such as strong domestic or international condemnation or loss of one's reputation as a trustworthy actor, may be recognized by the challenger, however, and may be deemed sufficient to dissuade him from such an attempt.)

A challenger who is considering resort to a *fait accompli* strategy does well to recognize that the adversary, although not committed to defend a particular status quo situation, may change his mind as soon as the *fait accompli* attempt occurs. This risk may give the challenger sufficient concern to decide against making use of the *fait accompli* strategy and to consider using a more cautious offensive strategy. On the other hand, the challenger may conclude that his quick and decisive action will change the status quo so quickly that the defender will not have time to muster the capabilities to resist the *fait accompli* action.

This, then, is the logic or rationale for choosing a *fait accompli* strategy for altering a status quo situation in one's favor. The policy dilemma of crisis management is to be resolved by a quick, decisive transformation of the situation that achieves the challenger's objective and avoids the risk of unwanted escalation. But, of course, *fait accompli* efforts may boomerang, as was the case with the Anglo-French-Israeli attack on Egypt in 1956 discussed by Jönsson in Chapter 9. The challenger may mistakenly assume that his adversary has written off the position he wishes to challenge. The challenger may overestimate his ability—as Khrushchev did in undertaking the secret missile deployment into Cuba—to achieve a quick, decisive transformation of the situation before the adversary can respond. Or, contrary to the challenger's expectations, the adversary may quickly reverse his policy and commit himself to defending the status quo after the effort at a *fait accompli* is launched and before it succeeds—as the United States did after the North Korean attack on South Korea in June 1950.

5. The Attrition Strategy

Under other conditions, a state may seek to change the status quo through the strategy of attrition. It may choose this strategy because it lacks the capacity for a *fait accompli* attempt or because conditions do not favor use of a *fait accompli*, blackmail, limited probe, or controlled pressure strategies. A highly motivated but relatively weak actor can adopt a guerrilla or terrorist form of attrition strategy in an effort to wear out a stronger, but possibly less strongly motivated adversary. A weak actor may also decide to engage in selective military operations (as Nasser did in the War of Attrition against Israel in 1969–1970) hoping to establish ground rules or a set of limitations on combat that cancel out the advantages of a stronger opponent and to sustain such operations over a relatively long period of time in order to force concessions from the opponent. Of course, the stronger opponent (as in the case of Israel's response to Nasser's attrition strategy in 1970 and Moscow's eventual response to Mao's attrition strategy in the 1969 border confrontation) may decide to stop observing the initial pattern of limitations and either escalate military operations in a way that is highly damaging to the initiator or respond with strong and credible threats to escalate the conflict.

DEFENSIVE CRISIS MANAGEMENT STRATEGIES

A number of strategies are available to a defender for thwarting the challenger's effort to change the status quo in his own favor. When the defender is sensitive to the possibility that his response may trigger unwanted escalation, he, too, experiences the fundamental policy dilemma of crisis management: He needs to take action to prevent damage to the interests that are challenged, but, at the same time, he wishes to avoid doing so in ways that could trigger escalation to war (or higher levels of warfare).

Seven different defensive strategies can be identified: (1) coercive diplomacy; (2) limited escalation of involvement to establish ground rules more favorable to the defender, plus efforts to deter an escalatory response by the opponent; (3) tit-for-tat reprisals without escalation, plus deterrence of escalation by the opponent; (4) accepting a "test of capabilities" within the restrictive ground rules chosen by the opponent that initially appear disadvantageous to the defender; (5) drawing the line; (6) conveying commitment and resolve in order to avoid miscalculation by the challenger; (7) time-buying actions and proposals that provide an opportunity to explore a negotiated settlement of the crisis that might satisfy some, if not all, of the challenger's demands.

1. Coercive Diplomacy[7]

The strategy of coercive diplomacy (or "compellance," as some prefer to call it[8]) employs threats of force or quite limited increments of force to persuade the opponent to call off or undo the encroachment in which he is engaged—to induce him, for example, to halt provocations or to give up territory he has seized.

Coercive diplomacy needs to be distinguished from pure military coercion. Coercive diplomacy seeks to persuade the opponent to cease his provocative, aggressive behavior rather than to bludgeon him into stopping it. In contrast to the crude use of force to repel the opponent, coercive diplomacy attempts to use threats of force (and possibly the exemplary use of quite limited force) to persuade him to back down. Thereby the defender hopes to demonstrate resolution and to emphasize the credibility of his determination to use more force, if necessary. The opponent is given an opportunity to stop or back off before the defender resorts to a military strategy for forcing him to do so.

Coercive diplomacy, therefore, is essentially a *diplomatic* strategy backed by the threat of force. To this end, the employment of threats or exemplary military actions must be closely coordinated with appropriate communications to the opponent. All-important signaling, bargaining, and negotiating dimensions, therefore, must be built into the strategy of coercive diplomacy.

Why is coercive diplomacy an attractive defensive strategy for crisis management? Its appeal lies in the possibility of defending threatened interests with little if any bloodshed, with fewer political and psychological costs, and with much less risk of unwanted escalation than would accompany the use of traditional military strategy for defending the interests at stake. The very same attractiveness of coercive diplomacy, however, can make it a dangerously beguiling strategy. Leaders of militarily powerful countries—like Lyndon B. Johnson, for example, in his unsuccessful use of air power against Hanoi in early 1965—are tempted to believe that they can, with little risk to themselves, intimidate weaker opponents into giving up their gains and their objectives. If, however, the opponent refuses to be intimidated and, in effect, calls the bluff of the coercing power, the latter must then decide whether to back off himself or to escalate the use of force.

It is important to identify the conditions necessary for successful employment of this strategy, for, in their absence, even a superpower can fail to intimidate a weak opponent and find itself drawn into a costly, prolonged conflict. Comparison of cases of successful coercive diplomacy (for example, Kennedy's use of this strategy in the Cuban Missile Crisis and Eisenhower's use of it against the British in the Suez Crisis of 1956) with unsuccessful ones (for example, the U.S. oil embargo against Japan in 1941, which boomeranged, provoking the attack on Pearl Harbor) has enabled researchers to identify a number of such conditions. Three in particular appear to be of critical importance: The coercing power must create in the opponent's mind (1) a sense of urgency for compliance with its demand; (2) a belief that the coercing power is more highly motivated to achieve its stated demand than the opponent is to oppose it; and (3) a fear of unacceptable escalation if the demand is not accepted.

However, the defender must recognize that what he demands of the opponent can affect the balance of motivation. If one demands a great deal, as the United States did in its diplomatic confrontation with Japan in 1941, the opponent's motivation not to comply will be strengthened. But if the coercing power can carefully limit its demands to what is essential for itself without damaging important interests of the opponent, then it is more likely to create an asymmetry of motivation that favors the success of the strategy.

The essentials and drawbacks of the strategy of coercive diplomacy have long been known, although its use in the European balance of power era was evidently not systematically articulated. Rather, it was part of the conventional wisdom of those who engaged in statecraft and diplomacy.[9] Coercive diplomacy bears a close resemblance to the ultimatums that were often employed in the conduct of European diplomacy. A full-blown ultimatum has three components: a specific, clear demand on the opponent; a time limit for compliance; and a threat of punishment for noncompliance that is both credible and sufficiently potent to convince the opponent that compliance is preferable. These three components of an ultimatum are not always fully present in efforts at coercive diplomacy. The demand on the opponent, for example, may lack clarity or specificity. It may not be accompanied by a specific time limit for compliance, and the coercing power may fail to convey a sense of urgency. The threat of punishment for noncompliance may be ambiguous, of insufficient magnitude, or lacking in credibility. Generally speaking, dilution of any of these components in the ultimatum may weaken its impact on the adversary's calculations and behavior.

There are several variants of coercive diplomacy. In addition to the full ultimatum version of the strategy already mentioned, there is what has been called the "try-and-see" approach. In this variant of the strategy, only the first element of an ultimatum—a specific and clear demand—is conveyed; the coercing power does not announce a time limit or attempt to create a strong sense of urgency for compliance. The try-and-see form is not uncommon; a coercing power often shies away from employing the ultimatum form for one reason or another. Instead, it takes limited action, as the United States did in attempting to pressure Japan for several years before Pearl Harbor and as Kennedy did in the early stage of the Cuban Missile Crisis. The coercing power then waits to see whether that action will suffice to persuade the opponent before threatening or taking the next step. There are several variants of the try-and-see strategy. In some circumstances, a gradual turning of the screw may be more appropriate than the ultimatum form.

Systematic study of cases of coercive diplomacy has shown that this strategy is highly context-dependent. This means that the strategy must be tailored in a rather exacting way to fit the unique configuration of each situation. But the special configuration of a crisis in which coercive diplomacy may be employed is not always clearly visible or correctly appraised by the policy maker, and, as a result, the strategy can easily fail. For this and other reasons, efforts to engage in coercive diplomacy rest heavily upon skill at improvisation. The policy maker must be able to blend the requirements of strong coercive diplomacy with several somewhat contradictory operational requirements of crisis management. Thus, although coercive diplomacy calls for creating a sense of urgency for compliance, it may be necessary to slow down the momentum of events in order to give the opponent time to digest the signals sent him. And, although coercive diplomacy requires conveying a threat of strong punishment, this warning must not give the impression of an imminent attack that might cause the opponent to launch a preemptive strike. The defender has to choose and time his actions carefully to make it possible for the opponent to appraise the evolving situation and to respond appropriately, and he must always leave the opponent with a way out of the crisis.

As these remarks suggest, coercive diplomacy must be sensitive to some of the important political and operational requirements of crisis management discussed in Chapter 4.

Generally speaking, the strategy of coercive diplomacy is in fact more difficult and problematical than is often thought to be the case. Leaders who consider using the strategy against opponents encroaching on their country's interests often erroneously assume that prevailing conditions favor its successful use, that the communication of their demands and threats will be clear and credible to the opponent, and that they are more highly motivated by what is at stake than the opponent.

Practitioners of coercive diplomacy also often mistakenly rely solely on threats of punishment for noncompliance with their demands instead of also offering positive incentives for compliance. They fail to recognize as clearly as President Kennedy did in the Cuban Missile Crisis that the objectives on behalf of which coercive diplomacy is exercised can sometimes be achieved only if one makes genuine, even substantial concessions. As our case study of the Cuban crisis pointed out, Kennedy and Khrushchev did finally negotiate and agree upon a quid pro quo that ended the missile crisis, Khrushchev agreeing to remove the missiles and bombers in return for Kennedy's pledge not to invade Cuba and to eventually remove the Jupiter missiles from Turkey.

Coercive diplomacy, then, is best conceived as a flexible carrot and stick strategy whereby what the stick cannot always achieve by itself, one can possibly obtain by adding a carrot. Thus, as already noted, in contrast to pure coercion, coercive diplomacy typically requires negotiation, bargaining, and compromise.

The immediate purpose of coercive diplomacy is to convey strong resolution to do what is necessary to protect one's interest. Bargaining and negotiation may be postponed until this tactical objective is achieved, but the willingness to do so must also be conveyed and implemented in a timely fashion at some point in the crisis. No ultimatum can be so final that concessions cannot be made to bring the crisis to a close before it escalates. The importance of timing is crucial in coercive diplomacy. An opponent must be permitted the opportunity to digest the situation as presented to him and to reflect carefully. If adequate time is not provided, his response may well be reckless and ill-considered. Responsibility for pacing events, for determining the appropriate sense of urgency, and for clear communications must be assumed by the nation that adopts this strategy. Feedback on one's initial actions as the crisis evolves must be carefully noted and considered in deciding what to do next. Without skillful orchestration of the strategy, events can easily backfire, producing more harm than good and making victims of all concerned.

Finally, it must be recognized that the outcome of coercive diplomacy depends not on one's absolute power but on those components of power that can be made relevant under the specific circumstances of a particular crisis. To be sure, a strong power has gross capabilities that could, if used, inflict tremendous damage on its opponent. But not all gross capabilities can be used in a crisis. More relevant are the more limited usable options that the leader of a strong power can threaten to turn to in support of coercive diplomacy. The state that engages in coercive diplomacy cannot have full control over the outcome because so much depends on the image of the situation the other side develops and on the conclusions it reaches as a result.

The fundamental danger of the strategy is related to this fact. What may be seen as an inexpensive policy may prove otherwise if the coercing power's bluff is called and action becomes necessary. Coercive diplomacy is a policy that must be rationally and cautiously implemented with an eye to all the dangers and to the limits of what may be obtained. It is a sharp tool—at times useful, but difficult to employ when one is faced with a recalcitrant or unpredictable opponent. Although this strategy often assumes an attraction that is difficult to resist, its apparent advantages must not make it a substitute for more manageable strategies when there are suitable alternatives.

2. The Strategy of Limited Escalation Coupled with Deterrence of Counterescalation

The initiator of a crisis who is concerned over the possibility of unwanted escalation can be expected to pose his challenge in ways that attempt to establish ground rules for the contest that will handicap the defender. Confronted by this situation, the defender—if he forgoes responding with coercive diplomacy or another of the available defensive strategies—may attempt to alter the ground rules favored by the challenger in order to obtain more favorable conditions for crisis bargaining. Accordingly, the defender may engage in limited, selective escalation designed to establish new, more advantageous ground rules and attempt to stabilize them by deterrence of counterescalation by the adversary.

Such a crisis takes on the character of competition for establishing favorable ground rules, for creating a pattern of limitations that will constrain further escalation, and for providing the boundaries within which bargaining to achieve an acceptable crisis outcome will take place. The jockeying for favored ground rules and any threats to escalate made for bargaining purposes will be accompanied by demands and offers and with efforts to persuade the other side—all part of the process of negotiating to achieve a mutually acceptable settlement.

As with other strategies, there are variants of this one. The variant chosen and the outcome will depend upon which offensive strategy the challenger has adopted, various conditions affecting the ability and willingness of the two sides to escalate, and their estimate of prospects and risks.

The War of Attrition case presented by Bar-Siman-Tov in Part Four offers striking examples of the use of this strategy by both sides. The Israelis, finding that their adherence to the restrictive ground rules of Nasser's opening attrition strategy was proving to be highly disadvantageous in terms of casualties incurred, escalated the conflict by engaging in deep penetration air attacks against Egyptian urban centers, which proved very costly to Nasser. Faced with a losing situation, Nasser persuaded the Soviets to engage in counterescalation. Major Soviet defense forces were deployed into Egypt in order to curb Israeli air attacks. The result was a stalemate that led eventually to curtailment of military operations by both sides.

An important variant of this strategy needs to be mentioned. Thus far we have referred only to what is commonly called "vertical escalation" within the geographical area of the crisis. Escalation can also occur when the defender takes actions to damage the challenger in other areas or threatens to do so. The term "horizontal escalation" is given to this variant of the strategy. A threat of broadening the conflict to other areas may be effective for crisis bargaining purposes without having to be implemented. Horizontal escalation is a way of altering or compensating for unfavorable local conditions. The threat of horizontal escalation may also be used to deter counterescalation by the opponent.

Stalin's partial blockade of Western access to West Berlin in 1948 may be regarded as an example of horizontal escalation. The blockade provided leverage for his use of coercive diplomacy to dissuade the Western Allies from proceeding with their unilateral policy for shoring up the economy of the three Western occupation zones and taking steps to unify Western Germany.

3. The Tit-for-Tat Strategy Coupled with Deterrence of Escalation by the Opponent

The defender may be unwilling to adopt the preceding strategy of limited escalation for various reasons, including a concern that it would lead to further, unwanted escalation. He may prefer a policy of carefully measured tit-for-tat reprisals for the provocations he is subjected to. This may be accompanied by an expression of willingness by the defender employing tit-for-tat reprisals to discuss the adversary's grievances and demands.

The reprisals may be chosen to match, but not exceed, the severity of the provocations. If such a restrained use of the tit-for-tat strategy is not successful, the defender—as did the Soviets in the 1969 border clash with the Chinese—may turn to a stronger version of the strategy of reprisal involving actions that are deliberately somewhat more punitive than the provocative actions of the adversary.

Examples of several variants of this strategy and different outcomes thereof are to be found in the long history of disagreements between the Soviet Union and the Western powers over Berlin and Germany.

If the tit-for-tat strategy is unsuccessful, the defender may decide to move to one of the two stronger strategies that have already been discussed. As noted in our case study of the Sino-Soviet border war of 1969, the Soviets finally shifted from a tit-for-tat reprisal strategy to a strong form of coercive diplomacy that evidently persuaded Mao to call off his border provocations.

4. The Test of Capabilities Strategy Coupled with Deterrence of Escalation by the Opponent

The defender may decide that using the strategy of limited escalation to secure more favorable ground rules is too risky or politically unacceptable. Confronted by a low-level, controlled challenge to the status quo, the defender may decide to accept a test of capabilities within the framework of the disadvantageous ground rules and limitations introduced by the carefully chosen opening action of the opponent. Even though these initial ground rules are clearly disadvantageous and seem to point to an unfavorable outcome of the crisis for the defender, he may decide to accept the challenge without, at least for the time being, escalating the conflict or resorting to coercive diplomacy.

In accepting a test of capabilities, the defender hopes that by dint of hard work, skill in improvisation, and efficient use of available resources, he may eventually succeed in reversing the expected outcome of the crisis, thereby transferring to the adversary the onerous decision of whether to engage in a risky escalation or accept the failure of his initiative.

To facilitate successful reversal of the expected outcome, the defender must also deter the adversary from escalating. To this end, the defender may alert and deploy combat forces and generate implicit or explicit threats (as Eisenhower did in the Offshore Islands Crisis of 1958), the purpose of which, however, is not to threaten escalation himself but to deter the frustrated adversary from doing so.

Examples of the successful use of the test of capabilities strategy (backed by deterrence of escalation by the adversary) are to be found in both the Berlin Blockade Crisis of 1948 and the Offshore Islands Crisis of 1958.

5. The Strategy of "Drawing a Line"

In some crises, the most appropriate and acceptable way of responding to an emerging threat to one's interests is to "draw a line" that identifies what action by the opponent would provoke a strong response. By doing so, the defender acts responsibly, not only to protect his most important interests but also in the interest of avoiding an escalation of the crisis that presumably neither side wants. Thereby, the danger of an inadvertent war is avoided.

Drawing a line, however, in effect conveys two messages—what you will *not* respond to as well as what will force you to act. Therefore, employment of this strategy often forces the defender to differentiate between major interests worth fighting for and lesser ones not worth the risk of combat. This is not always an easy or pleasant decision to make, and, under some circumstances, it may lead the defender either to reject this strategy altogether or to try to implement it in ways that blur the line and, therefore, possibly jeopardize its success. A possible disadvantage of drawing a line is that it facilitates the opponent's ability to make reliable risk calculations, making it easier for him to advance up to the line as well as clarifying the risks of going beyond it. But this requires that the line be drawn clearly and in a credible way. Faulty communication by the defender and misperception by the opponent are, therefore, among the vulnerabilities implicit in this strategy.[10]

Another vulnerability of this strategy is that the defender, after having conveyed what interests he will not defend, may change his mind, as the United States did after the North Koreans attacked South Korea in June 1950, and decide to defend them after all. The result will be, as in Korea, an inadvertent war neither side had wanted or expected.[11]

On the other hand, history provides many examples of successful use of the strategy of drawing the line, including crises in which the two superpowers have been indirectly involved. The Carter administration, in a quiet, serious diplomatic way, did so during the Ogaden Crisis of 1977–1978 in order to indicate that it would feel obliged to respond if Ethiopian forces moved from Ogaden into Somalia. The Soviet Union employed the strategy during a tense, war-threatening phase of the Lebanon Crisis in 1983 to indicate that while it would not respond to Israeli attacks on Syrian forces in Lebanon, it would be obliged to do so should the Israeli air force attack targets in Syria itself.[12]

6. Conveying Commitment and Resolve to Avoid Miscalculation by the Adversary

This familiar strategy needs little discussion. Conveying commitment and resolve, of course, is an important component of some of the other strategies already discussed. But under some circumstances, it is a strategy in and of itself. When developments indicate that the adversary may be getting ready to initiate a challenge of some kind to alter the status quo, the defender has an opportunity to discourage him from doing so. The possibility of such a move by the adversary may arise under different circumstances. For example, in the early stages of a crisis, as tension builds up there may be indications that the adversary will take some action to alter the status quo. The tension may have been deliberately created or exacerbated by the adversary by means of rhetorical statements and military preparations as part of a war of nerves strategy designed to elicit concessions and appeasement or to help justify the forthcoming action before public and world opinion. Or the possibility of a challenge to the status quo may emerge during a quiet period as the adversary makes secret preparations for a surprise initiative—for example, a *fait accompli* attempt.

In either of these two scenarios, the defender may receive high-confidence or low-confidence warnings that the adversary will take some action against the status quo. The critical question becomes: How shall the defender utilize the available warning, even when it is equivocal?

There are various uses to which available warning in situations of this kind can be put, which will be discussed shortly. But first it is useful to note that, for various reasons, the defender may downgrade the significance of warning indicators and derive false assurance that the adversary is not going to act. The problem of lack of receptivity to warning has received considerable attention, as noted in the chapter by Stan A. Taylor and Theodore J. Ralston, particularly in the literature on avoiding surprise attack. There are various psychological mechanisms imbedded in the dynamics of individual, small-group, and organizational behavior that often reduce receptivity to warning. This is especially likely when the action predicted by intelligence is something policy makers strongly prefer should not happen or are not prepared to deal with. Not only the individual mind but organizations as well are capable of engaging in various psychological stratagems for discrediting new information that challenges existing expectations, preferences, habits, or convenience. Discrepant information that challenges an existing mind-set is often required, in effect, to meet higher standards of evidence and to pass stricter tests to gain acceptance than new information that supports existing expectations and hypotheses.

All this is well known. Perhaps less well appreciated, although often of great significance, is another impediment to the acceptance of an unwelcome warning that can greatly reinforce the obstacles already mentioned. To take seriously a warning that the adversary may be preparing to challenge a status quo position may require policy makers to make decisions of a difficult, unpalatable character. The policy maker's anticipation of the difficult response he might have to make if he takes the warning seriously may produce a subtle feedback that reduces his receptivity to that very same warning.[13]

What, then, are the various uses to which warning, even of an equivocal character, can be put by the defender? The use of warning encompassed by the strategy under discussion is to convey commitment and resolution to oppose any forthcoming provocation or attack. If the defender has previously signaled a deterrence policy to protect the threatened status quo, this strategy can be used to reinforce that signal in case the adversary might be operating on the assumption that the previously announced deterrence policy was not seriously intended or had been eroded with the passage of time. Or, if the defender had not previously adopted a deterrence commitment, the warning now available gives him an opportunity to do so.[14]

Ways in which deterrence might be reinforced, however, need careful assessment, as they are not necessarily without risks and costs.[15] Alerting and deploying military forces to convey resolution may, under some circumstances, provoke undesirable countermoves by the adversary, which can lead to an unwanted, undesirable escalation of the crisis. Although such a development need not lead to war, it may preclude or make more difficult alternative, peaceful ways of dealing with the conflict of interests through diplomacy.

Even successful reinforcement of deterrence may entail important costs. It may harden the defender's commitment and make it more difficult for him, after the immediate crisis subsides, to recapture the political and diplomatic flexibility that will be needed to find a diplomatic solution to the problem.[16] Successful reinforcement of deterrence may also inflate the ideological dimensions of the overall conflict with an adversary. It may harden the adversary's conviction that the defender is unresponsive to his legitimate interest in changing the distasteful status quo. As a result, the frustrated adversary may resolve to prepare more effectively for the next round by acquiring additional capabilities and new options.[17]

We conclude, therefore, with the observation that the strategy of conveying commitment and resolve to avoid a miscalculation by the opponent, although often necessary and effective, may have one or another of the adverse consequences that have been noted here and therefore should be utilized with caution.

7. The Strategy of Buying Time to Explore a Negotiated Settlement

When facing the possibility that an adversary will challenge a status quo position, or when the adversary has already set into motion a slow-moving challenge, the defender may regard it in his best interest to try to buy time in order to explore the possibility of a mutually acceptable negotiated settlement. This, too, must be regarded as a crisis management strategy that seeks to protect (or to minimize the damage to) one's interests without triggering unwanted escalation. The history of diplomacy offers many instances of successful as well as unsuccessful use of this strategy. And diplomats and specialists in conflict mediation in many other fields as well often stress the importance of getting the antagonists to agree to a breathing spell to be used to explore the possibility of a peaceful, compromise settlement.

There are various circumstances in which this strategy may seem preferable to other defensive strategies, the more so when starting with this crisis management strategy does not exclude shifting to another one if it fails. Buying time for negotiations may recommend itself when the defender feels he is ill-prepared or otherwise handicapped for making effective use of other strategies or when he regards them as generating too great a risk of war. This strategy may also appeal to the defender when he perceives a distinct asymmetry of interests and motivation in favor of his adversary—that is, when what is at stake is genuinely more important to the other side. Buying time for negotiation may also be attractive to the defender when he sees the issue at hand as standing in the way of a major improvement in overall relations with the adversary, which he would welcome.

Thus, crises sometimes pose opportunities for advancing other important interests as well as for dealing with threats to immediate interests. If the threat to immediate interests can be defused through negotiation and accommodation, such a strategy can then open up new possibilities for substantial foreign policy gains. What this strongly implies, therefore, is that how one chooses to respond to a threat to a status quo position in which one has some interest should be judged from a broader strategic perspective.

The Berlin Blockade Crisis of 1948 offers an example of the defender initially resorting to this strategy. The hastily mounted Allied airlift to bring supplies to West Berlin was initially regarded as a time-buying action to give time for negotiations that might persuade Stalin to lift the blockade. When the negotiations failed, the United States and Britain turned to the strategy of accepting a test of capabilities. By dint of hard work, improvisation, and efficient use of resources, the Allies were able—contrary to their initially somber view of its potential—to convert the airlift into an effective instrument for resupply of West Berlin.

CONCLUSION

We have discussed various offensive strategies by which a challenger can move to alter the status quo in his own favor and various defensive strategies available to the defender. We have also suggested that the challenger must anticipate the defender's response in deciding which offensive strategy to choose. Similarly, the defender must gauge how the challenger, having chosen a particular strategy, will respond to his defensive strategy. Thus, the anticipated as well as the actual interactions between the strategies chosen by the two sides will channel the crisis in one direction or another, with both sides free to alter their initial strategies as the crisis proceeds.

Even though in crises of the kind under consideration both challenger and defender choose their strategies with a pronounced desire to avoid unwanted escalation as well as with a need to protect their interests, the sequence of interactions may lead to an inadvertent war.

NOTES

1. This *analytical* distinction between "offensive" and "defensive" strategies can become blurred in some historical situations. It should also be kept in mind that the distinction between "challenger" and "defender" also is opaque in some situations. Thus, the United States regarded itself as employing deterrence strategy to protect the status quo in the Taiwan Straits in the 1950s, but from the viewpoint of the People's Republic of China the United States was the "aggressor" because it was interfering in the Chinese civil war. In other words, each side regarding the other as being the challenger and itself as the defender. On this point, see Alexander L. George and Richard Smoke, *Deterrence in American Foreign Policy: Theory and Practice* (New York: Columbia University Press, 1974), chs. 9 and 12.

2. For a broad discussion of various reassurance strategies that can be employed by the defender as well as the challenger, see Janice Gross Stein, "Deterrence and Reassurance," in Philip E. Tetlock, Jo L. Husbands, Robert Jervis, Paul Stern, and Charles Tilly, eds., *Behavior, Society, and Nuclear War*, Vol. 2 (New York: Oxford University Press, 1991).

3. For brief accounts of these two crises, see George and Smoke, *Deterrence*, chs. 13 and 14.

4. This section draws on George and Smoke, *Deterrence*; see particularly pp. 540–543. According to their analysis the Soviet Union employed the limited probe strategy in the early phase of the Berlin blockade crisis of 1948–49 and in setting up the Berlin Wall in August 1961; the People's Republic of China employed this strategy in the early phases of the Taiwan Strait crisis of 1954–55 and the Offshore Islands crisis of 1958.

5. This section draws on George and Smoke, *Deterrence*; see particularly pp. 543–547. According to their analysis the Soviet Union employed the strategy of controlled pressure in several of the Berlin crises and in the latter phase of the Cuban missile crisis; the People's Republic of China employed controlled pressure in the latter phases of the Taiwan Strait crisis of 1954–55 and the Offshore Islands crisis of 1958.

6. This section draws on George and Smoke, *Deterrence*; see particularly pp. 536–540. Examples of successful faits accompli include the Soviet invasions of Hungary in 1956 and Czechoslovakia in 1968; and the U.S. invasion of Grenada. Examples of abortive fait accompli attempts include the North Korean effort to overrun South Korea in 1950, the Argentine invasion of the Falkland Islands, and the Anglo-French-Israeli military action against Egypt in 1956 discussed by Christer Jönsson in Chapter 9.

7. This section draws on A. L. George, D. K. Hall, and W. E. Simons, *The Limits of Coercive Diplomacy* (Boston: Little, Brown, 1971).

8. I prefer the term "coercive diplomacy" to characterize the defensive use to which "compellant" threats can be put. As generally employed, "compellance" covers offensive as well as defensive uses of such threats. I have used the term "blackmail" to refer to offensive uses of compellance threats.

9. Cf. Paul Gordon Lauren, "Ultimata and Coercive Diplomacy," *International Studies Quarterly*, 16 (1972): 131–165.

10. For an insightful analysis of how problems associated with "drawing a line" can contribute to miscalculated escalation, see Richard Ned Lebow, *Nuclear Crisis Management: A Dangerous Illusion* (Ithaca, N.Y.: Cornell University Press, 1987), pp. 104–109.

11. For a succinct analysis of the origins of the Korean War that advances this interpretation see George and Smoke, *Deterrence*, ch. 6.

12. On the Ogaden crisis, see Larry C. Napper, "The Ogaden War: Some Implications for Crisis Prevention," ch. 10 in A. L. George, ed., *Managing U.S.-Soviet Rivalry* (Boulder, CO: Westview Press, 1983).

13. For a further discussion and historical examples see George and Smoke, *Deterrence*, pp. 572–576.

14. Other uses to which warning can be put include: (1) a step-up in the acquisition of information bearing on the opponent's intentions and a review and reassessment of all existing intelligence indicators; (2) steps to reduce vulnerability and improve readiness of military forces to meet a variety of possible encroachments; (3) rehearsal of the decision problem that will arise if the adversary does challenge the status quo, including reassessment of the commitment and review of the adequacy and relevance of existing contingency plans.

15. Consideration of the various risks of deterrence strategy has led Janice Gross Stein and Richard Ned Lebow to emphasize the importance of various "reassurance" strategies to supplement or replace reliance on deterrence. (See Footnote 2.)

16. Thus, for example, the deterrence success of the Eisenhower administration in the Taiwan Straits crisis of 1954–55 hardened U.S. policy on precisely those relatively peripheral issues on which flexibility later on would have better served overall American interests. This crisis ended with the administration more firmly committed to the defense of Quemoy and Matsu, the offshore islands close to the Chinese mainland, than before and thereby set the stage for another offshore islands crisis in 1958. See George and Smoke, *Deterrence*, ch. 9 and 12.

17. The Berlin crisis of 1961 offers an example of this kind of hidden, delayed cost that deterrence success may entail. Kennedy's success in thwarting Khrushchev's desire for a change in Western policy on West Berlin by invoking American strategic superiority in the autumn of 1961 undoubtedly contributed to Khrushchev's decision the following year to place missiles in Cuba.

For additional discussion of the uses of warning and possible costs and risks of reinforcing deterrence see George and Smoke, *Deterrence*, pp. 576–580.

CHAPTER 17

The Role of Intelligence in Crisis Management

Stan A. Taylor
Theodore J. Ralston

National decision makers require intelligence information to alert them on a timely basis to potentially hazardous events and to allow them to manage crises as they occur. Some may believe that the very existence of a crisis demonstrates an intelligence failure. That is not the case. Not only is it unrealistic to expect that intelligence can correctly anticipate all potentially hazardous events, but the warning by intelligence of such occurrences may not be credited or acted upon by policy makers.[1] Nonetheless, the need for relevant and timely intelligence information to alert policy makers to untoward, threatening actions by other states or nonstate actors is self-evident, and institutional arrangements to provide it have a long history.

In 1947, the United States established a centralized civilian intelligence organization, the CIA, and gave it a virtual monopoly on access to the highest decision-making bodies. Since that time, the terrain between the policy-making apparatus and the intelligence agencies has been a major battleground in a bureaucratic war, the outcome of which shapes the role of intelligence in crisis management. Most significant, and often overlooked, is the fact that this battle has dominated the attention of every new administration during both its transition into office and its early days in office.

Animating much of this attention have been concerns about effective crisis anticipation and management. These concerns have led to a series of both structural and organizational changes made by each successive administration since 1948 in the so-called "intelligence community" (that group of eight separate agencies that provides intelligence to the appropriate foreign policy, diplomatic, and military organizations of the U.S. government).[2] The dominating role played by this concern is not surprising, given that the intelligence community itself grew out of what was

Uri Bar-Joseph, Alexander L. George, Edita Hanley, Ronald H. Hinckley, Mike Murdock, Adm. R. B. Inman, Gloria Duffy, and Valerie Hudson offered helpful comments on earlier versions of this paper.

widely seen as a failure of intelligence in the case of the Japanese attack on Pearl Harbor.

The intelligence and foreign policy bureaucracies of virtually all democratic governments must not only provide information to senior policy makers, they must also synthesize that information and provide continuity. Intelligence agencies provide part of the institutional memory that greases the revolving door that brings, potentially with every election, new faces into senior policy-making roles. In fact, the intelligence community and the foreign policy bureaucracy are perhaps the only sources of institutional memory for crisis management. Such sources do not exist at the policy-making level. A former senior member of the Carter National Security Council staff articulated this problem very clearly: "[T]he most staggering thing was walking into the White House during our first major crisis, wondering what to do, and then all of a sudden realizing that there are no rules, no books, and no procedures. One of your first thoughts is to ask the President; but the President doesn't know; he only knows what the staff tells him."[3]

At least since the Kennedy administration, an increasing number of senior policy makers have been appointed to important foreign policy positions, more for their domestic political knowledge and activities than for their understanding of foreign affairs. These new officials must be educated and initiated as well as briefed. Unfortunately, the skills most needed for successful crisis management come with experience and knowledge, both of which are "disturbingly inadequate at the highest levels of the American government."[4]

At the same time, the quality of intelligence available to new decision makers has suffered from a variety of collection, management, and institutional problems. Attention to critical analytic subjects within the intelligence agencies has waxed and waned, subject to the vagaries of budget changes, political fads, and "new" targeting priorities.[5] Personnel problems have also contributed to a deterioration of the quality of intelligence. Whether caused by inadequate recruitment or by frequent assignment changes that have prevented analysts and case officers from developing country and issue expertise, it is increasingly difficult to find intelligence personnel with rich, in-depth institutional memory.[6] The net effect has often been to lower the overall quality of intelligence on the antecedents of political or military crises, which is critical to the preventive mission of intelligence, and to lessen the quality of intelligence during crises.

CRISIS RESPONSIBILITIES OF INTELLIGENCE

In the context of the theme of this book—crisis management—it is worth noting that every state throughout history has come to look to its intelligence service for those tasks that are most critical and basic to its survival: (1) precrisis information on what both friends and enemies are doing; (2) advance warning of imminent attack, drastic adverse developments, or foreign policy opportunities; (3) traditional intelligence support during a crisis; and (4) postcrisis evaluations of crisis policy and behavior.[7] These four functions of intelligence in some ways conform to the natural stages of a crisis.[8]

Precrisis intelligence is often the most general of all intelligence. At the highest levels of the U.S. government, this information is contained in routine National

Intelligence Estimates (NIEs) or in Special National Intelligence Estimates (SNIEs). These documents often form the basis of White House, National Security Council (NSC), or congressional briefings.

The pre-onset stage of a crisis is a critical time for intelligence agencies. Clearly, decision makers want advance warning of probable attacks or seriously adverse developments. It is equally clear that such forecasts are exceedingly difficult to make, given the wide range of options available to an adversary, not to mention the possibility of a crisis developing in a "friendly" state. In the wake of the Iran crisis, a new national warning system has been set in place. Given the dramatic changes in the Soviet Union, central Europe, and Central America, it appears that the United States will continue to undergo crises but that these crises will not necessarily involve traditional and well-identified adversaries.[9]

Some experts have attempted to develop mathematical and statistical approaches to predict crisis-creating situations. All too often, however, these techniques are either misapplied or misunderstood and end up serving as tools for analyzing what went wrong after the fact.[10] Unfortunately, even an insightful forecast of a possible crisis may not get to policy makers, as there are many potential crises competing for their attention. In fact, intelligence analysts at the country or regional level have a fairly good track record of anticipating crisis situations.[11] In such cases, "the major problem is how to get this intelligence to the top decision-makers, such as those on the National Security Council, so that they have the benefits of familiarity with [it] prior to the outbreak of a crisis."[12]

The early stage of a crisis is, perhaps, the most difficult challenge for intelligence. Ambiguity and uncertainty reign, there is a dearth of real information, and speculation runs rampant. Decision makers have a habit of demanding instant answers to questions that should have been asked much earlier. Wide-ranging, and often contradictory, options for action are quickly conceived, hurriedly debated, modified, abandoned, and then resurrected.[13] Operations centers are mobilized, and collection resources are deployed or retargeted. Task forces are created in all the appropriate departments and agencies.

CAUSES OF MALFUNCTIONS

Perhaps the oldest and most frequently used metaphor to describe governments is that of a ship. Policy makers are seen as helmsmen steering the ship of state through the murky waters of international politics. If one can also describe the intelligence community as a second ship, then the metaphor of the two ships passing in the night, each unaware of the course of the other, is apt.

Obviously, intelligence does not always meet its full potential in crisis management. Since no intelligence agency publishes an annual report, the successes of intelligence are less well known than its failures, but they should not be forgotten. There are as many explanations of the failures as there are crises themselves. In some respects, every crisis is unique, and the role of intelligence in each crisis must be studied carefully. There are, however, a few general categories into which causes of malfunctions may be placed. The following categories are neither exclusive nor exhaustive but are intended to be illustrative. Although we are primarily interested in the U.S. crisis management system, we have drawn illustrations from the experiences of several countries.

Communication Problems

Communication failures are frequent causes of breakdowns in the intelligence–crisis management relationship. Even when essential and reliable information is available, it is often not received by decision makers in a timely and distortion-free manner. Communication is the glue that holds the policy-making and intelligence communities together. Good two-way communication between decision makers and intelligence providers is essential both for understanding crisis conditions and for conducting successful crisis management operations. There is another side to that coin: Because of poor communication, key indicators are missed and policies are made that can contribute to the onset, continuation, or escalation of crises.

Communication between decision makers and intelligence officers occurs formally and informally. In either case, the subtle transfer of ideas, attitudes, and biases is as important as the transfer of factual information. Moreover, communication is shaped by the ambience in which it occurs. That is, intelligence officers will communicate more completely and openly with decision makers whose policies they favor than they will with those whose policies they do not support. Among other things, it is this communication block that is created when policy makers and intelligence analysts disagree that sets the stage for unauthorized releases of classified information (leaks).

Gloria Duffy has documented the serious problems created when classified information was leaked in two separate crises involving the United States, Cuba, and the Soviet Union. In 1978, the Soviet Union shipped MIG-23 fighter interceptors to Cuba. While the Carter administration was trying to resolve the potential crisis diplomatically, leaks to Washington journalists nearly ruined the crisis containment efforts. Leaks combined with the prematurely authorized release of information further exacerbated the 1979 crisis involving the discovery of a so-called Soviet combat brigade in Cuba.[14]

Informal channels of communication often prove to be more significant than formal ones, particularly during crises. Formal reporting channels, official reporting agreements, and contingency operational plans are the first victims of terrorist bombs or dramatic hostile developments. The quality of communication between decision makers and intelligence agencies is, first and foremost, a function of their relations before the crisis.[15]

There are a variety of obstacles to effective communication between intelligence officials and decision makers. Overcompartmentation is one serious problem. Compartmentation occurs when intelligence information is classified into narrow categories, usually on the basis of collection sources. There may be an intelligence compartment for all information coming from a single overhead surveillance system or from a well-placed human source, and only decision makers and intelligence officers cleared for that compartment may receive that information. Obviously, this protects very tenuous and fragile sources of information, but it also creates communication problems when differential access to particularly sensitive classified information occurs within and between policy makers and the intelligence community.

For example, the widely held assumption that the Arabs would not start a war in 1973 or that, if they did resort to war, they would be defeated more quickly than they were in 1967 was not supported by compartmented information collected by the National Security Agency (NSA). However, to protect the secrecy of this information (which had resulted from successful codebreaking), it was not shared with senior analysts who were providing intelligence to the decision makers.[16] In another case, the full analytical resources of the intelligence community were not used when decisions were being made about the Bay of Pigs invasion. That is, analysts who had information about internal Cuban conditions that would have challenged some of the optimistic assumptions of the plan were kept from influencing those who were planning the invasion.[17]

In an earlier period, there is also evidence that U.S. policy makers facing the question of whether or not to drop an atomic bomb on Japan did not have access to all classified information, some of which may have influenced their decision.[18] "Wartime secrecy . . . imposed compartmentation on the policy process, which interfered with comprehensive evaluation of the alternative courses of action available to the United States for ending the war."[19]

More recently, Senate Intelligence Committee investigators found evidence that a senior intelligence agency analyst who was solely responsible for reports going to the highest levels about a sensitive problem in the South Pacific was completely unaware of compartmented intelligence being collected by another office in the same agency.[20]

The need for secrecy itself is an enemy of good communication. Special assistant to President Reagan for national security affairs, and also senior director of Reagan's Crisis Management Center (CMC), Richard Beal, reported that the secrecy requirements imposed during the invasion of Grenada meant that "there was a period of about 6 or 7 hours when we knew nothing."[21]

Just as information that is not known cannot be communicated, policy-making systems can also be clogged by an information overload. Prior to the 1973 war in the Middle East, the NSA had intercepted thousands of communications revealing Egyptian war plans. The sheer volume of these intercepts, however, meant that many key messages were never analyzed or seen by policy makers. According to Lawrence Eagleburger, at the time on Henry Kissinger's staff, "the problem is not one of quality, but of the inability of the system to digest it. The intelligence had clearly demonstrated that Sadat was going to begin the '73 war, but . . . this did not penetrate the system."[22]

This very problem, among other things, caused the Reagan administration to design a more sophisticated crisis management system geared to monitor multiple crisis spots around the world and to provide on-line, organized information to crisis managers.[23] Information technology can provide several means for improving communications between disparate groups and organizations during a crisis, but only when there is a positive inclination to use it. A combination of networks, graphics, and reasoning technology has proven useful in several public policy contexts through the use of issue-based information systems (IBIS).[24]

Bureaucratic Problems

The proliferation of both policy-making and intelligence agencies leads to bureaucratic problems at every stage of a crisis. Unique to the pre-onset stage is the problem of placing a noncrisis (or, more accurately, a potential crisis) sufficiently high on the list of intelligence priorities to occasion the collection and analysis of information about the relevant country or region. Contrary to popular opinion, intelligence agencies are subject to budgetary constraints very similar to those faced by all government agencies. They cannot place every country and region equally high on a priority list in order to prompt the collection of intelligence.

Policy makers must first transmit a "need to know" to an intelligence agency. Although this sounds quite simple, it is in fact complicated by bureaucratic politics. There are hundreds of officials with foreign policy decision-making responsibilities and often competing (if not conflicting) geographical and functional interests. Each demands immediate information about some international development but often remains unsure just what it is he or she needs to know.

This results in severe competition between policy makers to place their intelligence requirements higher on the priority list (called National Intelligence Topics) than the information required by others. Thus, information about developments that may erupt into a crisis in the near or distant future may be ignored because the office seeking that information was outmaneuvered on the National Intelligence Topics priority list.

Intelligence priority lists have been dominated over the last 40 years by interest in Soviet and Chinese strategic developments. During the 1970s, questions about international energy developments began to appear on the list. But the priority list problem is illustrated by the fact that prior to 1978, little interest was expressed in information about Iran before the overthrow of the shah and the seizure of the U.S. embassy.[25] Once a crisis erupts in a country or region, it quickly rises to the top of the priority list. Prior to the crisis, however, it is difficult to justify the diversion of scarce intelligence resources to that region, thus making it difficult to collect adequate intelligence about the region. And the ultimate irony is that even if by chance critical intelligence is discovered, it is often difficult to arouse the attention of policy makers whose agenda are occupied with other existing crises.

A variation of this problem occurs when a crisis calms down and, for political or financial reasons, it becomes difficult to justify continuing the heavy diversion of intelligence resources to the country or region in which the crisis arose now that it is apparently over. Duffy documents the disastrous effects of cutbacks in both technical and human resources devoted to Cuba during the Nixon and Carter administrations: "In the years following the Cuban missile crisis . . . U.S. intelligence coverage of Cuba was steadily eroded." This erosion, according to Duffy, contributed to the exacerbation of several crises.[26]

Of course, the most fragile link in the intelligence process occurs after the collection, analysis, and production stages are complete. Then senior policy makers must decide which of the large array of intelligence products they will read, believe, and act upon. Unfortunately, this decision is often driven by bureaucratic considerations. A key NSC official, for example, may have representatives from two or three intelligence agencies figuratively knocking at his or her door marketing intelligence products. Every agency has a special briefing team that competes to get information, often drawn from different and highly compartmented sources, to White House officials. What a policy maker sees, reads, and acts upon may often be determined by the quality of the salesmanship as much as by the quality of the intelligence. Few things are more dangerous than for one intelligence agency to be relied on at the exclusion of others during crises. As Allen S. Whiting notes in his case study of the Korean War (Chapter 7 above), policy makers need to "hear divergent [intelligence] viewpoints that can be weighed in advance of final decisions."

Competition between intelligence agencies for both political access and funds leads to other bureaucratic problems. Even though the director of central intelligence (DCI) has the authority to coordinate the various intelligence agencies, intense competition between these agencies still exists. A former DCI, Adm. Stansfield Turner, illustrated this competition when he suggested that the CIA reacted negatively (but in a typically bureaucratic fashion) to the NSA scoop of the so-called Soviet combat brigade in Cuba in 1978. According to Turner, the NSA had what appeared to be an intelligence scoop, and "the CIA and the others feigned a lack of interest in the report until it became obvious that it was too significant to ignore. That, I believe, is the only explanation for the CIA's dragging its feet in searching its files and discovering that it too knew there had been a brigade in Cuba for a long time. Most of all, though, everyone became defensive."[27]

Bureaucratic competition often occurs even within a given intelligence agency, sometimes at the expense of sound intelligence. According to one account, the long-standing rivalry between the operational directorate and the analytical directorate of the CIA left the senior analytical official unaware of operational plans for the Bay of Pigs operation in Cuba.[28]

The fact that virtually all intelligence analysts are located in agencies and bureaus, rather than at the level of senior policy makers, is also an organizational impediment to the sound use of intelligence during crises. As Richard Beal, director of the Reagan administration's Crisis Management Center, has pointed out, we spend a lot of money to support the collection and analysis of information, but when that information goes to senior policy makers, they become their own analysts. "We have very few analytic tools for the very high-level people."[29]

Bureaucratic procedures also influence the quality of intelligence. On the one hand, reliance on procedures that are overly bureaucratic—most notably, reporting through a strict and lengthy chain of command when time is of the essence—can delay needed intelligence. Bureaucratic frictions caused the delay of the U-2 flight that revealed the missiles in Cuba.[30] For another example, when the USS *Pueblo* was captured by North Korea, critical messages from the *Pueblo* took approximately two hours to be processed through the system and acted upon.[31] And in the 1989 invasion of Panama, policy makers could not obtain timely information due to rigid adherence to reporting procedures. The Reagan Crisis Management Center (CMC) attempted to overcome, at least partially, the timeliness problem by developing the ability to use immediately images from television news in briefing the president. In the case of the bombing of the marine barracks in Beirut, this allowed, when accompanied by maps and other information, a significant briefing to take place hours before the intelligence community was prepared to report to the White House.[32]

Further complicating matters, however, is the tendency of governments to create ad hoc procedures in crises. One manifestation of this tendency is the creation of ad hoc crisis task forces, which crop up in several different departments or agencies, follow separate rules and procedures, and sometimes even rely on different information sources. This both results from and reinforces the tendency to compartmentalize, a problem discussed earlier. Multiple task forces can be healthy if they contribute to diversity of views and provide a broader range of options for decision makers. They can also result in unnecessary duplication of effort, contribute to slowness and delay in decision making, and prevent a full and objective consideration of information.

It is also true that reliance on one centralized crisis center can weaken effective crisis management. A single center is usually dominated by the agency or department in which it resides and tends to rely on its own intelligence. The Reagan administration attempted to deal with this problem by creating a single White House CMC that tied into all agency electronic messages going to the White House. The intelligence agencies have also attempted to link all specialists within the intelligence community who are working on similar problems through an on-line communications computer network. Such efforts are commendable, but the normal bureaucratic tendency to protect turf and insulate against possible blame for failures tends to vitiate what these networks were created to achieve.[33]

The existence of multiple intelligence agencies, each competing for scarce resources and trying to enhance its own organization, also contributes—albeit indirectly—to another serious problem. That is, in assessing possible outcomes, intelligence analysts tend to emphasize worst case scenarios—the most damaging series of events that could occur. The logic driving this tendency is difficult to resist. Faced with competition from other analytical centers, no individual analyst or agency wants to incur the risk of being left with egg on its face. That is, no one wants to be caught having predicted a benign future if, in fact, the future should turn out to be very messy. Thus, the prudent response is to protect oneself by erring on the pessimistic side. If things turn out better than predicted, one merely breathes a sigh of relief and says, "at least we were prepared for the worst." If the worst comes to pass, the analyst merely says, "I told you so." Sophisticated policy makers, knowing of the worst case proclivities of intelligence analysts, may discount such warnings as examples of the "cry wolf" phenomenon; but this practice in turn creates the possibility that they will dismiss correct warnings of an actual attack.

In the absence of interagency competition, an analyst might be more willing to stick to moderate and statistically more likely interpretations and predictions. If something worse should occur, there would be fewer bureaucratic rivals waiting to dance on one's grave. Competition between Aman and Mossad (two Israeli intelligence agencies) contributed to several Israeli intelligence failures in the early 1950s. An Israeli scholar's explanation of highly pessimistic analyses is terse but apt: "Better, though, to be oversensitive than to be caught napping."[34]

If political leaders accept worst case scenarios as a basis for policy, the actions they take may evoke responses from other nations that, in turn, appear to justify the original bleak analysis. This type of self-confirming phenomenon operates not only with intelligence forecasts but can also occur when analysts have to interpret the meaning of ambiguous data. An almost inexorable urge toward worst case interpretation is built into the analytical process. This urge introduces a high degree of pessimism into the process. Even though policy makers try to overcome this tendency by asking for an array of forecasts and interpretations, the same pessimistic urges can be found at even the highest level of policy making as long as there are individuals and offices competing for influence and power.

One crisis described as being brought on, at least in part, by this phenomenon occurred in July 1988. The commander of the USS *Sides*, a part of the USS *Vincennes* battle group in the Persian Gulf, has suggested that the *Vincennes* might not have shot down the Iranian civil airliner had it not been for worst case scenarios presented by military intelligence analysts. "All of us," he wrote, "were done a grave disservice by an intelligence system that covered itself by forecasting every possible worst-case scenario. Crews of ships reporting to the Middle East Force in the summer months were noticeably on edge" as a result.[35] Indeed, the incident fourteen months before the downing of Iran Air Flight 655, in which the USS *Stark* was hit by two Exocet missiles fired by an Iraqi fighter in the Gulf, did much to influence the mind-set of the officers and crew of the vessels on patrol there. The subsequent finding by the U.S. navy of negligence on the part of the *Stark's* captain in failing to respond early enough to the threat posed by the assumed friendly Iraqi plane was noted by several participants in the investigation of the *Vincennes*–Iranian airliner incident. They regarded the finding as a contributing factor in the liberalization of the rules of engagement with respect to the policy of firing on assumed hostile aircraft.[36]

Bureaucratic competition between intelligence agencies has another interesting manifestation, which shows itself in competition between the CIA and the NSA over the use of raw intelligence derived from electronic surveillance. The problem stems from a sort of Gresham's Law in intelligence, according to which raw, technical intelligence drives out finished, analyzed intelligence. That is, the increasingly available raw intelligence collected through technical means tends to be seen as more immediate, more secret, more accurate, and more valuable than the same information after it has been analyzed.

What people say in secret conversations or communications is assumed to have greater meaning in and of itself without reference to the larger context in which such exchanges take place. This is a dangerous assumption because it assumes that a given communication between any set of individuals reflects, in fact, the totality of the policies and intentions of the governments of those individuals. Anyone who has seen the inside of any government's decision-making circle knows this is not true. A foreign intelligence service, for example, could have a hidden microphone on the president of the United States and still not know clearly what the United States was doing on the stage of world politics. How could they, when the president himself may not know?

The same is true of other large and technologically sophisticated nations, and it also appears to operate in the case of small revolutionary movements. In response to criticism about the failure of the CIA to predict the Khomeini revolution in Iran, former DCI Turner suggests that even Khomeini himself was surprised by developments.[37]

It must also be noted, that while the presence of multiple intelligence agencies can create bureaucratic problems, the existence of only one dominant agency can be equally hazardous. Raymond Cohen has documented the deleterious effect of this condition in Israel in the early 1950s; he concluded that "had military intelligence been balanced by equally powerful civilian agencies, enjoying similar resources, its biases would have been canceled out. But this was not the case."[38]

Psychological Impediments

This category of obstacles is large and is discussed frequently in the growing body of intelligence literature.[39] We are interested here in a more limited, but related, discussion of psychological obstacles that occur in the use of intelligence in crisis management.

A host of psychological forces influences cognitive processes, and many of these are accentuated in times of crisis. Existing beliefs and mental images tend to screen out or dilute the significance of new information, and pressures to conform to prevailing policy assumptions cause distortions in the evaluation of new information. In crises, however, few factors are more significant than stress. As Richard J. Heuer, Jr., has noted, "[I]f we consider the circumstances under which accurate perception is most difficult, we find these are exactly the circumstances under which intelligence analysis is generally conducted—dealing with highly ambiguous situations on the basis of information that is processed incrementally under pressure for early judgment."[40]

Crisis-induced stress significantly affects the intelligence process. Crisis intelligence tends to be more incremental than noncrisis intelligence. The demands of both time and urgency force bits and pieces of intelligence information to be dealt with immediately, as they become available and, perhaps, before they are analyzed. Under these conditions, "new information tends to be assimilated with existing data," and existing assumptions and plans tend to be reinforced.[41] T. L. Cubbage argues that Germany's failure to identify the location of the cross-channel invasion resulted from these conditions. The Germans, after careful and thorough research, predicted that the Allied invasion would occur in the Pas de Calais area. Once that was decided, virtually all subsequent intelligence was interpreted to fit that assumption.[42]

Stress also creates a "current events syndrome" in which policy makers are swept into the flow of events and both the demand for, and the supply of, intelligence tend to focus almost myopically on the latest piece of information, at the expense of placing intelligence into a context arrived at through systematic consideration of a body of integrated evidence. This syndrome was found to have been a significant cause of analytical problems in post mortems conducted by the intelligence community on the performance of intelligence during crises in the Middle East and Cyprus.[43]

Crisis conditions also enhance the significance of the psychological requirement for cognitive consistency as it operates in the intelligence process. Individuals cannot remake their perceptual world with every new cognitive cue, especially under crisis conditions. To do so would cause cognitive dysfunction. Striving to maintain cognitive balance or congruence allows one to fit new cognitive cues into a larger pattern. There is a powerful tendency to make new developments consistent with prevailing images and expectations as well as with desired outcomes. Intelligence analysts tend to see what they expect to see and sometimes what they want to see.

One of the primary reasons behind the failure of the British government to accept warnings of a Nazi-Soviet pact through most of 1939 was the inability of Foreign Office officials to accept evidence counter to their existing beliefs and assumptions.[44] In fact, according to Michael Handel, "The major causes of all types of surprise are rigid concepts and closed perceptions."[45]

Related to these obstacles is the tendency to believe that things will remain as they are. The perception that a particular area known for its stability is unlikely to become a major trouble spot has been the source of many intelligence and policy failures. The Korean crises in 1950 and 1977 are just two examples.[46] This view often reflects a misperception brought about by a failure to take warning indicators seriously, in part because to do so would require reconsideration of existing policy and the assumptions on which it is based, a task both psychologically and politically difficult.

As noted in Jack S. Levy's case study of World War I (Chapter 6), a key issue following the assassination of Archduke Ferdinand was the anticipated actions and policies of Great Britain, an issue critical to the definition of commitments by the various parties and to the escalation of the resulting conflict from a continental to a world war. The assumption of British neutrality reinforced Germany's declaration of support for Austria against Serbia. As Levy noted, "German perception of the strong likelihood of British neutrality emerges as the key to the escalation of all stages of the crisis."

Throughout July 1914, German policy makers based their actions on what turned out to be an incorrect and damaging assumption. In fact, the German assumption of British neutrality was made prior to the onset of the crisis in July and, indeed, was part of the mind-set of German political leaders as they drew up various contingency plans.

Intelligence deals with both intentions and capabilities. Not only were the Germans wrong in their perception of British neutrality, they were also wrong in their intelligence regarding British capabilities. The Germans viewed the British military as too incompetent and ineffective to make a difference, even if the British did intervene. Again, once this assumption was made, contrary information that did not fit this image was rejected, diluted, or reinterpreted so as to preserve the prevailing assumption.

The difficulty of adjusting long-held assumptions is illustrated in the observation of a long-time CIA veteran.

In reading the history and Agency-conducted postmortems of past international crises in a search for what might have gone wrong when intelligence failed to provide advance warning, I was struck by one common denominator running through the incidents in which the Agency performed inadequately. . . . [I]n each case bits and pieces of information [had been] collected in advance that should have alerted the intelligence analysts and policymakers to what was coming. But to find these germs of wheat in the abundant chaff and to understand their significance in time to affect decision making was not an easy job in the face of a preponderance of evidence pointing the other way. More important, *these intelligence gems usually contradicted the prevailing optimistic assumptions of the policymakers*[47] (emphasis added).

Some psychological influences on perceptions seem to be more controlling than others. The image of a hostile opponent will usually have a distortive effect on assessments of its intent, and these assessments of intent will usually shape perceptions of the opponent's capabilities. In the World War I case mentioned above, when German perceptions of the likelihood of British neutrality varied widely, it was perceptions of intent that shaped German behavior more than perceptions of capabilities.[48] In this case, the Germans tended to underestimate British capabilities because they assumed the British did not have hostile intentions.

Ideological and Political Obstacles

Ideological and political distortions occur when intelligence judgments are altered to suit the views of those receiving them or to further the interests of those reporting them. Distortions also occur when intelligence is excluded, withheld, or disguised, or when it is presented in a raw, unanalyzed, and misleading manner in order to curry the favor of policy makers. Such distortions may result from subtle, almost unconscious, misinterpretations of ambiguous information or from willful attempts to influence policy through intelligence judgments.

In any hierarchical organization, intelligence providers are tempted to "cook the intelligence to fit the policy-makers' recipes." And the climate created by this kind of intelligence may, directly or indirectly, affect crisis management. Although these events are not easily documented and are not the rule, two such examples have been reported. The first involved pressure from the White House to redraft a conclusion from a 1969 National Intelligence Estimate on Soviet strategic forces. The import of the conclusion was whether the Soviet Union had developed a first-strike capability for the SS-9 intercontinental ballistic missile (ICBM) through the use of MIRV technology (the original draft concluded that it had not and that the technology tested was not MIRVed). The new conclusion, that the Soviets had developed a first-strike capability, had a profound impact on the pending U.S. policy decision on whether to deploy its MIRVed missiles or seek to negotiate MIRV limits in a strategic Arms Limitation Treaty (SALT).

Similarly, having been told by the White House of the upcoming invasion of Cambodia in 1971 and ordered not to tell CIA analysts, the DCI chose not to forward to the White House, on the eve of the invasion, an important intelligence memorandum on Cambodia because it contained a pessimistic judgment on the possible consequences of a U.S. invasion. The reasons for the DCI's action are not clear, but the effect was to withhold an important judgment on a policy matter that would have been received unfavorably. When questioned about these two incidents, the DCI said, "One does not want to lose one's audience, and this is easy to do if one overloads the circuit."[49]

It is also possible for policy makers, particularly those with strong ideological preferences, to indicate that bad news (and those who bear it) is unwelcome. Policy makers have been known to exclude intelligence from playing an active role in crises. Ray S. Cline illustrates one such example, which occurred during the early

U.N.-requested ceasefire in the Middle East in October 1973. In this case, a military alert was called on the basis of a telephone conversation between Henry Kissinger and Richard Nixon without any analysis of the meaning of the events that occasioned the Soviet message, the message itself, or the possible global effects of the alert. This alert, in Cline's judgment, unnecessarily exacerbated the crisis and angered NATO members.[50]

Altering intelligence judgments to suit the perceived preferences of policy makers can be subtle or blatant. In his recounting of the Cuban Missile Crisis, Robert Kennedy reported that "personalities change when the President is present, and frequently even strong men make their recommendations on the basis of what they believe the President wishes to hear."[51] More blatant, however, were the efforts Kennedy also observed by senior policy makers to "exclude certain individuals from participating in a meeting with the President because they held a different point of view."[52]

It appears this is not merely a U.S. problem. Enrique H.G. Cavallini, in his review of the British-Argentine conflict over the Falkland-Malvinas islands, documents the disastrous effects created by the "concentration of power in the few military hands that controlled both the government and the intelligence community and the typical intelligence analyst's attitude to reflect their political premises and biases."[53]

International political interests can create a political climate that distorts or affects intelligence collection and reporting. For example, in an effort to gain access to Soviet listening posts in Iran, the United States made arrangements with the shah that lessened the CIA's ability to collect intelligence on domestic developments in Iran. Instead, the CIA would rely on the shah for that information, and, in return, the shah would "let you [the CIA] have all the telemetry and monitoring equipment up north that you want."[54] This agreement made it difficult to assess the domestic opposition to the shah, a development that hurt the ability of the United States to prepare for the Iranian revolution in 1979.

Domestic political conditions can have similar effects. In 1973, intelligence information that Egypt was preparing to attack Israel was downplayed or ignored because it would have forced Nixon to take a more interventionist role in the Middle East, a policy that Nixon was reluctant to take because of his tenuous domestic political situation. According to one observer, DCI James Schlesinger watered down information of this pending attack to protect Nixon's plan to encourage a diplomatic solution.[55]

CONCLUSION

We referred earlier to the relationship between intelligence and policy making in crises as resembling the two metaphorical ships that pass in the night, each unaware of the other. The metaphor is, of course, too strong. Intelligence has played a valuable and supportive role in the management, if not the prevention, of many crises. Unfortunately for scholars, those cases are not written about as much as those marked by intelligence failures. Ray S. Cline, for example, extols the role of intelligence in some aspects of the Cuban Missile Crisis.[56] And Richard Beal is quoted as praising the effective role of intelligence during the crisis surrounding the shooting down of the Korean airliner over Kamchatka in 1983 and a Middle East crisis in June and July, 1984.[57]

Nevertheless, problems do exist, some of which we have illustrated above. New administrations usually try to correct these problems through organizational fixes. These often fail for two reasons. In the first place, the problems frequently result not from structural or organizational arrangements but rather from managerial styles or poor personal relationships between policy makers and intelligence officers. Second, most of the organizational fixes are arrived at between the time immediately following a national election and the first days in office. Newly elected presidents are preoccupied with transition arrangements and are inundated with office seekers. Organizational changes developed during this period are often based more on campaign rhetoric and ideological predilections than on objective assessments of needs.

Some problems are more easily overcome than others. Communications problems brought about by technological inadequacies are not impossible to remedy. The crisis management system created for the Reagan administration was a move in the proper direction. Crisis gaming and simulations are also helpful. Since human relationships tend to take precedence over organizational prescriptions, especially in times of crisis, it is important for exercises to be conducted that will create, develop, and reinforce these relationships. As the head of the Scotland Yard Bomb Squad once said, "[W]hen the bomb goes off, all paper plans for dealing with the crisis go out the window."[58] Given the politically driven turnovers at the highest levels of policy making, these exercises must be repeated frequently.

There are several possible ways to ameliorate at least some bureaucratic problems. Whiting (Chapter 7) argues that, at least in the case of the Korean War, the White House would have been better served by hearing direct confrontations between senior analysts rather than relying on joint intelligence estimates that often resulted from bureaucratic bargaining and compromises. Some senior policy makers have also requested to see competing analytical products, not merely final compromise drafts.

Also helpful would be efforts to improve intelligence analysts' understanding of the policy-making process and policy makers' understanding of intelligence work. Our metaphor of two ships passing in the night fails to suggest that they often pass not only in ignorance but in anger. Policy makers are frustrated because they cannot get the kind of information they want, and intelligence personnel are angry that their analyses are unheeded. Both need to know more about the tradecraft of the other. It is too often true in all countries, as a recent review of Israeli intelligence pointed out, that "while most of the members of the intelligence community have expert knowledge of the enemy, their understanding of the Israeli political system itself is at best average."[59] There are U.S. analysts and collectors who know more about "the enemy" than they know about the policy-making process and milieu in their own country.

Both bureaucratic and political impediments would be moderated if there were greater consistency in the intelligence targeting process. When intelligence targets are taken from priority lists at the whim of individual policy makers, whole categories of important information may become extinct, only to be needed at a later time. All too often, the exigencies of military intelligence take precedence over those of political intelligence. As Duffy concludes after her investigation of U.S.-Cuban crises, "a category of intelligence may exist that is politically significant beyond its operational military importance."[60] Greater attention needs to be paid to nonstrategic intelligence topics—economic, agricultural, political, ecological, and so on. These are often the root causes of international crises. Perhaps the dramatic developments of the winter of 1989–1990 in the Soviet Union and Eastern Europe might encourage greater attention to what the Senate Intelligence Committee once called "New 'Strategic Problems' for the Future."[61]

Crisis data sets and more sophisticated information management systems are also needed. "The American government will spend billions of dollars developing information systems for the bottom and nothing for the top [the NSC, the president, etc.]."[62]

In addition to all of these considerations, it must be remembered that the greatest needs are to appoint informed persons to key posts and to maintain and cultivate a complete and comprehensive memory of past events. This may not prevent crises, but it may lessen their adverse impact and improve crisis management.

NOTES

1. See Richard K. Betts, *Surprise Attack: Lessons for Defense Planning* (Washington, D.C.: Brookings Institution, 1982) for one of the better discussions of this topic.

2. The Intelligence Community (IC) is usually described as containing the following agencies or parts of agencies: Central Intelligence Agency (CIA); Defense Intelligence Agency (DIA); National Security Agency (NSA); the various intelligence branches of the Armed Services; portions of the Federal Bureau of Investigation (FBI), specifically the counterintelligence sections of the FBI; certain bureaus or offices within the Department of State, the Department of the Treasury, and the Department of Energy; as well as usually unnamed offices for the collection of specialized national foreign intelligence.

3. Quoted in R. Jeffrey Smith, "Crisis Management Under Strain," *Science* 225 (August 21, 1984): 908.

4. See the discussion on this point in Chapter 1 in this volume.

5. See Allan E. Goodman, "Dateline Langley: Fixing the Intelligence Mess," *Foreign Policy* 57 (1984–85): 160–79 for a discussion of this. The *Annual Reports* of the Senate Select Committee on Intelligence also discuss these problems.

6. See Stansfield Turner, *Secrecy and Democracy: The CIA in Transition* (New York: Harcourt Brace, 1986), pp. 230–34, for a discussion of the absence of institutional memory, at least at the most senior intelligence levels, during the crisis over the Soviet combat brigade in Cuba.

7. The broadest surveys of intelligence throughout history are in Richard W. Rowan with Robert B. Deindorfer, *Secret Service: 33 Centuries of Espionage* (New York: Hawthorn Books, 1967) and Ronald Seth, *Encyclopedia of Espionage* (Garden City, N.Y.: Doubleday and Co., 1974).

8. This is adapted from William Ury and Richard Smoke, *Beyond the Hotline: Controlling a Nuclear Crisis* (A Report to the United States Arms Control and Disarmament Agency, Nuclear Negotiation Project, Harvard Law School, March 1984).

9. We are indebted to Ronald H. Hinckley for this point.

10. See, for example, Ted Robert Gurr, *The Conditions of Civil Violence: First Tests of a Causal Model* (Princeton, N.J.: Princeton University Press, 1967) for an early attempt and Stephen J. Andriole and Gerald W. Hopple, *Revolution and Political Instability: Applied Research Methods* (London: F. Pinter, 1984) for a more recent attempt.

11. See the comments about Korean and Vietnam specialists by Allen Whiting in his case study of the Korean War, Chapter 7, above.

12. The quotation is found on p. 3 of the final report of "The Asilomar Conference on Political-Military Decision-Making in Crisis Situations," sponsored by the U.S. Navy in April, 1986.

13. For a psychological explanation of why these kinds of responses are typical in foreign policy crises, see, Joseph H. de Rivera, *The Psychological Dimension of Foreign Policy* (Columbus, Ohio: Charles E. Merrill Publishing Co., 1968).

14. See Gloria Duffy, "Crisis Prevention in Cuba," in Alexander L. George, ed., *Managing U.S.-Soviet Rivalry: Problems in Crisis Prevention* (Boulder, CO: Westview Press, 1983), pp. 296 and 302. See also Stansfield Turner, *Secrecy and Democracy*, pp. 143–44 and 149–50 for his discussion of the damage caused by leakage.

15. We are indebted to Uri Bar-Joseph for this point.

16. John Ranelaugh, *The Agency: The Rise and Decline of the CIA* (New York: Simon and Schuster, 1986), p. 582.

17. Lyman B. Kirkpatrick, Jr., *The U.S. Intelligence Community* (Boulder, CO: Westview Press, 1985), p. 128.

18. Leon Sigal, *Fighting to a Finish: The Politics of War Termination in the United States and Japan, 1945* (Ithaca: Cornell University Press, 1988), p. 221.

19. Sigal, *Fighting to a Finish*, p. 290.

20. U.S. Senate, Select Committee on Intelligence, *Annual Report*, 95th Cong., 1st sess., May 18, 1977, Report No. 95–217, p. 16.

21. Quoted in Smith, "Crisis Management Under Strain," p. 908.

22. Ranelaugh, *The Agency*, p. 582.

23. The system is described in Smith, "Crisis Management Under Strain," p. 909.

24. Horst Rittel and W. Kunz, "Issues as Elements of Information Systems," Working Paper 131 (Stuttgart: Institut für Grundlagen der Planung I.A., University of Stuttgart, n.d.) and J. Conklin and M. Begeman, "IBIS: A Hypertext Tool for Team Design Deliberation," MCC Technical Report STP-016-88 (Austin, Texas: MCC, 1988).

25. See U.S. Congress, House, Permanent Select Committee on Intelligence, *Iran: Evaluation of U.S. Intelligence Performance Prior to November 1978* (96th Cong., 1st sess., 1979) for the background of this and Jeffrey T. Richelson, *The U.S. Intelligence Community* (Cambridge, MA: Ballinger Publishing Co., 1985), pp. 288–89 for a discussion of the priority list system. See also, Gary Sick, *All Fall Down: America's Tragic Encounter with Iran* (New York: Random House, 1985), pp. vii–viii.

26. Duffy, "Crisis Prevention in Cuba," p. 310.

27. Turner, *Secrecy and Democracy*, pp. 234–35.

28. See the evidence cited by Trumball Higgins, *The Perfect Failure: Kennedy, Eisenhower, and the CIA at the Bay of Pigs* (New York: W. W. Norton, 1987), p. 162.

29. Beal is quoted by his former coworker in the Reagan Crisis Management Center, Ronald H. Hinckley, in Hinckley's "National Security in the Information Age," *The Washington Quarterly* (Spring 1986): 128.

30. Graham T. Allison, *Essence of Decision* (Boston: Little, Brown, 1971), pp. 122–23.

31. See the comments of Admiral Bobby Inman in Hilliard Roderick, ed., *Avoiding Inadvertent War: Crisis Management* (Austin, TX: Lyndon B. Johnson School of Public Affairs, University of Texas at Austin, 1983).

32. Ronald H. Hinckley, "Information Technology and Foreign Policy," *Paradigms Revised: The Annual Review of Communications and Society* (1989): 69.

33. Organizational tinkering has improved coordination between intelligence agencies in recent years. During crises, however, bureaucratic self-protection tends to resurface. See Glenn P. Hastedt, "Organizational Foundations of Intelligence Failures," in Alfred C. Maurer and others, eds., *Intelligence: Policy and Process* (Boulder, CO: Westview Press, 1985), ch. 10, for a partial explanation. It also ought to be noted that the CMC established in the Reagan White House has been largely emasculated and turned into a message processing center. It certainly did not function as a crisis management center during the invasion of Panama.

34. Raymond Cohen, "Israeli Military Intelligence before the 1956 Sinai Campaign," *Intelligence and National Security* 3 (January 1988): 137.

35. The criticism was made by Cmdr. David R. Carlson in *Proceedings*, a publication of the U.S. Naval Institute. They were reprinted in *Harper's Magazine* (November, 1989), pp. 26–27. It ought to be noted that competition can also produce "best-case scenarios" in which agencies, in an attempt to gain access to policy makers, indulge in overly optimistic reporting.

36. *Washington Post*, January 15, 1989, Outlook, p. C1.

37. Turner, *Secrecy and Democracy*, pp. 116–17. In fact, at the time of the revolution several intelligence analysts hinted that the French did have an informant in Khomeini's entourage and that they were all surprised by developments.

38. Cohen, "Israeli Intelligence before 1956," p. 137.

39. The writings of Michael Handel, Richard Betts, Alexander George, Robert Jervis, Jack Levy, and others deal with, among other things, psychological problems in the intelligence process.

40. Richard J. Heuer, Jr., "Cognitive Factors in Deception and Counterdeception," in Donald C. Daniel and Katherine L. Herbig, eds., *Strategic Military Deception* (Elmsford, N.Y.: Pergamon Press, 1981), p. 40.

41. T. L. Cubbage, "German Misapprehensions Regarding Overlord: Understanding Failure in the Estimative Process," *Intelligence and National Security* 2 (July 1987): 157.

42. Cubbage, "Strategic and Operational Deception," p. 157.

43. U.S. Congress, Senate, Select Committee to Study Governmental Operations with respect to Intelligence Activities, *Foreign and Military Intelligence, Book 1, Final Report*, 94th Cong., 2d sess., 1976, pp. 272 ff.

44. D. Cameron Watt, "An Intelligence Surprise: The Failure of the Foreign Office to Anticipate the Nazi-Soviet Pact," *Intelligence and National Security* 4 (July 1989): 529.

45. See his "Avoiding Political and Technological Surprises in the 1980s" in Roy Godson, ed., *Intelligence Requirements for the 1980s: Analysis and Estimates* (London: Transaction Books, 1980), p. 85.

46. See Alexander L. George and Richard Smoke, *Deterrence in American Foreign Policy: Theory and Practice* (New York: Columbia University Press, 1974), pp. 140–183 for an illustration of this point.

47. Cord Meyer, *Facing Reality: From World Federalism to the CIA* (New York: Harper & Row, 1980), p. 227.

48. See, for example, L. L. Farrar, Jr., "The Limits of Choice: July 1914 Reconsidered," *Journal of Conflict Resolution* 16 (March 1972): 1–23.

49. Both incidents are reported in U.S. Senate, *Final Report*, pp. 73–83. It ought to be noted, however, that not every accusation of "cooked intelligence" is true. The Senate Intelligence Committee reported in 1978 that accusations that the CIA had altered judgments about Soviet oil production to aid President Carter's proposed energy plan were unfounded.

See the Committee's "The Soviet Oil Situation: An Evaluation of CIA Analyses of Soviet Oil Production," Staff Report, May 1978.

50. Ray S. Cline, "Policy Without Intelligence," *Foreign Policy* 17 (Winter 1974–75): 127.

51. Robert F. Kennedy, *Thirteen Days: A Memoir of the Cuban Missile Crisis* (New York: W. W. Norton, 1969), p. 33.

52. Kennedy, *Thirteen Days*, 116–17.

53. Enrique H.G. Cavallini, "The Malvinas/Falkland Affair: A New Look," *International Journal of Intelligence and Counterintelligence* 2 (Summer 1988): 213.

54. Ranelaugh is quoting an unnamed presidential intelligence adviser in his *The Agency*, p. 649.

55. Ranelaugh, *The Agency*, pp. 582–83.

56. Cline, "Policy Without Intelligence," p. 129.

57. Smith, "Crisis Management Under Strain," p. 908.

58. Personal interview, Senate Intelligence Committee Staff, April 27, 1977.

59. Gideon Doron and Reuven Pedatzur, "Israeli Intelligence: Utility and Cost-Effectiveness in Policy Formation," *International Journal of Intelligence and Counterintelligence* 3 (Fall 1989): 359.

60. Duffy, "Crisis Prevention in Cuba," p. 311.

61. U.S. Congress, Senate, Select Committee on Intelligence, *Annual Report*, (May 18, 1977), p. 12.

62. Smith, "Crisis Management Under Strain," p. 909, quoting Richard Beal, Director of the Reagan administration's Crisis Management Center.

CHAPTER 18

Crisis Bargaining Codes and Crisis Management

J. Philip Rogers

The provisional theory of crisis management described in Chapter 4 identified certain general principles for effective crisis management. When it comes to specific situations, however, different decision makers may interpret and apply the same general principles in very different ways. In a crisis, policy makers must develop an understanding of the nature and degree of threats to their country's interests, an estimate of the way the adversary views the situation, and a determination of the probable consequences of different courses of action designed to secure their objectives in this crisis. These complex, difficult judgments must be made with imperfect information under severe time pressures. That crisis decision making is, as a result, partly a phenomenological exercise is acknowledged by psychologists, most policy makers, and some political scientists. Reflecting back on his own extensive crisis experience, Henry Kissinger commented: "During fast moving events [of a crisis] those at the center of decisions are overwhelmed by floods of reports compounded of conjecture, knowledge, hope and worry. . . . Only rarely does a coherent picture emerge; in a sense, coherence must be imposed on the events by the decision-maker."[1]

But it is not enough to recognize in a very general way that subjective psychological factors can have an impact on crisis decision making; in order to use this insight in studying crisis management, a more sophisticated understanding is required.

In this chapter, I argue that all policy makers approach a given crisis with conscious or unconscious, vague or systematically developed beliefs about three key issues relevant to crisis bargaining: an image of the adversary, beliefs about the dynamics of crisis escalation and the best ways to control it, and bargaining rules of thumb for resolving the crisis on terms consistent with their country's interests. We refer to this constellation of beliefs for a particular policy maker as his or her "crisis bargaining code." These beliefs, it should be noted, do not constitute a fully articulated strategy that the policy maker applies in exactly the same fashion in every crisis. Instead, the crisis bargaining code should be thought of as a "cognitive prism" that in any particular crisis influences the way in which a policy maker interprets events and evaluates options.[2]

This chapter defines four types of crisis bargaining codes that U.S. policy makers adopt in crisis situations and then demonstrates how these different belief systems lead to different orientations toward crisis management. We discuss the impact of differing belief systems on the orientations and policy preferences of different U.S. policy makers faced with three different types of crises: (1) crises involving an adversary with nuclear weapons; (2) crises with an adversary armed with "terror" weapons (e.g., chemical); and (3) crises with an adversary armed only with conventional forces.

Crisis bargaining beliefs consist of general diagnostic and choice propensities that shape policy preferences in any particular crisis. It is important to recognize that situational variables in a crisis (such as what is at stake, available options, world and allied opinion, and domestic political factors) will affect a policy maker's final decisions. Nevertheless, on the basis of their differing crisis bargaining codes, one can often explain and predict, in a general sense, the relative responses of the different policy makers to a particular range of options.

A major concern of this chapter is the manner in which a policy maker's crisis bargaining beliefs might lead him or her to hold misperceptions or make miscalculations that could undermine efforts at effective crisis management. We demonstrate how each of these belief systems is vulnerable, under certain circumstances, to its own misperceptions and miscalculations. One general conclusion is that cognitive beliefs of this kind often operate on decision making in a less conscious, more context-dependent, and often more insidious fashion than is commonly understood. These beliefs can contribute to misperceptions and miscalculations insofar as they are inherently simplistic, insufficiently differentiated to deal with diverse crisis situations, or applied inappropriately.

One important finding is that the crisis bargaining codes operate somewhat differently when the policy maker is faced with different information problems: (1) information overload; (2) information deficits—that is, the lack of hard information on specific aspects of a decision; and (3) contradictory information, which necessitates weighing the relative merits of two contradictory reports of the same event. Precisely because the role of the crisis bargaining code is somewhat different in each of these cases, we argue that the dynamics of perception (or misperception) also differ.

In cases where major misperceptions or miscalculations occur, we contend that cognitive beliefs will vitiate efforts at effective crisis management in one or more of the following ways: (1) by producing perceptual distortions in the interpretation of the crisis situation that lead to an exaggeration of the degree of threat it poses; (2) by predisposing the policy maker to underestimate the risks of certain provocative actions; and (3) conversely, by predisposing the policy maker to take exclusively noncoercive actions, which may encourage the adversary to exploit the crisis.

This chapter builds on the existing literature on belief systems and cognitive decision making, but it differs in some significant respects.[3] First, although the notion of the "image of the adversary" (the primary element of other belief studies) remains a central element, we argue that more attention needs to be paid to cognitive beliefs about the nature of escalation in a crisis. Second, we find that some crisis bargaining codes include more than beliefs about the international system; they may also include decisional rules of thumb for information processing and general criteria for evaluating options. Third, we contend that in addition to verbal, prescriptive statements, some crisis bargaining beliefs may also be remembered and recalled in the form of historical analogies, bargaining metaphors, or semiconscious "scripts." Finally, we argue that the dynamics of the perceptual process are partly context-dependent in that the type of information problem the individual confronts may affect which parts of the belief system he or she brings to bear and the manner of their influence.

What all of this suggests is the importance of a renewed examination of cognitive beliefs and information processing in any attempt to make crisis management more effective in practice.

ELEMENTS OF THE CRISIS BARGAINING CODE AND CODE TYPES

A previous study by the author concluded that the belief systems of top-level U.S. policy makers always addressed, in some fashion and in varying degrees of sophistication, three pivotal crisis bargaining issues: (1) an image of adversary, including beliefs about the adversary's typical objectives, decision-making style, and typical bargaining strategy; (2) an image of crisis dynamics, including beliefs about the nature of crisis escalation and the manner in which a war might erupt in a crisis; and (3) general beliefs about the optimal mixture and timing of coercion, accommodation, and persuasion in an overall bargaining strategy.[4]

Policy makers often differ greatly in their beliefs about these three different aspects of bargaining. If an analyst has some idea of what a particular policy maker thinks about some of the more important aspects of this code, it should prove possible to predict (in a general sense) how that policy maker will interpret that information and (in a relative sense) the type of policy response he or she will tend to favor.

In fact I argue that it is possible to group crisis bargaining codes into four broad types: Type A; Type B (two subvariants: B–I and B–II); Type C; and Type D. Unlike most typologies, this one accords great significance to differences in the image of crisis dynamics, rather than to the image of the adversary alone.[5] Because the typology includes the additional dimensions of the image of crisis dynamics, it allows more differentiation than a simple hawk–dove dichotomy, which often misses key differences among hawks or among doves.[6]

Different crisis bargaining codes have different implications for the policy maker's choice of a strategy of crisis management in a particular crisis. For example, while all policy makers caught in a dangerous superpower confrontation would seek to avoid a nuclear war, policy makers and analysts would disagree over how best to resolve the crisis. The primary source of the difference can be found in their differing beliefs about the dynamics of the escalation process. In brief, the "ideal type" typology described below provides the basis for a more incisive and discriminating understanding of the manner in which different policy makers approach crisis management.[7]

Type A

Policy makers who follow this type of crisis bargaining code have an image of the adversary as almost exclusively aggressive in its objectives. Perhaps even more important than their image of the adversary is their image of crisis dynamics. For Type As, only intentional war is possible; they cannot even accept the possibility of an inadvertent war. Type As see crisis escalation as easily controllable even beyond the onset of limited nuclear exchanges and certainly controllable through very high levels of conventional combat.[8] They believe a crisis can escalate to war only when leaders on one side view the correlation of military forces as in their favor or when they see the other side as lacking resolve. As a result of this image of crisis dynamics, for the Type A policy maker, crisis management is reduced to efforts to anticipate and avoid gaps in one's military or intelligence capabilities and an insufficient demonstration of one's willingness to use force.[9]

Because of their extremely confident attitude toward control of unwanted escalation, Type As typically adopt a war-fighting approach to deterrence during a crisis. They tend to evaluate all changes in the rules of engagement and deployment of military forces in terms of their military utility rather than in terms of the problems they might pose for crisis management. A recent example of Type A individuals were those who held to the particular variant of maritime strategy favored by former Secretary of the Navy John Lehman.[10]

In those crises where they calculate that there is a fair possibility for military success, Type A policy makers will also tend to eschew coercive diplomacy—not to mention crisis management—and opt instead for a preemptive, military *fait accompli* as the best means of resolving the crisis.[11] For example, Type A policy makers favored bombing the Soviet missile sites in the 1962 Cuban Missile Crisis. If this tendency characterizes the behavior of Type A policy makers even in situations as intense as the Cuban Missile Crisis—with its serious risk of nuclear war—it is clear that their inclination toward decisive military action will be much more pronounced in nonsuperpower crises.

Type As tend to define objectives and evaluate success or failure in military rather than political terms and tend to dismiss or undervalue any potential negative political costs of U.S. actions. This tendency is illustrated by a debate in the winter of 1989–1990 over whether or not to deploy the nuclear-armed, "follow-on" Lance missile in West Germany. In this debate, Type A policy makers tended to evaluate the utility of deploying the modernized version of the Lance exclusively in terms of the additional military capability afforded by its increased range over that of the older Lance. They took this position despite the vehement, universal opposition in West Germany to the deployment of this missile, with German reunification appearing increasingly inevitable even at that early stage. (Warheads from the Lances would have fallen predominantly in what was then East Germany.)[12]

However, Type As do recognize the military (if not the political) constraints that militate against the use of force in most crisis circumstances. That is, they do examine the correlation of usable military forces both sides have at their disposal. If, in their estimation, there is little or uncertain probability that their preferred military action will be successful, the Type A policy maker will tend to favor strong, dramatic coercive actions rather than a *fait accompli*. Type As look with favor on the use of bluffs, and they see nothing inherently dangerous in the frequent use of nuclear threats as a means of coercion.

Of all four types, this approach to crisis bargaining poses the most serious threats to successful crisis management because of the propensity of Type A policy makers to be myopic about the political context of a crisis and the tenuous nature of crisis escalation. Moreover, this political myopia can pose problems for U.S. interests even when the United States moves beyond crisis management to the actual use of force, as it did in the Persian Gulf War. Had the war gone badly for the United States and its allies, a Type A policy maker might have seriously considered the use of tactical nuclear weapons against Iraqi forces, despite the negative long-term political consequences of such an action.

Type B

Type B policy makers would also be classified as hawks in the old vernacular, but they differ significantly from Type A hawks, primarily in their awareness of the political context of a crisis and in their image of crisis dynamics. Take the example of a crisis involving an adversary with nuclear or chemical weapons. Unlike Type As, Type Bs believe that at a particular point in the dynamics of such a crisis, one could speak meaningfully about inadvertent escalation to nuclear or chemical exchange. For the Type Bs, there is a brink or point beyond which control will become problematic. Contrast this with Type As' belief that crisis escalation can be reliably controlled not only throughout a crisis but into the actual onset of high levels of conventional combat and even during the initial nuclear or chemical exchanges. Type Bs, on the other hand, believe that it is quite possible for policy makers to effectively lose control of the escalation process, perhaps even before the actual onset of combat. That is, the Type B policy maker recognizes the possibility that certain actions may produce an unintended escalatory spiral that brings one side to the point where it mistakenly believes an attack is imminent and proceeds to launch a preemptive strike. A crucial point to recognize, however, is that Type B policy makers—in sharp contrast to the Type C and Type D policy makers described later—believe that they have a pretty good sense of the dynamics of the escalatory process and the type of actions that could lead to unwanted escalation. Precisely because of their confidence in their ability to identify and avoid, before it is too late, the point at which control is lost, Type B policy makers tend to be much more sanguine about coercive diplomacy than Type C and Type D policy makers.[13]

Type Bs believe that loss of control over the escalatory process can result not only from technical breakdowns but also because of the path that strategic interaction with the adversary can sometimes take. Given this image of crisis dynamics, Type Bs will specifically avoid those actions directed toward the adversary that could trigger inadvertent escalation. The salient question, then, centers on the nature of Type Bs' perceptions of precisely how unwanted escalation might occur, or, put another way, what they perceive as the cause of unwanted escalation. For superpower nuclear crises, there are two subvariant types of B policy makers with two different views as to escalation dynamics, the means by which control might be lost, and the policy responses this suggests.

Type B–I policy makers (for example, Richard Nixon and Henry Kissinger) are open to the use of both bluffs and nuclear threats. In fact, strong dramatic actions such as nuclear alerts are seen by these policy makers as sometimes being the safer course of action if they are taken early enough in the crisis.[14] The image of inadvertent escalation these policy makers hold is one in which both sides slide into the conflict through incremental, tit-for-tat responses, none of which seems particularly escalatory. Loss of control in a superpower crisis (which Type B–I policy makers see as resembling a game of bluff) occurs primarily because one's action does not suggest sufficient resolve early enough in the game.[15]

Type B–I policy makers tend toward the use of nuclear alerts in crises with another nuclear superpower for two reasons. First, as Kissinger has written, the suggestion that one will not even contemplate brandishing the nuclear sword is, for the Type B–I policy maker, more rather than less dangerous. It may lead another nuclear power to believe that one lacks real resolve to protect one's vital interests and open one to coercion by the other side.[16]

The second reason Type B–I policy makers assign utility and acceptable risks to nuclear alerts also derives from their image of crisis dynamics. For the Type B–I policy maker, inadvertent escalation to a nuclear war in a superpower conflict is more likely to occur through unintended conventional combat than through a nuclear threat. They believe this, first, because low-level conventional escalations are, in their judgment, erroneously seen by other policy makers as a relatively safe form of escalation, but, in fact, this tit-for-tat approach leads to the interactive, incrementally escalating process described earlier. Second, Type B–I policy makers believe it is much more difficult for the political decision maker to communicate with conventional forces and effectively control their actions in a prospective military confrontation than it is for him or her to control the nuclear forces under alert. Type B–I policy makers are also more sensitive than Type As to the tension between military and diplomatic logic. Faced with a choice between a conventional option with even a small probability of actual combat with the other superpower's conventional forces and the use of a nuclear threat, the Type B–I policy maker will often prefer the latter option because of the argument that a nuclear alert, particularly one involving land-based U.S. strategic forces, would be less susceptible to the pressures that would apply if a conventional force were out in the field and more exposed to attack.

In contrast, Type B–II policy makers (such as Dean Acheson) tend to believe that bluffing in general, and nuclear bluffing in particular, is difficult to accomplish and is quite dangerous. As Acheson put it, "sooner or later, someone will want to know if the statesman approaching the brink is bluffing."[17] Ironically, because of their fear of the dangers of coercive nuclear threats, Type B–II policy makers are often more willing then Type B–I policy makers to use conventional force to achieve a nonnuclear *fait accompli*. For the Type B–I policy maker, on the other hand, a nuclear threat is typically a less dangerous method of coercion than the use of conventional force when dealing with another superpower.

Despite these differences between Types B–I and B–II, however, the dominant belief of both is that *dramatic escalations are often safer than more incremental ones*. All Type Bs believe that incremental, small-step escalatory actions will be seen as timid and will tempt counterescalation. In short, all Type Bs believe that the most common cause of war in a crisis will be a failure to demonstrate resolve early and dramatically. The differences between Type B-I and B-II policy makers, so clear in superpower nuclear crises, are less pronounced during conventional crises, when both B-I and B-II policy makers tend to favor dramatic conventional escalation. Such escalation may make a coercive threat more credible, but as events leading to the Persian Gulf War demonstrated, at some point in the escalation, logistical problems, concern for troop morale, and other pressures could force the United States to move to the use of force before coercive diplomacy is given an adequate trial.

While Type B policy makers clearly hold a more realistic view of the stability of crisis situations than Type A policy makers do, on the whole they still have a high degree of confidence that inadvertent escalation in a crisis can be prevented by following their particular formulas or decision-making rules. Moreover, unlike Type A policy makers, Type B policy makers may include a "carrot" or accommodative measures as part of their crisis bargaining strategy. However, compared to the strategies of Type C and Type D, Type B policy makers put much greater emphasis on coercion, especially early in the crisis. And the method of coercion favored by Type B policy makers is likely to be much stronger. The central problem this approach to crisis bargaining poses for crisis management is the emphasis given to relatively strong, coercive actions in the initial phases of the crisis situation.[18]

Type C

Type C policy makers differ from all Type B policy makers in images of the adversary and of crisis dynamics. Type Cs believe it is often difficult to determine whether the objectives of the adversary in a particular crisis are primarily offensive or defensive. As a result, the interpretation Type Cs make about their adversary's objective in a crisis tends to be more influenced by the situational context.

With respect to the image of crisis dynamics, the most important difference between Type C policy makers and all other types is that Type Cs appear to have two images of the cause of war: One is based on a failure to demonstrate resolve and the other on spiraling escalation and responses to perceived provocations. While Type Bs also, in effect, have *two* images of how war breaks out, by far their dominant image and prime concern is that war might result from a failure to demonstrate resolve. Type Bs believe that there are relatively few paths to inadvertent war and that these paths are discrete and clearly marked. One can, in effect, avoid these slippery paths. In contrast, for the Type C policy makers, much more uncertainty surrounds the whole process; Type Cs believe there are many more paths to inadvertent war than Type Bs allow.[19]

As a result, Type C policy makers tend to be much less sanguine about controlling the crisis, particularly through the use of dramatic escalations. Type C policy makers believe that rather than constituting clear signals that contribute to crisis stability, such strongly coercive actions could set the inadvertent escalatory process in motion. Type C policy makers do not subscribe to the Type B beliefs that the brink can be recognized in advance and that one can exercise a high degree of control in a crisis up to this brink. As a result, when choosing between two coercive responses, the Type C policy maker will tend toward the more incremental coercive escalation rather than the more dramatic. The Type C policy maker also has an even stronger aversion to attempting a *fait accompli*. There are actually two reasons for this bias against the *fait accompli* and dramatic escalation. First, the fact that the Type C policy maker feels torn between two conflicting images of crisis escalation leads him or her to feel a great deal of uncertainty. Modest or low-level escalation is preferable because it is perceived to buy time for the policy maker to gather more information before choosing between alternative views. Robert McNamara's responses during the Cuban Missile Crisis are good examples of this point of view. Second, Type C policy makers favor the more incremental approach because it represents a compromise between the two images of war initiation. A low-level escalation signals resolve, so it presumably avoids giving the adversary a perception of U.S. weakness. At the same time, it demonstrates this resolve in a fashion that, it is hoped, least provokes the adversary. In fact, precisely because they have both a dual image of the adversary and a dual image of crisis dynamics, Type C policy makers have a strong propensity to opt for policy choices they believe reflect a middle course or compromise between these conflicting images.

For example, Type C policy makers assign great necessity and efficacy to mixed (that is, carrot and stick) strategies for influencing the adversary. In the mind of the Type C policy maker, this mixed bargaining strategy is the only way to steer safely through the perilously narrow passage between the Charybdis of inadvertent, spiraling escalation and the Scylla of appeasement. Type C policy makers are also more willing to compromise on nonessential issues, and they are more sensitive to situational variables.

In many respects, the Type C crisis bargaining code is the approach to crisis bargaining that poses the fewest problems for the theory of crisis management presented in this book. Nevertheless, there are potential problems for the effective practice of crisis management associated with the Type C policy maker. Since the problems for crisis management posed by Types A and B policy makers are somewhat more obvious, we will expand in greater detail on the problems the orientations of Type C policy makers might pose for crisis management.

First, as a result of their dual images of how war begins, and the resultant uncertainty they produce, Type Cs are more prone to procrastinate in making difficult decisions, even beyond the point where it is functionally useful for gathering information and carefully evaluating options. This can constitute a threat to effective crisis management in circumstances where the effective resolution of the crisis requires courageous and bold leadership.[20] A second dysfunctional consequence of their two-sided images and greater ability to see the complexity of issues is the fact that Type Cs are likely to experience greater stress in deciding what to do. As Jerrold Post suggests elsewhere in this book, stress can have severely debilitating effects on the quality of crisis decision making.[21] Third, the crisis behavior of Type C policy makers is subject to greater fluctuations, a propensity that may send confusing signals to the adversary. Finally, even their otherwise appropriate sensitivity to situational variables can have negative as well as positive consequences. On the positive side, conscious awareness of situational differences may enable the Type C policy maker to effectively tailor his or her response to the unique requirements of the situation. But, as will be noted later, susceptibility to situational influences does not necessarily imply a conscious, well thought out response to the situation.

Type D

The final type of crisis bargaining code is that held by Type D policy makers. This type of code involves a quite different image of the adversary, one that tends to err on the side of assuming the adversary operates solely from defensive motives. The Type D image of crisis dynamics emphasizes the idea that control is extremely problematic, if not impossible, in a crisis if one puts even modest emphasis on coercion. War would never (or only in extremely rare circumstances) occur because one did not demonstrate sufficient resolve; instead, war would result from the escalatory spiral created by coercive moves. Crisis management for this type of individual primarily involves ensuring that the crisis bargaining strategy and tactics emphasize accommodation. In fact, this type of policy maker would be hesitant to speak of crisis management or crisis bargaining at all. For these individuals, one's entire effort should be concentrated on crisis prevention. The problem is that some Type Ds can apply their own logic as rigidly across all situations as Type As or Type Bs do with theirs. In cases where the adversary does, in fact, have hegemonic objectives, this one-sided approach will ultimately exacerbate the crisis.

CRISIS BARGAINING BELIEFS AND DIFFERENT TYPES OF CRISES

It would be useful to illustrate the four types of bargaining codes by looking at how they might variously affect the evaluation of risks and options in three types of crises that might confront U.S. policy makers. There are a number of different dimensions along which one could divide crises. Here we focus on the interaction of crisis bargaining beliefs with the type of weapons and size of forces the adversary has at its disposal. We examine three types of crises: (1) nuclear crises between major powers; (2) crises involving smaller powers capable of delivering atomic, biological, or chemical weapons against civilian targets in the United States; and (3) "conventional" crises involving major or smaller powers.

The bipolar world, in which all post–WWII U.S. international crises have occurred, is rapidly giving way to a complex, multipolar international setting. While we may be witnessing the virtual end of an ideologically based tension between Marxist-Leninism and democratic liberalism, we are not, unfortunately, at the point where international crises—which could escalate to intentional or inadvertent war— are no longer possible. It is useful, therefore, to broaden our discussion of crisis management beyond an exclusive focus on U.S.-Soviet nuclear crises to an examination of crisis management involving a variety of adversaries with different objectives and military capabilities.

Nuclear Crises: Devolve or Centralize Control?

U.S.-Soviet crises are reasonably unlikely in the immediate future, barring an end to Soviet new political thinking in foreign policy, a large-scale Soviet military crackdown on independence movements near the borders with the West, or the emergence of a xenophobic Russian Republic as the remnant of a dismembered Soviet Empire. Nevertheless, as long as nuclear weapons exist, there is an ongoing chance of a crisis between the United States and another nuclear weapon state—including, but certainly not limited to, the Soviet Union or a nuclear-armed Russian Republic. To put it another way, the end of the Cold War does not eliminate the need to study nuclear crises and the peculiar constraints (including cognitive ones) these cases impose on effective crisis management.

A major dilemma would confront U.S. policy makers in the event of a severe crisis with another state armed with a sufficient number of nuclear-armed delivery systems to launch a surprise attack against U.S. nuclear C^3I (command-control-communication and intelligence) assets. Many analysts argue that there are two diametrically opposed objectives with respect to managing nuclear options during such a crisis. On the one hand, there is the need to preserve the credibility of one's deterrence. This requirement militates for such things as the devolution of launch authority early in the crisis. The problem with this perspective is that the possibility of an unauthorized launch is increased. On the other hand, the need to avoid unwanted escalation militates for continued tight political control. This can undermine deterrence, however, by making a decapitation strike by the nuclear adversary more attractive in a crisis.[22] The four different types of crisis bargaining codes (Types A, B, C, and D) respond quite differently to this dilemma.

Type As and B–Is. Because of their particular image of crisis dynamics, Type As simply do not recognize such a dilemma; they only see the possibility of a decapitation strike. Type As tend to favor a much more rapid and extensive devolution of the command and control of nuclear weapons in the event of a severe crisis. Type As might also favor a LOW (launch on warning) policy and a declaratory and operational nuclear policy that includes options for a preemptive damage limitation strike in the event a strike by another nuclear power is perceived as imminent. Type B–I policy makers would be much more sensitive to the sort of nuclear dilemma described above but would still often typically tend to err on the side of preserving the credibility of the deterrent at the expense of crisis stability. They might favor a damage limitation capability or perhaps a LUA (launch under attack) policy but would tend to oppose a LOW policy because they allow for the possibility of misperceptions at the brink.

Type B–IIs and Type Cs. Type B–II and Type C policy makers would probably respond to the dilemma in similar ways—that is, both would tend to err on the side of more rather than less control of nuclear options by the NCA (National Command Authorities). Both would be strongly opposed to a LOW or even a LUA policy.

Type Ds. Type Ds would respond to the problem in a straightforward manner—they would deny the existence of a dilemma. Type Ds would in all circumstances be so preoccupied with preserving crisis stability that they would ignore, or greatly minimize, threats to deterrence from a decapitation strike. Type Ds would simply assume the robustness of deterrence and focus exclusively on avoiding the appearance of impending offensive action.

Crises with Smaller States Armed with Chemical Weapons

There are some interesting parallels between nuclear crises and crises involving a small state armed with chemical or biological weapons (we put the emphasis on the much more probable chemical threat). There is an increasing risk that in future crises the United States may be confronted by a smaller state armed with ballistic missiles and chemical weapons. While the immense costs, the highly complex technical hurdles, and the relative ease of international monitoring have exercised major constraints on the proliferation of nuclear weapons to smaller states, these three constraints are not operative to the same degree when it comes to chemical weapons. For precisely this reason, chemical weapons have been referred to as the "poor states'" nuclear weapons.[23]

To understand how policy makers might react to this type of crisis, it is important to understand that chemical (and biological) weapons elicit a different sort of response than the threats from conventional weapons. There is a vague but highly generalized belief that such weapons are less humane than conventional weapons. Like nuclear weapons, chemical weapons share the dubious quality of breaking down the moral distinction between combatants and noncombatants. The damage from a single chemical weapon can be extensive, in both geographic scope and lethal effect.

Tight international controls would seriously retard the proliferation of ballistic missile technology but would not totally eliminate the threat. First, neither defense systems nor the nonproliferation regime can address the entire range of possible delivery options. Second, to eliminate fully the coercive effects of even a limited, poor-quality missile threat (such as Iraq's Scud missiles posed in the Gulf War), there must be widespread belief that defense systems are one hundred percent effective. Simply knocking a missile off course or out of the sky might not be enough if a functioning warhead could still fall on a civilian target. For all of these reasons, terror weapons may provide smaller states with significant coercive bargaining power—despite the fact that the military capabilities of these states may be much lower than those of the United States.

Against this background, I make the following general points. First, in the event of an explicit or clearly implied threat involving a chemical or biological attack against U.S. cities, the initial inclination of all types of policy makers would probably be to consider a preemptive U.S. attack against the other state's terror weapon systems if—and this is a big if—they were persuaded that there was a close to 100 percent probability for success in such an attack. For example, the threat of a terror weapons attack is likely to override—at the onset—the tendency of Type D policy makers to try diplomacy first.

Second, despite the fact that no type of policy maker would rule out a preemptive U.S. attack from the onset, the calculation of risk will be influenced partly by the images of crisis dynamics that each policy maker holds. In practice, what this is likely to mean is that as questions arise as to the chances for a near-perfect preemptive strike, Type C and Type D policy makers will tend to move rapidly away from their initial inclination toward preemption.

Third, in the much more probable crisis situations where there is no explicit or clearly implied threat by the adversary to use the chemical weapons it possesses, different crisis bargaining beliefs will tend to lead to different policy orientations. These differences will be roughly congruent with the differing responses of the four types of policy makers toward nuclear crises. For example, Type A policy makers would tend to be just as unconcerned about an inadvertent escalation to a chemical exchange as they would be about inadvertent nuclear exchange, while Type C and Type D policy makers would be very concerned about inadvertent escalation.

Finally, and most important, the first few confrontations between the United States and a smaller power armed with terror weapons will be more like the early U.S.-Soviet superpower crises rather than the later superpower crises of the 1970s, which is to say, the early crises involving chemical weapons will be very dangerous. This argument is based on the evolutionary development of U.S. and Soviet crisis behavior—an evolution that evinced a positive learning curve. With smaller powers, the rules of prudence we have seen emerge in U.S. and Soviet crisis behavior will not have had time to emerge.[24] Initially, at least, one or both parties might feel that their basic security interests may be threatened. Additionally, some of the adversaries will have a radically different culture than our own, which can increase the chances for misperceptions and miscalculation. In short, the possibility of inadvertent war in these cases is probably much higher than in many other types of crises.

The bargaining behavior of different types of policy makers may pose a variety of problems for crisis management in this new type of crisis. One danger comes from the tendency of Type C policy makers to fluctuate between tough and conciliatory responses. If the logic for the fluctuation is not clear to the adversary— that is, if the adversary does not understand that U.S. actions are directly tied to its own behavior—misperceptions and miscalculations are possible.

But the crisis bargaining propensities of Type A policy makers may be the most dangerous. The tendency of Type A policy makers to employ strong, coercive actions or undertake preemptive military actions, even when they have relatively limited political objectives, may make it very difficult for the adversary to believe its basic security interests are not threatened. The mutual confidence of both sides that their basic security interests will be respected is the sine qua non of crisis management; without it, efforts at crisis management will, at best, be problematic.

Conventional Crises

In international crises that do not involve nuclear or chemical weapons, the image of the adversary is much more important in determining policy responses than is the case in crises in which the United States is faced with the possibility of nuclear or chemical attack on its homeland. This image is particularly important in a conventional crisis involving a smaller power that does not have the military capability to attack the continental United States. It may also be important in conventional crises with a major power, although probably to a lesser degree. Second, most policy makers appear to envision different scenarios leading to conventional war or the unwanted escalation of low-intensity conflict, as contrasted with the nuclear or chemical war scenarios. Partly because of these different scenarios, but mostly because of the much lower costs of combat and escalation in a non-nuclear crisis, all four types of policy makers are likely to display a greater propensity to use *force* in non-nuclear crises.[25] Personality differences on the dimension of risk acceptance and risk aversion are more likely to be relevant in non-nuclear crises, given the much lower risks at stake.[26]

Nevertheless, in most non-nuclear crises, important differences remain in the policy responses of individuals with different crisis bargaining codes. Even in low-level crises, the image of crisis dynamics and beliefs about escalation can be important determinants of an individual's response. And the potential impact of these beliefs on a policy maker's preferences will increase when the adversary is a major conventional power. A key point of division is often over the utility of dramatic coercive escalation versus a limited or measured response. The response of Type A and Type B–II policy makers would be nearly identical in this instance. Both would favor a *fait accompli*, circumstances permitting. Type B–I policy makers would prefer a strategy of coercive diplomacy to alter the will of the adversary rather than a use of force to destroy all the adversary's capabilities (because the Type B–I policy maker is more predisposed to see potential problems with the *fait accompli*). If escalation of U.S. responses seems called for, all Type A and Type B policy makers would favor dramatic U.S. coercive actions over more measured, limited responses. According to this perspective, one should, in essence, give the adversary much more in return than one received from the adversary. Type C policy makers would tend to favor a mixed policy of carrot and stick, with situational variables determining which of the two would be given first and which would dominate. Any coercive military responses would be measured responses, carefully calculated not to escalate the crisis. Type D policy makers would put the emphasis on diplomacy or perhaps nonmilitary coercive responses (such as sanctions).

FORMS OF COGNITIVE REPRESENTATION

Beliefs may be categorized on the basis of substantive issue areas (as we did in the case of image of adversary, image of crisis dynamics, and optimal bargaining strategies), or they may be classified according to the form of their cognitive representation—that is, the manner in which beliefs about these issue areas are remembered or recalled. Forms of cognitive representation are important because they entail somewhat different dynamics of perception and misperception.

The beliefs that comprise a crisis bargaining code may be cognitively represented in at least three different forms. The first type is the most straightforward, as it involves beliefs that are consciously understood: descriptive and prescriptive verbal statements about the adversary, the problem of controlling escalation, and optimal bargaining tactics. In this case, a policy maker more or less consciously draws on these verbal statements to interpret information on the crisis and to generate and evaluate options for responding. Cognitive beliefs of this sort would include such rules as "bargain from strength."

However, recent cognitive psychological literature has drawn attention to the importance of several other ways in which beliefs may be cognitively represented.[27] These other types of beliefs play a more subtle role in information processing, and they typically come into play in a less conscious fashion; consequently, the policy maker is less aware that they are affecting his or her interpretation of the crisis and the generation and evaluation of different responses.

The type of belief that is activated in the least conscious manner is referred to in cognitive psychological literature as "scripts."[28] One defining characteristic of scripts is that they seem to be remembered and recalled in the form of a series of connected mental images rather than in the verbal statements of belief mentioned above. Scripts typically deal with a smaller subset of issues than is contained in an entire cognitive belief system. Scripts always depict causal relationships between different events or actions. Interpretation of causality is clearly a crucial task in effective crisis management. When crisis bargaining beliefs take the form of scripts, the quality of this interpretation can be impaired by three features that seem to be characteristic of many scripts: They tend to be oversimplified; they often carry strong emotional content that provides an unconscious motivation to suppress inconsistent information; and they are typically recalled and acted upon in a relatively unconscious fashion.[29]

One simpler way to think of the operation of scripts is given in the following illustration. The process begins when some dramatic event in the crisis situation automatically triggers an existing script. The series of causal events depicted in the script is then unconsciously viewed by the policy maker as one would perceive a related series of subliminal images in a film. This series of images conveys a simplistic, highly emotional scenario of what will happen under a particular sequence of events. For example, imagine being exposed to a series of vivid, subliminal images that begins with scenes depicting naive attempts to appease the Soviets and culminates in horrifying images of Soviet retribution against the citizens of Berlin. The fact that scripts are represented in mental images may account for their tendency to be more emotionally laden than other types of cognitive beliefs.

Analogies and metaphors are the third form in which cognitive beliefs may be represented in an individual's crisis bargaining code. These may be historical analogies deriving from previous international crises (for example, the Munich analogy), or they may be analogies or metaphors relating to more general situations (that is, the use of various tactics in poker as a metaphor for dealing with the bargaining situation). Analogies and metaphors represent a cross between consciously recalled verbal states of belief and the more semiconscious scripts. Certain lessons from a historical analogy or a metaphor may be consciously represented in the crisis bargaining code; however, the analogy or metaphor may affect decision making in ways the policy maker may not expect beyond these verbal statements of belief. Historical analogies can lead to misperceptions and miscalculations if they are used without careful attention to differences between the current situation and the historical analog.[30]

Like scripts, metaphors are recalled in the form of a mental image rather than as verbal statements.[31] Because metaphors, by definition, are farther removed from international relations than are historical analogies, their influence is more subtle and potentially more insidious. Actually, U.S. policy toward the Soviet Union has been replete with commonly used metaphors that may have entered, and in some cases distorted, the crisis bargaining codes of many policy makers. For example, the metaphor of falling dominos is a common image used to convey two arguments: (1) that relations between superpowers are a zero-sum game, and (2) that the "loss" of even a strategically unimportant state will ultimately affect the military balance because the chain reaction will proceed until it topples states strategically vital to the United States. So far, the metaphor is useful in illustrating two debatable—but at least plausible—assertions.

But metaphors are like icebergs (I could not resist the use of a metaphor myself)—the meaning that is intended represents only the visible portion of the meaning implied by the metaphor. The meanings hidden below the surface of a metaphor can contribute to misperception and miscalculation. This is the case because the nonisomorphic relationship between the metaphor and reality will sometimes produce, unconsciously, a distortion in the policy maker's perception of international events. For example, one of many nonisomorphic properties of the falling dominos metaphor is the implicit assumption of an equal propensity of all the dominos to fall. This may be true of dominos—arranged in a particular fashion—but it is clearly not true of states. If the falling dominos metaphor were to more accurately reflect international events, one would have to make some dominos much stronger than others (reflecting their different military capabilities), and one would have to create differing gaps between the dominos (reflecting the differential gain the adversary would achieve by toppling proximate states in different locations).

We are not suggesting that any policy maker would rely exclusively on such a simple metaphor in making bargaining decisions, nor are we suggesting that an intelligent policy maker would not recognize these differences if they were pointed out to him or her. But we do argue that operating under the severe time and information constraints of a crisis, even a highly intelligent policy maker may not be fully cognizant of the hidden meanings of a metaphor that is almost unconsciously activated during the crisis. In a crisis situation, a policy maker who employs the falling dominos metaphor might come to the erroneous conclusion that the fall of a particular state/domino is more imminent and more probable than even a worst case analysis of relative military capabilities would suggest.[32]

THE ROLE OF CRISIS BARGAINING BELIEFS IN MISPERCEPTION AND MISCALCULATION

While all policy makers must rely on their crisis bargaining codes to help make sense of the information they confront, sometimes these beliefs impose a procrustean bed into which crisis information is forced. Crisis bargaining codes pose problems for effective crisis management when they are inherently oversimplified, insufficiently differentiated to deal with unique crisis situations, or inappropriately applied. When this occurs, crisis bargaining beliefs can contribute to one or more of the following misperceptions or miscalculations: (1) an exaggeration of the degree of threat posed to U.S. interests, (2) a tendency to downplay the risks of certain provocative actions, or, conversely, (3) a tendency to exaggerate the risks of coercive action so much that only noncoercive actions are taken, which may encourage the adversary to exploit the crisis.

The first two problems are the most common; the policy maker tends to discard the principles of crisis management either because he or she erroneously concludes that the military logic of the situation demands drastic action or erroneously comes to believe that he or she can coerce the adversary at a lower risk than crisis management theory would suggest. Precisely how do such misperceptions and miscalculations occur?

The answer is not as simple as one might expect. Contrary to what older views in psychology asserted, many misperceptions are not the result of an internal motivation to act consistently with one's beliefs so as to avoid the unpleasant state of dissonance between beliefs and actions. It has subsequently been discovered that there are frequent exceptions to striving for consistency.[33] Nor is it particularly useful to suggest that misperceptions and miscalculations occur because some policy makers are generally "risk-aversive" while others are "risk-acceptive."[34] This distinction is less useful than it appears at first glance in accounting for miscalculations because, and this is the critical point, all policy makers do not calculate risk in the same fashion.[35] Instead, different policy makers calculate risks on the basis of very different crisis bargaining beliefs, in particular very different images of crisis dynamics. In a confrontation with an adversary armed with chemical or nuclear weapons, those policy makers who appear willing to take higher risks are really those who see less risk in their actions. In fact, they may see their strong, coercive actions as actually safer than more mixed responses. Policy makers can make serious misjudgments, even when they think they are open to discrepant information and even when they are seriously attempting to manage the crisis so that it does not escalate to war.

We argue that misperception occurs as a result of an abuse of one of three necessary information processing functions performed by the crisis bargaining code. Policy makers in a crisis can confront a variety of different information problems: (1) information overload, (2) decisions for which there is incomplete or no information, and (3) decisions for which there are contradictory interpretations of the same piece of information. The information processing role or function that crisis bargaining codes perform varies for each of these different information environments.

Faced with situations of information overload, the role of the crisis bargaining code is to provide certain cognitive shortcuts so that the policy maker can expeditiously make his or her way through the overwhelming amount of data and make a decision. Faced with situations of information deficits, the role of the crisis bargaining code is as gap filler. In the third instance, the role of the crisis bargaining code is as arbiter of contradictory information. We will now examine the manner in which these three necessary functions might be abused.

Information Overload
and the Cognitive Shortcut Function

In a crisis, policy makers are often deluged with a bewildering array of data, reports, and oral briefings. This might not be a problem were it not for the severe time pressures; in many instances, there is simply not enough time to study carefully all the reports or to listen attentively to all the briefings a policy maker could potentially receive.[36] At a bare minimum, during a serious crisis, policy makers are likely to receive several National Intelligence Situation Reports (NISRs), several Special National Intelligence Estimates (SNIEs), press clippings and short analyses from their own staffs, and at least one oral expert briefing for each day of the crisis.[37] Given the fact that policy makers (and their staffs) must attempt to assimilate the fairly technical and politically complex material contained in these reports and briefings in a relatively short period of time and must deal—even during a serious crisis—with issues outside of this crisis, this very conservative list of information demands is itself quite burdensome.

But if the crisis starts moving rapidly, as it often does, the problem of information overload can actually intensify. As the pace of events accelerates, hard-pressed analysts may not be able to produce formal reports soon enough and frequently enough to satisfy policy makers. (Actually, these formal reports are intended, in part, to mitigate the information overload problem by eliminating information of dubious or unconfirmed veracity, eliminating peripheral details and highlighting key points, and reducing the redundancy from the multiplicity of reports coming from different parts of the intelligence community.) Frantic to keep pace themselves with a fast-breaking serious crisis, policy makers may then ask to see more of the cable traffic or more raw intelligence input, as well as request additional ad hoc analyses generated by various subsets of the intelligence community or by experts on their own staffs. Ironically, modern technology has, in some respects, compounded rather than mitigated this problem. Policy makers now have access to computer networks that can instantly generate detailed background data on crisis hotspots. These computer-generated reports are in addition to, not in lieu of, the reports described above. The cumulative result is obviously a serious problem of information overload. Some of this information will be critically important, but much of it will be either redundant or relatively trivial. The problem, of course, is to separate the wheat from the chaff.

In this world of information overload, crisis bargaining codes operate as cognitive shortcuts by performing two necessary (though easily distorted) information processing functions. First, especially in the preliminary phase of attempting to define the situation, beliefs about the image of the adversary and the nature of escalation can have a major impact on how both policy makers and intelligence analysts determine the critical questions to be addressed. The role of the bargaining code is crucial because the choice of questions that are asked will itself have an impact on the definition of the problem. If the wrong questions are asked, the quality of the crisis decision making is impaired. Crisis bargaining codes can have a major impact on this orientation task.

Second, having defined what questions are critical, the policy maker must have some means for determining what types of data and what information sources are the most reliable means of answering these questions. Crisis bargaining codes can also have a major impact on this evidentiary task. The policy makers must also decide where to direct the focus of additional intelligence gathering and data assessment, given that they can only read so much of the material that is generated. The first type of perceptual error we will discuss—namely, the use of overly simplified or distorted cognitive shortcuts—can occur as a result of either the conscious application of certain decisional rules of thumb imbedded in a particular crisis bargaining code or the more unconscious activation of certain scripts by situational stimuli. In both cases, the result may be a dangerous degree of selective attention.[38]

One example of such misperception can be seen in the way Dean Acheson processed information during the Berlin Crisis of 1961. On June 4, 1961, during their summit meeting in Vienna, Nikita Khrushchev shocked President John F. Kennedy by presenting him with an ultimatum on Berlin that was interpreted as demanding forced withdrawal of the Western Allies from West Berlin. In this particular crisis, as in many crises, there were serious problems with information overload: Some of the information concerned the flow of refugees from East Germany, an exodus that was rapidly turning into a flood; but the information also dealt with a variety of other issues, such as Soviet and GDR (German Democratic Republic) military moves and nuclear blustering by Khrushchev going back to the onset of this particular Berlin Crisis in 1958. In interpreting this deluge of data, Acheson had to determine what information was critical for assessing Soviet objectives in the crisis: Was their primary concern defensive, or did they have hegemonic designs? Acheson ultimately concluded that the Soviets did have malign objectives—they were testing the resolve of the West to preserve the independence of West Berlin.

What is interesting is the apparent logic by which Acheson arrived at his conclusion. In order to simplify and focus on the task of interpreting Soviet objectives, Acheson appears to have drawn upon a long-standing decisional rule of thumb implicit in his crisis bargaining code. While Acheson frequently saw Soviet actions as motivated by offensive rather than defensive concerns, he also believed the Soviets might sometimes be motivated by what they considered requirements for their defensive security, as they had been in their actions against the revolution in Hungary in 1956. As a general rule, Acheson believed that in order to determine whether the Soviets had offensive objectives in any particular crisis, the most important index and the most important questions to ask concerned the tactics the Soviets were using in that crisis. Acheson believed Soviet actions in their invasion of Hungary in 1956 were typical of Soviet tactics in situations where they entertained no offensive designs against NATO (although obviously their attitude toward the Hungarian freedom fighters was anything but benign). Using this analogy as a base of comparison, Acheson believed that if the Soviet leaders thought their security interests were really threatened in a particular case, they would act dramatically, openly, and ruthlessly. In contrast, if the Soviets moved cautiously or surreptitiously in a crisis, Acheson believed their intentions in that case posed a real threat to U.S.-NATO interests.[39]

Acheson seems to have drawn on this decisional rule of thumb in concluding that Soviet leaders were pursuing offensive objectives in the 1961 Berlin Crisis that went far beyond the defensive concern of halting the flow of refugees. After all, this particular crisis had really begun in 1958 when Khrushchev initiated his first ultimatum on Berlin. Now it was early summer 1961, and the Soviets had still not responded with force despite the fact that the West largely ignored the first ultimatum. To Acheson, this sort of temporizing was not the usual response if Soviet leaders were sincerely worried about some aspect of their security. On the contrary, it suggested a wary, on-again, off-again probing of Western resolve. This decisional rule of thumb is not unreasonable; in fact, it is quite plausible. Nevertheless, because of his great reliance on this particular cognitive shortcut, Acheson virtually ignored absolutely critical information about the crisis: the reports about the exodus of refugees from East Germany to West Germany through Berlin. These reports were critical precisely because they provided a basis for an alternate interpretation of Soviet objectives.

What is important to see here is that Acheson did not discount this information on the refugees because he was totally closed to the idea that the Soviets might be concerned with defensive objectives in a particular crisis. Instead, the reason Acheson discounted the information on the refugees can be attributed to the particular cognitive shortcut he employed at this time. According to his own decisional rule of thumb, the information on the refugees was simply irrelevant for making the determination of Soviet objectives. On the basis of what we now know to be a faulty analysis of Soviet objectives in this crisis, Acheson advised President Kennedy to take a number of strong, coercive actions that might well have made subsequent attempts at crisis management quite difficult.[40]

Information Deficits: The Gap-Filling Role

The second manner in which crisis bargaining beliefs influence policy choice is through the gap-filling function. Sometimes the problem is not one of deciding what information to seek but simply that there are large gaps in the information that is available. This is particularly true with respect to assessments of probable outcomes and the manner in which a crisis is likely to unfold in the future under various contingencies. The gap-filling function seems to be most important when policy makers are assessing the degree of risk associated with different courses of action in a crisis. For these types of decisions, the problem is the inherent uncertainty about the consequences of different courses of action. Much of this uncertainty is likely to remain no matter how long and how thoroughly the policy maker researches the problem.

The psychological literature suggests that analogies and metaphors often serve as a common type of gap-filling device in dealing with decisions with intrinsic uncertainty.[41] Because of this uncertainty, recourse to analogies and metaphors is inevitable, and it may often be helpful. The question is not whether historical analogies should be allowed to play a role in decision making, but whether, when making use of them, the policy maker is sensitive to the possibility that the present situation is different in important respects from the historical case. This point is important, as the hasty application of a historical analogy, with parallels to only part of the present case, may skew the policy maker's perception of other aspects of the situation that are of critical importance in order to make the appropriate policy choices.[42]

Apart from historical analogies, it is possible that more general bargaining analogies may serve a gap-filling function regarding phenomena that are difficult to calculate. One bargaining metaphor that occurs in the crisis bargaining codes of some individuals is the poker metaphor. There is some tentative but plausible evidence that suggests that Richard Nixon's attitude toward poker may have influenced his general orientation toward crisis bargaining, crisis escalation, and risk assessment.[43]

The first lesson Nixon may have drawn from the poker analogy is that one gains bargaining power if one's actions are unpredictable. Unpredictability is an important, perhaps necessary, part of many different approaches to deterrence (for example, as part of the policy of flexible response). Nevertheless, according to at least one commentator, Nixon took unpredictable behavior several steps further.[44] A case may be made that Nixon saw great utility in appearing personally unpredictable and possibly even irrational to the adversary. In Nixon's approach, this meant seeking to gain and utilize a reputation for acting unpredictably at times and in an inordinately strong fashion, so that his actions would be viewed as incommensurate either with the limited stakes involved or with the actions of the adversary. Whether Nixon drew this lesson from a poker analogy cannot, of course, be definitely determined. What is clear is that Nixon repeatedly referred to poker to depict how one should act in international relations, including the utility of appearing unpredictable.

In *Six Crises*, Nixon contradicted the conventional wisdom of the day that Khrushchev was irrational (such as when he pounded his shoe on the podium at the U.N.) by asserting that Khrushchev simply knew how to use the adversary's fear of irrationality or emotionality for increasing the credibility of his threats and his bargaining leverage. Nixon paid Khrushchev his supreme compliment in this regard by declaring that his behavior proved that "Khrushchev would make a good poker player." Nixon strongly implied in this passage that he believed Khrushchev's approach to crisis bargaining was one that should be emulated.[45] Later, in *The Real War*, Nixon offered the following observation:

[I]nternational relations are a lot like poker—stud poker with a hole card. The hole card is all important because without it your opponent—the Soviet leader, for instance, has perfect knowledge of whether he can beat you. If he knows he will win he will raise you. If he cannot, he will fold and get out of the game. The United States is an open society. We have all but one of our cards face up on the table. *Our only covered card is the will, nerve, and unpredictability of the President—his ability to make the enemy think twice about raising the ante* (emphasis added).[46]

The poker analogy may also have influenced Nixon's beliefs about the process of escalation in an international crisis. Nixon seems to view unwanted, spiraling escalation in an international crisis as roughly analogous to a situation in which one's adversaries continue to stay in a poker hand in response to low raises on your part. In poker, if one is planning a bluff, frequently the safest strategy is to make a high raise rather than a modest one, for the latter might be seen as evidence of a lack of resolve. As a Type B-I policy maker, Nixon applied a similar logic to his assessment of the safest response in an international crisis. In the game of international crisis and nuclear brinkmanship (a form of bluffing), Nixon believed that in order to avoid a loss of control and an unwanted escalation to nuclear war, the safest response would be a strong, dramatic demonstration of U.S. resolve early in the crisis. This is consistent with his approval of the escalation of DefCon 3 in the 1973 Middle East Crisis—a fairly high-level alert given the relatively low-level importance of the stakes involved. Nixon and Kissinger clearly viewed this alert as the safest and most appropriate course of action.[47]

In summary, the image of crisis dynamics that forms part of an individual's crisis bargaining code is important to that individual's approach to risk assessment. If a policy maker believes that the world is highly stable and that inadvertent war is nearly or totally impossible, he or she might favor options that include a high degree of bluff, believing that one has everything to gain and little to lose from such an approach. On the other hand, a policy maker who tends to view the world as unstable might be more influenced by his or her estimation of the intrinsic value of the issues at stake, thereby opting for such actions as nuclear alerts only in those cases to which the policy maker assigned the highest importance for U.S. interests.

An illustration of the role the image of crisis dynamics can play in one's assignment of risk and estimations of the probable success of different options can be seen in the actions of Gen. Lucius Clay during the Berlin Wall Crisis of 1961. It is strongly evident in Clay's Type A crisis bargaining code that he viewed the international situation as stable, so much so that the idea of inadvertent war through loss of control was for Clay an oxymoron. However, Clay believed that not everyone accepted his image and that many people, including the Soviets, believed just the opposite. Clay sought to exploit the asymmetry between his own conception of crisis dynamics and what he saw as the Soviet perspective. He believed there was tremendous bargaining utility to be gained by taking actions that "kept the adversary off-guard."[48] Consequently, during the tense period shortly after the East Germans and Soviets had begun to build the wall across the city of Berlin, Clay recommended that Vice-President Johnson fly into Berlin along the prescribed corridor over East Germany above the 10,000 foot level. Such a recommendation might not seem so novel (in fact, Johnson soon did fly into Berlin, but below this altitude) were it not for the fact that, as part of a general policy of harassing the West Berlin missions, the Soviets had hinted that they might shoot down any Western planes that came in above this level. There seemed to be little consideration on Clay's part about the risks such action might pose for U.S.-Soviet relations, not to mention the personal risks for Lyndon Johnson.[49]

Contradictory Information: The Arbiter Role

The final type of information problem a policy maker can face in a crisis arises when he or she receives contradictory reports from different experts about the same item of information. Crisis bargaining codes operate in this instance in their arbiter role—again, performing a necessary function by coping with the problem of evaluating these opposing arguments. The fact that crisis bargaining beliefs will lead to certain policy inclinations is not necessarily unconstructive. The policy maker must employ some sort of criteria, derived partly from his or her crisis bargaining beliefs, to weigh the merits of differing interpretations and recommendations. However, if this evaluation process is conducted objectively, a decision will presumably not be made until after a reasonable period of time has elapsed in which both interpretations were carefully examined. Moreover, the rational use of the arbiter role of crisis bargaining beliefs also requires that the policy maker be receptive to subsequent information that might prove the initial choice incorrect.

But these requirements of a rational decision-making process are not always met. There are two typical types of abuses of the arbiter role of crisis bargaining beliefs.

One type of abuse occurs when there has been premature closure on an interpretation of contradictory or ambiguous information. When premature closure occurs, the policy maker has made no real attempt to examine the alternative points of view or to remain open to feedback, and in many cases there is good reason to question the quality of the criteria employed in the first place to evaluate the options. A second, less obvious abuse of the arbiter role of crisis bargaining beliefs occurs when the policy maker undertakes what amounts to an irrational compromise between the two conflicting interpretations.

Interestingly, policy makers who hold different types of beliefs will be prone to different abuses of the arbiter role. Those who hold Type A, B, or D crisis bargaining beliefs are more apt to err through premature closure, while policy makers who hold Type C beliefs are more vulnerable to irrational compromise. Because the first type of error—premature closure—is more readily understood, we will focus here on the second, more complex type of abuse of the arbiter role.

The Cuban Missile Crisis of 1962 stands out as a case in which most—but far from all—of the U.S. crisis decision making was fairly good. One major exception to the generally positive record, however, concerns the decision not to conduct further direct overflights of western Cuba, which was made prior to the onset of the crisis per se at a meeting of the COMCOR (Committee on Overhead Reconnaissance) on September 10, 1962. The decision ultimately proved to be a serious mistake because it was during the six-week cessation of reconnaissance that the Soviet missiles in Cuba were readied to the point that at least some may have had operational readiness for firing by the middle of October, when U.S. policy makers finally became aware of their presence.[50]

This serious intelligence failure was the product of many factors. One contributing factor was the fact that prior to the COMCOR decision, the U.S. intelligence community had issued an NIE (National Intelligence Estimate) that concluded that the Soviets probably would not undertake the high risk of introducing offensive missiles into Cuba. Based on past Soviet behavior, which indicated a reluctance to take high risks in the deployment of missiles, this was a reasonable estimate.[51] However, not everyone shared this point of view. Not only were congressional Republicans skeptical; more important, the director of the CIA, John McCone, took sharp exception to his own analysts. Director of Central Intelligence McCone argued on several occasions that the Soviets would probably attempt to deploy nuclear-armed MRBMs and IRBMS (medium-range and intermediate-range ballistic missiles) in Cuba.[52]

The September 5 overflight had produced no evidence of any Soviet ballistic missiles. What the overflight had confirmed, however, was that the Soviets were deploying SAMs (surface-to-air missiles, armed with conventional warheads), especially in the western portion of the island. McCone and others argued that SAM deployments were an obvious first step before the introduction of medium- and intermediate-range ballistic missiles, as the SAMs would provide protection for the ballistic missiles against air attacks. But other analysts disagreed, calling the SAMs merely a defensive measure against a U.S. air strike against Cuba. Everyone agreed that the SAMs could be very effective. That fact was driven home to the COMCOR policy makers just one day before their meeting, when, in an incident unrelated to Cuba, the PRC (People's Republic of China) shot down a U-2 flown by the Republic of China over PRC airspace.

On September 10, 1962, the members of COMCOR met to make a decision on whether or not to continue U.S. U-2 overflights of Cuba, with special attention paid to western Cuba. The decision had to be made on the basis of totally contradictory interpretations from the intelligence community of the significance of the Soviet SAM emplacements—undoubtedly a difficult task. The decision that COMCOR did make, however, was a curious one. It superficially appears to be a rational compromise between the conflicting interpretations, but on closer examination, it is clear that the decision was fatally flawed.

The decision called for a termination of direct overflights of those parts of Cuba where the SAM emplacements were concentrated (that is, especially, western Cuba). The supposed compromise or compensation for the lack of direct overflights would be that the U-2s would "dip" into Cuban airspace, outside the range of the SAMs, where they would take oblique or peripheral photos of western Cuba. Ostensibly, this compromise would prevent the loss of a U-2 while still permitting adequate air surveillance of the suspicious sites in western Cuba. The problem was that this plan simply did not permit real surveillance of the SAM-protected areas—the very parts of the island in which McCone and others (very presciently) argued that deployment of offensive missiles was most likely to occur.[53] In other words, COMCOR's decision ruled out the most important type of surveillance. The decision is even odder if one considers the fact that even the NIE report, which predicted that the Soviets would probably not deploy the missiles, still included a recommendation for a "continued alert" of the situation. This hedge was included in the NIE report because there was a widespread consensus in the intelligence community that if the Soviets took what the majority felt was the unexpected action of introducing the missiles, a continued U.S. alert would dramatically alter the Soviet ability to hit U.S. sites on short notice. Had the policy makers in COMCOR examined the decision for oblique photographs more carefully, and had they asked more questions about the ability of this angle of photos to adequately cover all of the island, they would have been more aware of the serious flaws in the option. The available evidence suggests that they did not seem to be aware of these problems. What accounts for this curious lapse?

One major factor that contributed to the failure to conduct the surveillance can be found in the role played by the crisis bargaining beliefs of Secretary of State Dean Rusk and Secretary of Defense Robert McNamara, the critical members of COMCOR in this particular situation. In sharp contrast to people like McCone, both Rusk and McNamara were Type C policy makers who held two images of war initiation in a crisis: One image suggested that if war occurred, it would come about because of a failure to be sufficiently prepared; and the second image suggested that war could occur inadvertently through spiraling escalatory moves.[54] One can see that these differing images would lead to differing policy inclinations toward the continuance of U-2 overflights: On the basis of the first image they would be inclined to favor direct overflights despite the risk of losing U-2s, while the second image would predispose them against direct overflights. There is good reason to believe that their inadvertent war image dominated (for reasons to be explained below) but that Rusk and McNamara still tried to convince themselves that they were satisfying the need for careful surveillance required by their other image of how wars are caused.

Certainly the news of the loss of the Chinese U-2 and the international tension it induced served to remind everyone that if the Soviets shot down a U.S. U-2 over Cuban airspace, it would seriously heighten the tension in this crisis. But the importance different policy makers attributed to this general conclusion and their own interpretation of what "heightened tension" might entail differed greatly as a function of their differing beliefs about the dynamics of escalation in a crisis.

For Rusk and McNamara, the immediacy of the Chinese U-2 incident and the international tension it created—occurring as it did only one day before the COMCOR decision—seems to have had great impact. This event probably served first to trigger Rusk's and McNamara's image of inadvertent war and then give this image the dominant role in their interpretation of the situation.

Undoubtedly, Rusk and McNamara were reassured by the majority view in the intelligence community that the Soviets probably would not deploy the missiles, but, as already noted, even the NIE estimate that articulated this view still cautioned for "continued alert." As typical Type C policy makers, however, Rusk and McNamara could not totally escape the policy inclinations that followed from contradictory images each one held of how war is initiated.

CONCLUSION

If cognitive factors are indeed the means by which policy makers impose coherence on crisis events, as Henry Kissinger and others suggest, then a more extensive study of these beliefs is clearly important in any attempt to improve the practice of crisis management. Such is the central premise of this chapter. Two questions follow from this premise: (1) Can one define a typology of cognitive beliefs relevant for crisis bargaining, and (2) how do these cognitive beliefs lead to misperceptions and miscalculations?

With respect to the first questions, we have argued that a fourfold typology of crisis bargaining beliefs, which gives central place to the image of crisis dynamics, has more explanatory and predictive utility than the older typologies based exclusively on the image of the adversary and the simplistic hawk/dove distinction.[55] In addition, we have defined the general bargaining strategies associated with each of these types, discussed the types of problems to which each of these types is vulnerable, and then made projections as to the likely responses of these four types in different kinds of crises.

A second major purpose of this chapter was to examine closely the precise manner in which cognitive beliefs might produce misperceptions or miscalculations. We have noted the relevance of a policy maker's use of scripts, historical analogies, and metaphors for crisis decision making and discussed potential decision-making errors associated with each. Finally, three general information processing functions of crisis bargaining beliefs were noted, and the potential abuses of each were examined.

Because of the inherent complexity involved in crisis decision making, it is evident that the practice of crisis management should be considered to be more of an art than a science. The conclusion that differing cognitive beliefs predispose those that hold them toward differing crisis management orientations, and the fact that each of the orientations is vulnerable, at times, to certain perceptual and information processing problems, does not diminish the importance of crisis management; but these observations should reinforce a sense of caution about the difficulty of making crisis management work in practice.

NOTES

1. Henry Kissinger, *White House Years* (Boston: Little, Brown, 1979), p. 617.
2. Crisis bargaining codes represent a particular type of the broader mental phenomena known as "cognitive schema" (the means by which all of us process information and make decisions in all aspects of life). One major conclusion of recent cognitive psychological literature is that our memory and the cognitive structures by which we process information are fragmented into a multiplicity of different issue-related "chunks," i.e., schema. For discussion of the more general concept of schema in the psychological literature see, e.g., S. Fiske and S. Taylor, *Social Cognition* (Menlo Park, CA: Addison-Wesley, 1985). Political scientists have taken this principle from cognitive psychology and applied it in different ways. For examples of the various applications and versions of the general concept of cognitive schema in the political science literature see R. Lau and D. Sears, eds., *Political Cognition* (Hillsdale, N.J.: Lawrence Erlbaum, 1985); and R. Axelrod, "Schema Theory: An Information-Processing Model of Perception and Cognition," *American Political Science Review* 67 (December 1973): 1248–1266.
3. The Crisis Bargaining Code Model differs from both the older "belief system" approaches and the new "attribution" approaches. For a more extensive discussion of these differences see P. Rogers, "The Crisis Bargaining Code Model: A Cognitive Schema Approach to Crisis Decision-Making," paper presented at the annual meeting of the International Studies Association, Washington, D.C., April 1987. For some examples of recent works which have applied cognitive psychology to crisis decision making see R. Jervis, *Perception and Misperception in International Politics* (Princeton: Princeton University Press, 1976); A. George, *Presidential Decision-Making in Foreign Policy: The Effective Use of Information and Advice* (Boulder, CO: Westview Press, 1980); R. N. Lebow, *Between Peace and War* (Baltimore: The Johns Hopkins University Press, 1981); R. Jervis, R. N. Lebow, and J. Stein, eds., *Psychology and Deterrence* (Baltimore: The Johns Hopkins University Press, 1985); R. Lebow, *Nuclear Crisis Management A Dangerous Illusion* (Ithaca: Cornell University Press, 1987); and J. Lebovic, *Dangerous Dilemmas* (New York: Columbia University Press, 1990).
4. This discussion of crisis bargaining codes is based on a recent study by the author which provides empirical support for the validity of elements of the typical crisis bargaining code, the typology of crisis bargaining types, and the explanatory utility and validity of the crisis bargaining code model. See P. Rogers, "The Crisis Bargaining Code Model: The Influence of Cognitive Beliefs and Processes on U.S. Policy-Making During Crises," unpublished Ph.D. thesis, University of Texas, Austin, 1986.
5. The image of the adversary is typically seen as the central organizing concept. See, e.g., Jervis, *Perception and Misperception in International Politics*, p. 58; G. Snyder and P. Diesing, eds., *Conflict Among Nations: Bargaining, Decision-Making and System Structure in International Crises* (Princeton: Princeton University Press, 1977), pp. 299–310; R. Leng, "Reagan and the Russians: Crisis Bargaining Beliefs and the Historical

Record," *American Political Science Review* 78 (June 1984): 338–355. O. Holsti developed a typology based on both image of adversary and role of conflict in the international system— the two aspects of the central belief in A. George's Operational Code Model. See O. Holsti, "The Operational Code as an Approach to the Analysis of Belief Systems," Final Report to the National Science Foundation: Grant No. SOC 75–15368, Duke University, 1977, pp. 156–160; and A. George, "The Operational Code: A Neglected Approach to the Study of Political Leaders and Decision-Making," *International Studies Quarterly* 13 (June 1969): 190–222 and "The Causal Nexus Between Cognitive Beliefs and Decision-Making Behavior: The Operational Code Belief System," in L. Falkowski, ed., *Psychological Models in International Politics* (Boulder, CO: Westview Press, 1978).

6. The importance of views on escalation is also incorporated into a recent book, G. Allison, A. Carnesale, and J. Nye, eds., *Hawks, Doves & Owls: An Agenda for Avoiding Nuclear War* (New York: W. W. Norton, 1985), pp. 209–212. Nye applies this bargaining typology in an analysis of decision making in the Cuban missile crisis. See J. Blight, J. Nye, and D. Welch, "The Cuban Missile Crisis Revisited," *Foreign Affairs* (Fall 1987): 170–188. However, I have argued elsewhere that this trichotomy (which is intended to be more prescriptive than explanatory) has several serious problems. First, it misrepresents the actual views of most doves on escalation in its claim that doves do not assume that accidental war and a loss of control are possible. An empirical examination suggests this simply is not the case. Allison, Carnesale, and Nye also miss several significant variations among hawks, especially with respect to their image of crisis dynamics. For an extended discussion see Rogers, "The Crisis Bargaining Code Model," pp. 180–182. For the classic work on escalation see R. Smoke, *War: Controlling Escalation* (Cambridge: Harvard University Press, 1977). Other recent works which examine different paths to inadvertent war include D. Frei, *Risks of Unintentional War* (Geneva: United Nations Institute for Disarmament, 1982) and Lebow, *Nuclear Crisis Management.*

7. The general principles of crisis management described elsewhere in this book have considerable empirical support. These general principles identify political and operational constraints that crisis management strategies must take into account. Within the framework of these general principles, there is room for considerable disagreement as to which strategies are the best, and over the critically important question of whether the primary threats to the goal of crisis management are political and psychological or more technical/communication problems. One must also expect differences among policy makers over how difficult it is to actually carry out any crisis management principles in practice. Differences in attitudes toward crisis management are discussed in A. Carter, J. Steinbrunner, and C. Zraket, eds., *Managing Nuclear Operations* (Washington, D.C.: Brookings, 1987).

8. This type of policy maker might accept the notion of a loss of control at some point high up in the escalatory process, say at some point during a nuclear exchange. Prior to a nuclear exchange this type of policy maker would accept fear of preemption as the primary trigger for launching nuclear weapons. Note, however, that according to this perspective, this fear would not necessarily motivate either nuclear threats or the intentional initiation of a conventional attack.

9. See also R. Pipes, "Why the Soviet Union Thinks It Can Fight and Win a Nuclear War," *Commentary* 64 (July 1977): 21–34. For discussion of some of the technical problems see A. Carter, "Communication Technologies and Vulnerabilities," in Carter, et al., *Managing Nuclear Options*, pp. 217–282.

10. See L. Brooks, "Naval Power and National Strategy: The Case for the Maritime Strategy," *International Security* 11 (Fall 1986): 58–88.

11. For the classic distinction between "force" and "coercion" see T. Schelling, *Arms and Influence* (New Haven: Yale University Press, 1966), pp. 1–32.

12. The Germans have a phrase to express the vehemence of their opposition: "The shorter the range, the deader the Germans." See A. Burley, "The Once and Future German Question," *Foreign Affairs* (Winter 1989/1990): 78.

13. See T. Schelling, *The Strategy of Conflict* (Cambridge: Harvard University Press, 1960), pp. 207–254.

14. See Snyder and Diesing, *Conflict Among Nations*, pp. 225–227; H. Kissinger, *Nuclear Weapons and Foreign Policy* (New York: Norton, 1969), p. 159, and *White House Years*, pp. 622–623.

15. See R. Nixon, *The Real War* (New York: Warner, 1980), pp. 253–257, and R. Nixon, *Six Crises* (New York: Doubleday, 1962), pp. 207, 262.

16. This is, of course, the basic thesis of *Nuclear Weapons and Foreign Policy*. While Kissinger's beliefs about the utility of limited nuclear war and "nuclear superiority" have fluctuated over time this basic premise has remained.

17. See D. Acheson, *Power and Diplomacy* (Cambridge: Harvard University Press, 1958), pp. 50–51.

18. It is important to recognize that a "high level" or "strong/dramatic" action is very much a relative, situation-specific phenomenon; i.e., the Type C policy maker will tend to favor the "lower" or incremental types of escalation and the Type A and B policy makers will tend to favor the "higher" or dramatic types of escalation, given the options discussed for a particular crisis.

19. See Lebow, *Nuclear Crisis Management*; Frei, *Risks of Unintentional War*; and Allison, et al., *Hawks, Doves & Owls*, for other scenarios.

20. See I. Janis and L. Mann, *Decision-Making: Psychological Analysis of Conflict, Choice and Commitment* (New York: Free Press, 1977), pp. 57–74.

21. See also O. Holsti and A. George, "The Effects of Stress on the Performance of Foreign Policy Decision-Makers," in C. Cotter, ed., *Political Science Annual: Individual Decision-Making*, Vol. 6 (Indianapolis: Bobbs-Merrill, 1975); and A. George, "The Impact of Crisis-Induced Stress on Decision-Making," paper read at the Institute of Medicine Symposium on the Medical Aspects of Nuclear War, National Academy of Sciences, Washington, D.C., September 20–22, 1985.

22. J. Steinbrunner, "Nuclear Decapitation," *Foreign Policy* 45 (Winter, 1981–1982): 16–28; J. Steinbrunner, "Choices and Tradeoffs," in A. Carter, J. Steinbrunner, C. Zreket, eds., *Managing Nuclear Operations*, pp. 535–554; B. Blair, *Strategic Command and Control* (Washington, D.C.: Brookings, 1985); and P. Bracken, *The Command and Control of Nuclear Forces*, (New Haven: Yale University Press, 1983).

23. For a discussion of the general threat of chemical weapons, and in particular, efforts to control them through arms control, see C. Flowerree, E. Harris, and J. Leonard, "Chemical Arms Control After the Paris Conference," in *Arms Control Today* (January/February, 1989).

24. See, e.g., A. George, "Incentives for U.S.-Soviet Security Cooperation and Mutual Adjustment," and "Factors Influencing Security Cooperation," in A. George, P. Farley, and A. Dallin, eds., *U.S.-Soviet Security Cooperation* (New York: Oxford University Press, 1988), pp. 641–676.

25. For an evaluation of the utility of coercion and low-intensity force in nonnuclear crises see B. Blechman and S. Kaplan, *Force Without War* (Washington, D.C.: Brookings, 1978).

26. B. Bueno de Mesquita, "The War Trap Revisited: A Revised Model," *American Political Science Review* 79 (March 1985): 156–177, assumes the utility of this distinction.

27. See, e.g., S. Fiske and S. Taylor, *Social Cognition*, pp. 5–35.

28. A script is defined in technical terms as "a hypothesized cognitive structure that, when activated, organizes comprehension of event-based situations." See R. Abelson,

"Psychological Status of the Script Concept," *American Psychologists* 36 (July 1981): 717. See also pp. 715–716, 718–719.

29. G. Bower, J. Black, and T. Turner, "Scripts in Text Comprehension and Memory," *Cognitive Psychology* 11 (April 1979): 177–220; R. Wyer and T. Srull, "Category Accessibility: Some Theoretical and Empirical Issues Concerning the Processing of Social Stimulus Information," in E. Higgins, Charles Herman, and M. Zanna, eds., *Social Cognition: The Ontario Symposium* (Hillsdale, N.J.: Lawrence Erlbaum, 1980); and Fiske and Taylor, *Social Cognition*, pp. 184–212.

30. For a discussion of the difference between metaphors and analogies see D. Snidal, "The Game Theory of International Politics," *World Politics* (October, 1985): 29–32. For examples of the use of analogy by historians and political scientists see e.g., E. May, *Lessons of the Past: The Use and Misuse of History in American Foreign Policy* (New York: Oxford University Press, 1973); and Jervis, *Perception and Misperception in International Politics*, pp. 266–281.

31. See G. Lakoff and M. Johnson, *Metaphors We Live By* (Chicago: University of Chicago Press, 1980), and J. Sapir and J. Crocker, eds., *The Social Use of Metaphor: Essays on the Anthropology of Rhetoric* (Philadelphia: University of Pennsylvania Press, 1977).

32. For a more extensive discussion see P. Rogers, "Metaphors and U.S. and National Security Policy: Cognitive and Political Linkages," unpublished paper, The George Washington University, Spring 1990.

33. For a distinction between the way in which the crisis bargaining code model, older belief system approaches, and new information-processing theories all attempt to explain misperception and miscalculation see Rogers, "Crisis Bargaining Code Model: A Cognitive Schema Approach." For excellent reviews of various paradigms in cognitive psychology see W. Bennett, "Perception and Cognition: An Information Processing Framework for Politics," in S. Long, ed., *The Handbook of Political Behavior*, Vol. 1 (New York: Plenum Press, 1981); and S. Taylor, "The Interface of Cognitive and Social Psychology," in J. Harvey, ed., *Cognition, Social Behavior and the Environment* (Hillsdale, N.J.: Lawrence Erlbaum, 1981). For some of the important contemporary theoretical and empirical literature in the field of cognitive psychology in addition to the cognitive schema literature cited previously see R. Nisbett and L. Ross, *Human Inference: Strategies and Shortcomings of Social Judgment* (Englewood Cliffs, N.J.: Prentice-Hall, 1980); and D. Kahneman, P. Slovic, and A. Tversky, eds., *Judgment Under Uncertainty: Heuristics and Biases* (New York: Oxford University Press, 1982).

34. For an article which assumes the importance of the risk-acceptance/risk-aversion distinction see Bueno de Mesquita, "The War Trap Revisited," 156–177.

35. This does not negate the point made by Tversky and others that there are common errors in calculations of risk and probability. This is the case because the cognitive schema that are called up on the basis of the common heuristics can differ significantly between people. It is on the basis of the schema that are elicited that people actually calculate risk and probability. See, e.g., D. Kahneman and A. Tversky, "Subjective Probability," in Kahneman, et al., *Judgment Under Uncertainty*, and Fiske and Taylor, *Social Cognition*.

36. The use of his immediate staff to generate "executive summaries" doesn't eliminate the problem. Staff resources are limited as well and the summarizing process itself takes time.

37. J. Richelson, *The U.S. Intelligence Community* (Cambridge: Ballinger, 1985), pp. 242–246.

38. See, e.g., L. McArthur, "What Grabs You? The Role of Attention in Impression Formation and Causal Attribution," in Higgins, et al., *Social Cognition: The Ontario Symposium*; C. Judd and J. Kulik, "Schematic Effects of Social Attitudes on Information-Processing and Recall," *Journal of Personality and Social Psychology* 38 (April 1980): 569–578.

39. For full documentation of sources for Acheson's crisis bargaining code see Rogers, "The Crisis Bargaining Code Model," appendix. By way of example, see Acheson, *Power and Diplomacy*, pp. 115–116.

40. Acheson's "Berlin Report" report is still classified, however the response to the report is widely documented. See, e.g., National Security Council, "Discussion at NSC Meeting, June 29, 1961, *National Security Files*, Box 81, Folder: "Germany-Berlin, 7/10/61," John F. Kennedy Presidential Library, Boston, Mass.; A. Schlesinger, *A Thousand Days: John F. Kennedy in the White House* (Boston: Houghton-Mifflin, 1965), pp. 355–356; and H. Catudal, *Kennedy and the Berlin Crisis: A Case Study in U.S. Decision-Making* (Berlin: Berlin-Verlag, 1980). In fact, Acheson was given a second chance and charged with writing a second report that would reflect the political aspects the first report missed. This report is entitled "Berlin: A Political Problem," August 1, 1961, *National Security Files* (NSF), Box 82, Folder: "Germany-Berlin, 8/1/61," JFK Presidential Library. Even this second report might be faulted for slighting such political problems as the refugee issue.

41. Lakoff and Johnson, *Metaphors We Live By*, pp. 226–246; M. Gick and K. Holyoak, "Schema Induction and Analytical Transfer," *Cognitive Psychology* 15 (April 1983): 1–38; and P. Tourangeau and R. Sternberg, "Aptness in Metaphor," *Cognitive Psychology* 13 (April 1981) 268–287.

42. May, *Lessons of History*, pp. 172–180. See also Richard Neustadt, *Thinking in Time* (New York: Free Press, 1986).

43. See, e.g., Nixon, *Six Crises*, pp. 207, 272–273.

44. See J. Gaddis, *Strategies of Containment* (New York: Oxford University Press, 1982), p. 300.

45. Nixon, *Six Crises*, p. 272.

46. Nixon, *The Real War*, pp. 253, 255, 257.

47. See Kissinger, *Nuclear Weapons and Foreign Policy*, p. 159, and *White House Years*, pp. 622–623.

48. See L. Clay, *Decision in Germany* (Garden City, N.Y.: Doubleday, 1950), pp. 372–374, for Clay's account of his own bargaining beliefs as reflected in his earlier actions in the 1948–1949 Berlin Wall Crisis.

49. L. Clay, *Oral History*, pp. 10–13. JFK Presidential Library; C. Cate, *The Ides of August: The Berlin Wall Crisis of 1961* (New York: Evans, 1978); and H. Catudal, *Kennedy and the Berlin Wall Crisis*, pp. 131–136.

50. See various intelligence reports for the various days of the Cuban crisis now available, e.g., CIA, "Untitled Report: SC-09540/62," October 21, 1962, *National Security Files*, Box 313, Folder: "NSC Meeting, No. 506, 10/21/62," JFK Presidential Library. See also R. Garthoff, "The Military Significance of the Soviet Missile Bases in Cuba," October 27, 1962 in *Intelligence Assessment and Policy-Making a Decision-Point in the Kennedy Administration* (Washington, D.C., Brookings, 1984). See also R. Garthoff, *Reflections on the Cuban Missile Crisis* (Washington, D.C.: Brookings, 1987), pp. 18–21; and J. Blight, J. Nye, and D. Welch, "The Cuban Missile Crisis Revisited," *Foreign Affairs* (Fall 1987): 170–188.

51. Secondary accounts of the still-classified NIE report attest to this. See Hilsman, *To Move a Nation* (Garden City, N.Y.: Doubleday, 1967), p. 172.

52. See J. McCone, *Oral History*, John F. Kennedy Presidential Library, Boston, Mass., pp. 10–12.

53. See R. Hilsman, *To Move a Nation*, pp. 170–174; A. George and R. Smoke, *Deterrence in American Foreign Policy* (New York: Columbia University Press, 1974), pp. 467–481; and U.S. Congress, Senate, Preparedness Investigating Subcommittee of Senate Committee on Armed Services, *Investigation of the Preparedness Program: Interim Report on the Cuban Military Buildup*, 88th Congress, 1st Session, May 9, 1963.

54. See Rogers, *Crisis Bargaining Code Model*, appendix, for full documentation. By way of example, see W. Kaufmann, *The McNamara Strategy*, (New York: Harper and Row, 1964), pp. 48, 60; and also Rusk's congressional testimony mentioned in W. Cohen, *Dean Rusk*, Vol. 14 in S. Bemis and R. Ferrell, eds., *The American Secretaries of State and Their Diplomacy* (Totowa, N.J.: Cooper Square, 1980), p. 37.

55. See Allison, Carnesale, and Nye, eds., *Hawks, Doves & Owls*, pp. 209–212; and Blight, Nye, and Welch, "The Cuban Missile Crisis Revisited," *Foreign Affairs* (Fall 1987), pp. 170–188. See fn. 7 above, and Rogers, "The Crisis Bargaining Code Model," pp. 180–182, for an extended discussion of problems with the hawk/dove/owl trilogy. Nevertheless, the work of Allison, et al. is a significant improvement over past works and clearly points in the same general direction as the Crisis Bargaining Code Model.

CHAPTER 19

Rules of Engagement

Scott D. Sagan

A policeman is on patrol along a downtown street on the night after a riot. He hears a loud bang coming from an alleyway—it could be a gunshot or a firecracker—and draws his pistol as he enters to investigate. Turning the corner he sees a dark figure in the shadows holding an object that is pointed directly at him. What should he do?

    A.)   Shout "Drop it or I'll shoot."
    B.)   Immediately fire his weapon at the figure.
    C.)   Fire a warning shot in the air.
    D.)   Drop his gun and slowly leave the alley.
    E.)   It depends.

The captain of a U.S. guided missile cruiser is on patrol along a naval blockade line. He is informed that an unidentified aircraft is rapidly approaching his ship. Although the aircraft has not turned on a fire control radar toward the cruiser, it is reportedly descending and does not respond to a radio warning to change course. What should he do?

    A.)   Continue issuing radio warnings.
    B.)   Launch a missile at the aircraft.
    C.)   Fire a warning shot in the direction of the aircraft.
    D.)   Contact higher authorities for further orders.
    E.)   It depends.

Both officers face similar dilemmas. If they immediately shoot first, they risk using unnecessary force, killing innocent individuals, and possibly triggering an escalation in violence. If they do not shoot, however, they risk their lives. What should they do?

If you answered "E.) It depends," you have chosen the position taken by both the San Francisco Police Department, when training officers about the force's general orders for the use of firearms, and the U.S. military, when training its

The author thanks the following individuals for comments on an earlier draft: Nathanial Beason, Joseph Bouchard, George Bunn, Bradd Hayes, Alexander George, W. Hays Parks, and Paul Stockton.

officers about rules of engagement (ROE), the set of directives given to commanders in the field to guide them on the circumstances and manner in which force may be used. For both the police and the military, appropriate action depends on, first, the specific rules given to the officers by higher authorities and, second, the personal judgment of the individual officer on the spot. All potential circumstances cannot be fully anticipated by central authorities, and such rules and regulations are therefore deliberately written in a flexible manner in order to balance the legitimate need for top-level guidance on appropriate action with the necessity for field-level judgments about specific conditions, threats, and opportunities.

A central problem for political authorities in the nuclear age has been how best to tailor military threats and uses of force to achieve limited political objectives without either unduly endangering one's own forces and their missions or producing undesired escalation against adversaries or innocent bystanders. This chapter examines how rules of engagement have been used as a management tool to increase the likelihood that military actions of subordinates will conform with the political intent of higher authorities. In most crises, tensions exist between the actions that appear to be most militarily prudent to officers in the field and those that are considered diplomatically appropriate by senior political officials. The first section of the chapter examines how rules of engagement are supposed to work, in theory, to help resolve such tensions. The subsequent section presents four historical case studies on the use of rules of engagement: the 1961 Bay of Pigs invasion, the 1962 Cuban Missile Crisis, the 1987 *Stark* incident, and the 1988 *Vincennes* incident. These case studies highlight the difficult task of integrating political objectives with military operations in crises and point to the existence of two mirror-image ROE problems: (1) those that can occur if rules of engagement are drawn too tightly, restricting military actions and limiting initiatives in ways that make U.S. forces excessively vulnerable to attack and reduce their ability to execute their mission; and (2) those that can occur if ROE are drawn too loosely, encouraging military activities with escalatory effects far beyond those desired by political authorities. In addition, a review of ROE in crisis management efforts helps identify the other situational factors—such as inadequate communications and training, perceptions of the enemy, and crisis-related stress—that can influence individual commanders' judgments about how to interpret the general rules in particular circumstances.

THE SCOPE OF THE RULES OF ENGAGEMENT

Rules of engagement are written to provide guidance to military commanders in the field on appropriate action under peacetime circumstances, in crises, and in the event of war. Two general categories of rules exist. First, many ROE documents describe a set of military actions that can be taken at the discretion of a commander under certain specified circumstances *unless* explicitly negated by new orders from higher authorities. Second, ROE documents may also spell out military activities that can be taken by a commander only *if* explicitly authorized at some later point by a higher command decision.[1] The first category of directives has been called "command by negation" provisions; the second set of directives constitutes "positive command" ROE provisions.[2] Most rules of engagement documents contain a mixture of both of these command elements.

ROE directives provide guidance on four central questions concerning the use of military force: (1) When can military force be used—that is, under what circmstances are units in the field authorized to initiate or continue the use of force, (2) where can military force be used—are there, for example, territorial restrictions placed on specific missions of operating units, (3) against whom should force be used under the circumstances defined above, and (4) how should military force be used to achieve the desired ends? Are commanders authorized to use any weapon under their control, for example, or are explicit orders from higher authorities required for the employment of specific munitions?

Providing an answer to each of these questions may appear simple. In ambiguous peacetime situations or in the fog of crisis or war, however, a number of complicating problems can emerge. A review of the areas covered by rules of engagement, with historical examples, illustrates the complexities involved.

When Should Force Be Used?

The question of when military force should be used, in its broadest sense of going to war, is a matter of national policy and not an ROE issue. In the more narrow sense, however, concerning when an individual military commander or field officer should use the forces under his immediate control, ROE becomes critical. At all times, U.S. military units retain the inherent right of self-defense under international law when, to use Daniel Webster's classic formulation, "necessity of that self-defense is instant, overwhelming and leaving no choice of means and no moment for deliberation."[3] Rules of engagement documents reflect, and do not create, this basic fact and often explicitly remind military officers that, as the Joint Chiefs of Staff (JCS) 1954 "Intercept and Engagement Instructions" stated, "nothing in these instructions shall be construed as preventing any responsible commander from taking such action as may be necessary to defend his command."[4] In addition, U.S. military units are often tasked with the responsibility for the defense of other military forces, U.S. citizens, and U.S. territory—what can be called "protective" or "national" self-defense—and this, too, is generally consistent with international law.[5]

Rules of engagement often provide a set of broad guidelines to help officers decide precisely when they should shoot in self-defense or to protect others. Three common issues are addressed in ROE efforts to set such boundaries. Together they can play a significant role in raising or lowering the threshold of violence.

The first issue is the definition of a hostile act. Does the right of self-defense come into effect, for example, if any enemy weapon has been launched at a unit or at the object it is protecting? Only if the target is actually hit? Only if there is reason to believe that the weapon was not fired accidentally? Is the laying of a mine a hostile act to a ship that has not yet entered the specific waters in question? What military activities constitute harassment, and where is the line drawn between harassment and hostility?

ROE enables central authorities to provide guidelines to their subordinates on such questions. Consider, for example, the following definition from the declassified 1954 JCS air defense interceptor rules:

Hostile Act. Any act by an aircraft openly committed with obvious intent to injure the United States shall be considered hostile. Further, any action by aircraft such as, but not limited to those examples listed below, committed within an area of air defense concern (the Continental United States and Coastal Air Defense Identification Zone)[6] shall be considered hostile unless previous notification is received that such actions are scheduled for operations or training within the specific area for the time at which they occur and clearance has been granted by appropriate authority.

    1. Aircraft releases bombs or fires guns, rockets or other weapons at any air, ground, or water target other than recognized weapons ranges.

    2. Aircraft conducts mine-laying operations.[7]

These directives reflect the JCS desire to encourage rapid response by U.S. interceptor pilots to any hostile act against themselves or other U.S. targets and yet to avoid unnecessary and undesirable attacks on lost Soviet aircraft or U.S. and allied forces conducting military exercises that might resemble attack operations. Considerable flexibility was also written into the rules, with such phrases as "[hostile acts] with obvious intent to injure" and "[acts] not limited to those examples listed below," in order to encourage effective use of commanders' personal judgment. Such specific definitions of a hostile act, coupled with caveats encouraging the use of professional judgment, are often included in U.S. ROE.

The second, and far more controversial, issue is the ROE definition of hostile intent. U.S. domestic law recognizes that self-defense can be anticipatory if it is beyond reasonable doubt that an attack is imminent and unavoidable. Many juries, for example, have pronounced a defendant in a murder case "not guilty" after determining that the defendant had no choice but to shoot someone who was about to kill him or her. Similarly, *U.S. Navy Regulations* clearly state that "the right of self-defense may arise in order to counter either the use of force or *an immediate threat of the use of force.*"[8] ROE can, however, significantly influence commanders' judgments about hostile intent by explicitly excluding such preemptive acts or, as is more common today given the lethality of modern weapons, by providing a specific set of operational indicators of hostile intent. Numerous actions could plausibly be interpreted as evidence of hostile intent—for example, failure to respond to warnings, maneuvering into a position from which an attack would be effective, aiming weapons, or "locking on" to a target with fire control radar[9]—and higher authorities may raise or lower the threshold of violence by providing relatively tight or relatively loose rules about when to engage in potential threats. ROE could suggest, for example, that repeated warnings should be issued before firing or that none is necessary; that many indicators of hostile intent are needed to justify shooting first or that only a single indicator is enough.

The rules of engagement provided to the U.S. Marines during the 1982–1984 Lebanon intervention illustrate the point. The marines in Beirut were originally issued wallet-sized ROE cards guiding them to use their weapons only "if you must act in immediate self-defense" and specifying "if you receive effective hostile fire direct your fire at the source."[10] In response to the April 1983 terrorist truck bombing of the U.S. embassy, however, new ROE were issued "to permit a Marine to fire if he 'perceived' hostile intent."[11] The new, more permissive rules of engagement nevertheless called for firing warning shots or disabling any vehicle that crossed an embassy barricade and only firing at the occupants if the vehicle would not then stop. If individuals crossed a barricade, the new ROE similarly required that warnings be issued in both French and Arabic before shots were fired.[12] Definitions of hostile intent can thus be fine-tuned to some degree, written in ways to encourage or discourage prompt reaction to specific warning indicators.

The third issue often addressed in such ROE is whether an operational commander has the authority to declare an enemy force hostile when it appears to present a continuing threat to his specific forces or to the United States.[13] Such authority can be held by senior commanders only or can be delegated to lower-echelon officers.[14] The purpose of such declarations is to provide additional flexibility for military commanders and enhance the ability of forces in the field to respond promptly to a major attack: Once an enemy force is declared hostile, field officers no longer are required to wait for individual hostile acts or signals of hostile intent before using their weapons.

Finally, as will be seen in the case studies that follow, military rules concerning when to use force are often adjusted under difficult crisis conditions. Rules of engagement can be altered automatically at higher states of military alert, for example, and crisis or wartime ROE may significantly differ from those that are normally operating in peacetime.[15] In addition, military commanders may receive supplementary rules of engagement, which are to come into effect only on particular crisis missions or only when their forces enter a particular area.

Where Can Force Be Used?

In a related effort to maximize the likelihood that military forces serve desired political objectives, rules of engagement may also provide guidance to field officers on where force should be used. There are many reasons why such geographical restrictions may be placed upon ROE for particular military missions. First, senior authorities may wish to minimize the risks of inadvertent escalation by setting mission boundaries for specific units. For example, an Alaskan buffer zone was in place in 1988, immediately adjacent to the USSR, to "prevent unintentional overflights of the Soviet Union airspace by [U.S.] military aircraft." U.S. interceptor aircraft could not enter this zone unless the pilots received specific authorization from higher authority, and they had to follow very strict transponder, navigation, and radio contact procedures while in the area.[16] The ROE for U.S. interceptor pilots in the 1950s also specified different procedures for treatment of identified Soviet military aircraft depending upon whether they had entered U.S. sovereign airspace or had only entered the coastal air defense identification zone. Aircraft with Soviet military insignias were to be considered hostile, and therefore subject to attack, if discovered inside U.S. airspace (and not obviously in distress or having received proper clearances from ground controllers); such aircraft observed in the coastal zone were not to be considered hostile unless they committed a hostile act or there was other intelligence (such as information that a major attack on the U.S. was underway) that led commanders to believe "beyond a reasonable doubt" that the planes had hostile intentions.[17]

In addition, geographical restrictions may be placed on ROE in order to minimize losses to neutral forces or territories in crises or in a war. Even against a wartime enemy, political authorities may use ROE to set restrictions on the geographic scope of violence, limiting the use of force, for example, to inside "maritime exclusion zones" or to forces at sea but not land targets, or to forces within one state's territory but not across a border.[18] ROE may also be used to protect friendly forces in a crisis or a war, for example, by creating air corridors for returning aircraft or "no attack" ocean area for friendly submarine forces.[19]

Geographical restrictions on ROE are also used to distinguish between self-defense and retaliation or reprisal. Although proportional self-defense is usually permitted in most circumstances, once an attacking force has broken off contact or returned to its own territory, it is no longer directly threatening the unit in question. Whether to retaliate or not in such a case is a political question that is properly under the jurisdiction of political authorities, not military commanders. Restricting U.S. forces' authority to enter foreign territorial waters or airspace is one common way of reinforcing political authorities' right to make decisions concerning any retaliatory actions.

There is often, however, a very fine line between retaliation and the continued use of force—or "hot pursuit"—to protect oneself or other friendly units. This ambiguity may force military commanders to use their professional judgment in determining the purposes and risks of action in any particular case. Different military officers facing identical situations may therefore respond differently in this regard, a point that was highlighted on congressional testimony over whether U.S. forces should have attacked the North Korean forces that captured the USS *Pueblo* in January 1968 after the North Koreans took the ship back into their territorial waters at the port of Wonson. In this case, the ROE clearly authorized "aggressive protective measures" including the "immediate pursuit" of attacking North Korean forces "when necessary and feasible" but also specified that pursuing U.S. forces *"will not penetrate territorial sea/airspace of communist countries."*[20] Yet although Adm. U.S.G. Sharp acknowledged to Congress that the ROE suggested that "once the *Pueblo* entered Wonson Harbor, any major U.S. counter-moves would then be of a retaliatory nature," he nevertheless maintained that U.S. forces should have attacked the *Pueblo*'s captors on their own authority, regardless of where they were, under the right of self-defense:

> Admiral Sharp: I would say they would have gone ahead and attacked.
> Mr. Bray: They would have the right under existing rules?
> Admiral Sharp: I don't think they would have worried about it. . . . I don't have a lawyer with me, Mr. Bray, but I am telling you what I would have done. . . . The rules don't make a bit of difference to me, and I would have done what I thought best.[21]

In short, as Adm. Thomas Moorer noted at the time, "it is often difficult factually to determine whether the self-defense situation still remains."[22]

Against Whom Should Force Be Used?

In many ambiguous situations short of war, information concerning the identity of potential enemies, friendly forces, neutral states, and belligerent powers in a local conflict could be of critical importance to field commanders. ROE documents, therefore, often identify and describe the forces, tactics, and anticipated behavior of such powers and provide guidance specifying against whom force should be used under authorized circumstances. Such rules of engagement can be tailored to maximize prompt defense against threatening forces while minimizing the danger of undesired action by U.S. forces against the forces of a less threatening country. To give an already cited example from the 1950s, the U.S. air defense interceptor rules specified that an aircraft bearing the military insignia of the Soviet Union was to be considered hostile if discovered inside U.S. territory, "unless it has received proper clearances or was obviously in distress."[23] No such presumption of hostility would apply to Soviet commercial planes or to aircraft from other countries discovered unexpectedly in U.S. airspace.

A more contemporary example of ROE concerning whom military force should be used against can be seen in U.S. naval aviation operations in the Gulf of Sidra in 1981. On August 18, 1981, the United States began a "freedom of navigation" exercise inside the Gulf of Sidra, which the Qadafi government claimed to be Libyan territorial waters. The ROE permitted U.S. aircraft to use force against Libyan planes under only two circumstances: first, if fired upon or second, if ordered by higher authorities to engage specific Libyan aircraft.[24] These rules thus defined a hostile act quite conservatively and did not encourage preemption in the event of signals of hostile intent. They did, however, provide guidance on who was to be attacked in the event that an individual Libyan aircraft fired at a U.S. fighter: Libyan fighters, like U.S. interceptors, often fly in pairs, and the ROE determined that if one of the Libyan planes shot at a U.S. aircraft, the other Libyan fighter in the formation was to be considered hostile, while any other Libyan ships or aircraft in the area were to be excluded.[25] Although numerous Libyan aircraft sorties were flown against the U.S. carrier task force on August 18, in each case U.S. fighters merely intercepted the Libyans and escorted them to the perimeter of the exercise area. On the next day, however, two Libyan Su-22 aircraft were being intercepted by two U.S. F-14s when one of the Libyan aircraft fired an air-to-air missile. The U.S. pilots quickly maneuvered to avoid the attack and, following their ROE, successfully pursued and shot down both Libyan aircraft. Other Libyan fighters and naval patrol boats in the vicinity were not declared hostile by the on-scene commander and were therefore not attacked.[26] Thus, in this 1981 incident, the ROE successfully encouraged U.S. forces to limit their response to directly related "partners" of hostile aircraft but not to attack other enemy units.[27]

How Should Military Force Be Used?

The degree to which rules of engagement should govern how military force should be used is a particularly controversial subject. Military officers writing about the proper use of ROE have in particular jealously guarded the individual commander's professional autonomy in making tactical decisions concerning the operations of the forces under his command. Thus, for example, Capt. J. Ashley Roach has maintained that "ROE should never be 'rudder orders': ROE should *not* delineate specific tactics, should *not* cover restrictions on specific systems operations, should *not* cover safety related restrictions, [and] should *not* set forth service doctrine, tactics or procedures."[28] Orders that "specify the tactics, weapons, and timing of military operations," Com. Bradd C. Hayes similarly argues, "are the province of the operational commander."[29]

While such views reflect an understandable aversion to excessive micromanagement of low-level military operations by senior authorities, they misrepresent the purpose and utility of rules of engagement in this area. Senior political and military leaders have often set both restrictions on the use of particular weapons and limits on specific tactics or the timing of operations in order to ensure that military operations serve the higher political interests of the state. While military commanders in the field may resent such ROE restrictions on their autonomy, senior political officials properly have full authority to make such important decisions.

The most obvious case in point concerns decisions to use nuclear weapons, which are properly the responsibility of the national Command Authority (NCA).[30] Despite the revolutionary character of these weapons, senior military commanders pressed for complete decentralization of nuclear command authority during the 1950s (arguing, for example, that "the decision to react must be delegated to those operational commanders in whose trust the command of atomic capable forces has been placed"[31]). The U.S. military, however, has come to accept the necessity of highly centralized control of nuclear forces today.

Civilian authorities also have, however, a strong and legitimate interest in managing how conventional weaponry is used in order to ensure that the use of military force serves political objectives. An example of such legitimate political ROE restrictions placed on the use of conventional military force can be seen in the April 1986 U.S. air strike against Libya. In late December 1985, in anticipation of a future presidential decision to attack Libya in the event of further terrorist acts by groups controlled by Colonel Qadafi, the JCS ordered that contingency plans for an air strike be developed with the following, quite minimal, guidance on the rules of engagement: "Use minimum force necessary for accomplishment of the mission and protection of friendly forces. Minimize civilian casualties and damage. Preemptive strikes against Libyan air defenses are not authorized."[32]

When subsequently briefed on these U.S. attack plans, President Reagan reportedly expressed his concern that "all possible precautions to avoid casualties or danger to civilians" be taken.[33] More detailed and more restrictive ROE were therefore drafted for the aircraft attacking Tripoli: In order to minimize collateral damage to the civilian populated areas, U.S. F-111 crews were instructed not to drop their bombs unless both of the aircrafts' target acquisition systems (an infrared night sight and a Pave Tack radar) were fully operable.[34] Following this ROE, two of the F-111s flew over the target but did not drop their bombs when the target acquisition systems failed to operate properly.[35] While currently available sources disagree on whether these restrictive ROE were instigated by the secretary of defense and the JCS or by subordinate military commanders, senior civilian authorities apparently fully approved of these highly restrictive ROE and were willing to sacrifice some degree of mission effectiveness in order to decrease expected collateral damage and minimize international opprobrium.[36] Indeed, according to Secretary of Defense Caspar Weinberger, "the President particularly applauded the Joint Chiefs' plan that required any pilot who might have any malfunction, or who was not sure of hitting his assigned target, to abort his mission."[37] Such ROE decisions, involving trade-offs between military effectiveness and broader political objectives, are legitimately the province of senior political authorities.

TYPE 1 AND TYPE 2 ROE FAILURES

Rules of engagement—whether delineating when, where, against whom, or how force is to be used—are designed to balance two competing requirements: the need to use force effectively to achieve the objective of an offensive or defensive mission, and the desire not to use military force in unnecessary circumstances or in an excessively aggressive manner. Serious ROE problems can therefore develop in either of two modes. Excessively tight ROE can contribute to a Type 1 or "weakness" error, in which a commander is not able to act effectively to complete his mission or to defeat an attack against his forces. Excessively loose ROE can contribute to a Type 2 or "escalatory" error, in which military force is used by an on-scene commander in a manner or to a degree that is deemed undesirable by national political authorities.

That a fundamental trade-off exists between preventing Type 1 errors and preventing Type 2 errors is easily understood by anyone who has a kitchen smoke detector or fire alarm. If the detector on the alarm is set too tightly, it will not go off until it is too late to evacuate the house or put out the fire; if the alarm is set too loosely, it will constantly go off when toast is burned or a dinner guest smokes a cigarette. The trick is to set the smoke detector at the right level so that neither of these errors is made.

This fundamental problem is made even more tricky in crisis management because ROE are meant to guide commanders' judgment about the appropriate uses of force, not to determine precisely when and how to respond to threats. ROE therefore can only encourage certain kinds of responses, but a myriad of other factors can—and often should—influence military commanders' judgments in this area. A commander's past experience, his knowledge about threats to his forces, his understanding of the mission and the potential adversary, and his level of stress can all affect his decisions concerning the use of force. The immense difficulty involved in the effort to ensure that appropriate military actions are taken in crisis situations is illustrated in the following brief case studies of how the rules of engagement were used in four important U.S. military operations.[38]

The Bay of Pigs

A brief review of the ROE provided to U.S. naval forces during the Bay of Pigs invasion in April 1961 provides insights into how senior authorities can use and misuse ROE in their attempt to control the use of force. The original ROE for the Bay of Pigs operation reflected the U.S. Atlantic Command's regular peacetime rules, which permitted a preemptive attack against any aircraft that maneuvered into a position indicating hostile intent and did not respond to repeated warnings to withdraw. Washington authorities, however, wanted to ensure that the U.S. forces escorting the Cuban Expeditionary Force (CEF) to the Bay of Pigs did not engage Cuban Air Force aircraft prematurely in order to limit U.S. involvement and permit the CEF to land on its own accord if at all possible. The JCS therefore issued the following special orders for Atlantic Command forces on April 7:

The "rules of engagement" are as follows:

1. Any unidentified aircraft approaching within radar range of Cuban Force ships and closing will be investigated.
2. If an investigation reveals the aircraft to be Cuban, the investigating aircraft will make *successive* close passes ensuring that Cuban aircraft is aware of his presence.
3. If Cuban aircraft maintains course too close to the Cuban Force ship(s) CAP (Combat Air Patrol) *will continue to make close passes* in an attempt to divert.
4. If Cuban aircraft insists in closing to take a position to attack the Cuban Force ship(s), the CAP aircraft will open fire *if the Cuban aircraft commences to fire* on the Cuban Force ship(s) *or if it opens its bomb bays and commences its bomb run.*[39]

Similar revised rules were also provided for encounters with Cuban surface ships or submarines in the area.[40] "In essence, the U.S. protecting forces could only open fire if the CEF was attacked," a JCS postmortem noted, "instead of opening fire when a Cuban ship or aircraft made a threatening move."[41] These rules were even further tightened just prior to the invasion, when strict geographical limitations on the escort protection mission were set by higher authorities: "In final form, the approved rules of engagement allowed the U.S. naval forces to open fire only if *they or the CEF were attacked while under escort*, and the escorting destroyers were *not to approach within 20 miles of Cuban territory.*"[42]

On the morning of the invasion, the JCS transmitted ROE guidance, formulated by officials at the White House, to the Commander in Chief of the Atlantic Command (CINCLANT) Adm. R.L. Dennison, stating that "U.S. aircraft shall attack if unfriendly aircraft makes aggressive move by opening bomb bay doors when headed toward ships to be protected or starts strafing run. Attacks will not be made by U.S. aircraft under any other condition."[43] Dennison was highly opposed to the severely restrictive nature of these ROE and greatly resented the fact that political authorities sent such detailed operational orders directly through the JCS to field forces. Dennison later complained about this ROE guidance "written at 1600 Pennsylvania Avenue": "It was really a tactical order addressed to me as Commander-in-Chief [of the Atlantic Command]. I wouldn't have sent the thing to a captain. It was not just what they wanted done, but exactly how to do it."[44]

Dennison acknowledged, however, that in the absence of such civilian-imposed ROE restrictions, he would have ordered U.S. aircraft to intercept and engage Cuban fighters far away from the invasion force, which would have undercut President Kennedy's political goal of limiting direct U.S. involvement.[45] The revised ROE, therefore, were critical in ensuring that U.S. forces, in accordance with Kennedy's desires, did not prematurely intervene in the invasion at the Bay of Pigs.

This high-level involvement in the details of operational ROE orders proved counterproductive two days later, however, when Kennedy was confronted with the imminent defeat of the rebel force and decided to permit limited U.S. carrier air intervention to support the Cuban exiles while still minimizing U.S. involvement.

At a White House meeting that ended at 2:46 A.M. on April 19, the president authorized an emergency one-hour combat air patrol mission from the carrier *Essex* and approved its ROE to protect CEF B-26 bombers attacking Castro's forces at the beach that morning. The hastily written orders were immediately issued to CINCLANT less than three hours before the mission was to begin: "Furnish air cover of 6 unmarked aircraft over CEF forces during period 0630 to 0730 local time 19 April to defend CEF against air attack from Castro forces. Do not seek air combat but defend CEF forces from air attack. Do not attack ground targets. Pilots carry as little identification as practicable. If necessary to ditch, ditch at sea."[46]

This was, as Arthur M. Schlesinger, Jr., later noted, "a somewhat tricky instruction."[47] Should U.S. forces wait for hostile acts, hoping their presence would scare off the Cuban Air Force pilots? Or should U.S. forces attack preemptively? Where should the intercepts take place? In the end, precisely how the U.S. Navy pilots would have implemented this vague order not to "seek air combat but defend the CEF forces from air attack" cannot be known, for the two forces failed to coordinate the timing of their missions in the confusion of the crisis. According to one account, however, the commanding officer of the flight of U.S. aircraft told his fellow pilots to shoot down any of Castro's planes trailing the CEF bombers, an assertive interpretation of the vague ROE.[48] In any event, the CEF bombers attacked the Bay of Pigs one hour before the *Essex* aircraft took off, and, without supporting air cover, two of the CEF planes were shot down. (One explanation offered for the timing error was that, in the haste of the crisis, there was a simple mixup between Nicaraguan and Cuban time zones.[49] Alternatively, it has been reported that the order to the *Essex* arrived late and that the U.S. planes were therefore launched well after the CEF bombers had left the area.[50])

President Kennedy's last-minute effort to save the invasion force, delicately balancing the need to support the CEF with the need to set limits on U.S. involvement, thus produced an utterly ineffective military operation. The rules of engagement were too vague; the timing restrictions were too tight. Confusing ROE and inadequate timing coordination instructions were the result of an attempt by top-level authorities to fine-tune a difficult military operation in the pressured moments of a crisis.

The Cuban Missile Crisis

The October 1962 Cuban Missile Crisis has been the most intensely studied confrontation of the nuclear era. The majority of studies on the crisis has focused on the decision-making process of the Kennedy administration and the intense strategic interaction between the Soviet Union and the United States. A smaller set of studies has concentrated explicitly on the management of the naval quarantine. These studies have emphasized, in particular, the degree to which Kennedy administration officials struggled to maintain control over where the quarantine line was set, which individual ships were to be intercepted, and how the vessels were to be boarded and searched.[51]

What role did ROE play in crisis management in October 1962? The special rules of engagement used during the Cuban quarantine were drafted by Joint Staff,

Navy Staff, and Atlantic Command officers and were officially approved by Secretary of Defense Robert McNamara before they came into effect.[52] The specific rules for intercepting vessels were issued by the JCS on October 23, the day before the quarantine came into effect: "In signifying his intent to stop a ship, the Commander of the intercepting ship will use all available communications, including international code signals, flag hoists, blinking lights, radio, loud speakers and other appropriate means. Failing this, warning shots across the bow should be fired. . . . Failing this, minimum force may be used, attempting if possible to damage only non-vital parts of the intercepted ship, such as the rudder, and attempting to avoid injury or loss of life.[53] These procedures were, fortunately, never implemented, as no Soviet military or merchant ships were ordered to attempt to run through the quarantine line.

ROE were also issued concerning appropriate responses to any attempt by Soviet or Cuban military forces to attack naval quarantine vessels or U.S. forces in Florida. Serious inconsistencies in the standing ROE in this area were quickly discovered and resolved by the JCS. In planning the quarantine of Cuba, senior political and military authorities determined that U.S. naval forces could not reasonably be expected to take the first hit from the lethally armed Cuban MIGs or Komar-class patrol boats. U.S. naval forces in the quarantine operation were therefore issued quite broad ROE that explicitly permitted anticipatory self-defense: "Any ships, including surface warships, armed merchant ships, or submarines, or any aircraft, *which take actions which can reasonably be considered as threatening* to a U.S. ship engaged in visit or search may be subjected to attack to the extent required to terminate the threat."[54] In contrast, however, U.S. Air Force air defense interceptors in Florida were issued ROE just prior to the crisis that explicitly prohibited similar anticipatory self-defense against Cuban aircraft: "Pilots employed against harassing aircraft should be thoroughly briefed that in the event Cuban aircraft harass our forces within the ADIZ (Air Defense Identification Zone) they will make their presence known to the harasser by flying close aboard. *However, firing is not authorized except in case of attack on our forces. It is imperative that the fighter pilot be positively certain that either he or aircraft that he has been dispatched to defend has actually been fired upon before he (the fighter) initiates an attack.*"[55]

These contrasting ROE were unacceptable on two counts: Not only would U.S. Air Force interceptors be extremely vulnerable to an attack in a highly volatile situation, but Cuban aircraft pilots might also be inadvertently misled by the lack of reaction, if they harassed an air force interceptor, into believing that they could also approach or harass U.S. Navy ships or aircraft with impunity. The JCS therefore altered the U.S. Air Force ROE in Florida to make them consistent with U.S. Navy ROE permitting anticipatory self-defense.[56] The new ROE specified that interceptors were to signal potentially hostile aircraft to land at a "non-critical airport" and permitted warning shots to be fired "in such a manner that the aircraft was not endangered but that the pilot would not fail to see it" if the plane continued toward the United States. If the plane did not respond, the regional air defense commander, who held the authority to declare a force "hostile," could authorize a conventional attack inside the Air Defense Identification Zone. For individual pilots, moreover, "pursuit, attack, and destruction of any Cuban naval craft or airplane, *attacking or attempting to attack* U.S. military shipping, aircraft or naval unit was authorized."[57] Although only non-nuclear use was authorized in this contingency, the JCS explicitly reminded the commanders of U.S. interceptor forces that "if the patterns of actions elsewhere in the NORAD/CONAD [North American Air Defense Command/Continental Air Defense] system indicated the existence of a Cuban and Sino-Soviet attack nuclear weapons could be used to destroy hostile aircraft."[58]

Although these civilian-approved ROE increased the likelihood that the surface quarantine and air defense operations would be successfully managed according to political objectives, the available evidence suggests that high-level authorities gave less sustained attention to the rules of engagement governing antisubmarine warfare (ASW) operations in the crisis. In an effort to balance the twin desires of protecting U.S. quarantine ships from Soviet submarines and not escalating the confrontation by initiating a military attack, Secretary of Defense McNamara approved special ASW ROE and so informed the Soviet Union: "U.S. forces coming in contact with unidentified submerged submarines will make the following signals to inform the submarine that he may surface in order to identify himself. . . . Quarantine forces will drop 4 to 5 harmless explosive sound signals which may be accompanied by the international code signal 'IDKCA,' meaning 'rise to surface.'. . . Submerged submarines, on hearing this signal, should surface on easterly course."[59]

These special procedures were designed to minimize the risk of an unnecessary attack on a Soviet conventionally armed submarine, while providing protection to U.S. surface forces on the quarantine line.[60] Promulgating revised ASW ROE was not, however, a simple matter in the middle of a complex operation. In the fog of crisis, for example, at least one destroyer captain involved in ASW activities failed to receive the new ROE and simply assumed that peacetime rules were still in effect.[61] This communications failure did not, in the end, negatively influence the crisis, as the peacetime ROE did not authorize dropping such signaling devices and thus were less aggressive than the special procedures approved in the crisis. Had peacetime ROE been more aggressive, however, such a communication breakdown in a crisis could have had serious escalatory consequences.

The majority of the U.S. naval forces in the quarantine area actively pursued all submarine contacts and, following the special ROE, sounded IDKCA on their underwater communications systems, dropped hand grenades or practice depth charges (PDCs) as signaling devices, and "rode" on top of the Soviet diesel submarines, which had to surface intermittently to recharge their batteries. Although there are no known incidents of ASW forces exceeding their ROE authority, it is not clear that the approved ROE were sufficiently safe so as to minimize the risks of an incident. It is worth noting, in particular, that one of the Soviet submarines pursued by U.S. forces was crippled during the operation and had to be towed back to the Soviet Union. Although it cannot currently be confirmed that the submarine damage was caused by U.S. ASW actions, one of the U.S. officers involved in the pursuit of the submarine believed a PDC might have caused the damage.[62] The failure of political and military authorities to review thoroughly the ASW ROE and to specify the size and the minimum acceptable range for the use of "harmless explosive sound signals" may thus have contributed to a military incident in the crisis that might otherwise have been avoided.[63]

The most serious example of faulty management of ROE during the Cuban Missile Crisis, however, is on the Soviet, not the U.S. side. Although full details are not available, some Soviet participants in the Cuban crisis have suggested that poorly managed rules of engagement were responsible for the Soviet shootdown of the U-2 reconnaissance aircraft over Cuba on October 27. At this point in the crisis, central Moscow authorities sought to avoid any military incident that might provoke a U.S. attack on Cuba, for, to quote from Soviet Defense Minister Rodion Malinovsky's telegram to local commanders denouncing their action, "an agreement for a peaceful way to deter an invasion of Cuba was already taking shape."[64] The rules of engagement for the Soviet air defense forces in Cuba, however, had apparently not been altered during the crisis, and, following standing orders "to fire on any aircraft that flies overhead in wartime," local commanders decided to shoot down the U.S. U-2 as soon as their surface-to-air (SAM) missiles became operational.[65] American officials did not know that the shootdown had been ordered by local commanders and, had the U.S. chosen to retaliate immediately against the SAM sites in Cuba, the loose ROE given the Soviet air defense would have been primarily responsible for serious unintended escalation. The wisdom of President Kennedy's decision not to retaliate immediately on October 27 is even more striking today, given the strong possibility that the U-2 shootdown was not intended by Soviet political authorities.

The *Stark* Incident

The difficulty of maintaining appropriate rules of engagement can also be seen in two more recent military incidents in the Persian Gulf. On the evening of May 17, 1987, the frigate USS *Stark*, on escort patrol duty protecting oil tankers in the Persian Gulf, was informed by a U.S. AWACS (Airborne Warning and Control System) plane that an Iraqi Air Force Mirage F-1 aircraft was approximately two hundred miles away, flying along the Saudi Arabian coast. The *Stark* picked up the fighter on its own air search radar when it was seventy miles from the ship. When the Mirage was approximately forty-three miles out, the *Stark* detected that the aircraft's radar had briefly locked onto the ship, and the *Stark's* radar operator requested permission of the tactical action officer (TAO) to broadcast a standard warning to the approaching fighter. He was told to wait, as the Mirage might turn away any minute, and the warning ("Unknown aircraft: this is U.S. Navy warship. . . . Request you state your intentions") was not broadcast until the plane was approximately twelve miles away. By this point, the Mirage had already fired an Exocet missile at the *Stark* and was in the process of firing a second. These missiles were not immediately identified by the *Stark's* air defense warning systems. A minute or two later, however, a second warning was issued, and the TAO ordered the *Stark's* primary defensive weapons systems—chaff launchers and the Phalanx gatling gun—to be readied for potential use. The order was too late. Before the systems were fully operable, the Exocet missiles hit the ship. Thirty-seven U.S. sailors were killed.[66]

What caused this tragedy? The incident sparked numerous investigations of the *Stark's* officers' behavior, the reliability of the warning and weapons systems, and the rules of engagement for U.S. forces in the Persian Gulf. The official U.S. Navy report on the attack, however, explicitly denied that excessively tight ROE were in any way responsible for the incident: "The Rules of Engagement that were in existence on 17 May 1987 were sufficient to enable *Stark* to properly warn the Iraqi aircraft, in a timely manner, of the presence of a U.S. warship; and, if the warning was not heeded, the Rules of Engagement were sufficient to enable *Stark* to defend herself against hostile intent and imminent danger without absorbing the first hit."[67] The fact that important changes were made in the ROE for U.S. Persian Gulf forces immediately after the *Stark* incident, however, belies this confident assessment that appropriate rules of engagement existed prior to May 17. The existing ROE, coupled with other communications that stressed the importance of avoiding provocative acts, bear at least a modicum of responsibility for the outcome of this incident.

What were the ROE in May 1987? Before entering into service on Persian Gulf patrols, all officers of U.S. Navy ships were briefed on the rules of engagement for the special Kuwaiti escort operation. There were many nonhostile aircraft in the Persian Gulf area, and yet there was also considerable risk that a deliberate Iranian attack or accidental attack by either of the belligerents in the Iran-Iraq War could take place. The ROE, therefore, attempted to balance these competing priorities.

The Persian Gulf ROE provided ships' commanders with full authority to use force against any aircraft that either committed a hostile act or displayed hostile intent. The aircraft of both belligerents (Iran and Iraq) and any unidentified planes were to be regarded as "potentially hostile." In addition, however, according to the congressional postmortem: "Potentially hostile contacts that appear to be approaching within specified distances of U.S. units should be requested to identify themselves and state their intentions. . . . Commanders are also directed not to stop if one attempt to attract the attention of an approaching contact has not elicited a response to their radio warnings. They should take graduated actions in attempting to attract the attention of the approaching contact, including training guns and firing warning shots."[68] Thus, although the *Stark* had "the technical authority"[69] to shoot down any potentially hostile plane that approached it with apparent hostile intent, the distance set for radio warning contacts, the rules for repeated attempts at warning and identification, and the suggestion to fire warning shots all guided officers toward quite conservative judgments concerning whether or when to attack preemptively.

Two related factors further encouraged officers to take a highly conservative position. First, U.S. policy supported Iraq against Iran in the war, and, despite the official guidance that both belligerents were to be treated as potentially hostile, it was common practice in the gulf to assume that Iranian aircraft, not Iraqi planes, posed the real danger to U.S. ships. U.S. AWACs aircraft, for example, regularly labeled Iraqi planes as "strike support general" rather than "potentially hostile" in their reports, and U.S. Navy commanders repeatedly permitted Iraqi Air Force jets to fly directly overhead once they had identified themselves.[70] Second, officers were explicitly told to place special emphasis on not causing a provocative and unnecessary shootdown. According to Capt. Glenn R. Brindel, the *Stark*'s reprimanded commander, officers were briefed on a previous incident in the Persian Gulf in which a U.S. ship had been misinformed about the identity of a civilian Iranian 747 and had come close to attacking the aircraft: "They highlighted it [the earlier incident] as something that had happened in the past and that the commanding officer of this ship was within a few seconds of firing a missile. . . . They told us: 'Nobody has fired at U.S. ships in the past; don't be trigger happy; there's a lot of civilian aircraft traffic; make sure you identify what you're firing at.' "[71]

The official navy investigation of the *Stark* disaster accurately identified warning and weapon system failures (including the failure of the *Stark's* air-search radar to detect immediately the launch of the Exocets) as well as the poor tactical judgments of individual officers (especially the errors of not sending a warning and identification request to the Iraqi aircraft earlier and not arming the antimissile and chaff launchers immediately upon receipt of ambiguous warning) that contributed to the disaster. The navy's report did not emphasize, however, that the ROE for Persian Gulf operations were immediately changed after the incident. These changes implicitly demonstrated the belief of higher authorities that the ROE had been excessively restrictive prior to the *Stark* attack.

Three particular changes in the ROE were immediately instituted. First, the definition of hostile intent was modified and clarified to encourage more prompt reaction to ambiguous warning. While previous ROE required that a set of indicators of hostile intent be considered prior to a preemptive response, officers were now encouraged to place greater emphasis on individual acts that might constitute hostile intent and were told that they had an unambiguous responsibility to defend themselves and their ships. After the *Stark* incident, Secretary of Defense Weinberger provided Congress with a description of the new ROE guidance. "Hostile intent: The threat of imminent use of force against friendly forces, for instance, any aircraft or surface ship that maneuvers into a position where it could fire a missile, drop a bomb, or use gunfire on a ship is demonstrating evidence of hostile intent. Also, a radar lock-on to a ship from any weapons system fire control radar that can guide missiles or gunfire is demonstrating hostile intent."[72] Second, the distance at which commanders were to begin interrogating and warning approaching aircraft, and engaging them if necessary, was set further away in order to prevent successful attacks on U.S. ships by long-range missiles.[73] Third, U.S. Navy ships were ordered to go immediately into "general quarters"—a high state of readiness with crew members at battle stations—whenever an aircraft or ship approached in a manner suggesting that an attack was possible.[74] This automatic alerting requirement also increased the capability of individual U.S. commanders to respond promptly to hostile acts or indicators of hostile intent against their ships.

These supplementary ROE significantly lowered the threshold at which the U.S. Navy would open fire against real or potential threats. The new ROE did not represent a fundamental reversal away from the guidance concerning preemption that existed prior to the *Stark* incident, but they did encourage U.S. commanders to respond more promptly and more vigorously to ambiguous warning. When coupled with subsequent events—the official letter of reprimand given to Captain Brindel, further Iraqi attacks against shipping in the gulf, and an increased number of hostile incidents between the United States and Iran—these ROE produced a situation in which U.S. officers were now more likely to err on the side of shooting too early rather than risk shooting too late.

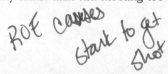

The *Vincennes* Incident

Throughout the year after the *Stark* incident, the Iran-Iraq War continued to simmer, and U.S. naval operations in the Persian Gulf increased in both scope and intensity. Between January and June 1988, Iran conducted forty-two attacks on tankers in the Persian Gulf, primarily through speedboat and frigate gunfire or naval mines, and Iraq launched twenty-seven attacks, primarily using missile-armed jets.[75] Until April 1988, the U.S. government resisted requests from Saudi Arabia and the United Arab Emirates to expand U.S. naval escort protection to non-U.S. flag ships in the gulf, but the escalating conflict produced a reconsideration in Washington. On March 6, U.S. helicopters on a reconnaissance mission were fired upon by Iranian forces, and on April 14, the *USS Samuel B. Roberts* was severely damaged when it struck what was believed to be an Iranian mine laid well outside the declared war-exclusion zone. In response, on April 18, the U.S. government ordered a significant retaliatory attack against Iranian oil platforms and a single Iranian ship in the southern gulf, and President Reagan personally approved a mid-battle request from the on-site commanders to attack other threatening Iranian naval vessels in the area. At the end of April, Secretary of Defense Frank Carlucci announced that the U.S. protective umbrella would be expanded to include any friendly or neutral vessel in the Persian Gulf outside of the war-exclusion zone.[76]

U.S. forces were explicitly warned of an increased likelihood of further Iranian military activities over the 4th of July weekend. On the morning of July 3, a U.S. helicopter from the *USS Vincennes*, investigating reports of Iranian gunboats challenging merchant ships in the area, was fired upon. The *Vincennes* immediately approached these gunships, and, after requesting and receiving permission from the commander of the Middle East force, the ship opened fire. During the subsequent surface engagement, a commercial Airbus, Iran Air Flight 655, took off from the joint military-civil Bandar Abbas airfield on the Iranian coast. This aircraft was misidentified by the *Vincennes* crew—although it was flying within the accepted commercial air corridor, continuously "squawking" the appropriate civilian signals from its IFF (Identification Friend or Foe) transponder[77] and correctly ascending to its assigned commercial route altitude. After the Airbus failed to respond to repeated radio warnings to change its course and stay clear from the *Vincennes*, Capt. Will Rogers III, acting fully within his ROE authority, ordered two Standard missiles to be launched against the aircraft. Iran Air Flight 655 was destroyed at an altitude of 13,500 feet, killing all 290 passengers and crew.[78]

What caused this incident? To what degree, if any, was the decision to loosen the rules of engagement for U.S. forces in the Persian Gulf after the 1987 *Stark* incident responsible for the 1988 shootdown of the Iranian airliner? Although there is relatively little disagreement over the facts surrounding the incident, considerable controversy continues over how to evaluate the evidence, and it is well beyond the scope of this chapter to assess the relative personal responsibility of the various U.S. officers involved or the broader responsibility of the Iranian government for stationing military aircraft near commercial aircraft. The issue here is a more limited one concerning the effectiveness of the U.S. ROE and on this question a more definite answer is possible. While it would be going too far to claim that the looser ROE caused the *Vincennes* incident, the evidence does suggest that revised ROE

[handwritten note: ROE too loose causes Iran flight 655 to be shot down]

encouraged the rash mind-set and the perceived necessity for rapid response that, when coupled with technical operator errors and psychological distortions of data, led to Captain Rogers's decision to destroy what he mistakenly believed was a hostile aircraft approaching his ship.

Three related factors contributed critically to the *Vincennes* incident. The first problem was an operator error that played a significant role in the misidentification of Iran Air Flight 655. As the Airbus took off from Bandar Abbas, the *Vincennes's* IFF interrogating instruments picked up both a common military signal (Mode II) and the appropriate civilian airliner signal (Mode III), apparently because of the proximity of the ascending Airbus to an Iranian military aircraft taking off soon thereafter. The *Vincennes's* readout instrument required that the "range gate" be moved manually with the target, however, which the operator did not do for a significant length of time. Thus, although Flight 655 continued to emit only Mode III signals throughout its flight, which were correctly picked up by other U.S. naval ships in the area, the *Vincennes* received both the military signal from Bandar Abbas and the commercial signals from the civilian airliner for enough time that the plane was identified as an "unknown-assumed enemy" and was soon believed to be an F-14 by the *Vincennes* crew.[79]

The failure to correct this initial mistake led directly to the second contributing factor to the tragedy: the emergence of a particularly strong case of the psychological phenomenon known as "scenario fulfillment." Human beings display a strong propensity to fit new information into their preexisting belief patterns. While some degree of this cognitive ability is absolutely necessary to permit individuals to make sense of ambiguous information, under many conditions—especially stressful situations—it can lead to "premature cognitive closure" and the psychological distortion or entire neglect of contradictory information.[80] This phenomenon apparently led to the critical misperceptions of information by a number of important crew members on the *Vincennes*. According to the official U.S. Navy investigation, the personnel responsible for further identification efforts "became convinced that track 4131 (the Airbus) was an Iranian F-14 after receiving the IDS report of a momentary Mode II"; despite the presence of correcting information coming to the *Vincennes* on other identification systems, the officers appear "to have distorted data flow in an unconscious attempt to make available evidence fit in a preconceived scenario."[81] This tendency to distort the evidence was particularly responsible for the critical misperception and erroneous reports of the *Vincennes's* tactical action officer that the Airbus was descending toward the ship, which is what would be expected if a hostile aircraft were attacking. In fact, the *Vincennes's* radar instruments were correctly reporting that the aircraft was rapidly *ascending*, which was what would be expected of a civilian airliner, but the officer unconsciously either simply inverted the accurate ascending altitude readouts into false descending information or misinterpreted diminishing range information (the Airbus was coming closer to the *Vincennes*, as the ship was directly under the commercial aircraft corridor) as decreasing altitude reports.[82]

These two pieces of false information—that a suspected Iranian F-14 was approaching, and that it was rapidly descending toward the ship—should be seen as the primary immediate causes of the shootdown, for when coupled with the aircraft's failure to respond to warning,[83] they led to Captain Rogers's decision that sufficient hostile intent was indicated under the then-current rules of engagement. This final factor—the ROE at the time—might therefore be best viewed as a permissive cause (or a necessary, but not sufficient, cause) of the incident. Prior to the attack on the *Stark*, U.S. ROE encouraged U.S. Navy commanders to wait until numerous signals of hostile intent were given before firing. One of the most critical of these signals, for example, was an aircraft's locking onto a ship with its fire control radar. By emphasizing that individual signals of hostile intent were sufficient to justify an attack, the post-*Stark* ROE decreased the importance of such indicators as fire control radar activities and thus lowered the threshold at which U.S. commanders were likely to fire.[84] If this ROE change had not occurred, it is possible, but by no means certain, that Rogers would have chosen not to shoot down the aircraft, for at no time had it or neighboring aircraft signaled any targeting radar emissions, nor had it responded when the *Vincennes* locked on with its radar.[85] Although the *Vincennes*'s crew might still have feared the possibility of an F-14 attacking with unguided iron bombs or perhaps even a Kamikaze attack, without the revised ROE emphasis on the importance of responding quickly to hostile threats, Rogers could have taken more time to review the evidence concerning hostile intent himself instead of relying on the misperceptions of his tactical action officer.[86]

The point here is not that the less restrictive post-*Stark* ROE definition of hostile intent produced by itself the shootdown of the Iran Airbus. After all, U.S. commanders in the immediate vicinity of the *Vincennes*—operating with the same ROE but without having the false altitude and transponder identification information—did not judge that the aircraft was a hostile threat to their ships. Nor is it accurate to state that the ROE were a political failure in the *Vincennes* case. After all, higher authorities decided after the *Stark* incident that it was worth taking an increased risk of a mistaken attack in the gulf in order to decrease the risk of another U.S. ship being struck, and the decision not to change the Persian Gulf ROE in any way after the *Vincennes* incident reflects continued high-level acceptance of the less restrictive rules.[87] It is accurate to state, however, that the new ROE contributed to the tragedy, even if the risks involved were accepted by higher officials.

CONCLUSION: ROE AND THE COMMANDER'S JUDGMENT

In any complex organization—whether a business corporation, a government bureaucracy, or a military command—there is an inevitable trade-off between centralized and decentralized decision making. For coordinating very simple tasks, leaders may rely upon standardized procedures or completely hierarchical decision making. As tasks become increasingly complex and the environment increasingly uncertain, however, efficient organizational leaders must increase the amount of discretionary authority given to lower-level officers. Such decentralization may be necessary, but it also inevitably raises the risk of inappropriate lower-level responses to rapidly changing circumstances.[88]

Military rules of engagement, combining top-level guidance with lower-level discretionary power, are an attempt to balance these competing requirements. ROE can, in theory, significantly increase the likelihood that the threshold and scope of violence in military operations are appropriate. Yet, this review of successful and failed attempts to use ROE has pointed to a number of potential operational difficulties that can seriously reduce the effectiveness of this crisis management tool. If civilian authorities do not thoroughly review or fully understand ROE, the resulting rules might not conform to political requirements. If ROE are not adjusted in a crisis, inappropriate military activities may be instigated by lower-level commanders. Yet, if rules are changed at the last minute, there might be inadequate time to communicate the changes to all relevant commanders. Finally, if unclear or contradictory ROE are issued to military forces, faulty signaling, undesired vulnerabilities, and inadvertent escalation might occur.

The existence of these potential problems is not surprising and, as was shown most prominently during the Bay of Pigs invasion and the Cuban Missile Crisis, the challenging task of setting the right ROE may require prolonged and detailed coordination between political and military authorities. Although military commanders might resent efforts that appear to them to be micromanagement, high-level authorities have legitimate interests in determining when, where, against whom, and how military force is used in crises. Yet, although political authorities might want to control every detail of a complex operation, military commanders have a legitimate need to maintain their ability to respond rapidly to changing circumstances. The inevitable tensions that emerge in this area can be diminished only through two-way education: Political officials and their staffs must be kept well informed about the risks and details of military operations, and military officials and their staffs must be kept well informed about the political objectives that underlie these activities.

Most discussions of rules of engagement end here: with calls for better communication, improved civilian understanding of military operations, and improved military sensitivity to political objectives. Although such steps may be necessary, it would be misleading to believe that the perfect set of ROE can be found to eliminate the dangers of overreaction or underreaction during any specific operation. The history of the *Stark* and *Vincennes* incidents, however, points to a more fatalistic conclusion about rules of engagement: Even if ROE are relatively well drafted and are fully understood by all relevant actors, they can nevertheless fail to produce the desired military action in the fog of crisis. The best ROE cannot *eliminate* the dangers of escalation or vulnerability; they can only reduce the likelihood of incidents and increase the likelihood that when incidents do occur, they will be of the sort (underreaction or overreaction) "preferred" by political leaders. Senior authorities can thus only pick their probable poison. Although senior authorities can encourage restraint or escalation through appropriate ROE, they cannot control the many situational factors that will also influence the decisions of on-scene military commanders. Senior authorities cannot, in short, determine the environment in which ROE guidance will be interpreted by military officers on the spot.

This is understandable and, indeed, in many respects fortunate, for authorities should not expect that centralized rules can supersede the professional judgments of competent field officers. Consider again the San Francisco policeman's scenario with which this chapter began. Rules can provide general guidance, but the specific appropriate action for the officer investigating explosive noises in a dark alley would depend on the answers to many unique questions that simply cannot be determined in advance. Is it the 4th of July weekend or New Years Eve in Chinatown? Precisely where were the recent riots in the area? Were children seen playing "cops and robbers" with toy guns in this neighborhood? How tall is the figure in the shadows?

Rules of engagement, no matter how well conceived, cannot substitute for good training and prudent judgment on the part of individual commanders in dangerous and ambiguous situations. Political authorities should make concerted efforts to adjust ROE to fit their political objectives prior to any military operation. But they should never expect perfection. Even the best ROE can never eliminate the elusive elements of risk and unpredictability that lie at the heart of crises and war.

NOTES

1. Alexander L. George, "Crisis Management: The Interaction of Political and Military Considerations," *Survival*, 26, 5 (September/October 1984), 227. For excellent analyses of rules of engagement see: Joseph F. Bouchard, "Use of Naval Force in Crises: A Theory of Stratified Crisis Interaction," Stanford University dissertation, Department of Political Science, 1988, pp. 235–290; Bradd C. Hayes, "Naval Rules of Engagement: Management Tools for Crises," RAND N-2963-CC, July 1989; D. P. O'Connell, *The Influence of Law on Sea Power* (Manchester, England: University of Manchester Press, 1975), pp. 169–180; J. Ashley Roach, "Rules of Engagement," *Naval War College Review*, 36, 1 (January–February 1983): 46–55; and W. Hays Parks, "Righting the Rules of Engagement," *U.S. Naval Institute Proceedings*, vol. 115/5/1035 (May 1989), pp. 83–93.

2. These ROE descriptive terms—"command by negation" and "positive command"—should not be confused with the similar terms commonly used to describe the two major functions of nuclear weapons command and control systems: to ensure that weapons are never used unless they are ordered to be used by the National Command Authority ("negative control"); and to ensure that the weapons will actually be launched if they are ordered to do so ("positive control"). On these concepts see Bruce G. Blair, *Strategic Command and Control: Redefining the Nuclear Threat* (Washington, D.C.: Brookings, 1986), passim; and John D. Steinbruner, "Choices and Tradeoffs," in Ashton B. Carter, John D. Steinbruner, and Charles A. Zraket, eds., *Managing Nuclear Operations* (Washington, D.C.: Brookings, 1987), pp. 538–546.

3. George Bunn, "International Law and the Use of Force in Peacetime: Do U.S. Ships Have to Take the First Hit?" *Naval War College Review*, 39, 3 (May/June 1986): 70.

4. Intercept and Engagement Instructions, November 23, 1954, 373.24 U.S., (9-8-49), S. 6, Geographic File, 1954–1957, p. 1, Records of the Joint Chiefs of Staff, Record Group 218, Modern Military Branch, National Archives (hereafter JCS followed by records year). According to Major Wallace Warriner, USMC, of the navy's Judge Advocate General's staff, "All rules of engagement contain a standard blurb that the commanding officer has the inherent right of self-defense." Quoted in Hayes, "Naval Rules of Engagement," p. 16. U.S. Army Air Defense Artillery officers training manuals state, for example, that in ROE, "the right of self-defense is always preserved" and that "the ultimate decision of whether to engage rests with the individual in charge of the weapon system." FM-44-1, *U.S. Army Air Defense Artillery Employment*, March 25, 1976, p. 6-1, Freedom of Information Act–Arms Race and Nuclear Weapons Research Project (hereafter FOIA–ARNWRP), Institute for Policy Studies, Washington, D.C. A similar reminder is included in the rules given to San Francisco policemen concerning the use of deadly force: "It is also the policy of this department that members shall not unnecessarily or unreasonably endanger themselves in

applying the firearms regulations below to actual situations." San Francisco Police Department, Order No. F-1 Revision, 8/24/84, Firearms Use Policy and Procedure, p. 1.

5. Bunn, "International Law and the Use of Force," p. 69.

6. U.S. sovereign air space extends twelve miles off U.S. shores. Currently, the Air Defense Identification Zone (ADIZ) ranges from there out to a variety of distances between 30 to 200 miles offshore. See Executive Proclamation 5928, December 27, 1988, *Federal Register*, vol. 54, no. 5, January 9, 1989, p. 777; Leonard Famiglietti, "Fighters Told Not to Shoot Air Space Violators," *Air Force Times*, September 26, 1983, p. 2.

7. Intercept and Engagement Instructions, November 23, 1954, p. 3. These rules of engagement were implemented by the Continental Air Defense Command in late 1954. According to Air Force documents, however, "it is worthy of note that the rules forwarded to CONAD were not approved by the Secretary of Defense." Rules of Engagement (Air Defense) Memorandum, October 31, 1956, p. 4, Papers of Nathan F. Twining, TS Files, Box 92, Library of Congress.

8. *U.S. Navy Regulations* (Philadelphia: Naval Publications Forms Center, 1973) paragraph 0915 (emphasis added), as quoted in Hayes, "Naval Rules of Engagement," p. 17.

9. Many, though not all, modern fire control radars have two modes of operation. When such a radar switches from a search mode (scanning the sky) to a tracking mode (concentrating the signal to follow an object), the target can often detect the change in radar signals. The object that has been "painted" or "locked-on" to by the radar thus knows that an immediate threat of attack is present. Whether this indicates hostile intent is, of course, a different matter.

10. Benis M. Frank, *U.S. Marines in Lebanon, 1982–1984*, History and Museums Division, HQ USMC (Washington, D.C.: U.S. Government Printing Office, 1987), p. 50.

11. Ibid., p. 63.

12. These restrictions apparently prevented an incident in at least one case in April 1983 when U.S. Marine guards fired warning shots, rather than shooting to kill, when two drunks drove through the barricade at the British embassy in Beirut. Ibid., p. 64. Unfortunately, these new ROE were not extended to the U.S. Marines at the Beirut International Airport (BIA) whose ROE suggested they should fire only if fired on. According to the Long Commission report "the Marines at BIA were conditioned by their ROE to respond less aggressively to unusual vehicular or pedestrian activity at their perimeter than were those Marines posted at the Embassy location." Report of the DOD Commission on Beirut International Airport Terrorist Act, October 23, 1983, p. 51.

13. The best discussion of this is Bouchard, "Use of Naval Force in Crises," pp. 264–266.

14. In the 1950s and 1960s, for example, CINCNORAD (Commander in Chief of the North American Air Defense Command) delegated the authority to declare an unidentified force of aircraft "hostile" down to subordinate commanders at the division level. Intercept and Engagement Instructions, November 23, 1954, p. 3.

15. For an example, see footnote 16 below.

16. See Craig Covault, "Alaska F-15 Capabilities Expanded," *Aviation Week and Space Technology*, May 16, 1988 p. 55. The quote is from Positive Control of Aircraft Operating in Airspace Adjacent to the Soviet Union, ANR/AAC Regulation 60–1, September 9, 1983, p. 1, FOIA-ARNWRP. The positive control rules for entering the buffer zone are in effect in peacetime, regardless of the Defense Condition (DEFCON) in effect. If, however, NORAD has declared an "Air Defense Warning RED" (meaning that an attack on the United States is imminent or taking place) or wartime rules of engagement have been declared, the buffer zone procedures are automatically cancelled.

17. Intercept and Engagement Instructions, p. 2 and p. 4. After the 1983 Soviet shootdown of flight KAL 007, U.S. officials stated that U.S. interceptor pilots are no longer

instructed to attack automatically any Soviet aircraft inside U.S. territory. Instead, they are to hold their fire unless 1) they have already been fired upon, 2) they are ordered to attack by higher authorities, or 3) if an obviously hostile situation, such as the outbreak of war, already exists. See Famiglietti, "Fighters Told Not to Shoot Air Space Violators," p. 2.

18. On wartime rules of engagement see Christopher Craig, "Falkland Operations II: Fighting by the Rules," *Naval War College Review*, 37, 3 (May-June 1984): 23–27; Douglas Kinnard, *The War Managers* (Hanover, NH: University of Vermont Press, 1977), pp. 51–55; and W. Hays Parks, "Rolling Thunder and the Law of War," *Air University Review*, 33, 2 (January-February 1982): 2–23.

19. See Hayes, "Naval Rules of Engagement," p. 17; and Norman Friedman, "The Rules of Engagement Issue," in E. F. Gueritz, Norman Friedman, Clarence A. Robinson, and William R. Van Cleave, eds., *NATO's Maritime Strategy: Issues and Developments* (Washington, D.C.: Pergamon-Brassey's), p. 42.

20. CINCPACFLT Instruction 003120.24A quoted in *Inquiry into the U.S.S. Pueblo and EC-121 Plane Incidents*, Hearings before the Subcommittee on the U.S.S. Pueblo of the Committee on Armed Services, House of Representatives, 91st Congress, 1st session, p. 718 (emphasis added.)

21. Ibid., p. 803 and pp. 805–806.

22. Ibid., p. 654. Also see pp. 717–719.

23. "Intercept and Engagement Instructions," p. 2.

24. Barrett Tillman, "The Gulf of Sidra Incident," letter, *U.S. Naval Institute Proceedings*, vol. 108/8/954, August 1982, p. 87; and David C. Martin and John Walcott, *Best Laid Plans, The Inside Story of America's War Against Terrorism* (New York: Harper and Row, 1988), pp. 68–72. For studies of the legal issues involved see Steven R. Ratner, "The Gulf of Sidra Incident of 1981," in W. Michael Reisman and Andrew R. Willard, eds., *International Incidents: The Law that Counts in World Politics* (Princeton, N.J.: Princeton University Press, 1988), pp. 181–201; and Dennis R. Neutze, "The Gulf of Sidra Incident: A Legal Perspective," *U.S. Naval Institute Proceedings*, vol. 108/1/947 (January 1982), pp. 26–31.

25. Tillman, "The Gulf of Sidra Incident," p. 87.

26. W. Hays Parks, "Crossing the Line," *U.S. Naval Institute Proceedings*, vol. 112/11/1005 (November 1986), pp. 43–44.

27. The ROE for subsequent Gulf of Sidra exercises were loosened by Secretary of Defense Caspar Weinberger to permit U.S. pilots to open fire on all threatening Libyan aircraft and ships if any one of them presented indications of hostile intent. See Caspar Weinberger, *Fighting For Peace: Seven Critical Years in the Pentagon* (New York: Warner Books, 1990), pp. 183–186.

28. Roach, "Rules of Engagement," p. 46.

29. Hayes, "Naval Rules of Engagement," p. 9. Also see, however, Parks, "Righting the Rules of Engagement," p. 86.

30. The 1971 Defense Department definition of the NCA was "the President and the Secretary of Defense or their duly deputized alternatives or successors." See Paul Bracken, "Delegation of Nuclear Command Authority" in Carter, et al., eds., *Managing Nuclear Operations* p. 363.

31. CINCLANT Memorandum to the Chief of Naval Operations, August 5, 1957, 00049/54, p. 2, Appendix to JCS 2019/245, Declassified Documents Reference Collection (hereafter DDRC) (Carrolton Press, 1980), no. 273A.

32. JCS message to USCINCLANT, USCINCEUR, et. al., DTG 312234Z December 85, FOIA-ARNWRP, pp. 1–2.

33. Weinberger, *Fighting for Peace*, p. 190.

34. "Targeting Terror: Operation Mad Dog," *The Sunday Times* (London), April 20, 1986, p. 25; Martin and Walcott, *Best Laid Plans*, p. 300; and Parks, "Righting the Rules of Engagement," p. 89.

35. Talking Paper for the CJCS, Subject: 14 April US Strike, FOIA-ARNWRP, p. 3; and Parks, "Righting the Rules of Engagement," p. 89. It has also been reported that another one of the F-111 crews, after having flown from England, dropped its bombs despite a failure of one of its targeting systems, which was a violation of the ROE, but nevertheless apparently hit the target. Martin and Walcott, *Best Laid Plans*, p. 309.

36. Weinberger refers both to "the Joint Chiefs' plan" and "*my* consequent requirement that all aircraft be 'fully operational' before dropping any bombs." Weinberger, *Fighting for Peace*, p. 190 and p. 198. A representative of the Joint Chiefs, however, stated in congressional testimony that this requirement was "not specifically required . . . by national guidance" but came into effect because "command elements of the executing forces interpreted the direction to limit collateral damage very conservatively." The ROE, however, were "reviewed and modified throughout the planning process and finally approved by the SecDef and the President." Draft JCS testimony to House Armed Services Committee, May 8, 1986, FOIA-ARNWRP, p. 18 and p. 11.

37. Weinberger, *Fighting for Peace*, p. 190.

38. For a detailed analysis of the use of ROE in an earlier crisis see the discussion of the 1958 Taiwan Straights Crisis in Bouchard, "Use of Naval Force in Crisis," pp. 424–494. For a detailed analysis of rules of engagement problems during the Vietnam War see "Vietnam Rules of Engagement Declassified," appearing in Congressional Record, March 6, 1985 (S2632–2641), March 14, 1985 (S2982–2990), March 18, 1985 (S3011–3018), and March 26, 1985 (S35110–3520). On the general subject of civil-military relations during crises, see Richard K. Betts, *Soldiers, Statesmen, and Cold War Crises* (Cambridge MA: Harvard University Press, 1977), passim.

39. CM-179-61, April 7, 1961, CJCS Lemnitzer to CINCLANT Dennison, Taylor Report, Annex 29, Enclosure F, pp. 2–3, Declassified Documents Reference Collection (hereafter DDRC) (Carrolton Press, 1985) no. 001624 (emphasis added).

40. The following ROE were issued against any unidentified submarine shadowing the escort force: "(1) request submarine identify itself; (2) if identity refused, repeat request stating its actions considered hostile and attack will be made if identity not given; (3) if identity still refused, assume submarine is attacking force and attack with all authorized means available until submarine surfaces and identifies itself (thereby coming under rules of engagement for surface ships), or the submarine is destroyed." JCS 2304/26. Memorandum for Admiral R.L. Dennison, April 1, 1961, Subject: "Bumpy Road," pp. 186–187, in DDRC 1985, no. 001624.

41. Commander G.A. Mitchell, undated memorandum, "Rules of Engagement Operation Bumpy Road," p. 2, DDRC 1985, no. 001624.

42. Maxwell Taylor Report, Memorandum 1, "Narrative of the Anti-Castro Cuban Operation Zapata," June 13, 1961, in *Operation Zapata* (Frederick, MD: University Publications of America, 1981), p. 31 (emphasis added).

43. JCS message 994247 Exclusive for Admiral Dennison, DDRC 001624 1985, tab G.

44. *The Reminiscences of Admiral Robert Lee Dennison*, U.S. Naval Institute, Oral History Collection, p. 352.

45. Ibid., p. 365.

46. JCS Message to CINCLANTFLT, 0334 R, April 19, 1961, Tab J. DDRC 1985, no. 001624.

47. Arthur M. Schlesinger, Jr., *A Thousand Days* (Boston: Houghton Mifflin, 1965), p. 278.

48. Wyden, *Bay of Pigs*, p. 243.

49. Schlesinger, *A Thousand Days*, p. 278.

50. See Wyden, *Bay of Pigs*, p. 242.

51. For analyses of the quarantine operation, including both surface ship and antisubmarine activities, see Graham Allison, *Essence of Decision* (Boston: Little Brown, 1971), pp. 117–132; Bouchard, "Use of Naval Force in Crises," pp. 405–708; Alexander L. George, "The Cuban Missile Crisis," in this volume; Forrest R. Johns, "The Naval Quarantine of Cuba, 1962," University of California, San Diego masters thesis, Department of History, 1984; and Scott D. Sagan, "Nuclear Alerts and Crisis Management," *International Security*, 9, 4 (Spring 1985): 106–118.

52. Dan Caldwell, ed., "Department of Defense Operations during the Cuban Missile Crisis," February 13, 1963, sanitized version reprinted in *The Naval War College Review*, 32, 4 (July-August 1979): 84; Bouchard, "The Use of Naval Force in Crises," p. 597 and p. 651.

53. JCS Message 6896 (hereafter JCS Message 6896), October 23, 1962, pp. 3–4, Maxwell Taylor Papers, National Defense University, Box 14.

54. JCS message 6896, p. 5 (emphasis added).

55. AF IN: 4267 (18 Sept. 62), Cuban Missile Crisis Collection, National Security Archives, Washington, D.C. (hereafter, NSA-CMCC) p. 2 (emphasis added).

56. *CINCLANT Historical Account of the Cuban Crisis*, NSA-CMCC, p. 52.

57. 26th Air Division (SAGE) Participation in the Cuban Crisis, October-December 1962, K-Div-26-HI, vol. 1, pp. 4–5, Air Force Historical Research Center, Maxwell AFB, AL (emphasis added).

58. *Chronology of JCS Decisions Concerning the Cuban Crisis*, NSA-CMCC, p. 50.

59. Navy message 252124Z October, NAVOCEANO, Wash D.C. to Sec. State, Box 41, Cuba Cables, 10/25/62, II, National Security Files, John F. Kennedy Library, Boston, MA. (Hereafter JFK Library). On October 24, McNamara requested that the State Department pass that message directly to the Soviet government. Message 240054Z October 62, Secretary of Defense to Secretary of State, NSA-CMCC. Also see, News Briefing, Assistant Secretary of Defense Arthur Sylvester, October 24, 1962, p. 6, NSA-CMCC and Caldwell, ed., "Defense Department Operations During the Cuban Missile Crisis," p. 87.

60. The Atlantic Command reported on October 23 that the "estimate(d) mission of these submarines (is) to contest, or be in a position to contest, (the) U.S. blockade." CINCLANT Message 232105Z October 1962, National Security Files, Box 40, Cuba Cables, vol. 4, 10/23/62, JFK Library. On October 27, CINCLANT advised the JCS that all Soviet submarines in the Western Atlantic were conventionally powered torpedo attack submarines noting that "there is no contact evidence of nuclear powered or missile configured subs in WESTLANT." United States Marine Corps Emergency Actions Center, "Summary of Items of Significant Interest," October 27, 1962, NSA-CMCC, p. 2.

61. Sagan, "Nuclear Alerts and Crisis Management," p. 115, fn. 38.

62. Bouchard, "The Use of Naval Force in Crises," p. 668, citing a letter from Captain Robert J. Wissman, operations officer for the *Essex* ASW force.

63. Although there are no known cases of Soviet submarine commanders mistaking these explosive sound signals for an attack operation, it is worth noting that such an incident did occur in the surface quarantine. On the night of October 24, 1962, a U.S. surveillance plane used a magnesium photoflash cartridge in order to photograph a Soviet tanker. The captain of the Soviet vessel reportedly misunderstood the activities, however, and radioed to Moscow that he was under attack. See Paul H. Nitze with Anne M. Smith and Steven L. Rearden, *From Hiroshima to Glasnost* (New York: Grove Weidenfeld, 1989), p. 231; and Bouchard, "The Use of Naval Force in Crises," pp. 642–643.

64. The Malinovsky telegram was read to the January 1989 Moscow conference on the Cuban Missile Crisis and is quoted in Bruce J. Allyn, James G. Blight, and David A. Welch, "Essence of Revision: Moscow, Havana, and the Cuban Missile Crisis," *International Security* 14, 3, (Winter 1989/90): 162.

65. Ibid., p. 161.

66. The two major sources on the incident are Rear Admiral Grant Sharp, "Formal Investigation into the Circumstances Surrounding the Attack on the USS *Stark* (FFG 31) on 17 May 1987" (sanitized version), (hereafter "Sharp Investigation Report"); and "Report on the Staff Investigation into the Iraqi Attack on the USS *Stark*," Committee on Armed Services, House of Representatives, 100th Congress, 1st session, June 1987, pp. 12–14 (hereafter "Armed Services *Stark* Report"). Also see Michael Vlahos, "The *Stark* Report," *U.S. Naval Institute Proceedings*, vol. 114/5/1023 (May 1988), pp. 64–67; and Hayes, "Naval Rules of Engagement," pp. 40–44.

67. "Sharp Investigation Report," p. 32.

68. "Armed Services *Stark* Report," p. 4.

69. "Technical authority" is the apt phrase used by the House Armed Services Committee report. Ibid., p. 1.

70. Ibid., p. 5.

71. Captain Glen R. Brindel, as quoted in Mark Thompson, "U.S. Almost Downed Jetliner in '85, *Starks'* Ex-captain Says," *San Jose Mercury News*, July 5, 1988, p. 7A.

72. Caspar W. Weinberger, "A Report to the Congress on Security Arrangements in the Persian Gulf," April 27, 1988, p. 17. Also see Hayes, "Naval Rules of Engagement," p. 42.

73. After the *Stark* incident, Lt. General Richard A. Burpee, Director of Operations for the JCS, told Congress that "now if (a captain) sees a threat, we are saying that if you feel an attack is imminent, you may engage him a little further out." Vernon A. Guidry, "U.S. Frigate Failed to Spot Iraqi Missiles," *Baltimore Sun*, May 20, 1987, p. 1.

74. "Armed Services *Stark* Report," p. 6; and John H. Cushman, "U.S. Navy Defense is on Hair Trigger on Escort in Gulf," *New York Times*, June 17, 1987, p. A8.

75. Ronald O'Rourke, "Gulf Ops," *U.S. Naval Institute Proceedings*, vol. 115/5/1035 (May 1989), p. 43.

76. The best sources on these 1988 operations in the Persian Gulf are Ibid pp. 42–50; Bud Langston, "The Air View: Operation Praying Mantis" and J.B. Perkins III, "The Surface View: Operation Praying Mantis," both in *U.S. Naval Institute Proceedings*, vol. 115/5/1035 (May 1989), pp. 54–65 and pp. 66–70; and Hayes, "Naval Rules of Engagement," pp. 44–54.

77. Modern military and civilian aircraft use electronic transponder devices which transmit specific identifying signals when "interrogated" by military or air traffic controllers' radars.

78. The primary source of evidence on the *Vincennes* incident is the sanitized version of the official Department of Defense investigation report. "Formal Investigation into the Circumstances Surrounding the Downing of Iran Air Flight 655 of 3 July 1988" (hereafter "*Vincennes* Report"). Also see Norman Friedman, "*Vincennes* Incident," *U.S. Naval Institute Proceedings*, vol. 115/5/1035 (May 1989), pp. 87–92.

79. "*Vincennes* Report," p. 47 and Friedman, "The *Vincennes* Incident," p. 73 and p. 79, fn. 7. The chairman of the Joint Chiefs, Admiral William Crowe, has argued that this was not "a critical error" since the *Vincennes* crew could still have believed that an attacker was camouflaging his identify by squawking Mode III. While certainly possible, such a belief is unlikely as was demonstrated by the fact that other U.S. ships which correctly picked up the Mode III signal did not assume that the aircraft was merely disguising itself

as a civilian airliner. CM-1485-88, August 18, 1988, Second Endorsement on Rear Admiral Fogarty's letter of July 28, 1988, p. 5.

80. The most thorough discussion of the psychological literature on this subject is Robert Jervis, *Perception and Misperception in International Politics* (Princeton NJ: Princeton University Press, 1976), pp. 117–202. Also see Alexander L. George, "The Impact of Crisis-Induced Stress on Decision Making," in Frederic Solomon and Richard Marston, eds., *The Medical Implications of Nuclear War* (Washington, D.C.: National Academy Press, 1986), pp. 529–552; Charles Lord, Lee Ross, and Mark Lepper, "Biased Assimilation and Attitude Polarization: The Effects of Prior Theories on Subsequently Considered Evidence," *Journal of Personality and Social Psychology*, 37, 11 (1979): 2098–2109; and Thomas Nash, "Human-Computer Systems in the Military Context," (Stanford University, Center for International Security and Arms Control, February 1990), pp. 16–21.

81. "*Vincennes* Report," p. 45.

82. Ibid., p. 48.

83. The reasons for the aircraft's failure to respond to repeated warnings remain uncertain. It is possible that the Iran Airbus did not receive the warning or chose to ignore it, believing it to be mere harassment. A plausible, alternative explanation, however, places responsibility on the faulty warning sent by the *Vincennes*: since the warning message did not include positional information on the ship or the aircraft, the pilot of Flight 655 may have believed the warning referred to another aircraft in the area. See Robert W. Covey, "The *Vincennes* Incident," letter, *U.S. Naval Institute Proceedings*, vol. 116/2/1044 (February 1990), p. 24.

84. The first clear sign of this lower threshold occurred on August 8, 1987, when a navy F-14 pilot fired a Sparrow missile against an Iranian fighter aircraft that had approached a U.S. reconnaissance plane while flying fast and low and failing to respond to radio warnings to stay clear of U.S. aircraft. The Sparrow was launched despite the fact that the Iranian military aircraft had not turned on its target-acquisition radar. This is a specific example of the loosening of the criteria for judging hostile intent after the *Stark* incident. See Hayes, "Naval Rules of Engagement," p. 45.

85. According to Commander David Carlson, the commanding officer of the USS *Sides* who has been especially critical of Rogers' decision: "Based on closest point of approach to the *Sides* (range *and altitude*), lack of any significant known F-14 antisurface warfare (ASUW) capability (speculation about the Harpoon aside), *lack of detected radar emissions*, and precedent, I evaluated the track as a non-threat." The missiles that could have been, at least in theory, used by an attacking F-14 (Maverick and modified Eagle or Harpoon missiles) would still have required some use of targeting radar to be effective. Here it is also important to note that, according to Carlson, contrary to rumors after the incident, the Iranian P-3 reconnaissance plane that had flown in the vicinity of the *Vincennes* had not been detected using targeting radar. David R. Carlson, "The *Vincennes* Incident," letter, *U.S. Naval Institute Proceedings*, vol. 115/9/1039 (September 1989), p. 89 (emphasis added) and p. 87.

86. Such a possibility was implicitly acknowledged by the Chairman of the Joint Chiefs in his press conference immediately after the shutdown:

Question: If we hadn't changed the rules in September, would he have held his fire, the skipper?

Admiral Crowe: Certainly the rules of engagement would not have been as specific in the authorities it granted him. I don't know whether he would have or not, under the old rules.

"Excerpts of News Briefing by Adm. William J. Crowe at Pentagon" *Washington Post*, July 4, 1987, p. A25. Also see C. Robert Zelnick, "A Harder Look at Captain Rogers' Judgment," *New York Times*, July 17, 1988, Section 4, p. 29.

87. Indeed, senior authorities continued to praise the new ROE after the *Vincennes* incident. In September 1989, for example, Admiral Crowe stated: "Incidently, now the world knows this, and nobody's treading on us now. We tell them, 'If you're within so many thousand yards (of a U.S. vessel) you're in jeopardy.' And even the Iranians stayed away from us (in the Persian Gulf)." P. J. Budahn, " 'Nobody's Treading on Us Now': Adm. Crowe," *Navy Times*, September 11, 1989, p. 14.

88. Jay Galbraith, "Information Processing Model," in Jay M. Shafritz and J. Steven Ott, eds., *Classics of Organization Theory* (Chicago: Dorsey Press, 1987), pp. 294–303. For important theoretical discussions also see Martin Landau and Russel Stout, "To Manage is Not to Control or the Folly of Type II Errors," *Public Administration Review*, 39, 2 (March-April 1979): 148–156; L. Peter Jennergren, "Decentralization in Organizations," in Paul C. Nystrom and William H. Starbuck, eds., *Handbook of Organizational Design*, Vol. 2 (Oxford: Oxford University Press, 1981), pp. 39–59; and Donald Chisholm, *Coordination Without Hierarchy: Informal Structures in Multiorganizational Systems* (Berkeley: University of California Press, 1989).

CHAPTER 20

The Impact of Crisis-Induced Stress on Policy Makers

Jerrold M. Post

A military investigation of the shooting down of an Iranian civilian airliner last month found that crew error arising from the psychological stress of being in combat for the first time was responsible for the disaster, Defense Department officials familiar with the inquiry said today.

The inquiry found that in the stress of battle, radar operators on the Vincennes *mistakenly convinced themselves that the aircraft they had spotted taking off from the airport in Bandar Abbas, Iran, was hostile and intended to attack the* Vincennes.

With the perceived threat fast approaching, they wrongly interpreted what they saw on their radar screens in a way that reinforced this preconceived notion. These misinterpretations were then passed on to Capt. Will C. Rogers III, the ship's commanding officer, and led him to conclude that his ship was in imminent danger.

Military psychologists say that soldiers and sailors in their first battle suffer immense stress before and during the fighting and may confuse perceptions with reality. Soldiers often shoot at shadows or at each other on their first night in a combat zone. Pilots in their first air engagements sometimes misread their instruments and fly in the wrong direction.

A navy officer who served with the Riverine forces in Vietnam said, "Stress can override your faculties. You see what you want to see and hear what you want to hear." Based on reports of what is contained in the investigation, this appears to have happened to some crew members aboard the Vincennes.

"Stress is something military medicine pays a lot of attention to," said a doctor at the Walter Reed Medical Center in Washington. "We concentrate on the effects of stress on individuals who have been exposed to prolonged periods of combat. We pay less attention to what is probably the highest stress point of all, the period immediately preceding and during first combat."

—Selected extracts from "Errors by a Tense U.S. Crew Led to Downing of Iran Jet," *New York Times*, August 3, 1988

No matter how well trained the military crew, in the stress of combat errors in perception and judgment occur that can have tragic consequences—a fact given pointed emphasis by the after-action report of the mistaken downing of an Iranian civilian airliner by the U.S. Navy combat frigate *Vincennes*. If this is true of well-trained military personnel in conventional combat, what of senior government officials in a nuclear environment? It is by definition a "first combat" of an extraordinary sort for which no prior training of a fully realistic character is possible; both the magnitude of the stresses upon the decision makers and the consequences of errors in judgment are incalculable.

Nevertheless, despite the obvious importance of thoroughly understanding all aspects of crisis decision making, there are important effects of crisis-induced stress on decision making that, for the most part, have been ignored or given only cursory attention. This chapter will endeavor to illuminate these effects. In particular, it will draw attention to the psycho-physiology of decision making under acute and prolonged stress, the interaction between personality and crisis behavior, the interaction between individual personalities and the decision-making group, and the interaction between personality and the organizational context. Indeed, as we will demonstrate in this chapter, it is at the nexus between these subsystems—the individual, the group, and the organization—that distortions of crisis decision making are most apt to occur.

The literature bearing on crisis decision making is extensive. In developing their highly useful conceptual framework for considering the effects of stress upon decision makers, Ole R. Holsti and Alexander L. George identify the three subsystems of the individual context, the small group context, and the organizational context, and emphasize the interrelationship among these three subsystems.[1] This chapter will systematically review theoretical material and experiential accounts bearing on the effects of crisis-induced stress upon individual decision makers and decision-making groups. Insofar as the individuals and decision-making groups operate in an organizational context, we will consider the manner in which the organizational culture affects their decision-making behavior in crisis situations. This chapter will give particular attention to the aspects of crisis decision making identified above that have not previously been thoroughly considered.

Scholars from different disciplines generally agree on what constitutes a crisis. The elements characteristically enumerated include a perceived threat to major values and some danger of a war. Moreover, crises often (although not always) have one or more other characteristics that are important, for they can add to the stress of the decision maker. They include time urgency, ambiguity or uncertainty, and surprise or uniqueness. Holsti, for example, finds two elements concerning which there is broad agreement—a severe threat to important values and finite time for coping with the threat—and adopts this as his working definition.[2] He also mentions the elements of surprise and probability of armed conflict, while T Hart identifies threat, urgency, and uncertainty.[3]

EFFECTS OF CRISIS-INDUCED STRESS ON INDIVIDUAL DECISION MAKERS

And since we live in an age in which individual reaction may bear on the fate of mankind for centuries to come, we must spare no effort to learn all we can and thus sharpen our responses.

—Richard Nixon[4]

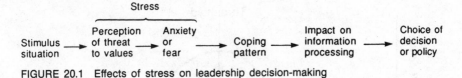

FIGURE 20.1 Effects of stress on leadership decision-making

The literature bearing on crisis decision making, including the role and performance of individual decision makers, is extensive.[5] The comprehensive review by Holsti, which builds on concepts identified in his earlier book *Crisis, Escalation, War*, is particularly clarifying, as he disaggregates four major analytic perspectives: the nation-state, the bureaucratic organization, the decision-making group, and the individual decision maker. He systematically considers different dimensions of each level of analysis, differentiating the character of decisions made in crises versus "normal" situations and analyzing constraints on rational decision making. But in considering the individual decision maker, he concludes that "the personality and other correlates of performance under stress are at best imperfectly understood."[6]

That this terrain is for the most part *terra incognita* is curious, for it is surely not as a consequence of overlooking the importance of personality as a variable in considering crisis reactions. F. Greenstein makes an important distinction between action dispensability and actor dispensability, and he particularly notes that crises are occasions when the performance of the actor will regularly be of central significance.[7] Likewise, S. Hook distinguishes between eventful and event-making leaders.[8] Margaret Hermann, in identifying eight conditions in which leader personality affects foreign policy decision making, gives important emphasis to the significance of crises.[9] In considering contributions to political behavior, M. Brewster-Smith considers the interaction of person and immediate situation.[10] Yet, in examining political behavior in crises, the consideration of person is, for the most part, undifferentiated. In particular, no systematic consideration has been given to the manner in which different personality structures will affect reactions to crises. We shall endeavor in at least some measure to reduce this deficiency in our understanding of crisis behavior by differentiating the role of person and personality.

Indeed, there is no one-to-one relationship between crisis, as defined by threat to national values, and stress, as experienced by the individual. What threatens one individual and, hence, becomes a source of stress for him or her may differ considerably from one individual to another. Consider, for example, Menachem Begin, for whom political conflict with the Arab world—being besieged from without—was like a tonic, but criticism from within Israel—particularly from within his own party—was a major source of stress. Thus, in stipulating threat as a characteristic of crises, from the individual perspective it should be amended to perceived threat. The flow chart from Alexander L. George shown in Figure 20.1 illustrates the importance of distinguishing between the properties of the stimulus situation and the perceptions of the actor.[11]

Several aspects of the sequence delineated by George are worth emphasizing. In particular, George identifies "perception of threat to values" as the first element following the initial stimulus. Whose values? While definitions of crisis characteristically refer to national values, as is noted in the Begin example cited above, there

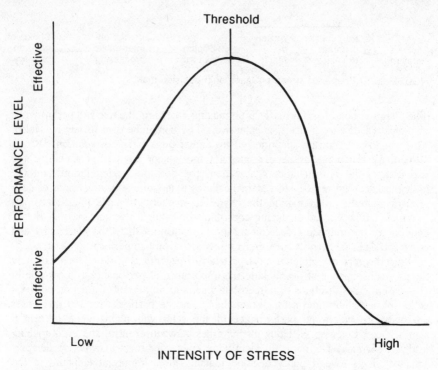

FIGURE 20.2   Relationship between stress and performance

may be a considerable discrepancy between the national values being threatened and personal values. Moreover, the term "coping pattern" in effect refers to the organized pattern of defense mechanisms. While the pattern of defenses precipitated by a crisis is not identical to the individual's characteristic pattern of defensive organization—personality—it is derivative. Under stress, characteristic defense patterns intensify. Thus, different personality types will react differently to stress, which is a major emphasis of this chapter.

Let us first consider in summary form aspects of individual crisis decision making at the level of the undifferentiated person—that is, without taking personality differences into account. It is important to emphasize that being under stress does not necessarily adversely affect performance. The feeling of being at the height of his powers that Richard Nixon describes during his periods of crisis has a foundation in the literature of social psychology. The early stress response has been demonstrated to improve performance, but as stress mounts, performance degrades. This is illustrated in the well-known "inverted U," as shown in Figure 20.2.

The manner in which performance degrades under conditions of continuing stress has been studied. Major attention has been directed to cognitive aspects of decision making and the role of belief structures, less to motivational aspects. In examining "hot" cognitive processes (the extremely useful term coined by R. P. Abelson[12] to characterize the quality of cognition in emergency situations), I. L. Janis has made major contributions to our understanding of decision making in general and crisis decision making in particular. In contrast to optimal decision making, what he terms "vigilant decision making," Janis has identified major patterns of impaired decision making that can affect the decision maker operating under the stress of crisis. Of particular importance are the patterns of defensive avoidance and hypervigilance.[13] Because of the anxiety attending making crucial decisions, some individuals will avoid decisional conflicts by unduly procrastinating or by not defining the situation as a crisis—hence, defensive avoidance. Hypervigilance, in contrast, is a much rarer state; it is a near panic-like state where there is a marked deterioration of judgment and impairment of cognitive efficiency.

There is essential agreement among all sources that a severely stressed individual is prone to suffer various types of impairment of cognitive functioning—perceptual distortions, exaggerated coping mechanisms, and flawed cognitive processes. Many of the following traits, which have been described as characterizing impaired decision making in crisis situations, are subsumed under the overarching patterns described by Janis:

1. a truncated time span, with major attention being devoted to the immediate and diminished attention to long-range consequences of the action;
2. a perceived requirement for decisional closure, which may in turn lead to premature action or, conversely;
3. in searching for certainty, a tendency to irrational procrastination;
4. cognitive rigidity—a tendency to maintain a fixed mind-set and not be open to new information;
5. a tendency to reduce cognitive complexity and uncertainty;
6. a reduction of the range of options considered;
7. in considering options, a tendency to "bolster,"—that is, to upgrade factors in favor of the favored action prescription and downgrade factors militating against;
8. a tendency to view the present in terms of the past;
9. a tendency to seek familiar patterns, to relate the critical events to mental schemata or scripts;
10. diminished creativity;
11. a tendency toward the fundamental attribution bias—to see the other's actions as being precipitated by internal (psychological) causes rather than external circumstances (example: my adversary's actions show he is malevolently out to destroy us, rather than that he is protecting himself from external threat; and
12. a corresponding tendency to fall into the actor-observer discrepancy—that is, to see the external situation as the cause of one's own behavior without attending to one's own internal psychological motivations.

CRISIS REACTIONS AND PERSONALITY STRUCTURE

Reflecting the imbalance in the literature discussed earlier, the majority of the reactions to crisis-induced stress that are catalogued above concern belief systems, cognition, and intellectual functioning. Emotional and interpersonal reactions also, of course, affect decision making in crisis situations, although they are less frequently addressed. By and large, however, the literature does not address the question of which leaders—leaders with what kinds of personality structure—are particularly apt to experience which kind of reaction and under what circumstances.

Let us consider the challenge of decision making in an atmosphere of ambiguity, a frequent feature of crisis situations. The tolerance of individuals for ambiguity varies considerably and is related to personality. An important example concerns individuals with compulsive personalities. Compulsive personality features, to a moderate degree, are frequently found in successful executives and leaders. Compulsive individuals are characteristically uncomfortable with uncertainty and handle ambiguous situations very differently from, for example, action-oriented individuals who react intuitively. The action-oriented decision maker who reacts viscerally—intuitively—will not be burdened in the same manner as the compulsive decision maker. The hazard for this type of decision maker is a premature decision to act, driven by the need to act and by discomfort with inaction, when judicious delay could provide a much more definitive assessment of the situation without unduly delaying a response—that is, rational procrastination as distinguished from irrational procrastination in search of certainty, which is the tendency of the compulsive decision maker.

At what point in an escalating crisis the leadership defines the situation as being of critical proportions is extremely important and can vary considerably depending upon a number of factors, including but not limited to the personality dispositions of the principal decision makers. Delay in diagnosing the criticality of a situation can, of course, have disastrous consequences, but to prematurely or incorrectly appraise a situation as critical can also have unfortunate consequences. Consider, for example, the Cuban Brigade Crisis of the Carter years, when intelligence information concerning the presence of a Soviet brigade in Cuba precipitated a crisis mentality in the government, which went into a crisis mode of operation. As an array of diplomatic and military moves was being considered at the highest levels, it was eventually recognized that the information was not new, that the Soviet unit was a construction brigade that had been present in Cuba for more than a decade assisting with a variety of engineering projects, and the "crisis" quickly disappeared.

EFFECTS OF CRISIS-INDUCED STRESS ON THE DECISION MAKING OF DIFFERENT LEADER PERSONALITIES

Three leader personality types will be discussed. On the basis of their cognitive, affective and interpersonal differences, their differing reactions to crisis situations will be characterized. Two of the personality types—the compulsive personality and the narcissistic personality—are frequently found in the ranks of leaders; the third, the paranoid personality, is found much less frequently in leadership ranks but is included because aberrant reactions of paranoid individuals under stress can have catastrophic consequences. In describing only these three personality types, there is no intent to suggest this is an all-inclusive typology. Moreover, the personality patterns as described are rarely found isolated from other personality traits. Indeed, well-balanced individuals are not easily categorized, for a measure of psychological health is the capacity to call upon a broad array of psychological coping mechanisms, or ego defenses, rather than be limited to a narrow repertory of ego defenses, as is the case in personality disorders.

Each of the three personality types described has a characteristic cognitive style. George has usefully observed that differing cognitive styles per se can contribute to the quality of decision making in the interval preceding a full-blown crisis when exaggerated coping mechanisms can be expected to be mobilized.[14]

Drawing upon D. Shapiro's depictions of the compulsive and paranoid cognitive styles, the following personality descriptions are also derived from the Diagnostic and Statistical Manual of the American Psychiatric Association (DSM III–R).[15] These descriptions are of severe personality disorders, not of healthy personalities. Indeed, it will be readily apparent that personality dysfunction of the magnitude described would be incompatible with sustained effective leadership. But to the extent that individuals do have significant compulsive, narcissistic, or paranoid elements in their personalities (as many successful individuals do), under stress these traits can be expected to magnify, and they can approach the extreme descriptions portrayed. Thus, in a crisis, when he perceives threats to values, the usually effective and basically psychologically healthy executive with many compulsive features in his personality makeup will tend to magnify his compulsive coping patterns and move in the direction of the full-blown compulsive personality described below.

The Compulsive Personality

Compulsive personality characteristics are frequently encountered in successful government and business executives, scientists and engineers, academic scholars, and military leaders. Indeed, core features of this personality type—organizational ability, attention to detail, and emphasis on rational process—often contribute to their success. For such individuals, there is a dominance of thinking over feeling, with a need to keep strong feelings—such as anxiety and anger—under control. Such individuals approach decision making on the basis of logical reasoning and reach solutions only after attempting to consider all aspects of the problem at hand.

Crises, however, do not easily lend themselves to such orderly thought processes, and, when these compulsive characteristics become intensified under pressure, they can become disabling and be manifested as preoccupation with detail, inability to see "the big picture," and indecisiveness. Under pressure to decide on the basis of only partial and imperfect information, a compulsive decision maker can become paralyzed with doubt (*folie du doute*), vacillating between alternatives and resembling Tevya in *Fiddler on the Roof*—"Well, on the one hand. . . , but, on the other hand. . . ." Because the compulsive personality suffers from an inordinate fear of making a mistake, he seeks to find that one extra fact that would help achieve certainty. Thus, the compulsive decision maker may procrastinate, reluctant to make a mistake, and this irrational procrastination in the quest for certainty can, in effect, become a decision to not act.

Moreover, during the final stages of decision making, the compulsive personality has a tendency to isolate himself, worrying "conscientiously" over the alternatives. His advisers become providers of information and sources of input but are not fully incorporated into the decision-making process. Thus, it is not uncommon for the compulsive decision maker to remain in this splendid isolation until he emerges to announce his decision, which is now final and not open to constructive criticism by his subordinates. Indeed, the rash subordinate who tries nevertheless to get his boss to reconsider may reap the whirlwind, for, with the decisional agony ended, the leader has experienced great relief and reopening the process would be to plunge again into an agony of indecision.

This decisional agony can be forestalled if there is a rule to apply, if there is a formula or standard operating procedure the situation seems to fit—hence the importance both of training and of psychological templates, which can facilitate high-quality decisions. But there is also the hazardous possibility that the compulsive decision maker, under stress, will shoehorn a unique situation into a familiar shape that has its own clear (but in this case inappropriate) procedural rules and thus make a flawed decision with dangerous consequences.

Even when the compulsive person does make a decision, after this agonizing doubt and anxious worrying over all of the possibilities and permutations, the decision itself is often not the product of the judicious weighing that has taken place but rather is the consequence of a frantic impulse, either because of a tight time limit or because of the need to end the tortured search for a decision. Decisional closure brings tangible relief, and therefore, as noted above, the subordinate who suggests an alternative after a decision has already been made may be dismissed without a real hearing. Not only will his suggestion probably receive short shrift, but he will probably provoke annoyance and even outright anger. Thus, it is very important for members of the compulsive leader's circle to weigh in before a decision is reached, for the ideas and judgments he arrives at after conscientious deliberation are overvalued by the compulsive; once he has reached his decision, the compulsive will react to criticism of it as he would to a personal attack.

It was observed earlier that the nexus of the individual personality and the decision-making group has the potential for generating considerable interference with optimal decision making. Unfortunately, much of the social psychology literature bearing on group decision making has little relevance to the realities of the political-military decision-making group. This literature, and the experimental situations from which it derives, characteristically assumes equality of the participants, but, in point of fact, in most decision-making groups, power is unequally distributed. Accordingly, the decision-making dynamics of such groups will be strongly affected by the manner in which participants relate to superiors, peers, and subordinates. Location in the interpersonal hierarchy is of great importance to compulsive individuals who are preoccupied with their relative status in dominant-submissive relationships. Indeed, many characteristics of the authoritarian personality are explained by these aspects of the compulsive personality. They can be extremely responsive to the wishes of their superiors and highly competitive with peers, and they may insist upon both peers and subordinates submitting to their will, tending to be oblivious to the resentment they create in others. Such behavior obviously can have a disruptive, harmful impact upon the group process of decision making.

The Narcissistic Personality

If the ranks of leaders were stripped of individuals with narcissistic personality features, they would be seriously depleted, for the upper levels of government and industry are filled with successful narcissists. After all, at one level narcissism is nothing more than extreme self-confidence, and the wedding of self-confidence and ability is what creates success.

But narcissism to an extreme can be disabling, and, as with the compulsive personality disorder, the personality flaws of the full-blown narcissistic character disorder are so severe as to be inconsistent with sustained effective leadership.[16] The differences, however, between individuals with significant narcissistic personality features and those with the full-blown character disorder are differences of degree, not of kind; under stress, mild narcissistic characteristics can become extreme and, temporarily, can resemble the full-blown picture.

In its most extreme form, the narcissistic personality is characterized by extreme self-centeredness, egocentricity, and self-absorption. As a consequence of developmental difficulties, the narcissist has emerged from childhood and adolescence with what is known as "the wounded self." Preoccupied with fantasies of unlimited success, because of the wounded self that underlies his grandiose facade, the narcissist seeks constant reassurance of his worth and accordingly has a strong need for admiration and for being in the limelight.

His interpersonal relationships are regularly disturbed, with an insensitivity to the needs of others and a tendency to interpersonal exploitiveness. Such individuals are often characterized as "sharks." They expect special treatment and expect others to do what they want, but they regularly ignore the rights and needs of others. Their primary loyalty is to themselves, and they accordingly have a difficult time sustaining loyal relationships over time. The reason for these interpersonal difficulties can be traced to the psychological development of the narcissist.

The narcissist is so self-absorbed that psychologically he does not experience the people in his environment—his subordinates and coworkers—as individuals in their own right with needs and wants of their own. Rather, he relates to them as extensions of himself. Their major psychological function is to maintain the narcissists's self-esteem. The narcissist continues to relate to other individuals, groups, and organizations as primary sources of self-esteem.

Some narcissistic leaders will so crave adulation that they surround themselves with individuals who learn that it is necessary to uncritically assure the leader of the excellence of his plans, and protect him from knowledge of public discontent and other criticisms of his policies. In effect, the self-esteem maintenance function dominates, and the leader has surrounded himself with sycophants. Even though he is psychologically "normal" according to all psychological tests and is fully in touch with psychological reality, a narcissistic leader who has selected his inner circle on this basis may be totally out of touch with political reality. There are reports that toward the end, this was true of Anwar el-Sadat. Despite his international success, he was extremely sensitive to criticism. When the Egyptian peasants rioted over the price of bread, an expression of their discontent with Sadat's economic policies, Sadat's advisers informed him of the bread riots but assured him they were caused by communist agitators.

Optimally, the adviser close to the narcissistic leader will manage both to shore up the leader's self-esteem and help him to appraise political reality accurately. Examples of such healthy advisory relationships include Theodore Sorensen and John F. Kennedy, Col. Edward House and Woodrow Wilson, and Louis Howe and Franklin D. Roosevelt. The foregoing is not meant to imply that Wilson, Kennedy, and Roosevelt were full-blown narcissistic characters, but a reading of relevant psychobiographic materials certainly suggests there were significant narcissistic elements in the personalities of each of these leaders. The quality of the special relationships they had with their close advisers was by all accounts healthy and candid. By no means sycophants, these advisers shored up the leaders' self-esteem while helping them to accurately gauge political reality.

Because the narcissist is so vulnerable under his grandiose facade, it is difficult for him to acknowledge ignorance and, accordingly, to accept information or constructive criticism of his ideas. This contributes to the tendency noted above for the narcissist to surround himself with sycophants who tell him what he wants to hear.

In contrast to the compulsive personality, who places high value on ideas and logical reasoning and whose decisions are often made in relationship to stable mental schemata or belief systems, for the narcissist, words and ideas are instrumental and are designed to enhance his own position. What he says is calculated for effect and does not reflect core beliefs. He can change his judgments rapidly and reverse his positions without a qualm of conscience, in response to the interpersonal environment, as circumstances change.

The conscience of the narcissist is dominated by self-interest. Nevertheless, his self-image is of a principled and scrupulous person who, if he has reversed himself, did so because of circumstantial changes. Thus, he communicates utter sincerity and trustworthiness, so the unwary can be completely taken in. The narcissist seems to be completely sincere, and indeed, at that moment, he is.

The narcissist places overly high value on his own judgments and tends to overestimate the probability of success for any plans he is formulating. Indeed, the narcissistic tendency to over-optimism may contribute to the overly optimistic group appraisals described by Janis under the rubric of "groupthink."[17]

Because of his difficulties in empathizing with others, he will have a difficult time putting himself into the mind of his adversary. Having a tendency to identity himself with the nation, he will have a difficult time in separating national interest from self-interest. Thus, for the narcissist, the operant questions are not "What are the threats to my country, and what can be done to counter them," but "How can I use this situation to enhance or protect my own reputation?"

In characterizing practitioners of "hardball politics," L. Etheredge is describing a variant of the narcissistic personality often encountered in the corridors of power.[18] For these individuals, image and career enhancement are always primary values.

Crises do not eclipse this personality tendency—to the contrary, for hardball politicians, crises are opportunities to seize the moment. It was probably the hardball narcissistic personality the cynical senior government official had in mind when he defined a crisis as "an optimal opportunity for a bureaucratic power player to gain senior level visibility and maximize his organizational position." Thus, as he went on to say, the primary interest for such an individual is who goes to the White House for the morning meeting. Since gaining access to power is a primary value for such an individual, knowledge becomes power—a precious commodity to be held tightly and used for one's own advantage.

These special characteristics of the narcissistic leader's psychology and interpersonal relationships have an important impact upon his leadership behavior and decision making in general, but particularly in crisis situations. Whether the narcissistic leader is surrounded by sycophants or has relationships with advisers who can find ways of assisting him in accurately assessing the nature of his adversary, in evaluating the completeness of his plans, and in making midcourse corrections, will be especially important in crisis situations.

The Paranoid Personality

The essential features of the paranoid personality are a pervasive and long-standing suspiciousness and mistrust of people in general. The paranoid is always expecting plots and betrayal and sees himself alone, surrounded by enemies. This derives in part from his exaggerated need for autonomy. In such a dangerous world, it is best to trust no one.

Suspiciousness is the sine qua non of the paranoid. Paranoid individuals are hypersensitive and easily slighted; they continually scan the environment for clues that confirm their original assumptions, attitudes, or biases. The suspicious person has something on his mind and constantly searches for ways to prove it. The goal of his search is to find evidence to confirm his conclusions. He seizes upon evidence that confirms his suspicions and rejects disconfirming evidence. The psychologically healthy individual can abandon his suspicions when he is presented with firm contradictory evidence. The paranoid, in contrast, has a fixed conclusion in search of evidence.

Paranoids tend to be rigid and unwilling to compromise. In a new situation, they tend to lose appreciation of the total context as they pursue their fixed conclusion of danger.

The paranoid will become hostile, defensive, and stubborn when presented with evidence that contradicts his suspicions. Trying to breach the rigidity of the paranoid can produce unfortunate consequences. Well-meaning attempts to reassure him or to reason with him will usually provoke anger, and the helpful one can himself become the object of suspicions and be seen as disloyal. This wary hypervigilance and readiness to retaliate often generate fear and uneasiness in others. One treads lightly and carefully around a paranoid and "walks on eggshells," lest one provoke his anger.

The paranoid's view of his adversary is both strong and central. The world is seen as highly conflictual and the adversary is seen as evil, an immutable threat to one's own and the national self-interests. An adversary's overture of friendship will be seen as confirmation of the adversary's treachery, as he tries to lull one's own side into a false sense of complacency. In a crisis situation, the paranoid will not see the adversary as being eager to avoid conflict but rather will attribute to him malevolent motivations and construct a worst case scenario. This in turn pushes the paranoid to preemptive action, for he is convinced that persuasion and compromise are impossible.

Fortunately, frank paranoids of the kind described above usually do not last long in a hierarchy, at least in an open society. More muted, often better controlled manifestations of these behaviors are seen in individuals who manage generally to function quite effectively, although the underlying personality gives a particular style to their behavior. Indeed, in a highly competitive bureaucracy, a touch of paranoia with its heightened readiness to see bureaucratic rivals around every corner can be adaptive and help the individual to survive the bureaucratic wars.

But, as noted earlier, under the stress of crisis pressures, paranoid personality traits of a moderate degree become exaggerated and can become dysfunctional. Thus, the somewhat suspicious individual, whose suspiciousness is not usually of pathological proportions, can, under stress, become frankly paranoid. Several journalistic and memoir accounts of the last days of the Nixon presidency suggest that there was serious concern within the inner circle that the effects of the stress of the Watergate Crisis on Nixon were so severe that his reactions could not be trusted, and emergency measures were instituted to limit his capability of instituting conflict. (In particular, procedural safeguards were instituted requiring additional validation by senior officials before direct orders by the commander-in-chief could be enacted.)[19]

In considering the relationships between personality styles and crisis-induced stress, we should not limit our attention to leaders in open societies—to principal U.S. and Western decision makers. What of their opposite numbers in closed societies? In a conspiratorial milieu, having paranoid traits is not only not dysfunctional, but it is necessary for survival. Stalin is an interesting case in point. To have failed to be on guard and plot conscious in the conspiracy-ridden Kremlin would have been to be out of touch with reality. Stalin's antennae for enemies were finely tuned. This additional edge of suspiciousness undoubtedly played a major role in his survival. But progressively, the ranks of identified enemies were swollen by imagined enemies. Moreover, the paranoid fears induced a self-fulfilling prophecy, for Stalin's paranoid political behavior toward imagined enemies created enemies in actuality. Robert C. Tucker's psychobiography of Stalin provides persuasive details concerning Stalin's state of mind at the end of his life.[20] At the time of the so-called "doctors' plot," there seems little doubt that Stalin was in a clinical paranoid state and that his fears were being manipulated by Lavrenti Beria to secure his own position and eliminate bureaucratic rivals.

When individuals with strong paranoid propensities, such as Stalin, occupy major leadership roles, their characteristic reactions can have major consequences for political behavior, especially in crisis situations. Consider Adolph Hitler in light of the foregoing discussion of paranoid dynamics, especially the characteristics of interpersonal relations. In particular, it is well to consider the interaction between an exaggeratedly paranoid Hitler and his officers, many of whom by all accounts had strongly authoritarian personality dispositions.

Accounts of Hitler under stress, both on the eve of the Normandy invasion and on other occasions as the political-military situation was further unraveling, are instructive. They suggest that the dynamics sketched above were very much in play. The greater the stress, the more rigidly Hitler held on to his construction of the world. To attempt to present him with new information or to persuade him to change his mind was not only to risk explosive wrath but even the possibility of expulsion from the ranks of advisers, court martial, or worse. This would inhibit even the most self-confident of advisers. But given the strong psychological need to please authority that characterized many of these individuals, the premium on not disturbing or angering the Führer took precedence over bringing fully to bear one's assessment of the situation. This example, while striking, is by no means unique. It emphasizes the point that in considering the effects of personality on crisis reactions, one must consider the interaction between different personalities in the decision-making hierarchy.

THE DECISION MAKER AND
HIS DECISION SUPPORT GROUP

> Representative Les Aspin, the Chairman of the House Armed Services Committee, asserted that a safety officer destroyed a Navy Trident 2 submarine missile by mistake. "There's always someone who doesn't get the word," Mr. Aspin said, "and in this incident it was the man with his finger on the button."
>
> —"Missile Blast Called Deliberate,"
> New York Times, October 14, 1988

The decision maker does not make his decisions in splendid isolation but, rather, in relationship to a chain of command. The interplay of personalities can significantly influence both the information on which the decision maker acts and the manner in which his decisions are implemented.

The following two examples illustrate subordinates who were inhibited because of a combination of bureaucratic and psychological reasons from getting the word to the principal decision maker.

In Victims of Groupthink, his study of the influence of group dynamics on decision making in the Bay of Pigs case, Janis provides an interesting illustration of the problems in reopening a decision when decisional closure has been reached by the principal decision maker and of the difficulties for the subordinate in groups in which power is distributed unequally. As the final countdown for the invasion of Cuba was proceeding, then-Undersecretary of State Chester Bowles expressed grave reservations to Secretary of State Dean Rusk about the wisdom of the plans. Rusk informed Bowles that the president had already made up his mind and that contrary opinions would not be welcome. Bowles felt unable to make his reservations known to Kennedy, and his opposition to the plan was only to surface after the operation so disastrously failed. While it was attributed to protocol, Bowles's reluctance to push the matter further in the face of Rusk's admonition can be seen to be deference to the superior authority of both Rusk and Kennedy.

Another example of the manner in which sensitivity to hierarchical relationships can adversely affect the quality of decisions is reflected in an episode that occurred in the crisis task force during a terrorist hostage crisis. The chair of the task force received an urgent cable from the field that required an immediate decision by officials at the senior policy-making level; lives were in jeopardy. The chair's immediate superior, the deputy assistant secretary, would normally have conveyed the message to the senior officials, but he could not be located. The chair delayed forwarding the cable for decision for some 45 minutes, not wishing to make an "end run" around his superior, the deputy assistant secretary. The chair of the crisis task force did not wish to place the deputy assistant secretary in the embarrassing position of having his superior, the senior policy official, know before he did. While fortunately the delay did not produce loss of life, what was uppermost on the chair's mind was avoiding embarrassing his boss and avoiding his boss's displeasure.

Both of the above circumstances have been characterized as demonstrating the manner in which sensitivity to hierarchical relationships can influence decision making. In neither circumstance is there any reason to believe that the key participants were suffering from a personality disorder. But in a decision node with a principal decision maker and his decision support staff or circle of advisers, all of the participants have personalities, and many of the personality traits described above will be present in varying degrees. It has been noted that individuals with significant compulsive traits tend to be especially concerned with hierarchical relationships. A subordinate with such personality features will be especially concerned with the reactions of the principal decision maker. The possibility of upsetting a somewhat paranoid leader or a vulnerable narcissistic leader is likely to magnify the anxiety of a highly deferential subordinate who has problems dealing with authority and who, accordingly, may well conceal adverse information rather than risk his superior's wrath.

There are important interpersonal implications of each of the personality types described above when the individual is acting in relation to superiors, peers, and subordinates. We have earlier observed that in the social science literature concerning group decision making, there is essentially no systematic examination of how decision groups with differential distribution of power and authority function. Adding further to the analytic complexity, there is no systematic consideration of how different personality types affect the function of such groups.

PSYCHOPHYSIOLOGIC CONSIDERATIONS

One of the most interesting and, at first blush, perplexing characteristics of reactions by an individual leader to crises concerns the discrepancy between subjective self-reports by the leader and objective descriptions by observers. The experience of the stress of crisis decision making is often described by the person engaged in it in the most glowing terms. A striking example is found in the introduction to Nixon's *Six Crises*. The sections of the text that particularly bear on psychophysiologic reactions to stress and Nixon's judgments on their salutary effects upon his decision making are highlighted in italics (added).

> From my own experience, the bigger the problem, the broader its consequences, the less does an individual think of himself. He has to devote his entire concentration

to the much larger problem which confronts him. *The natural symptoms of stress in a period of crisis do not become self-destructive as a result of his worrying about himself, but on the other hand, become positive forces for creative action. . . .*

No one really knows what he is capable of until he is tested to the full by events over which he may have no great control. [Nixon then goes on to describe some of the lessons he learned from his six crises, including confidence, coolness, courage, and experience.]

Courage—or putting it more accurately, lack of fear—is a result of discipline. Any man who claims never to have known fear is either lying or else he is stupid. But by an act of will he refuses to think of the reasons for fear and so concentrates entirely on winning the battle.

Experience is a vitally important factor. When a man has been through even a minor crisis, he learns not to worry when his muscles tense up, his breathing comes faster, his nerves tingle, his stomach churns, his temper becomes short, his nights are sleepless. He recognizes such symptoms as the natural and healthy signs that his system is keyed up for battle. Far from worrying when this happens, he should worry when it does not. Because he knows from experience that once the battle is joined, all these symptoms will disappear—unless he insists on thinking primarily of himself rather than the problem he must confront.

A man who has never lost himself in a cause bigger than himself has missed one of life's mountaintop experiences. Only in losing himself does he find himself. Only then does he discover all the latent strengths he never knew he had and which otherwise would have remained dormant.

Crisis can indeed be agony. But it is the exquisite agony which a man might not wish to experience again—yet would not for the world have missed.[21]

Some individuals may even seek out and create crises as a way of feeling a sense of mastery, of giving a channel to their own aggressive and combative instincts. Commenting on Nixon's reactions to crisis, J. D. Barber observes that for the "active-negative" Nixon, involvement in a crisis imbued him with a sense of power. Accordingly, Barber posits an adversarial crisis-seeking bent in Nixon.[22]

Gary Sick, the principal White House aide for Iran during the Iranian revolution and the hostage crisis, was by all accounts highly effective in his crucial National Security Council staff role. He has reflected on his experiences at that critical moment in our nation's history and has considered the effects of sustained crisis-induced stress on him and other principal decision makers. He has acknowledged that at times, the long hours and sustained pressure were debilitating. But he has also described aspects of his reactions during that prolonged crisis in terms reminiscent of Nixon's "mountaintop" experiences.[23] Sick served on the National Security Council staff under Presidents Ford, Carter, and Reagan, but he regarded the long days and nights when he was at the center of the Iran crisis as the very acme of his government service—an occasion when he functioned at the height of his powers—and other experiences paled by comparison.

The operational definition of crisis at the Department of State is any situation that calls into being a crisis task force. When a task force is created, key players from numerous bureaus within the department are recruited. Considered by many an onerous task, service on such task forces is sought after by others. They describe the excitement and high-tension involvement in glowing terms and are described by their peers as "action junkies." The choice of the term "action junkies" is not accidental, for they are seen as being addicted to the excitement of crises, and ordinary duties seem pale and lifeless by comparison.

The euphoric excitement and the feeling of being at the height of one's powers reported by Nixon, Sick, and the State Department task force members reflects in part the natural high that accompanies stress. It is in part a consequence of the discharge of adrenal hormones that is an important psycho-physiologic response to stress described by Hans Selye and others.[24] The same hormones that mobilize the body's defenses in a "fight-flight" pattern characteristically produce a heady euphoric feeling. Figure 20.3 is a version of Selye's illustration of the mind-body connection and reactions to stress updated by E. L. Rossi.[25]

Note particularly the central role of the adrenal glands, the endocrine glands that secrete adrenal steroids that play so central a role in the body's fight-flight reaction. Note that these steroids affect mental and emotional processes.

Let us now take a closer look at the relationship between increased levels of stress and the quality of an individual's performance. Indeed, early in a crisis, one's alertness is magnified, and there are data from physiological psychology that indicate certain kinds of performance may be improved. However, the so-called "inverted U," shown in Figure 20.2, usefully captures what experimental studies reveal—an early heightening of decision-making ability and performance that may be succeeded, if stress increases beyond a certain point, by a decline in judgment and performance. But the emotional effects of the discharge of corticosteroids (adrenal hormones) will convey a feeling of being at the height of one's powers, even when objective performance measures demonstrate the contrary. Adrenal hormones magnify feelings of mastery and optimism, a combination of feelings that can clearly lead to miscalculations. The subjective feeling and self-report of heightened abilities are to be distrusted.

Indeed, one of the characteristics of "group-think" identified by Janis is over-optimism concerning the likelihood of success. He offers a social psychological explanation for the over-optimism. Janis sees it as a consequence of unusually high group cohesion, a necessary condition for the concurrence-seeking that serves as a way of coping with the stress of crisis decision making.[26] The psycho-physiologic explanation of over-optimism presented here does not compete with that of Janis. Rather, it suggests that the observed over-optimism may be multiply determined. In addition to the social psychological explanation offered by Janis, it may also be the case, that the psycho-physiology of stress as well as the narcissistic over-evaluation earlier described contribute to this characteristic phenomenon and probably interact with it. Thus, it may well be that the adrenaline high produced by stress magnifies the already present tendency toward optimism in a consensus-seeking group of high-level decision makers abundantly endowed with narcissistic personality traits.

Other statements in Nixon's long discourse on the effects of crisis-induced stress on decision makers that, as we shall see, need to be distrusted, include the following:

When a man has been through even a minor crisis, he learns not to worry when his muscles tense up, his breathing comes faster, his nerves tingle, his stomach churns, his temper becomes short, his nights are sleepless. He recognizes such symptoms as

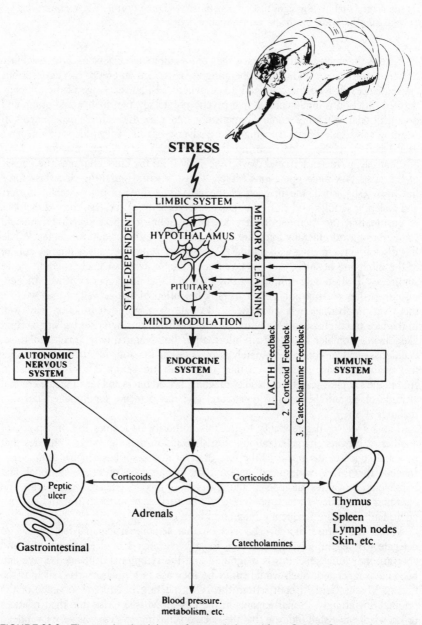

FIGURE 20.3   The psychophysiology of stress (adapted from Selye's General Adaptation Syndrome); *source:* reprinted by permission from Ernest L. Rossi, "Mind/Body Communication and the New Language of Human Facilitation," in *The Evolution of Psychotherapy,* Jeffrey K. Zeig, ed. (New York: Brunner/Mazel, 1989), p. 374.

the natural and healthy signs that his system is keyed up for battle. Far from worrying when this happens, he should worry when it does not.[27]

Nixon's statements to the contrary, the combination of sleeplessness and irritability that frequently affects individuals operating in crisis decision groups can have serious consequences. It is in the crisis task force, where 24-hour coverage of the critically defined situation is implemented, that psycho-physiology, personality, and group and organizational dynamics come dramatically into play. Individuals experienced in running crisis task forces, recognizing the adverse effects of sleep deprivation, have established procedures for ensuring that individuals serving on task forces have adequate sleep, recreation, and down time away from the emotional pressure cooker of the crisis task force operations center. Thus, when a round-the-clock task force has been established, the first job of the task force director is to establish rosters and watch schedules and shifts. A major responsibility of the task force director is to ensure that the members adhere to the discipline of these schedules; he will sometimes have to literally force the members to leave the operations center. While this discipline is effective with mid-level employees, senior officials will rarely adhere to the discipline of shifts, and the task force director, who is usually subordinate in stature, will often feel inhibited from insisting that his superior leave. Indeed, insofar as they are not only senior in rank but often in age as well, it may well be these very individuals who most need adequate sleep and can function least well in the face of fatigue. Stories abound of senior officials during crises walking around like "living zombies"—taking in information but being utterly unable to make decisions—with a consequent paralysis of decision making, for their subordinates feel unable to make decisions on their own while the senior officials are present. Add to the sleeplessness the irritability to which Nixon refers and recall the deferential attitude of certain personality types, and one has a recipe for impaired decision making.

The subject of deferentiality to irritable authority underlines the inaccuracy of another of Nixon's characterizations of crisis decision making. Nixon indicates that personal concerns disappear in the face of crisis and describes a noble selflessness. Indeed, there is a widespread notion that in the face of crisis, personal and bureaucratic rivalries disappear, and everyone pulls together to cope with the common emergency. In fact, nothing could be further from the truth, and bureaucratic fault lines are frequently magnified by a crisis.

When the nature of the crisis is such that senior participants feel unable to delegate to their juniors, the potential for adverse effects of sleep deprivation and aberrant individual reactions is magnified and the symptoms delineated above can become exaggerated. Such would surely be the case in a nuclear crisis, such as the Cuban Missile Crisis. Reports from the 1988 meeting in Moscow of some of the original Soviet and U.S. participants in the Cuban Missile Crisis and their relatives or knowledgeable staff indicate that the decision-making process was very far indeed from the idealized model of judicious governmental decision making many have considered the deliberations of the ExComm participants to be.[28] One of the participants described their thinking as badly flawed and indicated it was only a miracle that a disaster did not occur.

By the fourth or fifth day of the crisis, many were experiencing exhaustion and impaired reasoning processes. Anatoly Dobrynin's account of his meeting with Robert Kennedy, if correctly recalled by Nikita Khrushchev, is revealing: "Robert Kennedy looked exhausted. One could see from his eyes that he had not slept for days. He himself said that he had not been home for six days and nights. 'The President is in a grave situation,' Robert Kennedy said, 'and he does not know how to get out of it. We are under very severe stress.' "[29] Arthur Schlesinger reports Robert Kennedy's observation that the magnitude of the stress led Dean Rusk to have "a virtually complete breakdown mentally and physically."[30] (James G. Blight and David A. Welch's research leads them to disagree with this assessment of Rusk's reaction.[31])

Sleeplessness and irritability can have a further deleterious consequence. Sleeping pills may be turned to for insomnia, minor tranquilizers such as Valium for anxiety or irritability, and stimulants such as amphetamine compounds for fatigue. One particularly destructive sequence is to alternate so-called "downers" (sedative or tranquilizing medication) with "uppers" (stimulants). Each of these medication classes can affect reaction time, judgment, and other cognitive functions. For example, Halcyon, a frequently used sleeping pill, often produces retrograde amnesia. Among the initial effects of amphetamines, which make them attractive to a leader in a crisis situation, are an increase of alertness, lessened fatigue, feelings of well being, and lessened need for sleep. In a crisis, an individual who is "high" on amphetamines may be insufficiently cautious or unduly optimistic. Amphetamines cannot only give their takers a grossly overvalued sense of their own competence, but the feelings of well being can mount to the point of euphoria, exaltation, and grandiosity. Suspiciousness and irritability are frequently in evidence as well, and these stimulants can also produce paranoid reactions.

According to a *New York Times* investigative report, one of President Kennedy's personal physicians (who was later to lose his license for illegal distribution of amphetamines) assisted the president in abusing this potent drug.[32] Anthony Eden described himself as "living on Benzedrine" during the Suez Crisis. Irritable to the extreme, he would fly into rages at the very mention of Nasser's name, and his decision making was judged to be highly erratic.[33] Hitler's erratic reactions may well have been exacerbated by the concoction of medications prescribed to him by his physician, Dr. Morrell, widely viewed as a quack.[34] Morrell administered to Hitler more than 70 medications, including vitamins, bromides, barbiturates, cardiac stimulants, laxatives, steroids, and hormones from both the female placenta and the prostate of young bulls. Among other stimulants and sedatives, Hitler was taking Dr. Morrell's golden Vitamultin tablets, a concoction of methamphetamine and caffeine. Amphetamines alone would have had major deleterious effects on Hitler's decision making, but for his chronic sinusitis, he was receiving twice daily intranasal treatments of 10 percent cocaine solution as well as a cocaine inhalant. Thus, in the jargon of the street, Hitler was simultaneously on "speed" and "coke."

Because of the rank of the senior official, the physician may be loath to decline to prescribe the medications he requests or demands. In the midst of the Suez Crisis, with the very fate of the British empire resting on the prime minister's shoulders, it would be an intrepid physician who would resist his VIP patient's demand for Benzedrine.

In addition to taking prescription medications, individuals under stress may self-medicate, turning to alcohol to help them fall asleep and to calm their nerves. The question of alcohol abuse was raised prominently during the confirmation hearings for secretary of defense designate John Tower. Several senators indicated that the secretary of defense's position in the nuclear decision-making chain of command heightened the importance of whether he turned to alcohol under stress.

Heretofore in this chapter, only issues of personality and psycho-physiology have been considered. What are the effects of the aging process on crisis reactions? While "wisdom is with the aged, and understanding in length of days," in fact, rapid tactical decision making is difficult for individuals in their 60s and 70s, even if they are not hampered by significant illness. What, then, can be said about the decision-making ability of aged ailing individuals? What if such an individual is a major leader? What can be said about a decision-making group composed of aged leaders? Consider crisis decision making during the latter years of the Brezhnev era, when the average age of the Politburo was 73.5 years and several of the key leaders were manifestly suffering the incursions of age and probably suffering from moderate cerebral arteriosclerosis (hardening of the arteries of the brain). When the Korean airliner, the KAL-007, wandered into Soviet airspace, was the aging senior leadership involved in the decision that led to the shootdown?

A normal characteristic of the psychology of the later years is an increased urgency to make one's mark because of the perception of limited time available.[35] When the aging period is marked by an illness that affects mental processes, there may be an inhibition of judgment and an exaggeration of preexisting personality characteristics. In concert with increased urgency, these factors may have a major effect on political decision making, especially in a leader with dreams of glory.[36]

CONCLUSION

Despite Nixon's heroic claim of selflessness in the face of crisis, human vulnerability does not disappear in times of stress. To the contrary, while moderate levels of stress usually improve the performance of most individuals, at least initially, human frailties are magnified when acute, prolonged stress and fatigue are experienced. At the individual, group, and organizational levels, psychological fault lines are widened. And the greater the stress, the more magnified the responses.

Under stress, individuals become more like themselves—that is, their characteristic coping mechanisms become exaggerated: The characteristically suspicious individual, under stress, can become paranoid; the moderately compulsive individual can become paralyzed with indecision in his quest for certainty, which can lead to dangerous delay. At the interpersonal level, a leader's magnified irritability and tendency to become imperious and demanding can interact with the subordinate's need to please and to defer to authority. The result can be major distortions in communication and the syndrome of "groupthink." Conversely, irritability and exaggerated psychological reactions can contribute to a badly divided, fractious group. Nor do tensions and rivalries between groups and organizations necessarily disappear in the face of crises. The psycho-physiology of acute and chronic stress, which in turn can lead to abuse of prescription medications and alcohol, adds a further complicating dimension.

A war-threatening crisis or a conventional war that could escalate to nuclear confrontation would surely lead to massive stress. There is no reason to believe that the magnitude of the crisis would somehow immunize decision makers from the stress reactions described. Just as "soldiers and sailors in their first battle suffer immense stress before and during the fighting and may confuse perceptions with reality," so inevitably would senior officials experiencing the almost unimaginable level of stress of a nuclear crisis.

What are the implications—and prescriptions—that follow from this analysis? In the military, selection and training are the twin pillars for the identification and preparation of military officers responsible for decision making under combat stress.

- In selecting our leaders and senior civilian officials, a major criterion should be a demonstrated capacity for effective and judicious decision making under stress.
- Our leaders and senior officials should regularly participate in training simulations to become familiar with crisis decision making and to identify and remedy individual, group, and organizational vulnerabilities under stress.

Military psychologists note that such simulations can never fully prepare participants for combat because "the excitement factor is missing in such drills, because regardless of the realism of the simulation, it is just that, a simulation of the real thing," but, nevertheless, training simulations can make the unimaginable imaginable. Political-military simulations and exercises are regularly conducted by governments, East and West, but world leaders and their most senior officials are often too busy to participate. Yet, it is they who will be exercising that awesome responsibility should the unimaginable become reality. The very highest officials, including civilian officials, should be participating in such exercises within their own governments and alliances.

Moreover, we should now be considering what could not have been conceived of not too long ago—developing and conducting political-military exercises and war games in collaboration with our potential adversaries. By permitting the participants to see the distortions in decision making caused by crisis-induced stress, including the misinterpretations of the adversary's intentions, such exercises could have extremely constructive consequences in sensitizing the participants and helping to avoid inadvertent war.

NOTES

1. Ole R. Holsti and Alexander George, "The Effects of Stress on the Performance of Foreign Policy Makers," in C. P. Cotter, ed., *Political Science Annual: An International Review*, Vol. 6 (Indianapolis: Bobbs Merrill, 1975).

2. O. R. Holsti, "Foreign Policy Decision Makers Viewed Psychologically: 'Cognitive Process' Approaches," in J. N. Rosenau, ed., *In Search of Global Patterns* (New York: Free Press, 1976).

3. O. Rosenthal, P. T Hart, and M. Charles, *Coping with Crisis: The Management of Disasters, Riots, and Terrorism* (Springfield, Ill.: Thomas Books, 1989).

4. Richard M. Nixon, *Six Crises* (New York: Doubleday, 1960).

5. The manner in which flawed perceptions and decision making can contribute to international conflict has been a preoccupying concern of several authors. A few of the important contributions in this area are: R. Axelrod, ed., *Structure of Decision: The Cognitive Maps of Political Elites* (Princeton: Princeton University Press, 1976); J. Blight, "How Might Psychology Contribute to Reducing the Risk of Nuclear War?" *Political Psychology* 7, 4 (1986); J. Blight and D. Welch, *On the Brink: Americans and Soviets Re-examine the Cuban Missile Crisis* (New York: Hill and Wang, 1988); M. Bonham and M. G. Shapiro, "Mapping Structures of Thought," in I. N. Galhofer, W. E. Saris, and M. Melman, eds., *Different Text Analysis Procedures for the Study of Decision Making* (Amsterdam: Sociometric Research Foundation, 1986); M. Brecher, "Toward a Theory of International Crisis Behavior: A Preliminary Report," *International Studies Quarterly* 21 (1977): 39–74; Morton Deutsch, "The Prevention of World War III: A Psychological Perspective," *Political Psychology* 4, 1 (1983); Alexander George, "Assessing Presidential Character," *World Politics* 26, 2 (1974); "Adaptation to Stress in Political Decision Making: The Individual, Small Group and Organizational Contexts," in George V. Coelho, David A. Hamburg, John E. Adams, eds., *Coping and Adaptation* (New York: Basic Books, 1974); "The Causal Nexus Between Beliefs and Behavior and the Operational Code Belief System," in L. Falkowski, eds., *Psychological Models in International Politics* (Boulder, CO: Westview Press, 1979); "The Impact of Crisis-Induced Stress on Decision Making," in F. Soloman, ed., *The Medical Implications of Nuclear War* (Washington, D.C.: National Academy Press, 1986); Charles F. Hermann, *International Crises: Insights from Behavioral Research* (New York: Free Press, 1972); Margaret G. Hermann and Charles F. Hermann, "Maintaining the Quality of Decision Making in Foreign Policy Crises: A Proposal," in A. L. George, ed., *Towards More Soundly Based Foreign Policy: Making Better Use of Information*, Report to the Commission on the Organization of Government for the Conduct of Foreign Policy, Appendix D (Washington, D.C.: U.S. Government Printing Office, 1975); Margaret G. Hermann, "Indicators of Stress in Policy Makers During Foreign Policy Crises," *Political Psychology* 1 (1979): 27–46; Ole R. Holsti, *Crisis, Escalation, War* (Montreal: McGill-Queens University Press, 1972); Ole R. Holsti and A. L. George, "The Effects of Stress on the Performance of Foreign Policy-Makers," in C. P. Cotter, ed., *Political Science Annual: An International Review* (Indianapolis: Bobbs-Merrill, 1975); Ole R. Holsti, "Crisis Management," Paper presented to the eighth annual scientific meeting of the International Society for Political Psychology (Amsterdam: June 28–July 3, 1986); Robert Jervis, *Perception and Misperception in International Politics* (Princeton: Princeton University Press, 1976); Robert Jervis, Richard Ned Lebow, and Janice Gross Stein, *Psychology and Deterrence* (Baltimore: Johns Hopkins University Press, 1985); Richard Ned Lebow, *Between Peace and War: The Nature of International Crisis* (Baltimore: Johns Hopkins University Press, 1981) and *Managing Nuclear Crisis: A Dangerous Illusion* (Ithaca: Cornell University Press, 1987); Janice Gross Stein and R. Tanter, *Rational Decision Making: Israel's Security Choices, 1967* (Columbus: Ohio State University Press, 1980) and "Building Politics Into Psychology: The Misperception of Threat," *Political Psychology* 9, 2 (1988); P. Tetlock, "Psychological Research on Foreign Policy: An Overview," in L. Wheeler, ed., *Review of Personality and Social Psychology* 4 (Beverley Hills: Sage, 1983) and "Cognitive Perspectives on Foreign Policy," in S. Long, ed., *Political Behavior Annual* 1 (Boulder, CO: Westview Press, 1986), pp. 255–273; S. G. Walker, "The Motivational Foundations of Political Belief Systems: A Re-analysis of the Operational Code Construct," *International Studies Quarterly* 27 (1983): 179–201; and "Personality, Situation and Cognitive Complexity: A Revisionist Analysis of the Israeli Cases," *Political Psychology* 8, 4 (1987); T. C. Wiegele, "Decision Making in an International Crisis: Some Biological Factors," *International Studies Quarterly* 17 (1973): 295–335 and "Health and Stress During International Crisis: Neglected Input Variables in the Foreign Policy Decision-Making Process," *Journal of Political Science* 3 (1976): 139–

144; "Models of Stress and Disturbances in Elite Political Behaviors: Psychological Variables and Political Decision Making," in R. Robins, ed., *Psychopathology and Political Leadership* (New Orleans: Tulane Studies in Political Science, 1977); T. C. Wiegele and P. Plowman, "Stress Tolerance and International Crisis: The Significance of Biologically Oriented Experimental Research to the Behavior of Political Decision Makers," *Experimental Study of Politics* 3 (1974): 63–92 and "Presidential Physicians and Presidential Health Care: Some Theoretical and Operational Considerations Related to Political Decision Making," *Presidential Studies Quarterly* 44, 1 (Winter 1990): 71–89. The majority of these authors have focused on the role of cognitive factors and belief systems, with significantly less attention being devoted to affective influences.

D. Winter has developed measures of important drives associated with political behavior (need power, need affiliation, need achievement), in D. Winter and A. Stewart, "Content Analysis as a Technique for Assessing Political Leaders," in Margaret Hermann, ed., *A Psychological Examination of Political Leaders* (New York: Simon and Schuster, 1976); S. G. Walker has been exploring the relationship between drives and belief systems, in "The Motivational Foundations of Political Belief Systems: A Re-Analysis of the Operational Code Construct," *International Studies Quarterly* 27: 179–201; and Jerrold M. Post and Philip Rogers have been investigating the relationship between personality types and belief systems. "Personality and Belief Systems," a paper presented to the eleventh annual meeting of the International Society of Political Psychologists (ISPP), San Francisco, 1988.

6. Holsti, "Foreign Policy Decision Makers Viewed Psychologically: Cognitive Process Approaches."

7. F. Greenstein, *Personality and Politics* (Princeton: Princeton University Press, 1983).

8. S. Hook, *The Hero in History* (New Jersey: Humanities Press, 1943).

9. Margaret Hermann, "When Leader Personality Will Affect Foreign Policy: Some Propositions," in J. N. Rosenau, ed., *In Search of Global Patterns.*

10. M. Brewster-Smith, "A Map for the Analysis of Personality and Politics," *Journal of Social Issues* 24 (July 1968): 15–28.

11. A. George, "The Impact of Crisis-Induced Stress on Decision Making," in F. Soloman, ed., *The Medical Implications of Nuclear War* (Washington D.C.: National Academy Press, 1986), p. 33.

12. R. P. Abelson, "Computer Simulation of 'Hot' Cognition," in S. Tomkin and S. Messick, eds., *Computer Simulation of Personality* (New York: Wiley, 1963).

13. I. L. Janis, *Victims of Groupthink* (Boston: Houghton-Mifflin, 1972); I. L. Janis and L. Mann, *Decision Making: A Psychological Analysis Conflict, Choice and Commitment* (New York: Free Press, 1977); I. L. Janis, *Crucial Decisions* (New York: Free Press, 1989).

14. A. L. George, "Adaptions to Stress in Political Decision making: The Individual, Small Group, and Organizational Contexts," in G. V. Coelho, D. Hamburg, and J. E. Adams, *Coping and Adaption* (New York: Basic Books, 1974).

15. D. Shapiro, *Neurotic Styles* (New York: Basic Books, 1965).

16. O. Kernberg, *Borderline Conditions and Pathological Narcissism* (New York: Jason Aronson, 1975).

17. Janis, *Victims of Groupthink.*

18. L. Etheredge, "Hardball Politics: A Model," *Political Psychology* 1 (1979).

19. H. Kissinger, *The White House Years* (Boston: Little, Brown, 1979); B. Woodward and C. Bernstein, *The Final Days* (New York: Simon and Schuster, 1976).

20. Robert C. Tucker, *Stalin as Revolutionary 1879–1929: A Study in History and Personality* (New York: Norton, 1973).

21. Nixon, *Six Crises.*

22. J. D. Barber, *Presidential Character: Predicting Performance in the White House* (Englewood, NJ: Prentice-Hall, 1972).

23. Gary Sick, *All Fall Down* (New York: Penguin Books, 1986).

24. Hans Selye, *The Stress of Life* (New York: McGraw-Hill, 1976).

25. E. L. Rossi, "Mind/Body Communication and the New Language of Human Facilitation," in J. K. Zeigied, *The Evolution of Psychotherapy* (New York: Brunner-Mazel, 1987).

26. Janis, *Victims of Groupthink*.

27. Nixon, *Six Crises*.

28. Bruce J. Allen, James G. Blight, and David A. Welch, eds., *Proceedings of the Moscow Conference on the Cuban Missile Crisis, January 27, 28, 1989* (Cambridge, MA: Center for Science and International Affairs, Harvard University, December 1989).

29. N. Khrushchev, *Khrushchev Remembers* (Boston: Little, Brown, 1970).

30. A. Schlesinger, *Robert Kennedy and His Times* (New York, Ballantine, 1978).

31. J. Blight and D. Welch, *On the Brink: Americans and Soviets Reexamine the Missile Crisis* (New York: Hill and Wang, 1988).

32. B. Rensberger, "Amphetamines Used by a Physician to Lift Mood of Famous Patients," *New York Times*, December 4, 1972.

33. H. L'Etang, *Fit to Lead?* (London: Heinsmann Medical Books, Ltd., 1979); B. E. Park, *The Impact of Illness on World Leaders*, (Philadelphia: The University of Pennsylvania Press, 1986).

34. Ibid.

35. J. Post, "On Aging Leaders: Possible Effects of the Aging Process on the Conduct of Leadership," *Journal of Geriatric Psychiatry* 4 (1973) and "The Seasons of a Leaders Life: Influences of the Life Cycle on Political Behavior," *Political Psychology* 2, 3/4 (Fall/ Winter, 1980): 35–49.

36. J. Post, "Dreams of Glory and the Life Cycle: The Life Course of Narcissistic Leaders," *Journal of Political and Military Politics*, XXVI, 2.

PROSPECTS:
NEW CHALLENGES,
NEW OPPORTUNITIES

Introduction to Part Six

Alexander L. George

It is by now an often-repeated truism that dramatic and rapid changes in the international environment are creating an even more complex multipolar system that poses new problems for stability and that these developments call for the re-examination of traditional ways of viewing security and its requirements. In particular, the end of the Cold War, the transformation of East-West relations, and the internal changes within the Soviet Union offer much fresh encouragement that the two superpowers will be able to manage conflicting interests in the future without again plunging into war-threatening crises that might escalate to nuclear war. But, as noted in Chapter 1, inadvertent war involving the Soviet Union and the United States, while even less probable than before, remains a possibility that cannot be ignored.

Counterbalancing the favorable implications of the transition underway in East-West relations are developments elsewhere in the world that have ominous overtones. Other states and peoples, some of the them freed from the constraints and imperatives imposed on their behavior by the Cold War between the superpowers, can pursue their interests and foreign policy agendas in ways that are likely to heighten turbulence and conflict. Whether or not additional nuclear proliferation adds to the conflict potential of regional rivalries, the spread of chemical weapons, ballistic missile technology, and other types of advanced conventional weapons already poses grave threats to regional stability. And, as the U.S. response to Iraq's move into Kuwait demonstrated, the decline of superpower rivalry in some parts of the Third World does not mean that one or the other superpower will forego military intervention. Indeed, in some regional conflicts that affect their interests, the United States or the Soviet Union may be more willing to intervene militarily than in the past precisely insofar as the improvement in their relations makes it unlikely that such intervention would lead to a confrontation with the other superpower. It would be imprudent to ignore the likelihood of new threats and new uncertainties in the Third World. In particular, improved U.S.-Soviet relations and the partial retrench-ment of Soviet involvement in regional affairs may have unexpected implications for either exacerbating or alleviating the Arab-Israeli impasse.

In the chapter that follows, Phil Williams agrees with those who believe that the remarkable changes that have taken place in Eastern Europe and the Soviet

Union presage a much safer Europe, at least insofar as the likelihood of a major war is concerned. At the same time, however, post-Cold War Europe is likely to be much more unpredictable and subject to greater instability. In the past, the division of Europe into tacitly accepted spheres of influence, reinforced by a state of mutual deterrence, contributed to stability between the two blocs. But in the Europe that is emerging, the lines will be less clearly drawn and the limits of permissible behavior less well understood.

In the Europe of the Cold War, NATO gave priority to the deterrence of aggression against Western Europe and the prevention of crises that would seriously impinge on its security. Crisis management was not ignored, but, in part because confidence in managing crises was uncertain, the premium was placed on prevention. Planning for crisis management had a fairly low priority; the emphasis in NATO doctrine, force posture, and planning was to improve capabilities for responding to possible aggression.

In post-Cold War Europe, the probability of low-level violence is likely to be somewhat greater. As Williams puts it, "The single fault line between East and West has been replaced by a complex mosaic of ethnic and national rivalries that could lead to both civil strife and interstate conflicts in Central and Eastern Europe." The escalation potential of such conflicts cannot be ignored.

Consequently, Williams concludes, requirements for crisis management in Europe will be greater and more complex than in the past. To this end, he examines in some detail the need for developing new mechanisms for preventing a range of possible crises and for managing them when they occur. He considers how these objectives might be achieved either through changes in NATO or by the development of a Pan-European security arrangement through the Conference on Security and Cooperation in Europe (CSCE). He concludes that these two possibilities should be regarded as complementary rather than as mutually exclusive alternatives.

The improvement in superpower relations since the mid-1980s opened the way to what Kurt M. Campbell refers to in his chapter as U.S.-Soviet "military diplomacy." Earlier the Soviets had intermittently called for the expansion of military contacts, and, indeed, some voices in the West had urged that provision be made for regular conversations between military leaders of the two sides.

The Reagan-Gorbachev summit of December 1987 set into motion the beginning of military-to-military discussions that led in June 1989 to the signing of an agreement on "The Prevention of Dangerous Military Activities." This accord dealt with four potentially troublesome military activities: incursions by one side's forces across the other side's borders; use by one side of range-finding lasers capable of inflicting damage to personnel of the other side; ship and troop maneuvers in regions of high tension; and certain types of interferences with each other's command, communications, and control networks in peacetime. The agreement also instituted procedures to avoid and to defuse incidents that might arise from such activities. A Joint Military Commission was established that is to meet annually to discuss and deal with such problems.

The primary purpose of the military-to-military talks has been to find ways of avoiding accidental or inadvertent clashes and to help prevent misperceptions and misconceptions that could contribute to or aggravate crises. Campbell, who served as a member of the U.S. negotiating team, describes the history of the Dangerous Military Activities Agreement, indicates the present status of the military-to-military talks, and outlines a number of additional issues that might be placed on the agenda for future discussion. Clearly, the implementation and further development of these military-to-military contacts can play a constructive role in reducing the risks of accidental or inadvertent war. They can do so by preventing dangerous military practices, expanding crisis communications, removing unhelpful stereotypes that each side holds of the other, and providing a means for exploring potentially destabilizing doctrinal practices.

CHAPTER 21

Crisis Management in Europe: Old Mechanisms and New Problems

Phil Williams

The events of 1989 in Eastern Europe not only brought to an end the Cold War in Europe but marked a profound shift in the continent's strategic and military landscape. Long-standing fears that the Soviet Union might initiate a short-warning or a surprise attack disappeared as the Warsaw Pact disintegrated as an effective military alliance. In these circumstances, many observers concluded that the threat to Western security had disappeared and that relaxation and retrenchment were not only permissible and appropriate but—given the growing importance of other items on the policy agenda—absolutely essential. The reality, however, is less clear-cut, as the decline of the Soviet threat may be accompanied by the emergence of new risks and dangers. Although it is uncertain what these risks are, how serious they might be, or how they can be reduced or managed, it is certainly not inconceivable that the Europe of the 1990s and beyond could prove to be a more turbulent place than the Europe of the last 40 years. As John Mearsheimer has suggested, "The prospects of major crises, even wars, in Europe are likely to increase dramatically now that the Cold War is receding into history. The next forty-five years are not likely to be so violent as the forty-five years before the Cold War, but they are likely to be substantially more violent than the past forty-five years, the era that we may someday look back upon not as the Cold War but as the Long Peace."[1] In the Europe of the Cold War, there was a possibility—albeit remote—of large-scale conflict between the military blocs; in post-Cold War Europe, there is a somewhat larger probability of lower levels of violence, both at the interstate and the intrastate level. The single fault line between East and West has been replaced by a complex mosaic of ethnic and national rivalries that could lead to both civil strife and interstate conflict in Central and Eastern Europe. At the very least, therefore, the European state system will require procedures and mechanisms for both crisis prevention and crisis management.

The author thanks Alexander George, Scott Sagan, and Paul Hammond for their comments on an earlier draft of this chapter and Paul Stares for several helpful discussions of NATO crisis management.

The focus of this chapter is on crisis management in a future Europe. Before exploring this issue, however, it is helpful to delineate different approaches to crisis prevention and crisis management and to analyze the postwar security system in Europe in terms of the balance between prevention and management. Although the Cold War was punctuated by occasional crises, in Europe the system was predominantly oriented toward crisis prevention. The corollary of this—as is discussed below—is that in certain respects, crisis management mechanisms and procedures were flawed or inadequate. In a sense, this was tolerable because there was a fairly pervasive sense of stability in the system and there was an implicit assumption that crisis management capabilities were unlikely to be tested in any serious way. In the future, however, a capacity for crisis management may be more important than ever. This chapter will consider the main changes that have occurred in the security environment in Europe and identify the dangers that seem likely to arise in the future. It will then delineate the crisis management mechanisms that might be appropriate to the new Europe.

A FRAMEWORK FOR ANALYSIS

In thinking about both the existing security arrangements in Europe and possible alternatives, an analysis by Aaron Wildavsky entitled *Searching for Safety*, which deals with the question of the management of modern technologies, is both relevant and helpful.[2] Although there are some difficulties in translating Wildavsky's very general ideas about safety and risk into specific designs, some of his ideas might be relevant to the search for a manageable order in post-Cold War Europe.

Using studies related to coping with risk that have been done in other disciplines, Wildavsky argues that there is a crucial distinction between strategies of anticipation and strategies of resilience—a distinction that corresponds broadly with that between crisis prevention on the one hand and crisis management and escalation control on the other. The strategy of anticipation is defined as deterring or avoiding danger before it becomes threatening, while resilience can be understood in terms of coping, management, and learning mechanisms. With the former strategy, the main goal is to "predict and prevent potential dangers before damage is done," while the latter approach is based on the capacity to deal with "unanticipated dangers after they have become manifest." Whereas anticipation is designed to avoid or prevent shocks, resilience requires some kind of mechanisms for shock absorption: "The mode of resilience is based on the assumption that unexpected trouble is ubiquitous and unpredictable; and thus accurate advance information is in short supply." So learning from error (as opposed to avoiding error altogether) and reacting very rapidly are crucial to resilience. A capacity for buffering—that is, a generalized capacity to respond to the unknown—is also essential to strategies of resilience. Such strategies also draw upon the principle of redundancy, which allows for high rates of failure but is good at both error detection and error correction.[3]

Although Wildavsky has a clear preference for strategies of resilience, it is clear that each approach has its advantages and shortcomings. Wildavsky tends to dwell on the disadvantages of the anticipation strategy, contending that if the predictions or guesses of the anticipatory mode turn out to be wrong, those who are solely dependent on this mode will have no way of getting out of trouble or of responding to problems that have arisen in spite of all efforts to prevent or avoid them.[4] This argument is persuasive. At the same time, there are problems with excessive reliance on resilience. Although resilience offers greater chances of adapting to the unexpected, complete dependence on this kind of strategy or capacity would leave little room for error, would be enormously consuming of energy and resources, and would very quickly lead to an overload problem. In short, if no attempt is made to anticipate and fix the most obvious problems, there may be more problems than even a highly resilient system can cope with.

In practice, of course, there is some overlap between anticipation and resilience. This is not surprising. After all, crisis management activities are generally intended to prevent an existing crisis from escalating or being transformed into a more serious crisis of a different type. It is also clear that both types of approach or capability are needed and that, in crucial respects, they complement one another. Indeed, Wildavsky accepts that one of the central questions is: "What proportion of anticipation and of resilience (since we need both capacities) is desirable under which conditions?"[5] In international politics, this issue translates into a question about the balance between the capability for crisis prevention or crisis avoidance on the one hand and the capability for crisis management on the other. In this connection, it is clear that the more orderly and predictable the environment, the more appropriate are strategies of anticipation, while the more unpredictable the problems and dangers, the more important it is to have a capacity for resilience.[6] The implication is that in certain kinds of international systems, the emphasis can appropriately be placed on crisis prevention, while in other kinds of international systems there will have to be more reliance on crisis management. The argument here is that the Cold War system was of the former kind; the post-Cold War system is of the latter type.

THE POSTWAR SECURITY SYSTEM: THE PREEMINENCE OF CRISIS PREVENTION AND THE INADEQUACIES OF CRISIS MANAGEMENT

The Cold War system in Europe was based upon bipolarity—clear division between the rival blocs and their nuclear arsenals. Although this system was generally regarded as dangerous and in certain respects undesirable, it was in fact a highly stable system in which strategies of crisis prevention or anticipation were both appropriate and effective.

There were several reasons for this. In the first place, the environment was both simple and predictable. Europe was divided into rival blocs–NATO and the Warsaw Pact—clustered around the two superpowers, and although Berlin remained something of an anomaly, the alliance system both symbolized and accentuated basic acceptance of the physical division of the continent and a tacit understanding about the limits of permissible behavior. Second, there was a clear understanding of the costs and risks inherent in any major attempt to overturn the status quo. Although the Soviet domination of Eastern Europe was never accepted as legitimate in the United States, Washington was acutely aware that efforts at liberation and rollback would result in a major war. At the same time, there was a broad consensus in the West on what actions had to be taken to meet the Soviet threat to Western Europe. The United States and its European allies established institutional mechanisms for crisis prevention by making deliberate challenges to the system potentially very costly. Crisis prevention was to be achieved through deterrence of deliberate Soviet aggression. Modifying the environment through a strategy of anticipation came to mean influencing Soviet behavior through a strategy of deterrence. Moreover, during the 1960s, the strategy that was designed to achieve deterrence was modified in ways that made it increasingly robust and better able to cover a range of aggressive actions, including a large-scale but non-nuclear Soviet attack against Western Europe.

The stability of the system was also enhanced by the clearly delineated relationships between East and West and within the superpowers' spheres of influence. One consequence of this was what Wildavsky has described as patchiness—a quality that meant that instability or turbulence in one place did not spread.[7] Although there was a tight coupling between any Soviet action against Western Europe (including Berlin) and a firm military response by NATO, there was only a loose coupling between events in Eastern Europe and NATO reactions.[8] In effect, the tacit agreement on spheres of influence ensured that instability in Eastern Europe did not spread to Western Europe or become a spark for conflict between the blocs. The United States and its European allies disapproved of any Soviet intervention but did nothing to challenge Soviet predominance or to thwart Soviet efforts to maintain control over the states of Eastern Europe. In other words, the creation of the two blocs in Europe was accompanied by a tacit acceptance by the main participants of the rules of the game. Although the parallels are rarely drawn, Cold War Europe was in some respects akin to the European state system of the nineteenth century when, according to one analyst, "the powers drew demarcation lines, set limits and established ground rules for their competition in order to avoid misunderstandings and disputes."[9] Although the alliance system in postwar Europe was much simpler than the multipolar and flexible system of nineteenth-century Europe, the overall effect was much the same in that crises in the system were kept to a minimum.

Moreover, during the détente of the 1970s, these ground rules were developed and formalized in the Helsinki Agreement. Indeed, the Helsinki process or, to give it its full name, the Conference on Security and Cooperation in Europe (CSCE) was very similar in certain respects to the nineteenth-century concert system in which the rules were intended "to coordinate relations, minimize friction, avoid misperceptions and miscalculations, clarify respective interests, establish restraints, and make clear distinctions between legitimate and illegitimate ends and means in the pursuit of policy."[10] In order to achieve these objectives, there was an increasing emphasis on military transparency and on confidence and security building. Such measures were enshrined most fully in the Stockholm Agreement of 1986, which required at least 42 days advance notice of military maneuvers above certain levels as well as the exchange of annual calendars regarding military activities, provided for observation of notified activities, and had a limited provision for challenge on site inspections in specified areas. The agreement was designed to ensure that the capacity for crisis prevention through deterrence was accompanied by crisis prevention measures that were less abrasive and that dealt not with deliberate aggression but with inadvertent war or war through miscalculation or misunderstanding.

These efforts at confidence building suggest that the European security system as it existed from 1949 to 1989 was upheld primarily through strategies of anticipation. As Wildavsky has pointed out, one of the limitations of such an approach is that it is slow and dependent on correct information.[11] The security arrangements are designed primarily to prevent, not to respond. Although a capacity for response is necessary in order to ensure deterrence, if a large-scale response is required, then the system has either broken down or is in danger of doing so.

At the same time, it would be a mistake to believe that there was no capacity in the European security order for crisis management. Strategies of anticipation were accompanied by strategies of resilience. In addition to NATO's capacity for crisis prevention through deterrence, there was a reserve capacity for crisis management. Partly because faith in crisis management was uncertain, however, a premium was placed on prevention. Conversely, the concern with prevention meant that crisis management was not only considered a second-best solution but was so subordinated to deterrence that if a major challenge had arisen, some of the deterrence and defense mechanisms that came into play would have made the task of crisis management much more difficult.

Even in the best of circumstances, of course, crisis management involves difficult trade-offs and dilemmas. The problems are particularly formidable in a coalition of diverse governments such as NATO, where each member wants to resolve the trade-offs and dilemmas in ways that accord with its own distinct preoccupations, preferences, and interests. Yet at one level, the NATO crisis management system appears to be fairly elaborate.[12] It is a system in which considerable emphasis is placed on intelligence and warning, even though intelligence remains a matter of national responsibility with the NATO staff simply reviewing and evaluating data made available by the member nations, especially the United States. It is also a system built around formal procedures for consultation and decision making, with the North Atlantic Council and the Defence Planning Committee having crucial roles. The third component of the crisis management structure is the NATO alerts system. The precise details are classified, but it is possible to discern the broad outlines of the alert and mobilization procedures that would be followed in a major crisis.

One element enables the military to initiate certain measures as part of a counter-surprise strategy. This Counter Surprise Military System—state orange and state scarlet—is designed to allow the major NATO commanders to take protective measures if they believe attack is imminent. In a period where tension is increasing more gradually, commanders can move to military vigilance. This level of alert does not depend on rapid political decision and is within the prerogative of military commanders charged with ensuring the safety of their forces. According to a Western European Union report on crisis management, "military vigilance . . . can be ordered by any of the three major NATO commanders on their own initiative; this ensures that NATO Headquarters are manned twenty-four hours a day and that the staff is at full strength."[13] Military vigilance also leads to increased surveillance activity. If the situation looked particularly serious, then the Supreme Allied Commander Europe (SACEUR) could enhance the level of readiness and send a strong signal to the Soviet Union by beginning the reinforcement process with the dual-based forces from the United States. Such action could take place independent of the NATO system and allied agreement—although it would of course require a political decision by the U.S. president.[14]

In addition to these military measures and national responses, there are three formal levels of alert—simple alert, reinforced alert, and general alert—which are dependent upon political decisions made by the allies. As a Western European Union report noted, "Political authority from the Defence Planning Committee transmitted through the Military Committee is required for any of the three degrees of formal alert up to general alert which would involve large scale movement of assigned and reserve forces to their wartime positions and the call-up of reserves."[15] Central to the alert process has been the assumption that in a serious crisis in Europe, SACEUR would request a formal increase in alert levels and would go very quickly to a level of alert that would permit major reinforcement (going beyond simply the return of the Reforger forces) from the United States. Such a move would display resolve, demonstrate that NATO could not be divided, and minimize the likelihood of its being caught unprepared.[16]

These procedures suggest that NATO has balanced the capability for crisis prevention with an equally impressive capacity for crisis management. On closer inspection, however, it is clear that there are severe shortcomings in the NATO alert and crisis management system. The NATO alert system has never been tested, and, consequently, there is little evidence of learning from experience. While the fact that NATO forces never had to move to higher levels of alert was testimony to the degree of stability in Cold War Europe, it also means that there is little understanding of how the alliance would perform in a crisis. Nor has this been compensated for by the periodic NATO exercises, which have largely been seen as a way of testing procedures for going to war rather than for defusing a crisis and putting on the brakes.

Moreover, there are many uncertainties about the procedures themselves, especially about the point at which national authorities would actually allow the transfer of authority over their forces to SACEUR. This process—colloquially known in NATO as "the chop"—remains a matter for national discretion. Consequently, there is a considerable degree of flexibility but also considerable scope for uncoordinated actions. If different governments chop at different times or some refuse to chop at all, the whole process could be uncoordinated at best and chaotic at worst. The problems of coordination are likely to be worsened by the limited communication links between NATO headquarters and national capitals, by the gap between the formalities of multilateral diplomacy in the alliance and the realities of bilateral diplomacy between Washington and key allies, and by the coexistence of national alert procedures and NATO alert procedures. The result, as Paul Stares has pointed out, is that "NATO could react in an extremely ragged non-uniform manner that risks projecting a contradictory and highly ambiguous picture of its intentions to the Warsaw Pact."[17] Moreover, NATO's failure to realize that it was having this effect could itself increase the prospects for miscalculation or misunderstanding.

Another difficulty with the alert system is the inescapable tension between what Alexander L. George has called "the logic of military operations" and the "logic of diplomacy."[18] The task of the military is to ensure that if war comes, the forces are as well prepared as possible; the responsibility of the politicians and diplomats is to explore all possible avenues for avoiding hostilities. For the civilian leadership, crises are seen primarily in political terms, with actions or even inaction intended to convey messages to the adversary. For the military leadership, it is essential to be able to implement key roles and missions in the event of hostilities. The difficulty is that precautionary military measures might send unintended or undesirable signals, while refraining from necessary precautionary measures could signify weakness and encourage aggression. Moreover, restricting measures to increase military readiness in order to enhance crisis management might unduly reduce the ability of the military to implement defensive operations should the crisis result in hostilities. Indeed, the dilemmas that cause civil-military tensions are inherent in situations where there is a necessity to hedge against the failure of crisis management at the same time that strenuous efforts are being made to ensure that it does not fail.

In this connection, another more subtle problem is that the political leadership may approve military actions without fully understanding their scope and meaning or how threatening they might appear to the adversary. Civilian leaders rarely have a detailed grasp of military planning, of alert procedures, or of rules of engagement, and they might authorize actions they believe are carefully circumscribed, only to find that these actions jeopardize their control over events. Alexander George in Chapter 11 and Scott Sagan have shown clearly how during the Cuban Missile Crisis the Kennedy administration, when it authorized the U.S. Navy to engage in "surfacing and identification" procedures against Soviet submarines, failed to understand the zealousness with which the navy would act or the extent of its activities.[19] Sagan has also suggested that "many of the potentially dangerous developments in past crises occurred because civilian authorities did not thoroughly understand the military operations they were contemplating."[20] Bruce Blair has made a similar point, bemoaning the "poor knowledge of procedures at the apex of government."[21] This problem was perhaps even more serious in NATO than at the national level, and once again the fact that there was so little experience in managing the NATO alert system could have proved very troublesome—a shortcoming NATO's periodic exercises did little to overcome.

Both in these exercises and in its planning, NATO devoted considerable time and effort to the escalation process but gave insufficient attention to the de-escalation process and how this might be facilitated without thereby creating dangerous vulnerabilities. Preoccupation with the transition to war encouraged neglect of what Gen. J. T. Chain has called the "transition to peace."[22] Yet, as James A. Winnefeld has argued, "Backing away from the precipice warrants as much care as moving up to it."[23] If it makes sense to plan for a failure of crisis management, it also makes sense to plan for success and to think creatively about how forces might be stood down in ways that, if not completely reciprocal and symmetrical, at least create no new vulnerabilities as the crisis is winding down.

Before reversing direction, however, it is necessary to stop the escalation process. This is not simply a matter of political decision but also has an important organizational dimension. Although the alert and reinforcement system contains important gradations, it would require a major administrative and organizational effort, involving large numbers of men and materiel. Furthermore, once the process has been initiated, NATO's military leadership will be reluctant to see it interrupted or stopped. Even temporary halts in the process could create considerable dislocation and confusion. There are clearly problems, therefore, in both identifying and implementing what Paul Hammond has termed "preparations that do no harm," either by provoking the other side or by narrowing one's own options.[24]

The implication of the preceding analysis is that the NATO crisis management system has long contained serious flaws and imperfections. In a sense, this was tolerable because of the emphasis on crisis prevention in Europe. Planning for crisis management was a fairly low priority in a Europe in which major East-West crises seemed extremely remote. Moreover, insofar as NATO attempted to provide a hedge against the breakdown of this system, the hedge was intended to provide a reasonable capacity for military resistance. Consequently, the emphasis in crisis management was on preparation for war and not on the ways in which such preparations might encourage the very thing they were intended to avert.

The peacetime logic of deterrence was accompanied by the traditional war-fighting logic in the event that deterrence failed. The important exception to this was when crises occurred in Eastern Europe. Largely in an attempt to ensure that unrest and instability in Eastern Europe were not inadvertently coupled tightly with the security of Western Europe, NATO decided against any change in its alert status in response to Soviet military interventions. This decision was certainly carried out during the Soviet invasion of Czechoslovakia in 1968 when, as Richard Betts has pointed out, "nonprovocation took priority over hedging against an unlikely threat" and NATO did nothing to increase its readiness to meet a Soviet invasion of Western Europe.[25] Yet, in one sense, even this restraint was a reflection of the confidence NATO felt about the remoteness of a major East-West crisis in Europe. All things considered, therefore, it seems hardly an exaggeration to suggest that crisis management was really an orphan of the European security system. The Europe of the 1990s, however, is a Europe in which the capacity for crisis management might become more important.

BEYOND THE COLD WAR IN EUROPE: REDUCED THREAT, INCREASED DANGERS

The changes in the European security system were precipitated by a popular revolution in Eastern Europe that initiated a process of democratization and that has resulted in the virtual disintegration of the Warsaw Pact as a military alliance. The process of democratization is being accompanied not only by a process of demilitarization, which is manifested both in unilateral force reductions and in the negotiations on conventional forces in Europe, but also by a process of denuclearization. NATO has given up any idea of deploying a successor to Lance, and it seems very likely that negotiations on short-range nuclear systems and artillery will result in the removal of these systems from Europe by the mid or late 1990s. The other process that seems to be at work is a deepening of economic links, both within Western Europe and between Western Europe and Eastern Europe.

Most of these developments seem to presage a much safer Europe in which—if the changes become permanent—the likelihood of major conflict will be more or less eliminated. Indeed, there are those who would argue that the new Europe will transcend the war system that has characterized most of its history. This is all the more likely if the European community is able to provide sufficient support to the new governments of Eastern Europe to facilitate the emergence of liberal capitalist democracies able to meet the expectations of their populations for material progress commensurate with their greater political freedom and to prevent the emergence of policies that are characterized by nationalism and extremism.[26]

Such a positive outcome is not the only possibility, however. A second school of thought, which Jack Snyder has termed the Hobbesian pessimist view, is that Europe will revert to traditional patterns of conflict and rivalry.[27] This possibility cannot be excluded, especially when it is remembered that many of the factors that helped to maintain order and prevent crises in Cold War Europe have either disappeared or are undergoing a major transition. The European state system of the 1990s and beyond is one in which nuclear weapons are less relevant, in which the lines are less clearly drawn, and in which the limits of permissible behavior are less well understood than in Cold War Europe. Moreover, although the direct threat from premeditated Soviet aggression has declined considerably and will continue to do so during the 1990s, the danger of instability resulting from the decline of the Soviet Union may well increase.

In this more pessimistic view, there are three major questions on the security agenda: Will the dismantling of the Soviet empire become the dismantling of the Soviet Union? How will Europe respond to a reunited Germany? What will be the impact of the revival of Balkanization as a key theme in European politics? In the early 1990s, none of these issues has fully crystallized, nor are the appropriate responses entirely clear. Moreover, this very uncertainty and fluidity could prove to be enduring rather than temporary features of the European security system in the 1990s.

The future of the Soviet Union is one of the great imponderables that will affect the evolution of the European security system through the 1990s. A Soviet economy that goes into free fall, a conservative or military takeover, and a complete breakdown in the political fabric of the Soviet Union leading to civil war are just three of the possibilities that can no longer be safely excluded. None of this implies that the trends in Soviet domestic politics since the advent of Mikhail Gorbachev are completely reversible; it simply argues that the future direction of Soviet politics is far from certain and that future governments do not necessarily have to be communist to pose a challenge to Western Europe. Indeed, it is possible to conceive of a more conservative, nationalist, or militaristic government coming to power in the Soviet Union—with uncertain but probably adverse consequences for West European security.

Yet the changes have not only been in the internal politics of the Soviet Union. There have also been major alterations in military and geopolitical realities in Europe. The Soviet Union can no longer count on Eastern European military forces to assist in any conflict with NATO and may in fact have to include some of these forces in any assessment of likely opposition. The removal of Soviet forces from Poland, Hungary, and Czechoslovakia as well as from the territory of what was formerly East Germany will also provide NATO with an extended period of warning time. Indeed, the House Armed Services Committee concluded in a report published in July 1990 that the Soviet conventional threat to NATO had been greatly reduced and could not easily be reconstituted.[28] Yet even though a Soviet invasion of Western Europe has become a more remote possibility than ever, as Eastern Europe has been transformed from part of the Soviet security system to a potentially hostile buffer zone that Soviet forces would have to traverse before posing a direct threat to Western Europe, the Soviet Union will not cease to be a European power with historical sensitivities and security concerns that cannot be ignored.

If the Soviet Union does survive, either in its present form or in a truncated version, its military capabilities will remain significant, even after reductions in conventional forces. If, on the other hand, political and economic chaos results in revolution or civil war, this, too, could have important security implications for the West. The disintegration of a nuclear-armed state has no precedent; nor can it be faced with equanimity. This is not to imply that violence will spill over into Eastern let alone Western Europe; it is simply to suggest that there are some disconcerting questions such as who would have control of the strategic nuclear forces. An internal scenario—and one suggested by scapegoat theories—is that internal instability could encourage Soviet leaders to undertake foreign adventures in an attempt to unite or distract the country. Although it is hard to believe that a disintegrating Soviet Union could see an advantage in a major external adventure—especially one that incurs considerable risk—it is one more in a range of contingencies that cannot be completely excluded and therefore must be guarded against.

If there are question marks about the Soviet Union itself, there are additional uncertainties resulting from the removal of Soviet control from Eastern Europe. The democratization of Eastern Europe is not an unmitigated blessing in that the removal of Soviet control and Soviet military forces will permit a resurgence of ethnic and nationalist rivalries that were submerged but not eliminated during the Cold War era. Such contingencies as the disintegration of Yugoslavia or armed clashes between Romania and Hungary cannot be completely ruled out. One argument is that this does not really matter. These are contingencies that will not impinge on Western security, and the most appropriate policy response, therefore, is one of aloofness: Europe of the post-Cold War era is not the Europe of the early twentieth century, and a clash in the Balkans is not likely to lead to the same kind of chain reaction that precipitated the First World War. This is certainly an argument against oversimplified analogies with the Sarajevo Crisis. Yet it is not necessary to draw alarmist parallels with the European state system of 1914 or to become preoccupied with the prospect of another Sarajevo, in which a relatively trivial political spark ignites a massive conflict among the great powers, to be concerned over stability in Eastern Europe.

In fact, there are several reasons why instability in Eastern Europe could have serious implications for Western Europe. One is that it could result in large flows of refugees into Western Europe. An East European conflict could also provide the occasion for a confrontation between a declining and increasingly insecure

Soviet Union and a resurgent united, more assertive Germany—with unpredictable consequences. Neither Germany nor the Soviet Union is likely to be indifferent to large-scale violence and unrest on its doorstep, especially if the warring factions or states appealed to outside powers for help. In these circumstances, competitive intervention, either directly or indirectly, could not be ruled out.

Part of the problem here is the uncertainty over where the lines of demarcation and influence are drawn in the new Europe. What was unequivocally the Soviet sphere of influence during the Cold War could become a contested region. This would not be surprising, as Eastern Europe has long been an arena of great power rivalry between Germany and Russia. Although the postwar security system inhibited direct expression of that rivalry, there are far fewer obstacles or inhibitions preventing its re-emergence in the new Europe. Even in decline, the Soviet Union is unlikely to be indifferent to any actions by a reunified Germany that are reminiscent of German ambitions for control of Mitteleuropa. And while most of the signs in the first half of 1990 pointed to German-Soviet cooperation rather than confrontation, historically the relationship has fluctuated dramatically from alliance to enmity. Moreover, the revival of old security concerns over German power is already evident in Poland and may emerge more strongly in other East European states. In these circumstances, the Soviet Union could be perceived less as oppressor and more as protector.

The likelihood that the great powers would become entangled in conflict in Eastern Europe is all the greater because the violence would occur against a background of an uneasy power transition in Europe. The relationship between a declining Soviet Union and a vibrant, reunified Germany is likely to be a difficult one at best. In the event of instability, latent tensions and fears could all too easily come to the fore. It is not necessary, therefore, to treat Germany as inherently aggressive or expansionist to have some concerns about the impact of a reunited Germany on stability in Europe and especially on the prospects for containing turbulence in Eastern Europe. In the past, the European security system was characterized by what Wildavsky termed patchiness and what Charles Perrow, in a different context, termed loose coupling, and, as a result, instability in Eastern Europe did not spread to Western Europe. In the future, however, the prospect for localizing problems in this way may be far more problematic.

The danger would be increased in the event that the United States and its West European allies decided to provide some kind of security guarantees to East European states. A major problem with such a course is that it would appear as rollback under another guise, thereby greatly intensifying Soviet security concerns. Nevertheless, the fact that the spheres of influence in Europe are no longer as clearly delineated as in the past poses problems and, in certain circumstances, could increase the possibility of miscalculation. Put another way, it is no longer clear where the red lines are drawn on the strategic map of Europe.[29] Part of the confusion, of course, arises from having a reunified Germany that will be in NATO but no NATO forces deployed on the territory of what was formerly the GDR. On the other hand, should a crisis arise in Eastern Europe, Western forces might move eastward. It is possible to conceive of an East-West crisis, therefore, in which Soviet and Western troops confront one another across the Oder-Neisse line.

In short, post-Cold War Europe is far more unpredictable than the Cold War system and will become increasingly so as clear-cut alignments give way to more fluid and dynamic patterns. Moreover, the range of conflicts that could occur is much greater. The old crisis prevention regime based on tacit acceptance of sphere of influence—an acceptance undergirded by the operation of mutual deterrence and the fear that a crisis would result in inadvertent escalation—has given way to a complex vortex of uncertain relationships, fragile alignments, and resurgent tensions and rivalries. Nor are these problems likely to be offset by the fact that Europe might be regulated by a more formal arms control regime, especially if clear understanding of a few basic rules of prudence is replaced by somewhat less clear understanding of more formal and complex prescriptions and proscriptions.

In other words, in post-Cold War Europe, it is necessary to consider not only the residue of the East-West military confrontation but also the possibility that conflicts that have long been dormant or suppressed will come to the surface once again. It does not take a Cassandra or a Mearsheimer to predict that the new Europe will be both disorderly and potentially very unstable. The range of contingencies will be broader than during the Cold War, while crises could be more frequent and less predictable in both form and content. Consequently, the requirements for crisis management in Europe could prove to be more compelling than ever. At the same time, it is not feasible to plan against one or two major contingencies, in the way that was possible during the Cold War. Rather, it is necessary to have certain kinds of capabilities that will facilitate the task of crisis management in a variety of situations. In other words, it is necessary to build greater resilience into the system. Part of the difficulty, however, is that it is uncertain what the future security architecture of Europe will look like and who will be engaged in crisis prevention and crisis management.

ARCHITECTURE FOR CRISIS PREVENTION AND MECHANISMS FOR CRISIS MANAGEMENT IN THE NEW EUROPE

The implication of the preceding analysis is that the balance between the requirement and the capability for crisis prevention on the one hand and for crisis management on the other has shifted. The natural tendency—because of the new political climate—is to conclude that there is less need for crisis management than ever before, not because of faith in crisis prevention but simply because the threat to Western security problems has receded dramatically. Yet Wildavsky's analysis suggests that in circumstances where both stability and predictability are low, then strategies of resilience in crisis management are essential. Whereas in the past, anticipatory measures of crisis prevention helped to maintain a high level of stability, in a more dynamic and fluctuating situation, anticipation is likely to be less effective.

This is not to suggest that the new European architecture that is being widely discussed in the security policy community has no relevance for crisis prevention. Indeed, one of the major criteria for assessing any new architecture has to be its likely effectiveness in contributing to crisis prevention and in devising mechanisms for crisis management should crisis prevention fail. The difficulty in the current debate, however, is that both governments and analysts tend to be focusing on institutional structures without much sense of the purposes they are intended to serve. Moreover, too many prescriptions for a new architecture presume a degree of institutional tidiness and exclusiveness that is unlikely to be achieved.

Much of the debate has revolved around the respective merits of a reformed Atlantic Alliance compared with a pan-European security arrangement that could be embodied in the Conference on Security and Cooperation in Europe. Rather than treating these as alternatives, however, it would be preferable to regard them as complementary. This was recognized by NATO heads of government when, after their meeting in London in July 1990, they issued a declaration advocating the further development of the CSCE and suggesting that a conflict prevention center might be set up as part of this. While it is clear that both NATO and CSCE could contribute to crisis prevention and crisis management in Europe, there is also the danger that with an untidy institutional structure, there could be confusion about who does what.[30] It is important, therefore, to ensure that the respective crisis prevention and crisis management tasks of the two institutions are clearly specified, that they are mutually complementary rather than competitive, and that there is a clear understanding of who does what. Yet, this should not be too difficult. There are certain tasks for which one institution is clearly more suited than the other. Insofar as security in the new Europe will require a place for deterrence of deliberate aggression by the Soviet Union as a continued, if less salient, element in crisis prevention, then NATO is the obvious body to provide this. Insofar as there may be a role for peacekeeping forces in Europe as a way of ensuring that local conflagrations are contained, then NATO, in spite of the availability of small, rapid-response forces (such as the Allied Command Europe [ACE] mobile force), may be far less appropriate than CSCE. There is also clearly a place for enhanced communications in order to minimize the prospects for miscalculation or inadvertent clashes in the new Europe—and this could be provided at both the CSCE and NATO levels.

Both institutions, of course, would have to be adapted to the challenges that are likely to arise in the new Europe. The main roles for NATO would be to manage the residue of the East-West confrontation and to provide a forum for the United States to continue making a contribution to security and stability in Europe. By providing a continued, albeit not too overt, constraint on a united Germany, NATO could provide a degree of reassurance about Germany not only to the Soviet Union but also to the Poles, Hungarians, and even the French. Both for deterrence and for reassurance, therefore, a U.S. infrastructure commitment to NATO is essential. This can be accomplished at a much lower level of U.S. forces than has been deployed in Europe since 1951. The important thing is that there is some U.S. military presence as an indication of continued U.S. interest in European security. It is also necessary to maintain an infrastructure so that in the event the United States has to bring troops back to Europe in a crisis, there would be facilities and procedures for doing so. In addition, the United States has a crucial role to play in terms of its contribution to intelligence and warning and to command, control, and communications. The capabilities, here, however, might be modified and incorporated into a wider mechanism for monitoring military activity in Europe.

NATO very clearly has a continued role to play in the new European security system. At the same time, it will be a significantly different NATO in several ways. As suggested above, the level of standing ready forces will be much lower than currently exists, and it is unlikely that land-based nuclear missiles or nuclear artillery will be deployed in Europe. Perhaps most significant, the period of warning time in relation to any Soviet aggression will be measured in months rather than days or weeks. The fact that the Soviet Union would have to cross Eastern Europe and might encounter resistance in its forward movement has profoundly changed the requirements of NATO strategy. One result is that some of the shortcomings in NATO's alert and crisis management system, especially those that might exacerbate tension in a crisis, are less compelling. At the same time, as NATO revises its force planning and strategic doctrine and moves away from its previous dependence on nuclear weapons, it should also overhaul its crisis management machinery. This overhaul could take several forms.

In some ways, the first and most important need is for a shift in attitude. As discussed above, NATO has been so preoccupied with deterrence and with defense in the event that deterrence fails that crisis management has been neglected. Part of the task, therefore, is simply for NATO to think more imaginatively about a wide variety of crisis scenarios and their requirements in terms of NATO responses. As part of this conceptual shift, greater attention could be paid to the need for flexibility, to the need for a capacity to signal restraint as well as resolve, and to the ability to provide both reassurance and clarity in an inherently uncertain and fast-moving situation. Moreover, exercises should no longer be regarded as opportunities to test the machinery for going to war but rather as tests of the ability of NATO to contribute to maintaining the peace and defusing tension. Not only would this be more sensible, but it would also be more appropriate to the new Europe.

A second requirement, consistent with this new thinking, is that there should be greater potential for stopping and reversing any military preparations. As James A. Winnefeld has argued, de-escalation should be both planned for and practiced as much as escalation.[31] This has important consequences for U.S. reinforcement plans. There has to be a clear-cut capability for the reconstitution or regeneration of NATO and especially U.S. military capabilities in Europe—something that requires a continued U.S. capacity for rapid reinforcement and continued West European provision for host nation support. At the same time, these capabilities should be planned in accordance with Winnefeld's injunction about de-escalation. Reinforcement by the United States could be done on what might be termed a modular basis. This would provide maximum flexibility, allow for halting the process without creating confusion, and offer opportunities for political signaling of restraint without necessarily degrading military effectiveness.

The other advantage of this arrangement is that it would make reinforcement a more, rather than less, usable option in a crisis. With lower force levels, reinforcement from the United States would be more important than ever before, and even though the warning time would be far longer, this does not mean that the time will be effectively used. The decision to reinforce through the deployment of troops from the continental United States to Western Europe would be even more difficult in post-Cold War Europe than in the past. It would signal a reversal of direction in East-West relations and would certainly not be a decision that could be taken lightly. A modular approach to reinforcement that provided decision makers with maximum flexibility in a period of rising tension and allowed them to signal both resolve and restraint would be a more discriminating tool for crisis management than traditional reinforcement plans.

If there are certain things that NATO should do, there are also some things that should not be done. At the top of the list of actions to avoid is extending NATO security guarantees to the states of Eastern Europe. Insofar as this is a requirement for the European security system of the 1990s, it is better done through the Conference on Security and Cooperation in Europe than through NATO. Although it is tempting for NATO to offer fledgling democracies protection against any attempt by the Soviet Union to reimpose control, it is more sensible to treat Eastern Europe as a no-go zone for both the Soviet Union and NATO. The exceptions to this would be East Germany, which as part of a united Germany is also part of NATO (even though NATO troops will not be deployed there) and Poland, which may continue to host Soviet troops as an insurance against German revanchism. These exceptions might actually facilitate rather than inhibit the establishment of a de facto mutual no-go zone in the middle of Europe. Such a zone would help to prevent instability in the region from taking on the dimensions of an East-West crisis, thereby continuing to maintain the patchiness Wildavsky has identified as an important component of strategies of anticipation or crisis prevention. This zone would also preserve two of the most important features of the Cold War security system—its clarity and predictability.

Misunderstandings, of course, could still occur. In order to prevent them it is important that communications are improved both within the West and between the Soviet Union and the major Western powers. In a Europe in which instability, domestic turmoil, ethnic conflicts, and traditional rivalries seem likely to be far more of a problem than premeditated aggression by any of the major powers, mechanisms that facilitate communication and minimize the prospects for misperception or miscalculation could prove invaluable to both crisis prevention and crisis management.

One possibility would be to establish a direct communications link between the Soviet leadership and NATO headquarters. This would ensure timely communication in a crisis, reduce the risks of miscalculation or misunderstanding, and offer both sides a facility to provide explanations of military movements. Indeed, the installation of a hotline is a natural extension of the effort to establish a much more regulated military environment in Europe through the CFE (Conventional Forces in Europe) and CSCE processes. Insofar as procedures such as notification of maneuvers become standard, then a direct communications link would be a natural counterpart.

There might be objections to this, of course, on the grounds that the hotline would give the Soviet Union a *droit de regard* over Western Europe. Yet, this argument is hardly persuasive in a period when the Soviet Union is losing influence and trying to stave off not only continued decline but possible disintegration. Indeed, a Soviet Union that is feeling threatened could be particularly dangerous, and, insofar as the hotline offers a means of reassurance, its presence could prove a considerable asset in defusing tension.

Although the installation of a direct communications link might raise questions about responsibility at the NATO end—and there is something inherently problematic about a hotline between a sovereign political authority and an alliance headquarters—this problem is inherent in NATO crisis management procedures. In fact, the establishment of a direct communications link with Moscow might provide NATO with a reason for reassessing and overhauling its crisis management procedures and mechanisms and for establishing clearer understandings about the discretion national governments might be prepared to give it during periods of crisis. As a result, the NATO crisis management system might be rendered more efficient and effective. At the very least, there could be some discretionary arrangements whereby the secretary-general, with the approval of the North Atlantic Council, could send limited messages that are designed to clarify or explain the purpose of military movements. Although the deliberations at the NATO end could not be protracted if the hotline were to be used effectively, the fact that messages were being sent to Moscow directly from Brussels might concentrate NATO's collective political mind. Moreover, a natural corollary of the creation of a Moscow-Brussels hotline would be a systematic upgrading of the communication links between NATO headquarters and the national governments. This is something NATO should do regardless of a link with Moscow, as the communication lines to capitals would almost certainly suffer from overload during a crisis. With advances in telecommunications, there is no reason why the capacity of the Brussels-capitals links should not be greatly augmented.

The political hotline could also be accompanied by a direct communications link between the Soviet military and the NATO military leadership. In cases where there were unexplained military movements, violations of air space, or potential for clashes between rival forces, a direct communications link would provide a means of transmitting information that might help to clarify the situation and prevent inadvertent clashes or outbreaks of violence. A military-to-military hotline would have limited functions but would be a way of reducing the prospect of incidents such as the shooting down of KAL-007.

While an upgrading of NATO's capacity for crisis management is a necessary element in the adjustment to post-Cold War Europe, NATO's efforts in this direction could usefully be complemented by activities and mechanisms developed within the CSCE process. It might be possible, for example, to establish a series of agencies or centers, or a single center with multiple functions, that could deal with arms control monitoring and verification, with crisis prevention and crisis management, and with peacekeeping. Such a center or centers would be the operational arm of the CSCE.

A crisis prevention and crisis management center located either in Geneva or in Berlin (which arguably should be internationalized as much as possible as Germany moves toward reunification) would help to mitigate the traditional fears and rivalries the breakdown of the postwar framework in Europe has brought to the surface after being subsumed or held in check by the bloc system. Such a center would also be an important part of the communications network in the new Europe.

This center could be staffed on a multinational basis under CSCE and would have available a crisis control and monitoring force. The staff of the center could provide joint assessments on potential crisis management problems and establish a tradition of practical cooperation that could prove invaluable during a crisis. At the same time, the creation of a monitoring force to oversee arms control agreements would not only enhance confidence but provide an in-place force that could provide advance warning of any potential cross-border military activity and could also prove helpful in controlling and defusing a subsequent crisis. Indeed, the force could verify whether actions such as reductions in the level of alert status were in fact taking place, thereby facilitating the de-escalation process and ensuring that it occurred on a reciprocal basis. In addition, the center could provide the core of an efficient and effective communications system among the United States, the Soviet Union, Britain, France, and Germany. This could prove invaluable in a rapidly breaking crisis and help to minimize the likelihood of misunderstandings or miscalculation.

In addition, the center could have available a small, highly mobile, multinational peacekeeping force capable of being deployed rapidly to the scene of instability or conflict. Such a force would probably have to exclude any manpower contributions by the two superpowers or a reunited Germany but could be made up of units from other European states, perhaps on a rotating basis. It would also be a technologically intensive force, equipped not only with airborne surveillance capabilities but with remote sensors capable of detecting military activities by the belligerents. While the model for such a force would be the U.N. experience with peacekeeping, the units themselves would be European and would be part of a comprehensive regional approach to security. A European peacekeeping force could facilitate the management and control of ethnic or nationalist conflict in Eastern Europe, could act as an interposition force between opposing factions or states, could supervise truce agreements, and could patrol border or contested regions to ensure that no violations took place.[32] As with U.N. peacekeeping forces, this European force would be used "not in a fighting or enforcement role but interposed as a mechanism to bring an end to hostilities and as a buffer between hostile forces. In effect, it serves as an internationally constituted pretext for the parties to a conflict to stop fighting and as a mechanism to maintain a ceasefire."[33] It might provide an opportunity for mediation and would be a means of ensuring that conflicts in Eastern Europe were contained before they provided any temptations for the involvement of great powers on opposing sides.

There are, of course, problems and pitfalls with such a scheme. One objection is that some Western European governments will be reluctant to become too heavily engaged in Eastern Europe. Yet, it is clear that more traditional security tasks will be less demanding and less onerous in the future. Consequently, provision of forces for a multinational European peacekeeping force might appear attractive both to national military establishments concerned about declining budgets and eroding roles and missions and to governments concerned to show they are willing to share some of the responsibility for security in the new Europe. There might also be a certain amount of prestige attached to the peacekeeping function, although this could dissipate rapidly in the event that the force sustained serious casualties.

In addition to these practical and operational problems, there would also be difficulties regarding how the center was run, the mix of personnel, and the relationship between the center and the 35-nation CSCE forum. These difficulties are not insuperable, though. It might be possible, for example, to establish a small governing council of the crisis prevention and crisis management center drawn from the CSCE participants. This council could be composed of representatives of the United States, the Soviet Union, and the leading European governments, with some of the smaller states in Europe as revolving members. Although this would still be a complex arrangement, it would have the virtue of reflecting the real decision-making power and authority in Europe. Moreover, the center would be an integral part of a pan-European security architecture while also reflecting the fact that grand schemes for a new system in Europe are of little utility without the creation of mechanisms and procedures that would actually be used to manage conflicts and disputes within that system. An additional virtue of a scheme based around CSCE and a crisis or risk reduction center is that it gets away from more traditional schemes that approach security problems in Europe almost exclusively through the prism of East-West relations.

A multitiered arrangement in which security problems in Europe are handled by a reformed NATO and a crisis management center established in the CSCE framework would have several advantages. Not the least of these is that it would provide a capacity for resilience and improvisation—qualities that are essential where strategies of crisis prevention or anticipation are likely to have limited success. A scheme that provides a capacity for coping with the unexpected and the unanticipated would be eminently suited to a post-Cold War Europe in which the traditional restraints, understandings, and mechanisms that contributed to successful crisis prevention are no longer operating. The approach to Europe that Jack Snyder has characterized as Hobbesian pessimism should not become a doctrine of despair or resignation but a stimulus to creative thinking about how crises might be managed in an era when they might no longer be so easily prevented.

NOTES

1. John Mearsheimer, "Why We Will Soon Miss the Cold War," in *The Atlantic*, August 1990, pp. 35–50, at p. 35.
2. Aaron Wildavsky, *Searching for Safety* (New Brunswick: Transaction, 1988).
3. See ibid., especially pp. 77–79 and 118–120.
4. Ibid., p. 120.
5. Ibid., p. 77.
6. Ibid., p. 79.
7. Ibid., p. 117.
8. The notion of coupling as used here is taken, somewhat liberally, from Charles Perrow, *Normal Accidents* (New York: Basic Books, 1984), pp. 89–96.
9. P. G. Lauren, "Crisis Prevention in Nineteenth-Century Diplomacy," in A. L. George, ed., *Managing U.S.-Soviet Rivalry* (Boulder, CO: Westview, 1983), p. 43.
10. Ibid., p. 37.
11. Wildavsky, *Searching for Safety*, p. 119.
12. The fullest and most helpful account is Paul Stares's, in *Command Performance: The Neglected Dimension of European Security* (Brookings, forthcoming). I am extremely

grateful to Paul Stares not only for an opportunity to see this manuscript but also for many helpful discussions about NATO crisis management.

13. Assembly of the Western European Union, *Communications and Crisis Management in the Alliance*, Report by Mr. Watkinson, November 4, 1977, Document 757.

14. E. Klippenberg and F. Hussain, *NATO's Southern Region, The Mediterranean and the Persian Gulf: Problems of Command and Control*. Paper prepared for the European American Institute Workshop on NATO's Southern Flank, September 21–23, 1981, Naples, Italy, p. 9.

15. *Communications and Crisis Management in the Alliance*, p. 20.

16. As Scott Sagan points out in *Organizations, Accidents and Nuclear War* (forthcoming), this did not occur during the Cuban Missile Crisis. Even though U.S. forces in Europe went on alert, NATO forces did not. This was not a failure of the system, however, as the crisis was not European in origin or focus.

17. Stares, *Command Performance*.

18. A. L. George, "Crisis Management: The Interaction of Political and Military Considerations," *Survival* 26, 5 (September/October 1984): 224.

19. See S. Sagan, "Nuclear Alerts and Crisis Management," in *International Security* 9 (Spring 1985): 99–139 at p. 117.

20. Ibid., p. 138.

21. Bruce Blair, "Alerting in Crisis and Conventional War," in Ashton Carter, John Steinbruner, and Charles Zraket, eds., *Managing Nuclear Operation* (Washington, D.C.: Brookings, 1987), pp. 75–120 at p. 114.

22. J. T. Chain, "Political-Military Decision Making in the Atlantic Alliance: A Framework," in J. T. Chain, R. Dixon, and R. Weissinger-Baylon, *Decision Making in the Atlantic Alliance* (Menlo Park, CA: Strategic Decisions Press, 1987), p. 8.

23. James A. Winnefeld, *De-Escalation: The Stepchild of Crisis Management Analysis and Planning*, Rand Paper WD-4703-CC, December 1989.

24. Paul Hammond, "NATO Strategic Planning: Preparations That Do No Harm," in J. T. Chain, R. Dixon, and R. Weissinger-Baylon, *Decision Making in the Atlantic Alliance*, p. 24.

25. Richard Betts, *Surprise Attack* (Washington, D.C.: Brookings, 1982), p. 85.

26. On the importance of the internal domestic dimension see Jack Snyder, "Adverting Anarchy in the New Europe," *International Security* 14, 4 (Spring 1990): 5–41.

27. Ibid., p. 5.

28. See *The Fading Threat: Soviet Conventional Military Power in Decline*, Report of the Defense Policy Panel of the Committee on Armed Services, House of Representatives, 101st Congress, Second Session (July 9, 1990).

29. This phrase is drawn from a comment by Arnold Horelick, whose insights on this issue have been especially helpful.

30. I am grateful to Earl Gibbons for this point.

31. See James A. Winnefeld, *Crisis De-Escalation: A Relevant Concern in the "New Europe,"* Rand Paper WD-4885-CC, April 1990.

32. For a fuller and very helpful analysis see M.A. Browne, *United Nations Peacekeeping: Historical Overview and Current Issues*, Congressional Research Service, January 31, 1990.

33. B. Urquhart, quoted in ibid., p. 5.

CHAPTER 22

The Future of "Military Diplomacy" in U.S.-Soviet Relations

Kurt M. Campbell

In the more than four decades of U.S.-Soviet relations since the close of the Second World War and the onset of the Cold War, the militaries of the two superpowers have had an obscure history of periodic yet low-profile contacts and consultations.[1] However, since the first meeting between the chairman of the Joint Chiefs of Staff, Adm. William J. Crowe, and his Soviet counterpart, Chief of the Soviet General Staff Marshal Sergei F. Akhromeyev, in Washington during the Reagan-Gorbachev summit in December 1987, the two sides' militaries have engaged in unprecedented direct diplomacy on a host of issues. These range from operational arms control and military training to the larger questions of national strategy and doctrine. In important ways, this new development is a throwback to an earlier age when military men were more involved in diplomatic initiatives and the foreign policy process.[2]

A DEFINITION OF MILITARY DIPLOMACY

While traditionally there have been exchanges of military attachés between Moscow and Washington,[3] and military officers have figured prominently in civilian-led negotiations on strategic and conventional arms control,[4] this new phase of military involvement in foreign policy is a dramatic departure from postwar patterns.[5] Indeed, the development of "military diplomacy"—the establishment and evolution of a superpower military regime based on strictly reciprocal meetings, contacts, and negotiations—is one of the most unheralded yet potentially important factors in the future of U.S.-Soviet relations. As one commentator noted, the military negotiations "and the recent agreement on the Prevention of Dangerous Military Activities have

The author was a member of the U.S. negotiating team for the Dangerous Military Activities Agreement and was a Soviet/European specialist with the Joint Chiefs of Staff in 1989-1990. The views and opinions expressed in this chapter do not necessarily reflect those of the Joint Chiefs of Staff or the U.S. government.

been scorned by some experts as the 'junk food' of arms control. But the classical distinctions between reductions in arms and measures to build confidence and security have begun to blur. Both structural and operational arms control are parts of a larger process of political reassurance among adversaries."[6]

The first phase of U.S.-Soviet military diplomacy began in late 1987 and ran through the end of 1989, a period that coincided with the fall of communism in Eastern Europe, signs of increasing stress and dislocation inside the Soviet Union, and the end of Admiral Crowe's tenure as chairman of the Joint Chiefs of Staff. There were two twin tracks in the first so-called "two-year program" of military dialogue and discussion negotiated by Admiral Crowe and Marshal Akhromeyev: the establishment of a military working group to tackle the tough issues of dangerous military practices and a series of reciprocal visits between senior military officials. (These will be considered more fully in the following section.)[7] A follow-on program of military meetings was agreed to by the succeeding chairman of the Joint Chiefs, Gen. Colin Powell, and his opposite number, Gen. Mikhail Moiseyev, during the latter's visit to the United States in the fall of 1990.

The pattern of the progression of military diplomacy has to date been incremental and evolutionary, which, given the history of mutual distrust and the conflictual demands of preparing for war, is both prudent and wise. Any expansion in the scope of direct military contacts will inevitably raise sensitivities about the proper role of the military in making national policy and its impact on civil-military relations. Yet, for the military diplomacy regime to play a positive role in reducing the risks of accidental or inadvertent war in the turbulent period of realignment and rapprochement that lies directly ahead, it must demonstrate an ability to adapt to new and pressing circumstances and demands. The logical next steps for military diplomacy (such as more frequent meetings between U.S. and Soviet military commanders in a divided Germany) have been ambushed by the rapid pace of events in Europe. Many of the more traditional proposals involving confidence-building measures and limits on military exercises and maneuvers in the European theater are rapidly becoming obsolete in the face of dramatic changes in what was once the Eastern bloc. Certain notions of military and political parity, and the strict application of reciprocity in military matters that followed from these assumptions, have been called into question.

The next generation of military dialogue should, among other things, address the issue of the safety of Soviet nuclear stockpiles, the fundaments of future military doctrines, the potential military hazards associated with socialist transformations in the Soviet Union and Eastern Europe, the possibilities of military cooperation under the auspices of the United Nations, and the need for better communication at very early stages of crises. The regime must also adjust to the heightened sense of vulnerability shared by Soviet military elites as the "correlation of forces" in the international arena (to use the now unfashionable language of socialist internationalism) shifts suddenly and irreversibly against them. Indeed, if this evolving regime of U.S.-Soviet military diplomacy is to play a part in the emerging new political-military landscapes in the Soviet Union and Europe, it requires a fundamental rethinking of objectives and guidelines on both sides.

At the heart of the conundrum is an essential disparity between the domestic and international positions of the United States and the Soviet Union. The USSR is practicing a diplomacy of decline from superpower to big power status.[8] The Soviet Union is also facing increasingly serious challenges from obstreperous ethnic and nationalist groups, severe consumer shortages, and a host of other unpredictable political problems that plague its politicians. The status and the stature of Soviet armed forces are also increasingly threatened by public criticism, severe budget cutbacks, and morale problems, and it is doubtful whether the military could sustain a concerted conventional assault outside Soviet territory for any prolonged period. Soviet armed forces will, for the near future, face only two credible military missions: strategic nuclear operations of last resort and domestic or East European interventions. Given these two unpalatable extremes, Soviet military efforts in the immediate period will focus on designing a workable military strategy for the defense of the homeland under radically new conditions.[9] Soviet attention will also be devoted to developing procedures for an orderly military withdrawal from Eastern Europe. (Soviet strategists and logisticians have concentrated in the past on preparing plans for advancing, rather than for retreating, from Europe.) The only true experience the Soviets have had with orderly military retreat was in Afghanistan, and this holds little relevance for the current situation.

With the help of European allies, U.S. ideology and perseverance have led to a historic victory, and there is a powerful temptation to consider the possibility of a direct U.S.-Soviet military confrontation as now extremely remote. However, this chapter will argue that the chances of an inadvertent or accidental clash through misperception and mishandling have not diminished. As one commentator put it, "in this period of unprecedented change in the Soviet Union and in the world, the likelihood of unintended accidents is increasing. In times of transition, unexpected and unintended things happen, sometimes with dangerous consequences."[10] The process of military diplomacy can play a critical role in preventing dangerous military practices, expanding crisis communications, removing unhelpful stereotypes, exploring potentially destabilizing doctrinal practices, and building stronger domestic institutions.

This study of the potential of military diplomacy first defines the notion of a U.S.-Soviet military regime based on contacts and crisis communication rather than on combat. The next section describes the recent history and current status of military-to-military dialogue and diplomacy and discusses the procedures and practices that have shaped the conduct of relations to date. The subsequent section addresses the potential next steps and future roles of U.S.-Soviet military diplomacy with particular emphasis on how these should differ from previous steps. There will then be a treatment of some of the potential drawbacks of military diplomacy and the limits of confidence that are, in a sense, built into the relationship. Finally, the chapter attempts to advance a coherent and reasonable blueprint for the continuation of military diplomacy in this transitional age of U.S.-Soviet relations.

RECENT HISTORY AND CURRENT STATUS OF MILITARY DIPLOMACY

The genesis of early U.S.-Soviet military-to-military relations was World War II, when the United States extended lend-lease assistance to the USSR and U.S. soldiers were brought into contact with senior Soviet military officers and even staged joint operations.[11] However, the limited military cooperation quickly gave way to military confrontation after the war, as Soviet and U.S. forces faced off across a divided Europe. Military contacts were few and far between during the Cold War, a distance that has been reinforced by military incidents, domestic bureaucratic resistance, and appropriate concerns about the role of military personnel in the practice of foreign policy. Yet, exchanges of military visits between East and West have been encouraged, officially endorsed, and monitored by the Commission on Security and Cooperation in Europe as part of the Helsinki Final Act of 1976.[12] Despite this long-standing international support for more military contacts, the process of military dialogue has been hampered by a host of concerns. A review of the traditional restraints on, and reservations about, the expansion of military dialogue will help set the scene for a discussion of recent and potential future avenues for military diplomacy.

Throughout the postwar period, there has been a general resistance to the expansion of direct military-to-military contacts between the two sides. Indeed, what little U.S.-Soviet military dialogue we have seen since 1945 has been designed to restrict and constrain certain dangerous competition but not to eliminate it. Perhaps the most representative example of military diplomacy in the U.S.-Soviet context has been the 1972 Incidents at Sea Agreement.[13] The agreement, with its mandated yearly meetings of naval officers from both sides to discuss potential problems with the regime, has for nearly twenty years helped to avert potential dangerous incidents between U.S. and Soviet navies. According to Sean Lynn-Jones, "the success of the Incidents at Sea Agreement demonstrates that confidence building measures—constraints on military activities and improvements in communications that are intended to reduce the risk of inadvertent war or surprise attack—represent a workable alternative to traditional arms control proposals that impose quantitative or qualitative limits on weapons."[14]

Military diplomacy has been concerned with how forces are deployed and military operations conducted rather than with the reduction of the forces themselves. The primary purpose of military dialogue and discussion has been a mutual desire to avoid accidental or inadvertent clashes, improve mutual military confidence, and prevent or correct dangerous misconceptions. When soldiers have been involved in major talks with the Soviet Union, they have usually played a supporting role to civilians, and, until recently, the overall effect of military negotiations in the superpower relationship has been relatively modest. These limited and carefully conceived military relations reflect a traditional resistance on both sides to letting the uniformed elite play a direct role in the formulation and execution of diplomacy between the superpowers. For the United States, civilian primacy in diplomacy with other states and in the decision to use force is a basic tenet of democratic governments.[15] This principle has been publicly and profoundly demonstrated on many occasions in the postwar era, perhaps most memorably when President Truman relieved Gen. Douglas MacArthur of his command in Korea. All in all, however, the military has been an exemplar of institutional commitment, not only to the separation of military and civilian power but also to its own subordination to civilian authority.

Despite this history, or perhaps because of it, there has been a pattern of bureaucratic resistance—chiefly by the State Department and the civilian component of the Defense Department—to steps that would upgrade the military's diplomatic role. Some diplomats remain uneasy about the implicit message that high-level meetings and negotiations between senior U.S. and Soviet military officers send to the U.S. public and European allies. Civilian Pentagon officials are also uncomfortable abut the influence of military-to-military exchanges and contacts on troop morale. For instance, how will young crew members of a U.S. warship react to an outpouring of Soviet good will during a port call? Could the experience cloud their judgment and cause them to question orders in the event of military operations against Soviet ships at sea? According to this view, such meetings make it more difficult to sustain public support at home for defense spending and to maintain support abroad for alliance commitments. A more developed argument holds that the military is trained to fight wars, not to conduct diplomacy. A popular Washington quip has it that "in negotiations with the Soviets, it's better to have military personnel on tap, not on top." A parochial view—that conducting diplomacy with the Soviets is the sole prerogative of the State Department—also enters the picture. This bureaucratic territoriality is often expressed as a concern for diplomatic protocol.

Soviet military misdeeds and provocations in the international arena have been more of a problem than institutional or bureaucratic hindrances. The Soviet invasion of Afghanistan in 1980 finally ended the lingering climate of superpower détente that had prevailed since the late 1960s. Of direct importance to military contacts, the shooting death on March 24, 1985, of Maj. Arthur Nicholson, Jr., an officer detailed to the military liaison mission in Potsdam, seriously impeded the improvement of U.S.-Soviet military relations. Further, the Soviets' destruction of KAL-007 in September 1983 underscored their dangerous and provocative policy of regarding any intruding aircraft as hostile. As a result of these and other military incidents, the U.S. government restricted the already abbreviated military contacts between the two sides in the early 1980s. In 1987, before the first Crowe-Akhromeyev meeting, there was virtually no military dialogue between the two sides.

The Soviet Union had perhaps even more reason to be wary of expanding military dialogues and negotiations. Traditionally, a suspicious party apparatus has checked the power of the Soviet military. Joseph Stalin used the threat of Bonapartism as a reason to purge the senior military corps during the 1930s.[16] The senior party leadership has periodically dismissed General Staff chiefs for publicly disagreeing with government policies or for gaining too much influence in the decision-making bureaucracy. For example, Marshal Nikolai Ogarkov was dismissed as chief of the Soviet General Staff in 1984 amid reports of party leadership displeasure with his public pronouncements about adapting Soviet military procurement, armament, and strategy to the advancing technological conditions of warfare in the latter part of the twentieth century.[17] Perhaps more important, the Soviets have reason to be concerned about potential military uses of information gained from interaction between rival militaries. In the 1920s and early 1930s, the Soviet Union enjoyed close, though clandestine, military ties with Germany.[18] It has long been speculated that the German supreme command used information gleaned from this association in planning Operation Barbarossa, the invasion of the Soviet Union in 1941.

Given that so much of postwar Soviet thinking is based on the "objective lessons" of the Great Patriotic War, the recent Soviet interest in expanding military-to-military contacts with the United States represents a dramatic break with that tradition. The most important reason for this change follows from the promulgation of Soviet leader Mikhail Gorbachev's "new thinking" in Soviet security policy. Gorbachev has argued that political rather than military technical means have become the primary tools for guaranteeing the Soviet Union's security.[19] Indeed, he has gone so far as to suggest that political means may be the only way to secure the safety of the Soviet state. As one Sovietologist has written, "[T]his evolution towards political solutions is portrayed as a consequence of the military technologies of the 'nuclear-space' era: modern weapons make it impossible for states to defend themselves by military-technical means alone. War means catastrophe. Negotiations and diplomacy can buy the Soviet Union more security than could allocation of additional defense rubles."[20]

At the same time, the military's involvement in arms control has become a reasonable—even necessary—proposition in Soviet eyes. Given that the Soviet military traditionally has had responsibility for formulating military plans, designing force structures, and conducting threat assessments, it has played a disproportionately large role in the strategic analysis that supports Soviet arms control positions. That it would now become more involved during a much more ambitious period of arms control is only logical.

Yet recently, the military's monopoly on strategic thinking has been broken by greater involvement of the Ministry of Foreign Affairs and of think tanks associated with the Soviet Academy of Sciences. These rival institutions have offered alternative threat forecasts and arms control positions. The military has reacted to the relative decline of its bureaucratic clout by seeking to become more actively involved in U.S.-Soviet diplomacy. (This decline may turn out to be merely temporary.) The Soviet military has sought to gain bureaucratic influence in the Kremlin from high-profile dealings with Western interlocutors. For instance, Marshal Akhromeyev's position was enhanced by his personal involvement in arms control talks and his recent visits to the West for discussions with senior Western statesmen. Although Akhromeyev left his post as chief of the Soviet General Staff in December 1988, he now serves as Gorbachev's personal adviser on security matters. Even as Marshal Akhromeyev's foreign policy views grow increasingly hard line, he has still maintained a professed interest in the continuation of U.S.-Soviet military contacts. General Moiseyev does not command the power or prestige of previous Soviet chiefs of staff, but he has gained positive experience and exposure from his meetings with General Powell in Vienna and in the United States.

Changes in both the international environment and in the domestic bureaucracy have also increased the possibility and potential of active U.S. military participation in U.S.-Soviet diplomacy. Most important has been the 1986 Goldwater-Nichols Department of Defense Reorganization Act, which gave the chairman of the Joint Chiefs of Staff unparalleled influence for a military official in foreign and defense matters.[21] Indeed, one writer referred to Crowe as "the most powerful peacetime officer in American military history."[22] The power of the chairman only increased during General Powell's tenure. Crowe showed himself to be an adept politician and an able diplomat, and he has been a powerful advocate of better "uniformed communications" with the Soviet military and greater military involvement in the affairs of state.[23] Without his strong support for a comprehensive review of dangerous military activities involving Soviet and U.S. forces, the subsequent agreement on the prevention of such practices would not have been signed. Indeed, at the heart of the recent renewal of military dialogue and discussion is the unusual and unprecedented relationship between Admiral Crowe and Marshal Akhromeyev. Together with General Moiseyev, Marshal Akhromeyev's successor as chief of the Soviet General Staff, the two men helped create a consensus in their respective policy-making communities about the potential benefits of direct military dialogue. General Powell, who formerly served as national security council advisor to the president, not only maintained continuity but set a new professional standard for the role of chairman during his tenure in the Pentagon.[24]

The Soviets had intermittently pushed in the early 1980s for an expansion of military contacts, and, indeed, some academic voices in the West called for institutionalizing a military relationship between the two sides.[25] However, from the early to the mid-1980s, the only official contacts between the Soviet Union and the United States outside of normal diplomatic channels were the yearly meeting of naval officers as part of the Incidents at Sea Agreement and the ongoing communications through the military liaison missions in East and West Germany. Otherwise, the INF, SALT, and Comprehensive Test Ban talks were all stalled or discontinued, and ministerial exchanges between the Department of State and the Soviet Ministry of Foreign Affairs were severely curtailed. Furthermore, there was strict presidential guidance against even some simply ceremonial exchanges (such as U.S. military attachés in Moscow attending May Day festivities and parades), and the prospects for an enlargement of military contacts were dim without fundamental changes in the overall political relationship.

By the time of the Reagan-Gorbachev summit in December 1987, the political climate had changed enough for Crowe and Akhromeyev to meet in the former's office in the Pentagon on December 14, 1987. This was the first-ever private meeting between the highest ranking military commanders of the United States and the USSR. (Military and civilian leaders from the Department of Defense held brief meetings with their counterparts during the Vienna summit between President Jimmy Carter and General Secretary Leonid Brezhnev.) Both agreed during their historic meeting that the two sides' militaries should be prepared to play a more active role in the evolving political dialogue. Crowe and Akhromeyev believed that it would be fruitful, given the appropriate political environment, for the two militaries to begin some carefully chosen exchanges and contacts, such as war college visits, ship exchanges, sports contests, and perhaps reciprocal meetings of field commanders. They also favored joint discussions of military doctrine.

Crowe insisted that before this ambitious program could seriously be considered, the Soviet Union would have to address a number of U.S. concerns involving dangerous military practices. Marshal Akhromeyev responded that the Soviets were prepared for a full and frank discussion about any disputed area of Soviet doctrine or mode of military operations that would inhibit the course of the development of military rapprochement. Crowe suggested that this issue be addressed in detail by Secretary of Defense Frank Carlucci and Minister of Defense Dmitri Yazov when they met in March 1988. Both Crowe and Akhromeyev agreed that the civilian leadership would need to bless any further contacts or expansion of dialogue between the two sides' militaries.

When Secretary of Defense Carlucci met Minister of Defense Yazov in Berne, Switzerland, in March 1988 for a two-day ministerial discussion, it was—like Crowe and Akhromeyev's meeting in Washington—the first-ever summit of the two civilian heads of the U.S. and Soviet military establishments. (Yazov was recently made a marshal of the Soviet army, but the minister's portfolio is classified as a civilian task.) During the meeting, Carlucci and Yazov were able to explore heretofore uncharted political-military matters.

Yazov stated at the opening of the first session that the Soviet side was willing to hear U.S. concerns about perceived Soviet military misdeeds and dangerous activities. Carlucci was prepared with a list of incidents and practices with which the United States took issue. He began with the shootdown of KAL-007 as an example of the Soviet Union's treatment of all unidentified aircraft that happen to stray off course into Soviet territory as potentially hostile, a policy that, he said, had to stop if there were ever to be an improvement in military relations.[26] Second, in January 1987, the Soviets rammed a U.S. warship, the Aegis class cruiser USS Yorktown, while it was on a freedom of navigation exercise in the Black Sea off the Soviet coast; Carlucci stressed that the Soviets must stop the practice of ramming U.S. ships on peaceful missions designed to challenge the Soviet policy of intercepting ships transiting territorial waters.[27] Third, Carlucci cited incidents in which Soviet military personnel used lasers in a dangerous manner toward U.S. military personnel and equipment.[28] Fourth, Carlucci was concerned about the Soviets' occasional use of communication decoys and lures to confuse Western aircraft.[29] Fifth, Carlucci expressed hope that the United States and the Soviet Union could work out a set of ground rules for U.S. and Soviet forces operating in proximity in dangerous environments such as the Persian Gulf. He observed that on a number of occasions, Soviet ships and aircraft had intruded into U.S. operational areas and that this sort of activity could lead to an incident.[30]

Yazov agreed that each of these issues was worthy of further discussion and suggested that the two instruct the military heads of the Joint Chiefs of Staff and the Soviet General Staff to establish a working group to consider these questions as part of an enlarged program for military-to-military contracts. In press statements, the usually taciturn Yazov termed the meeting with Carlucci as "extremely substantive."[31] Carlucci concurred with Yazov's proposal, and, in July 1988, the Soviet chief of the General Staff, Marshal Akhromeyev, returned to the United States for a ten-day tour of the country. Crowe and Akhromeyev had ample opportunity for lengthy and detailed discussions about a whole range of issues. (Several State Department officials had initially sought to rein in Admiral Crowe and prohibit him from having anything more than general conversation with Marshal Akhromeyev.) At the end of Akhromeyev's tour, the two military leaders released a joint press report from Washington announcing the intention of the two sides' militaries to work more closely together.[32]

Specifically, the joint statement indicated that Crowe and Akhromeyev set out to establish a U.S.-Soviet military working group that would operate under their guidance to explore the issue of dangerous military activity in greater detail and to make recommendations. Among other things, the working group would review each side's capability to communicate expeditiously with elements of the military forces of the other side for the purpose of preventing dangerous military activity from occurring or continuing between those military forces. Further, the working group would consider whether types of dangerous military activity could arise that are not covered by specific existing arrangements and that should be made the subject of appropriate constraints or mutual understandings.

Both Akhromeyev and Crowe were sensitive to potential criticism that the military was becoming involved in political discussions.[33] They made clear in public statements and in private meetings within their respective bureaucracies that the working group would in no way replace or modify existing agreements, such as the 1972 Agreement on the Prevention of Dangerous Incidents on or over the High Seas or the 1947 Huebner-Malinin Agreement on Military-to-Military Liaison Missions in Germany. Both men stressed that the intent of the working group was simply to improve the professional relationship so that members of the military forces of the United States and the Soviet Union would be less at risk when operating in proximity in peacetime. In addition to a commitment to establish the Dangerous Military Activities working group, the two supreme military commanders signed an accord that set in motion an unprecented two-year period of military contacts, including war college meetings, ship visits, trips by historians, and sports exchanges.

After nearly a year of working-group-level negotiations conducted by Gen. George L. Butler from the U.S. Joint Chiefs of Staff and Gen. Anatoli Bolyatko of the Soviet General Staff, an agreement was set for signing during Admiral Crowe's return visit to the Soviet Union.[34] On June 12, 1989, Admiral Crowe and his new Soviet counterpart General Moiseyev, chief of the Soviet General Staff, signed a wide-ranging agreement aimed at reducing the likelihood of inadvertent war between the United States and the Soviet Union. The accord, entitled "The Prevention of Dangerous Military Activities," establishes a number of unprecedented presumptions and procedures to prevent the use of force in response to accidental military contacts and incidents.[35]

The agreement specifically mentions four types of potentially troublesome military activities: border or boundary incursions; use of range-finding lasers when armed forces are in proximity; ship and troop maneuvers in regions of high tension; and interference with command, communications, and control networks. Essentially, the Soviets had signed to avoid the very military practices listed by Carlucci during the meeting with Yazov in Berne. The document also provides procedures to prevent or, if necessary, defuse incidents arising from these activities, including direct communications between military commanders on the scene. The agreement also raises the possibility of both sides working in conjunction to designate an area of "special caution," such as the Persian Gulf during the Iran-Iraq War when significant U.S. and Soviet forces were operating in close proximity at a high alert status. Finally, both sides agreed to establish a Joint Military Commission made up of U.S. and Soviet officers to meet at least once a year to discuss any alleged or purported incidents and to exchange pertinent information. In addition to monitoring the existing agreement, the Joint Military Commission will also consider other potentially serious or dangerous military incidents that may arise from advances in military technology or the institution of new operational procedures. The U.S. and Soviet militaries have never before in their histories made such a sweeping pledge to avoid, terminate, and discuss dangerous military practices.[36]

The agreement is important for U.S.-Soviet relations, for it sets a precedent and a professional benchmark for the future involvement of military officers in the affairs of state. It is in many ways an organic document: Unlike an arms control treaty in which once the cuts are made, all that remains is to monitor, verify, and ensure mutual compliance with the treaty, the Dangerous Military Activities Agreement will require a tremendous amount of constant and ongoing attention by military personnel on both sides. Perhaps the most important legacy of the agreement is that hundreds of thousands of ground troops, pilots, sailors, and other military personnel will be trained in ways to avoid potentially dangerous military practices.

With the signing of the Dangerous Military Activities Agreement and the conclusion of the two-year program of military contacts, the first generation of U.S.-Soviet military exchanges and dialogue is complete, and we have now moved into the next stage of military diplomacy. General Moiseyev visited the United States in the fall of 1990 at the invitation of General Powell. Powell and Moiseyev had met for the first time in February 1990 at the Vienna Doctrine Seminar of the CSCE process. The fall meeting gave the two men the opportunity for extended conversation and debate, like Crowe and Akhromeyev before them.

This was Moiseyev's first visit to the United States, and he was shown several cities and a number of military installations, such as Ellsworth Air Force Base and Cheyenne Mountain at Colorado Springs.[37] During his visit, General Moiseyev briefed military and political leaders on the status of Soviet military withdrawals from Eastern Europe and domestic reforms involving the Soviet military. Moiseyev described in detail the Defense Ministry version of a proposal for military reform, which included the gradual introduction of contract service, the elimination of the political branch of the armed forces, and the scaling back of the military bureaucracy and the number of general officers in the force.[38] He also confirmed that Soviet authorities had moved tactical nuclear weapons from potential ethnic trouble spots around the Soviet Union.[39] Further, Moiseyev emphasized during a joint press interview with General Powell that the United States should allow economic sanctions to run their course against Iraq and not use force unless it was approved by the United Nations.[40] At the conclusion of the visit, Powell and Moiseyev announced a follow-on program of military contacts and exchanges that was intended to build on the first two-year military program.

It has been reliably reported that General Powell was initially cautious about establishing close contacts with the Soviet military, perhaps desiring to signal a careful and circumspect approach toward the Soviet armed forces. Yet accounts of the growing relationship between Powell and Moiseyev suggest a degree of continuity between past and present chiefs of staff. Since the substance and tone of the overall military relationship tend to flow from the personal and political relations of the two supreme military commanders, the outcome of their personal dialogue will have a direct impact on the future direction of military diplomacy.[41] Beyond the personal dimension, the next steps for military discussion and contacts will require both fine tuning and incremental advances of current programs, combined with fundamentally new directions of military exchange, if the regime is to remain relevant in the ever-changing international environment.

THE FUTURE OF MILITARY DIPLOMACY

The near-term future of the U.S.-Soviet military dialogue and exchange will differ fundamentally from the past, whether or not the actual substance of the program reflects such a change. Specifically, the primary parity of military means and political stability that has existed between the United States and the Soviet Union for a generation is increasingly suspect. The USSR is facing domestic upheavals of revolutionary proportions that will have a dramatic and drastic impact on Soviet armed forces. The Soviet Union cannot now with any confidence stage prolonged conventional military operations outside national boundaries. Yet, the tumult and change inside the USSR and in what was once the Soviet bloc can still raise the possibility of inadvertent or accidental war. One Estonian academician has expressed a fear that "a coming disintegration of the Soviet multinational empire is of concern to Western strategic analysts because the crisis of a superpower with thousands of nuclear warheads has a direct impact on the United States and the world in this interdependent age."[42] Indeed, a powerful argument can be mustered around the supposition that military misunderstandings are more likely and subsequently more dangerous during a period of profound hegemonic change, during which the USSR declines from superpower status, with domestic voices in favor of disunion inside the Soviet Union and anti-Soviet governments in power in Eastern Europe; and extremely large stocks of weapons and men under arms are transiting the European theater as a result of unilateral and negotiated pullbacks of Soviet troops and tanks from long-held positions in Eastern Europe.[43]

The greatest threats to inadvertent or accidental war between the United States and the Soviet Union come now from unforeseen events involving the Soviet military inside the USSR or in the surrounding Eastern European countries. The military diplomacy regime that has evolved between the two sides has focused on codifying means and mechanisms of operational arms control and crisis communication. The regime has looked to restrain dangerous military competition primarily in forward-deployed areas. Previous superpower showdowns and crises have occurred in third areas: either on the peripheries, in places such as Cuba, or in strategically important regions such as central Europe, where U.S. and Soviet forces have been heavily committed. However, future crises are much more likely to occur inside the Soviet empire of mutinous nationalities or in the surrounding countries of Eastern Europe.

Future U.S.-Soviet military contacts can serve as a vital conduit for communications and play a reassurance role in the turbulent period ahead. Military diplomacy can also be useful during periods of cooling relations between Washington and Moscow. To be successful, the regime must, however, evolve in some important ways. For the USSR, it will require a painful readjustment to the realities of its diminished power. Unpleasant and unpalatable possibilities, such as domestic nuclear terrorism, civil-military strife, armed insurrection, and a cataclysmic failure of central government and descent into civil war, now must be addressed. The United States must consider more seriously the merits of reassuring the USSR—particularly the Soviet military—through adjustments or explanations of its military strategy and doctrine. Further, just as direct assurances of noninterference in civil difficulties and disturbances have been communicated through personal meetings of U.S. and Soviet presidents and foreign ministers, the U.S. military should also carry the message to their opposite numbers.

There currently exists strong and far-reaching presidential guidance for the military-to-military program of contacts and exchanges between the United States and the Soviet Union. One of the primary goals has been to demonstrate to the USSR, through example and explanation, the role of the military in a democratic society. This objective will grow and permeate all aspects of U.S.-Soviet military relations in the future, as the USSR struggles to fashion new procedures for national security-making, a new model for a smaller, more professional military, and a new military strategy. The United States and the USSR moved ahead in the fall of 1990 during the Powell-Moiseyev summit with another two-year program of exchanges of military personnel and civilian professionals, incrementally building on the first two-year program. Several of the potential areas of military exchange listed below can easily be accommodated or incorporated into the already existing institutions of the present military regime. However, others will require serious discussion within the government and among allies before proceeding forward. Nevertheless, all of the following suggestions can play a positive role in helping to improve understanding and avoid potential conflicts in the new era ahead.

Crisis Communications: Codify and Integrate Procedures

Perhaps the most important area for further military exploration and discussion is in the realm of crisis communication. Several standing agreements between the United States and the USSR call for timely communication in the event of a military clash, nuclear accident, unauthorized use of military weaponry, or third party provocative attack. Some of these agreements include the 1972 Incidents at Sea Agreement, the 1971 Accidental Measures Agreement, and the 1989 Dangerous Military Activities Agreement.[44] There are also two U.S.-Soviet agreements that establish crisis communication links—the Direct Communications Link (DCL) or hotline, and the Nuclear Risk Reduction Centers (NRRC).[45] Furthermore, the NATO summit statement of June 1990 called for establishing a new crisis prevention and communication center for Europe as part of the CSCE process.[46]

Currently, there are essentially three agreed procedures for military personnel to communicate directly: through military attachés in Moscow and Washington, through the Nuclear Risk Reduction Centers, and between local commanders at the scene of an accidental clash or military misunderstanding (as stipulated by the Dangerous Military Activities Agreement). Given the proliferation of crisis prevention agreements and crisis communication procedures, it would be prudent to establish a U.S.-Soviet working group made up of government specialists and military officers to review current and potential future commitments and procedures in the realm of crisis communications.

There is an inherent tension between two competing visions of military involvement in crisis communication. A dominant civilian view is that the military should take preventive steps to avoid a military clash but should not be involved directly in crisis control after the outbreak of initial hostilities. This view holds that state-to-state communication in a crisis should be conducted and coordinated centrally by civilian leaders. However, an enlightened military view has it that many inadvertent or small skirmishes could well be contained at an early stage through prompt and timely communications, first between local commanders on the scene and then up the chain of command if necessary. This view holds that in the time it takes to assemble and brief a national security team in Washington, a minor misunderstanding that could be cleared up on the scene may escalate. This tension is inherent to the process of crisis control and will be a continuing feature in the debate about the merits of military involvement in crisis diplomacy.

There have been calls for making more use of the Nuclear Risk Reduction Center, beyond its current functions of notification of upcoming missile test launches and certain strategic military exercises and the passing of information relating to INF Treaty verification. There are also numerous ideas about how a European-wide crisis communication center should (and should not) operate. Embedded in many such proposals is a preference for facilitating greater military involvement in crisis communication, particularly in cases of inadvertent or accidental clashes. Since most crises involve the military, there is clearly scope for direct and carefully crafted communication between commanders on the scene to avoid unintended escalation. (This is actually mandated by the Dangerous Military Activities Agreement.) Indeed, in many cases, such as a potential U.S.-Soviet naval mishap at sea, the military commanders on the scene are the only authorities capable of directly defusing a tense situation during its initial phase.[47] Further, there should be mechanisms, such as the NRRC, to facilitate official communication and to gather and pass information at early stages of a crisis before a national-level crisis team can be constituted. These institutions should pose no reasonable threat to civilian control over crisis decision making, particularly if the procedures and guidelines for communication are well developed in advance. In any event, the issue of military involvement in crisis communication deserves more serious consideration by a U.S.-Soviet working group.

Doctrinal Discussions: Strengthening Bilateral and Multilateral Institutions

In the last two years, there have been two important vehicles for military exploration of doctrinal issues. Part of the first two-year program was a series of exchanges about military strategy and tactics between the National Defense University (NDU) and the Voroshilov General Staff Academy. In addition, in February 1990, the Confidence and Security Building Measures Conference of the CSCE process in Europe held a Doctrine Seminar in Vienna to discuss national defense strategies, European theater trends, military training techniques, and military budgeting procedures.[48] Both of these forums have provided unique opportunities to describe and explain military doctrines, and each should be institutionalized as part of a continuing military diplomacy regime. There is no plausible or prudent way to "negotiate" military doctrines, but a better understanding of the assumptions and objectives that drive national security decision making can help alleviate the threat of inadvertent or unintended war.

The NDU-Voroshilov exchanges have to date focused on more narrow, tactical questions of military practice. In the past, given the offensive character of Soviet military deployments, these discussions have had a decidedly European focus, with U.S. participants pressing their Soviet interlocutors about changes in Soviet defense forces brought on by the shift to "sufficient defense" as the watchword for military planning and preparations. Given the changes in the political geography of Eastern Europe, the talks should now give much more attention to sources of Soviet concern. Specifically, the NDU-Voroshilov meetings should strive to further explore and elicit Soviet concerns about naval strategy and practices. What, precisely, in the naval realm poses a threat to Soviet national interests? The United States has in the past dismissed Soviet calls for limitations on naval weapons, deployments, and operations, and the very appearance of U.S. intransigence and insensitivity to Soviet security concerns creates an atmosphere of distrust. Naval arms control may well not be in the U.S. national interest, but the United States must engage the USSR more openly on the subject. Further, the participation in the NDU-Voroshilov exchanges should increase from a small number of mid-level military specialists to include outstanding civilian specialists, perhaps from the Rand Corporation and universities. The Soviets should be encouraged to do the same. This joint participation of soldiers and civilians would raise the quality of dialogue considerably and help to educate civilian defense specialists in the USSR.

The Doctrine Seminar was also an unheralded success in that it brought the military leadership from all the CSCE participating states to Vienna.[49] It allowed the new governments of Eastern Europe the opportunity to unveil new national military strategies outside of the traditional coalition strategy of the Warsaw Pact. The Doctrine Seminar also offered an unprecedented opportunity for the United States and the Soviet Union, among others, to compare military doctrines, training procedures, and procurement and budgeting procedures. Given the momentous changes sweeping the Soviet Union and Eastern Europe, and the wild-card role the militaries will play in subsequent domestic and regional developments, it makes sense to institutionalize the Military Doctrine Seminar on a regular basis through this period of transition and transformation. Indeed, regular contacts between the militaries of East and West can set an example for civil-military relations in post-communist societies and perhaps reduce the possibility of Praetorian military intervention in domestic affairs.[50] The Doctrine Seminar can also serve as a functionalist building block in a future CSCE regime based on shared military information, agreed steps toward greater transparency, and a better understanding of military plans and priorities.

Finally, it would be prudent for the United States and the Soviet Union to establish military staff-to-staff talks between the Joint Chiefs of Staff and the Soviet General Staff. The meetings would offer the opportunity for a regular, discreet exchange of views on a wide variety to topics. Already, the Soviet Union has held military staff talks with West Germany as part of bilateral consultations toward German unification. Staff talks between the United States and the USSR represent a logical next step in the expanding dialogue between senior Soviet and U.S. officers and could easily be incorporated into a future program of military contracts and exchanges.

Dangerous Military Activities: The Role of the Joint Military Commission

The Dangerous Military Activities Agreement stipulates the formation of a U.S.-Soviet Joint Military Commission (JMC) of senior officers from the Joint Chiefs of Staff and the Soviet General Staff, which will meet regularly to discuss issues raised by or relating to the agreement. (The JMC will convene about once a year under normal circumstances; a meeting can be called by either side on short notice if necessary.) The JMC is modeled in some measure after the yearly meetings of U.S. and Soviet naval officers as part of the Incidents at Sea Agreement. The JMC will offer a unique forum for both sides' militaries to examine issues raised specifically by the agreement or to explore other matters mutually deemed to fall in the realm of dangerous military activity.

There are several aspects of the agreement that would benefit from more meticulous examination and exchange. Specifically, the agreement establishes the possibility of the United States and the USSR jointly declaring a "special caution area" when forces are operating in proximity in a region of high tension (such as the Persian Gulf). However, further exploration by the JMC is necessary to gain agreement on the potential characteristics of a special caution area and on procedures for declaring one. In the realm of U.S.-Soviet communications, the Joint Military Commission should also explore the possibility of using the Nuclear Risk Reduction Centers as a means of communicating during a crisis, should efforts at halting hostilities by local commanders on the scene prove ineffective. The JMC might also be usefully employed as a forum for one side to communicate dismay or concern about a military practice or policy of the other side. The JMC offers the participants an opportunity not only to monitor the existing treaty but also to jointly consider other potentially serious or dangerous military activities that are not spelled out in the agreement but that will invariably arise with advances in military technology or the implementation of new operational procedures.

Peacekeeping: Planning for Multilateral Military Operations

A number of successful Third World peacekeeping ventures in the past two years have renewed interest in and discussion about the future role of the United Nations and of peacekeeping in conflict management.[51] Both superpowers have traditionally been extremely wary of committing forces under international auspices and have strongly resisted greater involvement in peacekeeping endeavors. However, the superpowers have recently supported and been involved in several current U.N. peacekeeping operations, including the Good Offices Mission in Afghanistan and Pakistan; the Iran-Iraq Observer Group; the Assistance Group in Namibia; the Angola Verification Mission; and the Observer Group in Central America. Several of these operations involved monitoring crises and combatants, observing military withdrawals, verifying the fairness of elections, organizing relief shipments, and conducting narrowly defined military operations.[52]

The Soviet Union has taken a strong international lead in support of strengthening mulilateral military operations and procedures. In President Gorbachev's December 1988 speech to the United Nations, he stressed the USSR's commitment to improving U.N. peacekeeping capabilities. Soviet officials at the Ministry of Foreign Affairs have since actively campaigned to reinvigorate the Military Staff Committee (MSC), which has been moribund since 1947. The MSC actually was convened in New York during the initial military preparations for Operation Desert Storm in the Persian Gulf. As specified in the U.N. Charter, the MSC is composed only of senior military officers from the five permanent members of the Security Council. It is thereby subject to the Council's veto power and has hardly been an attractive institution to others, particularly troop contributors and financial powers. The United States in particular has not been eager to consider revamping the command and control of U.N. military operations. However, a resuscitated and redesigned MSC could in the future provide advice to the secretary-general about the military requirements of peacekeeping and might allow for greater cooperation in the military sphere between the United States and the USSR.

Given the at least prewar consensus of views between Moscow and Washington in favor of multilateral military involvement in the Persian Gulf, region, it is now possible to imagine Soviet and U.S. troops or ships serving in certain capacities together during an international crisis. The superpowers' initial diplomatic response to the Iraqi invasion of Kuwait in August 1990 demonstrates the possibility of much greater U.S.-Soviet military cooperation in the post–Cold War world. It would be propitious for the two sides' militaries to begin joint work on the future possibilities of multilateral military operations. Both sides would benefit from a detailed discussion about establishing clear guidelines for sending U.N. troops into a besieged Third World country or other high-tension area. There could also be useful talk about joint evacuation procedures in the event of a hostage situation, such as in Kuwait, or a dramatic decline of public order and safety, as in Liberia. This farsighted approach would be seen as a realistic and sober response to the emerging threats of the new world order: terrorism, nuclear proliferation, endemic civil wars, and hostage-taking on a massive scale. The realm of joint military action is still quite narrow today, but bilateral discussions can help facilitate future multilateral operations.

Nuclear Weapons Safety: Assuring Reliability and Control

There is increasing concern in the U.S. intelligence community and among Soviet defense intellectuals about the safety of Soviet nuclear weapons. Soviet press reports are replete with recent examples of huge quantities of military equipment stolen from Soviet bases inside the country and in Eastern Europe.[53] Soviet military spokesmen such as Marshal Akhromeyev have publicly stated that the Soviet nuclear arsenal is completely secure, and many Western specialists on the Soviet military believe that Soviet nuclear weapons stockpiles have not been threatened by domestic disturbances.[54] However, there has been at least one garbled and unconfirmed Western report of a breach of internal security at a Soviet military base with nuclear weapons.[55] In response, Sen. Sam Nunn has called for a review of U.S. nuclear weapons security and an exchange of information with the Soviet Union on the subject.[56]

Some aspects of nuclear weapons security would be appropriate for joint consideration in a military forum. In the 1960s and 1970s, the U.S. defense community discussed sharing information concerning nuclear safety procedures with the USSR, specifically technologies associated with Permissive Action Links.[57] Some have argued that this quiet dialogue should even expand to include shared guidelines for nuclear training.[58] However, the safety of Soviet nuclear weapons, particularly tactical artillery pieces and short-range systems, poses urgent concerns. The USSR by many accounts has moved and will continue to move very large numbers of these systems from outlying republics and from stockpiles in Eastern Europe to more secure sites inside the Russian republic in the near future. The United States has much more experience with safety techniques and technologies for transporting nuclear munitions as well as with sophisticated technical devices designed to prohibit inadvertent nuclear use. The United States should carefully weigh the merits and potential pitfalls of unilaterally sharing this information and technology with the Soviet Union. The model for this potential endeavor might be President Reagan's public commitment to share Strategic Defense Initiative (SDI) technology with the Soviet Union. Further, as part of any discreet dialogue about nuclear weapons security, there should be joint exploration of methods of communication during a nuclear weapons accident or hijacking.

Information and Data Exchanges: Building Stronger Civil-Military Institutions

The military dialogue between the United States and the USSR that may have the potential for effecting the greatest change in Soviet society involves the open exchange of military information. The Soviet military has traditionally had a monopoly on military plans, priorities, and budget data. Increasingly, there are rival voices within the Soviet elite—the research institutes associated with the Soviet Academy of Science, military specialists now with the Ministry of Foreign Affairs, and the newly configured committees on defense and intelligence matters in the Congress of Peoples' Deputies—that offer competing assessments and visions of Soviet national security. There is even a group of army officers elected to the Congress of Peoples' Deputies that is currently calling for, among other things, a much smaller, paid, professional Soviet army. Many of these groups are seriously hampered by a severe lack of access to information about the Soviet military. Indeed, because of the level of secrecy and compartmentalization inside the Soviet military, numerous Soviet officers also claim ignorance about many aspects of their own system.

The U.S. military should also make every effort to share information about the U.S. system of military procurement, command and control, and civilian rule and oversight. The USSR is currently redesigning its national security-making process and reconfiguring the Defense Council into a presidential system for the formulation and execution of state policy. Soviet specialists and spokesmen are particularly eager for information about how the United States and other states have designed their systems. Indeed, several officials in the Soviet Ministry of Foreign Affairs and the International Department asked a visiting delegation of U.S. military officers for any materials or memoirs about how President John F. Kennedy and Secretary of Defense Robert McNamara "civilianized" the Department of Defense in the early 1960s.[59] As the Soviets take further steps to reform the Ministry of Defense and the Soviet General Staff, they should have the benefit of understanding how the U.S. system of national security-making and civil-military affairs functions.

Data exchanges could also extend to sharing information on issues of mutual concern, such as environmental conditions. The U.S. Navy has recently undertaken a project with the Environmental Protection Agency to share information on the change in the thickness of polar ice obtained from samples taken over the last three decades in an effort to determine the rate of global warming.[60] Certainly the Soviet military has gathered similar data and information over the same period. These separate reference points could be combined into a definitive historical record. The Soviet military might also be in a position to share its recent findings on nuclear cleanups and contaminations in the aftermath of the Chernobyl reactor accident.

THE LIMITS OF MILITARY CONFIDENCE

The difficulty of establishing confidence between potentially hostile armies is an ancient problem. Perhaps the most eloquent formulation of the dilemma posed by armed diplomacy was reported by Xenophon in his chronicles of the Persian expedition 2400 years ago. He describes the mutual suspicion that arose between the Greek army departing Persia and the Persian army escorting them. The Greek general asked for an interview with his Persian counterpart and offered: "I observe that you are watching our moves as though we were enemies, and we, noticing this, are watching yours, too. On looking into things, I am unable to find evidence that you are trying to do us any harm, and I am perfectly sure that, as far as we're concerned, we do not even contemplate such a thing; so I decided to discuss matters with you, to see if we could put an end to this mutual distrust."[61] These sentiments could, with a few modifications, fit the rationale and record of U.S.-Soviet military diplomacy to date. However, a sobering reminder for current military leaders attempting to build trust and remove stereotypes is that the Persian expedition ended in war in spite of mutual assurances, timely communication, and attempts to convey and build confidence.

There are clear limits to the potential of a future military diplomacy regime. Indeed, a degree of mutual distrust and suspicion has returned to U.S.-Soviet relations, and the Soviet military is showing signs of siding with the resurgent hard-liners and conservatives in the Kremlin. Domestic unrest has increased dramatically, and the Soviet armed forces expressed grave reservations about the U.S. military presence and practices during the Gulf War. The ultimate responsibility of the armed forces is not to communicate during a crisis or to reassure a potential adversary but, rather, to be prepared to fight. This places inherent limits on the effects and extent of military-to-military dialogue and exchanges. Furthermore, there are clear bureaucratic lines and jurisdictions that would be difficult for the military to cross in the realm of direct U.S.-Soviet dialogue. For instance, the State Department initially was uncomfortable with Admiral Crowe's intention of talking about substantive issues with Marshal Akhromeyev during their first meetings, but these unreasonable objections were overcome and the two men were able to interact on a wide range of subjects.[62] Yet, there are certainly subjects that are better left to civilian interlocuters rather than military statesmen or working groups. Defining an agreeable framework for the future of the military contacts program will almost certainly involve considerable bureaucratic friction. To date, all major military-to-military initiatives have received the blessing of the National Security Council and the State Department. Indeed, there have been State Department and Defense Department representatives at every working group meeting held under the Incidents at Sea and Dangerous Military Activities agreements.

A number of past military contacts between U.S. and Soviet militaries have undermined, rather than advanced, the cause of mutual confidence. For example, the history of the military liaison missions in Germany is full of many examples of Soviet harassment and minor clashes.[63] The meetings of the military liaison missions have historically been tense and polemical. Indeed, some military agreements have had more to do with gaining information about the potential adversary than about gaining trust, and these conflicting desires have in the past—and can in the future—presented problems. There are clear drawbacks to several recent, and some proposed, contacts.

Reciprocal displays of military hardware have been a bonus for intelligence gathering, but these armed displays have often served to raise concerns rather than to reassure. For instance, during Marshal Akhromeyev's visit to the U.S. aircraft carrier USS *Theodore Roosevelt*, he viewed for the first time catapult landings and takeoffs of sophisticated fighter aircraft on a deck of a flat top. On his return to the USSR, Akhromeyev became the country's leading voice for extending arms control to sea, particularly to include battle carrier groups. Furthermore, when Secretary of Defense Carlucci was taken to see the new generation of Soviet strategic bombers, the *Blackjack*, during his visit to the USSR, he witnessed a flight test of two of these supersonic craft. Carlucci had no way of knowing it at the time, but one of the planes was experiencing serious engine failure on the ground before takeoff. The pilot requested senior Soviet commanders' permission to abort the mission. Nevertheless, the pilot was ordered into the air at great risk.[64] During an air show in the United States in July 1990, a Soviet pilot was allowed to fly in a navy Blue Angels F/A-18 fighter plane.[65] This sort of military "show and tell" had been put firmly off limits by Defense Department guidance, but an on-scene commander allowed the exchange to go ahead. Such exposure of the Soviets to our most advanced military hardware could have serious implications for U.S. security. During ship visits and air shows, there will often be strong temptations to demonstrate military equipment and technologies, but the effect of these displays can both undercut confidence and divulge classified technical or operational characteristics of sophisticated equipment. Sharing information on capabilities should be reserved only for our closest allies.

Finally, some Soviet proposals about joint troop training or exercises are obviously premature. Even with all the important changes and positive developments in U.S.-

Soviet relations, the USSR is still the only potential enemy the United States faces on a global scale. For the military diplomacy regime to survive, it must adapt to, and carefully negotiate around, the inherent contradictions of each side seeing the other as a limited partner and as a potential enemy. From the bureaucratic standpoint, the process is benefited by open and wide discussion of possible programs for military exchange, but it is better served by a centralized process of review and implementation of the overall contacts program. In the United States, the office of the chairman of the JCS and the Joint Chiefs of Staff, in close consultation with, and using clear guidelines from, the departments of State and Defense, should be responsible for the formulation and execution of U.S.-Soviet military dialogue and exchanges.

CONCLUSION: THE FUTURE OF MILITARY DIPLOMACY

Since the earliest days of the Cold War, the United States and the USSR have seen fit to regulate their rivalry through at least some level of military dialogue and exchanges. Over the last two years, both sides have advanced the institution of military diplomacy through a well-conceived plan of military contacts and working group meetings on dangerous military activities. The whole issue of military involvement in the affairs of state has raised important questions about the possible impact on civil-military affairs. However, with strong civilian oversight and proper interagency concurrence, the military diplomacy regime has advanced carefully and cautiously, with a subtle appreciation on the part of the U.S. government for the inevitable limits to military-to-military contacts. The regularized meetings of military specialists, the working-level discussions of dangerous military activities, the human dimension of the reciprocal ship visits, and the personal relationship that developed between Admiral Crowe and Marshal Akhromeyev have helped to establish a fledgling regime of military diplomacy.

The current climate of U.S.-Soviet rapprochement and reassessment coupled with the revolutionary changes sweeping the Soviet Union and Eastern Europe have opened up possibilities for greater involvement in the overall political relationship. Indeed, the very complexity and urgency of the issues concerned—the need to explore doctrinal issues, assure the safety of nuclear weapons, establish better crisis communications, avoid dangerous military practices, and build healthy civil-military institutions—demand the more active involvement of the military. The Soviet military—as one of the only organized, powerful, and enduring institutions in Soviet society—will play an important if not decisive role in the future of the country. Military diplomacy can help impart important values of democratic decision making to the national security system, such as the primacy of civilian rule over military authority and the desirability of military openness. Yet, these new responsibilities for the armed forces should not preempt or complicate civilian diplomacy with the USSR. Rather, the expansion of the scope and significance of military diplomacy should be seen as an increasingly necessary adjunct to traditional avenues of diplomacy.

NOTES

1. There is no systematic study of U.S.-Soviet military relations in the Cold War era, but episodes and aspects of this history are described in a range of sources. Since most of the official government files that touch on this history are still classified, military memoirs and personal accounts of the period are perhaps most illuminating. For instance, personal accounts of military contacts during the Eisenhower presidency can be found in Nathan F. Twining, *Neither Liberty Nor Safety* (New York: Simon and Schuster, 1982), pp. 552–555. Twining describes his visit to the USSR to view the Soviet airforce in 1956. For further material on the same visit of airforce officers, see Thomas S. Power, *Design for Survival* (New York: Coward-McCann, 1964), pp. 41–59. The tentative military diplomacy of the Cold War is also touched on by Maj. Gen. E. B. Atkeson, USA, Ret., *The Final Argument of Kings* (Fairfax, Virginia: Hero Books, 1988), pp. 245–250. There is a range of citations concerning military contacts in Germany in the immediate aftermath of World War II, including Frank Howley, *Berlin Command* (New York: Putnam's Sons, 1950); and Maxwell D. Taylor, *Swords and Plowshares* (New York: Norton, 1972), pp. 123–125. Some Soviet writers have also referred to military cooperation during and immediately after the war. See specifically, Gleb Baklanov, *Vstrecha Na Elbe* (Moscow: Novosti Press, 1988). Recent proposals for enlarging the military dialogue between East and West include, John A. Fahey and Philip S. Gillette, "Military Liaisons Between NATO and the Warsaw Pact," *US-Soviet Relations: An Agenda for the Future*, Foreign Policy Institute Briefs (Washington, D.C.: The Johns Hopkins University Foreign Policy Institute, 1988). For a full history of U.S.-Soviet military diplomacy since 1945, see the author's forthcoming *Soldiers as Statesmen* (1991 publication date).

2. European history is replete with examples of soldiers' involvement in the formulation and conduct of foreign policy. For instance, military conventions and general staff meetings were a significant feature of the shifting alliances and diplomatic maneuvering before World War I. This involvement was perhaps most apparent in the war-planning scenarios generated by Bismarck's Austro-German alliance of 1879, the Franco-Russian military meetings of 1892, and the Anglo-Russian Naval Convention of 1912. Yet, military diplomacy between the various rival European states rarely inhibited armaments programs or helped to build confidence and trust. Instead, these military exchanges often served as secret war planning sessions and are generally regarded as contributing to the deterioration rather than the maintenance of European security. The best and virtually the only thorough examination of the role of the soldier in statecraft is found in Alfred Vagts, *Defense and Diplomacy: The Soldier and the Conduct of Foreign Relations* (New York: King's Crown Press, 1956); and Vagts, *The Military Attache* (Princeton: Princeton University Press, 1967), pp. 15–36. There is also extensive material on the role of military representatives in interwar naval arms control. See for instance, Harold and Margaret Sprout, *Toward a New Order of Sea Power* (Princeton: Princeton University Press, 1940), pp. 57–67; Raymond O'Connor, *Perilous Equilibrium* (Kansas City: Kansas University Press, 1962), pp. 30–37; and a forthcoming excellent work, Emily Goldman "The Washington Treaty System: Arms Racing and Arms Control in the Inter-war Period," Ph.D. dissertation, Political Science Department, Stanford University, 1989.

3. For interesting early histories of military attachés in the Soviet Union, see Kemp Tolley, *Caviar and Commissars: The Experiences of a US Naval Officer in Stalin's Russia* (Annapolis, Maryland: Naval Institute Press, 1983); and Charles J. Weeks and Joseph O. Baylen, "Admiral Newton A. McCully's Missions in Russia, 1904–1921," *The Russian Review*, 33, 1 (January 1974): 63–79.

4. For an interesting account of military involvement in the SALT negotiations, see John Newhouse, *Cold Dawn: The Story of SALT* (New York: Holt Rinehart, 1973).

5. For a historical review of military involvement in negotiations and foreign policy, and the traditional inhibitions to this process, see Kurt M. Campbell, "The Soldiers' Summit," *Foreign Policy*, 75 (Summer 1989).

6. See Joseph S. Nye, "Arms Control After the Cold War," *Foreign Affairs* (Winter 1989/90), p. 44.

7. For a press account of the contacts program, see Bob Woodward and R. Jeffrey Smith, "US-Soviet Pact to Curb Incidents," *Washington Post*, June 7, 1989.

8. For an excellent exploration of the USSR's diplomatic retrenchment and national decline, see Stephen Sestanovich, "Gorbachev's Foreign Policy: A Diplomacy of Decline," *Problems of Communism* (January/February 1988), pp. 1–16; Paul Kennedy, *The Rise and Fall of the Great Powers: Economic Change and Military Conflict from 1500 to 2000* (New York: Random House, 1987); Francis Fukuyama, "The End of History," *The National Interest*, 16 (Summer 1989), pp. 3–18; and Seweryn Bialer, *The Soviet Paradox: External Expansion, Internal Decline* (New York: Alfred A. Knopf, 1986).

9. This trend is detailed in R. Hyland Phillips and Jeffrey I. Sands, "Reasonable Sufficiency: A Research Note," *International Security*, 13, 2 (Fall 1988): 164–178.

10. See Graham Allison, "US-Soviet treaty seeks to end policy of 'shoot first, ask questions later,' " *Boston Globe*, June 18, 1989.

11. For interesting histories of wartime cooperation, see Robert T. Jones, *The Road to Russia* (Oklahoma City: Oklahoma University Press, 1969); Raymond H. Dawson, *The Decision to Aid Russia, 1941* (Chapel Hill: University of North Carolina Press, 1959); and Richard C. Lukas, *Eagles East: The Army Airforce and the Soviet Union* (Tallahassee, FL: Florida State University Press, 1979).

12. For a review of the CSCE process and the military dimension of the Helsinki Final Act, see *First Semiannual Report by the President to the Commission on Security and Cooperation in Europe*, Report submitted to the Committee on International Relations (Washington, D.C.: U.S. Government Printing Office, 1976).

13. Sean Lynn-Jones, "A Quiet Success for Arms Control: Preventing Incidents at Sea," *International Security*, 9, 4 (Spring 1985): 154–184; and Sean Lynn-Jones, "Applying and Extending the USA-USSR Incidents at Sea Agreement," in Richard Fieldhouse, ed., *Security at Sea: Naval Forces and Arms Control* (Oxford: Oxford University Press, 1990), pp. 203–219.

14. See Sean Lynn-Jones, "Preventing Incidents at Sea," p. 154.

15. For the classic treatment on American civil-military relations, see Samuel P. Huntington, *The Soldier and the State: The Theory and Practice of Civil-Military Relations* (Cambridge: Harvard University Press, 1957).

16. Stalin's distrust of his generals is detailed throughout Seweryn Bialer, ed., *Stalin and His Generals: Soviet Memoirs of World War II* (New York: Pegasus, 1969).

17. See Dale R. Herspring, *The Soviet High Command, 1967–1989* (Princeton: Princeton University Press, 1990), pp. 166–208.

18. See John Erickson, *The Soviet High Command* (London: Macmillan, 1962); and Michael Gardner, *A History of the Soviet Army* (London: Pall Mall Press, 1966).

19. Many Sovietologists in the West see signs of stress and friction between the civilian Soviet leadership and the military about how best to defend the country. See Seweryn Bialer, "New Thinking and Soviet Foreign Policy," *Survival*, 30, 4 (July-August 1988), pp. 298–303.

20. See Steve Meyer, "The Sources and Prospects of Gorbachev's New Political Thinking on Security," *International Security*, 13, 2 (Fall 1988): 164–178.

21. See *Defense Organization: The Need for Change*, Staff Report to the Committee on Armed Services, United States Senate, 99th Congress, 1st Session, October 16, 1985,

Washington, D.C.; and the *Goldwater-Nichols Defense Department Reorganization Act of 1986*, 99th Congress, 2nd session, Washington, D.C.

22. Arthur T. Hadley, "Admiral Crowe: In Command," *New York Times Magazine*, August 7, 1988, p. 21.

23. For an excellent discussion of Crowe's views on this and other subjects, see Bob Woodward, "On the Admiral's Watch: William Crowe and the Shaping of the Modern Military," *Washington Post Magazine*, September 24, 1989.

24. See the description of General Powell in Andrew Rosenthal, "Military Chief: Man of Action and of Politics," *Washington Post*, August 17, 1990.

25. For instance, Joseph S. Nye, Jr. had proposed that the chairman of Joint Chiefs of Staff meet regularly with his Soviet counterpart to discuss military forces and doctrines. See Nye, "Restarting Arms Control," *Foreign Policy* 47 (Summer 1982), pp. 109–111.

26. For a good account of the downing of the 007, see Alexander Dallin, *Black Box: KAL 007 and the Superpowers* (Berkeley: University of California Press, 1985).

27. These freedom of navigation exercises have been controversial and hotly contested by the USSR. For a legal defense of U.S. policies in these matters, see the arguments of Capt. William L. Schachte, Judge Advocate General's Corps, USN, "The Black Sea Challenge," *Proceedings*, No. 114 (June 1988), p. 62.

28. Cases of "lasing" by Soviet forces against U.S. military units are described by Barry E. Fridling, "Lasers highlight policy blindspots," *Bulletin of the Atomic Scientists* (July/August 1988), pp. 36–39; "Blinding Lasers: The Need for Control," *Proceedings* (October 1988), p. 151; and "Russian Lasers Reported Aimed At US Planes," *New York Times*, October 3, 1987.

29. This practice of "beacon-luring," particularly the interference with U.S. MATC aircraft stationed in Turkey in the 1950s by Soviet radio lures, is described in Patrick J. McGarvey, *CIA: The Myth and the Madness* (New York: Penguin Books, 1973), p. 264.

30. These incidents are reviewed in Michael Dobbs, "New Pact Addresses Accidental Conflicts," *Washington Post*, June 13, 1989.

31. See "Yazov y Carlucci v Berne," *Krasnaya Zvezda*, March 18, 1988, p. 1.

32. In the joint statement, the U.S. chairman of the Joint Chiefs of Staff, and the Soviet chief of General Staff indicated their intent to pursue policies and actions which would assist the armed forces of the United States and the USSR in the avoidance of dangerous military activity in the vicinity of each other, and in the immediate termination of such activity, should it take place. To this end, the sides would also ensure the appropriate training and preparation of their respective armed forces. See the *Joint Statement by Admiral William J. Crowe, Jr. and Marshal of the Soviet Union Sergei F. Akhromeyev*, Washington, D.C., July 11, 1988.

33. To pointed suggestions that Admiral Crowe was involved in "negotiations" with the Soviets, he states in an interview: "I wasn't negotiating anything. But if better relations are to be achieved, the military should participate in and contribute to the process. If you say that only the State Department can talk to the Soviets, then, given the stakes, the multiplicity of contacts and the complexity of the issues, I must disagree. You know, senior military commanders deal all the time in diplomacy. The commanders in Europe and the Pacific go to country after country and are welcomed by heads of state and government officials and talk about a lot more than military affairs." See Bruce van Voorst, "William Crowe on the Soviets," *Time*, December 26, 1988. It was also clear from remarks by Akhromeyev after his U.S. visit, that military diplomacy was a sensitive subject in the USSR. In response to a question from a Soviet journalist, Akhromeyev said that "as regards military 'intervention' in solving foreign policy problems, you can't accomplish the paramount task of today—the prevention of war—without the military. This is why military leaders are active as never

before in the process that should lead to the prevention of war, to successful talks." See *FBIS*, Daily Report: Soviet Union, July 25, 1988.

34. For a review of the negotiations that led to the signing of the agreement see Kurt M. Campbell, "The Dangerous Military Activities Agreement," *Security Studies*, 1 (1991).

35. The full title is "Agreement Between the Government of the Union of Soviet Socialist Republics and the government of the United States of America on the Prevention of Dangerous Military Activities," The Joint Chiefs of Staff, Department of Defense, June 12, 1990.

36. The Dangerous Military Activities Agreement is discussed in the context of other U.S.-Soviet understandings to prevent conflict, in Francis Clines, "US-Soviet Accord Cuts the Risk of War," *New York Times*, June 13, 1989.

37. For press accounts of the Moiseyev visit, see Frank J. Murray, "Touring Soviet General Meets with Bush, Powell," *Washington Times*, October 3, 1990; and "19-Gun Salute Greets Soviet General," *Washington Times*, October 2, 1990.

38. There are currently two primary competing proposals for military reform in the USSR. Moiseyev described the more conservative approach favored by the Ministry of Defense and the Soviet General Staff. There is another version, often cited as the radical Supreme Soviet version, which calls for a smaller, all volunteer military, a civilian defense minister, and a unionized army that aims at protecting soldiers, sailors, and airmen from abuse.

39. See the analysis of Moiseyev's remarks in Michael Dobbs, "Soviets Moved Warheads, Top General Confirms," *Washington Post*, September 28, 1990.

40. Moiseyev was quoted as saying that "we cannot view the resolution of any crisis like this by means of using arms." See Michael R. Gordon, "Top Soviet General Tells US Not to Attack in Gulf," *New York Times*, September 28, 1990; and Gary Lee and Rick Atkinson, "Soviet General Warns of World War Risk," *Washington Post*, September 28, 1990.

41. There is an interesting personal dimension and dynamic to nearly every relationship that we have seen between senior Soviet and American commanders. Perhaps the most unusual and enduring relationship was the one established between General Eisenhower and Marshal Zhukov during the last year of the European campaign. The two had a rare camaraderie and mutual respect that at times seemed to transcend their political differences. For a description of their periodic contacts and correspondence between 1944 and 1957, see Stephen E. Ambrose, *Eisenhower: Soldier, General of the Army, President Elect, 1890–1952* (New York: Simon and Schuster, 1983).

42. See Andrus Pork, "Global Security and Soviet Nationalities," *Washington Quarterly*, 13, 2 (Spring 1990): 37.

43. For an excellent historical and theoretical appraisal of the perils associated with hegemonic decline and transitions, see Robert Gilpin, *War and Change in World Politics* (New York: Cambridge University Press, 1981); and for a possible militaristic Soviet response to global decline and 'regime pessimism,' see Edward Luttwak, *The Grand Strategy of the Soviet Union* (New York: St. Martin's Press, 1983).

44. See John Borawski, ed., *Avoiding War in the Nuclear Age: Confidence-Building Measures for Crisis Stability* (Boulder, CO: Westview Press, 1986).

45. See Barry M. Blechman, ed., *Preventing Nuclear War* (Bloomington: Indiana University Press, 1985).

46. The NATO declaration is printed in full in the *New York Times*, July 7, 1990; both Soviet Foreign Minister Shevardnadze and Czech President Havel have spoken about the possibility of establishing a crisis communications system as part of the CSCE framework. See Shevardnadze's speech in *FBIS*, May 7, 1990.

47. For a good discussion of the possibilities of avoiding U.S.–Soviet mishaps at sea, see William J. Durch, "Controlling High-risk US and Soviet Naval Operations," unpublished draft, Stimson Center, Washington, D.C., 1990.

48. See Peter Almquist, "Doctrine Dialogue: An East-West First," *Arms Control Today*, 20, 3 (April 1990); pp. 21–25.

49. See R. Jeffrey Smith, "East-West Open Talks on Defense," *Washington Post*, January 17, 1990; and A. Inyakov, "Seminar on Military Doctrine," *Krasnaya Zvezda*, November 19, 1989.

50. The prospects for military intervention in the domestic politics of Eastern Europe are described in Jack Snyder, "Averting Anarchy in the New Europe," *International Security*, 14, 4 (Spring 1990): 5–41.

51. For a discussion of the evolving U.S. and Soviet positions on peacekeeping, see Kurt M. Campbell and Thomas G. Weiss, "Superpowers and UN Peacekeeping," *Harvard International Review*, 7, 2 (Winter 1990): 22–26.

52. For a review of past and present U.N. peacekeeping operations, see Alan James, *Peacekeeping in International Politics* (London: Macmillan, 1990); John MacKinlay, *The Peacekeepers* (London: Unwin-Hyman, 1989); and Indar Jit Rikhye and Karl Skkjelsbaek, eds., *The United Nations and Peacekeeping: The Lessons of 40 Years of Experience* (London: Macmillan, 1990).

53. See for instance, Peter Schweizer, "Soviet Nationalists' Stolen Firepower," *Christian Science Monitor*, July 26, 1990.

54. Judge William Webster, the director of the CIA, has been quoted as saying that he believes that "the Soviets can hold up their end of the bargain" in protecting nuclear weapons. See Bill Gertz, "Soviet Rebels Storm an A-Bomb Facility," *Washington Times*, February 20, 1990.

55. This was reported in the above Gertz article; see also Robert C. Toth, "US Worried by Nuclear Security in Unstable Soviet Empire," *Los Angeles Times*, December 15, 1989.

56. Mellisa Healy, "Nunn Asks US-Soviet 'Fail-Safe Review' to Avert an Unwarranted Missile Launch," *Los Angeles Times*, February 11, 1990.

57. See Peter Stein and Peter Feaver, "Assuring Control of Nuclear Weapons: The Evolution of Permissive Action Links," *CSIA Occasional Paper Series*, No. 2, Harvard University (1987).

58. See Scott D. Sagan, *Moving Targets* (Princeton: Princeton University Press, 1989).

59. The book most often requested was Morton H. Halperin, *Bureaucratic Politics and Foreign Policy* (Washington, D.C.: Brookings Institution, 1974).

60. Patrick E. Tyler, "Senators Propose Shift of Defense Funds to Study Environment," *Washington Post*, June 29, 1990.

61. See Xenophon, *The Persian Expedition*, trans. by Rex Warner (New York: Penguin Books, Ltd., 1949), p. 82; this passage is also discussed by Thomas C. Schelling, "Confidence in Crisis," *International Security*, 8, 4 (Spring 1984): 55–66.

62. Walter Pincus, "Military-to-Military Talks on Force Cuts Suggested," *Washington Post*, July 25, 1988.

63. See Paul G. Skowronek, "US-Soviet Military Liaison in Germany Since 1947," unpublished Ph.D. thesis, Department of History, University of Colorado, 1976.

64. See "TU-160: Supersamoliot," *Krasnaya Zvezda*, June 3, 1990; and also Michael R. Gordon, "US Says Soviets Will Field Fewer of Its Latest Bombers," *New York Times*, June 5, 1990.

65. See "Clipping Angels' Goodwill," *Washington Post*, August 7, 1990.

PART SEVEN

FINDINGS AND RECOMMENDATIONS

Alexander L. George

This concluding part of the study draws together the major findings and implications of our research. As I stated in Chapter 2, the objectives of the study were to develop a better understanding of the types of inadvertent war and paths leading to it, to assess and refine the provisional theory of crisis management, and to formulate generic knowledge of the problems policy makers are liable to encounter in managing crises that have an escalation potential. Although the focus of the study has been on the possibility of inadvertent war between the United States and the Soviet Union, most of our findings and recommendations are relevant more broadly to the task of avoiding inadvertent wars between other states as well. We have attempted to formulate our findings in sufficiently general terms so that their applicability to other conflicts will be evident.

TYPES OF INADVERTENT WAR

In my effort to develop an analytical typology of different kinds of inadvertent war, I defined inadvertent war simply as a war neither side wanted or expected at the outset of the crisis. This definition is admittedly loose and not entirely free of ambiguity. It is intended to serve as a starting point for a detailed empirical analysis of historical cases that was designed to identify various pathways and processes that can lead to inadvertent war. Some scholars have suggested that all inadvertent wars are essentially alike and that no further differentiation among them is either necessary or useful. My own view is that even the imperfect typology of inadvertent wars I shall present here should be useful both for further analysis of this phenomenon and for policy making.

Several recent studies focused solely on different paths to nuclear war; the present study deals more broadly with the onset of conventional wars as well as possible nuclear conflicts. Also, the earlier studies did not clearly distinguish inadvertent war from other types of war. For example, *Hawks, Doves, & Owls* identified five different "general paths" to nuclear war. While two of them—

preemption and escalation of a conventional war—are consistent with my concept of inadvertent war, the distinctive nature and phenomenology of this type of war were not discussed in detail.[1] In another study, Richard Ned Lebow identified three "causal sequences" to nuclear war: preemption, loss of control, and miscalculated escalation.[2] Lebow refers to all of these as "undesired" wars, but his discussion does not clearly distinguish between accidental and inadvertent wars, both of which qualify as undesired wars. Wars that result from loss of control can be either accidental or inadvertent in nature.

I agree with Lebow's emphasis on the importance of "miscalculated escalation" as a causal factor in many undesired or inadvertent wars. There are, of course, many other causal factors as well, and these, too, could be identified; but it would be difficult to construct a useful typology of inadvertent wars based on factors that cause them, for a variety and multiplicity of causal factors are often at work in any path to war. More useful is the development of a typology that focuses on the character of decisions to initiate such wars—that is, the substantive reason why responsible central decision makers at some point during a crisis deliberately choose to initiate war. Even this task encounters difficulties; one of them is that elements of several rationales may combine to influence members of a policy-making group to initiate war. Nonetheless, it is useful for purposes of analysis to distinguish different rationales.

I have identified four substantive rationales for such decisions, and there may be additional ones that remain to be specified. Those I identify are (1) the "no acceptable alternative to war" rationale; (2) the preemptive war rationale; (3) the intracrisis preventive war rationale; and (4) the miscalculated *fait accompli* rationale. I will attempt to say just enough to characterize and illustrate each of these types before turning to the more interesting discussion of paths to inadvertent war.

1. The "No Acceptable Alternative to War" Rationale

This type of inadvertent war occurs frequently in history. At some point during the development of a crisis, top-level political authority on one side or the other arrives at the judgment that there is now no acceptable alternative to initiating war (or sharply escalating a low-level military engagement). In other words, initiation of war or major escalation of a small conflict is now seen as a rational choice, however reluctantly it may be undertaken.

One or another variant of this war-initiating rationale was evident in several of the cases presented in Part Two. Toward the end of the long crisis that eventuated in the Crimean War, British leaders decided on war with Turkey, feeling that a victory was needed to pacify an aroused public opinion and believing that it was necessary to restore the image of British naval superiority. In 1967, after miscalculating the impact of his escalation of the crisis, Gamal Abdel Nasser came to realize and to accept the fact that his repeated provocations of Israel would result in a war that he had not wanted or expected at the outset. Nasser's actions forced Israeli leaders to conclude, contrary to beliefs they had held early in the crisis, that they were left with no acceptable alternative to initiating war.

Sadat's decision to initiate war against Israel in 1973 reflected a judgment on his part that the unwillingness of either of the superpowers to use diplomatic avenues to address Egypt's grievances in the long-simmering Arab-Israeli conflict allowed him no alternative but to initiate war in the hope of catalyzing a change for the better.

The judgment that there is no acceptable alternative to war may not be fully justified or shared by all members of the policy-making group in each and every case, although in most of these cases it appears to have been a compelling belief that would have been difficult for top-level leaders to avoid. As Janice Gross Stein emphasized, domestic and strategic weakness can create psychological and political pressures on hard-pressed leaders that encourage them to believe they have no acceptable alternative to initiating or provoking war.

It is all the easier for leaders to persuade themselves of this when they are optimistic as to the chances of military success. In the Crimean case, as Richard Smoke has shown, the British were overly optimistic regarding the prospect of achieving the quick victory they initially expected. In the 1967 case, there is some evidence to indicate that as Nasser drifted toward war, he engaged in a certain amount of wishful thinking, encouraged by some dubious military estimates into believing he could win the war even though the Israelis would initiate it. As for the Israelis, their leaders were confident that they could win the war that Nasser forced upon them. In 1973, Sadat, it appeared, believed that Egypt and its allies would do well enough militarily to achieve his political objectives. Although, in fact, his expectations of military success proved to be excessively optimistic, the war did help alleviate the humiliation Egypt experienced in the 1967 war and did catalyze a change in diplomatic alignments that eventually led to the return of the Sinai to Egypt as a result of the Camp David Accord.

But leaders can adopt this rationale for initiating war even when they are quite sober or even somewhat pessimistic regarding the prospect of success. The Japanese decision to initiate war against the United States in 1941 is a case in point. The judgment that Washington had left Japan no acceptable alternative played an important role in the Japanese decision for war. Squeezed by Washington's effective oil embargo and faced by the U.S. demand for a diplomatic settlement that would require Japan to give up its aspirations for a sphere of influence in Asia, Japanese leaders experienced a sense of desperation. Backed into a corner and left with no line of honorable retreat, they perceived war as the only remaining alternative.

Still another variant of this type of inadvertent war has been recognized by strategic analysts. A state such as Israel cannot afford to remain in a state of mobilization for a prolonged period of time during a crisis because of the drain on its economy; at the same time, it cannot demobilize during an unresolved crisis for fear of undercutting its deterrence posture and its capacity for defense. This constraint can add to the pressure for initiating war when an acceptable diplomatic resolution of the dispute is not available within a reasonably short period of time.

2. The Preemptive War Rationale

This type of inadvertent war is a special, extreme variant of the "no alternative" case. For this reason and because so much concern has been expressed that a U.S.-Soviet nuclear war might occur in this fashion, I have decided to treat it as a distinct type of inadvertent war. Later I shall note that the path to preemptive war has distinctive elements that set it apart from the "no alternative" cases.

Of the five cases of inadvertent war discussed in Part Two, only World War I contains elements of this particular rationale for initiating war. (As Janice Gross Stein demonstrates, Israeli initiation of war during the tense crisis of 1967 resembles but does not really meet the exacting definition of preemptive war.) In 1914, Russian leaders, believing war to have become highly probable if not inevitable, felt that military considerations required them to initiate mobilization against Germany. In turn, the German decision to launch military operations against France and Russia was taken in the belief that Russian mobilization made a continental war inevitable and that it was imperative for Germany to seize the initiative, given the strategic assumption of its military leaders that Germany's chances for success in a two-front war rested on taking the offensive against France.

The preemption scenario has figured prominently in analyses of how nuclear war between the United States and the Soviet Union could come about. There is substantial agreement among analysts that a decision to initiate a war could be taken—however reluctantly—if during an escalating crisis or conventional war, political leaders either in Washington or Moscow came to hold three beliefs, whether or not these beliefs correctly reflected the situation. These three beliefs are: (1) a belief that the crisis has gotten out of control and that crisis management has broken down and cannot be restored; (2) a belief that war has become virtually inevitable and is imminent, making it urgent to quickly decide whether to accept a first strike by the opponent or to launch such a strike oneself; and (3) a belief that however damaging such a war would be, there is a premium on attacking first.[3]

So far as we know, and unlike the 1914 case, no U.S.-Soviet crisis has developed to a point at which all of these three beliefs entered into the consciousness of top decision makers. However, several of these beliefs did begin to emerge in President Kennedy's mind during the course of the Cuban Missile Crisis. As I noted in the analysis of this case in Chapter 11, the crisis reached its most dangerous point on Saturday, October 27. The president feared that the situation was getting out of hand, that his efforts at managing the crisis to avoid resort to military options were jeopardized by untoward developments, and that he might soon be confronted by irresistible pressure to authorize air strikes against missile sites in Cuba, which in turn might trigger a Soviet military response. Thus, the president was moving toward, although he had not as yet fully subscribed to, the first and second beliefs noted above. Kennedy's apprehension led him to decide to give something approximating an ultimatum to Khrushchev, coupled with the offer of a quid pro quo, in the hope of achieving a quick, mutually acceptable termination of the crisis.

I have emphasized that the three beliefs that could lead to a decision to launch a preemptive war need not be a correct evaluation of the situation confronting decision makers in the crisis. Of critical importance, therefore, is timely, reliable intelligence during the course of a tense and escalating crisis. The considerable difficulty of obtaining and making proper use of such intelligence is likely to be severely aggravated, if not altogether compromised, by psychological phenomena that can distort information processing and judgment in a highly stressful situation of this kind.[4]

3. The Intracrisis Preventive War Rationale

In this scenario, the decision to initiate war emerges from a judgment that the adversary's behavior in the crisis provides an opportunity and perhaps a useful cloak of legitimacy for launching what is in effect (although not necessarily acknowledged as such) a preventive war against an implacable opponent. Important in arriving at this judgment is the belief that even if the present crisis is resolved satisfactorily, the opponent will not only continue to threaten one's vital interests in the future but will do so more effectively than at the present time. Such a judgment may be supported by intelligence estimates forecasting that the enemy will become much stronger militarily in the future.

There is some evidence, cited by historians who place considerable blame on Germany for starting World War I, that some German leaders had for several years perceived a long-range threat in the growing Russian military power and that this sober expectation may have played a role in their preference for war during the 1914 crisis. And in the Pearl Harbor case, too, intracrisis preventive war reasoning was entertained by some Japanese military leaders who felt that conflict with the United States was inevitable in the long run and that it would be better to go to war before U.S. and British military capabilities became even greater.[5] In both the 1914 and Pearl Harbor cases, preventive war thinking was not the only motive for initiating war.

Establishing whether war was initiated on the basis of an intracrisis preventive war rationale is not always an easy task and requires careful analysis.[6] In her case study of the 1967 Arab-Israeli War, Janice Gross Stein considers, but rejects, the possibility that the Israeli decision to initiate war is an example of what we have referred to here as an intracrisis preventive war.

A preventive war motivation can also emerge in a crisis under a different set of circumstances. The temporarily stronger side may perceive prolongation of the crisis as an opportunity for the adversary to mobilize more of its own military potential and to secure the assistance of allies or world opinion. An expectation that the balance of military capabilities or diplomatic forces will shift decisively in favor of its weaker opponent if the crisis is prolonged may give the temporarily stronger side an incentive to initiate war before this can occur. A decision for war under these circumstances is more likely if it seems impossible or highly improbable that a favorable diplomatic settlement can be achieved before the balance shifts. A possible example of this kind of reasoning is Frederick the Great's decision to initiate the Seven Years War before a hostile coalition could be formed.[7]

4. The Miscalculated *Fait Accompli* Rationale

As I pointed out in the chapter on "Strategies for Crisis Management," the *fait accompli* strategy is resorted to in the expectation that it will achieve a desired change in the status quo in a quick, decisive way that will avoid war with an adversary. *Fait accompli* efforts, however, do not always succeed. The rationale for such an attempt may rest on a miscalculation of the adversary's probable response or of one's own ability to implement the *fait accompli* quickly and decisively; the result may be a war that the instigator of the *fait accompli* effort did not want or expect and that was forced on the adversary.

Several examples of this type of inadvertent war come to mind. As Jack S. Levy noted in his account of World War I, Austria-Hungary might possibly have succeeded in its military action against Serbia without Russian intervention had it acted more quickly and decisively, particularly if its territorial annexations were limited. The North Korean attack on South Korea in late June 1950 is often cited as an example of a *fait accompli* attempt that went awry because, quite unexpectedly, the United States reversed its earlier policy and quickly came to the assistance of the South Koreans. Similarly, the Argentine invasion of the Falklands rested on a *fait accompli* rationale that proved to rest on a miscalculation of the British response. The Argentine leaders neither wanted nor expected the war that followed.

5. Other Possibilities

It is possible that additional research will identify variants of inadvertent war in addition to the four mentioned above. One such possibility is that a state that is strongly motivated to bring about a favorable change in the status quo may assume that it will be able to do so peacefully through crisis diplomacy that relies on blackmail and coercive threats rather than military force. At the outset of the crisis, such a state neither wants nor expects a war, but the unexpected failure of its effort to pressure the opponent into accepting its demands confronts it with the choice between accepting the political and diplomatic costs of having its bluff successfully called or initiating war. Failures of the blackmail and coercive diplomacy strategies, as described in Chapter 16, create a policy dilemma that may be resolved by a decision to initiate war. Whether this scenario should be regarded as an additional type of inadvertent war or be accommodated as a variant of the "no acceptable alternative to war" rationale is unclear and perhaps less important than recognizing, as I did in Chapter 16, the risks and pitfalls of these two strategies.

PATHS TO INADVERTENT WAR

How and why, in a crisis, are the initial preference for avoiding war and the expectation that it will not occur altered so that inadvertent war results? What causal paths and developments lead to a change in these initial beliefs and preferences and lead one side to initiate or trigger a war?

We expect the paths to war to be different for each of the four types of inadvertent war. In addition, even for a particular type of inadvertent war, somewhat different paths to it are likely in different cases. Because the causal dynamics leading to inadvertent war can be so complex and variable, it will not be possible to arrive at simple generalizations as to how inadvertent wars occur. Let us take up in turn each of these four types and see what can be said as to the sequences that precede it.

As for the abortive *fait accompli*, at first glance it seems that the path to this type of inadvertent war should be relatively straightforward and perhaps simpler than the paths to the other three types. Further reflection, however, suggests this is likely to be the case only when the defender quickly mobilizes military resistance against the *fait accompli* effort. But there can be intervening developments. Implementation of a *fait accompli* may take longer than the challenger expected. Or for various reasons, the defender may not react immediately with military force; it may take him some time to decide whether and how to oppose the *fait accompli* or, as in the case of the British in the Falkland Islands case, to prepare and carry out a military response. It is also possible that the defender—again as in the case of the British—will first resort to coercive diplomacy to persuade the challenger to pull back before initiating a military response.

In several variants of this scenario, time will be available before war breaks out, and this will provide an opportunity to explore a peaceful resolution. Thus, a flawed *fait accompli* attempt does not necessarily lead to war. The two sides, or intermediaries on their behalf, may enter into negotiations to prevent it. However, the challenger may be unwilling or unable for political reasons to pull back; even the prospect of an unexpected war may not persuade him to do so, and his reluctance will be greater when he is relatively confident regarding the prospect of military success, although such confidence may not be justified and may be based on faulty intelligence or wishful thinking.

Finally, contextual factors may affect the emergence, development, and outcome of a *fait accompli* effort. A decision to try it may be made before, during, or after a diplomatic crisis. The consideration given to deciding whether to undertake a *fait accompli* may be time-compressed or stretched out over a considerable period of time. When the time to the decision is prolonged, there may be distinct opportunities for resolving the dispute peacefully before a *fait accompli* is attempted. This was certainly the case in the prolonged dispute over the Falklands between Britain and Argentina before the latter resorted to an invasion of the islands. There was time, too, for diplomatic efforts to settle the crisis before Iraq overran Kuwait in 1990, but they proved to be ineffectual. In other cases—for example, the North Korean effort to quickly overrun South Korea in June 1950—although ample time and considerable warning of a possible attack may be available, the possibilities for heading off a *fait accompli* can be meager because the differences between the two sides are fundamental and not easily bridged. In such cases, perhaps only a strong, credible deterrence effort can dissuade the challenger from attempting a *fait accompli*.

Another contextual factor can influence the path toward this type of inadvertent war. The challenger's discontent with the situation that prompts him to consider resort to the *fait accompli* strategy may be long-standing or may be a relatively recent development. His motivation to undertake the action may increase gradually over time or suddenly. He may be sensitive—as were the Argentine leaders—to mounting domestic pressures and be motivated to act out of political weakness.

Finally, we need to recognize that on occasion, resort to a *fait accompli* action may be based on incentives that closely resemble the rationale of the "no acceptable alternative to war" type of inadvertent war.

Turning to the "no alternatives" type, I noted earlier that there are quite a few variants that follow different paths to this type of inadvertent war. At the same time, however, it is difficult to provide a comprehensive listing of the many different events and developments in a crisis that can lead to this rationale for war. One or both sides may come to realize that the disagreement between them is more fundamental than they realized at first or that to avoid war will require greater concessions than they expected or are willing to make. One or the other side may escalate its objectives and increase its demands during the crisis, pushing the other side into the "no alternative" judgment. One or both sides, misreading the other side's perspective and the constraints under which it is operating, may engage in a miscalculated escalation of the crisis that triggers an unexpectedly strong response, either of war or of counterescalation. Other misperceptions and miscalculations may result in missed opportunities to resolve the dispute and further harden the position of the two sides. Signaling and communication between the two sides in the interest of avoiding war may lack clarity, consistency, credibility, or timeliness. Any of these developments or some combination of them may push one side to the view that no acceptable alternative to initiating war remains.

Of course, when incentives to avoid war are very strong on both sides and opportunities for doing so arise, skill in meeting the requirements of crisis management becomes the critical variable. The political and operational requirements for managing crises are particularly salient in such confrontations. Limiting one's objective to bare essentials and not escalating one's objectives during the course of the crisis may be essential if drifting into this type of inadvertent war is to be avoided. Also likely to be of critical importance are some of the operational requirements of crisis management: maintaining top-level political control over all diplomatic and military moves; integrating political and military actions into a coherent strategy; maintaining informed control over one's military forces by means of appropriate rules of engagement; slowing down the momentum of crisis developments to permit unhurried policy making and diplomatic communication with the other side; and last, but not least, leaving the opponent a way out of the crisis compatible with his basic interests so that he will not draw the conclusion that there is no acceptable alternative to initiating war.

On the other hand, when incentives to avoid a war are relatively weak on both sides, and when there are few opportunities for crisis management and these are neglected or misused, even reasonably adequate skills and capabilities for crisis management may not suffice to halt the drift to this type of inadvertent war.

As I observed earlier, preemptive war is a special, extreme variant of the type of inadvertent war that results from the "no alternative" rationale. Paths to preemptive war, too, can vary greatly in ways that resemble some of those associated with the "no alternative" case. However, distinctive in the path to preemption and what sets it apart from other "no alternative" cases is that at some point in the crisis, both sides have come so close to the brink that at least one side believes with near certainty—correctly or otherwise—that its adversary is taking steps to initiate war and, for that reason, decides to seize the initiative itself. Of course, preemptive scenarios can vary in other ways depending on contextual aspects of the crisis.

A decision to initiate a preventive war during a crisis could occur in a variety of scenarios. The path to such a war, too, is highly context-dependent. The idea of initiating a preventive war may come to the fore only during the course of the crisis, perhaps as a result of a shift in the power alignment within the state, which enables those who have favored a preventive war for some time finally to have their way. Another path to this type of war could be the realization by one side during the course of the crisis that in the future, the adversary will become much stronger or much more hostile. New intelligence may emerge regarding the adversary's growing capabilities and plans for further strengthening his forces, perhaps involving the development of a nuclear capability.

GENERIC PROBLEMS OF CRISIS MANAGEMENT

Another objective of the study was to identify various significant threats to crisis management experienced in the past, either those that contributed to the outbreak of war or those that, although present in a crisis and potentially troublesome, did not lead to war. Specific contributing factors and threats of this kind fall into a number of more general classes, and it is in this sense that I regard them as generic problems. Instances of these generic problems were described in the individual case studies. In the interest of brevity, the following discussion will not repeat specific details of triggers to escalation and threats to crisis management that were reported earlier in the study.

Problems of Strategy

The selection of an inappropriate strategy and inept implementation of strategy are among the major generic problems of crisis management. Strategies can be ineffectual or too risky for various reasons; implementation may be flawed in a number of different ways. Chapter 16 identified the particular vulnerabilities and risks to which each strategy is prone as well as its particular attractions and the conditions that, if present, might make it a viable choice. Quite obviously, much depends on the ability of policy makers to select a strategy that is appropriate to the character of the crisis, as well as that can be discerned, and one that offers a good chance of achieving crisis objectives without risking escalation to war.

Some strategies are much riskier than others. Of the five offensive strategies, least risky are the limited probe and controlled pressure initiatives. These two strategies recommend themselves as appropriately cautious choices in situations in which the defender has either clearly or ambiguously committed himself to defend a particular position; hence, if he is flagrantly challenged, the risk of war would be high. These two strategies give the challenger a good opportunity to monitor and control the risks. In contrast, the blackmail and *fait accompli* strategies are based, respectively, on the assumption that the defender will be too intimidated or insufficiently motivated to resist or that he will not respond with military action because he has made no prior commitment. If these assumptions prove to be incorrect, war may quickly follow. Unlike the limited probe and controlled pressure, blackmail and *fait accompli* strategies allow little opportunity to monitor and control their risks once either of these strategies is set into motion. The fifth offensive strategy, slow attrition, may entail low risks for a certain period of time, but, if attrition threatens to bleed the defender beyond a certain point, it may motivate him to undertake a major escalation. If the defender only threatens to do so, as did Moscow in its 1969 crisis with China, then the challenger has an opportunity to call off the attrition effort.

Turning to the seven defensive strategies, the least risky in terms of war, at least at the outset of a crisis, are the following: tit-for-tat, the test of capabilities, drawing a line, conveying commitment and resolve to avoid miscalculation, and time-buying proposals to explore negotiation. More immediately and more severely risky are the strategies of coercive diplomacy and limited escalation. The latter strategy works only when accompanied by effective deterrence of counterescalation by the opponent; when the strategy fails, as in several of the crises we studied (World War I, the Suez Crisis of 1956, and the Arab-Israel conflicts of 1967 and 1970), the result is a "miscalculated escalation" that may lead directly or eventually to war.

Coercive diplomacy is a particularly beguiling strategy for strong powers that suffer an encroachment from a weaker state because it seems to promise success without bloodshed or much expenditure of resources. Those who employ this strategy, however, often fail to consider whether the weaker opponent's strong motivation will compensate for its inferior capabilities. Coercive diplomacy is also a highly problematic strategy when one side uses it, as the Reagan administration did against Nicaragua, in conjunction with stringent demands that strengthen the opponent's motivation to resist. Coercive diplomacy was also the strategy the United States, backed by the U.N. Security Council, unsuccessfully employed to persuade Iraq to get out of Kuwait.

Thus far, the discussion has focused on the risk of war associated with different strategies. Of course, the failure of a strategy—even the risky blackmail and coercive diplomacy strategies—need not result in war, although generally failure results in other costs. We should also note the possibility that lower-risk strategies may bend so far to minimize the likelihood of escalation that they prove to be ineffective. There may be times, too, when a low-risk strategy will be interpreted as betraying weakness or irresolution by the adversary, who may then be encouraged to act in a bolder fashion than it otherwise would have.

Strategies also vary in difficulty of implementation. A strategy that looks good on paper may founder because of inept implementation. Strategies are seldom adequately assessed from this standpoint. All too often, the importance of implementation is recognized merely by noting that "skill" in carrying it out is necessary.[8] Implementation may suffer because, as in the Soviet effort to achieve surprise for the deployment of missiles into Cuba, organizational routines create unnecessary vulnerabilities that benefit the adversary. Similarly, as Levy noted, the Austro-Hungarian effort to achieve a *fait accompli* against Serbia failed in part because of cumbersome mobilization routines that required twelve to sixteen days before a military invasion could be undertaken. There is also the possibility that fragmented political authority and domestic political constraints may rob a strategy of consistent and effective implementation. Strategies may also fail when they depend on overly subtle signaling and require unusually timely and reliable communication between the adversaries.

Problems of Intelligence

The failure of intelligence to provide timely, reliable information about the onset of a crisis and its development, and the failure of policy makers to make use of available intelligence are among the major generic problems that can undermine efforts at crisis avoidance and crisis management. Impediments to good crisis intelligence, as Stan A. Taylor and Theodore J. Ralston noted, arise from communication problems between intelligence analysts and policy makers, from compartmentation of specialized intelligence in different parts of the intelligence community, from bureaucratic problems, and from various psychological and ideological-political impediments to processing intelligence and gaining a hearing for its findings.

The chronic problem of misperception and miscalculation deserves special emphasis. The maxim that "we must understand the other side's point of view," as Richard Smoke recalls in his study of the Crimean War, was already a cliché in 1852. Despite their awareness of this requirement for crisis management, intelligence analysts and policy makers frequently fail to understand the perspective and mind-set through which the adversary views the crisis situation. When one holds a flawed image of the opponent, it can lead to serious errors in estimating his intentions and in understanding how he views what is at stake, how he evaluates the threat to his interests, how he interprets the actions directed toward him, and how he evaluates the risks and possible gains of strategic and tactical options at his disposal. Striking examples of such flaws and their consequences were presented in our case studies of the Crimean War, World War I, the Suez Crisis of 1956, the Arab-Israeli conflicts, and the Cuban Missile Crisis; they have also occurred in other crises (such as the Japanese attack on Pearl Harbor and the Falklands Islands Crisis) that were not examined in this study. Specialized knowledge of the perspective and mind-set of an opponent is also often critical in determining whether efforts to signal and communicate with him are likely to be effective.

Intelligence specialists and political analysts who do have better insight into the mind-set and perspective of the opponent often are not brought into the deliberations of the top-level policy-making group. Consider the striking contrast between the important role played by Soviet expert Llewellyn Thompson, who participated in the deliberations of President Kennedy's advisory group in the Cuban Missile Crisis and helped to interpret Khrushchev's thinking, and the failure of top U.S. policy makers in November 1950 to grant a proper hearing to the State Department experts on China who warned that the threat of large-scale military operations by Chinese Communist forces should be taken seriously and urged that appropriate changes in U.S. policy should be undertaken.

Problems of Maintaining Informed Use of and Control over Military Forces

In any war-threatening crisis, central decision makers must know how to use military forces to support diplomatic efforts to achieve their objectives without, however, allowing military alerts, movements, and actions to contribute to unwanted escalation of the confrontation. Maintaining informed use and control over one's military forces is one of the most sensitive and difficult problems of crisis management.[9]

As I pointed out in Chapter 4, tension often emerges during a crisis between military doctrine and logic and the requirements of diplomacy. Military leaders understandably regard it as their highest priority and most urgent task when a crisis erupts to get ready to fight if war comes. On the other hand, when political leaders do not want the crisis to escalate to war, they consider it their most important task to explore all possibilities for avoiding war. They are, and should be, concerned over the possibility that some of the alert and readiness measures military logic dictates may send overly strong and unintended signals that provoke escalatory responses by the opponent. The right balance must somehow be struck between the imperatives of military logic and the logic of diplomacy. To be sure, if civilian leaders wish to use coercive threats as an instrument of their bargaining strategy, they may then authorize mobilization and deployments of military forces that deliberately threaten offensive operations. In such cases, military logic and the logic of coercive diplomacy move closer together, but the task of informed control over military forces in order to avoid unwanted escalation remains.

The need to make informed use and control of one's military forces in a war-threatening crisis makes special demands on top-level political authorities that they may not be equipped to meet. Civilian leaders do not ordinarily understand the complexities of military planning and operations or fully appreciate the possible consequences of imposing constraints on the alerting and movement of military forces. As is often noted, presidential-level intervention in matters of military strategy and tactics, however necessary and well-intentioned, raises the danger of micro-management of crises and adds to the dilemmas of crisis management.

On the other hand, civilian leaders may proceed to authorize military activities without fully comprehending the scope and significance of such operations or how such activities will be perceived by the opponent. Under these circumstances, informed control of one's military forces is lacking and may raise unanticipated threats to crisis management.

The proper military component of crisis management strategy will vary from case to case. Some aspects of a strategy for crisis management can easily incorporate standard military practices governing the management of combat forces and their missions. Other aspects of the strategy, however, must be tailored to the special demands of a particular crisis situation. Rules of engagement (ROEs) are the vehicle by means of which civilian leaders stipulate what various combat units are authorized to do under various conditions. In Chapter 19 Scott D. Sagan discussed the modalities of ROEs and the trade-offs that arise when decision makers must instruct combat units as to how they are to determine whether an occasion requires self-defense and what responses are permissible.

It is important to recognize that the ability of top-level political authorities to maintain informed control over the moves and actions of their military forces (the first of the operational requirements of crisis management) is sometimes jeopardized by the difficulty of keeping track of the large number and complexity of standing orders and ROEs that may come into effect at the onset of a crisis and as it intensifies. Therefore, timely arrangements and procedures must be in place to enable top political authorities to understand the implications of different ROEs and alerts for the task of crisis management.

All this is to warn that there are often severe limits on the possibility of transforming military force and threats of force into a highly refined, exquisitely discriminating instrument of diplomacy and crisis bargaining. Efforts to impose the operational requirements of crisis management on the management of military forces will often exacerbate the latent tension between competing diplomatic and military considerations. It is good to recognize that crisis management strategies often require novel concepts of military planning, military operations, and control of forces that may strain the experience, imagination, and patience of military professionals and civilians alike. There is clearly a critical need for developing concepts and planning guides that will better integrate political and military desiderata in strategies for crisis management.

Problems of Crisis Bargaining

Unless a confrontation is immediately terminated or quickly leads to war, a contest in crisis bargaining will take place. Crisis bargaining strategies vary depending on the mixture of three components of bargaining—persuasion, accommodative gestures and offers, coercive actions and threats—and the sequence in which these elements of bargaining are employed. The usefulness of conceptualizing crisis bargaining strategy in these terms was noted in our discussion of the Cuban Missile Crisis.

Alternative bargaining strategies are possible and should be considered by policy makers. I reject the rather widely held assumption that there is but one optimal bargaining strategy that is appropriate in all, or nearly all, crises. Many advocates of this view believe that one should always initiate bargaining by making coercive threats of some kind in order to convey resolution and defer offers of accommodation, if indeed any concessions are to be made, for a later stage of the crisis. My own view is that such a bargaining strategy is likely to be appropriate only under a special set of conditions that, for example, seems to have been present in the Cuban Missile Crisis. An optimal or appropriate strategy for crisis bargaining is also likely to vary depending on the psychological makeup of the opponent and the political constraints under which he operates.

Conveying resolution at the outset, by deeds as well as by words, may be necessary in some situations to forestall a possibly dangerous miscalculation by the opponent that he is dealing with a weak or irresolute adversary. Initial emphasis on coercive threats may also be appropriate in order to narrow the parameters for a bargained compromise; in other words, coercive threats, if credible, may provide bargaining leverage that will reduce the scope of concessions one will have to make to achieve an agreement and, at the same time, persuade the opponent to consider the need for concessions of his own.

In some situations and with some adversaries, however, initiating crisis bargaining by relying exclusively on coercive threats may backfire. If such threats lead the opponent to conclude that the demands made on him are rigid and nonnegotiable, he may decide that a mutually acceptable agreement to resolve the crisis is impossible and feel that he must either resort to coercive threats of his own or initiate military action. If both sides rely on naked, unqualified coercive bargaining strategies, the crisis can quickly assume the characteristics of the game of chicken, with all of the risks that entails.

In many situations, it may be advantageous to find ways early in the crisis of conveying a contingent willingness to consider accommodation to the more fundamental and legitimate interests of the adversary. A signal of this kind can be coupled with coercive pressure, of course, but willingness to listen to and discuss the merits of the adversary's case should also be conveyed.

I believe that persuasion should be an important component of one's bargaining strategy and that serious, nonpropagandistic efforts to explain and justify the position one takes in the crisis should come quite early in the bargaining. Persuasion of this kind should also include appropriate assurances regarding one's limited objectives. If the dialogue is conducted in a reasoned fashion by both sides, mutual efforts at persuasion may contribute to managing the crisis and finding a mutually acceptable solution.

It is difficult at this stage of research in crisis bargaining to go much further in identifying the conditions under which alternative bargaining strategies are likely to be most appropriate. Certainly the image one has of the opponent—how well one understands his general mind-set and perspectives, the values and beliefs with which he operates, the constraints on his decision making, and so forth—helps to form a judgment as to how the adversary views the crisis situation and how he can be influenced in the direction of an acceptable settlement. I need not belabor this point, as our discussion of intelligence problems called attention to the importance of being able to empathize with the adversary's way of thinking, perceiving, and calculating. Here I need add only that it is equally important to be aware of how one is viewed by the adversary. There is often a substantial difference between one's self-image and the image of oneself held by the opponent. Divergences of this kind can contribute greatly to serious miscommunication, misperception, and miscalculation.

An important contribution to the study of crisis management is the concept of "crisis bargaining codes" developed and illustrated in the chapter by J. Philip Rogers. As he indicates, a policy maker's approach to bargaining in a crisis is strongly influenced not only by the image he has of the opponent but also by his own general beliefs about optimal bargaining strategy and the dynamics of escalation. These beliefs have a significant influence on a policy maker's diagnosis of a crisis situation and his evaluation of options. Since such beliefs often take the form of assumptions that are not articulated, and since different members of a policy-making group often have different crisis bargaining codes, it may be useful in policy discussions to bring these assumptions out into the open and examine them before deciding what option to adopt.

Several other problems associated with crisis bargaining deserve mention. I have found that a serious tension exists between applying the strongest form of coercive diplomacy—namely, the variant of it that resembles an ultimatum—and some of the important operational requirements of crisis management. This tension was discussed in the chapter on strategies for crisis management and was illustrated in the chapter on the Cuban Missile Crisis.

When the structure of the crisis situation provides one side with certain advantages for crisis bargaining—as, for example, the advantage Soviet leaders enjoyed in the various Berlin crises because West Berlin was geographically isolated within East Germany—the temptation to ruthlessly exploit that advantage can lead to behavior that increases the risk of war. In 1948, Joseph Stalin seized the opportunity to impose a blockade of ground access to West Berlin, a move that did raise the possibility of a military response by the Western powers. Fortunately, when the Allied airlift showed signs of defeating his blockade, Stalin resisted the temptation to seriously interfere with it lest that lead to an escalation of the crisis. From the failure of Stalin's blockade in 1948–1949, his successor, Nikita Khrushchev, may have drawn the lesson that to limit himself to the threat of another blockade in 1958–1959 and in 1961 was safer than reimposing one and that such a threat might provide sufficient bargaining leverage for his purposes.

Success often whets the appetite. When one side gains a favorable position during a crisis, it may experience a temptation to ruthlessly exploit its advantage to secure even more important gains. To do so, however, can place the adversary in the difficult position of having to either back down or initiate force. The United States succumbed to just such a tempting opportunity after North Korean forces were routed in 1950, when it escalated its objective to liquidating the communist regime in North Korea and unifying the two Koreas by force of arms—a miscalculated escalation that brought the People's Republic of China into the war. A similar miscalculated escalation after achieving a modest success characterized Nasser's behavior in the 1967 crisis with Israel.

A number of analysts have spoken of a "basic rule of prudence," or tacit norm, that served to regulate and put a lid on crises involving the United States and the Soviet Union during the Cold War. The "rule" is, simply, that neither side should initiate the use of force against the military forces of the other superpower. The rationale for this rule is that any kind of shooting war between the two superpowers should be avoided, as it would raise the risk of escalation to nuclear war. But there is an important corollary to this basic rule of prudence that has not always been clearly recognized and fully honored. The corollary is that in order to avoid a shooting war, each superpower must resist the temptation to seize opportunities during a crisis to inflict too severe a defeat on the other side, a development that would place the disadvantaged superpower in the difficult position of having either to back down or consider the initiation of force in order to avoid a serious setback.[10]

Problems of Stress, Fatigue, Sleep Deprivation, and Medications

Another generic problem that poses severe threats to crisis management is the serious impairment of the psychological and physical well-being of officials who are involved in the crisis. Although such impairment may not occur frequently, awareness and alertness to this possibility are nonetheless necessary, particularly as it is often difficult to identify and to deal with. That crisis-induced stress and fatigue might activate latent psychological vulnerabilities or even borderline psychopathological tendencies in an individual are matters of legitimate and grave concern. These possibilities were discussed in Dr. Jerrold M. Post's chapter.[11]

Enough is known about the possible effects of crisis-induced stress, emotional and physical fatigue, sleep deprivation, the side effects of standard medications, and drug abuse to require that these sources of threat to crisis management should not be ignored. In addition, medical problems such as heart disease, hypertension, strokes, surgery, and cancer are known at times to produce deficits in the afflicted individual's performance of various cognitive functions—such as concentration, span of attention, memory, inventiveness, and deductive and inductive reasoning. It is important to recognize that illness can heighten one's vulnerability to crisis-induced stress. And more attention should be given to the very real possibility that the side effects of many medications can contribute to the impairment of cognitive functioning, perhaps more so when the individual is subjected to acute stress.

It is surely of critical importance for any policy-making group to find ways of identifying temporarily disabled officials and removing them from a primary decision-making role. Although this is an extremely sensitive matter, responsibility for addressing it cannot be avoided.

Pronounced sleep deprivation and disruption of an individual's circadian rhythms (that is the "biological clock") can also result in impaired cognitive functioning. This problem can also arise when sleep cycles are in conflict with a human being's natural circadian system; the results may be insomnia, emotional disturbance, and impaired information processing and judgment. (There has been speculation that pronounced sleep deprivation of key individuals may have contributed to the faulty decision-making process that led to the Challenger accident.)

After a day or two of sleep deprivation, use of stimulant medication, such as amphetamines, has been shown to reverse most of the documented performance impairment. This medication might be useful in a short-term situation, but the harmful potential of prolonged use of stimulants by crisis decision makers and other key personnel in the chain of command would be especially dangerous in the nuclear era, for it risks inducing a paranoid state of mind accompanied by greatly heightened impulsiveness and poor judgment.

The medical support system available to top policy makers in the past has functioned erratically and, at times, inadequately.[12] This system should be periodically reviewed and upgraded as necessary to provide comprehensive quality care for the treatment of organic illness and careful monitoring for possibly adverse side effects of medications. In addition, it should provide effective monitoring and advice with regard to dysfunctional effects of extreme stress, overwork, and inadequate sleep as well as appropriate counseling with respect to the adverse effects of over-reliance on sleeping pills and amphetamines.

Following well-known guidelines for maintaining the quality of the decision-making process during a crisis offers some safeguards against the harmful impact of these conditions. An additional safeguard is to ensure that participants in the decision-making group are thoroughly familiar with the general principles and requirements of crisis management and have been appropriately trained to apply these general principles to the special characteristics of the particular crisis with which they are forced to deal.

CRISIS MANAGEMENT THEORY RECONSIDERED AND AMPLIFIED

Our study has enabled me to refine and elaborate the provisional theory of crisis management with which I started. The case studies lend support to my initial hypothesis that the political and operational principles of the theory are not "requirements" in the strict sense of constituting necessary or sufficient conditions for successful management of war-threatening confrontations. At the same time, however, the case studies do support the more modest claim that whether these requirements are adequately met in a particular crisis can affect its outcome. The ability of decision makers on both sides to adhere reasonably well to these general principles favors, although it certainly does not guarantee, the possibility that they can cope with a crisis well enough to avoid war. Similarly, failure to adhere to them increases the likelihood of war. Our case studies also support the hypothesis that the causal importance of any one of these requirements varies in different crises, although the precise weight of any particular requirement cannot be established in a rigorous manner. Simple generalizations about the causal importance of different factors are not possible.

The most that can be concluded about the policy relevance and utility of my theory, therefore, is that it serves to identify those aspects of crisis management that are likely to make a difference. Awareness of relevant political and operational requirements should help sensitize policy makers to those aspects of their crisis behavior that can affect the outcome. These requirements also provide some guidance that can assist policy makers to deal with the fundamental dilemma of crisis management stressed so often in this study: namely, the need to find appropriate ways for protecting the most important interests engaged by the confrontation while avoiding actions that might trigger unwanted escalation to war. However, the guidance the theory provides is of a general character. Policy makers must adapt these general principles to the specific configuration of each particular crisis situation. This is a challenging task, as no two crises are exactly the same and each one can be expected to have distinctive characteristics that must be recognized and taken into account in fashioning a response.

For these reasons, the crisis management theory developed in this study is offered as an aid to the judgment policy makers must inevitably exercise in diagnosing and dealing with crisis situations; it is not a "recipe book" or a compilation of "rules" that can substitute for such judgment.

Let us turn now to important findings of the study that require placing the theory we have discussed into a broader, more comprehensive causal framework. Our research identified additional conditions and variables that can complicate and circumscribe the efficacy of crisis management. The Introduction to Part Two noted that not all diplomatic crises are equally "manageable"; some are particularly resistant to even the best efforts of statesmen to avoid war. In some crises, the conflicting interests and antagonisms of the two sides are so fundamental that they cannot be easily reconciled during the course of the crisis. War may occur because one or both sides reach the conclusion that it is desirable, or indeed necessary, to initiate war in order to achieve their objectives or to avoid an unpalatable outcome. War can occur, and in several of our cases did occur, because during the confrontation one side decided to embrace more ambitious objectives, thereby strengthening its adversary's motivation to resist, even at the cost of war. War can also occur in bitter confrontations of this kind because one or the other side makes a decision to escalate the crisis based on a miscalculation that the opponent will not counter with an escalation of its own or in the mistaken belief that it can control the risks of subsequent escalation.

It is important, therefore, not to exaggerate the potential of good crisis management practices for avoiding war and to pay attention to other variables that contribute to the likelihood of inadvertent war. The present study did so in several ways. Comparison of the cases of successful and unsuccessful crisis management encouraged one participant in the study, Phil Williams, to suggest a broader theoretical framework with which to understand the variation in crisis outcomes. This broader framework calls attention to the importance of three additional variables, not specified in our initial theory of crisis management, that supplement its focus on political and operational requirements of crisis management. These three variables are the incentive to avoid war, the opportunities for doing so during the crisis, and the level of skill and capabilities applied to crisis management. Comparison of the cases of successful and unsuccessful crisis management revealed considerable differences in these three variables, which helped to explain crisis outcomes. In other words, not only the ability but also the willingness of leaders to adhere to and satisfy the political and operational requirements of crisis management are significantly influenced by the strength or weakness of their incentives to avoid war, the presence of ample or few opportunities for doing so during the crisis, and the level of skill and capability they bring to the task.

How these variables differed in the crises we examined was discussed in the Introductions to Parts Two and Three. It suffices here to point out that in general, when incentives to avoid war are weak, favorable opportunities for crisis management are quite limited, and relevant skills are in short supply, then the likelihood of the crisis developing into war is appreciably higher. Conversely, as the case studies show, stronger incentives, better opportunities, and the exercise of relevant crisis management skills substantially increase the likelihood that war can be avoided.

Another finding of our study calls attention to additional complexities and obstacles that crisis management encounters when the confrontation involves more than two actors. Multiple actors were involved in quite a few of the eleven historical cases examined in this study. The analysis of these cases highlighted new challenges that arise in multi-actor crises and the special difficulties they pose for meeting the political and operational requirements of crisis management. These difficulties were evident in the older historical cases analyzed by Richard Smoke and Jack S. Levy; in the post–World War II era, they have been amply evident in Arab-Israeli conflicts in which the United States and the Soviet Union support rival regional actors. Both superpowers, it is true, have had important security interests of their own in the Middle East. But they have found it difficult to sort out and delimit their respective interests for various reasons having to do with the absence of a clear geographical line separating their predominant interests and the pervasive instability within the region. Moreover, in addition to the difficulty Moscow and Washington have experienced in recognizing and adjusting to each other's bedrock security interests in the Middle East, they have allowed the conflict potential of their relations in the area to be much accentuated by geopolitical considerations stemming from their Cold War global rivalry. The continuing conflict between Arab states and Israel offered the superpowers opportunities to make gains at each other's expense, a temptation that often could be controlled only when they perceived risks that involvement in the Arab-Israeli conflict might draw them into a shooting war with each other. This tension between opportunities and risks made the tasks of crisis avoidance and crisis management more complex for each of the superpowers and, at times, severely constrained their willingness and ability to cooperate in avoiding Arab-Israeli wars and in bringing them to an acceptable termination.

In brief, the basic policy dilemma of crisis management so often emphasized in this study has been experienced by Moscow and Washington in a special way in the Middle East. More specifically, each superpower experienced a tension between the desire—at times, the necessity—to lend meaningful support to its regional ally and, at the same time, a determination not to allow itself to be drawn into a dangerous, war-threatening confrontation with the other superpower.[13] This basic policy dilemma manifested itself in ways that were described in the case studies of the 1967, 1970, and 1973 Arab-Israeli wars. Efforts by a superpower patron to dissuade its regional client from initiating war failed in these cases because the superpower was not able to find a diplomatic solution to the grievance its client experienced. This was Washington's experience in the Arab-Israeli crisis of 1967 and Moscow's experience in the 1970 and 1973 cases. Similarly, Washington's inability to work out a diplomatic solution to the problem created by Nasser's nationalization of the Suez Canal Company in 1956 strengthened British and French incentives to resort to force.

The crises between their Middle East allies in 1967, 1970, and 1973 were in important respects more difficult to manage than crises in which the superpowers directly faced each other. Neither the Arab states nor Israel, typically, had much use for the political requirement of limiting their objectives or the means employed on their behalf in the interest of avoiding escalation. If an escalation promised gains, Arab and Israeli leaders were eager to undertake it, with or without the approval of their superpower patron. And, in fact, at times the superpower patron approved or condoned the escalation, seeing in it opportunities for gains of its own in addition to the advantages it might bring to its regional ally. Some of the important operational requirements of crisis management seemed hardly relevant to the regional actors. Neither the Arab states nor Israel displayed much interest in slowing down the momentum of events in a crisis in the interest of avoiding a war or its escalation. Similarly, given the acute zero-sum nature of their conflict, neither Arab nor Israeli leaders found much relevance in the crisis management principle that calls for leaving the adversary a way out compatible with its fundamental interests and honor.

Although the superpowers did not succeed in preventing these Arab-Israeli wars, they did manage to develop a tacit norm for regulating their own involvement in ways that would resolve the basic policy dilemma they experienced. Each superpower recognized the likelihood that the other superpower would intervene militarily in some way should it become necessary to do so in order to prevent its regional ally from suffering a catastrophic defeat. This tacit norm has, as its corollary, that the superpower backing the winning local actor in a conflict must pressure its ally to stop short of inflicting an overwhelming defeat on its opponent.

RECOMMENDATIONS

The end of the Cold War and the transformation underway in East-West relations offer much encouragement that Washington and Moscow should be able to manage conflicting interests and disputes in the future without again plunging into a war-threatening crisis that, if not managed effectively, could escalate to nuclear war. As I indicated in Chapter 1 and in Part Six, however, new challenges that may test their ability to cooperate in crisis avoidance and crisis management are likely to arise at the same time that new opportunities for doing so are emerging. The theory of crisis management presented in this study should be relevant and applicable both for strengthening mechanisms for cooperation in crisis avoidance and for managing any new crises that may arise. The relevance and flexibility of the theory derive from its generic character, as it is not tied to any particular crisis or any particular context. But for that very reason, the theory requires that policy makers adapt its general principles to the specific configuration of the particular crisis situation that confronts them.

It is appropriate, therefore, to conclude by restating some of the more important general principles of the theory together with presenting major recommendations.

• When conflicts of interest are simmering and threatening to erupt into a dangerous crisis, the superpowers should rely in the first instance on timely diplomatic communication and negotiation rather than engage in efforts to protect their interests by unilateral actions that are likely to provoke countermoves and crisis escalation.

• In peacetime as well as when embroiled in a dispute, the superpowers should avoid sudden or secret military deployments that affect the strategic or regional military balance, and they should forego foreign policy initiatives that seek to make major gains at each other's expense. Unless U.S. and Soviet leaders observe such restraints in their behavior toward each other, high-sounding declarations that they will forego use of force and threats of force against each other will remain hollow and brittle.

• Informed control and restraint of one's military forces is a critical requirement for effective crisis management. Top-level leaders on both sides must exercise informed and judicious control over all movements and alerts of combat forces. Leaders must be sensitive to and deal constructively with the tension that frequently exists in crisis situations between the imperatives of military logic and the requirements of diplomacy if they are to prevent unwanted escalation in crisis situations. Similarly, it is of the utmost importance that the rules of engagement given to combat forces be carefully chosen and monitored to reduce and control the risks of unwanted escalation.

• When a war-threatening crisis erupts, each side may find it necessary to take measures to reduce the vulnerability of its theater forces and to enhance its readiness to defend itself. However, at the same time, U.S. and Soviet leaders should take the greatest care to avoid alerts and deployments that are likely to be perceived by the other side as preparations for significant and imminent *offensive* operations. They should also avoid (or at least greatly minimize) the practice of using military alerts and deployments to signal resolution or to exert coercive pressure on the adversary for crisis bargaining purposes. In brief, there should be more use of diplomatic communication and less reliance on military signaling per se.

• The first objective of crisis management should be to terminate any U.S.-Soviet crisis promptly and effectively at its outset before it is allowed to escalate to dangerously high levels. Measures and actions to avoid an accidental or inadvertent nuclear war should not be geared exclusively to situations in which a crisis has already escalated to high-level alerts. However important it is to increase the reliability of warning systems, to eliminate the possibility of launch on false warning, to avoid or neutralize the effect of accidental or unauthorized actions and human errors, and to take other similar precautions, elementary prudence demands that maximal efforts be made to prevent a conflict of interest from developing into a tense U.S.-Soviet crisis that will severely test the two sides' ability to avoid accidental or inadvertent war.

• U.S. and Soviet leaders should discuss with each other in peacetime ways of preventing crisis escalation in different contexts, including regional conflicts in which they may be supporting rival regional actors.

• The time factor may be critical if efforts to avoid escalation and terminate a crisis are to have an opportunity to succeed. Accordingly, leaders on both sides must recognize the necessity to slow down the tempo and momentum of crisis developments. They may need to deliberately create pauses in crisis activity—as, for example, President Kennedy did in the Cuban Missile Crisis—in order to provide enough time for the two sides to exchange diplomatic communications and to give the leadership on both sides adequate time to assess the situation, make well-considered decisions, and respond to each other's proposals.

• It is essential that each side limit the objectives it pursues in a confrontation with the other and resist the temptation to inflict a damaging, humiliating defeat on its opponent if a superpower crisis is to be settled without escalation to dangerously high alert levels. While seeking to protect its own fundamental interests, each side must recognize the other side's legitimate interests and strive for a mutually acceptable formula for terminating the crisis.

• Since effective control and management of U.S.-Soviet confrontations may depend critically on the ability of the two sides to avoid misperceptions and miscalculations and to communicate rapidly and effectively with each other, it is highly desirable for Soviet and U.S. military and civilian specialists to discuss together problems of crisis stability, to identify types of behaviors that may threaten loss of control and trigger escalation pressures, and to consider and make provision for preventive and remedial measures.

• A great deal of essential knowledge and relevant experience has been gained from managing past U.S.-Soviet crises successfully. But the learning experience is virtually worthless unless the lessons and requisite skills are codified and institutionalized in each government. This body of knowledge and know-how must be transmitted quickly and effectively to new leaders and staff members who will have important crisis management responsibilities. It must be internalized by them by means of appropriate training, exercises, and rehearsals so that they will perform effectively the first time they are called upon to manage a crisis.

NOTES

1. Graham T. Allison, Albert Carnesale, and Joseph S. Nye, Jr., eds., *Hawks, Doves, & Owls* (New York: Norton, 1985). The other paths to nuclear war identified in this study were accidental war, surprise attack, and catalytic war.

2. Richard Ned Lebow, *Nuclear Crisis Management: A Dangerous Illusion* (Ithaca, N.Y.: Cornell University Press, 1987). In *Risks of Unintentional Nuclear War* (Totowa,

N.J.: Allanheld, Osmun & Co., 1983) Daniel Frei employs the term "unintentional" to refer generally to what we call inadvertent war but does not attempt to provide a typology of unintentional wars.

3. This and the following paragraph draw on A. L. George, "Crisis Management: The Interaction of Political and Military Considerations," *Survival*, 26, 5 (September/October 1984), pp. 229–230. Numerous other writers have called attention to the critical importance of these beliefs in the preemptive war scenario.

4. Robert Jervis provides an excellent discussion of various psychological factors that could contribute to the formation of the three beliefs that would encourage political leaders to consider initiating a preemptive war. See Ch. 5, "Psychological Aspects of Crisis Stability" in his *The Meaning of the Nuclear Revolution: Statecraft and the Prospect of Armageddon* (Ithaca and London: Cornell University Press, 1989).

5. Scott D. Sagan, "The Origins of the Pacific War," *Journal of Inter-disciplinary History* (Spring 1988): 342–344.

6. The phenomenon of preventive war and motives associated with it are incisively analyzed in Jack S. Levy, "Declining Power and the Preventive Motivation for War," *World Politics*, 40, 1 (October 1987): 82–197.

7. I am indebted to Jack Levy for calling this to my attention. See ibid, p. 92 (footnote 24) and p. 99 (footnote 37).

8. An exception to this is the detailed substantive analysis of the specific problems that must be dealt with "skillfully" in implementing the strategy of coercive diplomacy provided in A. L. George, D. K. Hall, W. E. Simons, *The Limits of Coercive Diplomacy* (Boston: Little, Brown, 1971), pp. 228–244.

9. This is a different problem, it should be recognized, from that of preventing military leaders from interfering with the *political* conduct of a crisis or with diplomatic efforts to manage it.

10. On "rules of prudence" in U.S.-Soviet relations see, for example, Graham T. Allison, William L. Ury, and Bruce J. Allyn, eds., *Windows of Opportunity: From Cold War to Peaceful Competition in U.S.-Soviet Relations* (Cambridge, MA.: Ballinger, 1989), Ch. 1, "Primitive Rules of Prudence"; and A. L. George, P. J. Farley, and Alexander Dallin, eds., *U.S.-Soviet Security Cooperation: Achievements, Failures, Lessons* (New York: Oxford University Press, 1988), pp. 583–585.

11. In addition, see Dr. Herbert Abrams's chapter, "Disabled Leaders, Cognition and Crisis," in *Accidental Nuclear War*, Proceedings of the Eighteenth Pugwash Workshop on Nuclear Forces (Toronto: Samuel Stevens, 1990). The discussion in these pages also draws on the "Workshop Summary" prepared by Alexander L. George and Kurt Gottfried that appears in the same volume.

12. See the detailed historical survey and analysis of the uneven workings of the White House medical support system in Thomas C. Wiegele, "Presidential Physicians and Presidential Health Care: Some Theoretical and Operational Considerations Related to Political Decision Making," *Presidential Studies Quarterly*, 20, 1 (Winter 1990): 71–89.

13. For an excellent general statement of this policy dilemma see Glenn H. Snyder, "The Security Dilemma in Alliance Politics," *World Politics*, 36, 4 (July 1984): 461–495.

The Persian Gulf Crisis, 1990–1991

Alexander L. George

Historians of the Persian Gulf War may well judge it to have been an "inadvertent war," as defined in this book. During the diplomatic crisis that led to the Iraqi invasion of Kuwait, neither Saddam Hussein nor the Kuwaiti, Saudi, and Egyptian leaders wanted or expected a war to result. Similarly, at that time neither Hussein nor President Bush expected that the dispute between the Arab states would lead eventually to a war between their two countries.

CRISIS MISMANAGEMENT

The first question historians are likely to raise, then, is whether the war that broke out in January 1991 could have been avoided by better crisis management. The data available at this time strongly suggest that war occurred because the Arab states mismanaged the crisis that had arisen in July as a result of Hussein's demands on Kuwait. The Iraqi president's demands may have been excessive, but they were not without legitimacy within the framework of Arab politics and the game of *realpolitik* in which he and other Arab leaders were engaged. As it turned out, Kuwaiti, Saudi, and Egyptian leaders who were negotiating with Hussein misjudged him and miscalculated his readiness to use force if not given greater concessions. (An alternative hypothesis, which I find less plausible, is that Hussein did not want a peaceful resolution of the dispute with Kuwait and advanced demands he knew would not be acceptable in order to have a pretext for initiating war.)[1] The Arab states opposing him may also have miscalculated in believing that if, contrary to their expectations, Hussein did send troops into Kuwait, he would be content to seize only the border area above the Rumaila oil field and perhaps the two islands at the mouth of Iraq's limited access to the Persian Gulf.

In fact, had Hussein indeed limited his military action to these more modest objectives, it is entirely likely that the crisis would have been resolved peacefully. There would have been no occasion for U.S. intervention and, at most, Hussein would have received a perfunctory slap on the wrist by the United Nations. Therefore, on top of the missed opportunity to avoid war occasioned by the Arab leaders' mismanagement of the diplomatic crisis, another opportunity for avoiding war was lost because of Hussein's miscalculation that he could occupy all of Kuwait without triggering U.S. intervention.

It should be noted that Hussein chose to achieve his goal by means of the strategy of a quick *fait accompli*. The rationale for the choice of this strategy and the risks associated with it were discussed in Chapter 16. The path to inadvertent war in this case, therefore, is that of the "miscalculated *fait accompli*" that was described in Part Seven.

THE ABORTIVE U.S. EFFORT TO DETER AN
IRAQI ATTACK ON KUWAIT[2]

For many months after Iraq's invasion of Kuwait there was considerable speculation that the Bush administration had failed to take intelligence indicators of a possible attack seriously enough to deter Saddam Hussein. Criticism of the administration received strong support from a transcript of the long conversation on July 25 between Hussein and U.S. Ambassador to Iraq April Glaspie. According to this transcript Ambassador Glaspie stated that she had "a direct instruction from the President to seek better relations with Iraq"; and later in the same conversation she stated that "we have no opinion on Arab-Arab conflicts, like your border disagreement with Kuwait."

The failure of the administration to deny the authenticity of the Iraqi transcript or to charge that it was doctored in some way to give a misleading account of Glaspie's remarks encouraged observers to look for additional indications that the administration had failed to see the need for an attempt to deter Saddam Hussein and had inadvertently encouraged him to believe that the United States would not become involved. It was not difficult to find indications in the public record that the administration may have been following a hands-off policy toward Iraq's dispute with Kuwait. Although Secretary of Defense Dick Cheney told journalists on July 19 that the U.S. commitment made during the Iran-Iraq war to come to Kuwait's defense if it were attacked was still valid, the import of his remarks was later diluted by the Department of Defense spokesperson. And on July 24 when Margaret Tutwiler, the State Department spokesperson, was asked whether the United States had any commitment to defend Kuwait, she answered: "We do not have any defense treaties with Kuwait, and there are no special defense or security commitments to Kuwait." Similarly, on July 31, in his testimony before a House Foreign Affairs subcommittee, Assistant Secretary of State for Near Eastern and South Asian Affairs John Kelly stated that "we have no defense treaty relationship with any Gulf country" and agreed that if Iraq attacked Kuwait the United States had no treaty that would obligate it to commit U.S. forces.

In fact, however, the Bush administration did make an effort to deter Hussein. Although the administration has not yet chosen to provide essential details of this effort, it is clear that in mid-July it became quite concerned over Saddam Hussein's intentions, saw the need for a strong deterrence effort, but then decreased its efforts for various reasons. It is also entirely likely that Ambassador Glaspie's confidential report to Washington of her conversation with Saddam Hussein conveyed a strong assurance that he would settle his dispute with Kuwait peacefully. It is also quite likely that her optimistic first-hand assessment of Hussein's intentions helped to calm Washington's concern about the danger of war until the CIA came forward on August 1 with intelligence indications that Iraqi forces would probably attack within 24 hours, but that they would possibly limit action to seizure of the oil field on the Iraq-Kuwait border and one of the two islands off the coast of Iraq.

Washington's concern over the possibility of an Iraqi attack against Kuwait was triggered by a bellicose speech by Saddam Hussein on July 17 in which he issued a naked threat to act if Kuwait did not meet his demands. The administration responded both publicly and privately to quickly improvise a strong deterrence effort. The Iraqi ambassador to the United States appears to have been told that the United States would defend its vital interests in the Gulf and would continue to support the sovereignty and integrity of the Gulf states. He was also told that although the United States would take no position on the issues dividing Iraq and Kuwait it would insist that this dispute be settled peacefully and without threat or intimidation. Washington also attempted to encourage friendly Arab states in the Gulf to join in vigorous diplomacy to this end. However, the Arab leaders held back, taking the position that the Iraqi-Kuwait dispute was an Arab matter that they could deal with and that Washington should not become involved. As a result, the U.S. attempt to mount a strong deterrence effort lost momentum and declined in credibility and potency, as is reflected in the statements by Tutwiler, Glaspie, and Kelly that have already been cited. In trying to shore up its deterrence effort the administration attempted, against the advice of the friendly Arab leaders who felt it would be provocative, to organize a joint U.S.-Arab show of military force to impress Hussein. Only the United Arab Emirates (U.A.E.) agreed to participate. A joint military exercise was announced on July 24—a U.S.-U.A.E. air force refueling exercise—and at the same time, it is reported, six warships of the U.S. Middle East task force were moved closer to Kuwait and the United Arab Emirates.

In her discussion with the Senate Foreign Relations Committee April Glaspie claimed that Hussein was impressed with the deterrent position the United States was taking and assured her that he would not resolve his problems with Kuwait by force. It was clear from the context of her discussion with the committee that Glaspie came away from the conversation with Hussein convinced that he had given up the idea of resorting to force, and that her confidential report to the State Department conveyed unqualified optimism that the Iraqi president had committed himself to a peaceful resolution of the dispute.

In retrospect, it is clear that it was difficult for Washington to mount a stronger deterrence effort for several reasons, some of them already noted. Instead of sending Hussein blunt and unequivocal statements that an invasion of Kuwait would be unacceptable and would be resisted by military force, Washington issued equivocal statements regarding its commitment to Kuwait. The repeated statement that the United States had no commitment to Kuwait weakened strong but highly general statements about defending U.S. interests in the Gulf and supporting the sovereignty and integrity of the Gulf states. Besides, the joint air refueling exercise hardly constituted a strong show of force. As a senior administration official explained to reporters, "We were reluctant to draw a line in the sand." Continuing, he added that he could not envisage at that time that the American public would have supported the deployment of U.S. troops over a dispute over twenty miles of desert territory. Besides, it could by no means be taken for granted that the local Arab countries would have allowed the stationing of U.S. troops on their territory. "The basic principle is not to make threats you can't deliver on. That was one reason there was a certain degree of hedging on what was said."[3]

This, then, is a case that illustrates some of the difficulties that efforts to employ deterrence strategy sometimes encounter and the limitations of the strategy as an instrument of foreign policy. Thus, what the United States was willing and able to do *after* the aggression against Kuwait, it was not able for various reasons to threaten to do on behalf of deterrence *before* the invasion occurred.

Another factor that in this case as in some others made it difficult to mount a stronger deterrence effort was U.S. policy at the time that a threat of aggression against a friendly state emerged. As a number of observers noted, the Bush administration's response to the July crisis in the Gulf was influenced by its standing policy of developing better relations with Hussein's Iraq. Some critics have disparaged the administration for having "cuddled up" to Saddam Hussein and, worse, for having engaged in appeasement. A more appropriate and fairer observation would be that the administration was operating on the premise that the best way to handle Hussein and to moderate his behavior was through offering conditional incentives and an improvement in relations in return for his cooperation—in other words, a diplomatic version of behavior modification. Washington was by no means unaware of Hussein's grandiose ambitions and that they might lead him some day to engage in aggression of some kind against neighboring states. But the administration hoped to influence him to moderate his goals and methods. April Glaspie's message from President Bush to Hussein, to which reference has already been made, should be seen in this context. President Bush later acknowledged that in the light of Iraq's invasion of Kuwait the U.S. policy of seeking improved relations with Hussein did not "make much sense."

Finally, it is quite possible that Hussein convinced himself that he need not worry about the possibility of a U.S. military response to an invasion of Kuwait and did not really need the additional assurance that he could draw from the statements of April Glaspie, Margaret Tutwiler, and John Kelly. Instead, Hussein may have sharply downgraded the possibility of U.S. intervention in the belief that Saudi Arabia and other Arab states would not agree to the deployment of U.S. forces on their territory. Such a belief was certainly not unjustified, but it proved to be wrong and was among the first of his many miscalculations. Other aspects of Hussein's image of the United States that will be mentioned later may have also operated to convince him that U.S. military intervention after he invaded and quickly occupied Kuwait was indeed a remote possibility that need not inhibit him.

THE FAILURE OF COERCIVE DIPLOMACY

To induce Hussein to get out of Kuwait the U.N. Security Council employed the strategy of coercive diplomacy. The attractiveness of this strategy and its uses and limitations have been outlined in Chapter 16. At first, the U.S.-led coalition backed its demand that Iraqi forces get out of Kuwait by imposing economic sanctions and proceeding to progressively tighten the embargo on Iraq's imports and exports. This is an example of the variant of coercive diplomacy that has been labeled "a gradual turning of the screw." The threat of resorting to military force, if necessary, remained in the background. It was understood from the beginning that economic sanctions, even though unusually tight in this case, would require considerable time to achieve maximum effectiveness and that it was uncertain whether and when they might induce Hussein to comply with the U.N. demands. Whether the embargo, if given more time, might have succeeded became a controversial, divisive issue in the United States after the administration moved in November to secure a new Security Council resolution authorizing the use of military force at some point after January 15, 1991. Washington also announced in November that an additional 200,000 soldiers would be sent to the Gulf to create an "offensive" option. Those who believe that sanctions might have eventually succeeded in persuading Hussein to accept the U.N. demands will regard this as another "missed opportunity" to avoid war.

Be that as it may, this development marked a significant shift in coercive diplomacy from a gradual turning of the screw via sanctions to an ultimatum backed by the threat of force. There were several reasons for this move to the stronger form of coercive diplomacy, among them the administration's fear that the international coalition might not hold together over the long period of time required for the embargo to have its full effect. Just as important, if not more so, were personality assessments of Hussein that had come to dominate the administration's thinking. According to psychological profiles of Hussein that circulated in Washington early during the crisis,[4] he was capable of retreat and could indeed be coerced into getting out of Kuwait, but this could be accomplished *only* if he were taken to the very brink of war and deprived of any alternative except the stark choice of backing down or being subjected to a devastating all-out war. Sanctions would not take Hussein to the brink and, therefore, they were not an adequate basis for the strategy of coercive diplomacy. Only the threat of war could enable coercive diplomacy to succeed. There is reason to believe that leading members of the administration subscribed to this image of Hussein and that they were rather confident at first that Hussein would back down when the deployment was completed and the coalition forces in the Gulf reached the stage of full combat readiness sometime in February.

The type of coercive strategy the administration attempted to use against Saddam was a diplomatic version of the well-known game of chicken. The United States deliberately set itself on a collision course with Hussein and tried to convince him that it had thrown away its steering wheel; therefore, a "crash" (that is, war) could be avoided only if he got off the road. To this end the administration repeatedly emphasized that the large offensive force being created in the Gulf could not be sustained for a long period of time and would have to be used sometime before the religious holiday of Ramadan in mid-March and certainly before the onset of hot summer weather in the Gulf. Coupled with this the administration insisted that there would be no negotiations, no weakening of the U.N. demands, and no "rewards for aggression." Thus, President Bush hoped to convince Hussein that the United States and its coalition partners were embarked on an irreversible course to the very brink of war, from which *they* could not and would not back off, and that all alternatives except capitulation or war were effectively denied him.

It would appear, however, that the administration ignored the fact that *both* sides can play the game of diplomatic chicken. As the January 15 deadline set by the Security Council resolution approached, the administration showed signs of increasing perplexity and frustration at indications that Hussein would not back down and instead seemed bent on calling its bluff. The administration also became aware that Hussein had options—for example, beginning a partial withdrawal from Kuwait—and that if he chose to exercise such options either before or just after January 15, he might well succeed in eroding the coercive pressure of the ultimatum and push the crisis into prolonged negotiations. It is entirely possible that historians will find evidence to support the hypothesis that although earlier the administration had indicated it would not be in a hurry to initiate war after the January 15 deadline, President Bush eventually decided to do so as soon as possible after that date because he was concerned that Saddam might at any moment announce a partial withdrawal from Kuwait or try in other ways to trap the allied coalition into negotiations. Some members of the press referred to this as the administration's "nightmare scenario."

Thus coercive diplomacy was tried and it failed. The question is, why did it fail? What "lessons" are scholars likely to draw from this case regarding the uses and limitations of the strategy of coercive diplomacy and, also, the risks of an ultimatum? As was noted in Chapter 16, the strategy of coercive diplomacy is attractive because it offers the possibility of achieving one's objectives without war. But coercive diplomacy assumes a type of simple, uncomplicated rationality on the part of the opponent. The assumption on which coercive diplomacy is based is that if the opponent is rational, he will surely see that it is in his interest to back down. This oversimplifies the roots of motivation and the considerations that may influence leaders who are the target of coercive diplomacy. The assumption of rationality is not sufficient for making a confident prediction as to what an opponent will do when subjected, as Hussein was, to an ultimatum. In this situation, one does not have to be irrational or a madman to refuse to knuckle under in the face of the threat of war. The assumption of rationality on which the strategy of coercive diplomacy relies must somehow take into account psychological, cultural, and political variables that can affect the opponent's response to an ultimatum.

We may recall in this connection that the strong U.S. ultimatum to Japan in the summer and autumn of 1941 boomeranged and provoked the attack on Pearl Harbor. Japanese leaders were aware that the prospects of winning a war with the United States were not at all favorable. But as they saw their predicament, the only alternative to war was to accept Washington's demand that Japan get out of China and give up its aspirations for a leading hegemonic position in Asia; and this was rejected as more distasteful than a risky war. A similar interpretation can be advanced that may possibly help to explain why Hussein did not accept the Bush administration's ultimatum even though he knew that war would follow. In addition, it would appear that Hussein's incentive to avoid war was not very strong. He seems to have operated with an image of the United States that encouraged him to believe that it could not tolerate the prospect of high casualties, and he was confident that his battle-hardened army could inflict heavy casualties.

One would like to believe that the fateful question of war or peace is not determined by psychological variables having to do with the personalities of leaders who are locked into a crisis of this kind. And yet there is reason to believe that in this crisis as well as previous ones, each leader's image of the other leader and each leader's image of himself do play at times a critically important role in the path to war or to peace. In the dangerous Cuban Missile Crisis in 1962, as was noted in Chapter 11, there is evidence that Khrushchev's *defective* image of Kennedy, whom he saw as being a weak, inexperienced opponent, played a role in the Soviet leader's miscalculation that he could get away with the deployment of missiles into Cuba. Paradoxically—and fortunately—the same type of psychological variable also played a critical role in the peaceful settlement of the crisis. This time it was Kennedy's *correct* image of Khrushchev as being an intelligent person who, if given sufficient time and evidence of U.S. determination, would realize he had miscalculated and would correct his mistake.

In the case of Hussein one of the influential psychological profiles of the Iraqi leader referred to earlier characterized him as indeed dangerous and ambitious, but not a madman. Once Hussein had embarked on his action against Kuwait, he could be expected to pursue his objective with determination; and in the face of opposition and pressure, Hussein would struggle all the harder to hold on. But, the psychological profile pointed out, a study of Hussein's behavior in the past also showed "a pattern of reversing his course" when he became convinced that he had miscalculated and that it was in his interest to retreat. This insight into Hussein's personality and past behavior strongly supported the Bush administration's belief that Hussein was capable of retreat if he were taken to the brink and given no alternative but to retreat or to face all-out war. However, the administration did not pay enough attention to another important point made in this psychological profile of Hussein—namely, *that he had to be given a way out that ensured his survival in power.* Otherwise, he would "stop at nothing" and would "use every weapon at his disposal" if he thought his survival in power was at stake.

Future historians are likely to ask whether instead of going to war with Iraq it would have been preferable for the United States and its allies to have given Hussein a better way out. Recall that toward the end of Cuban Missile Crisis, Kennedy gave Khrushchev the equivalent of an ultimatum that conveyed a credible threat that the United States would use force if necessary to get the Soviet missiles removed from Cuba. However, at the same time, the president coupled his ultimatum with two concessions that made it easier for the Soviet leader to comply with the demand. One concession was a commitment that the United States would not invade Cuba in the future; the other concession was a secret agreement by Kennedy to take the U.S. Jupiter missiles out of Turkey. In other words, even though Kennedy did give Khrushchev an ultimatum, the ultimatum was part of a carrot-and-stick type of coercive diplomacy.

In the Gulf crisis, on the other hand, the type of coercive diplomacy the Bush administration employed relied almost exclusively on the stick. Whereas Kennedy seriously negotiated with Khrushchev in order to reach a compromise solution to the missile crisis, the Bush administration rejected any negotiation with Hussein and any compromise settlement. Washington was not willing to go further than to give assurance that it would not attack Iraq if Hussein got out of Kuwait. On occasion administration officials referred to this assurance as a "carrot." But, although in this sense a door was left open for Hussein to escape, the Bush administration made it clear that there could be no "reward for aggression." It rejected any direct linkage of Hussein's withdrawal with a Middle East security conference or with a settlement of the dispute between Iraq and Kuwait that had triggered the conflict in early August. Nonetheless, had Hussein been willing to take the exit permitted him, he could have avoided the war that followed and survived. We must consider, therefore, why Hussein rejected this opportunity.

It is difficult to avoid the conclusion that in this case the strategy of coercive diplomacy was stretched to its limits and was unlikely to produce a peaceful settlement of the crisis. When a conflict with one's opponent is viewed in stark, zero-sum terms—a perception that both Bush and Hussein appeared to have had—then there is little interest on either side for a mutually acceptable compromise solution. In contrast, Kennedy and Khrushchev did not see their disagreement over the missiles in Cuba as a zero-sum conflict. Rather they believed that both the United States and the Soviet Union shared an interest in avoiding war, and they acted accordingly.

The zero-sum view of the conflict shared by Bush and Hussein, reinforced by the highly invidious image each had of the other, made each leader believe that war would be preferable to the concessions that he would have to make to secure a peaceful settlement. Moreover, each leader held an image of the costs, outcome, and consequences of war that was not distasteful enough to motivate him to seek a compromise settlement. President Bush could view the possibility of war, if his effort at coercive diplomacy failed, with a certain equanimity. Not only could war be accepted as necessary and just in order to punish a ruthless and evil aggressor, deter would-be aggressors in the future, and contribute to the development of a "new world order"; but war would offer other benefits as well. A war would provide an opportunity for the United States and its allies to destroy Iraq's weapons of mass destruction, sharply reduce its overall military capabilities, and thereby eliminate the basis of Hussein's ability to pursue hegemonic aspirations in the region—if not also get rid of Hussein himself (objectives that the United States could not embrace openly because they would approximate those of a preventive war, which the Security Council had not authorized). Moreover, the president was reasonably confident that the overwhelming military power of the coalition forces would secure victory with minimal casualties and erase for the American people the bad memory of the Vietnam War. All these considerations combined to powerfully reinforce the president's determination to back Hussein into a corner and to subject him to a humiliating defeat. When war became necessary to accomplish the objective, Bush did not shy away from it.

As for Hussein, he could more easily reject the January 15 ultimatum and call Bush's bluff because the Iraqi leader believed that the United States could not tolerate the heavy casualties that his ground forces would be able to inflict. Besides, if need be, Hussein was not averse to accepting heavy casualties and significant damage from air attacks to Iraq's military infrastructure and civil society. Finally, Hussein's motivation and judgment—and his many miscalculations—were influenced by an inflated image of himself as a hero with a mission to serve as the agent for the transformation of the Arab world.

Under these circumstances, there was little or no possibility that the strategy of coercive diplomacy could bring about a mutually acceptable peaceful resolution o this crisis. And, later, these same considerations served to defeat the last-minute Soviet effort to arrange a compromise settlement of the war before the U.S.-led coalition launched the powerful ground offensive that inflicted a catastrophic defeat on the Iraqi army. Nevertheless, although the strategy of coercive diplomacy had little chance of success in this case, the attempt to employ it in the hope of avoiding war was necessary for building and maintaining international and domestic support for the objective of liberating Kuwait. Ironically, the failure of coercive diplomacy was probably necessary in order to gain support for war when it became necessary as "the last resort."

NOTES

1. There is some evidence that Kuwaiti leaders, becoming increasingly apprehensive that Hussein might resort to force in the latter part of July, made a last-minute effort to finally offer some concessions that might appease him. Alexander Cockburn reports that in the Jidda mediation talks on August 1, the day before the invasion, "Kuwait agreed to write off Iraq's $15 billion war debt and to lease Warbah island to Iraq as an oil outlet for the Rumaila field" (Cockburn, *Wall Street Journal*, September 6, 1990). If this account is correct, it may have been a case of too little, too late. On the other hand, some historians may regard Hussein's rejection of the offer as evidence that he was bent on military aggression. Such an interpretation, however, has to contend with the fact that the last-minute Kuwaiti offer did not meet all of Hussein's demands and, also, that by then the Iraqi leader had already set into motion his invasion plans.

2. This account of the effort to deter Hussein from attacking Kuwait is reconstructed from a large number of public sources. Particularly useful were Don Oberdoerfer's "Missed Signals in the Middle East," *Washington Post*, Sunday, March 19, 1991, and April Glaspie's detailed statements to the Senate Foreign Relations Committee on March 20, 1991, a verbatim transcript of which was issued by the Federal News Service on the following day. Also useful was Glaspie's testimony before the Subcommittee on Europe and the Middle East, chaired by Lee Hamilton, of the House of Representatives Foreign Affairs Committee on March 21, 1991, a verbatim transcript of which was issued by the Federal News Service.

I have also drawn from the following sources: *New York Times*, September 23, 1990; Jim Hoagland, *Washington Post*, September 13, 1990; David Hoffman, *Washington Post*, September 24, 1990; Elaine Sciolino with Michael Gordon, *Washington Post*, September 23, 1990; Bruce W. Nelan, *Time*, October 1, 1990. Detailed excerpts from Saddam Hussein's conversation with April Glaspie, based on a transcript released by the Iraqi government, the authenticity of which was not challenged by the State Department, were published in the *New York Times*, September 23, 1990. See also Thomas L. Friedman, *New York Times*, March 22, 1991.

Important documentation remains classified: for example, the State Department's instructions to April Glaspie for her meeting with Hussein; the written U.S. note to Hussein that she mentioned in her appearance before the Senate Foreign Relations Committee; her cable to Washington reporting on her conversation with Hussein.

3. Quoted in Sciolino and Gordon, op. cit.

4. See, for example, Jerrold M. Post, "Saddam Hussein of Iraq: An Analysis of His Personality and Political Behavior," unpublished manuscript, September 14, 1990.

About the Book

Some wars are averted whereas others inadvertently erupt. Alexander George and his outstanding cast of contributors show us—through painstaking case study analysis—that neither outcome is accidental or inevitable. Crises of any sort can be managed poorly or well—but either way, crisis management is an essential part of the unfolding of events, deserving the attention of students, scholars, government officials, and others who must manage conflict.

For the first time, principles and strategies of crisis management are systematically drawn together in a single volume and applied to a variety of international confrontations. Alexander George begins and ends the book with pathbreaking formulations and assessments of crisis management theory, with specific reference to the Iraqi invasion of Kuwait. Three central sections of the book contain case studies of inadvertent war, wars that were avoided, and conflicts that involved superpower confrontation in the Middle East. Two additional sections analyze general aspects of crisis management and its prospects for the future. Sixteen contributors from academe, government, medicine, and business, in the United States and abroad, cover cases and topics ranging from World War I, Korea, and the Cuban Missile Crisis to the impact of stress on policy makers.

The volume goes a long way toward collecting and codifying the lessons of past war-threatening crises, with the goal of transmitting and institutionalizing a body of knowledge and experience that can help new leaders and their staffs manage international challenges—*before* they become crisis situations.

For a wide variety of college courses as well as for staff development and academic research, *Avoiding War* will become an indispensable resource on the theory, history, and future of crisis management.

About the Editor
and Contributors

Yaacov Bar-Siman-Tov is a senior lecturer in the Department of International Relations of the Hebrew University of Jerusalem. He is the author of *The Israeli-Egyptian War of Attrition 1969-1970: A Case Study of Limited Local War; Linkage in the Middle East: Syria Between Domestic and External Conflict, 1961-1970;* and *Israel, the Superpowers and the War in the Middle East.*

Kurt M. Campbell is assistant professor of public policy and international relations and assistant director of the Center for Science and International Affairs at the John F. Kennedy School, and serves as a special assistant to the Joint Chiefs of Staff in the Office of Political-Military Affairs. He received his Ph.D. in international relations from Oxford University and holds a certificate in Soviet studies from the Soviet University of Erevan. He is the author of *Soviet Policy Towards South Africa* and editor of *Gorbachev's Third World Dilemmas,* in addition to writing many articles on Soviet studies, military affairs, and international relations. Dr. Campbell was a member of the Joint Chiefs of Staff negotiating team for the talks with the Soviet military on Dangerous Military Activities.

Arthur A. Cohen received his B.A. in Chinese language and literature from the University of Chicago. He is the author of many articles on Chinese Communist policies and *The Communism of Mao Tse-tung* (1964). He was a senior analyst in the Directorate of Intelligence, Central Intelligence Agency.

M. Steven Fish is a candidate for the Ph.D. in political science at Stanford University. He has published articles in *Peace and Change* and *Diplomatic History.* He is writing his dissertation on social movements and the emergence of independent voluntary associations in the Soviet Union since 1985.

Alexander L. George is Graham H. Stuart Professor of International Relations (emeritus) at Stanford University. His first book, *Woodrow Wilson and Colonel House* (1956), written with his wife, Juliette L. George, is widely regarded as a classic study of the role of personality in politics. He is also the author or co-author of other books, including *Deterrence in Foreign Policy* (with Richard Smoke, 1974), which won the 1975 Bancroft Prize; *Presidential Decisionmaking in Foreign Policy* (1980); *Force and Statecraft* (with Gordon A. Craig, 1983); *Managing U.S.-Soviet Rivalry* (1983); and *U.S.-Soviet Security Cooperation* (with Philip J. Farley and Alexander Dallin, 1988).

Christer Jönsson is professor of political science, University of Lund, Sweden. He is the author of *Soviet Bargaining Behavior* (1979), *Superpower* (1984), *International Aviation* *and the Politics of Regime Change* (1987), and *Communication in International Bargaining* (1990), as well as several articles in scholarly journals and edited volumes.

Jack S. Levy is professor of political science at Rutgers University. He is author of *War in the Great Power System, 1495–1975* and has published articles in numerous scholarly journals and edited volumes. He is currently working on projects relating to domestic politics and war, the question of long cycles of war and peace, World War I, the Falklands/Malvinas War, and revision of his war data covering the last five centuries.

Jerrold M. Post is professor of psychiatry, political psychology, and international affairs at the George Washington University. The founder of the U.S. government's Political Psychology Center, he has published widely on the psychology of leadership and leadership decision making. Dr. Post received his M.D. from Yale University and his postgraduate training in psychiatry from Harvard University and the National Institute of Mental Health. He is co-author (with Robert Robins) of *The Captive King* (forthcoming), which deals with the effects of illness and disability on the political behavior of leaders.

Theodore J. Ralston serves as European technology analyst in the International Liaison Office of the Microelectronics and Computer Technology Corporation (MCC). Prior to joining MCC in 1983, Mr. Ralston was a member of the staff of Stanford University's Center for International Security and Arms Control. Earlier he served for seven years on the professional staff of the U.S. Senate Select Committee on Intelligence. Mr. Ralston received his B.S. in zoology and B.A. in history from the University of Washington in 1971 and his graduate degree in history and languages from Oxford University in 1974.

J. Philip Rogers is assistant professor of political science at the George Washington University. He has done research on nuclear and conventional arms control, superpower crisis management, and psychological factors in international crisis bargaining. His most recent publication, which will appear in Spring 1991, is an edited volume entitled *European Conventional Arms Control and European Security: The Search for Stability in an Era of Revolutionary Change.*

Scott D. Sagan is assistant professor of political science at Stanford University. He is the author of *Moving Targets: Nuclear Strategy and National Security* and co-author of *Living with Nuclear Weapons*. He has published numerous articles on crisis management and nuclear strategy.

Richard Smoke is professor of political science and research director of the Center for Foreign Policy Development at Brown University. He is co-editor (with Andrei Kortunov) of *Mutual Security: A New Approach to Soviet-American Relations* (1990). Earlier books include *War: Controlling Escalation; National Security and the Nuclear Dilemma;* and (with Alexander L. George) *Deterrence in American Foreign Policy: Theory and Practice.*

Janice Gross Stein is professor of political science at the University of Toronto. Her research interests include crisis prevention and management, deterrence, international negotiation, and the international politics of the Middle East. She is co-author (with Raymond Tanter) of *Rational Decision-Making: Israel's Security Choices, 1967* (1980) and (with Robert Jervis and Richard Ned Lebow) *Psychology and Deterrence* (1985). She recently edited *Getting to the Table: Processes of International Prenegotiation* (1989). She received her B.A. from McGill University, her M.A. from Yale University, and her Ph.D. from McGill.

Stan A. Taylor is chair of the Department of Political Science at Brigham Young University. A former staff member of the Senate Select Committee on Intelligence, Dr. Taylor received his Ph.D. from the Fletcher School of Law and Diplomacy. He is the author of *America the Vincible: U.S. Foreign Policy for the 21st Century* (forthcoming).

Allen S. Whiting is professor of political science at the University of Arizona. He has taught at Northwestern University, Michigan State University, and the University of Michigan; held positions at the Rand Corporation and the Department of State, Bureau of Intelligence and Research; and served as deputy principal officer at the American Consulate General, Hong Kong. He is the author of *Soviet Policies Toward China, 1917–1924; Siberian Development and East Asia: Threat or Promise?*; and many other books and articles.

Phil Williams is professor of international security at the Graduate School of Public and International Affairs, University of Pittsburgh, and director of research at the university's Ridgeway Center. He is author of *Crisis Management* and *The Senate and U.S. Troops in Europe* and co-editor of *Superpower Competition and Crisis Prevention in the Third World*.

Index